AIA

Professional 2 Level

Business and Financial Management

LEARNING & PRACTICE WORKBOOK

In this 2025 edition

- A **user-friendly format** for easy navigation
- **Exam-centred topic coverage**, directly linked to AIA's syllabus
- **Exam focus points** showing you what the examiner will want you to do
- Regular **fast forward** summaries emphasising the key points in each chapter
- **Questions** and **quick quizzes** to test your understanding
- **Exam question bank** containing exam-standard questions with answers
- **Mock exam** for real exam practice
- A full index

FOR EXAMS FROM MAY 2025

Second edition November 2024
ISBN 978 1 0355 2580 5
eISBN 978 1 0355 2608 6

British Library Cataloguing-in-Publication Data
A catalogue record for this book
is available from the British Library

Published by
BPP Learning Media Ltd
BPP House, Aldine Place
142-144 Uxbridge Road
London W12 8AA

learningmedia.bpp.com

Printed in the United Kingdom

Your learning materials, published by BPP Learning Media Ltd, are printed on paper obtained from traceable sustainable sources.

All rights reserved. No part of this publication may be reproduced, stored in a retrieval system or transmitted in any form or by any means, electronic, mechanical, photocopying, recording or otherwise, without the prior written permission of BPP Learning Media.

The contents of this book are intended as a guide and not professional advice. Although every effort has been made to ensure that the contents of this book are correct at the time of going to press, BPP Learning Media makes no warranty that the information in this book is accurate or complete and accept no liability for any loss or damage suffered by any person acting or refraining from acting as a result of the material in this book.

We are grateful to the Association of International Accountants for permission to reproduce past examination questions. The suggested solutions in the exam answer bank have been prepared by BPP Learning Media Ltd.

©
BPP Learning Media Ltd
2024

A note about copyright

Dear Customer

What does the little © mean and why does it matter?

Your market-leading BPP books, course materials and e-learning materials do not write and update themselves. People write them: on their own behalf or as employees of an organisation that invests in this activity. Copyright law protects their livelihoods. It does so by creating rights over the use of the content.

Breach of copyright is a form of theft – as well as being a criminal offence in some jurisdictions, it is potentially a serious breach of professional ethics.

With current technology, things might seem a bit hazy but, basically, without the express permission of BPP Learning Media:

- Photocopying our materials is a breach of copyright
- Printing our digital materials in order to share them with or forward them to a third party or use them in any way other than in connection with your BPP studies is a breach of copyright.

You can, of course, sell your books, in the form in which you have bought them – once you have finished with them. (Is this fair to your fellow students? We update for a reason.) But the e-products are sold on a single user license basis: we do not supply 'unlock' codes to people who have bought them second hand.

And what about outside the UK? BPP Learning Media strives to make our materials available at prices students can afford by local printing arrangements, pricing policies and partnerships which are clearly listed on our website. A tiny minority ignore this and indulge in criminal activity by illegally photocopying our material or supporting organisations that do. If they act illegally and unethically in one area, can you really trust them?

NO AI TRAINING. Unless otherwise agreed in writing, the use of BPP material for the purpose of AI training is not permitted. Any use of this material to "train" generative artificial intelligence (AI) technologies is prohibited, as is providing archived or cached data sets containing such material to another person or entity.

Contents

Page

Introduction

The introduction pages contain lots of valuable advice and information. They include tips on studying for and passing the exam, also the content of the syllabus and what has been examined.

How the BPP Learning Media Learning & Practice Workbook can help you pass – Help yourself study for your AIA exams – Syllabus – Command words and learning outcomes – The exam paper

Part A The financial environment
1 Financial management and financial objectives 3
2 Sources of finance..29
3 Capital markets and government policy..63

Part B Capital requirements and consequent costs
4 Strategic planning and financial management 89
5 Financial planning and forecasting..103
6 The cost of capital 135
7 Dividend policy 155

Part C The investment decision
8 Investment decisions...173
9 Risk and portfolio theory 207
10 The capital asset pricing model...225
11 Capital structure and advanced valuation techniques 243
12 Appraisal of overseas investment decisions..281

Part D Valuation and corporate change
13 Valuation of companies...299
14 Mergers and acquisitions..339
15 Corporate reorganisation..359

Part E International finance and interest rate risk
16 Foreign currency risk...375
17 Foreign currency risk: options..417
18 Interest rate risk..441
19 Swaps...467

Part F Working capital management
20 Management of working capital...479
21 The management of receivables and payables 497
22 The management of inventories and cash..525

	Page
Answers to end of chapter questions	551
Practice Exam question bank	599
Practice Exam answer bank	629
Exam question bank	671
Exam answer bank	699
Mock exam	739
Index	763

How the BPP Learning Media Learning & Practice Workbook can help you pass

> It provides you with the knowledge and understanding, skills and application techniques you need to be successful in your exams

This Learning & Practice Workbook has been targeted at the **Financial Management** syllabus.

- It is **comprehensive**. It covers the syllabus content. No more, no less.
- It is written at the **right level**. Each chapter is written with AIA's syllabus in mind.
- It is aimed at the **exam**. We have taken account of recent exams, guidance the examiner has given and the assessment methodology.

> It allows you to study in the way that best suits your learning style and the time you have available, by following your personal Study Plan (see page vii)

You may be studying at home on your own or you may be attending a course. You may like to read every word, or you may prefer to do a fast read through and learn through doing practice questions the rest of the time. However you study, you will find the BPP Learning Media Learning & Practice Workbook meets your needs in designing and following your personal Study Plan.

Help yourself study for your AIA exams

Exams for professional bodies such as AIA are very different from those you have taken at college or university. You will be under **greater time pressure before** the exam – as you may be combining your study with work. Here are some hints and tips.

The right approach

1 **Develop the right attitude**

Believe in yourself	Yes, there is a lot to learn. But thousands have succeeded before and you can too.
Remember why you're doing it	You are studying for a good reason: to advance your career.

2 **Focus on the exam**

Read through the Syllabus	This tells you what you are expected to know and is supplemented by **Exam focus points** in the text.
Study the Exam paper section	Past papers are likely to be good guides to what you should expect in the exam.

3 **The right method**

See the whole picture	Keeping in mind how all the detail you need to know fits into the whole picture will help you understand it better. • The **Introduction** of each chapter puts the material in context. • The **Syllabus content** and **Exam focus points** show you what you need to **grasp**.
Use your own words	To absorb the information (and to practise your written communication skills), you need to **put it into your own words**. • **Take notes**. • Answer the **questions** in each chapter. • Draw **mindmaps**. • Try **'teaching' a subject** to a colleague or friend.
Give yourself cues to jog your memory	The Learning & Practice Workbook uses **bold** to **highlight key points**. • Try **colour coding** with a highlighter pen. • Write **key points** on cards.

4 **The right recap**

Review, review, review	Regularly reviewing a topic in summary form can **fix it in your memory**. The Learning & Practice Workbook helps you review in many ways. • **Chapter roundups** summarise the 'Fast forward' key points in each chapter. Use them to recap each study session. • The **Quick quiz** actively tests your grasp of the essentials. • Go through the **Examples** in each chapter a second or third time.

Developing your personal Study Plan

BPP recommends that you follow a study plan. Planning and sticking to the plan are key elements of learning successfully. There are five steps you should work through.

Step 1 **How do you learn?**

What types of intelligence do you display when learning? You might be advised to brush up on certain study skills before launching into this Learning & Practice Workbook, but refer to the 'tackling your studies' section below which will help.

Step 2 **What do you prefer to do first?**

If you prefer to get to grips with a theory before seeing how it is applied, we suggest you concentrate first on the explanations we give in each chapter before looking at the examples and case studies. If you prefer to see first how things work in practice, read through the detail in each chapter, and concentrate on the examples and case studies, before supplementing your understanding by reading the detail.

Step 3 **How much time do you have?**

Work out the time you have available per week, given the following:

- The standard you have set yourself
- The other exam(s) you are sitting
- Practical matters such as work, travel, exercise, sleep and social life

Note your time available in box A.   A [   ] Hours

Step 4 **Allocate your time**

- Take the time you have available per week for this Learning & Practice Workbook shown in box A, multiply it by the number of weeks available and insert the result in box B.   B [   ]

- Divide the figure in box B by the number of chapters in this text and insert the result in box C.   C [   ]

Remember that this is only a rough guide. Some of the chapters in this book are longer and more complicated than others, and you will find some subjects easier to understand than others.

Step 5 **Implement**

Set about studying each chapter in the time shown in box C, following the key study steps in the order suggested by your particular learning style.

This is your personal **Study Plan**. You should try to combine it with the study sequence outlined below. You may want to modify the sequence to adapt it to your **personal style**.

Tackling your studies

The best way to approach this Learning & Practice Workbook is to tackle the chapters in order. Taking into account your individual learning style, you could follow this sequence for each chapter.

Key study steps	Activity
Step 1 **Topic list**	This topic list helps you navigate each chapter; each numbered topic is a numbered section in the chapter.
Step 2 **Introduction**	This sets your objectives for study by giving you the big picture in terms of the context of the chapter. The content is referenced to the syllabus, and Exam guidance shows how the topic is likely to be examined. The Introduction tells you **why** the topics covered in the chapter need to be studied.
Step 3 **Fast forward**	Fast forward boxes give you a quick summary of the content of each of the main chapter sections. They are listed together in the roundup at the end of each chapter to help you review each chapter quickly.
Step 4 **Explanations**	Proceed methodically through each chapter, particularly focusing on areas highlighted as significant in the chapter introduction, or areas that are frequently examined.
Step 5 **Key terms and Exam focus points**	• Key terms are definitions of important concepts that you really need to know and understand before the exam. • Exam focus points highlight areas or topics that may be examined.
Step 6 **Note taking**	Take brief notes, if you wish. Don't copy out too much. Remember that being able to record something yourself is a sign of being able to understand it. Your notes can be in whatever format you find most helpful; lists, diagrams, mindmaps.
Step 7 **Examples**	Work through the examples very carefully as they illustrate key knowledge and techniques.
Step 8 **Case studies**	Study each one, and try to add flesh to them from your own experience. They are designed to show how the topics you are studying come alive in the real world.
Step 9 **Questions**	Attempt each one, as they will illustrate how well you've understood what you've read.
Step 10 **Answers**	Check yours against ours, and make sure you understand any discrepancies.
Step 11 **Chapter roundup**	Review it carefully, to make sure you have grasped the significance of all the important points in the chapter.
Step 12 **Quick quiz**	Use the Quick quiz to check how much you have remembered of the topics covered and to practise questions in a variety of formats.
Step 13 **Question practice**	Attempt the quick quiz and end of chapter question(s) suggested at the very end of each chapter. These are designed for you to confirm some of the key concepts set out in each chapter. Some of these questions are designed to cover more than one topic area to develop your ability to apply syllabus learning. You can then attempt the questions related to this chapter which are contained in the question bank at the end of this Learning & Practice Workbook.

AIA Achieve Academy

AIA provides a distance learning course of study AIA Achieve Academy, which offers students the tools, resources and learning environment to study for the exams. The study tools include a course of study e-book, marked practice questions, marked mock exam paper and feedback and technical advice via an e-Tutor. Contact the Study Support team at: Achieve@aiaworldwide.com.

Moving on...

When you are ready to start revising, you should still refer back to this Learning & Practice Workbook.

- As a source of **reference** (you should find the index particularly helpful for this)
- As a way to **review** (the Fast forwards, Exam focus points, Chapter roundups and Quick quizzes help you here)

PQ Qualification Syllabus

The assessment requirements in the AIA exams at the Foundation, Professional 1 and 2 stages reflect a progression of cognitive levels which successful students are expected to demonstrate in satisfying each stage of the qualification. The levels progress from an emphasis on 'knowledge and comprehension' at the Foundation stage, to a predominance of 'application and analysis' at the subsequent Professional 1 and 2 stages and incorporate 'synthesis and evaluation' at the Professional 2 stage.

Indicative weightings for the cognitive levels at each stage of the qualification are defined in the following table.

Stage of qualification	Cognitive levels of learning*			Associated learning outcomes
	Knowledge and comprehension	Application and Analysis	Synthesis and evaluation	
Foundation Level	90%	10%	0%	Outcomes consistent with the International Education Standards Board (IAESB) standards
Professional 1 Level	50%	50%	0%	
Professional 2 Level	10%	70%	20%	

*The cognitive levels of learning are associated with the following:

'Knowledge and comprehension' refer to

The acquisition of concepts, ideas, terms, facts, practices and techniques in accounting and related disciplines and understanding of how they relate to the conduct, management, reporting and assessment of the activities of business and other organisations.

'Application and analysis' refer to

The ability to apply knowledge and comprehension to actual circumstances and situations and to identify constituent components involved (concepts, ideas, terms, facts, practices, and techniques) and the relationship between these elements.

'Synthesis and evaluation' refer to

The ability to bring together a variety of components in order to form a coherent whole, and to form judgements about the application of and value of those components in a particular context or for a particular purpose.

Professional 2 Level Syllabus

Business and Financial Management

The Business and Financial Management paper develops the student's knowledge and skills from those covered in the Management Accounting paper and Professional 1 Level, and the related elements of the Foundation level. It covers the financing and capital requirements of organisation, investment decisions, valuation, international aspects of finance and working capital management. The approach relates the work and contribution of the accountant to situations that are characterised by high levels of ambiguity, uncertainty and complexity.

The coverage of the paper is consistent with the relevant learning outcomes relating to financing, investment and valuation included in IES 2 Intermediate Standard for Finance and Financial Management.

In designing the syllabus and the related examination papers AIA has employed 'intended learning outcomes' as the means to communicate expectations to potential students and stakeholders and to inform the specification requirements to be tested in the assessment of students.

The use of learning outcomes:

- Is consistent with what is commonly acknowledged as good practice in the higher education sector; and

- Is consistent with the approach embodied in International Accounting Education Standards

At the Professional 2 Levels students are expected to demonstrate that they are able to achieve the following:

Intended Learning Outcomes[1] – Description of expectations	
Professional 2 level	At the Professional 2 level students are expected to demonstrate that they: • Can critically evaluate current issues and developments relevant to accounting and related practices • Are able to integrate knowledge, understanding and technical ability from different areas of accounting and related practices to analyse situations, make judgements and recommend actions • Understand fundamental principles and concepts underpinning accounting and related practices in organisations and can discuss the conceptual rationale that provides the basis for those practices • Understand the role of accounting and related practices within the financial and governance context of organisations • Are able to apply relevant regulations and standards in accounting, auditing, law and taxation • Know and can execute basic recording and measurement techniques relevant to accounting, management and assurance • Are able to analyse financial information and interpret it for the purpose of supporting decision making

---

[1] The description of the levels of proficiency supports the IAESBs use of learning outcomes in its International Education Standards (IESs) 2, 3, and 4.

Relationship to Qualification Structure

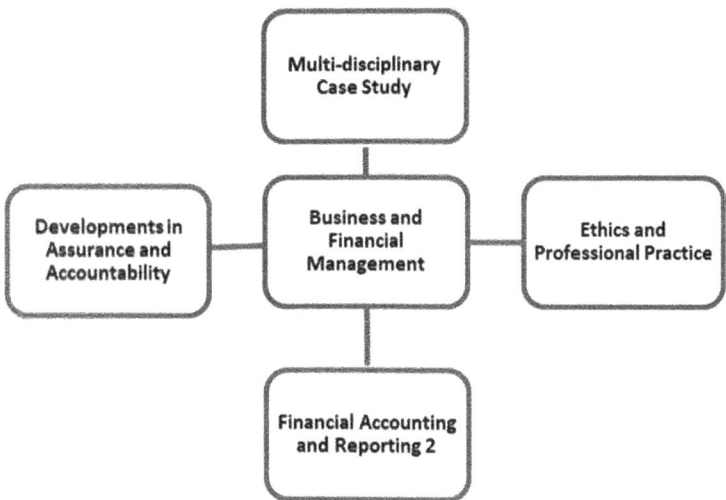

Aims

The aim of this paper is to develop and examine the candidate's ability:

- To determine the capital requirements of an organisation
- To apply in the context of financial decision making, a critical understanding of the deployment of financial resources and the long-term impact
- To analyse and evaluate the economic and financial consequences of strategic and operational decisions of business organisation, including those of a global level

Business and Financial Management Learning Outcomes

In order to successfully complete this paper candidates will demonstrate that they are able to:

1. Apply an understanding of the role of the financial manager in determining capital requirements, capital structure, dividend policy and its implications in the capital markets along with managing relationships with relevant stakeholders
2. Critically appraise long-term investments
3. Critically appraise corporate valuations and change
4. Critically appraise the economic and financial consequences of global company operations
5. Critically appraise the working capital management practices of organisations and make appropriate recommendations

Structure of the Paper

Assessment is by a three-hour 15-minute examination (including 15 minutes reading time) consisting of four compulsory questions.

Question 1 will contain a scenario-based question worth 40 marks. Three further questions, each worth 20 marks, will be set.

Normally approximately 70% of the paper will be computational. The remainder (approximately 30%) will be narrative discussion based. Individual questions may have both computational and essay elements.

Relationship to Qualification Structure

Business and Financial Management builds upon the knowledge required for the preceding Management Accounting paper at the Professional 1 Level and the Management Accounting and Business Management components at the Foundation Level Unit. It provides the basis for the subsequent Multi-disciplinary Case Study.

Ethics

Emphasis on ethical issues is made throughout the syllabus, many questions will have an ethical component and the coverage of the paper is consistent with the relevant learning outcomes in IES 4 Professional Values, Ethics and Attitudes.

Recommended reading

This reading list is recommended and not essential for your studies.

You can purchase any of the books listed quickly and easily on the AIA website www.aiaworldwide.com/books

AIA Magazine – International Accountant
ISSN: 14655144

AIA Learning & Practice Workbook
Business and Financial Management
Publisher: BPP Learning Media
ISBN: 9781509732142

Corporate Finance and Investment (9th Edition)
Authors: Pike, R and Neale, B, Linsley, P
Publisher: Pearson Education Limited
ISBN: 9781292208541

Corporate Financial Management (6th Edition)
Author: Arnold, G
Publisher: Pearson Education Limited
ISBN: 9781292140445

International Financial Management (10th Edition) (e-book version)
Author: Shapiro, A and Moles, P
Publisher: John Wiley & Sons
ISBN: 9781118929322

Command words

The following list contains active command words appropriate for use at the Professional 2 level of the AIA qualification. Reference to the command words is essential to understanding how the assessment is applied in AIA exams.

Cognitive Levels of Learning	Command Words	Definitions
Professional 2 Synthesis and Evaluation 20% Application and Analysis 70% Knowledge and Comprehension 10%	Appraise	Assess the worth, value, or quality of
	Assess	Determine the strength, weakness and significance
	Calculate/Compute	Select the appropriate method and techniques and apply your knowledge and understandings to work out and show how figures were arrived at
	Critically Analyse	Examine in detail using arguments for and against, and develop a view
	Develop	Elaborate or expand in detail
	Evaluate	Determine the value in light of arguments for and against
	Integrate	Combine information and/or standards and theory from different accounting disciplines or different parts of the case study to provide holistic professional recommendations or conclusions
	Justify	Demonstrate the correctness of an action, claim or conduct
	Prepare	To make or get ready for use
	Recommend	Advise the appropriate action in terms the recipient will understand
	Report	Give an account of the results of the investigation

PART A

The financial environment

Financial management and financial objectives

Topic list	Syllabus reference
1 The scope of financial management	LO1
2 Financial objectives and the relationship with corporate strategy	LO1
3 Non-financial objectives	LO1
4 Stakeholders in a company	LO1
5 The economic environment	LO1
6 Impact of taxation	LO1
7 Not for profit organisations	LO1
8 Financial management decisions	LO1

Introduction

Starting with this chapter and throughout this Text, we examine the work of the financial manager and the framework within which the financial manager operates. After introducing the **scope of financial management**, we consider the **objectives** of organisations.

1 The scope of financial management

FAST FORWARD

Financial management decisions cover **investment** decisions, **financing decisions** and **dividend** decisions.

1.1 What is financial management?

Financial management can be defined as the management of the finances of an organisation in order to achieve the financial objectives of the organisation. The usual assumption in financial management for the private sector is that the objective of the company is to **maximise shareholders' wealth**. Broadly, there are two aspects of financial management: **financial planning** and **financial control**.

1.2 Financial planning

The financial manager will need to **plan** to ensure that enough funding is available at the right time to meet the needs of the organisation for short, medium and long-term capital.

(a) In the short term, funds may be needed to pay for purchases of inventories, or to smooth out changes in debtors (receivables), creditors (payables) and cash: the financial manager is here ensuring that **working capital requirements** are met.

(b) In the medium or long term, the organisation may have planned purchases of **non-current assets** such as plant and equipment, for which the financial manager must ensure that **funding** is available.

The financial manager contributes to decisions on the uses of funds raised by **analysing financial data** to **determine uses** which meet the **organisation's financial objectives.** Is Project A to be preferred to Project B? Should a new asset be bought or leased?

1.3 Financial control

The **control** function of the financial manager becomes relevant for funding which has been raised. Are the various activities of the organisation meeting its objectives? Are assets being used efficiently? To answer these questions, the financial manager may **compare data** on **actual performance** with **forecast performance**. Forecast data will have been prepared in the light of past performance (historical data) modified to reflect expected future changes. Future changes may include the effects of economic development, for example an economic recovery leading to a forecast upturn in revenues.

1.4 Financial management decisions

The financial manager makes decisions relating to **investment**, **financing** and **dividends**.

Investments in assets must be **financed** somehow. Financial management is also concerned with the **management of short-term funds** and with how funds can be raised over the long term.

As part of the financing decision, the company may decide to retain profits for future investment. The other side of this decision is that if profits are retained, there is less to pay out to shareholders as dividends, which might deter investors. An appropriate balance needs to be struck in addressing the **dividend decision**: how much of its profits should the company pay out as dividends and how much should it retain for investment to provide for future growth and new investment opportunities?

We shall be looking at various aspects of the investment, financing and dividend decisions of financial management over the rest of the Learning & Practice Workbook.

Examples of different types of investment decision	
Decisions **internal** to the business enterprise	• Whether to undertake new projects • Whether to invest in new plant and machinery • Research and development decisions • Investment in a marketing or advertising campaign
Decisions involving **external parties**	• Whether to carry out a takeover or a merger involving another business • Whether to engage in a joint venture with another enterprise
Disinvestment decisions	• Whether to sell off unprofitable segments of the business • Whether to sell old or surplus plant and machinery • The sale of subsidiary companies

Question — Disposal of surplus assets

'The financial manager should identify surplus assets and dispose of them'. Why?

Answer

A surplus asset is one that earns no return for the business. The business is likely to be paying the 'cost of capital' in respect of the money tied up in the asset, ie the money which it can realise by selling it.

If surplus assets are sold, the business may be able to invest the cash released in more productive ways, or alternatively it may use the cash to cut its liabilities. Either way, it will enhance the return on capital employed for the business as a whole.

Although selling surplus assets yields short-term benefits, the business should not jeopardise its activities in the medium or long term by disposing of productive capacity until the likelihood of it being required in the future has been fully assessed.

2 Financial objectives and the relationship with corporate strategy

> **FAST FORWARD**
>
> **Strategy** is a course of action to achieve an objective. There are three main levels of strategy in an organisation.
>
> • Corporate: the general direction of the whole organisation
> • Business: how the organisation or its business units tackle particular markets
> • Operational/functional: specific strategies for different departments of the business

2.1 Strategy

Strategy may be defined as a course of action, including the specification of resources required, to achieve a specific objective.

Strategy can be **short term** or **long term**, depending on the time horizon of the objective it is intended to achieve.

This definition also indicates that since strategy depends on objectives or targets, the obvious starting point for a study of strategy is the **identification and formulation of objectives**.

Key term

> **Corporate strategy** is concerned with the overall purpose and scope of the organisation and how value will be added to the different parts (business units) of the organisation. **(Johnson, Scholes and Whittington)**

2.2 Corporate objectives

> **FAST FORWARD**
>
> **Corporate objectives** are relevant for the organisation as a whole, relating to key factors for business success.

Corporate objectives are those which are concerned with the firm as a whole. Objectives should be **explicit**, **quantifiable** and **capable of being achieved**. The corporate objectives outline the expectations of the firm and the strategic planning process is concerned with the means of achieving the objectives.

Objectives should relate to the **key factors for business success**, which are typically as follows.

- Profitability (return on investment)
- Market share
- Growth
- Cash flow
- Customer satisfaction
- The quality of the firm's products
- Industrial relations
- Added value

2.3 Financial objectives

> **FAST FORWARD**
>
> In financial management of businesses, the key objective is the **maximisation of shareholders' wealth**.

2.3.1 The prime financial objective of a company

The theory of company finance is based on the assumption that the objective of management is to **maximise the market value of the company's shares**. Specifically, the main objective of a company should be to maximise the wealth of its **ordinary shareholders**.

A company is financed by ordinary shareholders, preference shareholders, loan stock holders and other long-term and short-term creditors. All surplus funds, however, belong to the legal owners of the company, its ordinary shareholders. Any retained profits are undistributed wealth of these equity shareholders.

However, a company will need to ensure that, as it attempts to maximise shareholder wealth, it does not take undesirable actions such as:

- neglecting the importance of risk management
- behaving unethically, for example by using suppliers that employ unethical working practices
- creating waste or pollution that has a damaging environmental impact.

In any case, these actions may damage shareholder wealth in the **long-term** because of their impact on a company's stability and reputation.

This area is considered further in the discussion of sustainability in section 3.

2.3.2 Measuring wealth and value

If the financial objective of a company is to maximise the value of the company, and in particular the value of its ordinary shares, we need to be able to put values on a company and its shares. How do we do it? Three possible methods of valuation might occur to us.

Methods of company valuation	
Going concern basis	Based on the company's statement of financial position. Rising retained profits is an indication of potential dividends
Break-up basis	Only of interest if company is threatened with insolvency, or if individual assets are being sold to raise cash
Market values	Trading prices of stocks and shares, most relevant to financial objectives. Shareholders' return on investment comes from dividends received and increases in market value of shares (determined by expectations of future dividends)

The **wealth** of the shareholders in a company comes from **dividends** received and the **market value** of the shares. A shareholder's **return on investment** is obtained in the form of dividends received and capital gains from increases in the market value of his or her shares.

Dividends are most commonly paid by UK listed companies just twice a year at most, whereas a current market value is always known from share prices. There is also a theory that market prices are influenced strongly by expectations of what future dividends will be. So we might conclude that the wealth of shareholders in quoted companies can be **measured** by the **market value** of the shares.

2.3.3 How is the value of a business increased?

If a company's shares are traded on a stock market, the wealth of shareholders is increased when the share price goes up. The price of a company's shares will go up when the company makes attractive profits, which it pays out as dividends or re-invests in the business to achieve future profit growth and dividend growth. However, to increase the share price the company should achieve its profits without taking business risks and financial risks which worry shareholders.

If there is an increase in earnings and dividends, management can hope for an increase in the share price too, so that shareholders benefit from both **higher revenue** (dividends) and also **capital gains** (higher share prices). Management should set **targets** for factors which they can influence directly, such as profits and dividend growth.

Earnings are the profits attributable to equity (that is, to ordinary shareholders) after tax. Earnings per share (EPS) are the earnings attributable to each ordinary share.

2.3.4 Financial targets

In addition to targets for earnings, EPS, and dividend per share, a company might set other financial targets:

Examples of other financial targets	
Restriction on gearing	Ratio of debt: equity should not exceed a certain level or finance costs should not be higher than a certain percentage of profit from operations
Profit retentions	Dividend cover (Profit for the year: Dividends) should exceed a certain level
Profit from operations	Target profit from operations: profit margin, (level of profit as a percentage of revenue) or minimum return on capital employed
Cash generation	As well as generating profits, businesses need to generate enough cash to ensure they remain liquid
Value added	Creation of economic value for shareholders, to be discussed later in this text

LEARNING OUTCOME 1 THE FINANCIAL ENVIRONMENT AND CAPITAL REQUIREMENTS AND CONSEQUENT COSTS

These financial targets are not primary financial objectives, but they can act as subsidiary targets or constraints which should help a company to achieve its main financial objective without incurring excessive risks.

2.3.5 Short-term and long-term targets

Targets are usually measured over a year rather than over the long term, and it is the **maximisation of shareholder wealth** in the **long term** that ought to be the **corporate objective**. Short-term measures of return can encourage a company to pursue short-term objectives at the expense of long-term ones, for example by deferring new capital investments, or spending only small amounts on research and development or on training.

2.3.6 Multiple financial targets

A major problem with setting a number of **different financial targets** is that they might not all be consistent with each other, and so might not all be achievable at the same time. When this happens, some compromises will have to be accepted.

2.3.7 Example: Financial targets

Lion Grange has recently introduced a formal scheme of long range planning. Sales in the current year reached $10,000,000, and forecasts for the next five years are $10,600,000, $11,400,000, $12,400,000, $13,600,000 and $15,000,000. The ratio of net profit after tax to sales is 10%, and this is expected to continue throughout the planning period. Total assets less current liabilities will remain at around 125% of sales.

It was suggested at a recent board meeting that:

(a) If profits rise, dividends should rise by at least the same percentage

(b) An earnings retention rate of 50% should be maintained

(c) The ratio of long-term borrowing to long-term funds (debt plus equity) is limited (by the market) to 30%, which happens also to be the current gearing level of the company

You are required to prepare a financial analysis of the draft long range plan.

Solution

The draft financial plan, for profits, dividends, assets required and funding, can be drawn up in a table, as follows.

	Current Year $m	Year 1 $m	Year 2 $m	Year 3 $m	Year 4 $m	Year 5 $m
Sales	10.00	10.60	11.40	12.40	13.60	15.00
Net profit after tax	1.00	1.06	1.14	1.24	1.36	1.50
Dividends (50% of profit after tax)	0.50	0.53	0.57	0.62	0.68	0.75
Total assets less current liabilities	12.50	13.25	14.25	15.50	17.00	18.75
Equity (increased by retained earnings)	8.75	9.28	9.85	10.47	11.15	11.90
Maximum debt (30% of long-term funds, or 3/7 × equity)	3.75	3.98	4.22	4.49	4.78	5.10
Funds available	12.50	13.26	14.07	14.96	15.93	17.00
(Shortfalls) in funds *	0	0	(0.18)	(0.54)	(1.07)	(1.75)

* Given maximum gearing of 30% and no new issue of shares = funds available minus net assets required.

Dividends and gearing

Suggest policies on dividends, retained earnings and gearing for Lion Grange, using the data above.

Answer

The financial objectives of the company are not compatible with each other. Adjustments will have to be made.

(a) Given the assumptions about sales, profits, dividends and net assets required, there will be an **increasing shortfall of funds** from Year 2 onwards, unless new shares are issued or the gearing level rises above 30%.

(b) In Years 2 and 3, the shortfall can be eliminated by **retaining a greater percentage** of profits, but this may have a serious **adverse effect** on the share price. In Year 4 and Year 5, the shortfall in funds cannot be removed even if dividend payments are reduced to nothing.

(c) The **net asset turnover** appears to be **low**. The situation would be eased if investments were able to generate a higher volume of sales, so that fewer fixed assets and less working capital would be required to support the projected level of sales.

(d) If asset turnover cannot be improved, it may be possible to **increase the profit to sales ratio** by reducing costs or increasing selling prices.

(e) If a new issue of shares is proposed to make up the shortfall in funds, the amount of funds required must be considered very carefully. Total **dividends** would have to be **increased** in order to pay dividends on the new shares. The company seems unable to offer prospects of suitable dividend payments, and so raising new equity might be difficult.

(f) It is conceivable that extra funds could be raised by issuing new debt capital, so that the level of gearing would be over 30%. It is uncertain whether investors would be prepared to lend money so as to increase gearing. If more funds were borrowed, profits after interest and tax would fall so that the share price might also be reduced.

3 Non-financial objectives

FAST FORWARD

Non-financial objectives such as welfare, service provision, strengthening the brand of the company and fulfilment of social responsibilities are also important for businesses.

3.1 Importance of non-financial objectives

An enterprise may have important non-financial objectives, either because these objectives support the achievement of financial objectives (eg % items produced that are defective or the number of customer complaints) or because they reflect the growing importance of environmental, social and governance issues to shareholders, customers, suppliers and employees.

Non-financial objectives

Before looking at what follows, write out your own list of the various non-financial objectives which an enterprise might have.

Examples of non-financial objectives are as follows.

Non-financial objectives	
Welfare of employees	Competitive wages and salaries, comfortable and safe working conditions, good training and career development
Welfare of management	High salaries, company cars, perks
Welfare of society	Concern for environment
Provision of service to minimum standard	For example regulations affecting utility (water, electricity providers)
Responsibilities to customers	Providing quality products or services, fair dealing
Responsibilities to suppliers	Not exploiting power as buyer unscrupulously
Leadership in research and development	Failure to innovate may have adverse long-term financial consequences
Maintaining competitive position and market share	Preventing rivals from becoming too large and enjoying benefits of size such as economies of scale

One important aspect of non-financial performance relates to **sustainability** issues. The concept of **sustainable development** is defined in the Brundtland report as 'development that meets the needs of the present without compromising the ability of future generations to meet their own needs.'

Sustainable development recognises that without the environment, businesses and society could not exist and that businesses have a **corporate responsibility** to take the needs of their wider stakeholders into account.

One approach to measuring sustainability is to consider a company's performance across a range of environmental, social and governance issues. These are defined in the following table.

Definition of ESG objectives	
Environmental objectives	Relating to the company's impact on the environment eg waste, energy, pollution.
Social objectives	Relating to the how well a company treats its employees, customers, suppliers and local communities. This includes the company's policies on diversity, inclusion and human rights.
Governance objectives	Relating to how a company is governed, including internal controls, risk management and business ethics.

This framework is considered further in the remaining parts of Section 3.

3.2 The relationship between financial and non-financial objectives

Non-financial objectives do not negate financial objectives, but they do mean that the simple theory of company finance, that the objective of a firm is to maximise the wealth of ordinary shareholders, is too simplistic.

If a company only focusses on financial objectives, this may have a damaging impact on non-financial objectives. Here are a few examples based around the ESG framework:

Examples of the impact of financial performance measures on non-financial objectives	
Environmental objectives	Issues relating to the impact of a company's activities on the environment may be neglected leading to biodiversity loss, higher greenhouse gas (GHG) emissions etc

Examples of the impact of financial performance measures on non-financial objectives	
Social objectives	Issues relating to the rights, well-being and interests of people and communities may be overlooked, such as labour standards in the supply chain and workplace health and safety.
Governance objectives	Issues relating to how a company is governed, including executive pay and business ethics, will be relegated in importance. If financial targets are the only concern, then it is more likely that a company will start to take excessive risks (eg ignoring safety protocols in order to reduce costs) to achieve profit targets.

Financial factors may have to be compromised in order to satisfy non-financial objectives in the short term. However, in the long-term non-financial objectives are usually designed, at least in part, to support the financial objectives.

3.3 A framework for non-financial reporting

Key performance indicators (KPIs) are often used by management to measure a company's performance against its non-financial objectives. Companies can also report on KPIs in their annual reports in addition to the core financial statements. This is common for larger companies (and mandatory for UK quoted companies).

Companies can also report on their sustainability using key performance indicators covering a range of ESG indicators, for example:

Examples of the impact of ESG KPIs	
Environmental	<ul><li>Energy consumption</li><li>Total water consumption</li><li>Greenhouse Gas ("GHG") emissions</li><li>Waste generated</li><li>Pollutants and effluents released</li><li>Recycling: recycled materials used in production, recycled of end-of-life products</li></ul>
Social	<ul><li>Employee turnover overall, by department, by age and gender</li><li>Average training hours per employee split by gender, seniority and role</li><li>Occupational Health & Safety. Fatalities, high consequence injuries.</li><li>Employee satisfaction survey results</li><li>Supplier satisfaction survey results</li></ul>
Governance	<ul><li>Diversity of board directors by age, gender</li><li>Board member expertise</li><li>Number of staff trained in anti-bribery policies</li></ul>

Reporting of KPIs, sustainability reporting and integrated reporting are optional in most countries but mandatory for certain types of companies in certain counties and are increasingly seen as being important by investors and sometimes also by customers, suppliers and employees.

Exam focus point

Look out in investment appraisal questions for details of non-financial objectives. If a company is for example aiming to respect the interests of stakeholders and operate to the highest ethical standards, this could impact upon the investments it undertakes.

LEARNING OUTCOME 1 THE FINANCIAL ENVIRONMENT AND CAPITAL REQUIREMENTS AND CONSEQUENT COSTS

4 Stakeholders in a company

FAST FORWARD

> **Stakeholders** are individuals or groups who are affected by the activities of the firm. They can be classified as **internal** (employees and managers), **connected** (shareholders, customers and suppliers) and **external** (local communities, pressure groups, government).

Key term

> There is a variety of different groups or individuals whose interests are directly affected by the activities of a firm. These groups or individuals are referred to as **stakeholders** in the firms.

The various stakeholder groups in a firm can be classified as follows.

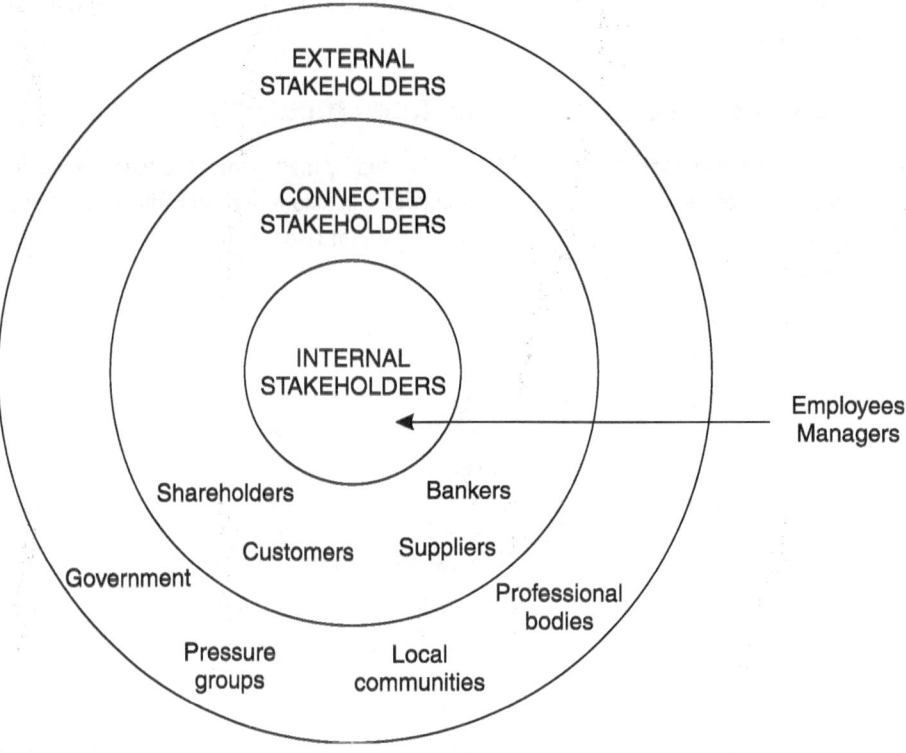

Exam focus point

> You may be told in a question that a company aims to respect the interests of stakeholders, and determines its policies in the light of that aim. You will see at various times in this text circumstances when stakeholder interests become particularly important, for example in a merger and acquisition situation.

4.1 Objectives of stakeholder groups

The various groups of stakeholders in a firm will have different goals which will depend in part on the situation of the organisation.

Stakeholder goals	
Shareholders	Providers of risk capital, aim to maximise wealth
Suppliers	Often other businesses, aim to be paid full amount by date agreed, but want to continue long-term trading relationship, and so may accept later payment
Long-term lenders	Wish to receive payments of interest and capital on loan by due date for repayment
Employees	Maximise rewards paid to them in salaries and benefits, also prefer continuity in employment
Government	Political objectives such as sustained economic growth and high employment
Management	Maximising their own rewards

Exam focus point: You might be asked to comment on a situation where the interests of different stakeholders diverge.

4.2 Stakeholder groups and strategy

The actions of stakeholder groups in pursuit of their various goals can exert influence on strategy. The greater the power of the stakeholder, the greater his influence will be. Each stakeholder group will have different expectations about what it wants, and the **expectations of the various groups may conflict**. Each group, however, will influence strategic decision-making.

4.3 Shareholders and management

Although ordinary shareholders (equity shareholders) are the owners of the company to whom the board of directors are accountable, the actual powers of shareholders tend to be restricted, except in companies where the shareholders are also the directors. The **day-to-day** running of a company is the responsibility of **management.** Although the company's results are submitted for shareholders' approval at the annual general meeting (AGM), there is often apathy and acquiescence in directors' recommendations.

Shareholders are often ignorant about their company's current situation and future prospects. They have no right to inspect the books of account, and their forecasts of future prospects are gleaned from the annual report and accounts, stockbrokers, investment journals and daily newspapers. The relationship between management and shareholders is sometimes referred to as an **agency relationship**, in which managers act as agents for the shareholders.

Key term

Agency relationship: a description of the relationship between management and shareholders expressing the idea that managers act as agents for the shareholder, using delegated powers to run the company in the shareholders' best interests.

However, if managers hold none or very few of the equity shares of the company they work for, what is to stop them from working inefficiently or not bothering to look for profitable new investment opportunities **or** giving themselves high salaries and perks?

One power that shareholders possess is the right to **remove** the **directors** from office. However shareholders have to take the initiative to do this, and in many companies, the shareholders lack the energy and organisation to take such a step. Even so, directors will want the company's report and accounts, and the proposed final dividend, to meet with shareholders' approval at the AGM.

Another reason why managers might do their best to improve the financial performance of their company is that managers' pay is often related to the size or profitability of the company. Managers in very big companies, or in very profitable companies, will normally expect to earn higher salaries than managers in smaller or less successful companies. There is also an argument for giving managers some **performance-related pay**, or providing incentives which are related to profits or share price.

The **advantages** of having a **wide range of shareholders** include the following:

(a) There is likely to be **greater activity** in the market in the firm's shares.

(b) There is less likelihood of one shareholder having a **controlling interest**.

(c) Since shareholdings are smaller on average, there is likely to be **less effect** on the **share price** if one shareholder sells his holding.

(d) There is a **greater likelihood** of a **takeover** bid being **frustrated**.

Disadvantages of a large number of shareholders include the following.

(a) **Administrative costs** will be **high**. These include the costs of sending out copies of the annual report and accounts, counting proxy votes, registering new shareholders and paying dividends.

(b) Shareholders will have **differing tax positions** and **objectives** in holding the firm's shares, which makes a dividend/retention policy more difficult for the management to decide upon.

4.4 Shareholders, managers and the company's long-term creditors

The relationship between long-term creditors of a company, the management and the shareholders of a company encompasses the following factors.

(a) Management may decide to raise finance for a company by taking out long-term or medium-term loans. They might well be taking **risky investment decisions** using outsiders' money to finance them.

(b) Investors who provide debt finance will rely on the company's management to generate enough net cash inflows to make **interest payments on time**, and eventually to repay loans.

However, long-term creditors will often take **security** for their loan, perhaps in the form of a fixed charge over an asset (such as a mortgage on a building). Debentures are also often subject to certain restrictive covenants, which restrict the company's rights to borrow more money until the debentures have been repaid.

If a company is unable to pay what it owes its creditors, the creditors may decide to **exercise their security** or to apply for the company to be **wound up**.

(c) The money that is provided by long-term creditors will be invested to earn profits, and the profits (in excess of what is needed to pay interest on the borrowing) will provide **extra dividends** or retained profits for the shareholders of the company. In other words, shareholders will expect to increase their wealth using creditors' money.

4.5 Shareholders, managers and government

The government does not have a direct interest in companies (except for those in which it actually holds shares). However, the government does often have a strong indirect interest in companies' affairs.

(a) **Taxation**

The government raises taxes on sales and profits and on shareholders' dividends. It also expects companies to act as tax collectors for income tax and VAT. The **tax structure** might influence investors' preferences for either dividends or capital growth.

(b) **Encouraging new investments**

The government might provide **funds** towards the cost of some investment projects. It might also encourage private investment by offering **tax incentives.**

(c) **Encouraging a wider spread of share ownership**

In the UK, the government has made some attempts to encourage more private individuals to become company shareholders, by means of **attractive privatisation issues** (such as in the electricity, gas and telecommunications industries) and tax incentives, such as individual savings accounts (ISAs) to encourage individuals to invest in shares.

(d) **Legislation**

The government also influences **companies**, and the **relationships** between shareholders, creditors, management, employees and the general public, through legislation, including the Companies Acts, legislation on employment, health and safety regulations, legislation on consumer protection and consumer rights and environmental legislation.

(e) **Economic policy**

A government's economic policy will affect business activity. For example, **exchange rate policy** will have implications for the revenues of exporting firms and for the purchase costs of importing firms. Policies on **economic growth, inflation, employment, interest rates** and so on are all relevant to business activities.

5 The economic environment

FAST FORWARD

Economic influences on the strategy of an organisation and the ability to achieve its objectives are **inflation, interest rates** and **exchange rates**. A financial manager would be expected to understand how economic factors can impact on an organisation and the effect on financial strategies. A financial manager will also be expected to manage the **financial risk** that these factors present.

5.1 Impact of inflation

Inflation can affect all the financial areas of a business and impact upon its **profit performance** in a variety of ways:

(a) The rate of inflation will **affect the prices** that a business must pay for all the factors of production and the prices that it is able to charge to its customers. It will therefore affect the level of reported profits.

(b) When inflation is high, **regular price reviews** will be necessary so as to ensure that there is no erosion of real returns. In times of low inflation it may be difficult to achieve any price increases due to a reduced level of inflationary expectations.

(c) Where there is a high level of inflation, there is also a **high level of uncertainty** about the future. This tends to make businesses wary of committing themselves to new long-term investments.

(d) Inflation places **pressure on cash flow**, particularly where the prices of raw materials are rising ahead of prices charged to customers. Even where sales prices do keep up, additional cash will still be required to cover the increased payments to suppliers that will have to be made in advance of monies being received in respect of credit sales.

(e) Companies may **increase their level of investment in inventory** as a hedge against anticipated price rises. This will also increase the amount of working capital required and restrict the funds available for new investment.

(f) Different approaches may need to be taken to **financial reporting** and evaluation methods, such as current cost accounting techniques, which make it easier to understand the changing performance of a company over time.

(g) The relationship between **inflation rates** and **interest rates** means that interest rates tend to rise during a period of inflation. This has implications both for the capital structure decisions and investment appraisal criteria used by companies.

5.2 Interest rates

Interest rates are an important element in the economic environment, and are of particular relevance for financial managers.

Interest rates are effectively the 'prices' governing lending and borrowing. The borrower pays interest to the lender at a certain percentage of the capital sum, as the price for the use of the funds borrowed. As with other prices, supply and demand effects apply. For example, the higher the rates of interest that are charged, the lower will be the demand for funds from borrowers.

(a) Interest rates **measure the cost of borrowing**. If a company wants to raise money, it must pay interest on its borrowing, and the rate of interest payable will be one which is 'current' at the time the borrowing takes place. When interest rates go up, companies will pay more interest on some of their borrowing (for example on bank overdrafts).

(b) Interest rates in a country **influence the foreign exchange value** of the country's currency.

(c) Interest rates act as a **guide to the sort of return** that a company's shareholders might want, and changes in market interest rates will affect share prices.

5.2.1 The general level of interest rates

Interest rates on any one type of financial asset will vary over time. In other words, the general level of interest rates might go up or down. The general level of interest rates is affected by several factors.

(a) **Need for a real return**

Investors normally want to **earn a 'real' rate of return** on their investment. The appropriate 'real' rate of return will depend on factors such as investment risk.

(b) **Inflation**

Nominal rates of interest should be sufficient to **cover expected rates of inflation** over the term of the investment and to provide a real return.

(c) **Uncertainty about future rates of inflation**

When investors are uncertain about inflation and therefore about what future nominal and real interest rates will be, they are likely to require **higher interest yields** to persuade them to take the risk of investing, especially in the longer term.

(d) **Liquidity preference of investors and the demand for borrowing**

Higher interest rates have to be offered to persuade savers to invest their surplus money. When the demand to borrow increases, interest rates will rise.

(e) **Balance of payments**

When a country has a continuing deficit on the current account of its balance of payments, and the authorities are unwilling to allow the exchange rate to depreciate by more than a certain amount, interest rates may have to be raised to **attract capital** into the country. The country can then finance the deficit by borrowing from abroad.

(f) **Monetary policy**

Since mid-1997, decisions over UK interest rate policy have been made by the Monetary Policy Committee of the Bank of England. The Bank of England influences very short-term money market rates by means of **open market operations**. Usually longer term money market rates, and then banks' base rates, will respond to the authorities' wish for interest rate changes. The purpose of influencing money market interest rates is to create a longer-term influence over the rate of inflation. One type of monetary policy is **Quantitative Easing**. In response to the 2008 financial crisis, the Bank of England adopted this policy which involves creating money to buy bonds from financial institutions. This aims to lower interest rates and therefore the cost of borrowing decreases, leading to increased spending, in order to bring inflation up to a target rate.

(g) **Interest rates abroad**

The rate of interest in one country will be influenced by **external factors**, such as interest rates in other countries and expectations about the exchange rate. When interest rates in overseas countries are high, interest rates on domestic currency investments must also be comparably high, if it is the intention to avoid capital transfers abroad and a fall in the exchange rate of the domestic currency.

Interest rate risk is the risk of a change in value of an interest-bearing loan or bond, arising from fluctuating interest rates. This is managed through a number of methods such as hedging the risk using interest rate options. This is covered later in the Text.

5.3 Impact of exchange rates

Exchange rates between different currencies on the world's foreign exchange markets are continually changing, and often by large amounts.

Foreign exchange rates are important for a business and its financial management because they affect:

- The cost of imports
- The value of exports
- The costs and benefits of international borrowing and lending

Changes in the value of a currency will affect the cost of goods from abroad. For example, if a consignment of goods is shipped from the USA to Germany and the invoice price is US$420,000:

- If the euro-dollar exchange rate is €1 = $1.50, the cost of the imports would be €280,000
- If the euro fell in value to €1 = $1.25, the cost of the imports would be higher, at €336,000

Changes in the value of a currency affect buying costs, companies and households alike, because a large proportion of the raw materials, components and finished goods that we consume is imported.

Exchange rates affect **exporting companies**, for similar reasons, because changes in exchange rates affect the price of exported goods to foreign buyers.

(a) **When the local currency, say the yen, goes up in value**, goods sold abroad by Japanese exporters, and invoiced in yen, will cost more to the foreign buyers (who must purchase yens with their own currency in order to pay).

(b) **When the yen falls in value,** goods sold abroad by Japanese exporters and invoiced in yen will become cheaper to foreign buyers.

To the extent that demand is influenced by price, the demand for exports will therefore vary with changes in the exchange rate.

Similarly if you are going on holiday or on a shopping trip abroad you will be interested in movements in the exchange rate. When you are buying currency, you want your own currency to appreciate as this means you will get more of the foreign currency for every unit of your own currency. For example, if £1 is worth $1.3089 and you purchased £500 worth of dollars, you would receive $654.45. However if sterling appreciated to £1 = $1.3300, you would receive $665.

However when you are exchanging foreign currency into your home currency, you want your home currency to depreciate. For example, if you came back from holiday with $50 and £1 = $1.3300, you would receive £37.59 ($50/$1.3300). If sterling depreciated to £1 = $1.3089, you would receive £38.20.

Currency risk is the risk of losses arising from fluctuating exchange rates. This is managed in a number of ways such as hedging using currency options. This is covered later in the Text.

6 Impact of taxation

FAST FORWARD

> Tax regulations are an important factor to consider in financial management. As part of maximising shareholder wealth, companies can take advantage of tax relief schemes, and have subsidiaries in countries with lower tax rates. Tax liabilities are an important factor in cash flow forecasts.

6.1 Domestic tax considerations

(a) Payment of taxes

The deadlines for payment of taxes needs to be factored into cash flow forecasts to ensure the entity has enough cash to meet the deadlines and avoid penalties. This will have an effect on a company's working capital management.

(b) Tax relief incentives

Companies can reduce their tax bill by taking advantages of tax relief schemes. For example, capital allowances (ie tax allowable depreciation) on purchases of equipment are deductible from a company's taxable profits.

Tax relief is also available for interest payments on debt finance, but not equity finance. This will be a factor in a company's financing decisions.

6.2 International tax considerations

(a) Reducing liability to international tax

A variety of approaches can be considered in order to minimise a company's liability to international tax. Some examples are given here, but in each if the approach can be easily challenged by tax authorities on the grounds of being aggressively abusive and contrived then it can't be part of an ethical or sustainable financial strategy and should not be considered.

Possible approaches	
Dividend payments	Tax considerations are a key reason for the dividend policies inside a multinational firm. For example, the parent company may reduce its overall tax liability by receiving larger amounts of dividends from subsidiaries in countries where undistributed earnings would otherwise be taxed.
Tax havens	Tax havens are countries with lenient tax rules or relatively low tax rates, which are often designed to attract foreign investment. Multinational companies may decide to shift profits to these low tax regimes for example, by exploiting transfer pricing, which is discussed below. Tax havens are discussed in further detail later in the Text.
Transfer pricing	Transfer pricing is charging for goods and services traded between group companies. This can be structured in such a way that reduces tax; whereby a company in the low tax regime charges fees, arguably at unrealistically high rates, to another group company in a higher tax jurisdiction, to effectively shift profits to the lower tax jurisdiction. For example, some companies have exploited the use of management charges and royalties between group companies to reduce tax. Company B in a low tax rate country could charge a high management fee to another group Company A in a high tax rate country. This effectively shifts profits from Company A to Company B, resulting in a lower tax charge on the profits. Many tax authorities have imposed limits on transfer prices to prevent these being exploited for tax. In a similar way, another example of profit shifting is intercompany loans. Company B in a low tax rate country could lend to Company A in a high tax rate country. Company B could charge a high rate of interest to Company A. Not only does this shift profits from Company A to Company B, it also means Company A can claim tax relief on interest payments (see thin capitalisation below).
Thin capitalisation	Excessive tax relief on interest payments is a result of thin capitalisation. A company that has a significantly higher level of debt compared to equity (normally from intra-group borrowings) than it could achieve on its own is described as thinly capitalised. This means that in theory, it can claim excessive tax relief on interest payments. However there are rules in many tax jurisdictions that limit the amount of interest that can be claimed for tax relief.

(b) General taxation issues

If a company makes investments abroad it will be liable to income tax in the home country on the profits made, the taxable amount being before the deduction of any foreign taxes. The profits may be any of the following.

- Profits of an overseas branch or agency
- Income from foreign securities, for example debentures in overseas companies
- Dividends from overseas subsidiaries
- Gains made on disposals of foreign assets

In many instances, a company will be potentially subject to overseas taxes as well as to local income tax on the same profits. However, this can be reduced by double taxation relief (DTR).

6.3 Double taxation relief (DTR)

Key term

> A **double taxation agreement** is an agreement between two countries which prevents income being taxed twice in both countries.
>
> **Witholding tax**, also called retention tax, is a governemnt requirement for the payer of an item of income to withold or deduct tax from the payment, and pay that tax to the government.

Typical provisions of double taxation agreements based on the OECD Model Agreement are as follows:

(a) DTR is given to taxpayers in their **country of residence** by way of a credit for tax suffered in the country where income arises. This may be in the form of relief for withholding tax only or, given a holding of specified size in a foreign company, for the underlying tax on the profits out of which dividends are paid.

(b) **Total exemption from tax** is given in the country where income arises in the hands of, for example:
  (i) Visiting diplomats
  (ii) Teachers on exchange programmes

(c) **Preferential rates of withholding tax** are applied to, for example, payments of rent, interest and dividends. The usual rate is frequently replaced by 15% or less.

(d) There are **exchange of information** clauses so that tax evaders can be chased internationally.

(e) There are **rules to determine** a person's residence and to prevent dual residence (tie-breaker clauses).

(f) There are **clauses** which render certain profits taxable in only one rather than both of the contracting states.

(g) There is a **non-discrimination clause** so that a country does not tax foreigners more heavily than its own nationals.

Case Study

Double taxation relief

Suppose the tax rate on profits in the Federal West Asian Republic is 20%, the UK company tax is 30%, and there is a double taxation agreement between the two countries.

A subsidiary of a UK firm operating in the Federal West Asian Republic earns the equivalent of £1 million in profit, and therefore pays £200,000 in tax on profits. When the profits are remitted to the UK, the UK parent can claim a credit of £200,000 against the full UK tax charge of £300,000, and hence will only pay £100,000 to the UK tax authorities, and therefore only pays £300,000 in total.

7 Not for profit organisations

FAST FORWARD

Not for profit and public sector organisations have their own objectives, generally concerned with achieving specified objectives effectively and efficiently.

7.1 Not for profit sectors

Although most people would know one if they saw it, there is a surprising problem in clearly defining what counts as a **not for profit (NFP) organisation**. Local authority services, for example, would not be setting objectives in order to arrive at a profit for shareholders, but nowadays they are being increasingly required to apply the same disciplines and processes as companies which are oriented towards straightforward profit goals.

Case Study

Oxfam operates around 700 shops in Britain, and these operate at a profit. The Royal Society for the Protection of Birds owns and operates an internet and mail order trading company which operates profitably and effectively.

The not for profit sector may involve a number of different kinds of organisation with, for example, differing legal status – charities, statutory bodies offering public transport or the provision of services such as leisure, health or public utilities.

The tasks of setting objectives and developing strategies and controls for their implementation can all help in improving the performance of charities and NFP organisations.

7.2 Objectives

The primary objective of many NFP organisations will be the effective provision of a service, not the creation of profit. This has implications for reporting of results. The organisation will need to be open and honest in showing how it has managed its budget and allocated funds raised. **Efficiency and effectiveness** are particularly important in the use of donated funds, but there is a danger that **resource efficiency** becomes more important than **service effectiveness**.

Here are some possible objectives for a NFP organisation:

(a) Surplus maximisation (equivalent to profit maximisation eg a charity shop)
(b) Revenue maximisation (as for a commercial business eg a charity shop)
(c) Usage maximisation (for example, leisure centre swimming pool usage)
(d) Usage targeting (matching the capacity available, for example, in a government-funded hospital)
(e) Full/partial cost recovery (minimising subsidy)
(f) Budget maximisation (maximising what is offered)
(g) Producer satisfaction maximisation (satisfying the wants of staff and volunteers)
(h) Client satisfaction maximisation (the police generating the support of the public)

Example: Performance measures for NFP

Although output of not for profit organisations is difficult to measure in a way that is generally agreed to be meaningful, it is not impossible. Outputs of a university might be measured in terms of the following.

Broader performance measures

- Proportion of total undergraduate population attending the university (by subject)
- Proportion of students graduating and classes of degrees obtained
- Amount of private sector research funds attracted
- Number of students finding employment after graduation
- Number of publications/articles produced by teaching staff

Operational performance measures

- Unit costs for each operating 'unit'
- Staff: student ratios; staff workloads
- Class sizes
- Availability of computers; good library stock
- Courses offered

7.3 Value for money

FAST FORWARD

> **Value for money** is getting the best possible combination of services from the least resources.

It is reasonable to argue that not for profit organisations **best serve society's interests** when the **gap** between the **benefits** they provide and the **cost** of providing those benefits is **greatest**. This is commonly termed **value for money** and is not dissimilar from the concept of profit maximisation, apart from the fact that society's interests are being maximised rather than profit.

Key term

> **Value for money** can be defined as getting the best possible combination of services from the least resources, which means maximising the benefits for the lowest possible cost.

This is usually accepted as requiring the application of economy, effectiveness and efficiency (sometimes known as the 3Es).

(a) **Economy** (spending money frugally)
(b) **Efficiency** (getting out as much as possible for what goes in)
(c) **Effectiveness** (getting done, by means of (a) and (b), what was supposed to be done)

More formally, these criteria can be defined as follows.

Key terms

> **Effectiveness** is the extent to which declared objectives/goals are met.
>
> **Efficiency** is the relationship between inputs and outputs.
>
> **Economy** is attaining the appropriate quantity and quality of inputs at the lowest cost to achieve a certain level of outputs.

7.4 Example: Economy, efficiency, effectiveness

(a) **Economy.** This dimension relates to the cost of inputs. Economy within a school could be measured, for example, by comparing average salaries per teacher with earlier years and budgets.

(b) **Efficiency.** The efficiency with which a school's IT laboratory is used might be measured in terms of the proportion of the school week for which it is used.

(c) **Effectiveness.** The effectiveness of a school's objective to produce quality teaching could be measured by the proportion of students going on to higher or further education.

8 Financial management decisions

FAST FORWARD

In seeking to attain the financial objectives of the organisation or enterprise, a financial manager has to make the following decisions:

- Investment
- Financing
- Dividends

8.1 Investment, financing and dividend decisions

Maximising the wealth of shareholders generally implies maximising profits consistent with long-term stability. It is often found that short-term gains must be sacrificed in the interests of the company's long-term prospects. In the context of this overall objective of financial management, there are three main types of decisions facing financial managers: **investment decisions**, **financing decisions** and **dividend decisions**.

In practice, these three areas are interconnected and should not be viewed in isolation.

8.2 Investment decisions

The financial manager will need to **identify** investment opportunities, **evaluate** them and decide on the **optimum allocation of scarce funds** available between investments.

Investment decisions may be on the undertaking of new **projects** within the existing business, the **takeover** of, or the **merger** with, another company or the **selling off** of a part of the business. Managers have to take decisions in the light of strategic considerations such as whether the business wants to **grow internally** (through investment in existing operations) or **externally** (through expansion).

The investment decision is covered in chapters 8 to 12 of this Learning & Practice Workbook.

8.3 Interaction of investment with financing and dividend decisions

Managers will need to consider whether **extra finance** will be required, and if it will be, what will be the consequences of obtaining it. They will have to consider the demands of **providers of finance**, particularly of equity shareholders who require **dividends**. Will equity shareholders be content with projects that maximise their long-term returns, or will they require a minimum return or dividend each year?

8.4 Financing decisions

Financing decisions include those for both the long term (**capital structure**) and the short term (**working capital management**).

The financial manager will need to determine the **source, cost** and effect on **risk** of the possible sources of long-term finance. A balance between **profitability** and **liquidity** (ready availability of funds if required) must be taken into account when deciding on the optimal level of short-term finance.

We shall look more at financing decisions in chapters 2, 6 and 11.

8.5 Interaction of financing with investment and dividend decisions

When taking financial decisions, managers will have to fulfil the **requirements of the providers of finance**, otherwise finance may not be made available. This may be particularly difficult in the case of equity shareholders, since dividends are paid at the company's discretion; however, if equity shareholders do not receive the dividends they want, they will look to sell their shares, the share price will fall and the company will have more difficulty raising funds from share issues in future.

Although there may be risks in obtaining extra finance, the long-term risks to the business of **failing to invest** may be even greater and managers will have to balance these up. Investment may have direct consequences for decisions involving the **management of finance**; extra working capital may be required if investments are made and sales expand as a consequence. Managers must be sensitive to this and ensure that a balance is maintained between receivables and inventory, and cash.

A further issue managers will need to consider is the **matching** of the **characteristics** of investment and finance. **Time** is a critical aspect; an investment which earns returns in the long term should be matched with finance which requires repayment in the long term.

8.6 Dividend decisions

Dividend decisions may affect the view that shareholders have of the long-term prospects of the company, and thus the **market value of the shares**. The dividend decision is covered in chapter 7.

8.7 Interaction of dividend with investment and financing decisions

The amount of surplus cash paid out as **dividends** will have a direct impact on **finance** available for **investment**. Managers have a difficult decision here; how much do they pay out to shareholders each year to keep them happy, and what level of funds do they retain in the business to invest in projects that will yield long-term income. In addition, funds available from retained profits may be needed if debt finance is likely to be unavailable, or if taking on more debt would expose the company to undesirable risks.

8.8 Impact of ESG on investment, financing and dividend decisions

We have already mentioned the growing importance of ESG issues to investors. To reflect this, a company should seek to embed ESG considerations throughout its financial management decision-making.

ESG has a number of potential implications for the investment, financing and dividend decisions.

Impact of ESG on key financial management decisions	
Investment decision	The potential impact of an investment on the environment (for example, energy consumption and pollution) is an important non-financial consideration in investment appraisal.
	This will be considered in Chapter 8.
Finance decision	Companies that transparently report ESG information are more likely to attract capital from ESG-focused investors.
	The potential use of 'green finance' should be a consideration in selecting appropriate sources of finance.
	This will be considered in Chapter 2.
Dividend decision	The potential impact of paying a dividend on sustainability will be considered in Chapter 7.

Chapter Roundup

- Financial management decisions cover **investment** decisions, **financing decisions** and **dividend** decisions.
- **Strategy** is a course of action to achieve an objective. There are three main levels of strategy in an organisation.
    - Corporate: the general direction of the whole organisation
    - Business: how the organisation or its business units tackle particular markets
    - Operational/functional: specific strategies for different departments of the business
- **Corporate objectives** are relevant for the organisation as a whole, relating to key factors for business success.
- In financial management of businesses, the key objective is the **maximisation of shareholders' wealth**.
- **Non-financial objectives** such as welfare, service provision and fulfilment of responsibilities are also important for businesses. **Sustainability issues** will often be important, and can be measured using KPIs covering Environmental, Social and Governance issues.
- **Stakeholders** are individuals or groups who are affected by the activities of the firm. They can be classified as **internal** (employees and managers), **connected** (shareholders, customers and suppliers) and **external** (local communities, pressure groups, government).
- Economic influences on strategy are **inflation, interest rates** and **exchange rates**. A financial manager would be expected to have a good understanding of how economic factors can impact on an entity and the effect on financial strategies. A financial manager will also be expected to manage the **financial risk** that these factors present.
- Tax regulations are an important factor to consider in setting financial strategy. As part of maximising shareholder wealth, companies can take advantage of tax relief schemes, and have subsidiaries in countries with lower tax rates. Tax liabilities are an important factor in cash flow forecasts.
- Not for profit and public sector organisations have their own objectives, generally concerned with achieving specified objectives effectively and efficiently.
- **Value for money** is getting the best possible combination of services from the least resources.
- In seeking to attain the financial objectives of the organisation or enterprise, a financial manager has to make the following decisions:
    - Investment
    - Financing
    - Dividends

    ESG issues should be considered in making each of these decisions.

LEARNING OUTCOME 1 THE FINANCIAL ENVIRONMENT AND CAPITAL REQUIREMENTS AND CONSEQUENT COSTS

Quick Quiz

1 Give a definition of financial management.

2 What three broad types of decision does financial management involve?

3 What main financial objective does the theory of company finance assume that a business organisation has?

4 If earnings per share fall from one year to the next, so will the level of dividends.

☐ True

☐ False

5 Tick which are stakeholder groups for a company (Tick all that apply).

Employees ☐

Ordinary shareholders ☐

The Board of Directors ☐

Trade creditors ☐

6 Which of the following is an example of a financial objective that a company might choose to pursue?

A Provision of good wages and salaries
B Restricting the level of gearing to below a specified target level
C Dealing honestly and fairly with customers on all occasions
D Producing environmentally friendly products

7 Which of the following decisions is not an investment decision?

A Whether to go ahead with an advertising campaign
B Whether to retain more profits for reinvestment in the business
C Whether to carry out a takeover of another company
D Whether to initiate a new research project

Answers to Quick Quiz

1. The management of the finances of an organisation in order to achieve the financial objectives of the organisation.
2. Investment decisions, financing decisions, dividend decisions.
3. To maximise the wealth of the company's ordinary shareholders.
4. False. Dividends may still be maintained from payments out of profits retained in earlier periods.
5. You should have ticked all four boxes.
6. B   This is a financial objective that relates to the level of risk that the company accepts.
7. B   This is the correct answer. Decisions on the level of retentions are financing decisions, not investment decisions.

    A   This is a decision that will involve the expenditure of funds in anticipation of earning additional profits. It is therefore an investment decision.

    C   A takeover would involve the outlay of additional funds with the aim of increasing group profits. It is therefore an investment decision.

    D   The research project would involve the outlay of funds now with the aim of increasing future company profits. It is therefore an investment decision.

End of chapter question

EarthCare (AIA November 2012)

EarthCare is a company that sells vegetarian food. It only sells food that is organic and it tries to promote healthy eating habits to its customers. It ensures suppliers are paid a fair price for all the food it purchases from them and prefers to buy from small, independent suppliers rather than from large multinational companies. It also tries to buy from local suppliers who are only a small distance from the company wherever possible, and avoids buying from countries with poor human rights records.

The company is a workers' co-operative which means that the company is jointly owned by all the workers. All workers are paid the same salary and there is not a conventional management structure. Work is carried out by self-managing teams of employees who will always perform more than one role within the company. This helps to broaden their skills and improves the morale of staff.

The company is aware of its impact on the environment and always tries to keep the impact to a minimum. The company uses renewable electricity and recycles as much waste as possible. Vehicles used by the company have tracking devices to ensure that the distance travelled is minimised.

The company has been in business for 30 years and has grown steadily, rather than rapidly, over this period.

Required

It is commonly stated in finance textbooks that the principal financial objective of a company's managers is to maximise the market value of the company's shares. You are required to critically analyse whether the likely financial and non-financial objectives of EarthCare have any connection to this objective of maximising the market value of the company's shares. **(20 marks)**

LEARNING OUTCOME 1 THE FINANCIAL ENVIRONMENT AND CAPITAL REQUIREMENTS AND CONSEQUENT COSTS

Sources of finance

Topic list	Syllabus reference
1 The financing decision	LO1
2 Short-term sources of finance	LO1
3 Debt finance	LO1
4 Venture capital	LO1
5 Equity finance and preference shares	LO1
6 Principles of capital structure	LO1
7 Green finance	LO1

Introduction

In this chapter we look at the financing decision and the distinction between short- and long-term sources of finance.

When sources of **long-term finance** are used, large sums are usually involved, and so the financial manager needs to consider all the options available with care, looking at the possible effects on the company in the long term.

If a company decides to raise new equity finance, it needs to consider which method would be best for its circumstances.

The use of ethical financial sources is also considered here, and is growing in importance (green finance).

1 The financing decision

Financing decisions include those for both the long term (**capital structure**) and the short term (**working capital management**). There are two main sources of long-term finance, debt and equity; this chapter will consider both.

1.1 Internal sources of finance

> **FAST FORWARD**
>
> Internal sources of finance include **retained earnings** and **increasing working capital efficiency**.

1.1.1 Retained earnings

Retained earnings is surplus cash that has not been needed for operating costs, interest payments, tax liabilities, asset replacement or cash dividends. For many businesses, the cash needed to finance investments will be available because the earnings the business has made have been retained within the business rather than paid out as dividends. This **interaction** of investment, financing and dividend policy is the most important issue facing many businesses.

Retained earnings **belong to shareholders** and are classed as **equity** financing.

A company may have substantial retained profits in its statement of financial position but no cash in the bank and therefore will not be able to finance investment from retained earnings.

1.1.2 Advantages of using retained earnings

(a) Retained earnings are a **flexible source** of finance; companies are not tied to specific amounts or specific repayment patterns.

(b) Using retained earnings does not involve a change in the pattern of shareholdings and no dilution of control.

(c) Retained earnings have no issue costs.

1.1.3 Disadvantages of using retained earnings

(a) Shareholders may be **sensitive** to the **loss of dividends** that will result from retention for reinvestment, rather than paying dividends.

(b) Not so much a disadvantage as a misconception, that retaining profits is a cost-free method of obtaining funds. There is an **opportunity cost** in that if dividends were paid, the cash received could be invested by shareholders to earn a return.

1.1.4 Increasing working capital management efficiency

It is important not to forget that an internal source of finance is the **savings** that can be generated from more efficient management of trade receivables, inventory, cash and trade payables. Efficient working capital management can reduce bank overdraft and interest charges as well as increasing cash reserves.

2 Short-term sources of finance

> **FAST FORWARD**
>
> A range of short-term sources of finance are available to businesses including **overdrafts, short-term loans, trade credit** and **operating lease finance**.

Short-term finance is usually needed for businesses to run their **day to day operations** including payment of wages to employees, inventory ordering and supplies. Businesses with seasonal peaks and troughs and those engaged in international trade are likely to be heavy users of short-term finance.

2.1 Overdrafts

Where payments from a current account exceed income to the account for a temporary period, the bank may agree to finance a deficit balance on the account by means of an **overdraft**. Overdrafts are the most important source of short-term finance available to businesses. They can be arranged relatively **quickly** and offer a level of **flexibility** with regard to the amount borrowed at any time, while interest is only paid when the account is overdrawn.

Overdrafts	
Amount	The bank specifies an overdraft limit. The overdrawn (negative) balance on the account cannot exceed this limit. The bank usually decides the limit with reference to the borrower's known income. Overdraft borrowing is through the borrower's normal business bank account.
Margin	Interest charged at the bank's administrative base rate plus a margin. This rate is usually higher than the rate for a short-term bank loan. Interest is calculated daily on the amount overdrawn and is charged to the borrower's account quarterly (or monthly). An additional fee may be charged for arranging a large-size overdraft facility.
Purpose	Generally to cover short-term deficits in cash flows from normal business operations. The borrower may not want to retain large amounts of cash in a bank account, earning no interest; therefore some negative cash balances may occur.
Repayment	Technically repayable on demand. If a bank ends an overdraft facility without warning, the borrower could face a risk of insolvency.
Security	Depends on size of facility. The bank may ask for security (collateral) but often does not.
Benefits	The customer has flexible means of short-term borrowing; the bank has to accept fluctuations in amount of lending.

By providing an overdraft facility to a customer, the bank is committing itself to providing an overdraft to the customer whenever the customer wants it, up to the agreed limit. The bank will earn interest on the lending, but only to the extent that the customer **uses the facility** and goes into their overdraft. If the customer does not go into their overdraft, the bank cannot charge interest.

The bank will generally charge a **commitment fee** when a customer is granted an overdraft facility or an increase in their overdraft facility. This is a fee for granting an overdraft facility and agreeing to provide the customer with funds if and whenever they need them.

2.1.1 Overdrafts and the operating cycle

Many businesses require their bank to provide financial assistance for normal trading over the **operating cycle**.

For example, suppose that a business has the following working capital position.

	$	$
Inventories and trade receivables		10,000
Bank overdraft	1,000	
Trade payables	3,000	
		4,000
Working capital		6,000

LEARNING OUTCOME 1 THE FINANCIAL ENVIRONMENT AND CAPITAL REQUIREMENTS AND CONSEQUENT COSTS

It now buys inventory costing $2,500 for cash, using its overdraft. Working capital remains the same, $6,000, although the bank's financial stake has risen from $1,000 to $3,500.

	$	$
Inventories and trade receivables		12,500
Bank overdraft	3,500	
Trade payables	3,000	
		6,500
Working capital		6,000

A bank overdraft provides support for normal trading finance. In this example, finance for normal trading rises from $(10,000 – 3,000) = $7,000 to $(12,500 – 3,000) = $9,500 and the bank's contribution rises from $1,000 out of $7,000 to $3,500 out of $9,500.

A feature of bank lending to support normal trading finance is that the amount of the overdraft required at any time will depend on the **cash flows of the business** – the timing of receipts and payments, seasonal variations in trade patterns, and so on. The purpose of the overdraft is to bridge the gap between cash payments and cash receipts.

2.1.2 Solid core overdrafts

When a business customer has an overdraft facility, and the account is always in overdraft, then it has a **solid core** (or **hard core**) overdraft. For example, suppose that the account of a company has the following record for the previous year.

Quarter to	Average balance $	Range $		$
31 March 20X5	40,000 debit	70,000 debit	–	20,000 debit
30 June 20X5	50,000 debit	80,000 debit	–	25,000 debit
30 September 20X5	75,000 debit	105,000 debit	–	50,000 debit
31 December 20X5	80,000 debit	110,000 debit	–	60,000 debit

These figures show that the account has been permanently in overdraft, and the hard core of the overdraft has been rising steeply over the course of the year.

If the hard core element of the overdraft appears to be becoming a **long-term feature** of the business, the bank might wish, after discussions with the customer, to convert the hard core of the overdraft into a **loan**, thus giving formal recognition to its more permanent nature. Otherwise annual reductions in the hard core of an overdraft would typically be a requirement of the bank.

2.2 Short-term loans

A **term loan** is a loan for a fixed amount for a specified period, usually from a bank. The loan may have a specific purpose, such as the purchase of an asset. It is drawn in full at the beginning of the loan period and repaid at a specified time or in defined instalments. Term loans are offered with a variety of **repayment schedules**. Often, the interest and capital repayments are predetermined.

The bank establishes a separate loan account for the loan, charging interest to the account and setting off loan payments against the balance on the account.

The main advantage of lending on a loan account for the bank is that it makes **monitoring** and **control** of the advance much easier, because the loan cash flows are recorded in a separate account. The bank can see immediately when the customer is falling behind with their repayments, or struggling to make the payments. With overdraft lending, a customer's difficulties might be obscured for some time by the variety of transactions on their current account.

(a) The customer knows what they will be **expected** to **pay back** at regular intervals and the bank can also predict its future income with more certainty (depending on whether the interest rate is fixed or floating).

(b) Once the loan is agreed, the **term of** the loan must be **adhered** to, provided that the customer does not fall behind with their repayments. It is not repayable on demand by the bank.

(c) Because the bank will be committing its funds to a customer for a number of years, it may wish to insist on **building certain written safeguards** into the loan agreement, to prevent the customer from becoming overextended with their borrowing during the course of the loan. A loan **covenant** is a condition that the borrower must comply with. If the borrower does not act in accordance with the covenants, the loan can be considered in **default** and the bank can demand payment.

2.3 Overdrafts and short-term loans compared

A customer might ask the bank for an overdraft facility when the bank would wish to suggest a loan instead; alternatively, a customer might ask for a loan when an overdraft would be more appropriate.

(a) In most cases, when a customer wants finance to help with **'day to day' trading** and cash flow needs, an **overdraft** would be the appropriate method of financing. The customer should not be short of cash all the time, and should expect to be in credit in some days, but in need of an overdraft on others.

(b) When a customer wants to **borrow** from a bank **for only a short period of time**, even for the purchase of a major fixed asset, such as an item of plant or machinery, an overdraft facility might be more suitable than a loan, because the customer will stop paying interest as soon as their account goes into credit.

2.3.1 Advantages of an overdraft over a loan

(a) The customer **only pays interest** when they are **overdrawn**.

(b) The bank has the **flexibility** to review the customer's overdraft facility periodically, and perhaps agree to additional facilities, or insist on a reduction in the facility.

(c) An overdraft can do the **same job** as a loan: a facility can simply be renewed every time it comes up for review.

Bear in mind, however, that overdrafts are normally repayable on demand.

2.3.2 Advantages of a loan for longer-term lending

(a) Both the customer and the bank **know** exactly what the **repayments** of the loan will be and how much **interest** is payable, and when. This makes planning (budgeting) simpler.

(b) The interest rate on the loan balance is likely to be lower than the interest charged on overdrawn balances. The comparative cost therefore depends on the size and duration of borrowing requirements.

(c) The customer does **not** have to **worry** about the bank deciding to reduce or withdraw an overdraft facility before they are in a position to repay what is owed. There is an element of 'security' or 'peace of mind' in being able to arrange a loan for an agreed term.

(d) Loans normally carry a **facility letter** setting out the precise terms of the agreement.

However, a **mix** of overdrafts and loans might be suggested in some cases. Consider a case where a business asks for a loan, perhaps to purchase a shop with inventory. The banker might wish to suggest a loan to help with the purchase of the shop, but that inventory ought to be financed by an overdraft facility. The offer of part-loan part-overdraft is an option that might be well worth considering.

2.3.3 Calculation of repayments on a loan

We can use an annuity table to calculate the repayments on a loan.

For example, a $30,000 loan is taken out by a business at a rate of 12% over 5 years. What will be the annual payment, assuming that payments are made every 12 months with the first payment due in twelve months' time and the loan provides for gradual repayment over the term of the loan?

The annuity factor for 12% over 5 years is 3.605. Therefore $30,000 = 3.605 × annual payment.

$$\text{Annual payment} = \frac{30{,}000}{3.605}$$

$$= \$8{,}321.78$$

2.3.4 The split between interest and capital repayment

A loan of $100,000 is to be repaid to the bank, over five years, in equal annual year-end instalments made up of capital repayments and interest at 9% pa.

$$\text{The annual payment} = \frac{\$100{,}000}{3.890} = \$25{,}707$$

Each payment can then be split between the repayment of capital and interest.

Year	Balance b/f $	Interest @ 9% $	Annual payment $	Balance c/f $
1	100,000	9,000	(25,707)	83,293
2	83,293	7,496	(25,707)	65,082
3	65,082	5,857	(25,707)	45,232
4	45,232	4,071	(25,707)	23,596
5	23,596	2,111*	(25,707)	

* Rounding difference

2.4 Trade credit

Trade credit is a major source of short-term finance for a business. Current assets such as raw materials may be purchased on credit, with payment terms normally varying from between 30 and 90 days. Trade credit therefore represents an interest-free short-term loan. In a period of high inflation, purchasing via trade credit will be very helpful in keeping costs down. However, it is important to take into account the **loss of discounts** suppliers offer for early payment.

Unacceptable delays in payment will worsen a company's **credit rating** and additional credit may become difficult to obtain.

2.5 Leasing

Rather than buying an asset outright, using either available cash resources or borrowed funds, a business may **lease** an asset. Leasing is a popular source of finance.

Leasing can be defined as a contract between **lessor** and **lessee** for hire of a specific asset selected from a manufacturer or vendor of such assets by the lessee. The lessor retains ownership of the asset. The lessee has possession and use of the asset on payment of specified rentals over a period.

Many lessors are financial intermediaries, such as banks and insurance companies. The range of assets leased is wide, including office equipment and computers, cars and commercial vehicles, aircraft, ships and buildings.

2.5.1 Sale and leaseback

A company which owns its own premises can obtain finance by selling the property to an insurance company or pension fund for immediate cash and renting it back, usually for at least 50 years with rent reviews every few years.

A company would raise more cash from sale and leaseback arrangements than from a mortgage, but there are significant **disadvantages**.

(a) The company **loses ownership** of a valuable asset which is almost certain to appreciate over time.

(b) The **future borrowing capacity** of the firm will be reduced, as there will be fewer assets to provide security for a loan.

(c) The company is **contractually committed** to occupying the property for many years ahead which can be restricting.

(d) The **real cost** is likely to be high, particularly as there will be frequent rent reviews.

3 Debt finance

> **FAST FORWARD**
>
> A range of long-term sources of finance are available to businesses including **debt finance**, **leasing**, **venture capital** and **equity finance**.

Long-term finance is used for major investments **and is usually more expensive and less flexible than short-term finance**.

3.1 Reasons for seeking debt finance

Sometimes businesses may need long-term funds, but may not wish to issue equity capital. Perhaps the current shareholders will be unwilling or unable to **contribute additional capital**; possibly the company does not wish to involve outside shareholders who will have more onerous requirements than current members.

Other reasons for choosing debt finance may include **lower costs** and **easier availability**, particularly if the company has little or no existing debt finance. Debt finance provides **tax relief** on interest payments, unlike dividend payments which are paid out of post-tax earnings, and receive no tax relief.

3.2 Sources of debt finance

If a company does wish to raise debt finance, it will need to consider what **type** of finance will be available. If it is seeking medium-term bank finance, it ought to be in the form of a **loan**. Bank finance is an important source of both short-term and longer-term debt for small companies.

If a company is seeking to issue bonds, it must decide whether to make an issue of 'conventional' bonds, or whether investors may be attracted by a different type of bond issue, such as convertible bonds.

3.3 Factors influencing choice of debt finance

> **FAST FORWARD**
>
> The choice of **debt finance** that a company can make depends on:
> - The size of the company; a public issue of bonds is only available to a large company
> - The duration of the required financing
> - Whether a fixed or floating interest rate is preferred (fixed rates are more expensive, but floating rates are riskier)
> - The security (collateral) that can be offered and the security that may be demanded by a lender

Later in this Text, we shall look in detail at the factors that determine the mix of debt and equity finance that a company chooses. For now, you need to bear in mind when reading this chapter the following considerations influencing what type of debt finance is sought.

(a) **Availability**

Only listed companies are able to make a public issue of bonds. With a 'public issue' the bonds are listed on a stock market. Most investors will not invest in bonds issued by small companies as they are perceived as high risk, and this means that smaller companies are only able to obtain significant levels of debt finance in the form of bank loans.

(b) **Credit rating**

Large companies may prefer to issue bonds if they have a strong credit rating. Credit ratings are given to bond issues by credit rating agencies. The credit rating given to a bond issue affects the interest yield that investors will require - the higher the grade, the lower the risk the bond is deemed to involve, and the lower the yield demanded by the investor. If a company's bonds would only be given a sub-investment grade rating ('junk bond' rating), the company may prefer to seek debt finance from a bank loan because the high risk associated with junk bond status would lead to investors demanding a very high yield, making this seem an unattractive source of finance.

(c) **Amount**

Bond issues are usually for large amounts. If a company wants to borrow only a small amount of money, a bank loan would be appropriate.

(d) **Duration**

If loan finance is sought to buy a particular asset to generate revenues for the business, the length of the loan should **match** the length of time that the asset will be generating revenues.

(e) **Fixed or floating rate**

Expectations of interest rate movements will determine whether a company wants to borrow at a fixed or floating rate. Fixed-rate finance may be more expensive, but the business runs the risk of adverse upward rate movements if it chooses floating rate finance. Banks may refuse to lend at a fixed rate for more than a given period of time.

(f) **Security and covenants**

The choice of finance may be determined by the assets that the business is willing or able to offer as **security**, and by the restrictions in **covenants** that the lenders wish to impose.

3.4 Bonds

> The term **bonds** describes various forms of long-term debt a company may issue, such as **loan notes**, which may be:
> - Redeemable
> - Irredeemable
>
> Bonds or loans come in various forms, including:
> - Floating rate loan notes
> - Zero coupon bonds
> - Convertible bonds

Key term

Bonds are long-term debt capital raised by a company for which interest is paid, usually half yearly and at a fixed rate. Holders of bonds are therefore long-term payables for the company.

3.4.1 Conventional bonds

Conventional bonds are fixed-rate redeemable bonds.

Bonds have a nominal value, which is the debt owed by the company, and interest is paid at a stated '**coupon**' on this amount. For example, if a company issues 10% bonds, the coupon will be 10% of the nominal value of the bonds, so that $100 of bonds will receive $10 interest each year. The rate quoted is the gross rate, before tax.

Unlike shares, debt is often issued **at nominal value**, ie with $100 payable per $100 nominal value, or close to nominal value. Bond prices are quoted per $100 nominal value of bonds, so a price of $98.65 means a market price of $98.65 per $100 nominal value.

Where the coupon rate is fixed at the time of issue, it will be set according to **prevailing market conditions** given the **credit rating** of the company issuing the debt. Subsequent changes in market (and company) conditions will cause the **market value** of the bond to fluctuate, although the coupon will stay at the fixed percentage of the nominal value.

Bonds issued by large companies are marketable, but bond markets are small. When a company issues new equity shares, the new shares rank equally with all existing equity shares, and can be bought and sold in the same market. In contrast, each bond issue is different, with its own interest rate and redemption date; the market for different bond issues by the same company cannot be combined. This is why equities may be extensively traded on a stock market, but bonds are not.

Key term

A **loan note** is the written acknowledgement of a debt incurred by a company, normally containing provisions about the payment of interest and the eventual repayment of capital.

(**Note**. For the purposes of your exam, debentures is simply another word for bonds or loan notes.)

3.5 Deep discount bonds

Key term

Deep discount bonds are bonds or loan notes issued at a price which is at a large discount to the nominal value of the notes, and which will be redeemable at nominal value (or above nominal value) when they eventually mature.

For example a company might issue $1,000,000 of bonds in 20X1, at a price of $50 per $100 of bond, and redeemable at nominal value in the year 20X9. The coupon rate of interest will be very low compared with yields on conventional bonds with the same maturity. For a company with specific cash flow requirements, the low servicing costs during the currency of the bond may be an attraction, coupled with a high cost of redemption at maturity.

Investors might be attracted by the **large capital gain** offered by the bonds, which is the difference between the **issue price** and the **redemption value**. However, deep discount bonds will carry a much **lower rate of interest** than other types of bond. The only tax advantage is that the gain gets taxed (as **income**) in one lump on maturity or sale, not as amounts of interest each year. The borrower can, however, **deduct notional interest** each year in computing profits.

The main benefit of deep discount bonds for a company is that the interest yield on the bonds is lower than on conventional bonds. However, it will have to pay a much larger amount at maturity than it borrowed when the bonds were issued. Deep discount bonds defer much of the cost of the debt.

3.6 Zero coupon bonds

> **Key term**
>
> **Zero coupon bonds** are bonds that are issued at a discount to their redemption value, but no interest is paid on them.

Zero coupon bonds are an extreme form of deep discount bond. For example, a company may issue zero coupon discount bonds at 75.00, pay no interest at all, but at maturity (say, five years later) redeem the bonds at 100.00. The investor gains from the difference between the issue price and the redemption value ($25 per $75 invested). There is an implied interest rate in the amount of discount at which the bonds are issued (or subsequently resold on the market).

(a) The advantage for borrowers is that zero coupon bonds can be used to **raise cash immediately**, and there is **no cash repayment** until redemption date. The cost of redemption is known at the time of issue. The borrower can plan to have funds available to redeem the bonds at maturity.

(b) The **advantage for lenders** is **restricted**, unless the rate of discount on the bonds offers a high yield. The only way of obtaining cash from the bonds before maturity is to sell them. Their **market value** will depend on the **remaining term** to maturity and **current market interest rates**.

The tax advantage of zero coupon bonds is the same as that of deep discount bonds (see 5.5 above).

Deep discount bonds and zero coupon bonds are not common. Companies must want to pay little or no interest and incur the main cost at redemption. Investors must have reasons for wanting to invest in these bonds, rather than in conventional bonds.

3.7 Convertible bonds

> **FAST FORWARD**
>
> **Convertible bonds** are bonds that give the holder the right to convert to other securities, normally ordinary shares, at a predetermined price/rate and time.

Convertible bonds are fixed-rate bonds. The coupon rate of interest is lower than on similar conventional bonds. They give the bond holders the right (but not an obligation) to convert their bonds at a specified future date into new equity shares of the company, at a conversion rate that is also specified when the bonds are issued.

For example, the conversion terms for a convertible bond may be that on 1 April 20X0, $100 of bonds can be converted into 40 ordinary shares, whereas on 1 April 20X1, the conversion rate is 45 ordinary shares per $100 of bonds. Once converted, convertible securities cannot be converted back into the original fixed return security.

If bond holders choose not to convert their bonds into shares, the bonds will be redeemed at maturity, usually at nominal rate.

3.7.1 The conversion value and the conversion premium

The current market value of ordinary shares into which a bond may be converted is known as the conversion value. The **conversion value** will be below the value of the bond at the date of issue, but will be expected to increase as the date for conversion approaches on the assumption that a company's shares ought to increase in market value over time.

Conversion value = Conversion ratio × market price per share
Conversion premium = Current market value – current conversion value

Question: Convertible debt

The 10% convertible bonds of Starchwhite are quoted at $142 per $100 nominal. The earliest date for conversion is in 4 years' time, at the rate of 30 ordinary shares per $100 nominal bond. The share price is currently $4.15. Annual interest on the bonds has just been paid.

Required

(a) Calculate the current conversion value.
(b) Calculate the conversion premium and comment on its meaning.

Answer

(a) Conversion ratio is $100 bond = 30 ordinary shares
Conversion value = 30 × $4.15 = $124.50

(b) Conversion premium = $(142 – 124.50) = $17.50 or $\frac{17.50}{124.50} \times 100\% = 14\%$

The share price will have to rise by 14% before the conversion rights become attractive.

3.7.2 The issue price and the market price of convertible bonds

A company will aim to issue bonds with the **greatest possible conversion premium**, as this will mean that for the amount of capital raised it will, on conversion, have to issue the lowest number of new ordinary shares. The premium that will be accepted by potential investors will depend on the company's growth potential and so on prospects for a sizeable increase in the share price.

Convertible bonds issued at nominal have a **lower coupon rate of interest** than similar conventional bonds. This lower interest rate is the price the investor has to pay for the conversion rights. It is, of course, also one of the reasons why the issue of convertible bonds is attractive to a company.

A (large) company may issue convertible bonds rather than conventional bonds in order to benefit from lower interest costs, even if this means having to issue new shares in the future, when profits and cash flows are stronger.

When convertible bonds are traded on a stock market, their **minimum market price** or **floor value** will be the price of conventional bonds with the same coupon rate of interest. If the market value falls to this minimum, it follows that the market attaches no value to the conversion rights.

The actual market price of convertible bonds will depend on:

- The **price of straight debt**
- The **current conversion value**
- The **length of time** before conversion may take place
- The **market's expectation** as to future equity returns and the risk associated with these returns

Most companies issuing convertible bonds expect them to be **converted**. They view the bonds as **delayed equity**. They are often used either because the company's ordinary share price is considered to be particularly depressed at the time of issue or because the issue of equity shares would result in an immediate and significant drop in earnings per share. There is no certainty, however, that the security holders will exercise their option to convert; therefore the bonds may run their full term and need to be redeemed.

3.7.3 Example: Convertible bonds

CD has issued 50,000 units of convertible bonds, each with a nominal value of $100 and a coupon rate of interest of 10% payable yearly. Each $100 of convertible bonds may be converted into 40 ordinary shares of CD in three years' time. Any bonds not converted will be redeemed at 110 (that is, at $110 per $100 nominal value of bond).

Estimate the likely current market price for $100 of the bonds, if investors in the bonds now require a pre-tax return of only 8%, and the expected value of CD ordinary shares on the conversion day is:

(a) $2.50 per share
(b) $3.00 per share

Solution

(a) Shares are valued at $2.50 each.

If shares are only expected to be worth $2.50 each on conversion day, the value of 40 shares will be $100, and investors in the debt will presumably therefore redeem their debt at 110 instead of converting them into shares.

The market value of $100 of the convertible debt will be the discounted present value of the expected future income stream.

Year		Cash flow $	Discount factor 8%	Present value $
1	Interest	10	0.926	9.26
2	Interest	10	0.857	8.57
3	Interest	10	0.794	7.94
3	Redemption value	110	0.794	87.34
				113.11

The estimated market value is $113.11 per $100 of debt. This is also the floor value.

(b) Shares are valued at $3 each.

If shares are expected to be worth $3 each, the debt holders will convert their debt into shares (value per $100 of bonds = 40 shares × $3 = $120) rather than redeem their debt at 110.

Year		Cash flow/value $	Discount factor 8%	Present value $
1	Interest	10	0.926	9.26
2	Interest	10	0.857	8.57
3	Interest	10	0.794	7.94
3	Value of 40 shares	120	0.794	95.28
				121.05

The estimated market value is $121.05 per $100 of debt.

3.8 Security

Bonds may be secured. Bank loans are often secured. **Security** may take the form of either a **fixed charge** or a **floating charge**.

Fixed charge	Floating charge
Security relates to specific asset/group of assets (land and buildings)	Security in event of default is whatever assets of the class secured (inventory/trade receivables) company then owns
Company can't dispose of assets without providing substitute/consent of lender	Company can dispose of assets until default takes place
	In event of default lenders appoint receiver rather than lay claim to asset

Investors are likely to expect a higher yield with **unsecured bonds** to compensate them for the extra risk. Similarly, a bank may charge higher interest for an unsecured loan compared with a similar secured loan.

3.9 The redemption of bonds

Key term

> **Redemption** is a term for the repayment of preference shares and bonds at maturity.

Bonds are usually redeemable. They are issued for a term of ten years or more, and perhaps 25 to 30 years. At the end of this period, they will 'mature' and become redeemable (at nominal value or possibly at a value above nominal value).

Most redeemable bonds have an earliest and a latest redemption date. For example, 12% Loan note 20X7/X9 is redeemable at any time between the earliest specified date (in 20X7) and the latest date (in 20X9). The **issuing company** can choose the date.

Some bonds do not have a redemption date, and are **'irredeemable'** or **'undated'**. Undated corporate bonds could be redeemed by the company if it wishes to pay off the debt, but there is no obligation on the company to do so.

There are some issues of undated government bonds.

3.9.1 How will a company finance the redemption of long-term debt?

There is no guarantee that a company will be able to raise a new loan to pay off a maturing debt. One item you should look for in a company's statement of financial position is the **redemption date** of current loans, to establish how much new finance is likely to be needed by the company, and when.

Occasionally, perhaps because the secured assets have fallen in value and would not realise much in a forced sale, or perhaps out of a belief that the company can improve its position soon, unpaid loan note holders may be persuaded to surrender their loan notes. In exchange they may receive an **equity interest** in the company or **convertible loan notes**, paying a lower rate of interest, but carrying the option to convert the loan notes into shares at a specified time in the future.

3.10 Tax relief on loan interest

As far as companies are concerned, debt capital is a potentially attractive source of finance because interest charges are an allowable expense for tax purposes. Interest charges **reduce the profits** chargeable to corporation tax. Dividend payments to shareholders do not attract tax relief. The after-tax cost of debt can therefore be much lower than the cost of equity.

(a) A new issue of bonds is likely to be preferable to a new issue of preference shares (preference shares are shares carrying a fixed rate of dividends).

(b) Companies might wish to **avoid dilution of shareholdings** and **increase gearing** (the ratio of fixed interest capital to equity capital) in order to improve their earnings per share by benefiting from tax relief on interest payments.

4 Venture capital

Key term

> **Venture capital** is risk capital, normally provided by a venture capital firm or individual venture capitalist, in return for an equity stake.

Venture capital is capital that is invested (or is available for investing) in private companies. The venture capital may be provided by a wealthy individual, or it may be provided by a venture capital firm that manages a venture capital fund. (A venture capital fund consists of money from investors for investing in private company equity.)

Venture capitalists seek to invest cash in return for shares in private companies with high growth potential. They seek a high return, which is often realised through a stock market listing.

Venture capital may be invested in young start-up companies, but is more commonly invested in small companies that already have a track record of business development and which need additional finance to grow. These companies may have borrowed as much money as their banks are prepared to lend, and do not have enough equity capital (from the existing owners or retained profits) to expand at the rate or scale required.

Venture capital organisations have been operating for many years. There is now quite a large number of such organisations. For example:

(a) The British Venture Capital Association is a regulatory body for all the institutions that have joined it as members.

(b) **Investors in Industry plc**, or the **3i group** as it is more commonly known, is the biggest and oldest of the venture capital organisations. It is involved in many venture capital schemes in Europe, Singapore, Japan and the US.

Venture capitalists want to invest in companies that will be successful.

The types of venture that the 3i group might invest in include the following:

(a) **Business start-ups**. When a business has been set up by someone who has already put time and money into getting it started, the group may be willing to **provide finance** to enable it to take the next step in its development.

(b) **Business development**. The group may be willing to **provide development capital** for a company which wants to invest in new products or new markets or to make a business acquisition, and so which needs a major capital injection.

(c) **Management buyouts**. A management buyout is the **purchase** of all or parts of a **business** from its owners by its managers.

(d) Helping a company where one of its owners wants to **realise all or part of their investment**. The 3i group may be prepared to buy some of the company's equity.

4.1 Venture capital funds

Some other organisations are engaged in the creation of **venture capital funds**. In these the organisation raises venture capital funds from investors and invests in management buyouts or expanding companies. The venture capital fund managers usually reward themselves by taking a percentage of the portfolio of the fund's investments.

4.2 Finding venture capital

When a company's directors look for help from a venture capital institution, they must recognise that:

(a) The institution will want an **equity stake** in the company.

(b) It will need convincing that the company can be successful (management buyouts of companies which already have a record of **successful trading** have been increasingly favoured by venture capitalists in recent years).

(c) It may want to have a **representative** appointed to the company's board, to look after its interests, or an **independent director**.

The directors of the company must then contact venture capital organisations, to try to find one or more which would be willing to offer finance. Typically, a venture capitalist will consider offering finance of $500,000 upwards. A venture capital organisation will only give funds to a company that it believes can succeed.

A venture capitalist may also agree to invest in some redeemable preference shares as well as equity, but will want a suitable proportion of the company's equity as part of the financing arrangement.

When a venture capitalist invests in new equity for a company, the company's bank may also be prepared to lend more, because the company is now seen as a lower credit risk.

A survey has indicated that around 75% of requests for venture capital are rejected on an initial screening, and only about 3% of all requests survive both this screening and further investigation and result in actual investments.

The venture capital organisation (VC) will take account of various factors in deciding whether or not to invest.

Factors in investment decisions	
The nature of the company's **product**	Viability of production and selling potential
Expertise in **production**	Technical ability to produce efficiently
Expertise in **management**	Commitment, skills and experience
The **market and competition**	Threat from rival producers or future new entrants
Future profits	Detailed business plan showing profit prospects that compensate for risks
Board membership	To take account of VC's interests and ensure that VC has say in future strategy
Risk borne by existing owners	Owners bear significant risk and invest significant part of their overall wealth

5 Equity finance and preference shares

> **FAST FORWARD**
>
> Equity finance is raised through the sale of **ordinary shares** to investors via a **new issue** or a **rights issue**.

5.1 Ordinary shares

Ordinary shares are issued to the owners of a company. Ordinary shares in many countries have a **nominal** or 'face' value, typically $1 or 50c. In some countries, equity shares no longer have a nominal value.

You should understand that the **market value** of a quoted company's shares bears **no relationship** to their nominal value except that, when ordinary shares are issued for cash, the issue price must be equal to or (more usually) more than the nominal value of the shares.

Ordinary shareholders have **rights** as a result of their ownership of the shares.

(a) Shareholders can attend company general meetings.

(b) They can vote on important company matters such as the appointment and re-election of directors; approving a takeover bid for another company, where the financing arrangements will involve a large new issue of shares; the appointment of auditors; or (possibly, as in the UK) approving the company's remuneration policy for senior executives.

(c) They are entitled to receive a share of any agreed dividend.

(d) They will receive the annual report and accounts.

(e) They will receive a share of any assets remaining after liquidation.

(f) They can participate in any new issue of shares, unless they agree to waive this right.

Ordinary shareholders are the ultimate bearers of **risk**, as they are at the bottom of the **creditor hierarchy** in a liquidation. This means there is a significant risk they will receive nothing after settlement of all the company's liabilities.

This high equity risk means that shareholders expect the **highest return** of long-term providers of finance, in the form of dividend yields, dividend growth and share price growth. The cost of equity finance is therefore always **higher** than the cost of debt.

5.2 Advantages of a stock market listing

FAST FORWARD — A company can obtain a **stock market listing** for its shares through a **public offer** or a **placing**.

There are certain advantages to obtaining a stock market listing.

(a) Enhanced public image and credibility.
(b) Access to a wider source of finance.
(c) To allow the original owners selling the holding to obtain funds for alternative investments.
(d) Improved marketability of shares.
(e) Original owners realising holding.
(f) Easier to seek growth by acquisition.

5.3 Disadvantages of a stock market listing

The owners of a company seeking a stock market listing must take the following disadvantages into account.

(a) There will be significantly greater **public regulation, accountability** and **scrutiny**. The legal requirements the company faces will be greater, and the company will also be subject to the rules of the stock exchange on which its shares are listed.
(b) A **wider circle of investors** with more exacting requirements will hold shares.
(c) There will be additional costs involved in making share issues, including **brokerage commissions** and **underwriting fees**.

5.4 Methods of obtaining a listing

An unquoted company that is becoming listed for the first time can issue shares on the stock market by means of:

- **An initial public offering (IPO)**
- **A placing**
- **An introduction**

5.4.1 Initial public offer

Key term — An **initial public offering (IPO)** is an invitation to apply for shares in a company based on information contained in a prospectus.

An **initial public offering (IPO)** is a means of selling the shares of a company to the public at large for the first time. When companies 'go public' for the first time, a **large** issue will probably take the form of an IPO. This is known as **flotation**. Subsequent issues are likely to be **placings** or **rights issues**, described later.

An IPO entails the **acquisition by an issuing house** (an investment bank acting for the company) of a large block of shares of a company, with a view to offering them for sale to the public and investing institutions.

An issuing house is usually an investment bank. It may acquire the shares either as a direct allotment from the company or by purchase from existing shareholders. In either case, the issuing house publishes an invitation to the public to apply for shares, either at a fixed price or on a tender basis. The issuing house **accepts responsibility** to the public, and gives to the issue the support of its own standing.

In an IPO, the company's shareholders may take the opportunity to sell some of their shares. They receive the money from these share sales. In addition, the company will issue new shares in the IPO to raise equity finance for investment.

5.4.2 A placing

A **placing** is an arrangement whereby, instead of offering the shares to the general public, the sponsoring investment bank arranges for most of the issue to be bought by a **small number of investors**, usually institutional investors such as pension funds and insurance companies.

5.4.3 The choice between an IPO and a placing

Is a company likely to prefer an IPO of its shares, or a placing?

(a) **Placings** are much **cheaper**. Approaching institutional investors privately is a much cheaper way of obtaining finance, and thus placings are often used for smaller issues.

(b) Placings are likely to be **quicker**.

(c) Placings are likely to involve **less disclosure** of **information**.

(d) However, most of the shares will be placed with a **relatively small number of (institutional) shareholders**, which means that most of the shares are **unlikely to be available for trading** after the flotation, and that **institutional shareholders** will have control of the **company**.

(e) When a company first comes to the market, there may be a restriction on the proportion of shares that can be placed, or a minimum proportion that must be offered to the general public.

5.4.4 A stock exchange introduction

By this method of obtaining a quotation, no shares are made available to the market, neither existing nor newly created shares; nevertheless, the stock market grants a quotation. This will only happen where shares in a large private company are already widely held, so that a market can be seen to exist. A company might want an **introduction** to obtain **greater marketability** for the shares, a known share valuation for inheritance tax purposes and easier access in the future to additional capital.

5.5 Costs of share issues on the stock market

Companies may incur the following costs when issuing shares:

- Underwriting costs (see below)
- Stock market listing fee (the initial charge) for the new securities
- Fees of the issuing house (investment bank), solicitors, auditors and public relations consultant
- Charges for printing and distributing the prospectus: (the prospectus is the document in which the company offers its shares for sale)
- Advertising in national newspapers

5.5.1 Underwriting

A company about to issue new securities in order to raise finance may decide to have the issue underwritten. **Underwriters** are financial institutions which agree (in exchange for a fixed fee, perhaps 2.25% of the finance to be raised) to buy at the issue price any securities which are **not subscribed** for by the investing public.

Underwriters **remove** the **risk** of a share issue's being undersubscribed, but at a cost to the company issuing the shares. It is not compulsory to have an issue underwritten. Ordinary offers for sale (IPOs) are likely to be underwritten, although rights issues may be as well.

5.6 Pricing shares for a stock market launch

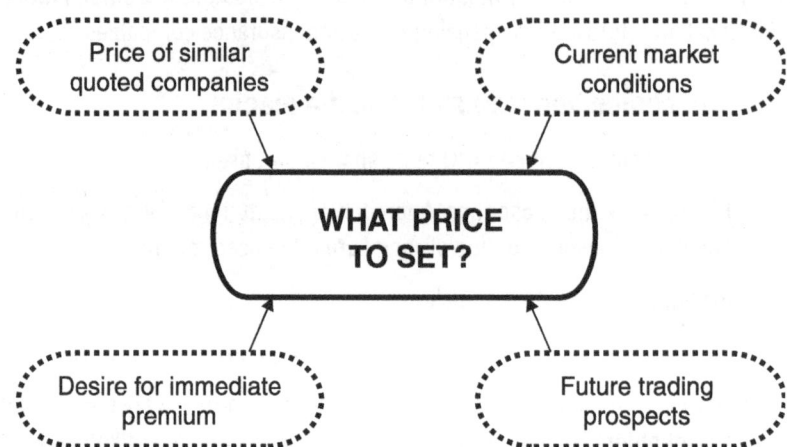

Companies will be keen to avoid **overpricing an issue**, which could result in the **issue** being **undersubscribed**, leaving underwriters with the unwelcome task of having to buy up the unsold shares. On the other hand, if the **issue price** is **too low** then the issue will be **oversubscribed** and the company would have been able to raise the required capital by issuing fewer shares.

The share price of an issue is usually advertised as being based on a certain P/E ratio, the ratio of the price to the company's most recent earnings per share figure in its audited accounts. The issuer's P/E ratio can then be compared by investors with the P/E ratios of similar quoted companies.

5.7 Rights issues

> **FAST FORWARD**
>
> A **rights issue** is an offer to existing shareholders enabling them to buy more shares, usually at a price lower than the current market price, and in proportion to their existing shareholding.

A **rights issue** provides a way of raising new share capital by means of an offer to existing shareholders, inviting them to subscribe cash for new shares in proportion to their existing holdings.

For example, a rights issue on a one for four basis at 280c per share would mean that a company is inviting its existing shareholders to subscribe for one new share for every four shares they hold, at a price of 280c per new share. A rights issue may be made by any type of company. The analysis below, however, applies primarily to listed companies.

The major advantages of a rights issue are as follows.

(a) Rights issues are **cheaper** than **IPOs** to the general public. This is partly because **no prospectus** is normally required, partly because the administration is simpler and partly because the cost of underwriting will be less.

(b) Rights issues are **more beneficial** to **existing shareholders** than issues to the general public. New shares are issued at a discount to the current market price to make them attractive to investors. A rights issue **secures** the **discount** on the market price for existing shareholders, who may either keep the shares or sell them if they wish.

(c) **Relative voting** rights are **unaffected** if shareholders all take up their rights.

(d) The finance raised may be used to **reduce gearing** in book value terms by increasing share capital and/or to pay off long-term debt which will reduce gearing in market value terms.

5.8 Deciding the issue price for a rights issue

The **offer price** in a rights issue will be lower than the current market price of existing shares. The size of the discount will vary, and will be larger for difficult issues. In the UK, however, the offer price must be at or above the **nominal value** of the shares, so as not to contravene company law.

A company making a rights issue must set a price which is **low enough** to **secure** the **acceptance** of shareholders, who are being asked to provide extra funds, but not too low, so as to avoid excessive dilution of the earnings per share.

5.9 Example: Rights issue (1)

Seagull can achieve a profit after tax of 20% on the capital employed. At present its capital structure is as follows.

	$
200,000 ordinary shares of $1 each	200,000
Retained earnings	100,000
	300,000

The directors propose to raise an additional $126,000 from a rights issue. The current market price is $1.80.

Required

(a) Calculate the number of shares that must be issued if the rights price is:
$1.60; $1.50; $1.40; $1.20.

(b) Calculate the dilution in earnings per share in each case.

Solution

The earnings at present are 20% of $300,000 = $60,000. This gives earnings per share of 30c. The earnings after the rights issue will be 20% of $426,000 = $85,200.

Rights price $	No of new share ($126,000 ÷ rights price)	EPS ($85,200 ÷ total no of shares) Cents	Dilution Cents
1.60	78,750	30.6	+ 0.6
1.50	84,000	30.0	–
1.40	90,000	29.4	– 0.6
1.20	105,000	27.9	– 2.1

Note that at a high rights price the earnings per share are increased, not diluted. The breakeven point (zero dilution) occurs when the rights price is equal to the capital employed per share: $300,000 ÷ 200,000 = $1.50.

5.9.1 The market price of shares after a rights issue: the theoretical ex-rights price

When a rights issue is announced, all existing shareholders have the right to subscribe for new shares, and so there are rights attached to the existing shares. The shares are therefore described as being **'cum rights'** (with rights attached) and are traded cum rights. On the first day of dealings in the newly issued shares, the rights no longer exist and the old shares are now **'ex-rights'** (without rights attached).

After the announcement of a rights issue, share prices normally **fall**. The extent and duration of the fall may depend on the number of shareholders and the size of their holdings. This temporary fall is due to **uncertainty** in the market about the consequences of the issue, with respect to future profits, earnings and dividends.

After the issue has actually been made, the market price per share will normally fall, because there are more shares in issue and the new shares were issued at a discount price.

In theory, the new market price will be the consequence of an adjustment to allow for the discount price of the new issue, and a theoretical ex-rights price can be calculated.

5.9.2 Example: Rights issue (2)

Fundraiser has 1,000,000 ordinary shares of $1 in issue, which have a market price on 1 September of $2.10 per share. The company decides to make a rights issue, and offers its shareholders the right to subscribe for one new share at $1.50 each for every four shares already held. After the announcement of the issue, the share price fell to $1.95, but by the time just prior to the issue being made, it had recovered to $2 per share. This market value just before the issue is known as the cum rights price. What is the theoretical ex-rights price?

Solution

Value of the portfolio for a shareholder with 4 shares before the rights issue:

	$
4 shares @ $2.00	8.00
1 share @ $1.50	1.50
5	9.50

So the value per share after the rights issue (or TERP) is 9.50/5 = $1.90.

5.9.3 The value of rights

The value of rights is the theoretical gain a shareholder would make by exercising their rights.

(a) Using the above example, if the price offered in the rights issue is $1.50 per share, and the market price after the issue is expected to be $1.90, the value attaching to a right is $1.90 − $1.50 = $0.40. A shareholder would therefore be expected to gain 40 cents for each new share they buy.

If they do not have enough money to buy the share themselves, they could sell the right to subscribe for a new share to another investor, and receive 40 cents from the sale. This other investor would then buy the new share for $1.50, so that their total outlay to acquire the share would be $0.40 + $1.50 = $1.90, the theoretical ex-rights price.

(b) The value of rights attaching to existing shares is calculated in the same way. If the value of rights on a new share is 40 cents, and there is a one for four rights issue, the value of the rights attaching to each existing share is 40 ÷ 4 = 10 cents.

5.9.4 The theoretical gain or loss to shareholders

The possible courses of action open to shareholders are:

(a) To **'take up' or 'exercise' the rights**; that is, to buy the new shares at the rights price. Shareholders who do this will maintain their percentage holdings in the company by subscribing for the new shares.

(b) To **'renounce' the rights** and sell them on the market. Shareholders who do this will have lower percentage holdings of the company's equity after the issue than before the issue, and the total value of their shares will be less.

(c) To **renounce part of the rights and take up the remainder**. For example, a shareholder may sell enough of their rights to enable them to buy the remaining rights shares they are entitled to with the sale proceeds, and so keep the total market value of their shareholding in the company unchanged.

(d) To **do nothing**. Shareholders may be protected from the consequences of their inaction because rights not taken up are sold on a shareholder's behalf by the company. If new securities are not taken up, they may be sold by the company to new subscribers for the benefit of the shareholders who were entitled to the rights.

Question — Rights issue

Gopher has issued 3,000,000 ordinary shares of $1 each, which are at present selling for $4 per share. The company plans to issue rights to purchase 1 new equity share at a price of $3.20 per share for every 3 shares held. A shareholder who owns 900 shares thinks that they will suffer a loss in their personal wealth because the new shares are being offered at a price lower than market value. On the assumption that the actual market value of shares will be equal to the theoretical ex-rights price, what would the effect on the shareholder's wealth be if:

(a) They sell all the rights
(b) They exercise half the rights and sell the other half
(c) They do nothing at all

Answer

Value of the portfolio for a shareholder with 3 shares before the rights issue

	$
3 shares @ $4.00	12.00
1 share @ $3.20	3.20
4	15.20

So the value per share after the rights issue (or TERP) is 15.20/4 = 3.80.

	$
Theoretical ex-rights price	3.80
Price per new share	3.20
Value of rights per new share	0.60

The value of the rights attached to each existing share is $\frac{\$0.60}{3} = \$0.20$.

We will assume that a shareholder is able to sell their rights for $0.20 per existing share held.

(a) If the shareholder sells all their rights:

	$
Sale value of rights (900 × $0.20)	180
Market value of their 900 shares ex rights (900 × $3.80)	3,420
Total wealth	3,600
Total value of 900 shares cum rights (× $4)	$3,600

The shareholder would neither gain nor lose wealth. They would not be required to provide any additional funds to the company, but their shareholding as a proportion of the total equity of the company will be lower.

(b) If the shareholder exercises half the rights (buys 450/3 = 150 shares at $3.20) and sells the other half:

	$
Sale value of rights (450 × $0.20)	90
Market value of their 1,050 shares, ex rights (× $3.80)	3,990
	4,080
Total value of 900 shares cum rights (× $4)	3,600
Additional investment (150 × $3.20)	480
	4,080

The shareholder would neither gain nor lose wealth, although they will have increased their investment in the company by $480.

(c) If the shareholder does nothing, but all other shareholders either exercise their rights or sell them, they would lose wealth as follows.

	$
Market value of 900 shares cum rights (× $4)	3,600
Market value of 900 shares ex rights (× $3.80)	3,420
Loss in wealth	180

It follows that the shareholder, to protect their existing investment, should either exercise their rights or sell them to another investor. If they do not exercise their rights, the new securities they were entitled to subscribe for may be sold for their benefit by the company, and this would protect them from losing wealth.

5.10 The actual market price after a rights issue

The actual market price of a share after a rights issue may differ from the theoretical ex-rights price. This will occur when:

5.10.1 Expected yield from new funds raised ≠ Earnings yield from existing funds

The market will take a view of how profitably the new funds will be invested, and will value the shares accordingly. An example will illustrate this point.

5.10.2 Example: Rights issue (3)

Musk currently has 4,000,000 ordinary shares in issue, valued at $2 each, and the company has annual earnings equal to 20% of the market value of the shares. A one for four rights issue is proposed, at an issue price of $1.50. If the market continues to value the shares on a price/earnings ratio of 5, what would the value per share be if the new funds are expected to earn, as a percentage of the money raised:

(a) 15%
(b) 20%
(c) 25%

How do these values in (a), (b) and (c) compare with the theoretical ex-rights price? Ignore issue costs.

Solution

The theoretical ex-rights price will be calculated first.

	$
Four shares have a current value (× $2) of	8.00
One new share will be issued for	1.50
Five shares would have a theoretical value of	9.50

Theoretical ex-rights price $= \dfrac{1}{4+1}((4 \times 2) + 1.50)$

$= \$1.90$

The new funds will raise 1,000,000 × $1.50 = $1,500,000.

Earnings as a % of money raised	Additional earnings $	Current earnings $	Total earnings after the issue $
15%	225,000	1,600,000	1,825,000
20%	300,000	1,600,000	1,900,000
25%	375,000	1,600,000	1,975,000

If the market values shares on a P/E ratio of 5, the total market value of equity and the market price per share would be as follows.

Total earnings $	Market value $	Price per share (5,000,000 shares) $
1,825,000	9,125,000	1.825
1,900,000	9,500,000	1.900
1,975,000	9,875,000	1.975

(a) If the additional funds raised are expected to generate earnings at the **same rate** as existing funds, the **actual market value** will probably be the **same** as the theoretical ex-rights price.

(b) If the new funds are expected to generate earnings at a **lower rate**, the **market value** will **fall** below the theoretical ex-rights price. If this happens, **shareholders** will **lose**.

(c) If the new funds are expected to earn at a **higher rate** than current funds, the **market value** should **rise** above the theoretical ex-rights price. If this happens, shareholders will profit by taking up their rights.

The decision by individual shareholders as to whether they take up the offer will therefore depend on:

- The **expected rate of return** on the investment (and the risk associated with it)
- The **return obtainable from other investments** (allowing for the associated risk)

5.11 New issues of shares for listed companies

A listed company can also raise new equity finance through a **public offer** or a **placing**. Usually these methods will be used as a method of refinancing or to finance growth. These methods of issuing shares will dilute the ownership of the existing shareholders. They are also more **expensive** as a method of raising equity finance than a rights issue, as the new issues can incur costs such as those covered earlier.

5.12 Stock split

A stock split occurs where, for example, each ordinary share of $1 each is split into two shares of 50c each, thus creating cheaper shares with **greater marketability**. There is possibly an added psychological advantage in that investors may expect a company which splits its shares in this way to be planning for substantial earnings growth and dividend growth in the future.

As a consequence, the market price of shares may benefit. For example, if one existing share of $1 has a market value of $6, and is then split into two shares of 50c each, the market value of the new shares might settle at, say, $3.10 instead of the expected $3, in anticipation of strong future growth in earnings and dividends.

A stock split changes the share capital but does not raise any new equity finance for the company. It also leaves the company's reserves (as shown in its statement of financial position) unaffected.

5.13 Scrip issue

A scrip issue occurs when a company issues new shares to existing shareholders in proportion to their existing holdings at no charge. The issue is made out of distributable reserves (retained profits).

A scrip issue, like a stock split, raises no extra finance for the company.

The difference between a stock split and a scrip issue is that a scrip issue converts equity reserves into share capital, whereas a stock split leaves reserves unaffected.

A company may make a scrip issue when it wants to pay a dividend to shareholders, but would prefer not to pay the dividend in cash. Scrip dividends are explained in Chapter 7.

5.14 Preference shares

Preference shares are shares which give the right to receive dividends (typically a fixed percentage of the nominal value of the shares) before any dividends can be paid to ordinary shareholders.

As a source of finance, preference shares have several advantages over debt capital.

(a) Dividends do not have to be paid if company performance is poor, whereas interest must be paid on debt capital regardless of profit.

(b) Preference shares are not secured on company assets.

(c) Preference shareholders usually have no voting rights so there is no dilution of control.

There is, however, a fairly significant disadvantage.

(a) Preference share capital is not as tax efficient as debt capital, as dividends paid are not tax deductible, whereas interest on debt is.

6 Principles of capital structure

FAST FORWARD

Capital structure refers to the way in which an organisation is financed, by a combination of the sources of finances discussed above: long-term capital (ordinary shares and reserves, preference shares, loan notes, bank loans, convertible loan stock and so on) and short-term liabilities, such as a bank overdraft and trade creditors. The mix of finance can be measured by **gearing** ratios.

The assets of a business must be financed somehow. When a business is growing, the additional assets must be financed by additional capital.

However using debt to finance the business creates financial risk. **Financial risk** can be seen from different points of view.

(a) **The company as a whole**

If a company builds up debts that it cannot pay when they fall due, it will be forced into liquidation.

(b) **Lenders**

If a company cannot pay its debts, the company will go into liquidation owing lenders money that they are unlikely to recover in full. Lenders will probably want a **higher interest yield** to compensate them for higher financial risk and gearing.

(c) **Ordinary shareholders**

A company will not make any distributable profits unless it is able to earn enough profit from operations to pay all its interest charges, and then tax. The lower the profits or the higher the interest-bearing debts, the less there will be, if there is anything at all, for shareholders.

Ordinary shareholders will probably want a **bigger expected return** from their shares to compensate them for a **higher financial risk**. The market value of shares will therefore depend on gearing, because of this premium for financial risk that shareholders will want to earn.

6.1 Suitability of financing

FAST FORWARD

Factors determining the **suitability** of capital structure include the **stability** of the company's situation, **matching of assets with funds**, **impact on shareholders**, the possibility of **international finance** and the **cost** and **flexibility** of sources available.

6.1.1 Amount provided

A basic issue is whether the proposed source of finance is **able to provide all** the required finance or whether a number of sources will be required. Use of a number of sources could mean that the mix of debt and equity can be adjusted; however there are the complications of having to **keep all the providers happy**, plus **potentially higher arrangement costs** from having to use several sources of finance.

6.1.2 Company circumstances

One determinant of how suitable the gearing mix is is the stability of the company. It may seem obvious, but it is worth stressing that debt financing will be more appropriate when:

- The company is in a **healthy competitive position**
- **Cash flows** and **earnings** are stable
- **Profit margins** are **reasonable**
- The **bulk of the company's assets** are **tangible**
- The **liquidity** and **cash flow position** is **strong**
- The **debt-equity ratio** is **low** in comparison to other companies in the same industry
- **Share prices** are **low**

6.1.3 Matching assets with funds

As a general rule, **assets that yield profits over a long period of time should be financed** by **long-term funds** whereas **working capital** should be **financed by shorter-term funds**.

In this way, the returns made by the asset will be sufficient to pay either the interest cost of the loans raised to buy it, or dividends on its equity funding.

If, however a long-term asset is financed by short-term funds, the company cannot be certain that when the loan becomes repayable, it will have enough cash (from profits) to repay it.

A company would not normally finance all of its short-term assets with short-term liabilities, but instead finance **short-term assets partly with short-term funding** and **partly with long-term funding**.

6.1.4 Long-term capital requirements for replacement and growth

A distinction can be made between long-term capital that is needed to finance the replacement of worn-out assets, and capital that is needed to finance growth.

Aims	Main funding sources
Maintenance of current level of operations	Internal sources
Growth	External finance

6.1.5 Signalling

Some investors may see the issue of debt capital as a sign that the directors are confident enough of the future cash flows of the business to be prepared to commit the company to making **regular interest payments** to **lenders**.

6.1.6 Clientele effect

When considering whether to change gearing significantly, directors may take into account changes in the profile of shareholders. If gearing does change significantly, the company may adjust to a **new risk-return trade off** that is unsuitable for many shareholders. These shareholders will look to sell their shares, whilst other investors, who are now attracted by the new gearing levels, may look to buy shares.

6.1.7 Domestic and international borrowing

If the company is receiving income in a foreign currency or has a long-term investment overseas, it can try to limit the **risk of adverse exchange rate movements** by matching. It can take out a long-term loan and use the foreign currency receipts to repay the loan. Similarly it can try to **match its foreign assets** (property, plant etc) by a **long-term loan** in the foreign currency. However if the asset ultimately generates home currency receipts, there will be a long-term currency risk.

In addition foreign loans may carry a lower **interest rate**, but the principle of **interest rate parity** (covered in Chapter 16) suggests that the foreign currency will ultimately strengthen, and hence loan repayments will become more expensive.

6.1.8 Cost and flexibility

Interest rates on longer-term debt may be higher than interest rates on shorter-term debt. However **issue costs** or **arrangement fees** will be **higher** for shorter-term debt as it has to be renewed more frequently.

A business may also find itself locked into **longer-term debt**, with adverse interest rates and large penalties if it repays the debt early. **Future expectations about interest rates** – the future shape of the yield curve – will therefore have a significant impact on the financing decision.

6.1.9 Taxation

The impact on the company's tax **overall tax position** will need to be considered, also how **tax efficient** the alternative sources of finance are.

6.1.10 Optimal capital structure and the cost of capital

When we consider the capital structure decision, the question arises of whether there is an optimal mix of capital and debt that a company should try to achieve. Under one view (the traditional view) there is an optimal capital mix at which the **average cost of capital**, weighted according to the different forms of capital employed, is **minimised**.

However, the alternative view of **Modigliani and Miller** is that the firm's overall **weighted average cost of capital** is **not influenced** by changes in its **capital structure**. Their argument is that the issue of debt causes the cost of equity to rise in such a way that the benefits of debt on returns are exactly offset. Investors themselves adjust their level of personal gearing and thus the level of corporate gearing becomes irrelevant. We shall discuss this debate further in Chapter 11.

6.2 Acceptability of capital structure

> **FAST FORWARD**
>
> The **acceptability** of the **proposed capital structure** will depend on director-shareholder attitudes to **risk**, also the **degree of control** they are willing to sacrifice, and the **costs** and **commitments** required for extra funding.

6.2.1 Risk attitudes

The choice of capital structure will not only depend on company circumstances, but the **attitudes** that directors and owners have towards the **principal risks**. This will include the risks that are specific to the business, more general economic risks, and also the risks of raising finance. **Foreign exchange risk** will need to be considered if the company is considering using international sources of finance. It could, for example, adversely affect the company's reputation if it made a rights issue that was not fully subscribed.

6.2.2 Loss of control

The directors and shareholders may be unwilling to accept the **conditions** and the **loss of control** that obtaining extra finance will mean. Control may be diminished whether equity or loan funding is sought:

(a) **Issuing shares** to outsiders may **dilute** the **control** of the existing shareholders and directors, and the company will be subject to greater regulatory control if it obtains a stock market listing.

(b) The price of additional debt finance may be **security** restricting disposal of the assets secured and **covenants** that limit the company's rights to **dispose of assets** in general or to pay dividends.

6.2.3 Costs

The directors may consider that the **extra interest costs** the company is committed to are too high; remember that companies are not legally obliged to pay dividends, although obviously if they don't do so, there may be an impact on the share price. On the other hand the effective **cost of debt** might be cheaper than the **cost of equity**, particularly if tax relief can be obtained.

The costs of **arranging new finance sources** may also be significant, particularly if the business is contemplating using a number of different sources over time.

6.2.4 Commitments

The interest and repayment schedules that the company is required to meet may be considered **too tight**. The collateral loan providers require may also be too much, particularly if the directors are themselves required to provide **personal guarantees.**

6.2.5 Present sources of finance

Perhaps it's easy to find reasons why new sources of finance may not be desirable, but equally they may be considered more acceptable than drawing on current sources. For example shareholders may be **unwilling to contribute further funds** in a rights issue; the business may wish to improve its relations with its suppliers, and one condition may be lessening its reliance on trade credit.

6.3 Feasibility of capital structure

> **FAST FORWARD**
>
> The mix of finance chosen must be **feasible;** companies may face **restrictions** in the finance available, and will not be able to commit to repaying too much at any one time.

Even if directors and shareholders are happy with the implications of obtaining significant extra finance, the company may not be able to obtain that finance.

6.3.1 Lenders' attitudes

Whether lenders are prepared to lend the company any money will depend on the company's circumstances, particularly as they affect the company's ability to generate **cash** and **security** for the loan.

6.3.2 Availability and popularity of finance

If the **stock market** is **depressed**, it may be difficult to raise cash through share issues, so major amounts will have to be borrowed. On the other hand specific sources of finance may be particularly appealing to investors.

How quickly amounts are available may also be an issue.

6.3.3 Future trends

Likely **future trends** of **fund availability** will be significant if a business is likely to require a number of injections of funds over the next few years. The business needs to consider how much current decisions may affect its ability to raise funds in the future.

6.3.4 Restrictions in loan agreements

Restrictions written into agreements on current loans may prohibit a business from taking out **further loans**, or may require that its gearing does **not exceed specified limits**.

6.3.5 Maturity dates

If a business already has significant debt repayable in a few years' time, because of **cash flow restrictions** it may not be able to take out further debt repayable around the same time.

7 Green finance

> **FAST FORWARD**
>
> **Green finance** refers to the financing of investments that provide environmental benefits, and is often used to describe the financing of investments that carry significant benefits in terms of meeting a company's ESG objectives.

Companies that are pursuing an environmental/sustainable agenda are likely to require finance to support investment in projects that provide environmental benefits such as reductions in pollution, reductions in greenhouse gas emissions and improved energy efficiency.

Green finance (sometimes referred to as ethical finance or sustainable finance) describes the financing of investments providing such environmental benefits.

7.1 Green bonds

A green bond is a type of fixed-interest bond used to raise money for **climate and environmental projects**. These bonds are typically secured and have the same credit rating as a company's other debt obligations.

Green bonds may come with tax incentives to encourage their use (eg no tax to pay on interest earned) which may mean that they can be issued by a company with a lower coupon rate.

Green bonds may also be cheaper because of rising demand for such bonds and because there is often a view that companies who have an ESG strategy are seen as better borrowers from a credit risk perspective due to their focus on the long term sustainability and business continuity.

To qualify for green bond status, they often need to be verified by a third party such as the Climate Bonds Standard Board, which certifies that the bond will channel finance to environmentally beneficial projects.

Over the past decade green bonds have increased in popularity dramatically.

7.2 Green loans

A green loan is a loan used to finance an environmentally sustainable project such as the construction of a windfarm. Some banks, often with government backing, specialise in financing green projects.

For example, in the UK, the Green Investment Bank (GIB) was launched in 2012 to finance investment in reducing greenhouse gas emissions, promoting efficiency in the use of natural resources, protection of the environment, and promoting environmental sustainability. The GIB was privatised in 2017 (now the Green Investment Group), but retains the same goals.

Like green bonds, green loans may potentially be cheaper than standard loans due to possible government incentives and high demand for this type of business from banks.

However, such loans often carry a higher administrative burden to the borrower, who will need to demonstrate compliance with the terms of the loan (ie that the finance has only been used on a specific green project, and that the green benefits of the project have been independently verified).

There may also likely be consequences to the borrower for breaching the ESG terms and the loan no longer being considered green, for example:

- A higher interest rate may be imposed
- The loan may need to be repaid

7.3 Sustainability linked loans

Sustainability Linked Loans (SLLs) are **loans for any purpose** (whether 'green' or not), with an in-built pricing mechanism that reduces the cost of the loan if the borrower achieves certain sustainable or ESG (environmental, social and governance) related targets.

The ability to utilise SLLs across a range of projects, rather than financing a single asset, has added to the attractiveness of this source of green finance and the use of SLLs has grown rapidly in recent years.

7.4 Green equity funds

Many stock markets produce an index of firms that satisfy social and environmental criteria.

For example, in the UK the London Stock Market have the FTSE4Good index. To be included in the FTSE4Good Indexes, companies must, for example, support human rights, make progress to become environmentally sustainable, and ensure good labour standards for their own company and for companies that supply them as well.

This helps investors to target investments in company with higher standards of behaviour in terms of social responsibility.

As with other forms of green finance, the reduction in risk from compliance with high ESG standards can mean the investors are happy with a lower return i.e. a reduction in the cost of equity.

Chapter Roundup

- Internal sources of finance include **retained earnings** and **increasing working capital efficiency**.
- A range of short-term sources of finance are available to businesses including **overdrafts**, **short-term loans**, **trade credit** and **operating lease finance**.
- A range of long-term sources of finance are available to businesses including **debt finance**, **leasing**, **venture capital** and **equity finance**.
- The choice of **debt finance** that a company can make depends on:
  - The size of the company; a public issue of bonds is only available to a large company
  - The duration of the required financing
  - Whether a fixed or floating interest rate is preferred (fixed rates are more expensive, but floating rates are riskier)
  - The security (collateral) that can be offered and the security that may be demanded by a lender
- The term **bonds** describes various forms of long-term debt a company may issue, such as **loan notes**, which may be:
  - **Redeemable**
  - **Irredeemable**

  Bonds or loans come in various forms, including:
  - **Floating rate loan notes**
  - **Zero coupon bonds**
  - **Convertible bonds**
- **Convertible bonds** are bonds that give the holder the right to convert to other securities, normally ordinary shares, at a predetermined price/rate and time.
- Equity finance is raised through the sale of **ordinary shares** to investors via a **new issue** or a **rights issue**.
- A company can obtain a **stock market listing** for its shares through a **public offer** or a **placing**.
- A **rights issue** is an offer to existing shareholders enabling them to buy more shares, usually at a price lower than the current market price and in proportion to their existing shareholding.
- **Capital structure** refers to the way in which an organisation is financed by a combination of the sources of finance discussed above; long-term capital (ordinary shares and reserves, preference shares, loan notes, bank loans, convertible loan stock and so on) and short-term liabilities, such as a bank overdraft and trade creditors. The mix of finance can be measured by **gearing** ratios.
- Factors determining the **suitability** of capital structure include the **stability** of the company's situation, **matching of assets and funds**, **impact on shareholders**, the possibility of **international finance** and the **cost** and **flexibility** of sources available.
- The **acceptability** of the **proposed capital structure** will depend on director-shareholder attitudes to **risk**, also the **degree of control** they are willing to sacrifice, and the **costs** and **commitments** required for extra funding.
- The mix of finance chosen must be **feasible**; companies may face **restrictions** in the finance available, and will not be able to commit to repaying too much at any one time.
- The use of **green finance** should be considered where a project delivers ESG benefits; this can include green bonds, green loans, sustainability-linked loans or the use of a green stock market index.

LEARNING OUTCOME 1 THE FINANCIAL ENVIRONMENT AND CAPITAL REQUIREMENTS AND CONSEQUENT COSTS

Quick Quiz

1. Identify four reasons why a company may seek a stock market listing.

2. A company's shares have a nominal value of $1 and a market value of $3. In a rights issue, one new share would be issued for every three shares at a price of $2.60. What is the theoretical ex-rights price?

3. Which of the following is least likely to be a reason for seeking a stock market flotation?

    A Improving the existing owners' control over the business
    B Access to a wider pool of finance
    C Enhancement of the company's image
    D Transfer of capital to other uses

4. Which of the following is not true of a rights issue by a listed company?

    A Rights issues do not require a prospectus.
    B The rights issues price can be at a discount to market price.
    C If shareholders do not take up the rights, the rights lapse.
    D Relative voting rights are unaffected if shareholders exercise their rights.

5. A company has 12% loan notes in issue, which have a market value of $135 per $100 nominal value. What is:

    (a) The coupon rate?
    (b) The amount of interest payable per annum per $100 (nominal) of loan note?

6. Convertible securities are fixed-return securities that may be converted into zero coupon bonds/ordinary shares/warrants. (Delete as appropriate.)

7. What is the value of $100 12% debt redeemable in three years' time at a premium of 20c per $ if the loan holder's required return is 10%?

8. Identify one advantage of a green bond compared to a conventional bond, and one disadvantage.

Answers to Quick Quiz

1. **Four** of the following **five**: access to a wider pool of finance; improved marketability of shares; transfer of capital to other uses (eg founder members liquidating holdings); enhancement of company image; making growth by acquisition possible.

2. $\frac{1}{3+1}$ (($3 \times 3) + \$2.60) = \$2.90$

3. A   Flotation is likely to involve a significant loss of control to a wider circle of investors.

4. C   Shareholders have the option of renouncing the rights and selling them on the market.

5. (a) 12%
   (b) $12

6. Convertible securities are fixed-return securities that may be converted into **ordinary shares**.

7.

Years			Discount factor 10%	Present value
		$		$
1-3	Interest	12	2.487	29.84
3	Redemption premium	120	0.751	90.12
Value of debt				119.96

8. Advantage (for example): high demand for this type of investment, possibility of low interest rate if seen to reduce a company's risk.

   Disadvantage (for example): money is tied to the finance of a specific project, high compliance costs.

End of chapter questions

1. Mrs Johnson (AIA May 2015)

Mrs Johnson trained as a designer and is considering setting up her own business. Her plan is to design a range of schoolbags suitable for children aged 11-16. She would outsource the manufacturing of the schoolbags and sell the bags online via the internet. She has prepared a simple business plan that forecasts profits for the next five years. The business plan projects small profits in the initial two years and increasing profits in the following three years. The business plan only shows projected revenues less projected costs; it does not include any figures relating to the funding options available to the business. Mrs Johnson needs to fund the business and she has thought of two options. A friend, who has successfully run her own business for the past twenty years, might be willing to buy an equity stake in the company. There have been no discussions as to the percentage of the company's equity that this friend would acquire should she provide the funding. Mrs Johnson would be the only other shareholder. The other funding option is to borrow the required amount from a bank. The bank she has approached has indicated that security would be required. Mrs Johnson could secure the bank loan on her own house and has no other security. Interest on the bank loan would be payable monthly.

Required

Mrs Johnson has asked you to prepare a report evaluating the proposed financing choices.   **(20 marks)**

2. Bryden Ltd (AIA May 2013)

Bryden Ltd is a company that grows and sells plants. The business was set up 15 years ago by a husband and wife, Mr and Mrs Bryden. They set up the business as they were very keen gardeners. They purchased a large plot of land and this is where they still continue to grow and sell the plants. The plot of land was purchased for £100,000 but it has risen in value. Today it is worth an estimated £950,000 as property developers have become very interested in purchasing the land. Bryden Ltd employs a small number of staff who all have a lot of expertise in growing plants. They have become very well known for the quality of their plants and people travel quite large distances to buy from Bryden Ltd.

One of the important risk factors that can affect plant sellers is whether they are able to anticipate what the next trend in plants will be. In the past Bryden Ltd has noted that if they are unsuccessful in this respect then operating profit can drop by 30%. The year ended 30 April 2013 can be categorised as an unsuccessful year as the company failed to predict the trend. The resulting profit was as follows:

BRYDEN LTD
SUMMARY OF THE STATEMENT OF COMPREHENSIVE INCOME FOR THE YEAR ENDED 30 APRIL 2013

	£'000
Revenue	800
Cost of sales	(355)
Gross profit	445
Operating expenses	(221)
Operating profit	224
Finance costs – interest payable	(0)
Profit before taxation	224
Taxation	(45)
Profit after tax	179

The company pays corporation tax at a rate of approximately 20%.

The sales of plants are not spread evenly throughout the year. Most plant sales are in the period March to May as this is the time of year for gardeners to plant.

The company currently has no debt finance and the two shareholders are Mr and Mrs Bryden.

They are thinking that they would like to expand the business significantly and to do this they would need further funding. They are considering raising £750,000 which they estimate would result in additional operating profit of £90,000 per year. This additional operating profit figure is assuming that they successfully predict the next trend for plants.

The £750,000 would be used to: (1) purchase additional greenhouses for growing more plants, (2) buy three more plots of land so that they can establish a total of four sales outlets and (3) finance additional working capital required for setting up the new sales outlets.

Mr and Mrs Bryden cannot decide whether to raise the £750,000 through debt at an interest rate of 9% or to take up the offer of a successful businesswoman who will provide the amount in return for a shareholding of 50% of the company.

Required

Mr and Mrs Bryden have asked you to prepare a report evaluating the proposed financing options. In evaluating the financing options you should:

(1) Provide any calculations that you consider appropriate.
(2) Advise of any further information that would be useful.
(3) Advise of any assumptions you have made. **(20 marks)**

Capital markets and government policy

Topic list	Syllabus reference
1 The flow of funds	LO1
2 Financial intermediation and credit creation	LO1
3 Commercial banks as providers of funds	LO1
4 Money markets and capital markets	LO1
5 The efficient market hypothesis	LO1
6 Competition policy	LO1
7 Government aid schemes	LO1
8 Corporate governance	LO1

Introduction

Having discussed the scope of financial management and the objectives of firms and other organisations, we now introduce the framework of **markets** and **institutions** through which the financing of a business takes place. We also look at some theoretical aspects of how this framework operates including the **efficient market hypothesis**, which tries to account for why share prices behave as they do. The chapter concludes by considering the broader economic environment within which organisations operate.

1 The flow of funds

FAST FORWARD

Within an economy, some people, firms and organisations will have money which is surplus to their needs (**surplus units**), while others have less money than they need for their spending requirements (**deficit units**). **Credit** involves lending money, and the transfer (usually in return for interest payments) of money from surplus units to deficit units.

Having discussed the main units of the economy and the reasons why there is a demand and supply of funds to the economy, we discuss now how **surplus units** are able to transfer surplus funds to **deficit units**, and how the deficit units can raise the requisite funds.

There are two ways in which the transfer of funds takes place. First, there is the direct way, in which economic units transact directly in an organised market. There are many markets that cater for all the needs of the economic units in terms of maturity or currency. A schematic approach of the flow of funds is shown as

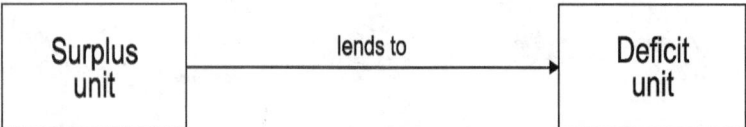

The second way of bringing together surplus and deficit units is through a **financial intermediary**. The intermediary provides a service to both the surplus unit and the deficit unit, by accepting surplus funds and making these funds available to a deficit unit.

The main advantage of financial intermediation is that it provides a way of channelling funds for large and small economic units. For example, a person might deposit savings with a bank, and the bank might use its collective deposits of savings to provide a loan to a company.

The two methods of channelling funds are shown schematically below.

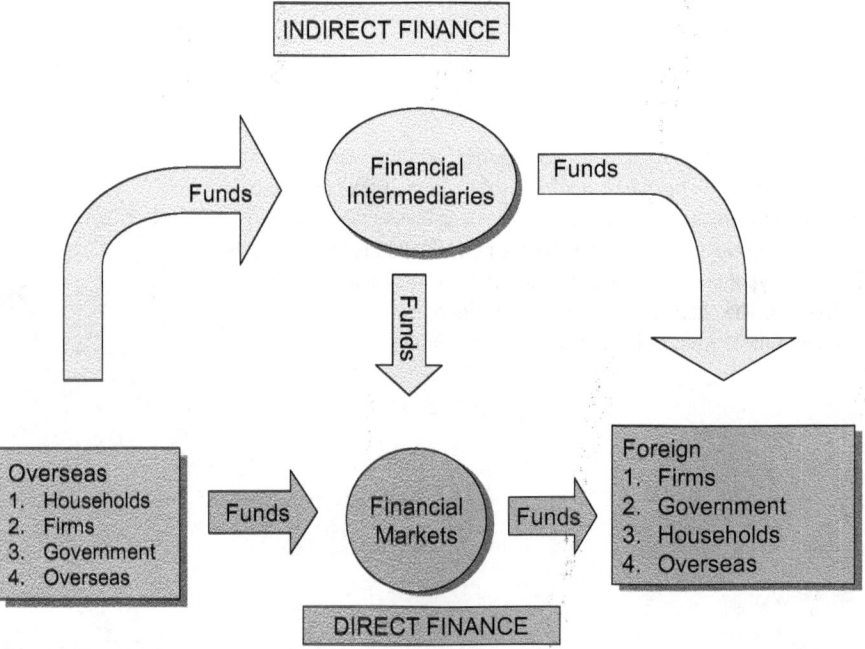

Figure 1 Flow of funds in an open economy, showing the role of financial intermediation

In the next sections we shall discuss the main financial intermediaries and financial markets in the financial system.

2 Financial intermediation and credit creation

FAST FORWARD

A **financial intermediary** links those with surplus funds (eg **lenders**) to those with funds deficits (eg potential **borrowers**) thus providing **aggregation** and **economies of scale**, **risk pooling** and **maturity transformation**.

2.1 Financial intermediation

Key term

Financial intermediary is a party bringing together providers and users of finance, either as broker or as principal.

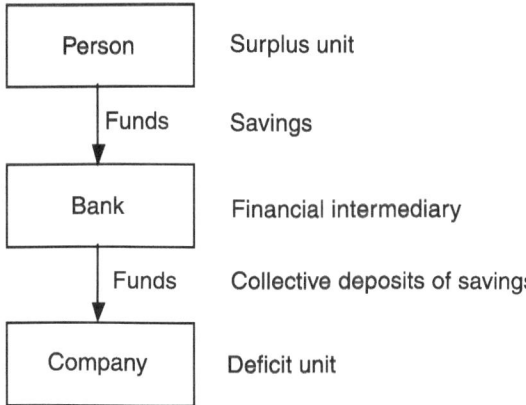

Not all intermediation takes place between savers and investors. Some institutions (such as the discount houses which intermediate between the Bank of England and the commercial banks) act mainly as **intermediaries** between **other institutions**. Financial intermediaries may also lend abroad or borrow from abroad.

Exam focus point

Bear in mind that **financial markets** and **institutions** are topic areas on which the examiner is not expected to set full questions. These topics could, however, be examined in subsections of a question.

2.1.1 Examples of financial intermediaries

- Commercial banks
- Finance houses
- Building societies
- Government national savings department
- Institutional investors eg pension funds and investment trusts

2.2 The benefits of financial intermediation

Financial intermediaries perform the following functions:

(a) They provide obvious and **convenient** ways in which a lender can save money. Instead of having to find a suitable borrower for his money, the lender can deposit his money with a financial intermediary. All the lender has to do is decide for **how long** he might want to lend the money, and **what sort of return** he requires, and he can then choose a financial intermediary that offers a **financial instrument** to suit his requirements.

(b) Financial intermediaries also provide a **ready source of funds** for **borrowers**. Even when money is in short supply, a borrower will usually find a financial intermediary prepared to lend some.

(c) They can **aggregate** or **'package'** the amounts lent by savers and lend on to borrowers in different amounts.

(d) **Risk** for individual lenders is reduced by **pooling**. Since financial intermediaries lend to a large number of individuals and organisations, any losses suffered through default by borrowers or capital losses are effectively pooled and **borne** as **costs** by the intermediary. Such losses are **shared among lenders in general**.

(e) By pooling the funds of large numbers of people, some financial institutions are able to give investors access to **diversified portfolios** covering a varied range of different securities, such as unit trusts and investment trusts.

(f) Financial intermediaries, most importantly, provide **maturity transformation**; ie they bridge the gap between the wish of most lenders for **liquidity** and the desire of most borrowers for **loans** over longer periods.

2.3 Bank deposits and the creation of money ('credit creation')

Banks create money when they lend because when a bank lends money, most of the money will find its way back into the banking system as **new customer deposits**. This means that the amount lent by the bank adds to the money supply.

Suppose, for example, that in a country with a single bank, a customer C deposits £100,000. The bank, we will assume, re-lends all these deposits to another customer D. This customer D uses the money he has borrowed to buy goods and services from firm Y. If firm Y, after receiving payment, then puts the money into its own account with the bank, the bank's deposits will have doubled.

Liabilities of the bank	£	Assets of the bank	£
Deposit of customer C	100,000	Loan to customer D	100,000
Deposit of firm Y	100,000		
	200,000		

This will enable the bank to re-lend more money (another £100,000), to bring its assets up to £200,000 and this in turn will create even more bank deposits. This cycle could go on and on, with the bank making more and more loans, and the people who are paid for goods and services bought with the loans putting all their receipts back into the bank as extra deposits. In short, **'every loan creates a deposit'**.

Extra bank lending (and building society lending) therefore has a dual effect. It **increases the money supply**. It **provides credit** which borrowers use to increase their amount of spending. Lending adds to spending in the economy.

Key term

Credit creation is the process whereby banks and other deposit-taking and lending institutions can, on the basis of an increase in reserve assets, expand the volume of lending and deposit liabilities by more than the initial increase in reserves.

3 Commercial banks as providers of funds

FAST FORWARD

Commercial banks can provide
- A payment mechanism
- Notes and coins
- Bank accounts
- Loans and overdrafts
- For individuals and businesses

An important grouping of financial intermediaries is the **commercial banks**, which include:

(a) The retail banks, which include the well known 'High Street' banks

(b) The wholesale banks, which offer services mainly to larger customers, including large companies. (The wholesale banks include merchant banks and overseas banks.)

3.1 The functions of the commercial banks

The functions of the commercial banks include the following.

(a) They provide a **payments mechanism** – a way in which individuals, firms and government can make payments to each other. The **'clearing system'** of the clearing banks enables individuals and firms to make payments.

(b) The banks are also a source from which individuals and firms can **obtain notes and coins**.

(c) They provide a place for individuals, firms and government to **store their wealth**. Banks compete with other financial institutions to attract the funds of individuals and firms.

(d) They act as **providers of funds** by lending money in the form of loans or overdrafts.

3.2 Bank borrowing

Borrowings from banks are an important source of finance to companies as well as to unincorporated businesses. Bank lending is mainly short-term to medium-term.

Short-term to medium-term borrowing may take various forms.

(a) An **overdraft**, which a company should keep within a limit set by the bank. Interest is charged (at a variable rate) on the amount by which the company is overdrawn from day to day.

(b) A **short-term loan.** This may last for up to three years.

(c) **Medium-term loans.** These are loans for a period of from three to ten years.

The rate of interest charged on medium-term bank lending to large companies will typically be a set margin above the rate at which banks lend to each other, with the size of the margin depending on the **credit standing** and **riskiness** of the borrower.

Lending to **smaller companies** will typically be at a margin **above the bank's base rate** and at either a variable or a fixed rate of interest.

Lending on **overdraft** is always at a **variable rate**.

A loan at a variable rate of interest is sometimes referred to as a **floating rate loan.**

Longer term bank loans will sometimes be available, usually for the purchase of property, where the loan takes the form of a mortgage.

LEARNING OUTCOME 1 THE FINANCIAL ENVIRONMENT AND CAPITAL REQUIREMENTS AND CONSEQUENT COSTS

4 Money markets and capital markets

FAST FORWARD

> The **capital markets** and **money markets** are markets for long-term and short-term capital respectively.
>
> A stock market (in the UK: the **main market** plus the **AIM**) acts as a **primary market** for raising finance, and as a **secondary market** for the trading of existing securities (ie stocks and shares).

The **capital markets**, being markets for long-term capital, are distinguished from the **money markets**, which are markets for:

- Trading short-term financial instruments
- Short-term lending and borrowing

Key terms

> **Short-term capital** is capital that is lent or borrowed for a period which might range from as short as overnight up to about one year, and sometimes longer.
>
> **Long-term capital** is capital invested or lent and borrowed for a period of five years or more.

There is a 'grey area' between long-term and short-term capital, which is lending and borrowing for a period from about a year up to about five years, which may be referred to as **medium-term capital**.

4.1 The money markets

The money markets are **operated** by the **banks** and other **financial institutions**. Although the money markets largely involve borrowing and lending by banks, some large companies and nationalised industries, as well as the government, are involved in money market operations. The building societies have also become major participants in the money markets since liberalisation of the building societies has allowed them to raise wholesale funds.

The primary market is known as the **official market**, the other markets as the **parallel** or **wholesale markets**.

Types of market	
Primary market	Approved institutions deal in financial instruments with the Bank of England (UK Central bank). The Bank of England uses trading to control short-term interest rates
Interbank market	Banks lend short-term funds to each other
Eurocurrency market	Banks lend and borrow in foreign currencies
Certificate of deposit market	Market for trading in Certificates of Deposit (negotiable instruments acknowledging deposits)
Local authority market	Local authorities borrow short-term funds by issuing and selling short-term debt instruments
Finance house market	Dealing in short-term loans raised from money markets by finance houses
Inter-company market	Direct short-term lending between treasury departments of large companies

4.2 The capital markets

Capital markets are markets for trading in long-term finance, in the form of long-term financial instruments such as equities and debentures. In the UK, the principal capital markets are:

(a) The Stock Exchange **'main market'** (for companies with a full Stock Exchange listing)
(b) The more loosely regulated 'second tier' **Alternative Investment Market (AIM)**

The Stock Exchange is also the market for dealings in **government securities**.

Firms obtain long-term or medium-term capital in one of the following ways.

(a) They may raise **share capital**. Most new issues of share capital are in the form of ordinary share capital. Firms that issue ordinary share capital are inviting investors to take an **equity stake** in the business, or to increase their existing equity stake.

(b) They may raise **loan capital**. Long-term loan capital might be raised in the form of a mortgage or debenture.

The stock markets serve two main purposes.

(a) As **primary markets** they enable organisations to **raise new finance**, by issuing new shares or new debentures. In the UK, a company must **have public company status** (be a plc) to be allowed to raise finance from the public on a capital market.

(b) As **secondary markets** they enable existing investors to **sell their investments**, should they wish to do so. The marketability of securities is a very important feature of the capital markets, because investors are more willing to buy stocks and shares if they know that they could sell them easily, should they wish to.

These are the main functions of a stock market, but we can add two more important ones.

(a) When a company comes to the stock market for the first time, and 'floats' its shares on the market, the owners of the company can **realise** some of the **value of their shares** in cash, because they will offer a proportion of their personally-held shares for sale to new investors.

(b) When one company wants to **take over** another, it is common to do so by issuing shares to finance the takeover. Takeovers by means of a share exchange are only feasible if the shares that are offered can be readily traded on a stock market, and so have an identifiable market value.

Question — Financial Times

Get hold of a copy of the Companies and Markets section of the weekday *Financial Times*, and look out for points relevant to your studies. Note the various share prices quotations on the Main Market and the AIM on the Share Service pages. This may help to put some of the topics covered here into context.

4.3 The Alternative Investment Market (AIM)

The London Stock Exchange launched the AIM in 1995 as a market for smaller, growing, companies that cannot qualify for or do not wish to join the Official List (or 'main market').

AIM companies might be new business 'start-ups' or well established family businesses, from high technology firms to traditional manufacturers. The AIM is designed to attract companies which wish to **cut the cost** of a **stock market** quotation.

4.3.1 Example: Capital markets

What advantages are there to a firm of:

(a) A listing on the main stock market?
(b) A listing on the Alternative Investment Market?
(c) Issuing bonds?

Solution

(a) The main stock market

Public profile, investor confidence (audited accounts, regular briefings, NEDs, three years of successful trading history), access to wider pool of equity finance, allows owners to realise some of their investment.

(b) The Alternative Investment Market

Lower membership fees and compliance requirements (no successful trading history or corporate governance requirements).

(c) Bonds

Bonds are a liquid investment, so will often be cheaper than a bank loan. A bond will be called in if its terms are breached; a bank may be more willing to renegotiate a loan whose terms have been breached (they hope to do more business with the company). Another advantage of bonds is that often they can be redeemed over a range of dates at the company's discretion.

4.4 Institutional investors

Institutional investors are institutions which have large amounts of funds which they want to invest, and they will invest in stocks and shares or any other assets which offer satisfactory returns and security or lend money to companies directly. The institutional investors are now the biggest investors on the stock market.

The major institutional investors in the UK are **pension funds**, **insurance companies, investment trusts**, **unit trusts** and **venture capital organisations**. Of these, pension funds and insurance companies have the largest amounts of funds to invest.

4.5 Fintech

FinTech (financial technology) can be thought of as the software and other modern technologies used by businesses to provide automated and improved financial services.

Changes in technology have helped to develop new financial institutions and new financial markets which are transforming financial services.

There are many examples of FinTech, but here we focus on how FinTech has impacted on financial institutions and financial markets.

4.5.1 Financial institutions

Challenger banks seek to offer a wide range of **online financial services** normally without the expense of maintaining a 'bricks and mortar' banking network. In 2015 Monzo was among the first so-called 'challenger' banks to launch in the UK; many more have followed since then.

More recently, challenger banks have targeted business customers, seeking to use their low cost base to offer competitive products and also offering more flexible services. For example:

- multi-currency accounts which allow business customers collect, store, convert and pay in a wide range of foreign currencies.
- using an app to allow currency hedging eg using forward contracts to fix the exchange rate (forward contracts are covered in Chapter 16).
- allowing greater visibility of the stage of payment of customer invoices (supply chain finance is covered in Chapter 21).

4.5.2 Financial markets

Another impact of FinTech has been to increase the availability of long-term finance by creating new financial markets such as the electronic platforms used for crowdfunding, peer to peer lending and security token offerings.

Fintech and financial markets	
Crowdfunding	Crowdfunding allows a company to access finance via an online crowdfunding platform (eg Kickstarter) to pitch for finance from a large number of potential investors.
	A successful pitch will require a well thought out business plan setting and a high-quality management team (in terms of their skills and experience).
	Crowdfunding is available to start-ups, as well as established companies, and can be a relatively quick process (sometimes taking as little as a couple of months).
	It is also a way of building awareness of a business and helping to attract customers.
	Some crowdfunding platforms offer both equity and debt finance (debt finance is also called peer to peer lending and was covered in Chapter 2).
Peer to peer lending	Peer-to-peer (or P2P) lending connects established businesses looking to borrow with investors who want to lend, usually via an online platform.
	This can result in cheaper loan finance compared to a bank loan because the lender is not having to support the cost of maintaining the infrastructure of a financial intermediary (eg the branch network).
	P2P lending can also be quicker to arrange than a bank loan because the process can be initiated and processed outside normal bank opening hours.
	P2P lending is not normally available to start-up companies because investors require an established trading history. Platforms usually require borrowers to have a trading track record, to submit financial accounts, and will perform credit checks as part of the credit assessment.
	The use of P2P lending has grown rapidly in recent years.
Security token offerings	Blockchain technology has facilitated the use of security token offerings to raise long-term finance.
	With a security token offering, an investor receives a token eg a share in exchange for payment made in a cryptocurrency such as Bitcoin.
	Historically there have been fewer regulations surrounding security token offerings compared to share issues. This has made them more attractive to companies as a way of raising long-term equity finance.

5 The efficient market hypothesis

FAST FORWARD

The **efficient market hypothesis** suggests that **share prices reflect** the **type of information** which is available to investors.

The UK and US stock markets are perhaps efficient capital markets. An 'efficient capital market' in this context is one in which:

(a) The prices of securities bought and sold **reflect all** the **relevant information** which is available to the buyers and sellers – in other words, share prices change quickly to reflect all new information about future prospects.

(b) **No individual dominates** the market.

(c) **Transaction costs** of buying and selling are **not so high** as to discourage trading significantly.

If the stock market is efficient, share prices should vary in a rational way.

(a) If a company makes a **profitable investment**, shareholders will get to know about it, and the **market price** of its shares will **rise** in anticipation of future dividend increases.

(b) If a company makes a **bad investment** shareholders will find out and so the **price** of its shares will **fall**.

(c) If **interest rates rise**, shareholders will want a **higher return** from their investments, so **market prices** will **fall**.

An efficient market is one in which the market prices of all the securities traded on it reflect all the available information. In such a market, there would be no possibility of 'speculative bubbles' in which share prices are pushed up or down by speculative pressure to unrealistically high or low levels. Investors will be reassured that the prices they pay for shares and loan stock are a **fair reflection** of value.

5.1 The definition of efficiency

Different types of efficiency can be distinguished in the context of the operation of financial markets.

Types of efficiency	
Operational	Minimisation of transaction costs such as commissions, interest rate margins and loan arrangement fees
Informational	Reflects ability of stock market to absorb information widely at minimum cost
Pricing	Market prices of all securities reflect all available information. It has three forms: • Weak • Semi-strong • Strong It arises out of operational and informational efficiency
Allocative	Direction of funds towards firms making best use of them, arises out of pricing efficiency

Under the **weak form** hypothesis of **market efficiency**, current share prices **reflect all information available from past changes in the price**.

Research to prove that the stock market displays weak form efficiency has been based on the principle that:

- If share price changes are random, and
- If there is no connection between past price movements and new share price changes,

then it should be possible to prove statistically there is no correlation between successive changes in the price of a share, that is, that **trends** in prices **cannot be detected**. Proofs of the absence of trends have been claimed in the work of various writers.

Semi-strong form tests attempt to show that the stock market displays semi-strong efficiency, by which we mean that current share prices reflect both:

- All **relevant information** about **past price movements** and their implications, and
- All **knowledge** which is **available publicly** in the financial press, annual accounts, company announcements.

Research in both the UK and the USA has suggested that market prices anticipate mergers several months before they are formally announced, and the conclusion drawn is that the stock markets in these countries **do** exhibit semi-strong efficiency.

Strong form efficiency means that share prices reflect all information available:

- From past price changes
- From public knowledge or anticipation, and
- From insider knowledge available to experts such as investment managers

If strong form efficiency applies, management should concentrate simply on **maximising** the **net present value** of its **investments.** It need not worry, for example, about the effect on share prices of financial results in the published accounts. Investors will make allowances for low profits or dividends in the current year if higher profits or dividends are expected in the future.

Exam focus point

> Market efficiency is likely to be tested in the context of how a company's assessment of market efficiency would influence the company's actions.

5.2 The implications of the efficient market hypothesis

If the strong form of the efficient market hypothesis is correct, a company's **real financial position** will be **reflected in its share price**. Its real financial position includes both its **current position** and its expected **future profitability**.

The implication for an investor is that if the market shows **strong form** or **semi-strong form** efficiency, he can **rarely spot shares** at a **bargain price** that will soon rise sharply in value. This is because the market will already have anticipated future developments, and will have reflected these in the share price. All an investor can do, instead of looking for share bargains, is to concentrate on building up a **good spread of shares** (a portfolio) in order to achieve a satisfactory balance between **risk and return**.

The main consequences of efficient markets for financial managers will be that they simply need to **concentrate** on **maximising the net present value** of the **company's investments** in order to maximise the wealth of shareholders. Managers need not worry, for example, about the effect on share prices of financial results in the published accounts because investors will make **allowances** for **low profits** or **dividends** in the current year if higher profits or dividends are expected in the future. A company's real financial position will be reflected in its share price.

If the market is strongly efficient, there is little point in financial managers attempting strategies that attempt to mislead the markets.

(a) There is no point for example in trying to identify a correct date when **shares** should be **issued**, since share prices will always reflect the true worth of the company – they will not be over or under valued at any point in time.

(b) The market will identify any attempts to **window dress the accounts** and put an optimistic spin on the figures.

(c) The market will decide what **level of return** it requires for the risk involved in making an investment in the company. It is pointless for the company to try to change the market's view by issuing different types of capital instruments.

Similarly if the company is looking to expand, the directors will be wasting their time if they seek as **takeover targets** companies whose shares are undervalued, since the market will fairly value all companies' shares.

Only if the market is semi-strongly efficient and the financial managers possess **inside information** that would significantly alter the price of the company's shares if released to the market could they perhaps gain an advantage. However, attempts to take account of this inside information may breach insider dealing laws.

5.2.1 Example: Efficient market hypothesis

Wallace Co announced yesterday that it plans to invest in a new project with a huge positive net present value. The share price in Wallace Co doubled yesterday after the announcement.

What type of market efficiency does this indicate?

Solution

This indicates a semi strong form efficient market as the share price in Wallace Co doubled after the news of the new project was made public.

Exam focus point

The examiner has noted that market efficiency is often poorly understood, so this topic will be examined frequently in this paper.

6 Competition policy

6.1 Regulation and market failure

FAST FORWARD

The government influences markets in various ways, one of which is through direct **regulation** (eg the **Competition and Markets Authority**).

Key term

Market failure is said to occur when the market mechanism fails to result in economic efficiency, and therefore the outcome is sub-optimal.

An important role of the government is the regulation of private markets where these fail to bring about an efficient use of resources. In response to the existence of market failure, and as an alternative to taxation and public provision of production, the state often resorts to regulating economic activity in a variety of ways. Of the various forms of market failure, the following are the cases where regulation of markets can often be the most appropriate policy response.

(a) **Imperfect competition**

Where one company's large share or complete domination of the market is leading to **inefficiency** or **excessive profits**, the state may intervene, for example through controls on prices or profits, in order to try to reduce the effects of this power.

(b) **Social costs**

A possible means of dealing with the problem of social costs or **externalities** is *via* some form of regulation. Regulations might include, for example, controls on emissions of pollutants, restrictions on car use in urban areas, the banning of smoking in public buildings, or compulsory car insurance.

(c) **Imperfect information**

Regulation is often the best form of government action whenever informational inadequacies are undermining the efficient operation of private markets. This is particularly so when consumer choice is being distorted.

(d) **Equity**

The government may also resort to regulation to **improve social justice**.

6.2 Types of regulation

Regulation can be defined as any form of state interference with the operation of the free market. This could involve regulating demand, supply, price, profit, quantity, quality, entry, exit, information, technology, or any other aspect of production and consumption in the market.

In many markets the participants (especially the firms) may decide to maintain a system of voluntary **self-regulation**, possibly in order to try to avert the imposition of government controls. Areas where self-regulation often exists include the professions (eg the Law Society, the British Medical Association and other professional bodies).

6.3 Monopolies and mergers

Key term

> In a pure **monopoly**, there is only one firm, the sole producer of a good, which has no closely competing substitutes.

A monopoly situation can have some advantages:

(a) In certain industries, it is arguably only by achieving a monopoly that a company will be able to benefit from the kinds of **economies of scale** (benefits of conducting operations on a large scale) that can minimise prices.

(b) Establishing a monopoly may be the best way for a business to **maximise its profits**.

However monopolies often have several adverse consequences:

(a) Companies can impose **higher prices** on consumers.

(b) The lack of incentive of competition may mean companies have **no incentive** to **improve their products** or **offer a wider range of products**.

(c) There is no pressure on the company to **improve the efficiency** of its **use of resources**.

In practice, government policy is concerned not just with situations where one firm has a 100% market share, but other situations where an organisation has a significant market share.

The Competition and Markets Authority can also be asked to investigate what could be called '**oligopoly situations**' involving explicit or implicit collusion between firms.

The investigation is not automatic. Once the case has been referred, the Competition and Markets Authority must decide whether or not the monopoly is acting '**against the public interest**'.

In its report, the Competition and Markets Authority will say if a monopoly situation has been found to exist and, if so, will make recommendations to deal with it. These may involve various measures.

- Price cuts
- Price and profit controls
- Removal of entry barriers
- The breaking up of the firm (rarely)

A prospective **merger** between two or more companies may be referred to the Competition and Markets Authority for investigation if a larger company will gain more than 25% market share and where a merger appears likely to lead to a substantial lessening of competition in one or more markets in the UK.

Again, referral to the Competition and Markets Authority is not automatic and, since the legislation was first introduced, only a small proportion of all merger proposals have been referred.

If a potential merger is investigated, the Authority again has to determine whether or not the merger would be against the public interest. As with monopolies, it will assess the relative benefits and costs in order to arrive at a decision.

Question — Competition and Markets Authority

Look through newspapers or on the Internet for a report on the activities of the Competition and Markets Authority. Why is the investigation being carried out and how was it initiated?

6.4 Restrictive practices

Some countries have legislation which deals with restrictive practices that distort, restrict or prevent competition. A notable example of a restrictive practice would be agreements with direct competitors resulting in them colluding to the disadvantage of the consumer (eg price-fixing agreements). The legislation may also deal with abuse of dominant position offences, such as predatory pricing (charging low prices to unfairly destroy competition) or refusing to supply so as to restrict competition.

6.5 Deregulation

Deregulation or 'liberalisation' is, in general, the opposite of regulation. Deregulation can be defined as the removal or weakening of any form of statutory (or voluntary) regulation of free **market activity**. Deregulation allows **free market forces** more scope to determine the outcome.

Deregulation, whose main aim is to introduce more competition into an industry by removing statutory or other entry barriers, has the following potential benefits:

(a) **Improved incentives for internal/cost efficiency**

Greater competition compels managers to try harder to keep down costs.

(b) **Improved allocative efficiency**

Competition keeps down prices closer to marginal cost, and firms therefore produce closer to the socially optimal output level.

In some industries it could have certain disadvantages, including the following:

(a) **Loss of economies of scale**

If increased competition means that each firm produces less output on a smaller scale, unit costs will be higher.

(b) **Lower quality or quantity of service**

The need to reduce costs may lead firms to reduce quality or eliminate unprofitable but socially valuable services.

(c) **Need to protect competition**

It may be necessary to implement a regulatory regime to protect competition where inherent forces have a tendency to eliminate it, for example if there is a dominant firm already in the industry, as in the case of British Telecom. In this type of situation, effective 'regulation for competition' will be required, ie regulatory measures aimed at maintaining competitive pressures, whether existing or potential.

6.6 Privatisation and denationalisation

> **FAST FORWARD**
>
> **Privatisation** is a policy of introducing private enterprise into industries which were previously state-owned or state-operated.

Privatisation takes three broad forms:

(a) The **deregulation of industries**, to allow private firms to compete against state-owned businesses where they were not allowed to compete before (for example, deregulation of bus and coach services)

(b) **Contracting out work** to **private firms**, where the work was previously done by government employees – for example, refuse collection or hospital laundry work

(c) **Transferring the ownership** of **assets from** the **state to private shareholders**

Privatisation can improve efficiency, in one of two ways:

(a) If the effect of privatisation is to **increase competition**, the effect might be to reduce or eliminate allocative inefficiency.

(b) The effect of denationalisation might be to make the **industries more cost-conscious**, because they will be directly answerable to shareholders, and under scrutiny from stock market investors.

There are other possible advantages of privatisation:

(a) Denationalisation provides an **immediate source of money** for the government.

(b) Privatisation reduces **bureaucratic and political meddling** in the industries concerned.

(c) It encourages **wider share ownership**. Denationalisation is one method of creating wider share ownership, as the sale of British Telecom, British Gas, British Rail and some other nationalised industries have shown in the UK.

There are arguments against privatisation too:

(a) State-owned industries are more likely to respond to the **public interest**, ahead of the profit motive. For example, state-owned industries are more likely to cross-subsidise unprofitable operations from profitable ones.

(b) Encouraging private competition to state-run industries might be **inadvisable** where significant economies of scale can be achieved by monopoly operations.

(c) There is also an argument that privatised businesses act as monopolists or oligopolists.

7 Government aid schemes

> **FAST FORWARD**
>
> The freedom of European governments to offer cash **grants** and other forms of direct assistance to business is limited by European Union policies designed to prevent the distortion of free market competition.

The government provides finance to companies in cash grants and other forms of official direct assistance as part of its policy of helping to develop the national economy, especially in high technology industries and in areas of high unemployment.

Government incentives might be offered on:

(a) A **regional basis**, giving help to firms that invest in an economically depressed area of the country

(b) A **selective national basis**, giving help to firms that invest in an industry that the government would like to see developing more quickly, for example robotics or fibre optics

In Europe, such assistance is increasingly limited by European Union policies designed to prevent the distortion of free market competition. EU member states' government powers to grant aid for modernisation and development are restricted.

8 Corporate governance

FAST FORWARD

Corporate governance is a fundamental internal control system ensuring the best interests of the company are served in the most efficient and effective manner.

Key term

Corporate governance: 'A set of relationships between a company's directors, its shareholders and other stakeholders. It also provides structure through which the objectives of the company are set, and the means of obtaining these objectives and monitoring performance are determined.'

(OECD, 2004: p.4)

Corporate governance: Is the system by which organisations are directed and controlled.

(Cadbury, 1992: p.15)

8.1 What is corporate governance?

Corporate governance aims to ensure that companies are run for the benefit of shareholders and/or stakeholders, depending on the view taken. Corporate governance issues are also relevant to not-for-profit organisations, ensuring that they are run in the best interests of beneficiaries. For corporate governance to be effective it must be embedded as a feature of the inherent business culture, ie the way business is conducted.

8.1.1 Example: Corporate governance

(a) What problems would you expect to see in an organisation with poor corporate governance?

(b) Assume you are a potential investor in a company – what controls would you want to see in place to ensure that investors' interests are protected and avoid the problems stated in part (a)?

Solution

Problems	Controls
• Dominance of the organisation by one individual	• Some control over who is appointed to the board, possibly a seat on the board for a major investor
• Ignoring rules and formal controls in place	
• Organisations run for the benefit of management, not shareholders or other stakeholders	• Reassurance that directors are of the right calibre via some form of scrutiny
	• A financial audit by a reputable firm
• Excessive pay and benefits	• Some control over pay and benefits for directors and full disclosure
• Lack of effective scrutiny by auditors and stakeholders	
	• Fines and/or punishments in the event that company directors do not comply

The following diagram illustrates the **11 core principles** that underlie most good corporate governance systems across the world.

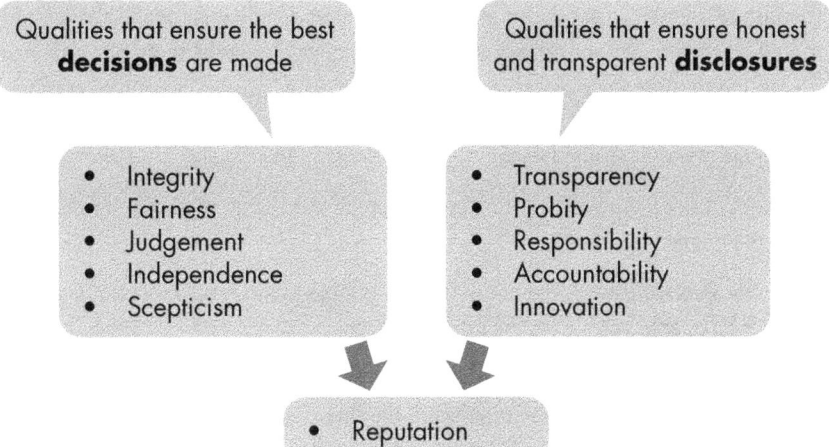

Definitions of each of these:

Integrity: Is concerned with straightforward dealing and completeness; high moral character; honesty.

Fairness: Is concerned with balance; respecting the rights and views of any group with a legitimate interest.

Judgement: Making complex decisions that enhance the organisation's prosperity.

Independence: Means being free from bias or undue influence; independence of mind and in appearance.

Scepticism: Means considering all parts of a business with an open mind; no preconceptions.

Transparency: Providing open and clear disclosure, including voluntary disclosure of reliable information.

Probity: Means being truthful and not misleading; avoiding disingenuous behaviour.

Responsibility: Acknowledgement of praise or blame; open management of errors and failures.

Accountability: Having to answer for the consequences of actions and knowing who that relates to.

Innovation: Change happens and governance must stay fit for purpose regardless.

Reputation: Other people's perceptions or expectations: a valuable asset of any organisation.

8.2 Regulatory guidance

8.2.1 Organisation for Economic Cooperation and Development

The Organisation for Economic Co-operation and Development (OECD) developed its Principles of Corporate Governance in 1998 and issued a revised version in April 2004. They are non-binding principles, intended to assist governments in their efforts to evaluate and improve the legal, institutional and regulatory framework for corporate governance in their countries.

They are also intended to provide guidance for stock exchanges, investors and companies. The focus is on stock exchange listed companies, but many of the principles can also apply to private companies and state-owned organisations. The OECD principles deal mainly with governance problems that result from the separation of ownership and management of a company. Issues of ethical concern and environmental issues are also relevant, although not central to the problems of governance.

8.2.2 International Corporate Governance Network

The International Corporate Governance Network (ICGN) issued its Global Governance Principles in 2014. The principles set out the corporate governance responsibilities that boards and institutional shareholders should adhere to. The purpose is to provide practical guidance that corporate boards can use when attempting to meet the expectations of investors. The ICGN believes that companies will only achieve value in the longer term if they effectively manage their relationships with stakeholders such as employees, customers, local communities and the environment as a whole.

Section A of the ICGN (2014) principles focuses on the role of corporate boards and emphasises the following points in particular:

1. **Responsibilities** – the board is accountable to shareholders and is duty bound to generate sustainable value over the long term
2. **Leadership and independence** – the board should offer independent leadership, with clear separation between the running of the board and the executive leadership of the company
3. **Composition and appointment** – the board should be effective, diverse, experienced and accountable for its actions
4. **Corporate culture** – the board should support ethical behaviour, supporting whistle-blowing if necessary
5. **Risk oversight** – the board should be proactive in overseeing and managing the company's risk management processes
6. **Remuneration** – should be transparent and aligned appropriately with risk and other objectives
7. **Reporting and audit** – should be robust, effective and independent (internal and external)
8. **General meetings** – the board should ensure that it follows procedures in respect of shareholder interactions ie notice of meetings, voting deadlines and voting mechanisms
9. **Shareholder rights** – should be protected and respected by directors

8.3 How is corporate governance achieved across the world?

8.3.1 Principles or rules?

Principles-based governance: Uses a broad series of ideas to set corporate governance behaviour, usually requiring 'comply or explain' disclosure (eg UK Corporate Governance Code).

Rules-based governance: A system based on inflexible rules that must be complied with, or else face sanctions from a regulator (eg Sarbanes-Oxley in the USA).

The big debate about corporate governance globally is whether the guidance should be in the form of principles or detailed rules and regulations.

	Principles-based approach	Rules-based approach
Features	Sets out broad principles (eg 'The Board should be effective') supported by guidance. Works on a **comply or explain** basis, with any departure from the specific provisions of codes requiring an explanation. Allows investors to decide if they agree that departure from the code is appropriate.	Organisations are required to comply with a detailed and rigid code. Non-compliance cannot be justified. A company has either succeeded or failed in complying. Investors tend to rely on a third party (eg SEC) to penalise the company for non-compliance.

	Principles-based approach	**Rules-based approach**
Benefits	Allows for greater flexibility and potential cost savings. Applies across different legal jurisdictions, which makes the governance of a multi-national business more effective. Forces both boards and shareholders to think about the consequence of governance arrangements.	Easier compliance with the rules, as they are unambiguous, and can be evidenced. Provides a consistent minimum standard of governance for investors' confidence.
Disadvantages	The principles are so broad that they are of very little use as a guide to best corporate governance practice. Investors cannot be confident of consistency in approach. Incorrectly viewed as voluntary.	Allows no leeway or deviation, irrespective of how illogical the situation is. Enforcement can be difficult for situations that are not covered explicitly in the rules.
Where you find them	Favoured in legal jurisdictions where the governing bodies of stock markets have had the prime role in setting standards for companies to follow.	Favoured in legal jurisdictions (and cultures) that lay great emphasis on obeying the letter of the law rather than the spirit of it.
Examples	UK Corporate Governance Code 2018	USA Sarbanes-Oxley Act (2002) (SOx)

LEARNING OUTCOME 1 THE FINANCIAL ENVIRONMENT AND CAPITAL REQUIREMENTS AND CONSEQUENT COSTS

Chapter Roundup

- Within an economy, some people, firms and organisations will have money which is surplus to their needs (**surplus units**), while others have less money than they need for their spending requirements (**deficit units**). **Credit** involves lending money, and the transfer (usually in return for interest payments) of money from surplus units to deficit units.

- A **financial intermediary** links those with surplus funds (eg **lenders**) to those with funds deficits (eg potential **borrowers**) thus providing **aggregation** and **economies of scale**, **risk pooling** and **maturity transformation**.

- **Commercial banks** can provide
    - A payment mechanism
    - Notes and coins
    - Bank accounts
    - Loans and overdrafts
    - For individuals and businesses

- The **capital markets** and **money markets** are markets for long-term and short-term capital respectively.

    A stock market (in the UK: the **main market** plus the **AIM**) acts as a **primary market** for raising finance, and as a **secondary market** for the trading of existing securities (ie stocks and shares).

    Fintech has increased the range of services offered by financial institutions and by financial markets.

- The **efficient market hypothesis** suggests that **share prices reflect** the **type of information** which is available to investors.

- The government influences markets in various ways, one of which is through direct **regulation** (eg the **Competition and Markets Authority**).

- **Privatisation** is a policy of introducing private enterprise into industries which were previously stated-owned or state-operated.

- The freedom of European governments to offer cash **grants** and other forms of direct assistance to business is limited by European Union policies designed to prevent the distortion of free market competition.

- Corporate governance is a fundamental internal control system ensuring the best interests of the company are served in the most efficient and effective manner.

Quick Quiz

1. For short-term borrowing, a company will go to the **money markets/capital markets**. (Which?)

2. (a) From which does the **demand** for capital markets funds come: Individuals/Firms/Government? (Delete any that do not apply.)

   (b) From which does the **supply** of capital markets funds come: Individuals/Firms/Government? (Delete any that do not apply.)

3. Identify five types of capital market intermediaries.

4. Is the Stock Exchange a money market?

5. Which of the following is not a function of the London Stock Exchange?

   A Enabling organisations to raise new finance
   B Enabling shareholders to realise the value of their shares
   C Enabling companies to become public companies
   D Enabling takeovers by share exchanges

6. The semi-strong form of the hypothesis implies that share prices will reflect information such as earnings forecasts and announcements of acquisitions.

   ☐ True

   ☐ False

7. Which of the following statements is true of the Alternative Investment market (AIM)?

   A AIM shares are treated as quoted for tax purposes.

   B Companies wishing to have their shares traded on AIM must meet eligibility criteria in terms of size and profitability.

   C There are more obligations to issue shareholder circulars than on the main market.

   D There are no Stock Exchange requirements for the percentage of shares in public hands.

8. What is meant by efficiency in the context of the efficient market hypothesis?

9. Give four reasons for government intervention in markets.

10. According to the theories of supply-side economists, what will happen if the market is freed from government intervention?

11. What is corporate governance?

Answers to Quick Quiz

1. Money markets.

2. (a) and (b): You should have deleted none.

3. Any five of: banks; building societies; insurance companies; pension funds; unit trust companies; investment trusts; Stock Exchanges; venture capital organisations.

4. No. The Stock Exchange is a capital market, not a money market.

5. C   Not every public company is listed on the London Stock Exchange.

6. True.

7. D   This is the correct answer. There are no minimum requirements, although if too few shares are freely available there will be no realistic market price.

    A   AIM shares are treated as unquoted for tax purposes, meaning that a number of reliefs are available to investors.

    B   There are no eligibility criteria for new entrants.

    C   This is incorrect; public announcements will generally be sufficient.

8. Efficiency in processing information in the pricing of stocks and shares.

9. (a) Imperfect competition
   (b) Social costs/externalities
   (c) Imperfect information
   (d) Equity

10. The free market will automatically generate the highest level of national income and employment available to the economy.

11. The system by which companies are directed and controlled

End of chapter question

Crowther Systems plc (AIA May 2008, amended)

Imagine that you are the financial controller of Crowther Systems plc; a company producing and selling billing and information management systems.

The company has acquired a large and expanding share of a growing market but is not really performing financially. The share price has been stagnant for three years; the company does not have the cash to pay a reasonable dividend and is burdened by high levels of debt at uneconomic rates of interest.

The consensus of opinion amongst the shareholders is that you are to blame for this situation. The main criticism levelled at you is that you do not appear to really understand the financial markets. You consider this criticism to be unfair and are convinced that the main reason for the company's dilemma is the fact that the 'markets' do not really appreciate its true potential. The shareholders' meeting is due to take place shortly and you anticipate some difficult questions.

Required

Produce brief reports to provide answers to the following potential questions.

(a) Describe the main Financial Markets and what overall economic roles do they fulfil? **(4 marks)**

(b) Describe financial intermediaries and the role do they play in enabling financial markets to operate effectively? **(8 marks)**

(c) Explain the efficient market hypothesis? Advise in what way, if any, could you use the EMH to support your case? **(8 marks)**

(Total 20 marks)

PART B

Capital requirements and consequent costs

Strategic planning and financial management

Topic list	Syllabus reference
1 Planning issues	LO1
2 Planning and strategy	LO1
3 Financial controls	LO1

Introduction

Having discussed business objectives, in this chapter we focus on how a business decides its strategies and draws up plans to implement them. We then focus on alternative strategies for growth.

This chapter provides perspectives on the key decisions companies have to take and indicates how strategic decisions are taken. Bear in mind when reading this chapter that major financial management decisions will be subject to all stages of the strategic development process.

LEARNING OUTCOME 1 THE FINANCIAL ENVIRONMENT AND CAPITAL REQUIREMENTS AND CONSEQUENT COSTS

1 Planning issues

> **FAST FORWARD**
>
> Planning decisions will depend upon the extent to which the organisation is pursuing **short- or long-term objectives**, and whether planning is driven from the **top** of an organisation or its **lower** levels.

1.1 Trade-offs between short-term and long-term objectives

Objectives may be **long-term** and **short-term**. A company that is suffering from a recession in its core industries and making losses in the short term might continue to have a primary objective in the long term of achieving a steady growth in earnings or profits, but in the short term, its primary objective might switch to survival.

Just as there may have to be a **trade-off** between different objectives, so too might there be a need to make trade-offs between short-term and long-term (S/L) objectives.

In practice, managers' performance is usually judged by short-term achievements.

(a) Middle and senior management are expected to achieve **budget targets**, and are criticised if they do not.

(b) The board of directors of a public company are expected by City analysts to achieve a **certain growth in profits and earnings** per share each year. If they do not, the share price will be marked down, and the board will be criticised for poor corporate results.

Since performance is often judged by short-term achievements, it is hardly surprising that the natural tendency for managers is to sacrifice longer-term aims in order to achieve short-term targets. In some situations, this might be the 'right' thing to do; in others, it might be a short-sighted and ultimately bad decision.

1.1.1 Sacrifice of long-term objectives

Decisions which involve the sacrifice of longer-term objectives include:

(a) **Postponing or abandoning capital expenditure projects**, which would eventually contribute to (longer-term) growth and profits, in order to protect short-term cash flow and profits.

(b) **Cutting research and development expenditure** to save operating costs, and so reducing the prospects for future product development.

1.2 'Top-down' and 'bottom-up' planning

The development of corporate planning can be seen as a response to the existence of **bottom-up planning systems**.

(a) In a **'bottom-up' organisation**, information is accumulated at lower levels of the enterprise and consolidated as it is passed up through the organisation, with a summary covering the overall position being prepared for top levels of management. Management may react only on the basis of the limited options which seem to be available on the basis of the information which is presented to them.

(b) A **top-down planning system**, in contrast, is based on the idea that strategic directives emanating from the top management flow down through the organisational structure.

An example of a **bottom-up** organisation is a conglomerate in which there are many disparate subsidiaries, all having autonomy and not being linked by a synergistic relationship.

Disadvantages of bottom-up planning in an organisation include the following:

(a) **Overall control** may become **difficult**.
(b) There may be a **number** of **separate objectives** which become difficult to reconcile.
(c) There may be a lack of sense of direction in the organisation as a whole.

Top-down planning recognises the position that top management has the ultimate managerial responsibility for the overall direction of the enterprise, and for providing a framework within which decision making by managers at lower levels in the organisation can operate.

Nevertheless the 'top-down' principle should probably not be taken too far: planning should, where practicable, involve a wide range of people in the organisation and not just top managers or specialist planners.

2 Planning and strategy

> **FAST FORWARD**
>
> Strategic planning is centred on the **preparation** of a **long-term plan of action** to achieve organisational objectives.
>
> The **rational model** suggests that strategic planning involves **strategic analysis, choice** and **implementation**.

2.1 Long-term strategic planning

Key term

Long-term strategic planning may be defined as the formulation, evaluation and selection of strategies for the purpose of preparing a long-term plan of action to attain objectives.

Drucker defines strategic planning as having three aspects:

(a) 'The continuous process of **making present risk-taking decisions** systematically and with greatest knowledge of their futurity' (ie their future effect)

(b) '**Organising systematically** the efforts needed to carry out these decisions'

(c) '**Measuring the results** of these decisions ... through organised, systematic feedback'

2.1.1 Characteristics of strategic plans

- They are written down.
- They are circulated to interested parties in the organisation.
- They specify the outcomes (eg where the business wishes to be in five years' time).
- They specify how these are going to be achieved.
- They trigger the production of operational plans lower down the hierarchy.

2.1.2 The rational model

The rational model of strategic planning is a logical and comprehensive approach. It attempts to consider all relevant information and options. It is iterative; there is a planning cycle (usually annual) in which the results of one cycle become an input into the next.

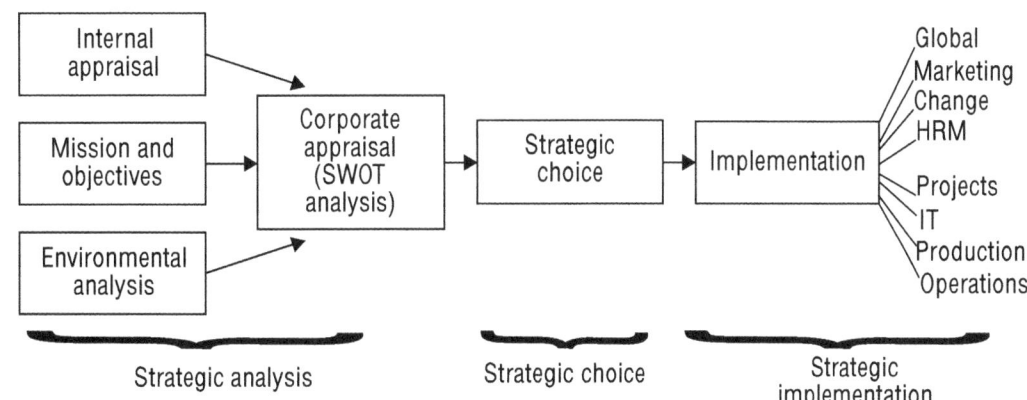

2.1.3 The planning period

Planners must decide what the **planning period** ought to be. The planning period ought to be the period of time which is **most suitable for planning requirements** and which enables the decision making and control processes to be most effectively exercised. The most suitable length for the planning period varies with circumstances. For example, forestry requires a period of many years whereas clothing manufacture may require only a few months.

2.2 Strategic analysis

Strategic analysis is concerned with understanding the strategic position of the organisation in the widest terms.

(a) The organisation operates within its **environment**. This has political/legal, economic, social and technological (PEST) aspects. The environment contains both **threats** and **opportunities**.

(b) The **resources** of the organisation (its **strengths** and **weaknesses**), how it adds value and its **distinctive competences** (what it does best or uniquely) must be matched to opportunities.

(c) **Mission and objectives**. The firm sets goals. The expectations of **stakeholder groups** must be considered. For example, if the organisation is financed by venture capitalists, a strategy might require sufficient growth generation to allow them to recover their investment.

2.2.1 Example: Strategic analysis

Susan Grant is in something of a dilemma. She has been invited to join the board of the troubled Marlow Fashion Group as a non-executive director, but is uncertain as to the level and nature of her contribution to the strategic thinking of the Group. Susan has approached the consultancy firm for which you work and has requested a short report to help her better understand the Marlow Fashion Group's current position. She has provided you with the following information:

Exhibit 1 – History of the group

The Marlow Fashion Group was set up by a husband and wife team a number of years ago in an economically depressed part of Ecuria, a developed country in Western Europe. They produced a comprehensive range of women's clothing built round the theme of traditional style and elegance. The Group had the necessary skills to design, manufacture and retail its product range. The Marlow brand was quickly established and the company built up a loyal network of suppliers, workers in the company factory and franchised retailers spread around the world.

Marlow Fashion Group's products were able to command premium prices in the world of fashion. Rodney and Betty Marlow ensured that their commitment to traditional values created a strong family atmosphere in its network of partners and were reluctant to change this.

Unfortunately, changes in the market for women's wear presented a major threat to Marlow Fashion. First, women had become a much more active part of the workforce and demanded smarter, more functional outfits to wear at work. Marlow Fashion's emphasis on soft, feminine styles became increasingly dated. Second, the tight control exercised by Betty and Rodney Marlow and their commitment to control of design, manufacturing and retailing left them vulnerable to competitors who focused on just one of these core activities.

Third, there was a reluctance by the Marlows and their management team to acknowledge that a significant fall in sales and profits were as a result of a fundamental shift in demand for women's clothing. Finally, the share price of the company fell dramatically. Betty and Rodney Marlow retained a significant minority ownership stake, but the company has had a new chief executive officer every year since.

Required

Using the information provided in Exhibit 1, write a short report to Susan Grant identifying and explaining the strategic strengths and weaknesses in the Marlow Fashion Group.

Solution

To: Susan Grant

From: A consultant

Strategic strengths and weaknesses in Marlow Fashion Group

This report looks at the strengths which are helping Marlow Fashion Group (Marlow) achieve its commercial success, and the weakness that are hindering it. It is also important to note that features of a company that have historically been **strengths can shift to become weaknesses as the competitive environment changes** over time, meaning that the company needs a strategic turnaround in order to survive. This appears to be the case with Marlow.

Strengths

Market position and reputation. Marlow has successfully developed a niche market for its products, based around traditional style and elegance. This enabled it to expand successfully, and developed Marlow as a worldwide brand with a reputation for design excellence and quality.

Premium prices. Marlow's reputation for quality has enabled it to charge premium prices for its clothes. The ability to sustain a high price premium is important in retaining the profitability of the company.

Supplier relationships. Marlow has built up a strong relationship with its suppliers. This relationship with the suppliers is important in maintaining the quality of the clothes produced, and so has facilitated the brand's reputation and global expansion of the group.

Loyal network of franchise partners. Marlow has created a strong family atmosphere among its network of retail partners around the world. As with the strong supplier relationships, this network has also helped facilitate the global expansion of the group.

Weaknesses

Outdated business model. The business model which has served Marlow well in the past is no longer appropriate to the fashion world in which they are now competing.

Lack of outsourcing, and high cost base. The competitive environment in which Marlow operates is becoming increasingly competitive. Therefore clothing retailers are increasingly looking to outsource the manufacture of their clothes. However, the approach pursued by Marlow prevents this, and means that the company's **cost base is higher** than it should be, because the company is failing to benefit from any economies of scale which outsourced providers enjoy. Consequently, Marlow's costs are also likely to be higher than its competitors, reducing its profitability.

Unclear strategy. One of Marlow's strengths was the niche position and brand reputation it established for itself. However, the changes in its environment have now led to some uncertainty as to whether Marlow Fashion is a brand, a manufacturer, a retailer or an integrated fashion company. It is likely that to be successful in the future, Marlow will need to **identify its core competences** and focus only on its core activities.

Outdated styles. Women's tastes in clothing have also changed and Marlow's emphasis on soft, feminine styles has become outdated. Consequently, demand for the clothes they sell has declined, and this has prompted a **significant fall in Marlow's sales and profits**.

Narrow product range. Although Marlow produces a comprehensive range of women's clothing, it is all built round the theme of traditional style and elegance. This means that Marlow's products are **over-concentrated** in one style, and therefore extremely vulnerable to a fall in demand as styles change.

Resistance to change. The tight control which Rodney and Betty Marlow exerted over product design has **prevented recognition of the changes in consumer tastes**, meaning the company has continued to produce the type of designs that served it well in the past, rather than the designs which consumers now want.

This resistance to change can also be seen in the management team's reluctance to accept that the significant fall in sales and profits reflects the shift in demand for women's clothing.

Lack of awareness of competitive environment. It is possible that the failure to adapt product design and manufacturing processes to keep pace with current trends may be as much due to Rodney and Betty Marlow not being aware of the current trends as them resisting change. Either way, the failure to produce clothes which current tastes demand is causing a significant fall in sales.

Rapid turnover of CEOs. Marlow has had a new chief executive officer every year. A succession of CEOs of this nature is indicative of a company which is performing poorly – with each new CEO being brought in to try to turn around its fortunes.

Conclusion

The changes in the market for women's wear have caused Marlow to move from a strategically sound position to one where it now needs a swift strategic turnaround. Its products and markets have changed, and its value chain no longer delivers any distinctive value to its customers. These issues need addressing urgently to try to reverse the decline in the company's sales and profitability.

2.3 Strategic choice

Strategy development has three phases:

(a) **Strategic options generation**

A variety of options can be set up for consideration. The aim is to build on the firm's capabilities and exploit market opportunities.

(b) **Strategic options evaluation**

Each option is then examined on its merits and considered with regard to suitability, feasibility and acceptability.

Suitability	Decisions should have strategic logic, and be consistent with long-term strategy
Feasibility	Availability of financial and non-financial resources, viability of planned production and sales levels and generation of sufficient returns to compensate suppliers of finance
Acceptability	Shareholders concerned with strategy of maximising profits, other financial stakeholders want commitments to them to be met, all stakeholders concerned with risk levels and financial viability

At times there may be a conflict between what is **suitable strategically**, and what is **acceptable to stakeholders** and **feasible** in the light of **available resources**.

(c) **Strategy selection**

A strategy is chosen, according to the evaluation above. This process is strongly influenced by the **values** of the managers concerned.

2.4 Implementation

The chosen strategy is embodied in a corporate plan. From this, plans for operations are developed. The diagram below relates the corporate strategy to the activities of the sales force.

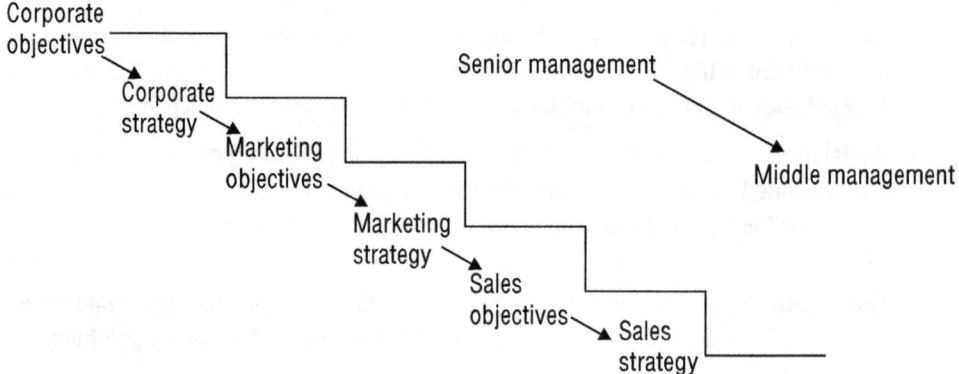

2.5 Strategic cash flow planning

Strategic cash flow planning ensures that **sufficient funds** are available for investment, and that **surplus funds** are used to best advantage.

In order to survive, any business must have an adequate inflow of cash. Cash flow planning at a strategic level is similar to normal cash budgeting, with the following exceptions.

(a) The **planning horizon** (the furthest time ahead plans can be quantified) is longer.

(b) The **uncertainties** about future cash inflows and cash outflows are much greater.

(c) The business should be able to respond, if necessary, to an **unexpected need** for cash. Where could extra cash be raised, and in what amounts?

(d) A company should have planned cash flows which are consistent with:

  (i) Its **dividend payment policy**, and
  (ii) Its policy for **financial structuring, debt and gearing**

Question — Financing and strategic targets

Suppose that WXY plc had the following statement of financial position at 31 December 20X8.

	£
Non-current assets	3,500,000
Current assets less current liabilities	500,000
	4,000,000
Share capital	500,000
Reserves	1,600,000
Long-term 10% debt	1,900,000
	4,000,000

The company's strategic planners have formulated the following policies.

(a) By the end of the next year (31 December 20X9), gearing should not exceed 100% – ie long-term debt should not exceed the total of share capital and reserves.

(b) The company shall pay out 50% of its profits as dividend to shareholders.

The following estimates have been made.

(a) Each £10,000 of assets generates profits of £2,000 pa, before interest.
(b) The current market cost of debt capital is 10% pa.

The company would like to invest a further £500,000 but does not intend to make a share issue to raise the finance. Advise its management. Could it borrow the money and still achieve its strategic targets by the end of 20X9? (Ignore taxation and non-current asset depreciation.)

Answer

The company's strategic aims **can** all be achieved, without a new share issue, even though it is already near the gearing limit it has set itself, of 100%.

A further £500,000 investment in capital would yield extra annual profits of £100,000 pa before interest.

LEARNING OUTCOME 1 THE FINANCIAL ENVIRONMENT AND CAPITAL REQUIREMENTS AND CONSEQUENT COSTS

Without a share issue, the £500,000 would have to be raised as a loan at 10%, raising the total company debt to £2,400,000 and total assets at the beginning of the year to £4,500,000.

		£
(1)	Profits before interest in 20X9 (£4,500,000 × 20%)	900,000
(2)	Interest (10% of £2,400,000)	240,000
(3)	Profits before dividend	660,000
(4)	Dividend (NB: taxation ignored)	330,000
(5)	Retained profits	330,000

Statement of financial position at 31 December 20X9

	£
Total assets (depreciation ignored)	
At 31.12.X8	4,000,000
New investment	500,000
Retained profits	330,000
	4,830,000
Financed by	
Share capital	500,000
Reserves	1,930,000
Debt capital	2,400,000
	4,830,000

The company's gearing would just about remain below the maximum target limit of 100%.

Exam focus point

> The information on sources of finance and the finance decision which was covered in Chapter 2, is also relevant to this section of the syllabus on capital requirements.

2.5.1 New investments/product developments

Investments in new projects, such as new product developments, use up cash in the short term, and it will not be for some years perhaps that significant profits and cash inflows are earned from them.

One aspect of strategic cash flow planning is to try to achieve a balance between the following.

(a) **Making and selling products** which are still in their **early stages of development**, and are still 'soaking up' cash

(b) **Making and selling products** which are **'cash cows'** – ie established products which are earning good profits and good cash inflows

2.5.2 Cash surpluses

A company should try to plan for adequate cash inflows, and be able to call on 'emergency' sources of cash in the event of an unforeseen need, but it might be unwise to hold too much cash.

When a company is **cash-rich**, it can invest the money, usually in short-term investments or deposits, such as the money market, to earn interest. However, for companies which are not in financial services or banking, the main function of money is to be spent. A cash-rich company could do one of the following.

(a) **Plan to use the cash**, for example for a project investment or a takeover bid for another company

(b) **Pay out the cash** to shareholders as **dividends**, and let the shareholders decide how best to use the cash for themselves

(c) **Re-purchase its own shares**

2.6 Strategic fund management

> **FAST FORWARD**
>
> **Strategic fund management** involves asset management to make **assets available for sale** if **cash deficiencies** arise.

Strategic fund management is an extension of cash flow planning, which takes into consideration the ability of a business to overcome unforeseen problems with cash flows, recognising that the assets of a business can be divided into three categories.

(a) Assets which are needed to carry out the **'core' activities** of the business. A group of companies will often have **one or several main activities**, and in addition will carry on several peripheral activities. The group's strategy should be primarily to develop its main activities, and so there has to be enough cash to maintain those activities and to finance their growth.

(b) Assets which are **not essential for carrying out** the main activities of the business, and which could be **sold off** at **fairly short notice**. These assets will consist mainly of short-term marketable investments.

(c) Assets which are not essential for carrying out the main activities of the business, and which could be **sold off to raise cash**, although it would probably take time to arrange the sale, and the amount of cash obtainable from the sale might be uncertain. These assets would include: long-term investments (for example, substantial shareholdings in other companies); subsidiary companies engaged in 'peripheral' activities, which might be sold off to another company or in a management buyout; and land and buildings.

If an unexpected event takes place which threatens a company's cash position, the company could also meet the threat by:

(a) **Working capital management** to **improve cash flows** by reducing inventory and receivables, taking more credit, or negotiating a higher bank overdraft facility

(b) **Changes to dividend policy**

3 Financial controls

3.1 Levels of control

> **FAST FORWARD**
>
> Levels of planning include:
> - **Strategic planning** – deciding on objectives, resources and policies
> - **Tactical control** – obtaining resources and using them effectively and efficiently
> - **Operational control** – ensuring that specific tasks are carried out effectively and efficiently

Robert Anthony in *Planning and Control Systems* defined three levels or tiers of control. We have discussed **strategic planning** above; Anthony's definition is given below along with his definition of tactical and operational control.

Key terms

Strategic planning and control is 'the process of deciding on objectives of the organisation, on changes in these objectives, on the resources used to attain these objectives, and on the policies that are to govern the acquisition, use and disposition of these resources'.

Tactical or management control is 'the process by which managers assure that resources are obtained and used effectively and efficiently in the accomplishment of the organisation's objectives'.

Operational control is 'the process of assuring that specific tasks are carried out effectively and efficiently'.

Management control is sometimes called **tactics** or **tactical planning**. Operational control is sometimes called **operational planning**.

The controls identified by Anthony impact upon key financial management decisions such as:

	Investment	Financing	Dividend
Strategic	Selection of products and markets Required levels of profitability Purchase of non-current assets fundamental to the business	Target debt/equity mix	Capital growth or high dividend payout
Tactical	Other non-current asset purchases Efficient use of resources Effective use of resources Pricing	Lease v buy	Scrip or cash dividends
Operational	Working capital management	Working capital management	N/A

3.2 Strategic control

As we have seen strategic plans are those which set or change the objectives, or strategic targets of an organisation. They include such matters as the required levels of company profitability, the purchase and disposal of subsidiary companies or assets, and whether employees should share in company profits.

3.3 Tactical control

Control at a strategic level, and the **review of strategic plans**, should therefore be an iterative process, with **revised forecasts** for the future being an important part of the control information.

Tactical control includes such activities such as the following:

- Preparing budgets of production, inventory levels
- Establishing departmental measures of performance (eg return on capital employed)
- Developing a product for launching in the market
- Planning advertising and marketing campaigns
- Establishing a line of authority structure for the organisation

3.4 Tactical and strategic control compared

The dividing line between **strategic planning** and **tactical planning** is not a clear one. Matters such as the optimum siting of a transport depot, for example, include issues ranging from the strategic to the tactical. Nevertheless, there is a basic distinction between the two levels of decision.

(a) The decision to **launch a new brand** of calorie-controlled frozen foods is a **strategic** plan (business strategy), but the **choice of ingredients** for the frozen meals involves a **tactical** control decision.

(b) A decision that the **market share** for a product should be 25% is a strategic plan (competitive strategy), but the **selection of a sales price** of £2 per unit, supported by other marketing decisions about sales promotion, direct sales effort etc to achieve the required market share, would be a series of **tactical** control decisions.

Tactical control tends to be carried out in a series of **regular planning and comparison procedures** (annually, monthly or weekly). For example, a budget is usually prepared annually, and control reports issued every month or four weeks. Strategic planning, in contrast, might be irregular and occur when opportunities arise or are identified.

3.5 Conflict between tactical and strategic control

It is quite common for strategic plans to be in conflict with the shorter-term objectives of management control. Examples are as follows:

(a) It might be in the long-term interests of a company to buy more expensive or technologically advanced machinery to make a product, in the expectation that when market demand for the product eventually declines, customers will buy from producers whose output is of a slightly better quality – ie made on better machinery. In the short run, however, new and expensive machinery will incur higher depreciation charges and therefore **higher unit costs** for the same volume of production.

(b) Similarly, it may be in the long-term interests of a company to invest in research and development, in spite of the costs and loss of profits in the short term.

3.6 Operational control

The third and lowest tier in Anthony's hierarchy of decision-making consists of **operational control** decisions. As we have seen, it is the task of ensuring that **specific tasks** are carried out effectively and efficiently. Just as 'management control' plans are set within the guidelines of strategic plans, so too are 'operational control' plans set within the guidelines of both strategic planning and management control.

3.7 Operational control and tactical control compared

Whereas tactical information for management control is often expressed in money terms, operational information, although quantitative, is more often expressed in terms of units, hours, quantities of material and so on. **Management control** decisions are generally taken by managers senior in the organisation to those who take operational control decisions.

Management control reports are often prepared monthly (although sometimes annually, or weekly). **Operational control** is exercised during and after the completion of individual tasks – ie more frequently. In the case of automated production, control is exercised minute by minute.

LEARNING OUTCOME 1 THE FINANCIAL ENVIRONMENT AND CAPITAL REQUIREMENTS AND CONSEQUENT COSTS

Chapter Roundup

- Planning decisions will depend upon the extent to which the organisation is pursuing **short- or long-term objectives,** and whether planning is driven from the **top** of an organisation or its **lower** levels.
- Strategic planning is centred on the **preparation** of a **long-term plan of action** to achieve organisational objectives.
- The **rational model** suggests that strategic planning involves **strategic analysis, choice** and **implementation**.
- **Strategic cash flow planning** ensures that **sufficient funds** are available for investment, and that **surplus funds** are used to best advantage.
- **Strategic fund management** involves asset management to make **assets available for sale** if **cash deficiencies** arise.
- Levels of planning include:
    - **Strategic planning** – deciding on objectives, resources and policies
    - **Tactical control** – obtaining resources and using them effectively and efficiently
    - **Operational control** – ensuring that specific tasks are carried out effectively and efficiently

Quick Quiz

1. In what type of organisation is information accumulated at the lower levels of the enterprise and consolidated as it is passed up through the organisation?
2. What, according to Johnson and Scholes, are the characteristics of a strategic decision for an organisation?
3. What are the main characteristics of strategic plans?
4. What does PEST stand for?

Answers to Quick Quiz

1. A bottom-up organisation

2. Scope; Environment; Matching; Effect on operations; Values and expectations; Implications for change

3. (a) They are written down.
   (b) They are circulated to interested parties in the organisation.
   (c) They specify the outcomes.
   (d) They specify how the outcomes are going to be achieved.
   (e) They trigger the production of operational plans lower down the hierarchy.

4. Political/legal
   Economic
   Social
   Technological

End of chapter question

Strategic management

Advise how strategic management differs from operational management.

(20 marks)

LEARNING OUTCOME 1 THE FINANCIAL ENVIRONMENT AND CAPITAL REQUIREMENTS AND CONSEQUENT COSTS

Financial planning and forecasting

Topic list	Syllabus reference
1 Ratio analysis	LO1
2 Comparison of accounting figures	LO1
3 Other information from companies' accounts	LO1
4 Predicting business failure	LO1
5 Cash flow planning and forecasting	LO1
6 Financial planning	LO1
7 Uncertainty	LO1

Introduction

In this chapter, we concentrate on the practical aspects of planning and performance analysis. The measures discussed can be useful support to business valuation. Section 4 discusses business failure.

The ratio analysis covered in the early part may seem familiar but the examiner expects you to be rigorous, so pay particular attention to the limitations of the processes carried out, also the other information to be considered. You may be asked to prepare a plan, so go carefully through the steps required, as well as noting how plans are used.

1 Ratio analysis

> **FAST FORWARD**
>
> **Ratios** provide a means of systematically analysing financial statements. They can be grouped under the headings **profitability**, **liquidity**, **gearing** and **shareholders' investment**. It is important to calculate **relevant ratios** and to take into account the **limitations** of **ratio analysis**.

1.1 Uses of ratio analysis

Businesses carry out ratio analysis in order to **measure the progress of the enterprise** and of individual subsidiaries, so that managers know how well the company concerned is doing. The financial situation of a company will also obviously affect its share price. Is the company profitable? Is it growing? Does it have satisfactory liquidity? Is its gearing level acceptable? What is its dividend policy?

The key to obtaining meaningful information from ratio analysis is **comparison**: comparing ratios over time within the same business to establish whether the business is improving or declining, and comparing ratios between similar businesses to see whether the company you are analysing is better or worse than average within its own business sector.

A vital element in effective ratio analysis is understanding the **needs of the person** for whom the ratio analysis is being undertaken. **Investors** for example will be interested in the **risk and return** relating to their investment, so will be concerned with dividends, market prices, level of debt v. equity etc. **Suppliers** and **loan creditors** are interested in receiving the payments due to them, so will want to know how liquid the business is. **Managers** are interested in ratios that indicate how well the business is being run, and also how the business is doing in relation to its **competitors**.

> **Exam focus point**
>
> Try not to be too mechanical when working out ratios, and think constantly about what you are trying to achieve. You will only obtain credit in the exam for calculating ratios that are relevant.

1.2 Limitations of ratio analysis

Although ratio analysis can be a very useful technique, it is important to realise its limitations.

(a) **Availability of comparable information**

When making comparisons with other companies in the industry, industry averages may hide **wide variations** in figures. Figures for 'similar' companies may provide a better guide, but then there are problems identifying which companies are similar, and obtaining enough detailed information about them.

(b) **Use of historical/out of date information**

Comparisons with the previous history of a business may be of limited use, if the business has recently undergone, or is about to undergo, **substantial changes**. In addition, ratios based on published accounts suffer from the disadvantage that these accounts are filed some months after the end of the accounting period. Comparisons over time may also be distorted by **inflation**, leading to assets being stated at values that do not reflect replacement costs, and revenue increasing for reasons other than more sales being made.

(c) **Ratios are not definitive**

'Ideal levels' vary industry by industry, and even they are not definitive. Companies may be able to exist without any difficulty with ratios that are rather worse than the industry average.

(d) **Need for careful interpretation**

For example, if comparing two businesses' liquidity ratios, one business may have higher levels. This might appear to be 'good', but further investigation might reveal that the higher ratios are a result of higher inventory and receivable levels which are a result of poor working capital management by the business with the 'better' ratios.

(e) **Manipulation**

Any ratio including profit may be distorted by **choice of accounting policies**. For smaller companies, working capital ratios may be distorted depending on whether a big customer pays, or a large supplier is paid, before or after the year-end.

(f) **Ratios lack standard form**

For example, when calculating **gearing** some companies will include bank overdrafts, others exclude them.

(g) **Other information**

Ratio analysis on its own is not sufficient for interpreting company accounts, and there are other items of information that should be looked at. We shall consider this further below.

> **Exam focus point**
>
> Bear these limitations in mind when calculating and interpreting ratios, as examiners' reports give many examples of misapplication of ratio analysis, and over-simplistic and misleading interpretations.
>
> In the exam you should calculate each ratio clearly, showing the figures used, and then indicate if there are any significant distortions.

1.3 Broad categories of ratios

Ratios can be grouped into the following four categories:

- Profitability and return
- Debt and gearing
- Liquidity: control of cash and other working capital items
- Shareholders' investment ratios (or 'stock market ratios')

The Du Pont system of ratio analysis involves constructing a pyramid of interrelated ratios like that below.

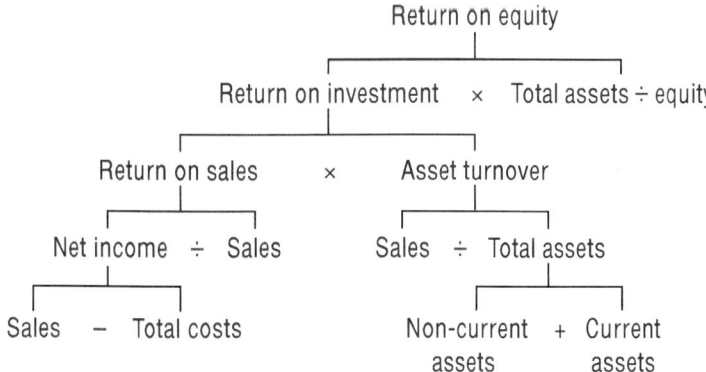

Such **ratio pyramids** help in providing for an overall management plan to achieve profitability, and allow the interrelationships between ratios to be checked.

LEARNING OUTCOME 1 THE FINANCIAL ENVIRONMENT AND CAPITAL REQUIREMENTS AND CONSEQUENT COSTS

Exam focus point

> Although you will have encountered most or all of the ratios that we are about to define before, make sure you know how to calculate them in the exam. Whenever a question that involves the calculation of ratios is set, the examiner's report highlights that many students get basic calculations wrong. One suggestion is to list all the ratios you need to know on a single sheet of paper and go through that sheet over and over again.

1.4 Profitability and return: the return on capital employed (ROCE)

A company ought of course to be profitable, and obvious checks on **profitability** are:

- Whether the company has made a profit or a loss on its ordinary activities
- By how much this year's profit or loss is bigger or smaller than last year's profit or loss

It is impossible to assess profits or profit growth properly without relating them to the amount of funds (the capital) employed in making the profits. An important profitability ratio is therefore **return on capital employed (ROCE)**, which states the profit as a percentage of the amount of capital employed. **Profit** is usually taken as PBIT, and **capital employed** is shareholders' capital plus long-term liabilities and debt capital. This is the same as total assets less current liabilities.

The underlying principle is that we must compare like with like, and so if capital means share capital and reserves plus long-term liabilities and debt capital, profit must mean the profit earned by all this capital together. This is PBIT, since interest is the return for loan capital.

$$\text{Thus ROCE} = \frac{\text{Profit on ordinary activities before interest and taxation (PBIT)}}{\text{Capital employed}}$$

Capital employed comprises shareholders' funds plus 'creditors: amounts falling due after more than one year' plus any long-term provisions for liabilities and charges.

1.4.1 Evaluating the ROCE

What does a company's ROCE tell us? What should we be looking for? There are three comparisons that can be made.

(a) The **change** in ROCE from one year to the next

(b) The **ROCE** being **earned** by other companies, if this information is available

(c) A comparison of the ROCE with **current market borrowing rates**

　(i) What would be the cost of extra borrowing to the company if it needed more loans, and is it earning a ROCE that suggests it could make high enough profits to make such borrowing worthwhile?

　(ii) Is the company making a ROCE which suggests that it is making profitable use of its current borrowing?

1.5 Analysing profitability and return in more detail: the secondary ratios

We may analyse the ROCE, to find out why it is high or low, or better or worse than last year. There are two factors that contribute towards a return on capital employed, both related to revenue.

1.5.1 Profit margin

A company might make a high or a low profit margin on its sales. For example, a company that makes a profit of 25c per $1 of sales is making a bigger return on its revenue than another company making a profit of only 10c per $1 of sales.

1.5.2 Asset turnover

Asset turnover is a measure of how well the assets of a business are being used to generate sales. For example, if two companies each have capital employed of $100,000, and Company A makes sales of £400,000 a year whereas Company B makes sales of only $200,000 a year, Company A is making a higher revenue from the same amount of assets. This will help Company A to make a higher return on capital employed than Company B.

Profit margin and asset turnover together explain the ROCE, and if the ROCE is the primary profitability ratio, these other two are the secondary ratios. The relationship between the three ratios is as follows.

Profit margin × Asset turnover = ROCE

$$\frac{\text{PBIT}}{\text{Sales}} \times \frac{\text{Sales}}{\text{Capital employed}} = \frac{\text{PBIT}}{\text{Capital employed}}$$

It is also worth commenting on the **change in turnover** from one year to the next. Strong sales growth will usually indicate volume growth as well as revenue increases due to price rises, and **volume growth** is one sign of a prosperous company.

1.6 Debt and gearing ratios

Debt ratios are concerned with how much the company **owes in relation to its size** and whether it is getting into heavier debt or improving its situation.

(a) When a company is heavily in debt, and seems to be getting even more heavily into debt, banks and other would-be lenders are very soon likely to refuse further borrowing and the company might well find itself in trouble.

(b) When a company is earning only a **modest profit** before interest and tax, and has a **heavy debt burden**, there will be very little profit left over for shareholders after the interest charges have been paid.

1.6.1 The debt ratio

The debt ratio is the ratio of a company's total debts to its total assets.

(a) **Assets** consist of non-current assets at their balance sheet value, plus current assets.
(b) **Debts** consist of all current and non-current liabilities.

You can ignore long-term provisions and liabilities, such as deferred taxation.

There is no absolute rule on the **maximum safe debt ratio**, but as a very general guide, you might regard 50% as a safe limit to debt. In addition, if the debt ratio is over 50% and getting worse, the company's debt position will be worth looking at more carefully.

1.6.2 Capital gearing

Capital gearing is concerned with the amount of debt in a company's **long-term** capital structure. **Gearing ratios** provide a long-term measure of liquidity.

$$\text{Gearing ratio} = \frac{\text{Prior charge capital (long-term debt)}}{\text{Prior charge capital} + \text{equity (shareholders' funds)}}$$

Prior charge capital is long-term loans and preference shares (if any). It does not include loans repayable within one year and bank overdraft, unless overdraft finance is a permanent part of the business's capital.

1.6.3 Operating gearing

Operating gearing is concerned with the relationship in a company between its **variable/fixed cost operating structure** and its profitability. It can be calculated as the ratio of **contribution** (sales minus variable costs of sales) **to PBIT**. The possibility of rises or falls in sales revenue and volumes means that operating gearing has possible implications for a company's business risk.

1.6.4 Interest cover

The **interest cover** ratio shows whether a company is earning enough profits before interest and tax to pay its interest costs comfortably, or whether its interest costs are high in relation to the size of its profits, so that a fall in profit before interest and tax (PBIT) would then have a significant effect on profits available for ordinary shareholders.

$$\text{Interest cover} = \frac{\text{PBIT}}{\text{Interest charges}}$$

An interest cover of two times or less would be low, and it should really exceed three times before the company's interest costs can be considered to be within acceptable limits. Note it is usual to exclude preference dividends from 'interest' charges.

1.6.5 Cash flow ratio

The **cash flow ratio** is the ratio of a company's net annual cash inflow to its total debts:

$$\text{Cash flow ratio} = \frac{\text{Net annual cash inflow}}{\text{Total debts}}$$

(a) **Net annual cash inflow** is the amount of cash which the company has coming into the business each year from its operations. This will be shown in a company's cash flow statement for the year.

(b) **Total debts** are short-term and long-term creditors, together with provisions for liabilities and charges.

Obviously, a company needs to earn enough cash from operations to be able to meet its foreseeable debts and future commitments, and the cash flow ratio, and changes in the cash flow ratio from one year to the next, provides a useful indicator of a company's cash position.

1.7 Liquidity ratios: cash and working capital

Profitability is of course an important aspect of a company's performance, and debt or gearing is another. Neither, however, addresses directly the key issue of liquidity. **A company needs liquid assets so that it can meet its debts when they fall due.**

Liquidity is the amount of cash a company can obtain quickly to settle its debts (and possibly to meet other unforeseen demands for cash payments too). **Liquid funds** consist of:

(a) **Cash**

(b) **Short-term investments for which there is a ready market,** such as investments in shares of other companies. (Short-term investments are distinct from investments in shares in subsidiaries or associated companies)

(c) **Fixed term deposits** with a bank or building society, for example six month deposits with a bank

(d) **Trade receivables.** (These are not cash, but ought to be expected to pay what they owe within a reasonably short time)

(e) **Bills of exchange receivable.** (Like ordinary trade receivables, these represent amounts of cash due to be received soon)

5: FINANCIAL PLANNING AND FORECASTING

If an analysis of a company's published accounts is to give us some idea of the company's liquidity, profitability ratios are not going to be appropriate for doing this. Instead, we look at **liquidity ratios** and **working capital turnover ratios**.

Knowledge brought forward from earlier studies

Liquidity ratios

- The **current ratio** is defined as:

    $$\frac{\text{Current assets}}{\text{Current liabilities}}$$

- In practice, a current ratio comfortably in excess of 1 should be expected, but what is 'comfortable' varies between different types of businesses.

- The **quick ratio**, or **acid test ratio**, is:

    $$\frac{\text{Current assets less inventory}}{\text{Current liabilities}}$$

- This ratio should ideally be at least 1 for companies with a slow inventory turnover. For companies with a fast inventory turnover, a quick ratio can be less than 1 without suggesting that the company is in cash flow difficulties.

- An excessively large current/quick ratio may indicate a company that is **over-investing in working capital**, suggesting poor management of receivables or inventories by the company.

- We can calculate **turnover periods** for inventory, receivables and payables (receivables and payables days). If we add together the inventory days and the receivables days, this should give us an indication of how soon inventory is convertible into cash. Both receivables days and inventory days therefore give us a further indication of the company's liquidity.

Question — Ratios

Calculate liquidity and working capital ratios from the accounts of a manufacturer of products for the construction industry, and comment on the ratios.

	20X8 £m	20X7 £m
Revenue	2,065.0	1,788.7
Cost of sales	1,478.6	1,304.0
Gross profit	586.4	484.7
Current assets		
Inventories	119.0	109.0
Receivables (Note 1)	400.9	347.4
Short-term investments	4.2	18.8
Cash and equivalents	48.2	48.0
	572.3	523.2
Current liabilities: amounts falling due within one year		
Loans and overdrafts	49.1	35.3
Corporation taxes	62.0	46.7
Dividend	19.2	14.3
Payables (Note 2)	370.7	324.0
	501.0	420.3
Net current assets	71.3	102.9

LEARNING OUTCOME 1 THE FINANCIAL ENVIRONMENT AND CAPITAL REQUIREMENTS AND CONSEQUENT COSTS

Notes

		20X8 £m	20X7 £m
1	Trade receivables	329.8	285.4
2	Trade payables	236.2	210.8

Answer

	20X8		20X7	
Current ratio	$\frac{572.3}{501.0}$ = 1.14		$\frac{523.2}{420.3}$ = 1.24	
Quick ratio	$\frac{453.3}{501.0}$ = 0.90		$\frac{414.2}{420.3}$ = 0.99	
Receivables payment period	$\frac{329.8}{2,065.0} \times 365$	= 58 days	$\frac{285.4}{1,788.7} \times 365$	= 58 days
Inventory turnover period	$\frac{119.0}{1,478.6} \times 365$	= 29 days	$\frac{109.0}{1,304.0} \times 365$	= 31 days
Payables' turnover period	$\frac{236.2}{1,478.6} \times 365$	= 58 days	$\frac{210.8}{1,304.0} \times 365$	= 59 days

As a manufacturing group serving the construction industry, the company would be expected to have a comparatively lengthy receivables turnover period, because of the relatively poor cash flow in the construction industry. It is clear that the company compensates for this by ensuring that they do not pay for raw materials and other costs before they have sold their inventories of finished goods (hence the similarity of receivables and payables turnover periods).

The company's current ratio is a little lower than what we would expect the average to be in the construction industry but its quick ratio is better than the expected average and very little less than the current ratio. This suggests that inventory levels are strictly controlled, which is reinforced by the low inventory turnover period. It would seem that working capital is tightly managed, to avoid the poor liquidity which could be caused by a high receivables turnover period and comparatively high payables.

Payables turnover is ideally calculated by the formula:

$$\frac{\text{Average payables}}{\text{Credit Purchases}} \times 365$$

However, it is rare to find purchases disclosed in published accounts and so cost of sales serves as an approximation. The payables turnover ratio often helps to assess a company's liquidity; an increase in payables days is often a sign of lack of long-term finance or poor management of current assets, resulting in the use of extended credit from suppliers, increased bank overdraft and so on.

Exam focus point

Most marks in exams are for interpretation and discussion of the shortcoming of ratios. Your answer should suggest further information that would be of value.

1.8 Stock market ratios

The final set of ratios to consider are the ratios which help equity shareholders and other investors to assess the value and quality of an investment in the ordinary shares of a company.

You have covered the computations of stock market ratios in your previous studies, and the formulae for the main ones are summarised below. We shall then consider their significance in the analysis of performance.

> **Knowledge brought forward from earlier studies**
>
> Stock market ratios
>
> - **Dividend yield** = $\dfrac{\text{Dividend per share}}{\text{Market price per share}}$
>
> - **Interest yield** = $\dfrac{\text{Interest payable}}{\text{Market value of loan stock}}$
>
> - **Earnings per share** = $\dfrac{\text{Profit after tax and preference dividends}}{\text{Number of ordinary shares in issue}}$
>
> - **Price/Earnings ratio** = $\dfrac{\text{Market value per share}}{\text{Earnings per share}}$
>
> - **Dividend cover** = $\dfrac{\text{Earnings available for distribution to ordinary shareholders}}{\text{Actual dividend for ordinary shareholders}}$

Exam focus point

Ratio analysis remains an important technique in this paper; the examiner has highlighted lack of knowledge of even simple ratios as a basic weakness of many candidates.

Investors are interested in:

- The value (market price) of the securities that they hold
- The return that the security has obtained in the past
- Expected future returns
- Whether their investment is reasonably secure

1.8.1 Dividend and interest yields

In practice, we usually find with quoted companies that the **dividend yield** on shares is less than the interest yield on debentures and loan stock (and also less than the yield paid on gilt-edged securities). The share price generally rises in most years, giving shareholders **capital gains**. In the long run, **shareholders** will want the **return on their shares**, in terms of **dividends received** plus **capital gains**, to exceed the return that investors get from fixed interest securities.

Exam focus point

Note that the interest yield, which is the **investor's** rate of return, is different from the coupon rate payable by the company as the nominal value of the loan stock. (Many students confuse these.)

1.8.2 Earnings per share (EPS)

EPS is widely used as a measure of a company's performance and is of particular importance in comparing results over a period of several years. A company must be able to sustain its earnings in order

LEARNING OUTCOME 1 THE FINANCIAL ENVIRONMENT AND CAPITAL REQUIREMENTS AND CONSEQUENT COSTS

to pay dividends and re-invest in the business so as to achieve future growth. Investors also look for **growth** in the EPS from one year to the next.

Question
Earnings per share

Walter Wall Carpets plc made profits before tax in 20X8 of $9,320,000. Tax amounted to $2,800,000.

The company's share capital is as follows:

	$
Ordinary share (10,000,000 shares of $1)	10,000,000
8% preference shares	2,000,000
	12,000,000

Required

Calculate the EPS for 20X8.

Answer

	$
Profits before tax	9,320,000
Less tax	2,800,000
Profits after tax	6,520,000
Less preference dividend (8% of $2,000,000)	160,000
Earnings	6,360,000
Number of ordinary shares	10,000,000

EPS   63.6c

EPS must be seen in the context of several other matters.

(a) EPS is used for **comparing the results** of a company over time. Is its EPS growing? What is the rate of growth? Is the rate of growth increasing or decreasing?

(b) Is there likely to be a significant **dilution** of EPS in the future, perhaps due to the exercise of share options or warrants, or the conversion of convertible loan stock into equity?

(c) EPS should not be **used blindly** to compare the earnings of one company with another. For example, if A plc has an EPS of 12c for its 10,000,000 10c shares and B plc has an EPS of 24c for its 50,000,000 25c shares, we must take account of the numbers of shares. When earnings are used to compare one company's shares with another, this is done using the P/E ratio or perhaps the earnings yield.

(d) If EPS is to be a reliable basis for comparing results, it must be **calculated consistently**. The EPS of one company must be directly comparable with the EPS of others, and the EPS of a company in one year must be directly comparable with its published EPS figures for previous years. Changes in the share capital of a company during the course of a year cause problems of comparability.

Note that EPS is a figure based on **past data**, and it is easily manipulated by changes in accounting policies and by mergers or acquisitions.

1.8.3 Price/earnings ratio

The P/E ratio is, simply, a measure of the relationship between the **market value** of a company's shares and the **earnings** from those shares.

The value of the P/E ratio reflects the market's appraisal of the shares' future prospects. In other words, if one company has a higher P/E ratio than another it is because investors either expect its earnings to **increase faster** than the other's or consider that it is a **less risky** company or in a more 'secure' industry.

As we shall see later in the text, one approach to assessing what share prices ought to be, which is often used in practice, is a P/E ratio approach:

(a) The relationship between the EPS and the share price is **measured** by the **P/E ratio**.

(b) There is no reason to suppose, in normal circumstances, that the P/E ratio will vary much over time.

(c) So if the EPS goes up or down, the share price should be expected to move up or down too, and the new share price will be the new EPS multiplied by the constant P/E ratio.

For example, if a company had an EPS last year of 30c and a share price of $3.60, its P/E ratio would have been 12. If the current year's EPS is 33c, we might expect that the P/E ratio would remain the same, 12, and so the share price ought to go up to $12 \times 33c = \$3.96$.

Changes in the P/E ratios of companies over time will depend on several factors.

(a) If **interest rates go up**, investors will be attracted away from shares and into debt capital. Share prices will fall, and so P/E ratios will fall.

(b) If **prospects** for **company profits improve**, share prices will go up, and P/E ratios will rise. Share prices depend on expectations of future earnings, not historical earnings, and so a change in prospects, perhaps caused by a substantial rise in international trade, or an economic recession, will affect prices and P/E ratios.

(c) **Investors' confidence** might be changed by a variety of circumstances, such as:

    (i) The prospect of a change in government
    (ii) The prospects for greater exchange rate stability between currencies

1.8.4 The dividend cover

The dividend cover is the number of times the actual dividend could be paid out of current profits and indicates:

(a) The **proportion** of distributable profits for the year that is being **retained** by the company

(b) The level of **risk** that the company will **not be able to maintain the same dividend** payments in future years, should earnings fall

A high dividend cover means that a high proportion of profits are being retained, which might indicate that the company is investing to achieve earnings growth in the future.

2 Comparison of accounting figures

FAST FORWARD

Ratio analysis often forms the basis of comparisons with performance over time or with other companies. Comments on a company based on such ratios are far more likely to be right than comments based on a casual read through of a set of accounts.

2.1 Results of the same company over successive accounting periods

Useful comparisons over **time** include:

- **Percentage growth** in **profit** (before and after tax) and percentage growth in turnover
- Increases or decreases in the debt ratio and the gearing ratio

- **Changes** in the **current ratio**, the inventory turnover period and the receivables payment period
- **Increases** in the **EPS**, the dividend per share, and the market price

The principal advantage of making comparisons over time is that they give some indication of progress: are things getting better or worse? However, there are some weaknesses in such comparisons.

(a) The effect of **inflation** should not be forgotten.

(b) The progress a company has made needs to be set in the context of **what other companies have done**, and whether there have been any **special environmental or economic influences** on the company's performance.

2.1.1 Allowing for inflation

Ratio analysis is not usually affected by **price inflation**, except as follows:

(a) **Return on capital employed (ROCE)** can be misleading if non-current assets, especially property, are valued at **historical cost net of depreciation** rather than at current value. As time goes by and if property prices go up, the non-current assets would be seriously undervalued if they were still recorded at their historical cost.

(b) Some growth trends can be misleading, in particular the **growth in sales revenue**, and the **growth in profits or earnings**.

2.2 Comparisons between different companies in the same industry

Making comparisons between the results of different companies in the same industry is a way of assessing which companies are outperforming others.

(a) Even if two companies are in the **same broad industry** (for example, retailing) they might not be direct competitors. For example, in the UK, the Kingfisher group (which owns DIY stores such as B&Q) does not compete directly with the Arcadia group (which owns clothing stores such as Burton and Topshop). Even so, they might still be expected to show **broadly similar performances** in terms of growth.

(b) If two companies are **direct competitors**, a comparison between them would be particularly interesting.

Comparisons between companies in the same industry can help investors to rank them in order of desirability as investments, and to judge relative share prices or future prospects. It is important, however, to make comparisons with caution: **a large company and a small company in the same industry might be expected to show different results**, not just in terms of size, but in terms of:

(a) **Percentage rates of growth** in sales and profits

(b) **Percentages of profits re-invested.** (Dividend cover will be higher in a company that needs to retain profits to finance investment and growth)

(c) **Non-current assets.** (Large companies are more likely to have freehold property in their balance sheet than small companies)

2.3 Comparisons between companies in different industries

Useful information can also be obtained by comparing the financial and accounting ratios of companies in different industries. An investor ought to be aware of how companies in one industrial sector are performing in comparison with companies in other sectors. For example, it is important to know:

(a) Whether sales growth and profit growth is higher in **some industries** than in others (For example, how does growth in the financial services industry compare with growth in heavy engineering, electronics or leisure?)

5: FINANCIAL PLANNING AND FORECASTING

(b) How the **return on capital employed** and **return on shareholder capital compare** between different industries

(c) How the **P/E ratios and dividend yields** vary between industries

3 Other information from companies' accounts

> **FAST FORWARD**
>
> As well as ratios, **other information** can be used to analyse a company's performance and identify possible problem areas. This will include information relating to **non-current assets** and **financial obligations, contingencies** and **events after the reporting period**.

3.1 The revaluation of non-current assets

Non-current assets may be stated in the statement of financial position at cost less accumulated depreciation. They may also be revalued from time to time to a current market value to avoid understatement of current value. When this happens:

(a) The increase in the value of the non-current asset is matched by an increase in the **revaluation reserve**

(b) **Depreciation** in subsequent years is based on the revalued amount of the asset, its estimated residual value and its estimated remaining useful life

3.2 Share capital and share issues

The **capital and reserves** section of a company's accounts contains information which appears to be mainly the concern of the various classes of shareholder. However, because the shareholders' interest in the business acts as a **buffer for the creditors** in the event of any financial problems, this section is also of some importance to creditors.

For example, if a company has increased its total share capital and reserves in the year:

(a) Did it do so by **issuing new shares** resulting in a higher allotted share capital and share premium account?

(b) Did it do so by **revaluing some non-current assets**, resulting in a higher revaluation reserve?

(c) Did it make a substantial profit and **retain a good proportion of this profit** in the business resulting in a higher income statement balance?

A **scrip issue** might also be of some interest. It will result in a **fall** in the **market price** per share. If it has been funded from a company's reserves, a scrip issue would indicate that the company recognised and formalised its long-term capital needs by now making some previously distributable reserves non-distributable.

If a company has **issued shares in the form of a dividend**, are there obvious reasons why this should be so? For example, does the company need to retain capital within the business because of poor trading in the previous year, making the directors reluctant to pay out more cash dividend than necessary?

3.3 Financial obligations

Financial obligations of a company may also be significant, and the timescale over which these become or could become repayable should be considered.

Examples are:

(a) Levels of **redeemable debt**

(b) **Earn out arrangements**

(c) **Potential or contingent liabilities,** such as liabilities under unresolved legal cases or insurance claims

(d) **Long-term commitments** (eg the Private Finance Initiative in the UK)

3.4 Debentures, loans and other liabilities

Two points of interest about debentures, loans and other liabilities are:

- Whether or not loans are **secured**
- The **redemption dates** of loans

For debentures and loan stock which are **secured**, the details of the security are usually included in the terms of a trust deed. Details of any **fixed or floating charges against assets** must be disclosed in a note to the accounts.

In analysing a set of accounts, particular attention should be paid to some significant features concerning **debenture or loan stock redemption**. These are:

(a) The closeness of the redemption date, which would indicate how much finance the company has to find in the immediate future to repay its loans. It is not unusual, however, to repay one loan by taking out another, and so a company does not necessarily have to find the money to repay a loan from its own resources.

(b) The **percentage interest rate** on the loans being redeemed, compared with the **current market rate of interest**. This would give some idea, if a company decides to replace loans by taking out new loans, of the likely increase (or reduction) in interest costs that it might face, and how easily it might accommodate any interest cost increase.

3.5 Contingencies

Contingencies are conditions which exist at the year end where the outcome will be confirmed only on the occurrence or non-occurrence of one or more uncertain future events.

Contingencies can result in contingent gains or contingent losses. The fact that the condition **exists at the year end** distinguishes a contingency from an event after the reporting period.

Some of the **typical types of contingencies** disclosed by companies are as follows:

- Guarantees given by the company
- Discounted bills of exchange
- Uncalled liabilities on shares or loan stock
- Lawsuits or claims pending
- Tax on profits where the basis on which the tax should be computed is unclear

Again, knowledge of such contingencies will enhance the quality of the information used in analysis.

3.6 Events after the reporting period

Key term

> **Events after the reporting period** are those events both favourable and unfavourable which occur between the year end and the date on which the financial statements are approved by the board of directors.

The following are examples of events after the reporting period which should normally be disclosed:

- Mergers and acquisitions
- The issue of new shares and debentures

- The purchase and sales of major non-current assets and investments
- Losses of non-current assets or inventories as a result of a catastrophe such as fire or flood
- The opening of new trading activities
- The closure of a significant part of the trading activities
- A decline in the value of property and investments held as non-current assets
- Changes in exchange rates (if there are significant overseas interests)
- Government action, such as nationalisation
- Strikes and other labour disputes
- The augmentation of pension benefits to employees

Knowledge of such events allows the analyst to 'update' the latest published figures by taking account of their potential impact.

> **Exam focus point**
>
> You should try to develop a mental checklist of areas where accounts can be distorted, whether intentionally or unintentionally. These may include:
>
> - Asset values
> - Off balance sheet items
> - Equity restructuring
> - Loan terms
> - Events after the reporting period

4 Predicting business failure

> **FAST FORWARD**
>
> Business failure can be predicted by using a number of financial variables, or by models such as **Argenti's model**, which emphasises defects, mistakes and symptoms.

4.1 Financial stability

The analysis of financial ratios is largely concerned with the efficiency and effectiveness of the use of resources by a company's management, and also with the financial stability of the company. Investors will wish to know:

- Whether additional funds could be lent to the company with reasonable safety
- Whether the company would fail without additional funds

4.2 Liquidity ratios

One method of predicting business failure is the use of **liquidity ratios** (the current ratio and the quick ratio). A company with a current ratio well below 2:1 or a quick ratio well below 1:1 might be considered illiquid and in danger of failure. Research seems to indicate, however, that the current ratio and the quick ratio and trends in the variations of these ratios for a company, are poor indicators of eventual business failure.

4.3 Corporate failure models

Beaver conducted a study which found the following.

- The **worst predictor** of failure is the current ratio (current assets/current liabilities).
- The **best predictor** of failure is cash flow borrowings.

Other writers have put forward alternative models designed to predict whether a business will fail. From historical data on a wide range of actual cases, **Argenti** developed a model which is intended to predict the likelihood of company failure.

Factors in Argenti's model	
Defects	Autocratic chief executive
	Passive board
	Lack of budgetary control
Mistakes	Over-trading (expanding faster than cash funding)
	Gearing – high bank overdrafts/loans
	Failure of large project jeopardises the company
Symptoms	Deteriorating ratios
	Creative accounting – signs of window-dressing
	Declining morale and declining quality

4.4 Weaknesses of financial information

There are the following problems in using available **financial information** to predict failure:

(a) **Significant events** can take place between the end of the financial year and the publication of the accounts. An extreme example of this would be the collapse of the Barings merchant bank. A further feature of the Barings case that is worthy of comment is the fact that the factors that led up to the collapse were essentially internal to the business and would never have become apparent in the published accounts.

(b) The information is essentially **backward looking** and takes no account of current and future situations. An extreme example would be a business producing bananas in a country that suffers a hurricane. There would be nothing in their previous published accounts to predict the effect on their businesses of the hurricane.

(c) The underlying financial information may not be reliable.

The use of **creative, or even fraudulent, accounting** can be significant in situations of corporate failure. Similarly, the **pressure to deliver earnings growth** may result in companies making poor decisions that eventually lead to their downfall.

4.5 Other indicators of financial difficulties

You should not think that **ratio analysis of published accounts** is the only way of spotting that a company might be running into financial difficulties. There are other possible indicators too.

4.5.1 Other information in the published accounts

Some information in the published accounts might not lend itself readily to ratio analysis, but still be an indicator of financial difficulties, for example:

- Very **large increases** in **intangible non-current assets**
- A **worsening net liquid funds** position, as shown by the funds flow statement
- Very large **potential or contingent liabilities**
- Important events after the reporting date
- **Excess** of **current liabilities** over **current assets**
- Imminent **debt repayment** and **limited cash resources**

4.5.2 Information in the chair's report, the directors' report and the audit report

The **report of the chair** or chief executive that accompanies the published accounts might be very revealing. Although this report is not audited, and will no doubt try to paint a rosy picture of the company's affairs, any difficulties the company has had and not yet overcome will probably be discussed in it. There might also be warnings of problems to come in the future. The **audit report** itself may indicate difficulties.

4.5.3 Information in the press

Newspapers and financial journals are a source of information about companies, and the difficulties or successes they are having and the **markets** in which they operate. There may be reports of strikes, redundancies and closures.

4.5.4 Credit ratings

Ratings from specialist agencies or banks may be useful.

4.5.5 Published information about environmental or external matters

There will also be published information about matters that will have a direct influence on a company's future, although the connection may not be obvious. Examples of external matters that may affect a company adversely are:

- **New legislation**, for example on product safety standards or pollution controls, which affect a company's main products
- **International events**, for example political disagreements with a foreign country, leading to a restriction on trade between the countries
- **New and better products** being launched on to the market by a competitor
- A big **rise in interest rates**, which might affect a highly-geared company seriously
- A big **change in foreign exchange rates**, which might affect a major importer or exporter seriously

5 Cash flow planning and forecasting

> **FAST FORWARD**
>
> **Cash forecasting** should ensure that sufficient funds will be available when needed, to sustain the activities of an enterprise at an acceptable cost.
>
> **Cash deficits** will be funded in different ways, depending on whether they are short or long-term. Businesses should have procedures for investing **surpluses** with appropriate levels of risk and return.

5.1 Cash forecasting

Key term

A **cash budget** (or **forecast**) is a detailed budget of estimated cash inflows and outflows incorporating both revenue and capital items.

Cash forecasts (or budgets) provide an early warning of liquidity problems, by estimating:

- How much cash is required
- When it is required
- How long it is required for
- Whether it will be available from anticipated sources

A company must know **when** it might need to borrow and **for how long**, not just **what amount** of funding could be required.

However, cash budgets and cash flow forecasts on their own do not give full protection against a cash shortage and enforced liquidation of the business by creditors. There may be **unexpected changes in cash flow patterns**. When unforeseen events have an adverse effect on cash inflows, a company will only survive if it can maintain adequate cash inflows despite the setbacks. **Strategic fund management** is an extension of cash flow planning, which takes into consideration the ability of a business to overcome unforeseen problems with cash flows.

5.2 Deficiencies

Any forecast **deficiency** of cash will have to be funded by:

(a) **Borrowing**. If borrowing arrangements are not already secured, a source of funds will have to be found. If a company cannot fund its cash deficits it could be wound up.

(b) The firm can make arrangements to **sell any short-term financial investments** to raise cash.

(c) The firm can delay payments to creditors, or pull in payments from debtors. This is sometimes known as **leading and lagging**.

Because cash forecasts cannot be entirely accurate, companies should have **contingency funding**, available from a surplus cash balance and liquid investments, or from a bank facility. The approximate size of contingency margin will vary from company to company, according to the cyclical nature of the business and the approach of its cash planners.

Forecasting gives management time to arrange its funding. If planned in advance, instead of a panic measure to avert a cash crisis, a company can more easily choose when to borrow, and will probably obtain a lower interest rate.

5.3 Forecasting a cash surplus

Many cash-generative businesses are less reliant on high quality cash forecasts. If a **cash surplus** is forecast, having an idea of both its size and how long it will exist could help decide how best to invest it.

5.4 Cash forecasts based on the statement of financial position

> **FAST FORWARD**
>
> **Forecasts** based on the statement of financial position can be used to assess the scale of funding requirements or cash surpluses expected over time, and to act as a check on the realism of cash flow based forecasts.

The forecast is produced for **management accounting purposes** and so not for external publication or statutory financial reporting. **It is not an estimate of cash inflows and outflows**. A number of sequential forecasts can be produced, for example, a forecast of the statement of financial position at the end of each year for the next five years.

As an estimate of the company's statement of financial position at a future date, the forecast is used to identify either the **cash surplus** or the **funding shortfall at the forecast date**.

Forecasts based on the statement of financial position have **two other uses**:

(a) **As longer-term (strategic) estimates**, to assess the scale of funding requirements or cash surpluses the company expects over time

(b) To act as a **check on the realism** of cash flow-based forecasts. (The estimated statement of financial position should be **roughly** consistent with the net cash change in the cash budget, after allowing for approximations in the statement of financial position forecast assumptions)

5.4.1 Estimating a future statement of financial position

A statement of financial position estimate calls for some prediction of the amount/value of each item in the company's statement of financial position, **excluding cash and short-term investments**, as these are what we are trying to predict. A forecast is prepared by taking each item in the statement of financial position, and estimating what its value might be at the future date. The assumptions used are critical, and the following guidelines are suggested:

(a) **Intangible non-current assets (gross book value) and long term investments**

These should be taken at their current value unless there is good reason for another treatment.

(b) **Non-current asset purchases and disposals**

An estimate will be required. Revaluations can be ignored as they are not cash flows.

(c) **Current assets**

Estimates of **inventories** and **receivables** can be based on fairly simple assumptions, and can be made in any of the following ways:

(i) **Same as current amounts**. This is unlikely if business has boomed.

(ii) **Increase by a certain percentage**, to allow for growth in business volume. For example, the volume of receivables might be expected to increase by a similar amount.

(iii) **Decrease by a certain percentage**, to allow for tighter management control over working capital.

(iv) Assume to be a **certain percentage** of the company's estimated **annual revenue** for the year.

(v) The firm can assume that the **operating cycle** will more or less **remain the same**.

(d) **Current liabilities**

Some itemising of current liabilities will be necessary, because no single set of assumptions can accurately estimate them collectively.

(i) **Trade payables and accruals** can be estimated in a similar way to current assets, as indicated above.

(ii) Current liabilities include **bank loans** due for repayment within 12 months. These can be identified individually.

(iii) **Bank overdraft facilities** might be in place. It could be appropriate to assume that there will be no overdraft in the forecast statement of financial position.

(iv) **Taxation**. Any corporation tax payable should be estimated from anticipated profits and based on an estimated percentage of those profits.

(v) **Dividends payable**. Any ordinary dividend payable should be estimated from anticipated profits, and any preference dividend payable can be predicted.

(vi) **Other payables** can be included if required and are of significant value.

(e) **Long-term payables**

Long-term payables are likely to consist of long-term loans, bond issues, debenture stock and any other long-term finance debt.

(f) **Share capital and reserves**

With the exception of the income statement reserves (retained profits), the estimated figures for share capital and other reserves should be the same as their current amount, unless it is expected or known that a new issue of shares will take place before the year end.

LEARNING OUTCOME 1 THE FINANCIAL ENVIRONMENT AND CAPITAL REQUIREMENTS AND CONSEQUENT COSTS

(g) **Retained profits**

An estimate is required of the change in the company's **retained profits** in the period up to the year end. This reserve should be calculated as:

(i) The existing value of the income statement reserve

(ii) **Plus** further **retained profits** anticipated in the period to the year end date (ie post tax profits minus estimated dividends)

The various estimates should now be brought together into a statement of financial position. The figures on each side of the statement of financial position will not be equal, and there will be one of the following.

(a) A surplus of share capital and reserves over net assets (total assets minus total creditors). If this occurs, the company will be forecasting a **cash surplus**.

(b) A surplus of net assets over share capital and reserves. If this occurs, the company will be forecasting a **funding deficit**.

5.4.2 Example: Alpha Ltd

Alpha Ltd has an existing statement of financial position and an estimated statement of financial position in one year's time before the necessary extra funding is taken into account, as follows.

	Existing £	Existing £	Forecast after one year £	Forecast after one year £
Non-current assets		100,000		180,000
Current assets	90,000		100,000	
Short-term payables	(60,000)		(90,000)	
Net current assets		30,000		10,000
		130,000		190,000
Long-term payables		(20,000)		(20,000)
Deferred taxation		(10,000)		(10,000)
Total net assets		100,000		160,000
Share capital and reserves				
Ordinary share capital		50,000		50,000
Other reserves		20,000		20,000
Retained earnings		30,000		50,000
		100,000		120,000

The company is expecting to increase its net assets in the next year by £60,000 (£160,000 – £100,000) but expects retained profits for the year to be only £20,000 (£50,000 – £30,000). There is an excess of net assets over share capital and reserves amounting to £40,000 (£160,000 – £120,000), which is a **funding deficit**.

The company must consider ways of obtaining extra cash (eg by borrowing) to cover the deficit. If it cannot, it will need to keep its assets below the forecast amount, or to have higher short-term payables.

A revised projected statement of financial position can then be prepared by introducing these new sources of funds. This should be checked for realism (eg by **ratio analysis**) to ensure that the proportion of the statement of financial position made up by non-current assets and working capital, and so on, is sensible.

6 Financial planning

FAST FORWARD

Forecast financial statements can be constructed for a period of several years, from first year data, given certain assumptions.

As part of a business' risk analysis, different forecasts should be prepared with **changing financial or business variables**. The links between these variables and the figures in the forecasts may not be straightforward.

6.1 Financial plans

As well as preparing a cash flow plan, businesses will want to prepare more wide-ranging financial plans covering quantifiable targets for all financial objectives.

Financial plans may cover a **number of years**, perhaps three to five years, or ten years, or even longer. Financial plans should be a part of the overall **strategic plan** of the organisation.

With good financial planning, a business can assess in advance:

(a) Just **how much finance** it needs for **long-term investment** and **short-term cash flow needs**

(b) Whether it is likely to have **surplus cash**, and if so for how long and what can best be done with the surplus cash when it arises

(c) How any required finance should be **raised**

(d) Whether the company is likely to be **profitable** and to achieve its main and subsidiary financial objectives, for example to carry out its policy of a 10% annual growth in dividends

6.2 The business plan and forecasting

Financial plans will be based on forecasts.

Question — Definite variables

See if you can identify the different types of forecast on which financial plans may be based before looking at the remainder of this paragraph.

(a) **Environmental forecasts** are needed to assess future economic and political events which will influence an organisation's prospects. Economic factors might include the rate of growth in the economy, the rate of inflation, foreign exchange rates and the level of interest rates.

(b) **Market or industry forecasts** can be formulated within the framework of environmental forecasts. These forecasts will cover the likely rate of growth or decline in an industry or market, technological changes which might alter product design or production methods, the possible break-up of a market into separate segments and so on. An organisation ought to be aware of the likely conditions in the markets and industries where it operates, and plan accordingly.

(c) **Forecasts for the organisation** itself can then be prepared within the framework of market and industry forecasts. Forecasts can be made for sales; costs and profits; new product development; the work force; and finance needs.

6.3 Constructing financial plans

(a) The **assumptions** made should be **reasonable** and clearly stated.

(b) Plans should be **consistent** with each other, so that **short-term plans link** with longer-term plans, financial plans link with non-financial (eg staffing level) plans.

LEARNING OUTCOME 1 THE FINANCIAL ENVIRONMENT AND CAPITAL REQUIREMENTS AND CONSEQUENT COSTS

(c) Plans should be in an **appropriate format**. Some plans will be very close in format to financial accounts, containing an income statement, statement of financial position and statement of cash flows. Others will be more of a summary, or contain more detail than statutory accounts in certain aspects, for example operating cash flows.

(d) **Appropriate plans** should be **prepared** for different parts of the business. Full plans should be prepared for each component (division, segment) of the business.

(e) It should be possible to **revise** the plans in the light of changed circumstances in the same way that forecasts are updated.

6.4 Further steps in the financial planning process

(a) Establishing the **financial requirements** of the business plan and arranging to secure the necessary funding from the most appropriate sources

(b) **Monitoring and review** of the business plan against actual events

6.5 Example: Business plan

Lion Grange has recently introduced a formal scheme of long range planning. At a meeting called to discuss the first draft plans, the following estimates emerged.

(a) Units sold in the current year reached 10,000, and forecasts for the units to be sold over the next five years are 10,600, 11,400, 12,400, 13,600 and 15,000.

(b) Sales price is forecast to be $1,000 per unit.

(c) Total operating costs this year are $9 million and are 20% variable and 80% fixed.

(d) Total assets less current liabilities will remain at around 135% of sales.

It was also suggested that:

(a) If profits rise, dividends should rise by at least the same percentage.

(b) An earnings retention rate of 50% should be maintained.

(c) The ratio of long-term borrowing to long-term funds (debt plus equity) is limited (by the market) to 30%, which happens also to be the current gearing level of the company.

Prepare a financial analysis of the draft long range plan and suggest policies for dividends, retained earnings and gearing (the level of debt).

Solution

The draft financial plan, for profits, dividends, assets required and funding, can be drawn up in a table, as follows.

	Current year $m	Year 1 $m	Year 2 $m	Year 3 $m	Year 4 $m	Year 5 $m
Sales (price x units sold)	10.00	10.60	11.40	12.40	13.60	15.00
Variable costs	1.80	1.91	2.05	2.23	2.45	2.70
Fixed costs	7.20	7.20	7.20	7.20	7.20	7.20
Net profit after tax	1.00	1.49	2.15	2.97	3.95	5.1
Dividends (50% of profit after tax)	0.50	0.75	1.07	1.48	1.98	2.55
Total assets less current liabilities (135% of sales)	13.50	14.31	15.39	16.74	18.36	20.25
Equity (increased by retained earnings)	9.45	10.20	11.27	12.75	14.73	17.28

	Current year $m	Year 1 $m	Year 2 $m	Year 3 $m	Year 4 $m	Year 5 $m
Maximum debt (30% of long-term funds)	4.05	4.29	4.62	5.02	5.51	6.08
Funds available	13.50	14.49	15.89	17.78	20.24	23.36
Shortfalls in funds, given Maximum gearing of 30% and no new issue of shares = funds available minus total assets less current liabilities	0.00	(0.18)	(0.50)	(1.04)	(1.88)	(3.11)

These figures show that the financial objectives of the company are not compatible with each other, and adjustments will have to be made.

(a) Given the assumptions about sales, profits, dividends and net assets required, there will be an increasing shortfall of funds from Year 1 onwards, unless new shares are issued or the gearing level rises above 30%.

(b) In most years, the shortfall can be eliminated by retaining a greater percentage of profits, but this may have a serious adverse effect on the share price. In Year 5, the shortfall in funds cannot be removed even if dividend payments are reduced to nothing.

(c) Asset turnover appears to be low. The situation would be eased if investments were able to generate a higher volume of sales, so that fewer non-current assets and less working capital would be required to support the projected level of sales. If asset turnover cannot be improved, it may be possible to increase the profit to sales ratio by reducing costs or increasing selling prices.

(d) No allowance has been made for the purchase of extra non-current assets, which may be needed to support the forecast sales growth. This may be difficult to finance due to the forecast shortfall in cash that is forecast.

(e) If a new issue of shares is proposed to make up the shortfall in funds, the amount of funds required must be considered very carefully. Total dividends would have to be increased in order to pay dividends on the new shares. The company seems unable to offer prospects of suitable dividend payments, and so raising new equity might be difficult.

(f) It is conceivable that extra funds could be raised by issuing new debt capital, so that the level of gearing would be over 30%. It is uncertain whether investors would be prepared to lend money so as to increase gearing. If more funds were borrowed, profits after interest and tax would fall so that the share price might also be reduced.

6.6 Gap analysis

FAST FORWARD

Gap analysis establishes the differences between an organisation's **targets** and its **expected achievements**.

Gap analysis is 'the comparison of an entity's ultimate objective with the sum of projections and already planned projects', with the purpose of establishing:

(a) What are the organisation's **targets for achievement** over the planning period?

(b) What would the organisation be **expected to achieve** if it **'did nothing'**? In other words, if it did not develop any new strategies, but simply carried on in the current way with the same products and selling to the same markets.

There will be a difference between the targets in (a) and expected achievements in (b). This difference is the 'gap'. New strategies will then have to be developed which will close this gap, so that the organisation can expect to achieve its targets over the planning period.

6.7 Errors in the forecast

A forecast cannot be expected to guarantee accuracy and there must inevitably be some latitude for error. If possible, the error should be quantified in either of the following two ways:

- By predicting the profit and **estimating likely variations**
- By providing a **probability distribution for profits**

7 Uncertainty

FAST FORWARD

Uncertainty in forecasts can be modelled by asking **what if questions**, **preparing a probability distribution** and **preparing pessimistic, optimistic** and **most likely forecasts**.

7.1 Problems with uncertainty

The main problem with planning and forecasting, especially in the longer term, is **uncertainty**. Forecasts about economic events and changes in a market or an industry will be very difficult to make, and planners must accept that even the best forecasts will not be wholly accurate.

(a) A sales forecast might be for an annual growth of 10% in sales for the next five years. But how reliable are the assumptions made?

(b) Similarly, a company might forecast that on the assumption that the exchange rate of sterling against the US dollar falls by 5% next year, export sales will rise by 8%. How can exchange rate movements be forecast accurately, and so how reliable is this forecast?

Managers should make forecasts based on **realistic assumptions** so as to be able to compare actual and expected performance.

7.2 Dealing with uncertainty

Planners should also try to assess the consequences of forecasts being inaccurate. Methods of assessing uncertainty are as follows.

7.2.1 Ask 'what if' questions

A forecast is prepared, based on certain assumptions. The forecaster or planner can then carry out **sensitivity analysis** by finding the answers to questions such as the following:

- What if sales growth is only 5% a year, not 10%?
- What if costs rise by 5% more than anticipated?
- What if the introduction of a new project is held up by 12 months?

Sensitivity analysis will be covered in detail in Chapter 9.

7.2.2 Prepare a probability distribution of possible outcomes

An alternative technique for assessing uncertainty is to prepare a probability distribution for the range of different possible outcomes

A probability distribution could be prepared for any key variable in the business plan, such as wage levels, raw material costs, productivity levels, interest rates, foreign exchange rates, sales and so on. From the probability distributions, forecasts can be prepared for:

- The expected value of (for example) sales or profits
- The probability distribution of (for example) sales or profits

5: FINANCIAL PLANNING AND FORECASTING

7.2.3 Preparing pessimistic, optimistic and most likely forecasts

A forecast can be prepared for each of three possible outcomes:

- **The worst** that might happen
- **The best** that might happen
- **The most likely** outcome that might happen

7.2.4 Simulations

A simulation model could be constructed by assigning a range of random number digits to each possible value for each of the uncertain variables. The random numbers must exactly match their respective probabilities. This is achieved by working upwards cumulatively from the lowest to the highest cash flow values and assigning numbers that will correspond to probability groupings.

7.2.5 Example: Simulation model

The following probability estimates have been prepared for a proposed project.

	Year	Probability	$
Cost of equipment	0	1.00	(40,000)
Revenue each year	1-5	0.15	40,000
		0.40	50,000
		0.30	55,000
		0.15	60,000
Running costs each year	1-5	0.10	25,000
		0.25	30,000
		0.35	35,000
		0.30	40,000

The cost of capital is 12%. Assess how a simulation model might be used to assess the project's NPV.

Solution

A simulation model could be constructed by assigning a range of random number digits to each possible value for each of the uncertain variables. The random numbers must exactly match their respective probabilities. This is achieved by working upwards cumulatively from the lowest to the highest cash flow values and assigning numbers that will correspond to probability groupings, as follows.

Revenue				Running costs		
$	Prob	Random numbers		$	Prob	Random numbers
40,000	0.15	00 – 14	*	25,000	0.10	00 – 09
50,000	0.40	15 – 54	**	30,000	0.25	10 – 34
55,000	0.30	55 – 84	***	40,000	0.35	35 – 69
60,000	0.15	85 – 99		40,000	0.30	70 – 99

* Probability is 0.15 (15%). Random numbers are 15% of range 00 – 99.
** Probability is 0.40 (40%). Random numbers are 40% of range 00 – 99 but starting at 15.
*** Probability is 0.30 (30%). Random numbers are 30% of range 00 – 99 but starting at 55.

For revenue, the selection of a random number in the range 00 and 14 has a probability of 0.15. This probability represents revenue of $40,000. Numbers have been assigned to cash flows so that when numbers are selected at random, the cash flows have exactly the same probability of being selected as is indicated in their respective probability distribution above.

Random numbers would be generated, for example by a computer program, and these would be used to assign values to each of the uncertain variables.

LEARNING OUTCOME 1 THE FINANCIAL ENVIRONMENT AND CAPITAL REQUIREMENTS AND CONSEQUENT COSTS

For example, if random numbers 37, 84, 20, 01, 56 and 89 were generated, the values assigned to the variables would be as follows.

	Revenue			Costs	
Calculation	Random number	Value $		Random number	Value $
1	37	50,000		84	40,000
2	20	50,000		01	25,000
3	56	55,000		89	40,000

A computer would calculate the NPV many times over using the values established in this way with more random numbers, and the results would be analysed to provide the following.

(a) An **expected NPV** for the project
(b) A **statistical distribution** pattern for the possible variation in the NPV above or below this average

The decision whether to go ahead with the project would then be made on the basis of **expected return** and **risk**.

7.2.6 Statistical models

You should be aware that multi-variate statistical models can be used to predict likely outcomes given interdependent variables. However, for the purposes of this paper, you do not need to know about the detail of these models.

7.2.7 Certainty equivalents

Using certainty equivalents involves restating estimated future cash flows conservatively to reflect uncertainty. For example, if it is felt an income of £100,000 is very likely, it might be assigned a value of £90,000 in decision making. If the income were much less certain, it would be assigned a lower value – say £15,000. These adjustments are subjective. They can be undertaken by applying **certainty equivalent factors** to cash flows and in the previous example the factors would be 0.90 and 0.15 respectively. Typically, these factors would be lower the further into the future the cash flows occur to reflect increased uncertainty. The certainty equivalent factors are also subjectively estimated. Once restated, certainty equivalents have been effectively converted to a risk-free equivalent and can be discounted, in theory, at a risk free rate. The key drawback with this method is the subjective nature of the adjustment process.

7.2.8 Example: Certainty equivalents

Tiger Co, whose cost of capital is 10%, is considering a project with the following expected cash flows.

Year	Cash flow $	Discount factor 10%	Present value $
0	(10,000)	1.000	(10,000)
1	7,000	0.909	6,363
2	5,000	0.826	4,130
3	5,000	0.751	3,755
			NPV = +4,248

The project seems to be worthwhile. However, because of the uncertainty about the future cash receipts, the management decides to reduce them to 'certainty-equivalents' by taking only 70%, 60% and 50% of the years 1, 2 and 3 cash flows respectively. The risk-free rate is 5%.

On the basis of the information set out above, assess whether the project is worthwhile.

Solution

The risk-adjusted NPV of the project is as follows.

Year		Cash flow: certainty equivalents $	Discount factor at risk-free rate of return 5%	Present value $
0		(10,000)	1.000	(10,000)
1	(7,000 × 0.70)	4,900	0.952	4,665
2	(5,000 × 0.60)	3,000	0.907	2,721
3	(5,000 × 0.50)	2,500	0.864	2,160
				NPV = (454)

The project's certainty-equivalent NPV is negative. This means that the project is too risky and should be rejected.

The disadvantage of the 'certainty-equivalent' approach is that the amount of the adjustment to each cash flow is decided **subjectively**.

7.3 Dealing with uncertainty

Companies may make **contingency plans**, for what should be done in the event that something occurs in the future that has not been allowed for in the main plan.

Companies may also **protect themselves** whenever possible against **adverse change**, by means of **risk management**. Companies can, at a cost, protect themselves against adverse movements in interest rates or foreign exchange rates. We shall look in some detail at risk management in later chapters.

7.4 Risk adjusted discount rate

This would involve:

(a) Assessing the risk of a project. Perhaps it can be assigned to a **risk class**.

(b) **Adjusting** the **discount rate** to the account of the risk. This can be done on an arbitrary basis, or methods such as **portfolio theory**, the **Capital Asset Pricing Model** or **Arbitrage theory** (all of which we shall discuss in later chapters) can be used.

LEARNING OUTCOME 1 THE FINANCIAL ENVIRONMENT AND CAPITAL REQUIREMENTS AND CONSEQUENT COSTS

Chapter Roundup

- **Ratios** provide a means of systematically analysing financial statements. They can be grouped under the headings **profitability**, **liquidity**, **gearing** and **shareholders' investment**. It is important to calculate **relevant ratios** and to take into account the **limitations** of **ratio analysis**.

- **Ratio analysis** often forms the basis of comparisons with performance over time or with other companies. Comments on a company based on such ratios are far more likely to be right than comments based on a casual read through of a set of accounts.

- As well as ratios, **other information** can be used to analyse a company's performance and identify possible problem areas. This will include information relating to **non-current assets** and **financial obligations**, **contingencies** and **events after the reporting date**.

- Business failure can be predicted using a number of financial variables, or by models such as **Argenti's model**, which focus on qualitative factors such as emphasising defects, mistakes and symptoms.

- **Cash forecasting** should ensure that sufficient funds will be available when needed, to sustain the activities of an enterprise at an acceptable cost.

- **Cash deficits** will be funded in different ways, depending on whether they are short or long-term. Businesses should have procedures for investing surpluses with appropriate levels of risk and return.

- **Forecasts** based on the statement of financial position can be used to assess the scale of funding requirements or cash surpluses expected over time, and to act as a check on the realism of cash flow based forecasts.

- **Forecast financial statements** can be constructed for a period of several years, from first year data, given certain assumptions.

- As part of a business' risk analysis, different forecasts should be prepared with **changing financial or business variables**. The links between these variables and the figures in the forecasts may not be straightforward.

- **Gap analysis** establishes the differences between an organisation's **targets** and its **expected achievements**.

- Uncertainty in forecasts can be modelled by asking **what if questions**, **preparing a probability distribution** and **preparing pessimistic, optimistic** and **most likely forecasts**.

Quick Quiz

1. Identify terms (A) to (F) to complete the equation.

   Profit margin × Asset turnover = ROCE

   $$\frac{(A)}{(B)} \times \frac{(C)}{(D)} = \frac{(E)}{(F)}$$

2. Complete the following in respect of capital gearing.

   $$\text{Gearing ratio} = \frac{(A)}{(B)+(C)}$$

3. Complete the following.

   $$\text{Interest cover} = \frac{(A)}{(B)}$$

4. $$\frac{\text{Current assets less inventory}}{\text{Current liabilities}} = ?$$

5. **Fill in the blanks**, using the terms in the box

   $$\text{Dividend yield} = \frac{(1)}{(2)} \times 100\%$$

   $$\text{Interest yield} = \frac{(3)}{(4)} \times 100\%$$

   $$\text{EPS} = \frac{(5)}{(6)}$$

   $$\text{P/E ratio} = \frac{(7)}{(8)}$$

   $$\text{Dividend cover} = \frac{(9)}{(10)}$$

   - Gross dividend per share
   - Loan stock market value
   - Number of shares
   - Earnings available for distribution
   - Share price
   - Earnings attributable to one share
   - Profit after tax
   - Gross interest
   - Actual dividend

6. Identify three weaknesses of corporate failure models.

7. Give three methods of funding a deficiency of cash.

8. Give three methods of measuring uncertainty in forecasts.

LEARNING OUTCOME 1 THE FINANCIAL ENVIRONMENT AND CAPITAL REQUIREMENTS AND CONSEQUENT COSTS

Answers to Quick Quiz

1. (A) PBIT
   (B) Sales
   (C) Sales
   (D) Capital employed
   (E) PBIT
   (F) Capital employed

2. (A) Prior-charge capital
   (B) Prior-charge capital
   (C) Equity

3. (A) PBIT
   (B) Interest charges

4. Quick or acid test ratio

5. (1) Gross dividend per share
   (2) Share price
   (3) Gross interest
   (4) Loan stock market value
   (5) Profit after tax
   (6) Number of shares
   (7) Share price
   (8) Earnings attributable to one share
   (9) Earnings available for distribution
   (10) Actual dividend

6. Choose from any of the following:
   (a) They relate to the past
   (b) They share the limitations of accounting
   (c) Accounting figures are published after a delay
   (d) Measures are subject to manipulation
   (e) The definition of corporate failure is unclear

7. (a) Borrowing
   (b) Selling short-term financial investments
   (c) Leading and lagging payables and receivables

8. (a) Ask what if questions
   (b) Prepare a probability distribution of possible outcomes
   (c) Prepare pessimistic, optimistic and most likely forecasts

End of chapter questions

1. Ben Hawk (AIA November 2014)

Ben Hawk set up an advertising agency 15 years ago. It is a London-based agency and focuses on working with clients in the transport industry to develop and implement their advertising, marketing and branding strategies. The agency has grown over the fifteen year period and has developed a good reputation for the work it produces. This has helped it to attract high calibre and creative staff which is important in the advertising industry. However, Ben is also aware that these staff can easily move to other advertising agencies should they decide they want to.

The profits trend for the agency shows a steadily increasing profit level generally. However, Ben also knows that companies in the transport industry will move agency if they feel that the service they are receiving is not of high quality. He is also aware that the transport industry is affected by the strength of the overall economy. Therefore, if the economy weakens this will adversely affect profits of transport companies and they are likely to reduce their advertising and marketing expenditure.

The current gearing ratio for the advertising agency (measured by the ratio of long-term debt to equity) is 40% and this compares to an industry average of 42%. The turnover for the agency in the last twelve months was £4m. The agency's offices are owned rather than rented. Ben is keen that the agency grows further and he would like to expand by setting up offices in other major cities in Europe. He is considering approaching one of the banks to ascertain whether they will provide additional borrowings to fund this expansion. Ben's ambition is to double the agency's turnover in the next three years and this would require him to almost double his borrowings. Prior to setting up the agency, Ben had gained extensive experience of advertising and marketing through working for other advertising agencies in a wide variety of roles. The principal reason he set up his own agency is that he is highly entrepreneurial and wanted to run his own business. He currently owns all the equity of the business.

Required

Prepare a report advising Ben on the issues that may be raised if he approaches a bank for additional borrowings. You should include in your report advice on additional information that is needed from Ben before he can approach the bank to ask for the additional borrowings. **(20 marks)**

2. Southern Drive plc (AIA May 2005)

Southern Drive plc is a manufacturing company. A summary of its latest financial statements is given below:

STATEMENT OF COMPREHENSIVE INCOME FOR YEAR END 31 DECEMBER 20X4

	£'000	£'000
Revenue		8,250
Cost of Sales*		5,106
Gross Profit		3,144
Variable Operating Expenses*	244	
Fixed Operating Expenses	1,772	2,016
Profit before Interest and Tax		1,128
Interest		204
Profit before tax		924
Tax		231
Profit after tax		693

*Cost of Sales and Variable Operating Expenses vary directly with revenue.

LEARNING OUTCOME 1 THE FINANCIAL ENVIRONMENT AND CAPITAL REQUIREMENTS AND CONSEQUENT COSTS

STATEMENT OF FINANCIAL POSITION AS AT 31 DECEMBER 20X4

	£'000
Net Assets	5,076
Long-Term Debt	(1,390)
	3,686
Capital and Reserves*	3,686

*Including 6,000,000 ordinary shares at 25p each.

The company is planning a major upgrading of its manufacturing facilities. This will cost £2 million and will reduce both cost of sales and variable operating expenses by 20% and enable the company to increase revenue by 15% per annum. Fixed operating costs will increase by £210,000 per annum. The upgrading will be financed by additional long-term debt at a rate of 8%.

The company pays tax at 25%.

Required

(a) Evaluate the effect of the upgrading on the company's operating gearing, financial gearing and earnings per share. **(11 marks)**

(b) Evaluate the effect on the ordinary shareholders of the company if, after the upgrading, revenue was to fall by 20% instead of increasing by 15%. **(4 marks)**

(c) Briefly discuss the relationship between business risk, operating gearing, financial gearing and a company's cost of capital. **(5 marks)**

(Total 20 marks)

The cost of capital

Topic list	Syllabus reference
1 The cost of capital	LO1
2 The cost of equity	LO1
3 The cost of debt	LO1
4 The weighted average cost of capital	LO1
5 WACC and share values	LO1

Introduction

Every source of finance has a **cost**. In deciding how to finance a company, the costs of all sources must be considered.

Financial managers also need a **cost of capital** to use when making investment decisions. A weighted average might seem a reasonable cost to use, but you should appreciate the arguments against, as well as those for, using it.

Work carefully through this chapter making sure you understand how the different calculations are carried out, as they are basic techniques in this paper.

1 The cost of capital

> **FAST FORWARD**
>
> The **cost of capital** is the rate of return that the enterprise must pay to satisfy the providers of funds, and it reflects the riskiness of providing funds.

1.1 Aspects of the cost of capital

The cost of capital has two aspects to it:

(a) The **cost of funds** that a company raises and uses, and the return that investors expect to be paid for putting funds into the company.

(b) It is therefore the **minimum return** that a company should make on its own investments, to earn the cash flows out of which investors can be paid their return.

The cost of capital can therefore be measured by studying the returns required by investors, and then used to derive a discount rate for DCF analysis and investment appraisal.

1.2 The cost of capital as an opportunity cost of finance

The cost of capital is an **opportunity cost of finance**, because it is the minimum return that investors require. If they do not get this return, they will transfer some or all of their investment somewhere else. Here are two examples:

(a) If a bank offers to lend money to a company, the interest rate it charges is the **yield** that the bank wants to receive from investing in the company, because it can get just as good a return from lending the money to someone else. In other words, the interest rate is the opportunity cost of lending for the bank.

(b) When shareholders invest in a company, the returns that they can expect must be sufficient to persuade them not to sell some or all of their shares and invest the money somewhere else. The yield on the shares is therefore the **opportunity cost** to the **shareholders of not investing somewhere else**.

1.3 The cost of capital and risk

The cost of capital has three elements:

Cost of capital	
Risk-free rate of return	Return required from a completely risk free investment, eg yield on government securities
Business risk premium	Increase in required rate of return due to uncertainty about future and business prospects
	Varies between firms and projects undertaken by same firm
Financial risk premium	Danger of high debt levels, variability in equity earnings after payments to debt capital holders

Because different companies are in different types of business (varying business risk) and have different capital structures (varying financial risk) the cost of capital applied to one company may differ radically from the cost of capital of another.

2 The cost of equity

FAST FORWARD

The **dividend valuation model** can be used to estimate a cost of equity, on the assumption that the market value of share is directly related to the expected future dividends on the shares.

Expected **growth in dividends** can be allowed for, using Gordon's growth model.

2.1 The cost of ordinary share capital

New funds from equity shareholders are obtained from:

- New issues of shares
- Cash deriving from retained earnings

Both of these sources of funds have a cost.

- Shareholders will not subscribe to **new issue of shares** unless the return on their investment is attractive.

- **Retained earnings** also have a cost, the dividend forgone by shareholders.

2.2 The dividend valuation model

Ignoring share issue costs, the cost of equity, both for new issues and retained earnings, could be estimated by means of a **dividend valuation model**, on the assumption that the **market value** of shares is **directly related** to **expected future dividends** on the shares. If the future dividend per share (D_1) is expected to be **constant** in amount then the ex dividend share price (P_0) will be calculated by the formula:

$$P_0 = \frac{D_1}{(1+Ke)} + \frac{D_1}{(1+Ke)^2} + \frac{D_1}{(1+Ke)^3} + \ldots = \frac{D_1}{Ke}, \text{ so } Ke = \frac{D_1}{P_0}$$

where: Ke is the cost of equity D_1 is the annual dividend per share, starting at Year 1 and then continuing annually in perpetuity

2.2.1 Share issue costs

The issue of shares, whether to the general public or as a rights issue, costs money and these costs should be considered in investment appraisal. Two approaches have been suggested.

(a) **Deduct issue costs as a year 0 cash outflow** of the project or projects for which the share capital is being raised. The issue costs would not affect the cost of equity capital.

(b) Calculate the cost of new equity with the **formula**:

$$Ke = \frac{D_1}{P_0 - X}$$

where X represents the issue costs. Thus, if the issue price of a share is £2.50, issue costs are 20p per share, and new shareholders expect constant annual dividends of 46p, the cost of new equity would be:

$$\frac{46}{(250-20)} = 0.2 = 20\%$$

Approach (a) is recommended.

2.3 The dividend growth model (Gordon's growth model)

Shareholders will normally expect dividends to **increase year by year** and not to remain constant in perpetuity.

Key term

> The **fundamental theory of share values** states that the market price of a share is the present value of the discounted future cash flows of revenues from the share.

The market value given an expected constant annual growth in dividends would be:

$$P_0 = \frac{D_0(1+g)}{(1+K_e)} + \frac{D_0(1+g)^2}{(1+K_e)^2} + \dots$$

where: P_0 is the current market price (ex div)

D_0 is the current net dividend

K_e is the shareholders' cost of capital

g is the expected annual growth in dividend payments, expressed as a proportion.

This formula can be adapted for an uneven growth rate of dividends. Capital growth through increases in the share price will arise from changed expectations about future dividend growth, or changes in the required return.

Exam focus point

> Remember that the net dividend should be used, as a company must achieve significant profits from the investments it undertakes to pay shareholders the net dividends they require out of after-tax profits.

It is often convenient to assume a constant expected dividend growth rate in perpetuity. The formula above then simplifies to:

$$P_0 = \frac{D_0(1+g)}{(K_e - g)}$$

and

$$K_e = \frac{D_0(1+g)}{P_0} + g$$

This is equivalent to the following equation.

Exam formula

> $$K_e = \frac{D_1}{P_0} + g$$
>
> where D_1 is the dividend in year 1, so that $D_1 = D_0(1+g)$.

Question — Cost of equity capital

A share has a current market value of 96p, and the last dividend was 12p. If the expected annual growth rate of dividends is 4%, calculate the cost of equity capital.

Answer

$$\text{Cost of capital} = \frac{12(1+0.04)}{96} + 0.04 = 0.13 + 0.04 = 0.17 = 17\%$$

2.4 Estimating the dividend growth rate

Formula to learn

The dividend growth rate, g, can be estimated in one of two ways.

(a) Reviewing the pattern of past dividend growth.

(b) Using the equations $g = rb$ or $\sqrt[n]{\dfrac{\text{dividend in year x}}{\text{dividend in year x} - n}} - 1$

As many companies try to have a stable dividend policy, (a) will often be a reasonable choice. Of course, both methods could be used, and if they give similar results, g can be selected with confidence. Remember however, that long-term dividend growth has to be supported by long-term increases in cash earnings.

The dividend growth model is sometimes called **Gordon's growth model**.

2.5 Example: Cost of capital (1)

The dividends and earnings of Hall Shores plc over the last five years have been as follows:

Year	Dividends £	Earnings £
20X1	150,000	400,000
20X2	192,000	510,000
20X3	206,000	550,000
20X4	245,000	650,000
20X5	262,350	700,000

The company is financed entirely by equity and there are 1,000,000 shares in issue, each with a market value of £3.35 ex div.

(a) What is the growth rate over the last four years?
(b) What is the cost of equity?
(c) What implications does dividend growth appear to have for earnings retentions?

Solution

The dividend growth model will be used.

(a) Dividends have risen from £150,000 in 20X1 to £262,350 in 20X5. The increase represents four years' growth. (Check that you are aware that there are four years' growth, and not five years' growth, in the table.) The average growth rate, g, may be calculated as follows:

Dividend in 20X1 × $(1 + g)^4$ = Dividend in 20X5

$(1 + g)^4 = \dfrac{\text{Dividend in 20X5}}{\text{Dividend in 20X1}}$

$= \dfrac{£262,350}{£150,000} = 1.749$

$1 + g = \sqrt[4]{1.749} = 1.15$

$g = 0.15 = 15\%$

(b) The growth rate over the last four years is assumed to be expected by shareholders into the indefinite future, so the cost of equity, is:

$\dfrac{D_0(1+g)}{P_0} + g = \dfrac{0.26235(1.15)}{3.35} + 0.15 = 0.24 = 24\%$

(c) Retained profits will earn a certain rate of return and so growth will come from the yield on the retained funds. It might be assumed that g = br where r is the yield on new investments and b is the proportion of profits retained for reinvestment.

In our example, if we applied this assumption the future annual growth rate would be 15% if br continued to be 15%. If the rate of return on new investments averages 24% (which is the cost of equity) and if the proportion of earnings retained is 62.5% (which it has been, approximately, in the period 20X1 – 20X5) then g = br = 62.5% × 24% = 15%.

2.6 Private companies and the cost of equity

The cost of capital cannot be calculated from market values for **private companies** in the way that has been described so far, because the shares in a private company do not have a quoted market price. Since private companies do not have a cost of equity that can be readily estimated, it follows that a big problem for private companies which want to use DCF for evaluating investment projects is how to select a cost of capital for a discount rate.

Suitable approaches might be:

(a) To **estimate** the **cost of capital** for **similar public companies**, but then add a further premium for additional business and financial risk

(b) To **build up a cost of capital** by adding estimated premiums for business risk and financial risk to the risk-free rate of return

3 The cost of debt

> **FAST FORWARD**
>
> The **cost of debt** is the return an enterprise must pay to its lenders.
>
> For **irredeemable debt**, this is the (post-tax) interest as a percentage of the ex interest market value of the loan stock (or preference shares).
>
> For **redeemable debt**, the cost is given by the internal rate of return of the cash flows involved.

3.1 Estimating the cost of debt

Estimating the cost of fixed interest or fixed dividend capital is much easier than estimating the cost of ordinary share capital because the interest received by the holder of the security is fixed by contract and will not fluctuate.

The **cost of debt capital already issued** is the **rate of interest** (the internal rate of return) which **equates the current market price** with the **discounted future cash receipts** from the security.

3.2 The cost of irredeemable debt

Ignoring taxation for the moment, in the case of **irredeemable debt** (or **preference shares**) the future cash flows are the interest (or dividend) payments in perpetuity so that $P_0 = \dfrac{I}{K_d}$.

3.3 After-tax cost of irredeemable debt capital

The interest on debt capital is an allowable deduction for purposes of taxation. This tax relief on interest ought to be recognised in DCF computations. One way of doing this is to include tax savings due to interest payments in the cash flows of every project. A simpler method, and one that is normally used, is to allow for the tax relief in computing the cost of debt capital, to arrive at an 'after-tax' cost of debt.

Formula to learn

$$Kd = \frac{i}{P_0}(1-t)$$

where   Kd   is the after-tax cost of irredeemable debt capital
         i   is the annual interest payment
         P_0 is the current market price of the debt capital ex interest (that is, after payment of the current interest)
         t   is the rate of corporation tax.

3.4 Example: Cost of capital (2)

Therefore if a company pays £10,000 a year interest on irredeemable debenture stock with a nominal value of £100,000 and a market price of £80,000, and the rate of corporation tax is 30%, the cost of the debentures would be:

$$\frac{10,000}{80,000}(1 - 0.30) = 0.0875 = 8.75\%.$$

The higher the rate of corporation tax is, the greater the tax benefits in having debt finance will be compared with equity finance. In the example above, if the rate of tax had been 40%, the cost of debt would have been, after tax:

$$\frac{10,000}{80,000}(1 - 0.40) = 0.075 = 7.5\%.$$

3.5 The cost of redeemable debt

The cost of redeemable debt has to be calculated by **trial and error** using an IRR. The best trial and error figure to start with in calculating the cost of redeemable debt is to take the cost of debt capital as if it were irredeemable and then add the annualised capital profit that will be made from the present time to the time of redemption.

If the debt is **redeemable** then in the year of redemption the interest payment will be received by the holder as well as the amount payable on redemption.

The **capital repayment** is **not** allowable to tax, however there is tax relief on the interest.

Exam focus point

Calculation of the cost of redeemable and irredeemable debt are important techniques, so make sure you do not confuse the two.

3.6 Example: Cost of capital (3)

Owen Allot plc has in issue 10% debentures of a nominal value of £100. The market price is £90 ex interest. Ignoring taxation, calculate the cost of this capital if the debenture is:

(a) Irredeemable
(b) Redeemable at par after ten years

Solution

(a)   The cost of irredeemable debt capital is $\frac{i}{P_0} = \frac{£10}{£90} \times 100\% = 11.1\%$

LEARNING OUTCOME 1 THE FINANCIAL ENVIRONMENT AND CAPITAL REQUIREMENTS AND CONSEQUENT COSTS

(b) The cost of debt capital is 11.1% if irredeemable. The capital profit that will be made from now to the date of redemption is £10 (£100 – £90). This profit will be made over a period of ten years which gives an annualised profit of £1 which is about 1% of current market value. The best trial and error figure to try first is, therefore, 12%.

Year		Cash flow	Discount factor 12%	PV £	Discount factor 11%	PV £
0	Market value	(90)	1.000	(90.00)	1.000	(90.00)
1–10	Interest	10	5.650	56.50	5.889	58.89
10	Capital repayment	100	0.322	32.20	0.352	35.20
				(1.30)		4.09

The approximate cost of debt capital is, therefore, $(11 + \frac{4.09}{(4.09 - -1.30)} \times 1) = 11.76\%$

The cost of debt capital estimated above represents the cost of **continuing to use the finance** rather than redeem the securities at their current market price. It would also represent the **cost of raising additional fixed interest capital** if we assume that the cost of the additional capital would be equal to the cost of that already issued. If a company has not already issued any fixed interest capital, it may estimate the cost of doing so by making a similar calculation for another company which is judged to be similar as regards risk.

3.7 The cost of floating rate debt

If a firm has **floating rate debt**, then the cost of an equivalent fixed interest debt should be substituted. 'Equivalent' usually means **fixed interest debt** with a **similar term to maturity** in a firm of similar standing.

3.8 The cost of convertible securities

The cost of fixed interest securities which are convertible into ordinary shares, would be calculated by finding the **IRR** which **equates** P_0 with the **present value of the future cash flows.** These include the cash flows relating to the conversion (which is assumed to take place). If the cost of capital found by treating the convertibles as non-convertible debentures is higher, that higher cost should be used on the basis that the debenture holders will choose not to convert, so as to secure the higher rate of return for themselves.

3.8.1 Example: Cost of capital (4)

Some 8% convertible debentures have a current market value of £106 per cent. An interest payment was made recently. The debentures will be convertible into equity shares in three years time, at a rate of four shares per £10 of debentures. The shares are expected to have a market value of £3.50 each at that time, and all the debenture holders are expected to convert their debentures.

What is the cost of capital to the company for the convertible debentures? Corporation tax is at 30%. Assume that tax savings occur in the same year that the interest payments arise.

Solution

Year	Item	Cash flow £	Try 12% Discount factor	PV £	Try 15% Discount factor	PV £
0	Current MV	(106.00)	1.000	(106.00)	1.000	(106.00)
1–3	Interest less tax (i(1–t))	5.60	2.402	13.45	2.283	12.78
3	Value of shares on conversion (40 × £3.5)	140.00	0.712	99.68	0.658	92.12
				7.13		(1.10)

6: THE COST OF CAPITAL

$$\text{Cost of capital} = 12\% + \left[\frac{7.13}{(7.13 - -1.10)} \times (15-12)\right]\%$$

$$= 12\% + 2.6\% = 14.6\%$$

3.9 The cost of short-term funds

The cost of short-term funds such as bank loans and overdrafts is the current interest being charged on such funds adjusted for the tax saving on interest

4 The weighted average cost of capital

FAST FORWARD

The **weighted average cost of capital** can be used to evaluate a business's investment projects if:

- The project is **small relative** to the company.
- The **existing capital structure** will be maintained (same financial risk).
- The **project** has the **same business risk** as the company.

4.1 Computing a discount rate

We have now looked at the costs of individual sources of capital for a company. But how does this help us to work out the **cost of capital** as a whole, or the **discount rate** to apply in DCF investment appraisals?

The correct cost of capital to use in investment appraisal is the **marginal cost** of the funds raised (or earnings retained) to finance the investment. The weighted average cost of capital (WACC) might be considered the most reliable guide to the marginal cost of capital, but only on the assumption that the company continues to invest in the future, in projects of a standard level of business risk, by raising funds in the same proportions as its existing capital structure.

4.2 General formula for the WACC

A general formula for the weighted average cost of capital is:

$$\text{WACC} = Ke_g\left(\frac{E}{E+D}\right) + Kd\left(\frac{D}{E+D}\right)$$

where Ke_g is the cost of equity
Kd is the pre-tax cost of debt
E is the market value of equity in the firm
D is the market value of debt in the firm

The above formula has the weakness of ignoring taxation. Bringing in corporation tax, we should calculate the cost of debt net of tax, where the tax rate is t, as follows:

Exam formula

$$\text{WACC} = Ke_g\left(\frac{E}{E+D}\right) + Kd(1-t)\left(\frac{D}{E+D}\right)$$

Exam focus point

If you are given a pre-tax cost of debt, and no details about the nature of the debt, then you can assume that it is irredeemable.

4.3 Example: Weighted average cost of capital

Prudence plc is financed partly by equity and partly by debentures. The equity proportion is two thirds of the total. The cost of equity is 18% and that of debt 12%. A new project is under consideration which will cost £100,000 and will yield a return before interest of £17,500 a year in perpetuity. The project will be financed 2/3 equity: 1/3 debt. Show whether the project should be accepted by:

(a) Calculating the NPV of the investment
(b) Calculating the return to equity

Solution

(a) Since the financing of the project is the same as the company's current financing mix, it is reasonable to assume that its marginal cost of funds equals its WACC. The weighted average cost of capital is as follows:

	Proportion	Cost	Cost × proportion
Equity	2/3	18%	12%
Debt	1/3	12%	4%
		WACC	16%

The present value of the future returns in perpetuity can be found using the WACC as the discount rate, as follows:

$$\text{Present value of future cash flows} = \frac{\text{Annual cash flow}}{\text{Discount rate}} = \frac{£17,500}{0.16} = £109,375$$

The **NPV of the investment** is £109,375 − £100,000 = £9,375.

(b) Another way of looking at the investment shows how using the WACC as the discount rate ensures that equity shareholders' wealth is increased by undertaking projects with a positive NPV when discounted at the WACC.

The amount of finance deemed to be provided by the debenture holders will be $1/3 \times £100,000 = £33,333$. The interest on this will be 12% × £33,333 = £4,000, leaving £13,500 available for the equity shareholders. The return they are receiving based on their 'investment' of £66,667 will be as follows.

$$\text{Return to equity} = \frac{£13,500}{£66,667} = 0.2025 \text{ or } 20.25\%$$

As this return exceeds the cost of equity capital, the project is acceptable.

4.4 Weighting equity and debt

In the last example, we simplified the problem of **weighting the different costs of capital** by giving the proportions of capital. Two methods of weighting could be used.

(a) Weights could be based on **market values** (by this method, the cost of retained earnings is implied in the market value of equity).

(b) Weights could be based on **book values**.

Although the latter are often easier to obtain they are of doubtful economic significance. It is, therefore, more meaningful to use market values when data are available. However there are some exceptions, such as:

(a) For unquoted companies estimates of **market values** are likely to be extremely **subjective** and consequently book values may be used.

(b) When using market values it is **not possible** to **split the equity value between share capital and reserves** and only one cost of equity can be used. This does, however, remove the need to estimate a separate cost of retained earnings.

Exam focus point

If you are not given the market value of debt, you can usually assume that loans are stated at market value. Remember also to use ex dividend and ex interest market values.

Question — Weighted average cost of capital

The management of Custer Ackers plc are trying to decide on a cost of capital to apply to the evaluation of investment projects. The company has an issued share capital of 500,000 ordinary £1 shares, with a current market value cum div of £1.17 per share. It has also issued £200,000 of 10% debentures, which are redeemable at par in two years' time and have a current market value of £105.30 per cent, and £100,000 of 6% preference shares, currently priced at 40p per share. The preference dividend has just been paid, and the ordinary dividend and debenture interest are due to be paid in the near future.

The ordinary share dividend will be £60,000 this year, and the directors have publicised their view that earnings and dividends will increase by 5% a year into the indefinite future. The non-current assets and working capital of the company are financed by the following.

	£
Ordinary shares of £1	500,000
6% £1 Preference shares	100,000
Debentures	200,000
Reserves	380,000
	1,180,000

Required

Advise the management. Ignore inflation, and assume corporation tax of 30%. Assume also that tax savings occur in the same year as the interest payments to which they relate.

Note. The cost of capital of a security is the IRR which equates the current market value of the security with its expected future cash flows. The statement of financial position (accounting) values of the securities and reserves should be ignored.

Answer

(a) **Equity.** Given a 5% annual increase in dividend in perpetuity, the cost of equity capital may be estimated as:

$$\frac{60,000(1+0.05)}{585,000 - 60,000^*} + 0.05 = 0.17 = 17\%$$

* MV of ordinary shares ex div

(b) **Preference shares.** The cost of capital is $\frac{6p}{40p} \times 100\% = 15\%$

(c) **Debentures.** The cost of capital is the IRR of the following cash flows. £95.30 is the ex-interest value (105.30 – 10)

Year	Cost £	Interest £	Tax relief £	Net cash flows £
0	(95.30)			(95.30)
1		10	(3.00)	7.00
2	100.00	10	(3.00)	107.00

LEARNING OUTCOME 1 THE FINANCIAL ENVIRONMENT AND CAPITAL REQUIREMENTS AND CONSEQUENT COSTS

	Net cash flow £	Try 10% Discount factor	PV £	Try 8% Discount factor	PV £
	(95.30)	1.000	(95.30)	1.000	(95.30)
	7.00	0.909	6.36	0.926	6.48
	107.00	0.826	88.38	0.857	91.70
			(0.56)		2.88

The IRR is approx $8\% + \dfrac{2.88}{(2.88 - -0.56)} \times (10-8)\% = 9.67\%$

(d) **Weighted average cost of capital**

Item	Market value £	Cost of capital	Product £
Ordinary shares*	525,000	17%	89,250
Preference shares	40,000	15%	6,000
Debentures*	190,600	9.67%	18,431
	755,600		113,681

* ex div and ex interest

$$\text{WACC} = \dfrac{113,681}{755,600} = 0.150 = 15.0\%$$

(e) The management of Custer Ackers plc may choose to add a premium for risk on top of this 15% and apply a discount rate of, say, 18% to 20% in evaluating projects.

4.5 Arguments for using the WACC

The weighted average cost of capital can be used in investment appraisal if we make the following assumptions.

(a) The project is **small relative to the overall size** of the company.

(b) The weighted average cost of capital reflects the company's **long-term future capital structure**, and capital costs. If this were not so, the current weighted average cost would become irrelevant because eventually it would not relate to any actual cost of capital.

(c) The project has the same degree of **business risk** as the company has now.

(d) New investments must be financed by new **sources of funds**: retained earnings, new share issues, new loans and so on.

(e) The cost of capital to be applied to project evaluation reflects the **marginal cost of new capital** (see below).

Key term

Business risk (or **systematic risk**) is risk arising from the existing operations of an enterprise (eg relating to macroeconomic factors) which cannot be reduced by diversification of investments.

4.6 Arguments against using the WACC

The arguments against using the WACC as the cost of capital for investment appraisal (as follows) are based on criticisms of the assumptions that are used to justify use of the WACC.

(a) New investments undertaken by a company might have different **business risk** characteristics from the company's **existing operations**. As a consequence, the return required by investors might go up (or down) if the investments are undertaken, because their business risk is perceived to be higher (or lower).

(b) The finance that is raised to fund a new investment might substantially change the capital structure and the perceived **financial risk** of investing in the company. Depending on whether the project is financed by equity or by debt capital, the perceived financial risk of the entire company might change. This must be taken into account when appraising investments.

(c) Many companies raise **floating rate debt capital** as well as **fixed interest debt capital**. With floating rate debt capital, the interest rate is variable, and is altered every three or six months or so in line with changes in current market interest rates. The cost of debt capital will therefore fluctuate as market conditions vary. Floating rate debt is difficult to incorporate into a WACC computation, and the best that can be done is to substitute an 'equivalent' fixed interest debt capital cost in place of the floating rate debt cost.

Exam focus point

You may be able to pick up a number of marks for discussing the pros and cons of WACC and observing that taking on a new project may alter the cost of capital. Remember that it can only be used to appraise projects if the business and financing risk remain the same.

4.7 Marginal cost of capital approach

FAST FORWARD

If **new investments** are financed by new **sources of funds**, a **marginal cost of capital** approach should be used.

The **marginal cost of capital approach** involves calculating a marginal cut-off rate for acceptable investment projects by:

(a) **Establishing rates of return** for **each component** of capital structure, except retained earnings, based on its value if it were to be raised under current market conditions

(b) **Relating dividends or interest** to these values to obtain a marginal cost for each component

(c) **Applying the marginal cost** to **each component** depending on its proportionate weight within the capital structure and adding the resultant costs to give a weighted average

The current weighted average cost of capital should arguably be used to evaluate projects where a company's **capital structure** changes **only very slowly** over time; then the marginal cost of new capital should be roughly equal to the weighted average cost of current capital.

Where **gearing levels fluctuate significantly**, or the finance for a new project carries a **significantly different level of risks** to that of the existing company, there is good reason to seek an alternative marginal cost of capital.

Note that the marginal cost of capital approach outlined above only takes into account the **incremental financing costs** of the new project. The financing of a major project may change the risk profile of the existing capital structure, in which case the **adjusted present value (APV) method**, discussed later in this Text, is likely to be more appropriate.

LEARNING OUTCOME 1 THE FINANCIAL ENVIRONMENT AND CAPITAL REQUIREMENTS AND CONSEQUENT COSTS

5 WACC and share values

FAST FORWARD

If WACC is unchanged, a company's value should increase in a strongly efficient market by the **NPV** of projects undertaken plus the **equity** funds invested to finance the project.

5.1 Interaction of cost of capital and dividends

Suppose that a company relying on equity as its only source of finance wishes to invest in a new project. If the money is raised by issuing new share capital to the existing shareholders and the inflows generated by the new project are used to increase dividends, then the project will have to show a positive net present value (NPV) at the shareholders' marginal cost of capital, because otherwise the shareholders would not agree to provide the new capital.

The gain to the shareholders after acceptance of the new project will be the **difference** between the **market value** of the **company before acceptance** of the new project and the **market value** of the company **after acceptance** of the new project less the amount of funds raised from the shareholders to finance the project.

The market value of the shares will increase by:

$$\frac{A_1}{(1+K_e)} + \frac{A_2}{(1+K_e)^2} + \frac{A_3}{(1+K_e)^3} + \ldots - \text{(Cost of project)}$$

where: A_1, A_2 are the additional dividends at Years 1, 2 and so on
K_e is the shareholders' marginal cost of capital

This is the **NPV** of the project.

5.2 Investment and gearing

The situation becomes more complex when gearing is introduced. You may encounter a scenario similar to the following.

5.3 Example: Geared company

Trubshaw plc is financed 50% by equity and 50% by debt capital. The cost of equity is 20% and the cost of debt is 14%. Ignoring tax, this means that Trubshaw's WACC is 17%.

The company currently pays out all its profits as dividends, and expected dividends are £800,000 a year into the indefinite future.

A project is under consideration which would cost £1,200,000. The company's mix of finance will remain unchanged after the financial results of the project, and the finance needed to fund it, have been taken into account. It would increase annual profits before interest by £340,000. The costs of equity and debt capital would be unchanged.

(a) What is the NPV of the project?
(b) By how much would the value of equity increase if the project is undertaken?

Solution

(a) The NPV of the project is as follows.

Year	Cash flow £	Discount factor 17%	Present value £
0	(1,200,000)	1.0	(1,200,000)
1–∞	340,000	1/0.17	2,000,000
		NPV	800,000

6: THE COST OF CAPITAL

(b) The market value of the company as a whole will increase by £2,000,000, which is the project's NPV **plus the cost** of the investment. Of this, £1,000,000 will be debt capital and £1,000,000 will be equity.

To maintain the 50:50 debt:equity ratio, the cost of the investment will be financed by £1,000,000 debt capital and £200,000 equity. It would not be financed by £600,000 of each. This is because the NPV of £800,000 will add to the value of equity **only,** not to the value of the debt capital.

If new equity of £200,000 is issued, the NPV of £800,000 will increase the market value of equity by £1,000,000 in total, which matches the new loan capital of £1,000,000.

The increased value of equity can be proved as follows:

	£
Annual profit from project, before interest	340,000
Less interest cost (£1,000,000 × 14%)	140,000
Increase in annual profits and dividends	200,000
Cost of equity	÷20%
Increase in the market value of equity	£1,000,000

This example therefore illustrates that given an unchanged WACC, the value of equity will be increased by the NPV of any project which is undertaken (plus the extra funds invested in equity, in this case £200,000) with the NPV calculated using a discount rate equal to the WACC.

Chapter Roundup

- The **cost of capital** is the rate of return that the enterprise must pay to satisfy the providers of funds, and it reflects the riskiness of providing funds.

- The **dividend valuation model** can be used to estimate a cost of equity, on the assumption that the market value of share is directly related to the expected future dividends on the shares.

- Expected **growth in dividends** can be allowed for, using Gordon's growth model.

- The **cost of debt to the company** is the return an enterprise must pay to its lenders adjusted for the tax relief the company receives on interest payments. .

- For **irredeemable debt**, this is the (post-tax) interest as a percentage of the ex div market value of the loan stock (or preference shares).

- For **redeemable debt**, the cost is given by the internal rate of return of the cash flows involved.

- The **weighted average cost of capital** can be used to evaluate a company's investment projects if:
    - The project is **small relative** to the company
    - The **existing capital structure** will be maintained (same financial risk)
    - The **project** has the **same business risk** as the company

- If **new investments** are **financed** by new **sources of funds**, a **marginal cost of capital** approach should be used.

- If WACC is unchanged, a company's value should increase in a strongly efficient market by the **NPV** of projects undertaken plus the **equity** funds invested to finance the project.

Quick Quiz

1. **Fill in the blanks**

   Cost of capital = (1) _____ + (2) premium for _____ risk + (3) premium for _____ risk.

2. State **four** assumptions of the dividend valuation model.

3. Where a company's capital structure changes only slowly over time, undertaking investments which offer a return above the WACC will increase the value of shareholders' capital.

   ☐ True

   ☐ False

4. A share has a current market value of 120p and the last dividend was 10p. If the expected annual growth rate of dividends is 5%, calculate the cost of equity capital.

5. What is the formula for the after-tax cost of irredeemable debt capital?

6. When using market values in a weighted average cost of equity calculation, the values used need to be split between share capital and reserves.

   ☐ True

   ☐ False

7. What type of risk arises from the existing operations of a business and cannot be diversified away?

8. In the marginal cost of capital approach, how is the marginal cut-off rate for acceptable investment calculated?

LEARNING OUTCOME 1 THE FINANCIAL ENVIRONMENT AND CAPITAL REQUIREMENTS AND CONSEQUENT COSTS

Answers to Quick Quiz

1. (1) Risk-free rate of return
   (2) Business
   (3) Financial

2. Four of the following.
   (a) Dividends from new project will be of same risk as existing
   (b) No other reason for cost of capital to increase
   (c) Shareholders have perfect information
   (d) Ignore taxation
   (e) Shareholders have some marginal cost of capital
   (f) No issue costs for new shares

3. True

4. $\dfrac{10(1+0.05)}{120} + 0.05 = 13.75\%$

5. $K_d = \dfrac{i}{P_0}(1-t)$

6. False. It is not possible to split the equity value, and only one cost of equity can therefore be used.

7. Systematic or business risk

8. (a) Establishing rates of return for each component of capital structure except retained earnings
   (b) Relating dividends or interest to these values to obtain a marginal cost for each component
   (c) Applying marginal cost to each component, weighting cost and adding resultant costs to give a weighted average

End of chapter questions

1. Fragrance plc (AIA November 2012)

Fragrance plc makes a range of perfumes. The perfumes it produces are considered a luxury item and are very expensive to buy. The company would like to diversify its activities and is considering whether to commence manufacturing a range of soap and shampoo products that are inexpensive and would have a mass market appeal. Fragrance plc currently has a beta factor of 1.2 and the directors have ascertained that the beta factor of another company that manufactures soaps and shampoos is 0.85.

If the company was to decide to do this it would have to raise additional finance of £20m and it would do this by borrowing long-term debt. At present the company is financed as follows:

The company has 20 million shares in issue. The current market value of one share is £1.36.

The recent history of dividend payments is:

Total dividend just paid	£1.138m
Total dividend one year ago	£1.121m
Total dividend two years ago	£1.105m
Total dividend three years ago	£1.088m

The company is also financed by long-term debt which has an interest rate of 6% and is irredeemable. This debt has a market value of £30m and a nominal value of £25m. The company pays corporation tax at a rate of 22%.

Required

(a) Calculate the existing weighted average cost of capital for Fragrance plc. You should use the dividend growth model to calculate the cost of equity. **(10 marks)**

(b) The board of directors of Fragrance plc is concerned that raising the additional finance may increase the current weighted average cost of capital. Therefore, the directors have asked you to prepare a report that advises them of the possible impact that this diversification strategy may have upon the weighted average cost of capital. **(10 marks)**

(Total 20 marks)

2. Chan Wai Merchandising Company (AIA November 2009)

The Chan Wai Merchandising Company (CWM) is listed on the Hong Kong Stock Exchange and is financed as follows:

	HK$
Ordinary Shares of HK$10	2,000,000
6% Debentures 2012	500,000
Retained Profits	380,000
	2,880,000

The ordinary shares have a market value of HK$50 and the company is not expected to pay a dividend. The shares have a beta factor of 1.2. The current risk free rate in Hong Kong is 3% and the estimated required market return, 13%.

The debentures have a current market value of HK$105 per HK$100 nominal and are due for redemption in exactly three years. The interest has just been paid.

The company is considering a plan to expand and diversify into a new line of business. The company has evaluated the investment of HK$1,500,000 using its current weighted average cost of capital and decided to raise the new funds required externally. It is being suggested by some of the directors that the company

LEARNING OUTCOME 1 THE FINANCIAL ENVIRONMENT AND CAPITAL REQUIREMENTS AND CONSEQUENT COSTS

should raise the funds by issuing new debt. They believe that this will have the effect of reducing the company's weighted average cost of capital and so make the new investment even more profitable than they have forecast. However the company accountant is not of the same opinion and has raised doubts over this belief.

Required

(a) Calculate the present weighted average cost of capital for CWM based on current market values.

(9 marks)

(b) Discuss why the accountant may have doubts about the expected effect of a new issue of debt on the company's cost of capital. **(5 marks)**

(c) Discuss the company's use of its existing weighted average cost of capital to evaluate the new investment. **(6 marks)**

(Total 20 marks)

Dividend policy

Topic list	Syllabus reference
1 Dividends and retentions	LO1
2 Dividend growth and market value	LO1
3 Theories of dividend policy	LO1
4 Practical aspects of dividend policy	LO1
5 Scrip dividends, scrip issues and stock splits	LO1
6 Share repurchases	LO1

Introduction

In this chapter, we deal with the question of how much should be paid out by a company to its shareholders in the form of **dividends**. What is the effect of dividend policy on share prices? What are the practical influences on dividend policy, including the effects of taxation? Should dividends be paid in the form of cash or shares?

We also consider the reasons for companies purchasing their own shares and other methods of reorganising share capital.

1 Dividends and retentions

Retained earnings are an important source of finance for companies, and financial managers should take account of the proportion of earnings that need to be retained as opposed to being paid as dividends.

1.1 Use of retained earnings

As we saw in Chapter 2, funds generated from **retained earnings** are an important source of finance for UK companies. For any company, the amount of earnings retained within the business has a direct impact on the amount of dividends. Profit re-invested as retained earnings is profit that could have been paid as a dividend.

1.2 Importance of dividend levels

A company must restrict its self-financing through retained profits because shareholders should be paid a **reasonable dividend**, in line with realistic expectations, even if the directors would rather keep the funds for re-investing. At the same time, a company that is looking for extra funds will not be expected by investors (such as banks) to pay generous dividends, nor over-generous salaries to owner-directors.

In practice, shareholders will usually be obliged to accept the dividend policy that has been decided on by the directors, or otherwise to sell their shares. In law shareholders can vote to reduce the size of the final dividend but not to increase it.

Case Study

Zero dividend policy

Amazon

Amazon has followed a policy of successfully reinvesting its earnings to create a dominant market position. Because of its high fixed cost base, Amazon has aimed to keep its financial gearing low (it is virtually zero). A consequence of this is that up to 2020 Amazon has never paid a dividend. This does not mean that its shareholders have lost out because, as a consequence of the investments in its value chain, Amazon's shares have generated a return of over 30% per year over the past ten years through the increase in its share price.

2 Dividend growth and market value

The **dividend growth model** suggests that share prices are a function of the rate of dividend change, although the position may be complicated by shareholders' tax position.

2.1 Dividend policy and share prices

The purpose of a dividend policy should be to maximise shareholders' wealth, which depends on both current dividends and capital gains. Capital gains can be achieved by retaining some earnings for reinvestment and dividend growth in the future.

According to what can be termed the **'residual theory'**, maximisation of shareholder wealth will be achieved by applying the following rules.

- If a company can identify projects with positive NPVs, it should invest in them.
- Only when these investment opportunities are exhausted should dividends be paid.

2.2 Growth in dividends

Remember we stated earlier that the rate of growth in dividends is sometimes expressed, theoretically, as:

g = rb

where g is the annual growth rate in dividends
       r is the rate of return on new investments
       b is the proportion of profits that are retained

2.3 Example: Dividend growth

(a) If a company has a payout ratio of 40%, and retains the rest for investing in projects which yield 15%, the annual rate of growth in dividends could be estimated as 15% × 60% = 9%.

(b) If a company pays out 80% of its profits as dividends, and retains the rest for reinvestment at 15%, the current dividend would be twice as big as in (a), but annual dividend growth would be only 15% × 20% = 3%.

2.4 An approach to dividend policy, based on fundamental analysis of share values

A theoretical approach to dividend and retentions policy can be based on the fundamental theory of share values. We will make the following assumptions:

(a) The market value of a company's shares depends on the **size of dividends paid**, the **rate of growth in dividends** and the **shareholders' required rate of return**.

(b) The rate of growth in dividends depends on **how much money** is **reinvested** in the company, and so on the rate of earnings retention.

(c) Shareholders will want their company to pursue a **retentions policy** that maximises the value of their shares.

Formula to learn

$$P_0 = \frac{D}{K_e} \quad \text{or} \quad P_0 = \frac{D_0(1+g)}{(K_e - g)}$$

2.5 Example: Dividend growth model

Tantrum plc has achieved earnings of £800,000 this year. The company intends to pursue a policy of financing all its investment opportunities out of retained earnings. There are considerable investment opportunities, which are expected to be available indefinitely. However, if Tantrum plc does not exploit any of the available opportunities, its annual earnings will remain at £800,000 in perpetuity. The following figures are available:

Proportion of earnings retained	Growth rate in earnings	Required return on all investments by shareholders
%	%	%
0	0	14
25	5	15
40	7	16

The rate of return required by shareholders would rise if earnings are retained, because of the risk associated with the new investments.

What is the optimum retentions policy for Tantrum plc? The full dividend payment for this year will be paid in the near future in any case.

Solution

Since $P_0 = \dfrac{D_0(1+g)}{(r-g)}$

the market value cum dividend is given by:

$$\text{MV cum div} = \dfrac{D_0(1+g)}{(r-g)} + D_0$$

We are trying to maximise the value of shareholder wealth, which is currently represented by the cum div market value, since a dividend will soon be paid.

(a) If retentions are 0%, the market value cum dividend is given by:

$$\text{MV cum div} = \dfrac{800{,}000}{0.14} + 800{,}000$$

$$= £6{,}514{,}286$$

(b) If retentions are 25%, the current dividend will be £600,000 and:

$$\text{MV cum div} = \dfrac{600{,}000(1.05)}{(0.15 - 0.05)} + 600{,}000$$

$$= £6{,}900{,}000$$

(c) If retentions are 40%, the current dividend will be £480,000 and:

$$\text{MV cum div} = \dfrac{480{,}000(1.07)}{(0.16 - 0.07)} + 480{,}000$$

$$= £6{,}186{,}667$$

The best policy (out of the three for which figures are provided) would be to retain 25% of earnings.

2.6 Dividend policy and shareholders' personal taxation

If not all shareholders have the same tax rates and after tax cost of capital, there might not be an optimum policy which satisfies all shareholders. By what is referred to as the **clientele effect**, companies may attract particular types of shareholders seeking particular dividend policies.

Key term

> The term **clientele effect** describes the tendency of companies to attract particular types of shareholders because of their management organisation and policies, particularly dividend policies.

A further problem occurs when income from dividends might be taxed either more or less heavily than capital gains. Note that in the UK, individuals have an **annual capital gains** exemption which is not available for setting against income, and companies are taxed on capital gains but not on dividend income.

Since the purpose of a dividend policy should be to maximise the wealth of shareholders, it is important to consider whether it would be better to pay a dividend now, subject to tax on income, or to retain earnings so as to increase the shareholders' capital gains (which will be subject to capital gains tax when the shareholders eventually sell their shares).

3 Theories of dividend policy

FAST FORWARD

> **Modigliani and Miller's theories** suggest that dividend policy is irrelevant to shareholder wealth in perfect capital markets. Given the imperfections in real-world markets and in taxation policies, the position is not so clear.

3.1 Residual theory

A **'residual' theory** of **dividend policy** can be summarised as follows:

- If a company can identify projects with positive NPVs, it should invest in them.
- Only when these investment opportunities are exhausted should dividends be paid.

3.2 Traditional view

The **'traditional' view** of dividend policy, implicit in our earlier discussion, is to focus on the effects on share price. The price of a share depends upon the mix of dividends, given shareholders' required rate of return, and growth.

3.3 Irrelevancy theory

In contrast to the traditional view, **Modigliani and Miller (MM)** proposed that in a tax-free world, shareholders are indifferent between dividends and capital gains, and the value of a company is determined solely by the 'earning power' of its assets and investments.

MM argued that if a company with investment opportunities decides to pay a dividend, so that **retained earnings** are **insufficient** to finance all its investments, the shortfall in funds will be made up by **obtaining additional funds** from outside sources. As a result of obtaining outside finance instead of using retained earnings:

Loss of value in existing shares = Amount of dividend paid

In answer to criticisms that certain shareholders will show a preference either for high dividends or for capital gains, MM argued that if a company pursues a consistent dividend policy, 'each corporation would tend to attract to itself a clientele consisting of those preferring its particular payout ratio, but one clientele would be entirely as good as another in terms of the valuation it would imply for the firm'.

3.4 The case in favour of the relevance of dividend policy (and against MM's views)

There are strong arguments against MM's view that dividend policy is irrelevant as a means of affecting shareholder's wealth.

(a) **Differing rates** of **taxation** on **dividends** and **capital gains** can create a **preference** for a **high dividend** or one for **high earnings retention**.

(b) **Dividend retention** should be **preferred** by companies in a period of **capital rationing**.

(c) Due to imperfect markets and the possible difficulties of selling shares easily at a fair price, shareholders might need **high dividends** in order to have funds to **invest** in **opportunities** outside the company.

(d) **Markets** are **not perfect**. Because of transaction costs on the sale of shares, investors who want some cash from their investments should prefer to receive dividends rather than to sell some of their shares to get the cash they want.

(e) Information available to shareholders is **imperfect**, and they are not aware of the **future investment plans** and **expected profits** of their company. Even if management were to provide them with profit forecasts, these forecasts would not necessarily be accurate or believable.

(f) As a consequence of imperfect information, companies are normally expected at least to **maintain the same level of dividends** from one year to the next. Failure to maintain the dividend level would undermine investors' confidence in the future.

(g) In practice, undertaking a new investment project with a positive NPV will not immediately increase the market value of shares by the amount of the NPV because markets do not show **strong-form efficiency**. It is only gradually, as the profits from the investment begin to show, that the market value of the shares will rise.

(h) Perhaps the strongest argument against the MM view is that shareholders will tend to **prefer a current dividend** to future capital gains (or deferred dividends) because the future is more uncertain.

Don't forget that even if you accept that dividend policy will have some influence on share values, there may well be other, more important influences.

4 Practical aspects of dividend policy

FAST FORWARD

Companies generally **smooth out dividend payments** by adjusting only gradually to changes in earnings: large fluctuations might **undermine investors' confidence**.

The dividends a company pays may be treated as a **signal** to investors. A company needs to take account of different clienteles of shareholders in deciding what dividends to pay.

4.1 Limitations and restrictions on dividend policy

So far, we have concentrated on theoretical approaches to establishing an optimal dividend and retentions policy. A practical approach to dividends and retentions should take various factors into consideration.

(a) The **need to remain profitable**. Dividends are paid out of profits, and an unprofitable company cannot for ever go on paying dividends out of retained profits made in the past.

(b) The **law on distributable profits**.

(c) Any **dividend restraints** which might be imposed by loan agreements.

(d) The **effect of inflation**, and the need to retain some profit within the business just to maintain its operating capability unchanged.

(e) The company's **gearing level**. If the company wants extra finance, the sources of funds used should strike a balance between equity and debt finance. Retained earnings are the most readily available source of growth in equity finance.

(f) The company's **liquidity position**. Dividends are a cash payment, and a company must have enough cash to pay the dividends it declares.

(g) The ease with which the company could raise **extra finance** from sources other than retained earnings. Small companies which find it hard to raise finance might have to rely more heavily on retained earnings than large companies.

If a company wants extra finance to invest, retained earnings can be obtained without incurring transaction costs. Costs of raising new share capital can be high, and even bank borrowings can be quite expensive.

4.2 Environmental, Social, and Governance (ESG) Considerations

When setting dividend policy it is important that consideration is given to the impact this will have on the organisation's broader ESG goals.

ESG considerations when setting dividend policy.	
Environmental	Favouring reinvestment over high dividends can facilitate funding for environmentally sustainable projects. When a company chooses to reinvest profits rather than pay out high dividends, it can allocate more resources towards initiatives such as reducing carbon emissions, improving energy efficiency, and developing green technologies. This reinvestment can lead to long-term environmental benefits, enhancing the company's sustainability profile and contributing positively to global environmental goals.
	Conversely, prioritising dividends over sustainable investments might divert resources from crucial environmental initiatives. Companies that focus on maintaining high dividend payouts may find themselves with limited funds to invest in necessary environmental projects. This can result in missed opportunities to adopt more sustainable practices, potentially leading to negative environmental impacts and damaging the company's reputation among increasingly eco-conscious consumers and investors.
	By adopting a dividend policy that balances shareholder returns with reinvestment in sustainable projects, companies can support both financial stability and environmental sustainability.
Social	Investing profits back into the business rather than paying out high dividends can also enhance a company's social initiatives. By reinvesting, companies can fund employee development programmes, improve workplace conditions, and support fair labour practices. This also enables contributions to community development projects, such as local education and healthcare, fostering positive relationships with the community and improving the overall social footprint of the company. Such investments not only boost employee morale and productivity but also strengthen the company's reputation as a socially responsible entity.
	If there is insufficient investment in employee welfare this can result in lower job satisfaction and higher turnover rates. Additionally, neglecting community engagement can weaken the company's social ties and damage its reputation among stakeholders.
Governance	The pressure to maintain high dividend payouts can lead to poor governance practices.
	When companies prioritise dividends excessively, they may cut corners in crucial areas such as internal controls, compliance, and risk management to free up funds. This can result in weakened oversight, increased vulnerability to fraud, and potential regulatory violations.
	Such shortcuts not only undermine the company's governance framework but also risk damaging its reputation and eroding stakeholder trust.

4.3 Dividends as a signal to investors

Key term

Signalling is the use of dividend policy to indicate the future prospects of an enterprise.

LEARNING OUTCOME 1 THE FINANCIAL ENVIRONMENT AND CAPITAL REQUIREMENTS AND CONSEQUENT COSTS

Although the market would like to value shares on the basis of underlying cash flows on the company's projects, such information is not readily available to investors. however, the directors do have this information. The dividend declared can be interpreted as a **signal** from directors to shareholders about the strength of underlying project cash flows.

As stated above investors usually expect a **consistent dividend policy** from the company, either a fixed or increasing dividend in money or real terms, or less commonly, a constant or increasing proportion of its equity as dividends. A **large rise or fall in dividends** in any year can have a marked effect on the company's share price. A cut in dividends may be treated by investors as signalling that the future prospects of the company are weak. Thus, the dividend which is paid acts, possibly without justification, as a signal of the future prospects of the company.

The signalling effect of a company's dividend policy may also be used by management of a company which faces a possible **takeover**. The dividend level might be increased as a **defence** against the takeover; investors may take the increased dividend as a signal of improved future prospects, thus driving the share price higher and making the company more expensive for a potential bidder to take over.

> **Exam focus point**
>
> You should make a point of showing in exam answers, where it is relevant, that you appreciate the signalling effect of dividends.

5 Scrip dividends, scrip issues and stock splits

> **FAST FORWARD**
>
> **Scrip dividends** are dividends in shares rather than in cash.
>
> **Scrip issues** are new shares issued by turning retained earnings into cash.
>
> **Stock splits** involve splitting individual shares into a number of shares.

5.1 Scrip dividends

> **Key term**
>
> A **scrip dividend** is a dividend payment which takes the form of new shares instead of cash. Effectively, it converts profit reserves into issued share capital.

When the directors of a company would prefer to retain funds within the business but consider that they must pay at least a certain amount of dividend, they might offer equity shareholders the choice of a cash dividend or a scrip dividend of more shares in the company.

Recently **enhanced scrip dividends** have been offered by a number of companies. With enhanced scrip dividends, the value of the shares offered is much greater than the cash alternative, giving investors an incentive to choose the shares.

5.2 Scrip issues

> **Key term**
>
> A **scrip** or **bonus issue** (also known as a **capitalisation issue**) involves the issue of new shares to existing shareholders in proportion to their existing holdings. Such an issue has the effect of reducing the retained earnings (income statement) account and increasing the called up share capital account.

Obviously there is no raising of cash, nor any increase in the value of shareholders' equity. Whether there is any point to the process (other than reducing the price per share and hence possibly increasing share trading liquidity) is open to debate. If there is, then it is because there are associated 'signals' that commonly accompany the scrip issue, eg perhaps that the dividend per share is to be maintained on the increased number of shares and hence the directors believe future company cashflows will be favourable.

5.3 Stock splits

Key term

A **stock split** occurs where, for example, each ordinary share of £1 each is split into two shares of 50p each.

This process creates **cheaper shares with greater marketability**. There is possibly an added psychological advantage, in that investors may expect a company which splits its shares in this way to be planning for substantial earnings growth and dividend growth in the future. As a consequence, the market price of shares may benefit, at any rate in the short term.

The difference between a stock split and a scrip issue is that a **scrip issue converts equity reserves into share capital**, whereas a **stock split leaves reserves unaffected**. Both are popular with investors as they are seen as likely to lead to increased dividends. Scrip dividends can, however, lead to tax complications for individual investors.

Question — Dividend policy

Ochre plc is a company that is still managed by the two individuals who set it up 12 years ago. In the current year, the company acquired plc status and was launched on the second tier Alternative Investment Market (AIM). Previously, all of the shares had been owned by its two founders and certain employees. Now, 40% of the shares are in the hands of the investing public. The company's profit growth and dividend policy are set out below. Will a continuation of the same dividend policy as in the past be suitable now that the company is quoted on the AIM?

Year	Profits £'000	Dividend £'000	Shares in issue
4 years ago	176	88	800,000
3 years ago	200	104	800,000
2 years ago	240	120	1,000,000
1 year ago	290	150	1,000,000
Current year	444	222 (proposed)	1,500,000

Answer

Year	Dividend per share	Dividend as % of profit
4 years ago	11.0	50%
3 years ago	13.0	52%
2 years ago	12.0	50%
1 year ago	15.0	52%
Current year	14.8	50%

The company appears to have pursued a dividend policy of paying out half of after-tax profits in dividend. This policy is only suitable when a company achieves a stable EPS or steady EPS growth. Investors do not like a fall in dividend from one year to the next, and the fall in dividend per share in the current year is likely to be unpopular, and to result in a fall in the share price.

The company would probably serve its shareholders better by paying a dividend of at least 15p per share, possibly more, in the current year, even though the dividend as a percentage of profit would then be higher.

6 Share repurchases

> **FAST FORWARD**
> Purchase by a company of its own shares can take place for various reasons and must be in accordance with any **requirements of legislation**.

6.1 Why buy back the company's shares?

UK legislation gives companies rights to **buy back shares from shareholders** who are willing to sell them, subject to certain conditions.

Knowledge brought forward from earlier studies

A UK company can purchase or redeem its own shares from either:

(a) Distributable profits; or
(b) The proceeds of a new issue of shares.

unless as a result of the purchase only redeemable shares are left.

There are two methods of making such a purchase:

(a) A market purchase is a purchase under the normal arrangements of a recognised investment exchange.
(b) An off-market purchase is any other purchase, usually by private treaty.

A private limited company may redeem or purchase its shares out of capital by a 'permissible capital payment'.

- General authority must be given by the articles.
- Capital can only be used to 'top up' distributable profits or the proceeds of a new issue, where such resources are insufficient. A capital redemption reserve may be required.

A complex procedure is prescribed to ensure that the company does not make itself insolvent.

For a **smaller private company** with few shareholders, the reason for buying back the company's own shares may be that there is no immediate willing purchaser at a time when a shareholder wishes to sell shares. For a public company, share repurchase could provide a way of withdrawing from the share market and 'going private'.

Larger public companies also sometimes repurchase their own shares. Recently, for instance, a number of the privatised UK electricity companies have made significant share repurchases having gained shareholder approval to do so at the companies' annual meetings.

Repurchase of own shares is common among US companies and is gaining popularity in the UK. However, the practice remains rare in the rest of Europe.

6.2 Benefits of share repurchase

(a) Finding a **use for surplus cash**, which may be a 'dead asset'.

(b) **Increase** in **earnings per share** through a **reduction** in the **number of shares** in issue – this should lead to a higher share price than would otherwise be the case, and the company should be able to increase dividend payments on the remaining shares in issue.

(c) **Increase in gearing**. Repurchase of a company's own shares allows debt to be substituted for equity, so raising gearing. This will be of interest to a company wanting to increase its gearing without increasing its total long-term funding.

(d) **Readjustment of the company's equity base** to more appropriate levels, for a company whose business is in decline.

(e) Possibly **preventing a takeover** or enabling a quoted company to withdraw from the stock market.

6.3 Disadvantages of share repurchase

(a) It can be **hard to arrive** at a **price** which will be fair both to the vendors and to any shareholders who are not selling shares to the company.

(b) A repurchase of shares could be seen as an **admission** that the **company cannot make better use** of the funds than the shareholders. However, the market may take the contrary view, and see share repurchases as a sign that the company has more cash and more earnings potential than previously believed.

(c) Some **shareholders** may **suffer** from being taxed on a capital gain following the purchase of their shares rather than receiving dividend income.

LEARNING OUTCOME 1 THE FINANCIAL ENVIRONMENT AND CAPITAL REQUIREMENTS AND CONSEQUENT COSTS

Chapter Roundup

- **Retained earnings** are the most important single source of finance for companies, and financial managers should take account of the proportion of earnings that need to be retained as opposed to being paid as dividends.
- The **dividend growth model** suggests that share prices are a function of the rate of dividend change, although the position may be complicated by shareholders' tax position.
- **Modigliani and Miller's theories** suggest that dividend policy is irrelevant to shareholder wealth in perfect capital markets. Given the imperfections in real-world markets and in taxation policies, the position is not so clear.
- **The size of dividend payout** will have an **impact** on the ability to enhance **environmental, social, and governance (ESG) practices**. Reinvesting earnings into sustainability initiatives can strengthen the company's ESG profile, fostering long-term value creation and stakeholder trust.
- Companies generally **smooth out dividend payments** by adjusting only gradually to changes in earnings: large fluctuations might **undermine investors' confidence**.
- The dividends a company pays may be treated as a **signal** to investors. A company needs to take account of different clienteles of shareholders in deciding what dividends to pay.
- **Scrip dividends** are dividends in shares rather than in cash.
- **Scrip issues** are new shares issued by turning retained earnings into cash.
- **Stock splits** involve splitting individual shares into a number of shares.
- Purchase by a company of its own shares can take place for various reasons and must be in accordance with any **requirements of legislation**.

Quick Quiz

1. What reasons are there in favour of using funds from retained earnings to finance new investments?

2. **Fill in the blank**

   $g = r b$.

   Annual dividend growth rate = Rate of return on new investments × _____ .

3. **Fill in the blank**

   Particular companies may attract particular types of shareholders. This is called the _____ effect.

4. Give a definition of 'signalling' in the context of dividends policy.

5. **Fill in the blank**

   A _____ is a dividend payment which takes the form of new shares instead of cash.

6. Is the main advantage of bonus issues that existing shareholders have to pay less cash for shares than they would do if they bought the shares on the stock market?

7. A private company can redeem or purchase its shares out of capital by a permissible capital payment.

   ☐ True
   ☐ False

8   What is the market value of a share where the current year's dividend was £2.00, the expected dividend growth rate is 5% and the shareholders' required rate of return is 10%?

LEARNING OUTCOME 1 THE FINANCIAL ENVIRONMENT AND CAPITAL REQUIREMENTS AND CONSEQUENT COSTS

Answers to Quick Quiz

1. (a) No need for recourse to shareholders or others
   (b) No issue costs
   (c) No possibility of change in control from issue of new shares
   (d) Financial and taxation position of shareholders

2. The proportion of profits that is retained

3. Clientele

4. The use of dividend policy to indicate the future prospects of an enterprise

5. Scrip dividend

6. No. No cash is involved. A bonus issue reduces retained earnings and increases called up share capital.

7. True

8. $P_0 = \dfrac{D_0(1+g)}{(r-g)} = \dfrac{2.00(1+0.05)}{0.1-0.05} = £42$

7: CORPORATE DIVIDEND POLICY

End of chapter question

Henderson Logitech Ltd (AIA November 2005)

Henderson Logitech Ltd is a private company and 100% of its shares are owned by members of the Henderson family. The company is considering a stock market listing and is currently undergoing a preliminary feasibility study by its merchant bank. The aspect currently being considered is the company's likely dividend policy after listing. Henderson Logitech's earnings and dividends for the last five years are shown below.

Year	Profit after tax	Dividend per share
	£'000	£
2000	900	1.08
2001	950	1.14
2002	1,800	2.16
2003	3,600	4.32
2004	5,300	6.36

The company has had 500,000 shares in issue for the last five years. The directors would like to increase the number of shares by 450,000 for the flotation with all the family members retaining their present shareholdings. The directors are, however, concerned that the family is unlikely to agree to the flotation unless they receive assurances that the company's current dividend policy is unlikely to change.

A mixture of retained earnings and debt has funded the company's growth. The merchant bank has expressed some concern at the company's high gearing level.

Required

(a) Evaluate Henderson Logitech's recent dividend policy and discuss whether or not you consider it will be suitable after the company is listed. **(8 marks)**

(b) Henderson Logitech is forecasting earnings growth of 20% per annum for the next three years but then expects that it will level off to 10% per annum for the foreseeable future. The merchant bank estimates Henderson's equity cost of capital to be approximately 14%.

Calculate a reasonable share price for a flotation, if dividends were to continue to grow at the same rate as earnings. **(7 marks)**

(c) Advise whether or not you consider it likely that the company would successfully float at that price. **(5 marks)**

(Total 20 marks)

LEARNING OUTCOME 1 THE FINANCIAL ENVIRONMENT AND CAPITAL REQUIREMENTS AND CONSEQUENT COSTS

The investment decision

Investment decisions

Topic list	Syllabus reference
1 Capital investment appraisal	LO2
2 Allowing for inflation in DCF	LO2
3 Allowing for taxation in DCF	LO2
4 Non-financial factors	LO2
5 Real options	LO2
6 International investment appraisal	LO2
7 Tackling overseas investment appraisal questions	LO2

Introduction

In this chapter, we begin our coverage of investment and decision-making by revising some of the principles of appraising a project.

Make sure you come away from this chapter fully confident not only of the basic methods, but also how to deal with inflation and taxation.

You **must** also be able to identify relevant and non-relevant costs.

In the last section we cover how to approach an international investment appraisal.

LEARNING OUTCOME 2 THE INVESTMENT DECISION

1 Capital investment appraisal

> **FAST FORWARD**
>
> The **payback method** of project appraisal and the **ARR/ROCE/ROI method** of project appraisal are popular appraisal techniques despite their limitations.
>
> There are two methods of using **discounted cash flow** to appraise investment projects, the NPV method and the IRR/DCF yield method.
>
> The **NPV method** of project appraisal is to accept projects with a positive NPV.
>
> The **IRR method** of project appraisal is to accept projects whose IRR (the rate at which the NPV is zero) exceeds a target rate of return. The IRR is estimated either from a graph or using interpolation.
>
> The formula to apply is IRR $\approx a + \left[\left(\dfrac{A}{A-B} \right) \times (b-a) \right] \%$.

1.1 Reasons for capital investment

Most **capital investment decisions** will have a direct effect on future profitability, either because they will result in an **increase in revenue** or because they will bring about an increase in efficiency and a **reduction in costs**. Whatever level of management authorises a capital expenditure, the proposed investment should be properly **evaluated**, and found to be **worthwhile**, before the decision is taken to go ahead with the expenditure.

1.2 Differences between capital and revenue expenditure

Capital expenditures differ from day to day **revenue** expenditures in that:

(a)   They often involve a **bigger outlay** of money.

(b)   The benefits will **accrue over a long period of time**, usually well over one year and often much longer, so that the benefits cannot all be set against costs in the current year's income statement.

1.3 Planning capital investments

The planning steps in the process of developing a new programme of capital investment are as follows:

- Identification of an investment opportunity
- Consideration of the alternatives to the project being evaluated
- Acquiring relevant information
- Detailed planning
- Taking the investment decision

1.4 Evaluating capital investments

The principal methods of evaluating capital projects are as follows:

(a)   The **return on investment method**, or **accounting rate of return** method

(b)   The **payback** method

(c)   Discounted cash flow (DCF):

   (i)   The **net present value** method (NPV)
   (ii) The **internal rate of return** method (IRR)

Of these, DCF should be by far the most important, although (a) and (b) are used more in practice by small and medium-sized firms.

The principles and mechanics of these methods were covered in your earlier studies. Before we go on to look at the more advanced aspects, and their application to international investment appraisal, we briefly revise the main points here, followed by some questions for you to brush up your knowledge.

Knowledge brought forward from earlier studies

The accounting rate of return (ARR) method of investment appraisal

- This method uses **financial accounting based figures** in arriving at a rate of return on a project, which is compared with a target rate of return to decide on its acceptability.

- There are various **definitions** of the ARR, the most common of which is

    $$\text{ARR} = \frac{\text{Estimated average annual profits, after depreciation, before interest and tax}}{\text{Average book value of capital employed}}$$

- The main disadvantages of the ARR are that it uses **subjective accounting profits** rather than cash flows; it does not take account of the **timing** of flows, and it can be computed under **various definitions**, which makes comparisons difficult.

The payback method of investment appraisal

- The **payback period** is the time required for the cash inflows from a capital investment project to equal the cash outflows.

- The payback should not be used as the sole appraisal method, as it ignores the cash flows after the payback period, but may be used as a **first screening method**, particularly when applied to risky projects.

- The payback period may be estimated by computing the **accumulated cash inflows** year by year until the initial capital investment is covered.

Discounted cash flow (DCF) methods of investment appraisal

- **DCF** is an appraisal technique which uses **cash flows**, takes account of both the **time value** of money and also the **total cash flow** over a project's life, and is thus a method superior to both the ARR and payback methods.

- The time value of money (why £1 now is worth more than £1 in the future) arises from considerations of **investment opportunities, risk** and **inflation**.

- **Basic discounting** of cash flows using an appropriate opportunity cost of capital principally takes account of the first of these considerations, although the method can be adapted to take account of both risk and inflation, as we shall see later.

- The cash flows used in DCF methods are those that are **relevant** – the **changes** in **future cash** flows of the business that will arise as a result of undertaking the project.

- There are two methods of applying the DCF technique to project appraisal: net present value **(NPV)** and internal rate of return **(IRR)**.

- The **NPV** approach applies a **specific discount rate** to the cash flows of the project to arrive at an **absolute** measure, the NPV, which, if positive, implies the project is acceptable.

- The **IRR** approach is to calculate the **discount rate at which the NPV of the project would be zero**, indicating the maximum cost of capital at which the project would be viable. Provided the investing business's cost of capital is less than this, the project may be accepted.

LEARNING OUTCOME 2 THE INVESTMENT DECISION

Knowledge brought forward from earlier studies

Formula to learn

- The IRR is found approximately by using interpolation, using the results from NPV computations at two different discount rates.

$$IRR \approx a + \left[\left(\frac{A}{A-B}\right) \times (b-a)\right]\%$$

where a = lower discount rate used with NPV = A
b = higher discount rate used with NPV = B

Soft and hard capital rationing

- When capital for investments is in restricted supply, a choice must be made between projects that all have a positive NPV.

- **Soft or internal capital rationing** is where capital is rationed by constraints within the business (which might include management reluctance to raise further capital and thus dilute EPS or allow in new outside shareholders).

- **Hard or external capital rationing** is where external forces limit the amount of capital available to a business (for example government policies on credit).

Single-period capital rationing

- If projects/investments are not divisible, the feasible combination of projects that give the highest total NPV should be selected.

- If projects/investments are divisible, the projects for selection should be ranked in descending order of their profitability indexes (PI).

Formula to learn

- $PI = \dfrac{\text{NPV of future net cash flows}}{\text{Current outlay}}$

Multi-period capital rationing

- If capital rationing is in more than one time period, a linear programming (LP) model can be set up to establish which projects to select.

Question — Accounting rate of return

A company has a target accounting rate of return of 20% (using the definition given above), and is now considering the following project.

Capital cost of asset	£80,000
Estimated life	4 years
Estimated profit before depreciation	
Year 1	£20,000
Year 2	£25,000
Year 3	£35,000
Year 4	£25,000

The capital asset would be depreciated by 25% of its cost each year, and will have no residual value. Should the project be undertaken?

Answer

	£
Total profit before depreciation over four years	105,000
Total profit after depreciation over four years	25,000
Average annual profit after depreciation	6,250
Original cost of investment	80,000
Average net book value over the four year period $\frac{(80,000 + 0)}{2}$	40,000

The average ARR is 6,250 ÷ 40,000 = 15.625%.

The project would not be undertaken because it would fail to yield the target return of 20%.

Question
Net present value

LCH Ltd manufactures product X which it sells for £5 a unit. Variable costs of production are currently £3 a unit, and fixed costs 50p a unit. A new machine is available which would cost £90,000 but which could be used to make product X for a variable cost of only £2.50 a unit. Fixed costs, however, would increase by £7,500 a year as a direct result of purchasing the machine. The machine would have an expected life of four years and a resale value after that time of £10,000. Sales of product X are estimated to be 75,000 units a year. If LCH Ltd expects to earn at least 12% a year from its investments, should the machine be purchased? (Ignore taxation.)

Answer

Savings are 75,000 × £(3.00 – 2.50) = £37,500 a year.

Additional costs are £7,500 a year.

Net cash savings are therefore £30,000 a year.

It is assumed that the machine will be sold for £10,000 at the end of Year 4.

Year	Cash flow £	PV factor 12%	PV of cash flow £
0	(90,000)	1.000	(90,000)
1	30,000	0.893	26,790
2	30,000	0.797	23,910
3	30,000	0.712	21,360
4	40,000	0.636	25,440
		NPV	+7,500

The NPV is positive and so the project is expected to earn more than 12% a year and is therefore acceptable.

Question
Discounted cash flow

Elsie Ltd is considering the manufacture of a new product which would involve the use of both a new machine (costing £150,000) and an existing machine, which cost £80,000 two years ago and has a current net book value of £60,000. There is sufficient capacity on this machine, which has so far been under-used.

LEARNING OUTCOME 2 THE INVESTMENT DECISION

Annual sales of the product would be 5,000 units, selling at £32 a unit. Unit costs would be as follows.

	£
Direct labour (4 hours at £2)	8
Direct materials	7
Fixed costs including depreciation	9
	24

The project would have a five-year life, after which the new machine would have a net residual value of £10,000. Because direct labour is continually in short supply, labour resources would have to be diverted from other work which currently earns a contribution of £1.50 per direct labour hour. The fixed overhead absorption rate would be £2.25 an hour (£9 a unit) but actual expenditure on fixed overhead would not alter.

Working capital requirements would be £10,000 in the first year, rising to £15,000 in the second year and remaining at this level until the end of the project, when it will all be recovered. The company's cost of capital is 20%. Ignore taxation.

Is the project worthwhile?

Answer

Working

		£
Years 1–5	Contribution from new product	
	5,000 × £(32 – 15)	85,000
	Less contribution forgone	
	5,000 × (4 × £1.50)	30,000
		55,000

Year	Equipment £	Working capital £	Contribution £	Net cash flow £	Discount factor 20%	PV of net cash flow £
0	(150,000)	(10,000)		(160,000)	1.000	(160,000)
1		(5,000)		(5,000)	0.833	(4,165)
1–5			55,000	55,000	2.991	164,505
5	10,000	15,000		25,000	0.402	10,050
					NPV =	10,390

The NPV is positive and the project is worthwhile, although there is not much margin for error. Some risk analysis of the project is recommended.

Note. The discount factor 2.991 applied to the annual contribution is an example of an **annuity factor**, which can be used for a series of equal annual cash flows where the first cashflow occurs at time 1 Annuity factors may be found from the table or from the formula, both given in the Appendix at the end of this Text.

Question   Internal rate of return

A company is trying to decide whether to buy a machine for £80,000 which will save £20,000 a year for five years and which will have a resale value of £10,000 at the end of Year 5. What would the IRR of the investment project be?

8: INVESTMENT DECISIONS

Answer

The return on investment is $\dfrac{20{,}000 - \text{depreciation of } 14{,}000}{\frac{1}{2} \text{ of } (80{,}000 + 10{,}000)} = \dfrac{6{,}000}{45{,}000} = 13.3\%$

A rough way to calculate the first rate to be used in the IRR calculation is to take (2/3 × return on investment). Two thirds of 13.3% is 8.9% and so we can start by trying 9%.

The IRR is the rate for the cost of capital at which the NPV = 0.

Year	Cash flow £	PV factor 9%	PV of cash flow £
0	(80,000)	1.000	(80,000)
1–5	20,000	3.890	77,800
5	10,000	0.650	6,500
		NPV	4,300

This is fairly close to zero. It is also positive, which means that the IRR is more than 9%. We will try 12% next.

Year	Cash flow £	PV factor 12%	PV of cash flow £
0	(80,000)	1.000	(80,000)
1–5	20,000	3.605	72,100
5	10,000	0.567	5,670
		NPV	(2,230)

This is fairly close to zero and negative. The IRR is therefore greater than 9% but less than 12%. We shall now use the two NPV values to estimate the IRR, using the formula given above.

Internal rate of return = $9 + \left[\dfrac{4{,}300}{4{,}300 - -2{,}230} \times (12 - 9)\right] = 10.98\%$ say 11%

Exam focus point

You need to read investment appraisal questions very carefully to make sure you have identified all relevant details, particularly timing of cash flows.

1.5 Other formulae

You may also find the following formulae useful:

(a) For **non-annual cash flows**, the period interest rate r is related to the annual interest rate R by the following formula.

$r = \sqrt[n]{1+R} - 1$

where n is the number of periods per annum.

For example, if the annual interest rate is 18%,

the monthly interest rate $r = \sqrt[12]{1.18} - 1 = 0.0139$, ie 1.39%

(b) **Changes in interest rate** can be reflected as in the following example.

In Years 1, 2 and 3, the interest rate is 10%, 12% and 14% respectively.

LEARNING OUTCOME 2 THE INVESTMENT DECISION

Then, Year 3 discount factor $= \dfrac{1}{(1+r_1)(1+r_2)(1+r_3)}$

$= \dfrac{1}{1.10 \times 1.12 \times 1.14} = 0.712$

(c) The value of a constant annual cash flows to infinity (this is also known as a perpetuity) = Cash flow × 1/r

Exam focus point

> The examiner has commented that many candidates use the formula 1/1 + r, not 1/r to calculate cash flows to infinity.

1.6 NPV or IRR?

FAST FORWARD

> When compared with the NPV method, the **IRR method** has a number of **disadvantages**.
> - It **ignores** the **relative size** of investments.
> - It is difficult to use if a project has **non-conventional cashflows** or when deciding between **mutually exclusive projects**.

Given that there are two methods of using DCF, the NPV method and the IRR method, the relative merits of each method have to be considered. Which is better?

The main advantage of the IRR method is that the information it provides is more easily understood by managers, especially non-financial managers. For example, it is fairly easy to understand the meaning of the following statement.

> 'The project has an initial capital outlay of £100,000, and will earn a yield of 25%. This is in excess of the target yield of 15% for investments.'

It is not so easy to understand the meaning of this statement.

> 'The project will cost £100,000 and have an NPV of £30,000 when discounted at the minimum required rate of 15%.'

In other respects, the IRR method has serious disadvantages.

(a) It might be **tempting to confuse** the IRR and the accounting ROCE. The accounting ROCE and the IRR are two completely different measures. If managers were given information about both ROCE (or ROI) and IRR, it might be easy to get their meanings and significance mixed up.

(b) It **ignores the relative size** of investments. Both the following projects have an IRR of 18%.

	Project A	Project B
	£	£
Cost, Year 0	350,000	35,000
Annual savings, Years 1-6	100,000	10,000

Clearly, Project A is bigger (ten times as big) and so more profitable but if the only information on which the projects were judged were to be their IRR of 18%, Project B would seem just as beneficial as Project A.

(c) If the cash flows from a project are **not conventional** (with an outflow at the beginning resulting in inflows over the life of a project) there may be more than one IRR.

This could be very difficult for managers to interpret. For example, the following project has cash flows which are not conventional, and as a result has two IRRs of approximately 7% and 35%.

Year	Project X
	£'000
0	(1,900)
1	4,590
2	(2,735)

(d) The IRR method should **not be used to select** between **mutually exclusive projects**. This follows on from point (b) and it is the most significant and damaging criticism of the IRR method.

1.7 Problems with the net present value method

The net present value method is the soundest method for appraising investment but it does have the following limitations.

- Some managers find it conceptually quite **difficult** (see below).
- A discount rate **needs to be chosen.**
- It **ignores** the **value** of real or embedded options (see later in this chapter).
- It is based on the assumption that **risk** is **totally time-dependent**.

Exam focus point

A weakness with many NPV calculations in exams is that they only cover one or two years rather than the life-time of the investment.

1.8 Relevant costs in NPV calculations

FAST FORWARD

Relevant costs of investment appraisal include **opportunity costs, working capital costs** and wider costs such as **infrastructure** and **human development costs. Non-relevant costs** include **past costs** and **committed costs**.

Relevant benefits from investments include not only **increased cash** flows, but also **savings and better relationships with customers and employees**.

The cash flows that should be considered in NPV calculations are those which arise as a **consequence** of the investment decision under evaluation.

1.8.1 Non-relevant costs

Cash flows that are not relevant include:

- Any costs incurred in the **past**
- Any **committed costs** which will be **incurred regardless** of whether or not an investment is undertaken
- **Centrally-allocated overheads** that are not a consequence of undertaking the project

Depreciation and other non-cash adjustments to profits are also not relevant.

The **annual profits** from a project can be calculated as:

Incremental contribution earned

minus

Any incremental fixed costs which are additional cash items of expenditure (that is, ignoring depreciation and so on).

LEARNING OUTCOME 2 THE INVESTMENT DECISION

Finance-related cash flows are normally **excluded** from project appraisal exercises because the **discounting process takes account** of the **time value** of money, that is the opportunity cost of investing the money in the project.

(a) If you included the cash inflow from, say, a loan, then the cash outflows of the interest payments and the loan repayment would also have to be included.

(b) These flows would all be **discounted at the cost of capital**, (which we assume is the same as the cost of the loan) and they would reduce to a zero net present value. They would therefore have had no effect on the NPV and are thus deemed irrelevant to the appraisal.

Finance-related cash flows are **only relevant if they incur a different rate of interest from that which is being used as the discount rate**. For example, a company may be offered a loan at a preferential rate below that which it uses for its discount rate and so the inclusion and discounting of the loan's cash flows produces a different NPV.

Dividend payments should also be **ignored** as they represent a distribution of the benefits of the project, rather than a **cash flow** influencing its appraisal.

1.8.2 Relevant costs

There are, however, other cash flows to consider. These might include the following:

(a) **Opportunity costs**

These are the costs incurred or revenues lost from diverting existing resources from their best use. For example if a salesman, who is paid an annual salary of £30,000, is diverted to work on a new project and as a result existing sales of £50,000 are lost, the opportunity cost to the new project will be the £50,000 of lost sales. The salesman's salary of £30,000 is **not** an opportunity cost since it will be incurred however the salesman's time is spent.

(b) **Taxation**

The extra **taxation** that will be payable on extra profits, or the reductions in tax arising from capital allowances or operating losses in any year.

(c) **Disposal proceeds**

The residual value or disposal value of equipment at the end of its life, or its disposal cost should be included.

(d) **Working capital**

If a company invests £20,000 in working capital and earns cash profits of £50,000, the net cash receipts will be £30,000. Working capital will be released again at the end of a project's life, and so there will be a cash inflow arising out of the eventual realisation into cash of the project's inventories and receivables in the final year of the project.

> **Exam focus point**
>
> If working capital is £20,000 Year 0 and £30,000 in Year 1, the **increase** (£10,000) is shown in the net present value calculation as an outflow.

(e) **Infrastructure costs**

Infrastructure expenditure may include computer equipment and costs of installing communications.

(f) **Marketing costs**

Marketing expenditure may be substantial, particularly of course if the investment is in a new product or service. They will include the costs of market research, promotion and branding and the organisation of new distribution channels.

(g) **Human resource costs**

Human resource costs include training costs and the costs of reorganisation arising from investments.

1.9 Relevant benefits

The benefits from a proposed investment must also be evaluated. These might consist of benefits of several types.

(a) **Savings** because assets used currently will no longer be used. The savings should include:

   (i) Savings in **staff costs**
   (ii) Savings in **other operating costs**, such as consumable materials

(b) Extra **savings** or revenue benefits because of the improvements or enhancements that the investment **might** bring:

   (i) **More sales revenue** and so additional contribution
   (ii) **More efficient system operation**
   (iii) Further savings in **staff time**, resulting perhaps in reduced future staff growth

(c) Possibly, some one-off revenue benefits from the **sale of assets** that are currently in use, but which will no longer be required

Some benefits might be **intangible**, or impossible to give a money value to.

(a) Greater **customer satisfaction**, arising from a more prompt service (eg because of a computerised sales and delivery service)

(b) Improved **staff morale** from working with higher-quality assets

(c) **Better decision making** may result from better information systems

> **Exam focus point**
>
> The examiner has commented that many students are unable to distinguish relevant and non-relevant costs.

2 Allowing for inflation in DCF

2.1 Effects of inflation

FAST FORWARD

> (1 + money rate of return) = (1 + real rate of return) × (1 + rate of inflation)
>
> **Real cash flows** (ie adjusted for inflation) should be discounted at a **real discount rate**.
>
> **Money cash flows** should be discounted at a **money discount rate**.

In our revision of the DCF approach to investment appraisal so far we have not considered the effect of inflation.

Inflation may affect both the cash flows of the project and the rate at which they are discounted – the higher the expected rate of inflation, the higher will be the required return.

LEARNING OUTCOME 2 THE INVESTMENT DECISION

> **Knowledge brought forward from earlier studies**
>
> ### DCF and inflation
>
> - In an inflationary environment, cash flows in a project may be given in **money terms** (the actual cash that will arise) or **real terms** (in today's values).
>
> - Similarly, the required rate of return on an investment may be given as a **money** rate of return (including an allowance for a general rate of inflation) or as a **real** rate of return (the return required over and above inflation).
>
> - The two rates of return and the inflation rate are linked by the equation:
>
>   **Formula to learn**
>
>   1 + money (nominal) rate of return = (1 + real rate)(1 + inflation rate)
>
>   or (1 + n) = (1 + r) (1 + i)
>
>   If cash flows are given in money terms, the money rate should be used to discount them; if the flows are in real terms, the real rate of return may be used to discount them.
>
> - If some of the cost or revenues relating to the project **inflate at rates different from the general rate of inflation** built into the money required return, it is **not** appropriate to discount real flows at the real rate. **Money flows must be computed**, by applying the relevant rates of inflation to the real flows, which must then be discounted at the money required return.
>
> - Real rates can be converted to nominal rates by using the equation Real cash flow $\times (1 + i)^n$ where n is the number of years of inflation, and i is the inflation rate.

Question — Inflation

Rice Ltd is considering a project which would cost £5,000 now. The annual benefits, for four years, would be a fixed income of £2,500 a year, plus other savings of £500 a year in Year 1, rising by 5% each year because of inflation. Running costs will be £1,000 in the first year, but would increase at 10% each year because of inflating labour costs. The general rate of inflation is expected to be 7½% and the company's required money rate of return is 16%.

Is the project worthwhile? (Ignore taxation.)

Answer

The cash flows at inflated values (nominal cash flows) are as follows:

Year	Fixed income £	Other savings £	Running costs £	Net cash flow £
1	2,500	500	1,000	2,000
2	2,500	525	1,100	1,925
3	2,500	551	1,210	1,841
4	2,500	579	1,331	1,748

The NPV of the project is as follows.

Year	Cash flow	Discount factor	PV
	£	16%	£
1	(5,000)	1.000	(5,000)
2	2,000	0.862	1,724
3	1,925	0.743	1,430
4	1,841	0.641	1,180
Intern	1,748	0.552	965
			+ 299

The NPV is positive and the project would appear to be worthwhile.

2.2 Expectations of inflation and the effects of inflation

When managers evaluate a particular project, or when shareholders evaluate their investments, they can only guess at what the rate of inflation is going to be. Their expectations will probably be wrong, at least to some extent, because it is extremely difficult to forecast the rate of inflation accurately. The only way in which uncertainty about inflation can be allowed for in project evaluation is by **risk** and **uncertainty** analysis and obtaining contingency funds.

3 Allowing for taxation in DCF

3.1 Effects of taxation

FAST FORWARD

In investment appraisal, tax is often assumed to be payable **one year in arrears,** but you should read the question details carefully.

Tax allowance details should be checked in any question you attempt.

So far, in looking at project appraisal, we have also ignored **taxation**. However, payments of tax, or reductions of tax payments, are cash flows and ought to be considered in DCF analysis. Again the basics were covered in your previous studies.

Exam focus point

The tax rules might be simplified for an examination question and, as mentioned earlier, you should read any question carefully to establish what tax rules and rates to use.

Typical assumptions which may be stated in questions are as follows:

(a) Corporation tax is payable in the **year following** the one in which the taxable profits are made. Thus, if a project increases taxable profits by £10,000 in Year 2, there will be a tax payment, assuming tax at (say) 30%, of £3,000 in Year 3.

This is not always the case in examination questions. Look out for questions which state that tax is payable in the same year as that in which the profits arise.

(b) Net cash flows from a project should be considered as the taxable profits arising from the project (unless an indication is given to the contrary).

LEARNING OUTCOME 2 THE INVESTMENT DECISION

3.2 Capital allowances

Capital allowances are used to reduce taxable profits, and the consequent reduction in a tax payment should be treated as a cash saving arising from the acceptance of a project.

Writing down allowances are allowed on the cost of **plant and machinery** at the rate of 25% on a **reducing balance** basis. Thus if a company purchases plant costing £80,000, the subsequent writing down allowances would be as follows.

Year		Capital allowance £	Reducing balance (RB) £
1	(25% of cost)	20,000	60,000
2	(25% of RB)	15,000	45,000
3	(25% of RB)	11,250	33,750
4	(25% of RB)	8,438	25,312

When the plant is eventually sold, the difference between the sale price and the reducing balance amount at the time of sale will be treated as:

- A taxable profit if the sale price exceeds the reducing balance, and
- A tax-allowable loss if the reducing balance exceeds the sale price

Exam focus point

> Examination questions often assume that this loss will be available immediately, though in practice the balance less the sale price continues to be written off at 25% a year as part of a pool balance unless the asset has been de-pooled.

The cash saving on the capital allowances (or the cash payment for the charge) is calculated by multiplying the allowance (or charge) by the corporation tax rate.

3.2.1 Assumptions about capital allowances

Assumptions about **capital allowances** could be **simplified** in an exam question. For example, you might be told that capital allowances can be claimed at the rate of 25% of cost on a straight line basis (that is, over four years), or a question might refer to 'tax allowable depreciation', so that the capital allowances equal the depreciation charge.

There are two possible assumptions about the time when capital allowances start to be claimed.

(a) It can be assumed that the first claim for capital allowances occurs at the start of the project (**at Time 0**) and so the first tax saving occurs one year later (**at Time 1**).

(b) Alternatively, it can be assumed that the first claim for capital allowances occurs later in the first year, so the first tax saving occurs one year later, that is, **Time 2**.

You should state clearly which assumption you have made. Assumption (b) is more prudent, because it defers the tax benefit by one year, but assumption (a) is also perfectly feasible. It is very likely, however that an examination question will indicate which of the two assumptions is required.

3.3 Example: Taxation

A company is considering whether or not to purchase an item of machinery costing £40,000 in 20X5. It would have a life of four years, after which it would be sold for £5,000. The machinery would create annual cost savings of £14,000.

The machinery would attract writing down allowances of 25% on the reducing balance basis which could be claimed against taxable profits of the current year, which is soon to end. A balancing allowance or charge would arise on disposal. The rate of corporation tax is 30%. Tax is payable one year in arrears. The after-tax cost of capital is 8%. Assume that tax payments occur in the year following the transactions.

Should the machinery be purchased?

Solution

The first capital allowance is claimed against Year 0 profits.

Cost: £40,000

Year	Allowance		Reducing balance (RB)	
	£		£	
(0) 20X5 (25% of cost)	10,000		30,000	(40,000 – 10,000)
(1) 20X6 (25% of RB)	7,500		22,500	(30,000 – 7,500)
(2) 20X7 (25% of RB)	5,625		16,875	(22,500 – 5,625)
(3) 20X8 (25% of RB)	4,219		12,656	(16,875 – 4,219)
(4) 20X9 (25% of RB)	3,164		9,492	(12,656 – 3,164)

	£
Sale proceeds, end of fourth year	5,000
Less reducing balance, end of fourth year	9,492
Balancing allowance	4,492

Having calculated the allowances each year, the tax savings can be computed. The year of the cash flow is one year after the year for which the allowance is claimed.

Year of claim	Allowance	Tax saved	Timing of tax payment/saving
	£	£	
0	10,000	3,000	1
1	7,500	2,250	2
2	5,625	1,688	3
3	4,219	1,266	4
4	7,656	2,297	5
	35,000 *		

*Net cost £(40,000 – 5,000) = £35,000

These tax savings relate to capital allowances. We must also calculate the extra tax payments on annual savings of £14,000.

The net cash flows and the NPV are now calculated as follows:

Year	Equipment	Savings	Tax on savings	Tax saved on capital allowances	Net cash flow	Discount factor	Present value of cash flow
	£	£	£	£	£	8%	£
0	(40,000)				(40,000)	1.000	(40,000)
1		14,000		3,000	17,000	0.926	15,742
2		14,000	(4,200)	2,250	12,050	0.857	10,327
3		14,000	(4,200)	1,688	11,488	0.794	9,121
4	5,000	14,000	(4,200)	1,266	16,066	0.735	11,809
5			(4,200)	2,297	(1,903)	0.681	(1,296)
							5,703

The NPV is positive and so the purchase appears to be worthwhile.

3.3.1 An alternative and quicker method of calculating tax payments or savings

In the above example, the tax computations could have been combined, as follows:

Year	0	1	2	3	4
	£	£	£	£	£
Cost savings	0	14,000	14,000	14,000	14,000
Capital allowance	10,000	7,500	5,625	4,219	7,656
Taxable profits	(10,000)	6,500	8,375	9,781	6,344
Tax at 30%	3,000	(1,950)	(2,512)	(2,934)	(1,903)

The net cash flows would then be as follows:

Year	Equipment	Savings	Tax	Net cash flow
	£	£	£	£
0	(40,000)			(40,000)
1		14,000	3,000	17,000
2		14,000	(1,950)	12,050
3		14,000	(2,512)	11,488
4	5,000	14,000	(2,934)	16,066
5			(1,903)	(1,903)

The net cash flows are exactly the same as calculated previously.

> **Exam focus point**
>
> In exams tax allowances should be treated in either of the following ways.
>
> (a) Deduct tax allowable depreciation to arrive at taxable profit; calculate taxable profit and add back tax allowable depreciation **or**
>
> (b) Deduct **tax** on capital allowances **separately** from taxable cash flows.

3.4 Taxation and DCF

The effect of taxation on capital budgeting is theoretically quite simple. Organisations must pay tax, and the effect of undertaking a project will be to increase or decrease tax payments each year. These incremental tax cash flows should be included in the cash flows of the project for discounting to arrive at the project's NPV.

When **taxation is ignored** in the DCF calculations, the discount rate will reflect the **pre-tax rate of return** required on capital investments. When taxation is included in the cash flows, a post-tax required rate of return should be used.

If there is inflation and tax in a question, remember that tax flows do not get inflated by an extra year even though they may be paid one year later.

Question — Taxation

A project requires an initial investment in machinery of £300,000. Additional cash inflows of £120,000 at current price levels are expected for three years, at the end of which time the machinery will be scrapped. The machinery will attract writing down allowances of 25% on the reducing balance basis, which can be claimed against taxable profits of the current year, which is soon to end. A balancing charge or allowance will arise on disposal.

The rate of corporate tax is 50% and tax is payable one year in arrears. The pre-tax cost of capital is 22% and the rate of inflation is 10%. Assume that the project is 100% debt financed.

Required

Assess whether the project should be undertaken.

Answer

Post-tax:

Year	Purchase £	Inflation factor	Cash flow after inflation £	Tax on cash inflow £	(W1-3) Tax saved on capital allowances £	Net cash flow £	Discount factor 22 (1-0.5) 11%	Present value £
0	(300,000)	1.000	(300,000)			(300,000)	1.000	(300,000)
1		1.100	132,000		37,500	169,500	0.901	152,720
2		1.210	145,200	(66,000)	28,125	107,325	0.812	87,148
3		1.331	159,720	(72,600)	21,094	108,214	0.731	79,104
4				(79,860)	63,281	16,579	0.659	(10,926)
							NPV =	8,046

Workings

1 Writing down allowance (Initial cost £300,000)

Year		WDA £	Reducing balance (RB) £
0	(25% at cost)	75,000	225,000
1	(25% of RB)	56,250	168,750
2	(25% of RB)	42,188	126,562
3	(25% of RB)	31,641	94,921

2 Balancing allowance

	£
Sale proceeds, end of third year	
RB, end of third year	94,921
Balancing allowance	94,921

3 Tax saved on capital allowances

Year of claim	Allowance claimed £	Tax saved £	Timing of tax saving
0	75,000	37,500	1
1	56,250	28,125	2
2	42,188	21,094	3
3	126,562	63,281	4
	300,000		

4 Non-financial factors

As well as financial considerations, any decision support information provided to management should also incorporate non-financial considerations. These factors can be assessed through a suitability, acceptability, and feasibility framework, ensuring a comprehensive evaluation of potential investments.

4.1 Suitability

Suitability refers to how well a proposed investment aligns with the **strategic objectives** and core values of the organisation. This involves evaluating whether the investment supports long-term goals, **enhances competitive advantage**, and fits within the overall strategic plan.

For example, a firm will want to target its investments to address its key opportunities (eg target growth areas) and threats (eg from rivals or technological trends). Investments that are not aligned to a firm's key opportunities and threats may be rejected as being unsuitable.

4.2 Acceptability

Acceptability concerns the expectations and reactions of **stakeholders** to the proposed investment.

Investment appraisal techniques will be useful in analysing whether shareholders are likely to find the risk and financial return of a project **acceptable**. However, there are likely to be other important stakeholders and it will be necessary to analyse the acceptability of a project to them by assessing the **social, ethical, and environmental implications** of the project, each of which can significantly influence stakeholder support and the project's long-term success.

This will involve considering the following non-financial factors:

(i) **Impact on Employee Morale:** Most investments affect employees' prospects, sometimes for the better, sometimes for the worse. For example, a new cafeteria for employees would have a favourable impact, enhancing job satisfaction and productivity. Conversely, automation investments might lead to job redundancies, negatively impacting morale.

(ii) **Impact on the Community**: Investments can have significant effects on the local community, particularly in terms of job creation or loss, and the potential displacement of small businesses. A project leading to a large-scale loss of jobs can harm the community, whereas one that creates employment opportunities can be seen positively.

(iii) **Impact on the Environment:** The environmental impact of an investment is crucial in today's context of increased ecological awareness. Projects such as the opening of a new mine or developing products that produce environmentally harmful waste can tarnish an organisation's image and reputation, affecting long-term growth and survival prospects. Environmental impacts can also directly affect project cash flows due to fines, legal costs, and cleanup expenses.

(iv) **Ethical Issues:** Some investments might be legal but might not align with the ethics and code of conduct demanded by various stakeholder groups. For example, projects involving exploitative labour practices or those contributing to significant environmental degradation may face public backlash and lose stakeholder support.

(v) **Learning and Development:** Investments, particularly those advancing technology, provide opportunities for learning and innovation. For instance, investment in AI managed computerised equipment can revolutionise a production process, enabling better use of highly technical production methods and fostering a culture of continuous improvement.

4.3 Feasibility

Feasibility examines whether the organization has the **capability** to implement the proposed investment.

There is a financial aspect to feasibility analysis because a project will need to be assessed in terms of whether there are sufficient cash resources to finance the project without damaging knock-on effects on other investment plans or on the proposed dividend. Consideration should also be given to the impact of using any debt finance that is proposed for use in financing a project on gearing (which is considered in Chapter 11).

There is also a non-financial aspect to feasibility analysis which involves evaluating the availability of **resources, technology, and expertise** that are required for the project.

4.4 Impact of non-financial factors on investment appraisal

The main implication of the use suitability / acceptability / feasibility (or SAF) analysis is that it raises the possibility that a project with a positive NPV may still be rejected because, although financially acceptable, it is deemed to be **unsuitable**, **unacceptable** on non-financial criteria or is considered **not feasible**.

5 Real options

Real options attempt to incorporate flexibility to adapt decisions in response to unexpected market developments. It is argued that traditional methods such as NPV fail to accurately capture the economic value of investments in an environment of widespread uncertainty and rapid change. The real options method applies financial options theory (covered in Section 6 of Chapter 17) to quantify the value of this flexibility.

5.1 Option to follow-on

A follow-on option is a strategic option when the investment opportunity leads to follow-on wealth-generating opportunities by utilising the technological know-how or brand strength that has been created by an investment to make follow-on investments either in the same market or in a linked industry.

For example, investing in an emerging new market at an early stage in that market's life cycle may not offer immediately attractive returns but allows a company to create the brand name an know-how to rapidly increase its scale as and when market growth accelerates.

Often, investments that involve buying new equipment carry an option to follow on because this could enable an organisation to develop experience and skills with the latest technology, which may allow follow-on opportunities that would otherwise have been unavailable.

5.2 Option to abandon

An abandonment option refers to the ability to abandon the project at a certain stage in its life. If large sums are being spent, and prospects do not appear healthy, an abandonment option may be available. If the benefit streams from a project are highly uncertain, an option to abandon the project could be highly valuable, reducing the riskiness of the project is reduced and increasing the expected NPV.

This type of option is affected, for example, by the type of equipment needed for the project and the terms on which the equipment is acquired. If equipment is readily resalable, this gives a more valuable abandonment option than if the equipment is highly specialised with no prospective second-hand purchasers.

An option to abandon also exists in projects that have a series of clearly identifiable stages, because managers can consider an option to abandon at each stage.

An option to abandon may also occur because the assets can be switched to another use (eg the production of another product); this latter example is sometimes called an option to redeploy. An example of this is a sports stadium that can be quickly and easily reconfigured for different types of sporting events, to meet changing demand.

5.3 Option to wait

An option to wait is a timing option which allows resolution of uncertainty. Investments are rarely 'now or never' opportunities, but we do need to consider the cash flows forgone in the period of postponement. The cost of this is balanced against the value of waiting.

For example, the possibility of 'doing nothing for a year' may be more valuable than a stated alternative because it will allow the resolution of the uncertainty surrounding legislation or to see if development status is granted on land.

5.4 Valuing real options

Real options can add value to projects, and should be taken into account in investment appraisal.

Option theory provides a means for businesses to take into account:

(a) **Initial costs and benefits**
(b) The **present value of future benefits** and costs
(c) The **variability of future benefits** and costs
(d) The **timescale** directors are allowed to make the decision
(e) The **cost of capital**

We discuss the formulae used to value options (such as the 'Black-Scholes model') in Chapter 17, but the formulae based on using the above variables to value options are not examinable.

The following example gives an overview of how real options can be valuable, and therefore should be taken into account in investment appraisal. Although the **valuation is difficult**, even a rough estimate is better than no estimate at all.

5.5 Example: real options

Libby Co is considering a 3-year project that has an initial cost of $10,000. Depending on the economic cycle, the cash inflows will either be $6,000 per year or $3,000 per year. There is a 60% probability that the cash flows will be $6,000 per year. The cost of capital is 10%.

This means that there is an expected cash flow per year of (6,000 × 0.6) + (3,000 × 0.4) = $4,800.

The NPV of this project is therefore:

Year	Cash flow $	Discount factor	Present value $
0	(10,000)	1.000	(10,000)
1–3	4,800	2.487	11,938
			1,938

Wait option

However, suppose that economic conditions after the first year are expected to remain the same for the **foreseeable future**. This means that Libby Co could wait one year to see which scenario occurs and then launch the project. This would give the following NPVs.

Best case

Year	Cash flow $	Discount factor	Present value $
1	(10,000)	0.909	(9,090)
2–4	6,000	2.261*	13,566
			4,476

Worst case

Year	Cash flow $	Discount factor	Present value $
1	(10,000)	0.909	(9,090)
2–4	3,000	2.261*	6,783
			(2,307)

* 4-year annuity factor – 1 year = 3.170 – 0.909 = 3.170 – 0.909 = 2.261

There is considerable value in the option to wait, in this case, because the NPV is increased by $4,476 – $1,938 = $2,538 as the downside risk is **eliminated** by waiting, as in the worst-case scenario the project would not commence.

Abandonment option

Alternatively, if the project is started now, there may be the option to abandon the project after one year when the machinery used can be sold for $6,000.

This option to abandon would create the following possibilities **at the end of year 1.**

Year (T_0 is now end of first year, when the decision is taken)	Cash flow $	Discount factor	Present value $
0	6,000	1.000	6,000
1	(6,000)	0.909	(5,454)
2	(6,000)	0.826	(4,956)
			(4,410)

Year	Cash flow $	Discount factor	Present value $
0	6,000	1.000	6,000
1	(3,000)	0.909	(2,727)
2	(3,000)	0.826	(2,478)
			795

This shows that if the cashin flows are only $3,000 per year, then the abandonment option should be taken as this has a positive NPV.

The abandonment option can then be incorporated into the NPV of the project as follows.

The expected value of the cash flows can be calculated as follows (including the scrap value for abandoning the project).

	Year 1			Year 2			Year 3	
Probability	$	EV	Probability	$	EV	Probability	$	EV
0.6	6,000	3,600	0.6	6,000	3,600	0.6	6,000	3,600
0.4	9,000	3,600	0.4	–	–	0.4	–	–
		7,200			3,600			3,600

The NPV would then be

Year	Cash flow $	Discount factor	Present value $
0	(10,000)	1.000	(10,000)
1	7,200	0.909	6,545
2	3,600	0.826	2,974
3	3,600	0.751	2,704
			2,223

The option to abandon has increased the overall NPV by $2,223 – $1,938 = $285.

5.6 Impact of real option theory on investment appraisal

Real options can add value to projects, so it follows that a project that has been evaluated without considering the value of real options may have significantly undervalued its NPV.

Projects initially evaluated as having a negative NPV may therefore still be accepted once the value of real options is taken into account.

6 International investment appraisal

6.1 Foreign project appraisal

FAST FORWARD

> Complications in DCF appraisals of international investments include **exchange rates**, **differing inflation rates**, **withholding taxes** and **restrictions on remittances**.

Multinational capital budgeting can be based on similar concepts to those used in the purely domestic case which we have examined earlier in this Learning & Practice Workbook.

6.2 The techniques for foreign project appraisal

Depending upon the information which is available, two alternative NPV methods are available. Both methods produce the NPV in domestic currency terms. For a UK company investing overseas, we can:

(a) **Convert** the **project cash flows** into **sterling** and then **discount** at a **sterling discount rate** to calculate the NPV in sterling terms, or

(b) **Discount the cash flows** in the **host country's currency** from the project at an **adjusted discount rate** for that currency and then **convert the resulting NPV** at the spot exchange rate.

There are, however, some special considerations in the international case, including the following.

(a) Exchange rates may change over time. The examiner may require you to predict the future rate using **purchasing power parity theory**.

(b) For the purpose of assessing how expected **performance** compares with potential performance, it is necessary to compare the project's net present value with those of similar host country projects. This involves measuring the cash flows in terms of the **currency of the host country**.

(c) A foreign project also needs to be evaluated on its net present value in respect of the **funds which can be remitted to the parent**. The purpose of this second stage is to evaluate whether the cash flow remitted justifies the cash invested from the home country.

(d) Cash flows from the subsidiary may come about through a variety of means, including **licensing fees** and **payments for imports** from the parent company.

(e) The possibility of **differing national rates of inflation** needs to be taken into account.

(f) The effects of **different tax systems** may need to be considered.

(g) **Terminal values** are often **difficult to estimate**.

Exam focus point

Remember that determining an appropriate risk-adjusted required rate of return for a foreign project is often complicated by the perceived **political** and **foreign exchange risks**. The range of possible expected outcomes may become so wide that it becomes difficult to produce a credible discounted cash flow analysis that calculates a single expected net present value.

6.3 Example: Overseas investment appraisal

Bromwich plc, a UK company, is considering undertaking a new project in Horavia. This will require initial capital expenditure of H$1,250m, with no scrap value envisaged at the end of the five-year lifespan of the project. There will also be an initial working capital requirement of H$500m, which will be recovered at the end of the project. Pre-tax net cash inflows of H$800m are expected to be generated each year from the project.

Company tax will be charged in Horavia at a rate of 40%, with depreciation on a straight-line basis being an allowable deduction for tax purposes Horavian tax is paid at the end of the year following that in which the taxable profits arise.

There is a double taxation agreement between the UK and Horavia, which means that no UK tax will be payable on the project profits.

The current H$/£ spot rate is 336, and the Horavian dollar is expected to appreciate against the £ by 5% per year.

A project of similar risk recently undertaken by Bromwich plc in the UK had a required post-tax rate of return of 16%.

Should the Horavian project be undertaken?

Solution

Method 1 – conversion of flows into sterling and discounting at sterling discount rate

Time	0	1	2	3	4	5	6
H$m flows							
Capital	(1,750)					500	
Net cash inflows		800	800	800	800	800	
Taxation (W1)			(220)	(220)	(220)	(220)	(220)
	(1,750)	800	580	580	580	1,080	(220)
Exchange rate (W2)	336	319	303	288	274	260	247
£m flows	(5.21)	2.51	1.91	2.01	2.12	4.15	(0.89)
16% df	1	0.862	0.743	0.641	0.552	9,476	0.410
PV	(5.21)	2.16	1.42	1.29	1.17	1.98	(0.36)

NPV = £2.45m

Workings

1. Taxation

	H$m
Net cash inflow	800
Less depreciation (1,250/5)	(250)
	550 @ 40% = H$220m

2. Exchange rate

   Current spot = H$336/£. If the H$ is *appreciating* against the £, this means that the H$ is getting more valuable in terms of £, ie there will be more £ per H$ or less H$ per £.

   Thus in one year's time the H$/£ rate will fall by 5%, to 95% × 336 = 319, etc.

Method 2 – discounting foreign cash flows at an adjusted discount rate

If we are to keep the cash flows in H$, and they need to be discounted at a rate that takes account of both the domestic discount rate (16%) and the rate at which the exchange rate is expected to decrease (5%). This is in fact an application of the **interest rate parity theorem** which is covered in later chapters:

$$(1 + \text{Horavian interest rate}) = (1 + \text{UK interest rate}) \times \frac{\text{Forward rate H\$/£}}{\text{Spot rate H\$/£}}$$

$$1 + i_H = \frac{319}{336} (=0.95) \times 1.16 = 1.10$$

Thus the adjusted discount rate is 10%

Discounting the H$ flows at this rate:

Time	0	1	2	3	4	5	6
H$m flows							
Capital	(1,750)	800	580	580	580	1,080	(220)
10% df	1	0.909	0.826	0.751	0.683	0.621	0.564
PV	(1,750)	727.1	479.1	435.6	396.1	670.7	(124.1)

NPV = H$834.6

Translating this present value at the spot rate gives H$834.6/336 = **£2.48m**

This method is useful if the currency flows are annuities and the adjusted discount rate is a round number, as the computation can be reduced by the use of annuity tables.

6.4 Using purchasing power parity to predict exchange rates

You may need to forecast the exchange rate in the exam using parity theories (this will be considered in more detail in Chapter 16).

Exam focus point

Exam papers in recent years have favoured the purchasing power parity method over the interest rate parity method in predicting future exchange rates.

If the rate of inflation is higher in one country than in another country, the value of its currency will tend to weaken against the other country's currency. **Purchasing power parity theory** attempts to explain changes in the exchange rate exclusively by the rate of inflation in different countries. The theory predicts that the exchange value of a foreign currency depends on the **relative purchasing power** of each currency in its own country and that spot exchange rates will vary over time according to relative price changes. This is sometimes referred to as the **law of one price**.

Key term

Purchasing power parity theory: the theory that, in the long run at least, exchange rates between currencies will tend to reflect the relative purchasing powers of each currency.

Formally, purchasing power parity is expressed in the following equation.

$$\frac{S_t - S_0}{S_0} = \frac{i_f - i_{uk}}{1 + i_{uk}} \quad \text{or} \quad S_t = S_0 \times \frac{1 + i_f}{1 + i_{uk}}$$

where S_0 is the current foreign currency spot exchange rate (at time 0)
  S_t is the expected spot rate at time t
  i_f is the expected inflation in the foreign country to time t (expressed as a decimal)
  i_{uk} is the expected inflation in the home country to time t (expressed as a decimal)

Formula to learn

Purchasing power parity $\quad \dfrac{i_f - i_{uk}}{1 + i_{uk}}$

6.4.1 Example: Purchasing power parity

A UK company is expecting to receive a net cash inflow of Malaysian ringgits in one year's time. The current spot rate is MYR4.92 to the £. It is expected that the exchange rate will change in the future, and it has been estimated that the inflation rate in the UK will be 1.5% per year and the inflation rate in Malaysia will be 1% per year. Predict what the exchange rate is likely to be in one years' time.

Solution

Using purchasing power parity, sterling is the numerator and ringgit is the denominator. So the expected future MYR to the £ exchange rate in one year is given by:

$$\text{Year 1: } 4.92 \times \dfrac{1.01}{1.015} = 4.90$$

In two years, the rate is expected to be:

$$\text{Year 2: } 4.90 \times \dfrac{1.01}{1.015} = 4.88$$

In the exam you will continue to forecast the exchange rate for the life of the project.

7 Tackling overseas investment appraisal questions

Because of the various complications that can come up in a question dealing with overseas investment appraisal, it is best to use a standard layout.

				Time			
Foreign currency cash flows	0	1	2	3	4	5	
Sales receipts		X	X	X	X		
Costs		(X)	(X)	(X)	(X)		
Foreign currency taxable profit		X	X	X	X		
Taxation			(X)	(X)	(X)	(X)	
Tax on writing down allowances		X	X	X	X		
Capital expenditure	(X)						
Scrap value					X		
Tax on scrap value						(X)	
Terminal value					X		
Tax on terminal value						(X)	
Working capital	(X)	(X)	(X)	X	X		
	(X)	X	X	X	X	(X)	
Exchange rates	X	X	X	X	X	X	
Sterling cash flows							
Invested in/remitted from foreign country	(X)	X	X	X	X	(X)	
Additional UK tax			(X)	(X)	(X)	(X)	
Additional UK expenses/income			(X)	(X)	(X)	(X)	
UK tax effect of UK expenses/income			X	X	X	X	
Net sterling cash flows	(X)	X	X	X	X	(X)	
Discount factors @ UK%	X	X	X	X	X	X	
Present values	(X)	X	X	X	X	(X)	

LEARNING OUTCOME 2 THE INVESTMENT DECISION

You may need workings for:

(a) Incremental UK tax

(b) Writing down allowances

(c) As an alternative to tax on writing down allowances, tax allowable depreciation is deducted after costs to arrive at foreign currency taxable profits, and added back after the taxation charge has been deducted

Question   Foreign investment

Donegal plc is considering whether to establish a subsidiary in Ruritania, at a cost of Ruritanian $2,400,000. This would be represented by non-current assets of $2,000,000 and working capital of $400,000. The subsidiary would produce a product which would achieve annual sales of $1,600,000 and incur cash expenditures of $1,000,000 a year.

The company has a planning horizon of four years, at the end of which it expects the realisable value of the subsidiary's non-current assets to be $800,000. It expects also to be able to sell the rights to make the product for $500,000 at the end of four years.

It is the company's policy to remit the maximum funds possible to the parent company at the end of each year.

Tax is payable at the rate of 35% in Ruritania and is payable one year in arrears.

Tax allowable depreciation is at a rate of 25% on a straight-line basis on all non-current assets.

Administration costs of £100,000 per annum will be incurred each year in the UK over the expected life of the project.

The UK taxation rate on taxable profits made in Ruritania and remitted to the UK, and on UK income and expenditure is 30%, payable one year in arrears.

The Ruritanian $:£ exchange rate is 5:1.

The company's cost of capital for the project is 10%.

Calculate the NPV of the project.

Answer

$'000 cash flows	0	1	2	3	4	5
			Time			
Sales receipts		1,600	1,600	1,600	1,600	
Costs		(1,000)	(1,000)	(1,000)	(1,000)	
Tax allowable depreciation		(500)	(500)	(500)	(500)	
$ taxable profit		100	100	100	100	
Taxation			(35)	(35)	(35)	(35)
Add back tax allowable depreciation		500	500	500	500	
Capital expenditure	(2,000)					
Scrap value					800	
Tax on scrap value (W1)						(280)
Terminal value					500	
Tax on terminal value						(175)
Working capital	(400)				400	
	(2,400)	600	565	565	2,265	(490)
Exchange rates	5:1	5:1	5:1	5:1	5:1	5:1

8: INVESTMENT DECISIONS

£'000 cash flows	0	1	Time 2	3	4	5
From/(to) Ruritania	(480)	120	113	113	453	(98)
Additional UK tax (W2)			(6)	(6)	(6)	(84)
Additional UK expenses/income		(100)	(100)	(100)	(100)	
UK tax effect of UK expenses/income			30	30	30	30
Net sterling cash flows	(480)	20	37	37	377	(152)
UK discount factors	1	0.909	0.826	0.751	0.683	0.621
Present values	(480)	18	31	28	257	(94)

NPV = (£240,000), therefore the company should not proceed.

Working 1

Tax is payable on $800,000 as tax written down = $2,000,000 − (4 × $500,000) = 0

Working 2

Years 1-3

$ taxable profit = $100,000
At 5:1 exchange rate = £20,000
Tax at 30% = £6,000

Year 4

$ taxable profit = $100,000 + $800,000 + $500,000
            = $1,400,000
At 5:1 exchange rate = £280,000
Tax at 30% = £84,000

Exam focus point

Investment appraisal questions are likely to be tested for a significant number of marks which permits the examiner to introduce a number of complexities, and allow a number of marks for discussion of the factors affecting the decision process. These include:

- Whether the assumptions made about the figures in the calculations are realistic.
- Other data that would be helpful.
- The need to apply sensitivity analysis or simulations using different assumptions.
- The effect of using a different timeframe to assess the investment.
- The possibility of using other techniques including real options.

You should also raise the issues of whether the investment is compatible with current strategy, the risks involved and whether other investments may be better.

Chapter Roundup

- The **payback method** of project appraisal and the **ARR/ROCE/ROI method** of project appraisal are popular appraisal techniques despite their limitations.

- There are two methods of using **discounted cash flow** to appraise investment projects, the NPV method and the IRR/DCF yield method.

- The **NPV method** of project appraisal is to accept projects with a positive NPV.

- The **IRR method** of project appraisal is to accept projects whose IRR (the rate at which the NPV is zero) exceeds a target rate of return. The IRR is estimated either from a graph or using interpolation.

  The formula to apply is $IRR \approx a + \left[\left(\frac{A}{A-B} \right) \times (b-a) \right]\%$.

- When compared with the NPV method, the **IRR method** has a number of **disadvantages**.
  - It **ignores** the **relative size** of investments.
  - It is difficult to use if a project has **non-conventional cashflows** or when deciding between **mutually exclusive projects**.

- **Relevant costs** of investment appraisal include **opportunity costs**, **working capital costs** and wider costs such as **infrastructure and human development costs**. Non-relevant costs include **past costs** and **committed costs**.

- **Relevant benefits** from investments include not only **increased cash flows**, but also **savings** and **better relationships with customers and employees**.

- In practice many businesses use the simpler, easy to understand methods, although some are developing strategic investment appraisal techniques.

- (1 + money rate of return) = (1 + real rate of return) × (1 + rate of inflation)

- **Real cash flows** (ie adjusted for inflation) should be discounted at a **real discount rate**.

- **Money cash flows** should be discounted at a **money discount rate**.

- In investment appraisal, tax is often assumed to be payable **one year in arrears**, but you should read the question details carefully.

- **Tax allowance** details should be checked in any question you attempt.

- **Non-financial factors** should also be considered; the suitability, acceptability, feasibility (SAF) framework is useful here.

- **Real options** (to follow-on, abandon or wait) can add value to projects, and should be considered to ensure that project's NPV has not been undervalued by failing to consider these options.

- Complications in DCF appraisals of international investments include **exchange rates**, **differing inflation rates**, **withholding taxes** and **restrictions on remittances**.

Quick Quiz

1. Identify the steps involved in a new programme of capital investment.

2. What is the time required for the cash inflows from a capital investment project to equal the cash outflows?

3. What is defined as 'a periodic payment continuing for a limitless period'?

4. Match up each term with the appropriate definition.

   Terms

   (A) Net terminal value

   (B) Net present value

   (C) Present value

   Definitions

   (1) The value obtained by discounting all cash outflows and inflows of a capital investment project at a chosen target rate of return or cost of capital.

   (2) The cash equivalent now of a sum of money receivable or payable at a stated future date, discounted at a specified rate of return.

   (3) The cash surplus remaining at the end of a project after taking account of interest and capital repayments.

5. Group the following items that occur in investment appraisal question under the following headings:

	Include in investment appraisal	Exclude from investment appraisal
Depreciation	☐	☐
Sunk costs	☐	☐
Opportunity costs	☐	☐
Allocated costs and revenues	☐	☐
After tax incremental cash flows	☐	☐
Effect of tax allowances	☐	☐
Dividend/interest	☐	☐
Working capital requirements	☐	☐

6. Which equation links the money rate of return and the real rate of return?

7. Are cash flows that are given in terms of today's pounds being given in money or real terms?

8. What are the non-financial issues that should be considered before accepting a project?

9. What are the three types of real option?

10. What alternative methods of foreign project appraisal can produce an NPV in domestic currency terms?

Answers to Quick Quiz

1. (a) Identification of an investment opportunity
   (b) Consideration of the alternatives to the project being evaluated
   (c) Acquiring relevant information
   (d) Detailed planning
   (e) Taking the investment decision

2. The payback period

3. A perpetuity

4. (A) (3)
   (B) (1)
   (C) (2)

5.
Include in **investment appraisal**	**Exclude** from **investment appraisal**
• Opportunity costs	• Depreciation
• After tax incremental cash flows	• Sunk costs
• Effect of tax allowances	• Allocated costs and revenues
• Working capital requirements	• Dividends/interest

6. 1 + money (nominal) rate of return = (1 + real rate) (1 + inflation rate)

7. Real terms

8. Suitability, acceptability and feasibility criteria should be applied to ensure adequate consideration of non-financial issues.

9. Options to follow-on, wait, and to abandon

10. (a) Convert the project cash flows into sterling and then discount at a sterling discount rate
    (b) Discount the cash flows in the host country's currency from the project at an adjusted discount rate for that currency, and then convert the NPV at the spot exchange rate

End of chapter questions

1. Mrs Grand (AIA May 2013)

Mrs Grand is a UK-based business woman who has experience of setting up a number of successful companies. She is considering a new venture which would involve selling handbags. She has not had previous experience of retail businesses. The handbags she intends selling have just become highly fashionable. She has found a suitable shop for rent on a four-year lease. The yearly rental is £45,000 payable in advance at the start of each year. New fixtures and fittings would have to be purchased for the shop at an estimated cost of £40,000. Mrs Grand's intention would be to close the business after the four-year period. She has estimated that the fixtures and fittings could be sold at the end of the four years for £6,000.

She would import the handbags from a Malaysian company and has estimated that the number of handbags sold over the next four years would be as follows:

	Projected number of handbags sold
Year 1	2,100
Year 2	2,400
Year 3	2,500
Year 4	2,800

These estimates of projected sales were provided by a market research company. The cost of employing the market research company was £12,000 and this payment is now due.

Mrs Grand would have to pay for the handbags in Malaysian ringgits (MYR) and she has estimated that the average cost of each handbag would be MYR275. She would purchase the same number of handbags as she estimates will be sold each year. The Malaysian company would require payment for these purchases to be made at the start of each year. She intends selling the handbags at an average selling price of £130.

The current spot rate is MYR4.92 to the £. It is expected that the exchange rate will change in the future, and it has been estimated that the inflation rate in the UK will be 1.5% per year and the inflation rate in Malaysia will be 1% per year.

Mrs Grand would employ a manager for the shop on a salary of £30,000 per year. She would also employ two other members of staff paying each a salary of £16,000 per year. She estimates that she would pay £11,000 per year for heating and lighting the shop. She estimates that advertising the handbags will cost £5,000 per year payable at the start of each year.

Tax would be payable for the business one year in arrears and at a rate of 20%. If the net cashflow for any year is negative then you should assume that zero tax will be paid on this cashflow, and that the negative cashflow will be used to reduce the next available positive cashflow when calculating tax on that positive cashflow.

When evaluating previous business ventures Mrs Grand has used a discount rate of 12%.

Required

(a) Prepare calculations to evaluate whether it is worthwhile for Mrs Grand to set up the new venture. State any assumptions you have made in your calculations. **(16 marks)**

(b) Advise Mrs Grand of any potential risks that may be associated with this venture. **(12 marks)**

(c) Mrs Grand is aware that different stakeholders in the company will have different objectives. Advise Mrs Grand who the principal stakeholders are in her business and of any difficulties there may be in satisfying the objectives of these stakeholders. **(12 marks)**

(Total 40 marks)

LEARNING OUTCOME 2 THE INVESTMENT DECISION

2. Mr Li (AIA May 2012)

A Hong Kong-based businessman, Mr Li, is considering whether to buy a franchise. He has spent some time looking at different franchise opportunities and is most interested in 'The Coffee Company' franchise. The Coffee Company has been established for three years and is based in the UK. It currently has 65 franchisees operating under The Coffee Company name in the UK, compared to 72 franchisees operating in the UK 12 months ago. During the last 12 months The Coffee Company has been offering franchise opportunities overseas as the company is keen to expand this aspect of their business. This would be the first franchise agreement in Hong Kong.

The Coffee Company was set up by a wife and husband who had had no previous business experience in coffee shops, although they have both had some prior business experience in the car industry. The wife has a background in accounting and the husband has a background in sales. The wife and husband do not run any Coffee Company shops; instead they are focused upon building up the number of franchisees. To differentiate themselves from other coffee shops, Coffee Company shops only sell coffee and biscuits.

Mr Li has no business experience in coffee shops either. His current business is manufacturing bricks for the construction industry. The Coffee Company provides initial training in how to run a coffee shop. Normally, they would provide a week's training shortly prior to the opening of the franchise. However, The Coffee Company has stated that in this case they can only offer three days training because of the travel time required to visit Hong Kong. The Coffee Company has said that it will be able answer any queries by email or telephone. The Coffee Company will provide advertising literature to Mr Li that is currently used by its UK franchisees.

The franchise agreement between Mr Li and The Coffee Company states:

1. An amount of £40,000 must be paid by Mr Li at the outset to The Coffee Company. This fee is to cover for use of The Coffee Company logo and to purchase fixtures and fittings that are standard in all Coffee Company outlets.

2. A fee amounting to 5% of turnover of the franchise must be paid by Mr Li to The Coffee Company each year. The fee must be paid at the end of each year and it must be paid in pounds sterling.

3. Mr Li must purchase all coffee and biscuits from The Coffee Company. The cost of purchasing the coffee is 10 pence per cup and the cost of purchasing each biscuit 20 pence. The payment for these purchases is to be made at the end of each year in pounds sterling.

4. The advertising literature that the Coffee Company will provide must be paid for by Mr Li. This will cost £5,000 per year. This amount is payable at the start of each year in pounds sterling.

5. Mr Li is responsible for finding suitable premises.

Mr Li has found premises that he considers suitable for a coffee shop. These premises would cost HK$500,000 per year to rent. The rent would be payable at the end of each year. The shop would sell different types of coffee and different types of biscuit. The average selling price for a cup of coffee would be HK$15 and the average selling price for a biscuit would be HK$10. Mr Li had hoped that he would be given assistance in projecting the likely level of future sales by The Coffee Company. However, they have not provided any assistance and Mr Li has estimated that sales over the next four years would be as follows:

	Number of cups of coffee sold	Number of biscuits sold
Year 1	90,000	60,000
Year 2	100,000	75,000
Year 3	120,000	80,000
Year 4	120,000	80,000

Mr Li has estimated that staff costs each year will total HK$1,150,000 and other costs will total HK$8,000 per year.

Assume that corporation tax is payable in Hong Kong at a rate of 15% and based on the net cashflow for each year. Corporation tax is payable one year in arrears. If the net cashflow for any year is negative then you should assume that zero tax is to be paid on this cashflow, and that the negative cashflow can be carried forward and deducted from future positive cashflows when calculating corporation tax.

Mr Li estimates that the value of the coffee shop at the end of Year 4 would be equivalent to the pre-tax net cashflow in Year 4 multiplied by a factor of 6.

The current spot rate is HK$12.82 to the £. The exchange rate is expected to change in the future, and it has been estimated that the inflation rate in the UK will be 2.5% per year and the inflation rate in Hong Kong will be 2% per year.

If Mr Li decides to buy the franchise then he will need to obtain a bank loan to finance the venture. He is aware that the bank will require him to have prepared a business plan. As a part of this business plan Mr Li will need to have considered any risks that might be associated with the venture.

Required

Mr Li is aware that he really needs some further advice and you have been asked to:

(a) Prepare an NPV calculation to evaluate whether it is worthwhile for Mr Li to buy the franchise. You should assume a discount rate of 12%. State any assumptions you have made in your calculations.

(17 marks)

(b) Prepare a report for Mr Li advising him of any potential risks he should be aware of before approaching the bank for a loan. **(13 marks)**

(c) Explore how the management of debtors, creditors and stocks may differ in respect of Mr Li's current business and this new venture he is considering. **(10 marks)**

(Total 40 marks)

LEARNING OUTCOME 2 THE INVESTMENT DECISION

Risk and portfolio theory

Topic list	Syllabus reference
1 Risk	LO2
2 Uncertainty	LO2
3 Portfolio theory	LO2

Introduction

This chapter examines how risk can be viewed by managers and also by shareholders.

From a management viewpoint it is essential that it is understood that the financial projections that underpin NPV analysis are estimates and may be wrong. Before accepting a positive NPV project it is therefore important to examine the risk that this NPV is not achieved. A distinction can be made here between understanding the **risk** of different outcomes (which can be quantified using probabilities) and the **uncertainty** of a project NPV (which cannot be quantified using probabilities). We will also describe a number of different **attitudes to risk** that will affect investment decision making.

From a shareholder viewpoint, portfolio theory explains the idea the importance of shareholders creating **diversified portfolios.** This chapter explains the benefits of portfolio diversification, and the relevance and limitations of **portfolio theory.**

1 Risk

FAST FORWARD

Risk arises where there are several possible outcomes and, based on past relevant experience, **probabilities can be assigned to the possible outcomes.**

Risk exists where a decision maker has knowledge that several different future outcomes are possible, the probabilities of which are known, or can be estimated, usually due to past experience.

1.1 Expected values

Where there is **risk**, a range of possible future outcomes can be **quantified** (eg best, worst and most likely) and probabilities assigned to them and an **expected value** or weighted average of these outcomes can be calculated.

In the absence of any information about a particular risk attitude (covered later in this chapter) it can be assumed that a decision maker, when faced with a number of alternative decisions, will select the one with the **best expected value** (EV).

1.2 Example: Expected Values

Harry Co is choosing between two mutually exclusive projects. The NPV of these projects in $m depends on the rate of growth of the economy over the next five years. Forecast NPV for scenarios of low, average and high growth are shown below along with the probabilities of each growth scenario.

Probability	Forecast	Project A NPV $m	Project B NPV $m
0.25	Low growth	1.00	−8.00
0.50	Medium growth	2.50	4.00
0.25	High growth	4.00	16.00

Expected values can be calculated as follows:

Project A: $(1 \times 0.25) + (2.5 \times 0.50) + (4 \times 0.25) = \underline{\mathbf{2.50}}$

Project B: $(-8 \times 0.25) + (4 \times 0.50) + (16 \times 0.25) = \underline{\mathbf{4.00}}$

Project B has a higher expected value and would therefore be chosen on the basis of this technique.

However, if the company is risk averse (see later section on risk attitudes), it may be deterred from project B by the 25% chance of a negative NPV.

1.2.1 Problems with the expected value method

There are a number of possible problems with using expected values in making investment decisions.

Problems with the expected value method	
Unreliable estimates of probabilities	If similar investment decisions have been taken before then it may be possible to estimate the probabilities of the outcome of such investments. However, investment opportunities are often one-offs and as a result the probabilities used to estimate the expected value of the investment will be unreliable.

Problems with the expected value method	
An expected value may not be a possible outcome	If an NPV has been calculated based on an expected value for sales (for example), then the evaluation of the investment is more complicated if the expected value is not a possible outcome. For example, if sales will be 110,000 units if an investment succeeds and 10,000 units if it fails, and there is a 50% chance of each outcome, then the expected value for sales is 110,000 × 0.5 + 10,000 × 0.5 = 60,000. However, it is not meaningful to base the NPV analysis on an expected value for sales of 60,000 units if this level of sales is not seen as being a possible outcome.
Expected values do not consider the range of possible outcomes	If a company has a neutral attitude to risk, it can be assumed that it will select an investment that is forecast to create the highest expected net present value. However, if a company is especially risk-averse or if it is risk-seeking (in the hope of high returns) the company's decision making would be influenced by this risk attitude (see next section).

1.3 Attitude to risk

Risk appetite or attitude is the amount of risk (or uncertainty) an organisation is willing to take on, or is prepared to accept, in pursuing its strategic objectives.

Decision-makers may be **risk seekers**, **risk neutral** or **risk averse**.

A decision maker is **risk neutral** if they are concerned with what will be the **most likely outcome**. A risk-neutral decision maker will be concerned with the most likely outcome, using **expected values.** However, not all decision-makers are risk neutral and will not base their decision-making on the most likely outcome as calculated by expected values.

A **risk seeker** is a decision maker who is interested in trying to secure the best outcomes, no matter how small the chance that they may occur. This attitude may reflect the values of the decision maker and may also be affected by any incentives that are based on ambitious performance targets being hit. Venture capitalists often encourage a risk-seeking attitude because they are often highly ambitious in their growth targets.

A **risk-averse** decision maker acts on the assumption that the worst outcome might occur. This attitude may result from a business being under cash flow pressure, so that it cannot afford an unexpected drop in cash flow (ie it has a low **risk capacity**). One reason for this may be that the business has high financial gearing and has interest payments that need to be made.

Risk seekers and risk-averse decision-makers will need different methods to support their differing attitudes to risk.

1.3.1 Risk attitude and decision making

Risk attitude will influence the method used to evaluate decisions.

Decision-making techniques for different risk attitudes	
Risk seeker	Risk seekers will want to make decisions that are based on making the maximum possible return (regardless of the probability of this). **Maximax** is the name given to the technique that looks at the best possible results from each decision option and selects the option that gives the best possible result.

Decision-making techniques for different risk attitudes	
Risk averse	Risk-averse decision makers will want to minimise downside risk by selecting the option that gives the best of the worst outcomes (regardless of the probability of the worst outcomes occurring).
	Two techniques may be used here:
	1. **Maximin** is the name given to the technique that looks at the worst possible results from each decision option and selects the option that gives the best possible of these worst case scenario results.
	2. **Minimax regret** may also be appropriate; this is where a decision is chosen that minimises the impact of it turning out to be the wrong decision (ie minimises regret). This involves considering the maximum regret a decision-maker would have they have selected the incorrect project to invest in; the project selected will be the one that minimises this level of maximum regret.

Example: Maximax, Maximin and Minimax regret

Harry Co (continuation of previous example) is choosing between two mutually exclusive projects. The NPV of these projects in $m depends on the rate of growth of the economy over the next five years. Forecast NPV for scenarios of low, average and high growth are shown below along with the probabilities of each growth scenario.

Forecast	Project A NPV $m	Project B NPV $m
Low growth	1.00	−8.00
Medium growth	2.50	4.00
High growth	4.00	16.00

If Harry was not risk neutral then expected values would not be relevant, which is why no probabilities are being considered here.

If Harry was a risk seeker, the **maximax** criteria would be appropriate.

The best case outcome for Project A is $4m, and for project B it is $16m. On this basis, Project B delivers the best maximum return and would be selected.

If Harry was **risk-averse**, the **maximin** criteria would be appropriate.

The worst case outcome for Project A is $1m, and for project B it is $−8m. On this basis, Project A delivers the best worst-case return and would be selected.

If Harry was **risk-averse**, the **minimax regret** criteria could also be appropriate.

Forecast	Project A NPV $m	Project B NPV $m	Regret NPV $m
Low growth	1.00 best decision	−8.00	If B is chosen the regret would be the difference between the two NPVs ie $9m
Medium growth	2.50	4.00 best decision	If A is chosen the regret would be the difference between the two NPVs ie $1.5m

Forecast	Project A NPV $m	Project B NPV $m	Regret NPV $m
High growth	4.00	**16.00 best decision**	If A is chosen the regret would be the difference between the two NPVs ie $12m

The maximum regret associated with Project A is the higher of $1.5m and $12m ie $12m

The maximum regret associated with Project B is $9m

Project B's maximum regret is lower than Project A's maximum regret so project B is chosen.

Exam focus point

Exam questions may expect you to infer which is the most appropriate technique to use, given the risk appetite of an organisation.

2 Uncertainty

FAST FORWARD

Uncertainty arises where there are several possible outcomes and **no information** (eg experience) **upon which to create probabilities** so the degree of uncertainty **cannot be quantified.**

Uncertainty exists when the future is unknown and the decision maker has no past experience on which to base predictions of change. There are therefore a number of possible outcomes but the probability of each outcome is not known.

Uncertainty can be described to managers to assist in decision making using sensitivity analysis.

2.1 Sensitivity analysis

Sensitivity analysis evaluates what percentage change would be required in the value of a single variable (eg sales revenue), for the NPV of a project to fall (or rise) to zero ie how much a single project variable would have to change by in order for the investment decision to change.

Sensitivity analysis therefore **provides an indication of which variables a project's NPV is most sensitive to.**

Management should review the variables where a small change in value would alter the investment decision, to assess whether or not there is a strong possibility of these changes occurring.

Management should also pay particular attention to controlling those variables to which the NPV is particularly sensitive, once the decision has been taken to accept the investment.

A simple approach to calculating sensitivity is as follows:

$$\frac{\text{Project NPV}}{\text{Present value of project variable}} \times 100$$

The lower the percentage, the more sensitive the NPV is to that project variable, as the variable would need to change by a smaller amount to make the project non-viable.

2.2 Example: Sensitivity analysis

Kenney Co is considering a project which required an initial investment of $7 million and is expected to result in sales of 100,000 units per year at a selling price of $65 and a variable cost per unit of $20. Kenney Co has a cost of capital of 8%.

The present value (PV) of each these variables has been calculated as follows:

Time	Discount factor 8%	PV of initial investment $000s	PV of variable costs $000s	PV of sales revenue $000s	PV of net cash flow $000s
0	1.000	(7,000)			(7,000)
1	0.926		(1,852)	6,019	4,167
2	0.857		(1,714)	5,571	3,857

The project has a positive NPV of +$1,024 (000) and therefore would appear to be worthwhile.

The project's IRR has been estimated as 18.5%.

Tax can be ignored

The sensitivity of the project to changes in a number of variables can be assessed by calculating what would need to have to these variables to change the project NPV from $1,024,000 to 0.

Sensitivity to the initial investment:

Sensitivity = (1,024/7,000) × 100 = 14.6%

This means that the project will only just provide the required investment return if the cost of the investment is 14.6% higher than estimated, assuming all other variables are unchanged.

Sensitivity to sales volume:

Sales volume will affect the value of **sales revenue and variable costs (ie contribution)**.

Sensitivity = (1,024/(11,590 − 3,566)) × 100 = 12.8%

The project will only just provide the required investment return if sales volume is 12.8% lower than estimated, assuming all other variables are unchanged.

Sensitivity to the selling price:

This will affect the value of **sales revenue only**.

Sensitivity = (1,024/11,590) × 100 = 8.8%

The project will only just provide the required investment return if the sales price is 8.8% lower than estimated, assuming all other variables are unchanged.

Sensitivity to variable costs:

Sensitivity = (1,024/3,566) × 100 = 28.8%

The project will only just provide the required investment return if variable costs per unit are 28.8% higher than estimated, assuming all other variables are unchanged.

Sensitivity to the cost of capital:

The project's IRR is 18.5% which is 10.5% above the cost of capital of 8%.

The cost of capital can therefore increase by (10.5% / 8%) × 100 = 135% before the NPV becomes negative.

Discussion of results

The elements to which the NPV appears to be most sensitive are the selling price followed by the sales volume. Management should pay particular attention to these factors so that they can be carefully monitored.

Note that tax was ignored in this illustration. If tax is given in a question, the sensitivity analysis should be performed on the **post-tax** present value of the cash flows.

2.2.1 Problems with sensitivity analysis

There are a number of possible problems with sensitivity analysis:

(a) The method requires changes in each key variable to be **examined one at a time**, but management is more interested in the combination of the effects of changes in two or more key variables. Looking at factors in isolation is unrealistic since they are often interdependent.

(b) Sensitivity analysis does not examine the **probability** that any particular variation in the value of a variable, such as costs or revenues, might occur.

3 Portfolios and portfolio theory

> **FAST FORWARD**
>
> **Portfolio theory** takes account of the fact that many investors have a range of investments that are unlikely all to change values in step. The investor should be concerned with his or her overall position, not with the performance of individual investments.
>
> **Correlation** measures the degree to which the returns on investment vary with each other.

3.1 Individual and company portfolios

From the viewpoint of an **individual investor**, risk is often managed by the creation of a **portfolio**. A portfolio is a collection of different investments that make up an investor's total holding.

A portfolio might also be created by a **company** through its investments in different capital projects.

Portfolio theory, is concerned with establishing guidelines for individual investors building up a portfolio of stocks and shares, or for companies building a portfolio of projects.

Factors in the choice of investment	
Security	Maintenance of capital value.
Liquidity	If made with short-term funds, should be convertible into cash with short notice.
Return	Obtain highest return compatible with safety.
Spreading risks	Spread risks over several investments, so losses on some offset by gains on others.
Growth prospects	Investment in steadily growing businesses.

3.2 Portfolios: Expected return and risk

When an investor has a portfolio of securities, they will expect the portfolio to provide a certain return on their investment. The **expected return** of a portfolio will be a weighted average of the expected returns of the investments in the portfolio, weighted by the proportion of total funds invested in each.

For example, if 70% of the portfolio relates to a security which is expected to yield 10% and 30% to a security expected to yield 12%, the portfolio's expected return is (70% × 10%) + (30% × 12%) = 10.6%

LEARNING OUTCOME 2 THE INVESTMENT DECISION

The **risk** in an investment, or in a portfolio of investments, is the risk that the **actual return** will **not be the same** as the **expected return**. The actual return may be higher, but it may be lower.

A prudent investor will want to avoid too much risk, and will hope that the actual returns from their portfolio are much the same as what they expected them to be. The risk of a security, and the risk of a portfolio, can be measured as the **standard deviation of expected returns**, given estimated probabilities of actual returns.

3.3 Example: Portfolios (1)

Suppose that the return from an investment has the following probability distribution.

Return X %	Probability p	Expected value px
8	0.2	1.6
10	0.2	2.0
12	0.5	6.0
14	0.1	1.4
		11.0

The expected return is 11%, and the standard deviation of the expected return is as follows. The symbol $\bar{x}$ refers to the expected value of the return, 11%.

Return X %	$x - \bar{x}$ %	p	$p(x-\bar{x})^2$
8	−3	0.2	1.8
10	−1	0.2	0.2
12	1	0.5	0.5
14	3	0.1	0.9
		Variance	3.4

Standard deviation = $\sqrt{3.4}$ = 1.84%

Thus, the expected return is 11% with a standard deviation of 1.84%.

The risk of an investment might be high or low, depending on the nature of the investment. **Low risk** investments usually give **low returns**. **High risk** investments might give **high returns**, but with more risk of disappointing results. So how does holding a **portfolio** of investments affect expected returns and investment risk?

Exam focus point

> In the exam you may need to **explain** the meaning of, or interpret the value of, standard deviation but **calculation of standard deviation (or correlation) will not be required**.

3.4 Correlation of investments

Portfolio theory states that individual investments cannot be viewed simply in terms of their risk and return. The relationship between the return from one investment and the return from other investments is just as important. The relationship between investments can be one of three types.

3.4.1 Positive correlation

When there is positive correlation between investments, if one investment does well it is likely that the other will do well. Thus if you buy shares in one company making umbrellas and in another which sells raincoats you would expect both companies to do badly in dry weather.

9: PORTFOLIO THEORY

3.4.2 Negative correlation

If one investment does well the other will do badly, and vice versa. Thus if you hold shares in one company making umbrellas and in another which sells ice cream, the weather will affect the companies differently.

3.4.3 No correlation

The performance of one investment will be independent of how the other performs. If you hold shares in a mining company and in a leisure company, it is likely that there would be no relationship between the profits and returns from each.

This relationship between the returns from different investments is measured by the correlation coefficient. A figure close to +1 indicates high positive correlation, and a figure close to –1 indicates high negative correlation. A figure of 0 indicates no correlation. If investments show high negative correlation, then by combining them in a portfolio overall risk would be reduced. Risk will also be reduced by combining in a portfolio investments which have no significant correlation.

3.5 The standard deviation of a portfolio

The standard deviation of the returns from a portfolio of two investments can be calculated using the following formula.

Exam formula

$$\sigma_p = \sqrt{\sigma_a^2 x^2 + \sigma_b^2 (1-x)^2 + 2x(1-x)p_{ab}\sigma_a\sigma_b}$$

where σ_p is the standard deviation of a portfolio of two investments, A and B

σ_a is the standard deviation of the returns from investment A

σ_b is the standard deviation of the returns from investment B

σ_a^2, σ_b^2 are the variances of returns from investment A and B (the squares of the standard deviations)

x is the weighting or proportion of investment A in the portfolio

p_{ab} is the correlation coefficient of returns from investment A and B

3.6 Example: Portfolios (2)

Security A and Security B have the following expected returns:

Probability	Security A return	Security B return
0.1	15.00%	10.00%
0.8	25.00%	23.75%
0.1	35.00%	50.00%

The expected return from each security is as follows:

Probability	Security A return %	EV %	Security B Return %	EV %
0.1	15	1.5	10	1
0.8	25	20.0	23.75	19
0.1	35	3.5	50	5
	Expected return =	25.0	Expected return =	25.0

The standard deviation of security A and B has been calculated as:

Security A: 4.472%
Security B: 9.287%

Security B therefore offers the same expected return as security A, but at a greater risk.

We will use this example to calculate the standard deviation of the returns from **a portfolio of 50% Security A and 50% Security B** using the formula given at the start of this section.

(a) When there is perfect positive correlation between the returns from A and B, $p_{ab} = 1$

$$\sigma_p = \sqrt{[(4.472^2 \times 0.5^2) + (9.287^2 \times 0.5^2) + (2 \times 0.5 \times 0.5 \times 1 \times 4.472 \times 9.287)]}$$
$$= \sqrt{[5 + 21.56 + (0.5 \times 4.472 \times 9.287)]}$$
$$= 6.88\%$$

The standard deviation of the portfolio is 6.88%

The expected return is 25% as both parts of the portfolio are expected to give this return.

(b) When there is perfect negative correlation between returns from A and B, $p_{ab} = -1$

$$\sigma_p = \sqrt{[(4.472^2 \times 0.5^2) + (9.287^2 \times 0.5^2) + (2 \times 0.5 \times 0.5 \times -1 \times 4.472 \times 9.287)]}$$
$$= \sqrt{[5 + 21.56 - (0.5 \times 4.472 \times 9.287)]}$$
$$= 2.41\%$$

Again, the expected return is 25% as both parts of the portfolio are expected to give this return.

(c) When there is no correlation between returns from A and B, $P_{ab} = 0$

$$\sigma_p = \sqrt{[(4.472^2 \times 0.5^2) + (9.287^2 \times 0.5^2)]}$$
$$= \sqrt{[5 + 21.56]}$$
$$= \sqrt{[5 + 20 + 0]}$$
$$= 5.15$$

The standard deviation of the portfolio is 5.15%

Again, the expected return is 25% as both parts of the portfolio are expected to give this return.

This illustrates that, for a rational risk averse investor it would be more attractive to have a portfolio made up of investments that have negative correlation since it offers the same return but with lower risk as measured by the standard deviation of the portfolio.

Exam focus point

In the exam you may need to compare the levels of risk and return of different portfolios. You may meet the situation where one portfolio has a higher risk and higher return level than another. Unless you know what the investors' preferences are, you may have to say that you can't tell which portfolio the investors will choose.

3.7 Portfolio theory and financial management

Our discussion of portfolio theory has concentrated mainly on portfolios of stocks and shares. Investors can reduce their investment risk by diversifying, **but what about individual companies choosing a range of businesses or projects to invest in?**

Just as an investor can reduce the risk of variable returns by diversifying into a portfolio of different securities, a company can reduce its own risk and so stabilise its profitability if it invests in a portfolio of **different projects** or **operations**, assuming that any positive correlation between returns is weak.

3.7.1 Advantages of diversification

(a) **Internal cash flows** will become **less volatile**. This makes it less risky to service the company's current level of debt and may consequently allow the company to make use of more debt without additional risk. This could reduce the cost of capital generally, increasing the wealth of shareholders.

(b) Diversification into foreign markets may enable shareholders to reduce the level of their **risk** where exchange controls or other barriers to direct investment exist. The diversifying company can enable this to occur by investing in markets which have a combination of risk and return which shareholders would not otherwise be able to obtain.

(c) A diversified company may have a lower probability of **corporate failure** because of the reduced total risk for the company. This will reduce the likely impact of insolvency costs.

3.7.2 Limitations of diversification

(a) A company may employ people with **particular skills**, and it will get the best out of its employees by allowing them to stick to doing what they are good at. A manager with expert knowledge of the electronics business, for example, might not be any good at managing a retailing business. Not all managers can adapt successfully to running a diversified business.

(b) When companies try to grow, they will often find the best opportunities to make extra profits in industries or markets with which they are **familiar**. If a market opens up for say, a new electronic consumer product, the companies which are likely to exploit the market most profitably are those which already have experience in producing electronic consumer products.

(c) Conglomerates are **vulnerable to takeover bids** where the buyer plans to 'unbundle' the companies in the group and sell them off individually at a profit, particularly because their returns will often be mediocre rather than high, and so the stock market will value the shares on a fairly low P/E ratio. Separate companies within the group would be valued according to their individual performance and prospects, often at P/E ratios that are much higher than for the conglomerate as a whole.

(d) Except where restrictions apply to direct investment, investors can probably reduce investment risk **more efficiently** than companies. They have a wider range of investment opportunities. Investments with uncorrelated or negatively correlated returns will be easier to identify.

Exam focus point

The point that shareholders can achieve diversification more easily and at less cost than a company is important; if shareholders do hold diversified portfolios then this has implications for understanding the type of risk that they are exposed to; this idea is developed in the capital asset pricing model in the next chapter.

3.8 Limitations of portfolio analysis for the financial manager

Portfolio analysis is useful for diversifying through the firm's investment decisions. Applied to the selection of investment proposals, portfolio theory has a number of limitations.

(a) **Probabilities** of different outcomes must be estimated: fairly easy for (eg) machine replacement; more difficult for (eg) new product development.

(b) **Shareholders' preferences between risk and return** may be difficult to know and **personal tax issues** may impact.

(c) Portfolio theory is based on the idea of managers assessing the relevant probabilities and deciding the combination of activities for the business. Managers have their job security to consider, while the shareholder can easily buy and sell securities. Managers may therefore be more risk-averse than shareholders, and this may distort managers' investment decisions (the '**agency problem**' – see Chapter 1).

(d) Projects may be of such a **size** that they are not easy to divide in accordance with recommended diversification principles.

(e) The theory assumes that there are **constant returns to scale**, in other words that the percentage returns provided by a project are the same however much is invested in it. In practice, there may be economies of scale to be gained from making a larger investment in a single project.

(f) Other aspects of **risk** not covered by the theory may need to be considered, eg bankruptcy costs.

3.9 International diversification of risk

A portfolio which is diversified internationally should in theory be less risky than a purely domestic portfolio. This is of advantage to any risk-averse investor. As with a purely domestic portfolio, the extent to which risk is reduced by **international diversification** will depend upon the degree of correlation between individual securities in the portfolio. The lower the degree of correlation between returns on the securities, the more risk can be avoided by diversification.

Most studies suggest that major capital markets are positively correlated with each other but that the correlation coefficients are in the range 0.5 to 0.8 ie significantly less than perfectly positively correlated. This creates significant opportunities for risk reduction through diversification.

A number of factors explain this, including the following:

(a) Different countries are often at **different stages of the trade cycle** at any one time.

(b) **Monetary, fiscal and exchange rate policies** differ internationally.

(c) Different countries have **different endowments of natural resources** and different industrial bases.

(d) Potentially **risky political events** are likely to be localised within particular national or regional boundaries.

(e) Securities markets in different countries differ considerably in the **combination of risk and return** which they offer.

3.10 International portfolio diversification – problems

Despite the potential benefits of international diversification there often remains a domestic bias among many types of investor, which can be attributed to a number of barriers to international investment, including the following:

(a) **Legal restrictions** exist in some markets, limiting ownership of securities by foreign investors.

(b) **Foreign exchange regulations** may prohibit international investment or make it more expensive.

(c) **Double taxation** of income from foreign investment may deter investors.

(d) There are likely to be higher **information and transaction costs** associated with investing in foreign securities.

(e) Some types of investor may have a parochial **home bias** for domestic investment.

(f) The risk of a change in exchange rates adversely affecting the investment's returns (**currency risk**).

Chapter Roundup

- **Risk** can be quantified in investment appraisal by using expected values. This technique is most suitable to risk-neutral decision-makers. Other techniques are needed for risk-averse decision-makers (maximin and minimax regret) and risk-seeking decision-makers (maximax).

- **Uncertainty** can be described using sensitivity analysis, which looks at the change that would be required in a single variable to change the investment decision.

- **Portfolio theory** takes account of the fact that many investors have a range of investments that are unlikely all to change values in step. The investor should be concerned with their overall position, not with the performance of individual investments.

- **Correlation** measures the degree to which the returns on investment vary with each other.

- Both individuals and firms diversify their investments. Individuals have **portfolios of shares** and firms have **portfolios of business operations** and **investments**. **Diversification** is equally an important consideration for the financial manager in making investment decisions.

- Reasons why companies should not diversify too far include their **lack of expertise in other industries** and **unfamiliarity with markets**. In particular diversification by investors is easier to achieve than diversification by companies.

LEARNING OUTCOME 2 THE INVESTMENT DECISION

Quick Quiz

1. Sensitivity analysis allows for uncertainty in project appraisal by assessing the probability of changes in the decision variables.

   ☐ True

   ☐ False

2. Minimax regret means that the decision-making will choose the project that has best worst case scenario, since this will minimise regret.

   ☐ True

   ☐ False

3. Identify five main factors an investor should consider in selecting investments.

4. If investments show high negative correlation, combining them in a portfolio will reduce risk overall.

   ☐ True

   ☐ False

5. Match each of A, B and C to its equivalent: one of 1, 2 or 3.

A	the expected return of a portfolio		1	the correlation coefficient of expected returns
B	relationship between returns from different investments		2	the standard deviation of expected returns
C	the risk of a portfolio		3	a weighted average of expected returns on portfolio investments

9: PORTFOLIO THEORY

Answers to Quick Quiz

1. False

    Sensitivity analysis does not assess the probability of changes in the decision variables.

2. False

    Minimax regret involves considering the maximum regret a decision-maker would have they have selected the incorrect project to invest in; the project selected will be the one that minimises this level of maximum regret. What is described in the question is Maximin.

3. Security; liquidity; return; risk; growth prospects

4. True

5. A3; B1; C2

LEARNING OUTCOME 2 THE INVESTMENT DECISION

End of chapter questions

1. Craxon

Craxon Co is appraising an investment project which has an expected life of four years and which will not be repeated.

Forecast sales and production volumes, and total nominal variable costs, have already been forecast, as follows:

Year	1	2	3	4
Sales and production (units)	300,000	500,000	800,000	600,000
Nominal variable cost ($'000)	4,770	8,400	14,160	11,460

Incremental overheads of $800,000 per year in current price terms will arise as a result of undertaking the investment project. A large proportion of these overheads relate to energy costs which are expected to increase sharply in the future because of energy supply shortages, so overhead inflation of 10% per year is expected.

The initial investment of $10m will attract tax-allowable depreciation on a straight-line basis over the four-year project life. The rate of corporation tax is 30% and tax liabilities are paid in the year in which they arise. Craxon Co has traditionally used a cost of capital of 11% per year for investment appraisal.

Scrap value of $1m is expected to arise at the end of 4 years.

There is some uncertainty about what price can be charged for the units produced by the investment project, as this is expected to depend on the future state of the economy. The following forecast of selling prices and their probabilities has been prepared:

Future economic state	Weak	Medium	Strong
Probability of future economic state	40%	45%	15%
Selling price in current price terms	$24 per unit	$30 per unit	$40 per unit

These selling prices are expected to be subject to annual inflation of 4% per year, regardless of which economic state prevails in the future.

Required

(a) Calculate the expected net present value of the investment project and comment on its financial acceptability. **(9 marks)**

(b) Explain how a company's attitude to risk would impact on the relevance of expected values in investment appraisal. **(5 marks)**

(c) Critically discuss if sensitivity analysis will assist Craxon Co in assessing the risk of the investment project.

(6 marks)

(Total = 20 marks)

2. Samson Conglomerates (AIA November 2009, amended)

The managing director of Samson Conglomerates has decided to establish a new subsidiary for the manufacture and sale of shoes. He has decided to form the subsidiary from the purchase of two existing companies both based in his own country. He has a finite amount to invest and has used 40% of this amount in purchasing ACom and 60% in purchasing BCom. The following are his estimates of the probability of the likely returns each company will give for the next year.

Possible annual rates of return		Probability of occurrence
ACom	BCom	
12%	15%	0.2
15%	20%	0.6
18%	25%	0.2

Because the two businesses are operating in the same markets he is expecting the correlation between the returns on the two companies to be virtually perfectly positive (ie +1).

The standard deviation of ACom's returns has been estimated as 1.90% and BCom's as 3.16%.

The managing director is also considering, alternatively, the purchase of two other companies – DCom and ECom. These two companies operate in completely different markets. DCom sells gourmet food products and ECom is a small bank. He expects that the return from DCom and ECom will be about the same as from ACom and BCom. But he expects that the standard deviation on DCom/ECom to be much lower than that for ACom/BCom.

Required

(a) Calculate the expected annual return and standard deviation from the portfolio of ACom/BCom.
(9 marks)

(b) Briefly explain, with reference to appropriate theory, why the standard deviation on DCom/ECom is expected to be lower than from ACom/BCom. **(7 marks)**

(c) Briefly discuss the advantages and disadvantages of diversification. **(4 marks)**

(Total 20 marks)

LEARNING OUTCOME 2 THE INVESTMENT DECISION

The capital asset pricing model

Topic list	Syllabus reference
1 Systematic and unsystematic risks	LO2
2 CAPM and beta factors	LO2
3 CAPM and portfolios	LO2
4 CAPM and investments	LO2
5 The arbitrage pricing model	LO2

Introduction

The **Capital Asset Pricing Model (CAPM)** brings together aspects of topics covered in other chapters: portfolio theory, share valuations and the cost of capital.

Make sure you can explain what **systematic** and **unsystematic risk** are and how CAPM can be used to measure **required returns** taking account of systematic risk.

LEARNING OUTCOME 2 THE INVESTMENT DECISION

1 Systematic and unsystematic risks

FAST FORWARD

> The **risk** involved in holding securities (shares) divides into **risk specific** to the company (unsystematic) and risk due to **variations** in **market activity** (systematic).
>
> **Unsystematic or business risk** can be diversified away, while **systematic or market risk** cannot. Investors may mix a diversified market portfolio with risk-free assets to achieve a preferred mix of risk and return.
>
> The required return on shares includes a **risk premium** in respect of **systematic risk** only.

1.1 Uses of the capital asset pricing model (CAPM)

(a) Trying to establish the 'correct' **equilibrium market** value of a company's shares

(b) Trying to establish the cost of a **company's equity** (and the company's average cost of capital), taking account of the risk characteristics of a company's investments, both business and financial risk

The CAPM thus provides an approach to establishing a cost of equity capital which is an alternative to the dividend valuation model. It relates risk to return.

1.2 Types of risk

Whenever an investor invests in some shares, or a company invests in a new project, there will be some risk involved. The actual return on the investment might be better or worse than that hoped for. To some extent, risk is unavoidable (unless investors settle for risk-free securities such as gilts).

Provided that investors diversify their investments in a suitably wide portfolio, the investments which perform well and those which perform badly should tend to cancel each other out, and much risk can be diversified away. In the same way, a company which invests in a number of projects will find that some do well and some do badly, but taking the whole portfolio of investments, average returns should turn out much as expected.

Key term

> **Market** or **systematic risk** is risk that cannot be diversified away. **Non-systematic** or **unsystematic risk** applies to a single investment or class of investments, and can be reduced by diversification.

(a) Risks that can be diversified away are referred to as **unsystematic risk** (a risk unique to the operations of an individual firm or sector).

(b) Some investments are by their very nature more risky than others. This has nothing to do with chance variations up or down in actual returns compared with what an investor should expect. This inherent risk – the **systematic risk** or **market risk** – cannot be diversified away (see Figure 1).

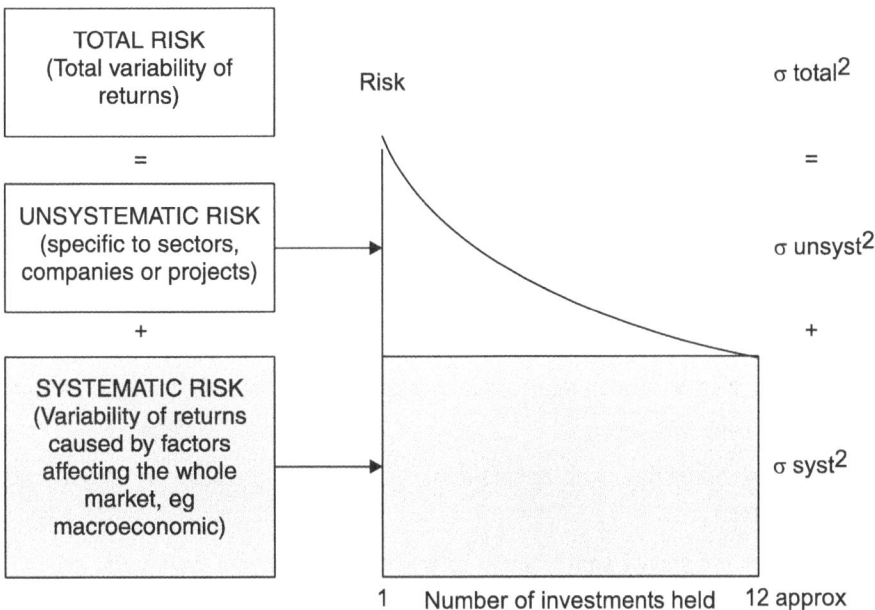

Figure 1

Systematic risk must be accepted by any investor, unless he invests entirely in risk-free investments. In return for accepting systematic risk, an investor will expect to earn a **return** which is **higher** than the return on a risk-free investment.

The amount of systematic risk in an investment varies between different types of investment. The systematic risk in the operating cash flows of a tourism company which will be highly sensitive to consumers' spending power might be greater than the systematic risk for a company which operates a chain of supermarkets.

Exam focus point

Common errors on this topic in exams include:

- Assuming risk-averse investors wish to eliminate risk. Risk-averse investors are prepared to accept risk, in exchange for higher returns
- Failing to link the risks of an investment with its returns
- Mixing up systematic and unsystematic risk

1.3 Systematic risk and unsystematic risk: implications for investments

If an investor holds shares in just a few companies, there will be some unsystematic risk as well as systematic risk in his portfolio, because he will not have spread his risk enough to diversify away the unsystematic risk. To eliminate unsystematic risk, he must build up a well-diversified portfolio of investments. If an investor holds a **balanced portfolio** of all the stocks and shares on the stock market, he will incur **systematic risk** which is exactly equal to the **average systematic risk** in the stock market as a whole.

Shares in individual companies will have systematic risk characteristics which are different to this market average. Some shares will be less risky and some will be more risky than the stock market average.

1.4 Systematic risk and the CAPM

The capital asset pricing model is mainly concerned with how **systematic risk is measured** (using **beta factors**) and with how systematic risk affects required returns and share prices.

LEARNING OUTCOME 2 THE INVESTMENT DECISION

CAPM theory includes the following propositions:

(a) Investors in shares require a return in **excess** of the **risk-free rate**, to compensate them for systematic risk.

(b) Investors should **not require** a **premium** for **unsystematic risk**, because this can be diversified away by holding a wide portfolio of investments.

(c) Because systematic risk varies between companies, investors will require a **higher return** from shares in those companies where the **systematic risk** is **greater**.

The same propositions can be applied to **capital investments by companies**.

(a) Companies will want a return on a project to **exceed** the **risk-free rate**, to compensate them for systematic risk.

(b) **Unsystematic risk** can be **diversified away**, and so a premium for unsystematic risk should not be required.

(c) Companies should want a **bigger return** on projects where **systematic risk is greater**.

1.5 Market risk and returns

Market risk (systematic risk) is the **average risk** of the **market as a whole**. Taking all the shares on a stock market together, the total expected returns from the market will vary because of systematic risk. The market as a whole might do well or it might do badly.

1.6 Risk and returns from an individual security

In the same way, an individual security may offer prospects of a return of x%, but with some risk (business risk and financial risk) attached. The return (the x%) that well-diversified investors will require from the individual security will be higher or lower than the market-return, depending on whether the security's systematic risk is greater or less than the market average.

A major assumption in CAPM is that there is a **linear relationship** between the return obtained from an individual security and the average return from all securities in the market.

1.7 Example: CAPM

The following information is available about the performance of an individual company's shares and the stock market as a whole.

	Individual company	Stock market as a whole
Price at start of period	105.0	480.0
Price at end of period	110.0	490.0
Dividend during period	7.6	39.2

The return on the company's shares (r_j) and the return on the 'market portfolio' of shares (r_m) may be calculated as:

$$\frac{\text{Capital gain (or loss) + dividend}}{\text{Price at start of period}}$$

$$r_j = \frac{(110 - 105) + 7.6}{105} = 0.12 \qquad r_m = \frac{(490 - 480) + 39.2}{480} = 0.1025$$

A statistical analysis of 'historic' returns from a security and from the 'average' market may suggest that a linear relationship can be assumed to exist between them. A series of comparative figures could be prepared (month by month) of the return from a company's shares and the average return of the market as a whole. The results could be drawn on a scattergraph and a 'line of best fit' drawn (using linear regression techniques) as shown in Figure 2. (Note that returns can be negative. A share price fall represents a capital loss, which is a negative return.)

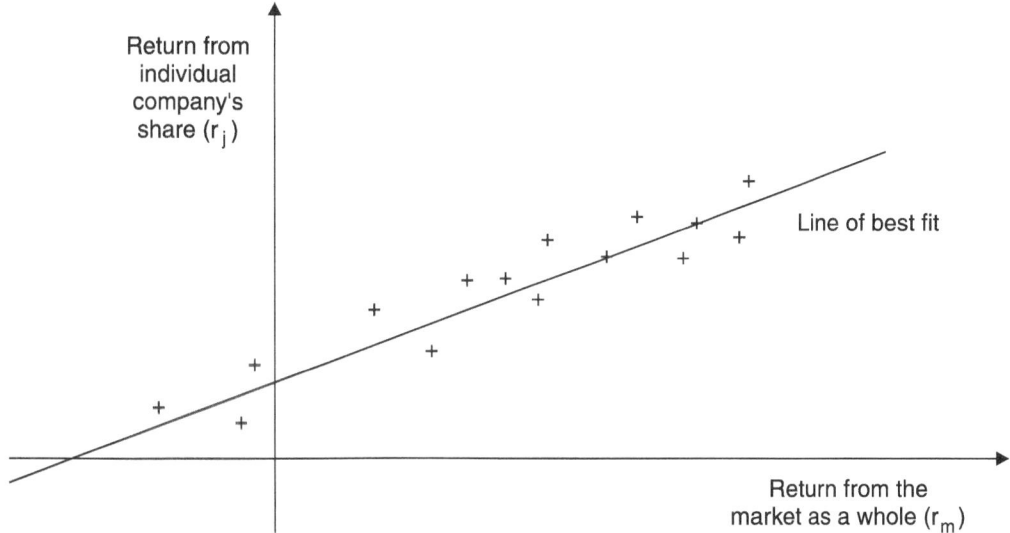

Figure 2

This analysis would show three things:

1   The return from the security (r_j) and the return from the market as a whole will tend to rise or fall together.

2   The return from the security may be higher or lower than the market return. This is because the systematic risk of the individual security differs from that of the market as a whole. The graph above corresponds to a security which is riskier than the market (higher returns).

3   The scattergraph may not give a good line of best fit, unless a large number of data items are plotted, because actual returns are affected by unsystematic risk as well as by systematic risk.

The conclusion from this analysis is that individual securities will be either more or less risky than the market average in a fairly predictable way. The measure of this relationship between market returns and an individual security's returns, reflecting differences in systematic risk characteristics, can be developed into a beta factor for the individual security.

2 CAPM and beta factors

FAST FORWARD

The **beta factor** measures a share's volatility in terms of **market risk.**

2.1 The beta factor and the market risk premium

Key term

A share's **beta factor** is the measure of its volatility in terms of market risk.

The beta factor of the **market as a whole** is **1.0**. Market risk makes market returns volatile and the beta factor is simply a basis or yardstick against which the risk of other investments can be measured.

For example, suppose that returns on shares in XYZ plc tend to vary twice as much as returns from the market as a whole, so that if market returns went up 3%, say, returns on XYZ plc shares would be expected to go up by 6% and if market returns fell by 3%, returns on XYZ plc shares would be expected to fall by 6%. The beta factor of XYZ plc shares would be 2.0.

LEARNING OUTCOME 2 THE INVESTMENT DECISION

Thus if the average market return rises by, say, 2%, the return from a share with a beta factor of 0.8 should rise by 1.6% in response to the **same conditions** which have caused the market return to change. The **actual return** from the share might rise by, say, 2.5%, or even fall by, say, 1%, but the difference between the actual change and a change of 1.6% due to general market factors would be attributed to unsystematic risk factors unique to the company or its industry.

It is an essential principle of CAPM theory that **unsystematic risk** can be **cancelled out** by **diversification**. In a well-balanced portfolio, an investor's gains and losses from the unsystematic risk of individual shares will tend to cancel each other out.

2.2 Beta levels

Risk free investments (government securities) have $\beta = 0$. Shares with $\beta > 1$ will do better than the market portfolio in a rising market, worse if the market is falling. Beta values are normally between 0 and 2.5.

2.3 CAPM: Betas and returns

FAST FORWARD

> The CAPM is based on a comparison of the **systematic risk** of **individual investments** with the **risks of all shares** in the **market**.

The CAPM makes use of the principle that returns on shares in the **market** as a whole are **expected** to be **higher than** the **returns on risk-free investments**. The difference between market returns and risk-free returns is called an **excess return**. For example, if the return on British Government stocks is 9% and market returns are 13%, the excess return on the market's shares as a whole is 4%.

The difference between the risk-free return and the expected return on an individual security can be **measured** as the excess return for the market as a whole multiplied by the **security's beta factor**.

Thus:

(a) If shares in DEF plc have a beta of 1.5 when the risk-free return is 9% and the expected market return is 13%, then the expected return on DEF plc shares would exceed the risk-free return by $(13 - 9) \times 1.5 = 6\%$ and the total expected return on DEF shares would be $(9 + 6)\% = 15\%$.

(b) If the market returns fall by 3% to 10%, say, the expected return on DEF plc shares would fall by $1.5 \times 3\% = 4.5\%$ to 10.5%, being $9\% + (10 - 9) \times 1.5\% = 10.5\%$.

2.4 The CAPM formula

The capital asset pricing model is a statement of the principles explained above. It can be stated as follows:

Exam formula

$$E(r_j) = r_f + (E(r_m) - r_f) \beta_j$$

where
- $E(r_j)$ is the expected return from an individual security or project
- r_f is the risk-free rate of return
- $E(r_m)$ is the expected return from the market as a whole
- β_j is the beta factor of the individual security or project
- $E(r_m) - r_f$ is the market premium for risk

The essence of this equation is for every beta, a required return can be calculated. Remember that the beta can be of anything; a share, a debt or a project. The principle is the same; given a beta, we can find a return.

Question CAPM

The expected market return ($E(r_m)$) is 12% and the risk-free rate of return is 9%. Deancourt plc's beta factor is 0.8. Calculate the cost of equity for Deancourt plc.

Answer

Cost of Deancourt plc equity = 9% + (12 − 9) × 0.8
= 11.4%

Exam focus point

A common mistake when using the formula is to take ($r_m - r_f$) to the power of beta, rather than multiplying it by the beta factor.

2.5 Alpha values

FAST FORWARD

The **alpha value** is a measure of a share's **abnormal return**.

Key term

A share's **alpha value** is a measure of its abnormal return, which is the amount by which the share's returns are currently above or below the required return, given the level of systematic risk.

The alpha value can be seen as a measure of how wrong the CAPM is.

Alpha values:

(a) Reflect only temporary, abnormal returns, if CAPM is a realistic model
(b) Can be positive or negative
(c) Over time, will tend towards zero for any individual share, and for a well-diversified portfolio taken as a whole will be 0
(d) May exist due to the inaccuracies and limitations of the CAPM

Exam focus point

In the exam you may be asked to compare the required return (calculated by CAPM) with the expected current return of the portfolio, and hence calculate the alpha value.

If the **alpha value** is **positive**, investors who don't hold shares will be tempted to buy them (to take advantage of the abnormal return), and investors who do hold shares will want to hold on to them so share prices will rise. If the **alpha value** is **negative**, investors won't want to buy them, and current holders will want to sell them, so share prices will fall.

Exam focus point

In the exam you may need to identify which share has the largest alpha value and hence is the most attractive investment.

2.5.1 Example: Alpha values

ABC plc's shares have a beta value of 1.2 and an alpha value of +2%. The market return is 10% and the risk-free rate of return is 6%.

Required return 6% + (10 − 6) × 1.2% = 10.8%

Current return = expected return + alpha value
= 10.8% + 2% = 12.8%

2.6 Alternatives to alpha values

2.6.1 Excess return to beta

This is useful for a well-diversified investor, measured by:

$$\frac{\text{Investment return} - \text{risk free rate}}{\text{Investment beta}}$$

2.6.2 Total risk

This is more appropriate for an investor who is not well-diversified, measured by:

$$\frac{\text{Investment return} - \text{risk free rate}}{\text{Standard deviation of returns}}$$

2.7 The CAPM and share prices

The CAPM can be used not only to estimate expected returns from securities with differing risk characteristics, but also to **predict the values of shares**.

2.7.1 Example: CAPM

Company X and Company Y both pay an annual cash return to shareholders of 34.048 pence per share and this is expected to continue in perpetuity. The risk-free rate of return is 8% and the current average market rate of return is 12%. Company X's β coefficient is 1.8 and Company Y's is 0.8. What is the expected return from Companies X and Y respectively, and what would be the predicted market value of each company's shares?

Solution

(a) The expected return for X is 8% + (12% − 8%) × 1.8 = 15.2%
(b) The expected return for Y is 8% + (12% − 8%) × 0.8 = 11.2%

The dividend valuation model can now be used to derive expected share prices.

(c) The predicted value of a share in X is $\frac{34.048p}{0.152}$ = 224 pence

(d) The predicted value of a share in Y is $\frac{34.048p}{0.112}$ = 304 pence

The actual share prices of X and Y might be higher or lower than 224p and 304p. If so, CAPM analysis would conclude that the share is currently either overpriced or underpriced.

Question — Expected return

The risk-free rate of return is 7%. The average market return is 11%.
(a) What will be the return expected from a share whose β factor is 0.9?
(b) What would be the share's expected value if it is expected to earn an annual dividend of 5.3p, with no capital growth?

Answer

(a) 7% + (11% − 7%) × 0.9 = 10.6%

(b) $\frac{5.3p}{10.6\%}$ = 50 pence

2.8 Problems with applying CAPM in practice

FAST FORWARD

Problems of CAPM include **unrealistic assumptions** and the **required estimates being difficult to make**.

(a) The need to determine the **excess return** ($E(r_m) - r_f$). (Forecast, rather than historical, returns should be used, although historical returns are used in practice.)

(b) The need to determine the **risk-free rate.** (A risk-free investment might be a government security. However, interest rates vary with the term of the lending.)

(c) **Errors** in the **statistical analysis** used to calculate β values.

(d) Beta factors based on historical data may be a poor basis for future decision-making. Evidence from a US study suggests that stocks with high or low betas tend to be fairly stable over time, but this may not always be so.

(e) Beta values may change over time, for example if luxury items produced by a company become regarded as necessities, or if the cost structure (eg the proportion of fixed costs) of a business change.

(f) The CAPM is also unable to forecast accurately returns for **companies with low price/earnings ratios** and to take account of **seasonal** 'month-of-the-year' or 'day-of-the-week' effects which appear to influence returns on shares. Beta factors measured over different timescales may differ.

(g) Financial managers should preferably use betas for industrial sectors rather than individual company betas, as measurement errors will tend to cancel each other out.

(h) CAPM fails to take into account the ways in which returns are paid; investors may have a preference for dividends or capital gains.

Some experts have argued that calculating betas by means of complicated statistical techniques often overestimates high betas, and underestimates low betas, particularly for small companies. Sometimes equations are used to adjust betas calculated statistically, such as:

Adjusted β = 0.5 (statistically calculated β) + 0.5

This sort of equation increases betas that are less than 1 and lowers betas higher than 1.

Exam focus point

The assumptions and limitations of CAPM are key discussion topics in this paper.

Question

Beta factor

(a) What does beta measure, and what do betas of 0.5, 1 and 1.5 mean?
(b) What factors determine the level of beta which a company may have?

Answer

(a) **Beta measures** the systematic risk of a risky investment such as a share in a company. The total risk of the share can be sub-divided into two parts, known as systematic (or market) risk and unsystematic (or unique) risk. The systematic risk depends on the sensitivity of the return of the share to general economic and market factors such as periods of boom and recession. The capital asset pricing model shows how the return which investors expect from shares should depend only on systematic risk, not on unsystematic risk, which can be eliminated by holding a well-diversified portfolio.

LEARNING OUTCOME 2 THE INVESTMENT DECISION

Beta is calibrated such that the average risk of stock market investments has a beta of 1. Thus shares with betas of 0.5 or 1.5 would have half or 1½ times the average sensitivity to market variations respectively.

This is reflected by higher volatility of share prices for shares with a beta of 1.5 than for those with a beta of 0.5. For example, a 10% increase in general stock market prices would be expected to be reflected as a 5% increase for a share with a beta of 0.5 and a 15% increase for a share with a beta of 1.5, with a similar effect for price reductions.

(b) The beta of a company will be the **weighted average** of the beta of its shares and the beta of its debt. The beta of debt is very low, but not zero, because corporate debt bears default risk, which in turn is dependent on the volatility of the company's cash flows.

Factors determining the beta of a company's equity shares include:

(i) **Sensitivity** of the company's **cash flows** to economic factors, as stated above. For example, sales of new cars are more sensitive than sales of basic foods and necessities.

(ii) The company's **operating gearing**. A high level of fixed costs in the company's cost structure will cause high variations in operating profit compared with variations in sales.

(iii) The company's **financial gearing**. High borrowing and interest costs will cause high variations in equity earnings compared with variations in operating profit, increasing the equity beta as equity returns become more variable in relation to the market as a whole. This effect will be countered by the low beta of debt when computing the weighted average beta of the whole company.

3 CAPM and portfolios

FAST FORWARD

The **expected return** of a portfolio of shares can be calculated by calculating the weighted beta of the portfolio and using CAPM.

3.1 Beta factors of portfolios

Just as an individual security has a beta factor, so too does a portfolio of securities.

(a) A portfolio consisting of all the **securities** on the **stock market** (in the same proportions as the market as a whole), excluding risk-free securities, will have an expected return equal to the expected return for the market as a whole, and so will have a **beta factor of 1**.

(b) A portfolio consisting entirely of **risk-free securities** will have a beta factor of **0**.

(c) The beta factor of an investor's portfolio is the **weighted average** of the **beta factors** of the securities in the **portfolio**.

3.2 Example: Beta factors and portfolios

A portfolio consisting of five securities could have its beta factor computed as follows:

Security	Percentage of portfolio	Beta factor of security	Weighted beta factor
A plc	20%	0.90	0.180
B plc	10%	1.25	0.125
C plc	15%	1.10	0.165
D plc	20%	1.15	0.230
E plc	35%	0.70	0.245
	100%	Portfolio beta =	0.945

If the risk-free rate of return is 12% and the average market return is 20%, the required return from the portfolio using the CAPM equation would be 12% + (20 – 12) × 0.945% = 19.56%

The calculation could have been made as follows:

Security	Beta factor	Expected return $E(r_j)$	Weighting %	Weighted return %
A plc	0.90	19.2	20	3.84
B plc	1.25	22.0	10	2.20
C plc	1.10	20.8	15	3.12
D plc	1.15	21.2	20	4.24
E plc	0.70	17.6	35	6.16
			100	19.56

3.3 CAPM and portfolio management

Practical **implications of CAPM theory for an investor** are as follows:

(a) He should decide what **beta factor** he would **like to have** for his portfolio. He might prefer a portfolio beta factor of greater than 1, in order to expect above-average returns when market returns exceed the risk-free rate, but he would then expect to lose heavily if market returns fall. On the other hand, he might prefer a portfolio beta factor of 1 or even less.

(b) He should seek to invest in shares with **low beta factors** in a **bear market**, when average market returns are falling. He should then also sell shares with high beta factors.

(c) He should seek to invest in shares with **high beta factors** in a **bull market**, when average market returns are rising.

3.3.1 International CAPM

The possibility of international portfolio diversification increases the opportunities available to investors.

If we assume that the international capital market is a **fully integrated market** like an enlarged domestic market, then we have an international CAPM formula as follows:

$E(r_j) = r_f + [E(r_w) - r_f]\beta_w$

where $E(r_w)$ is the expected return from the world market portfolio and β_w is a measure of the world systematic risk.

This analysis implies that the risk premium is proportional to the world systematic risk, β_w, and that investors can benefit from maximum diversification by investing in the world market portfolio consisting of all securities in the world economy. New risk and return combinations may be available.

In practice, such complete diversification will of course not be practicable. However, significant international diversification can be achieved by the following methods:

- Direct investment in companies in different countries
- Investments in multinational enterprises
- Holdings in unit trusts or investment trusts which are diversified internationally

3.3.2 Segmentation and integration

The international picture may be complicated by market segmentation. Segmentation is usually caused by government-imposed restrictions on the movement of capital, leading to restricted capital availability within a country or other geographical segment. Therefore:

- Returns on the same security may differ in different markets
- Some investments may only be available in certain markets

In a segmented market the parent company of a international group would use its own country's risk-free rate and market return in CAPM calculations.

In practice the situation that a multinational company faces will often not be completely integrated nor completely segmented. In this situation a multinational can use CAPM to estimate a local cost of equity and a world cost of equity, and use a cost of equity that is somewhere in between the two.

3.4 Limitations of the CAPM for the selection of a portfolio

Under the CAPM, the return required from a security is related to its systematic risk rather than its total risk. If we relax some of the assumptions upon which the model is based, then the total risk may be important. In particular, the following points should be considered.

(a) The model assumes that the **costs of insolvency** are **zero**, or in other words, that all **assets** can be **sold** at **going concern prices** and that there are no selling, legal or other costs. In practice, the costs of insolvency cannot be ignored. Furthermore, the risk of insolvency is related to a firm's total risk rather than just its systematic risk.

(b) The model assumes that the **investment market** is **efficient**. If it is not, this will limit the extent to which investors are able to eliminate unsystematic risk from their portfolios.

(c) The model also assumes that **portfolios are well diversified** and so need only be concerned with systematic risk. However, this is not necessarily the case, and undiversified or partly-diversified shareholders should also be concerned with unsystematic risk and will seek a total return appropriate to the total risk that they face.

4 CAPM and investments

FAST FORWARD

CAPM can be used to produce a **cost of capital** for an **investment project**, based on the systematic risk of that investment.

4.1 The use of CAPM for capital investment decisions

CAPM can also be used to determine the required return of a capital investment.

4.2 Example: Required return

Panda plc is all-equity financed. It wishes to invest in a project with an estimated beta of 1.5. The project has significantly different business risk characteristics from Panda's current operations. The project requires an outlay of £10,000 and will generate expected returns of £12,000.

The market rate of return is 12% and the risk-free rate of return is 6%.

Required

Estimate the minimum return that Panda will require from the project and assess whether the project is worthwhile, based on the figures you are given.

Solution

We do not need to know Panda's weighted average cost of capital, as the new project has different business characteristics from its current operations. Instead we use the capital asset pricing model so that:

Required return = 6 + 1.5(12 − 6)
= 15%

Expected return = $\dfrac{12{,}000 - 10{,}000}{10{,}000}$

= 20%

Thus the project is worthwhile, as expected return exceeds required return.

The CAPM produces a required return based on the expected return of the market, expected project returns, the risk-free interest rate and the variability of project returns relative to the market returns.

Its main advantage when used for investment appraisal is that it produces a **discount rate** which is based on the **systematic risk** of the individual investment. It can be used to compare projects of all different risk classes and is therefore superior to an NPV approach which uses only one discount rate for all projects, regardless of their risk.

The model was developed with respect to securities; by applying it to an investment within the firm, the company is assuming that the shareholder wishes **investments** to be evaluated as if they were securities in the capital market and thus assumes that all shareholders will hold diversified portfolios and will not look to the company to achieve diversification for them.

4.3 Limitations of using CAPM in investment decisions

(a) It is hard to estimate returns on projects under **different economic environments**, market returns under different economic environments and the probabilities of the various environments.

(b) The CAPM is really just a **single period model**. Few investment projects last for one year only and to extend the use of the return estimated from the model to more than one time period would require both project performance relative to the market and the economic environment to be reasonably stable.

In theory, it should be possible to apply the CAPM for each time period, thus arriving at successive discount rates, one for each year of the project's life. In practice, this would exacerbate the estimation problems mentioned above and also make the discounting process much more cumbersome.

(c) It may be **hard** to **determine** the **risk-free rate of return**, **systematic risk** and **expected return** on the market portfolio if that is volatile.

(d) **Complications in decision-making** (the need to consider other stakeholders' or the financial managers' own interests) cannot be modelled easily.

Problems in using the model for investment appraisal in an international context arise from the fact that where the company is raising funds and operating in a number of countries, it may be difficult to establish exactly what the **risk-free** and **market rates of return are**. The problems of estimation increase when the economic situation in more than one country has to be taken into account. In practice, an international company will normally base its calculations on conditions in its home country.

5 The arbitrage pricing model

FAST FORWARD

The **arbitrage pricing model** assumes that the return on securities is based on a number of independent factors.

5.1 CAPM and APM

Exam focus point

What is important here is to be aware that there are other models apart from the CAPM, and to know the benefits and limitations of the arbitrage pricing model relative to the CAPM.

The CAPM is seen as a useful analytical tool by financial managers as well as by financial analysts. However, critics suggest that the relationship between risk and return is more complex than the linear relationship assumed in the CAPM. One model which could replace the CAPM in the future is the **arbitrage pricing model** (APM).

5.2 Factors influencing APM

Unlike the CAPM, which analyses the returns on a share as a function of a single factor – the return on the market portfolio, the APM assumes that the return on each security is based on a number of **independent factors**.

The actual return r on any security is shown as:

$r = E(r_j) + \beta_1 F_1 + \beta_2 F_2 \ldots + e$

where $E(r_j)$ is the expected return on the security
β_1 is the sensitivity to changes in factor 1
F_1 is the difference between actual and expected values of factor 1
β_2 is the sensitivity to changes in factor 2
F_2 is the difference between actual and expected values of factor 2
e is a random term

Factor analysis is used to ascertain the factors to which security returns are sensitive. Four key factors identified by researchers have been:

- Unanticipated inflation
- Changes in the expected level of industrial production
- Changes in the risk premium on bonds (debentures)
- Unanticipated changes in the term structure of interest rates

It has been demonstrated that when no further arbitrage opportunities exist, the expected return $E(r_j)$ can be shown as:

$E(r_j) = r_f + \beta_1(r_1 - r_f) + \beta_2(r_2 - r_f) \ldots$

where r_f is the risk-free rate of return

r1 is the expected return on a portfolio with unit sensitivity to factor 1 and no sensitivity to any other factor

r2 is the expected return on a portfolio with unit sensitivity to factor 2 and no sensitivity to any other factor

5.3 APM in practice

With the APM, the CAPM's problem of identifying the market portfolio is avoided, but this is replaced with the problem of **identifying** the **macroeconomic factors** and their risk sensitivities. As is the case with the CAPM, what empirical evidence is available is inconclusive and neither proves nor disproves the theory of the APM. Both the CAPM and the APM do however provide a means of analysing how risk and return may be determined in conditions of competition and uncertainty.

10: THE CAPITAL ASSET PRICING MODEL

Chapter Roundup

- The **risk** involved in holding securities (shares) divides into **risk specific** to the company (unsystematic) and risk due to **variations** in **market activity** (systematic).
- **Unsystematic or business risk** can be diversified away, while **systematic or market risk** cannot. Investors may mix a diversified market portfolio with risk-free assets to achieve a preferred mix of risk and return.
- The required return on shares includes a **risk premium** in respect of **systematic risk** only.
- The **beta factor** measures a share's volatility in terms of **market risk**.
- The CAPM is based on a comparison of the **systematic risk** of **individual investments** with the **risks of all shares** in the **market**.
- The **alpha value** is a measure of a share's **abnormal return**.
- Problems of CAPM include **unrealistic assumptions** and the **required estimates being difficult to make**.
- The **expected return** of a portfolio of shares can be calculated by calculating the weighted beta of the portfolio and using CAPM.
- CAPM can be used to produce a **cost of capital** for an **investment project**, based on the systematic risk of that investment.
- The **arbitrage pricing model** assumes that the return on securities is based on a number of independent factors.

Quick Quiz

1 Which of the following is unsystematic risk, and which systematic risk?

   A   Risks specific to sectors, companies or projects
   B   Risk caused by market or macroeconomic factors

2 Which type of risk is reflected by which model? (Answer Yes/No in each case)

	Systematic	Unsystematic risk
Dividend valuation model	(1) Y/N	(2) Y/N
CAPM	(3) Y/N	(4) Y/N

3 Is unsystematic risk measured using beta factors?

4 Define the terms in the CAPM formula: $Ke = R_f + [R_m - R_f]\beta$

5 Only an individual security can have a beta factor – not a portfolio of investments. True/False?

6 What is a share's alpha value?

7 Give three assumptions that lie behind the proposition in the capital asset pricing model that a security's return is related to its systematic risk.

8 What is the main difference between CAPM and the arbitrage pricing model?

Answers to Quick Quiz

1. A = Unsystematic risk   B = Systematic risk

2. (1)Y, (2)Y, (3)Y, (4)N

3. No. Beta factors measure systematic risk.

4. K_e = the cost of equity/expected return on a security
   R_m = the return from the market as a whole
   $[R_m - R_f]$ = market premium
   R_f = the risk-free rate of return
   β = the beta factor of the security

5. False

6. An alpha value is a measure of a share's abnormal return.

7. The costs of insolvency are zero; The investment market is efficient; Individual portfolios are well-diversified.

8. CAPM analyses returns on shares as a function of the return on the market portfolio. The arbitrage pricing model assumes that returns are influenced by a number of independent factors.

End of chapter questions

1. Core plc (AIA May 2012)

Core plc is a listed company specialising in the construction of office accommodation. The company is currently financed by both debt and equity as follows:

The company has 160m shares in issue and the current market value of each share is £2.45.

The company has a long-term loan that is irredeemable. This loan has a nominal value of £450m and a market value of £480m. The interest rate on this loan is 5.5%.

The company has just paid a dividend of 14.0 pence per share. The dividends paid in the recent past have been as follows:

	Dividend per share
Dividend paid one year ago	13.4 pence
Dividend paid two years ago	12.6 pence
Dividend paid three years ago	12.1 pence

The equity beta for Core plc is 1.15

The tax rate applicable to the company is 20%

The risk-free rate is 4% and the expected return from the market is 8.5%

Core plc is considering expanding by acquiring another company, Oxton plc. Oxton plc manufactures office furniture and has an approximate market value of £90m. Core plc would raise additional borrowings to fund the acquisition. Oxton plc has a similar gearing level to Core plc and its equity beta is estimated to be 1.35. The directors of Core plc did attempt an acquisition that would have diversified the company's operations into a very different business area in the recent past. However, shareholder reaction to this venture was very mixed and the directors decided not to go ahead with the plan.

Required

(a) Calculate the weighted average cost of capital (WACC) for Core plc using the dividend growth model to calculate the cost of equity. **(8 marks)**

(b) Calculate the weighted average cost of capital (WACC) for Core plc using the capital asset pricing model to calculate the cost of equity. **(4 marks)**

(c) Advise the directors whether it is appropriate for Core plc to assess the net present value of the project using its current weighted average cost of capital (WACC) given the above circumstances.
(8 marks)

(Total 20 marks)

2. Hesco and Asarco (AIA November 2008)

Hesco is a large UK based supermarket with stores located in fifteen different countries. Its dividend yield is 2.2% based on its current share price of 390p. Its dividend has grown by an average of 9% per year for the last five years – which is just slightly lower than that of the earnings per share over the same period. Hesco's share price has more or less doubled over the last five years and has a beta factor of 0.83.

Asarco is a company providing facilities management and engineering services. It has a beta factor of 0.90. Its dividend yield is 1.1% based on its current share price of 449p. The dividend has grown by an average of 16.5% per year for the last five years – which is lower than the earnings per share at 22% per year over the same period. Asarco's share price has increased by more than five times over the last five years.

Required

(a) Analyse the basic differences in the theories underlying the Capital Asset Pricing Model and the Dividend Valuation Model. **(6 marks)**

(b) Assuming that the current risk free rate of return and the required market return are 5% and 13% respectively calculate the cost of capital for both companies using both the Capital Asset Pricing Model and the Dividend Valuation Model. **(10 marks)**

(c) Analyse the figures you have produced in b) and explain which of the two models is likely to be most applicable to each company in the above scenario? **(4 marks)**

(Total 20 marks)

LEARNING OUTCOME 2 THE INVESTMENT DECISION

Capital structure and advanced valuation techniques

Topic list	Syllabus reference
1 Financial risk, gearing and the cost of capital	LO2
2 Choosing a capital structure	LO2
3 Traditional theory of gearing	LO2
4 Modigliani Miller (MM) theory without taxation	LO2
5 Modigliani Miller theory adjusted for taxation	LO2
6 The adjusted present value method	LO2
7 Adjusted cost of capital	LO2
8 CAPM and MM combined – geared betas	LO2

Introduction

This chapter begins by considering what determines a company's choice of capital structure.

We then move on to consider the impact of capital structure on the cost of capital. The practical application of this comes in Sections 6-8 where we consider various ways of incorporating the effects of changing capital structure into cost of capital and net present value calculations.

LEARNING OUTCOME 2 THE INVESTMENT DECISION

1 Financial risk, gearing and the cost of capital

FAST FORWARD

Financial gearing or **leverage** is the increased variability of earnings resulting from having debt in the capital structure.

1.1 Financial gearing

A high level of debt creates financial risk. The **financial risk** of a company's capital structure can be measured by a gearing ratio. The method of calculating a gearing ratio which is appropriate for investment evaluation is one based on market values. **Capital gearing** can be measured as:

$$\frac{\text{Market value of debt (including preference shares)}}{\text{Market value of equity + market value of debt}} \text{ or } \frac{D}{D+E}$$

Because of the financial risk associated with gearing, higher gearing will increase the rate of return required by ordinary shareholders, and may also affect the yield required by long-term creditors. It follows that a company's gearing level could have a bearing on its weighted average cost of capital.

Knowledge brought forward from earlier studies

Practical limits to financial gearing

Financial gearing can reach very high levels, with companies preferring to raise additional capital for expansion by means of loans rather than issuing new equity, but there are limits.

- Restrictions on further borrowing might be contained in the debenture trust deed for a company's current debenture stock in issue
- Occasionally, there might be borrowing restrictions in the Articles of Association
- Lenders might want **security** for extra loans which the would-be borrower cannot provide
- Lenders might simply be unwilling to lend more to a company with high gearing/low interest cover
- Extra borrowing beyond a safe level will cost more in interest. Companies might not be **willing** to borrow at these rates

Policies to lower a company's financial gearing ratio might include the following:

- Revaluation of non-current assets (to boost book values)
- Place a value on brands, if any
- Tighten control over working capital
- Issue more shares

1.2 Gearing, project appraisal and the source of funds to finance a new project

A project which has a positive NPV when its cash flows are discounted at the WACC might be financially harmful to shareholders if it is financed in the wrong way. This suggestion can be taken one step further.

If a project is viable (has a positive NPV) when it is discounted at the current WACC, then it would be worthwhile provided that the new funds which are raised to finance it leave the company's WACC unchanged.

1.3 Gearing and shareholders' investment decisions

The value of equity is related, not only to the size of dividends and the cost of equity, but also to the weighted average cost of capital. We will assume that a shareholder would be prepared to accept a change in the gearing of a company, and therefore a change in the required rate of return for equity, provided that the effect of this change in gearing would be to increase the value of his shares, or at the very least to leave them unchanged.

2 Choosing a capital structure

> **FAST FORWARD**
>
> **Static trade-off theory** states that the debt-equity choice of finance decision will be determined by where a company is in relation to its ideal structure.
>
> **Pecking order theory** states that firms will prefer to use retained earnings, then debt, then equity to minimise issue costs, respond to investor preferences and send positive messages to the stock market.

2.1 Investments financed by retained profits

If for some reason there is a limit to the number of new shares that a company can issue to its shareholders and a company could undertake many projects with positive net present values, then **reducing its dividend payment** would **increase the supply of capital** available. Even though in the short term dividends will be reduced, this will be more than compensated for in the long term by the fact that extra cash inflows generated by the investments will **increase dividends** in the future. Indeed, it can be argued that no dividends should be paid until all projects with positive net present values have been financed.

In this situation, the shareholders would benefit from a sudden rise in the price equal to the net present value of the new project as soon as the project was accepted. This would only happen if there is a **strong form efficient market**, or if **dividend forecasts** are **published** and are **believed**. Furthermore, shareholders do not necessarily make rational decisions, so market values may not in practice respond to changes in future dividend expectations.

2.2 Traditional and static trade-off theory

Even if an optimum capital structure exists in theory, it is another issue whether managers aim towards it in practice. Various views backed by studies of businesses practices have been put forward.

The **static trade-off** view develops the traditional theory and states that firms will aim for an **ideal capital structure**, and will issue debt or equity depending on what their current position is in relation to their ideal position.

However, it seems that the **most successful** companies in some industries are those that have the **lowest gearing**. The companies that most actively seek a return to target optimum capital structure are often those with a very high level of debt who are not the leading participants in their markets.

It appears also that some companies will be prepared to move away from their ideal capital structure by issuing debt to take advantage of **large and profitable investment opportunities**, but will move back towards their optimum structure in the longer term.

2.3 Pecking order theory

Pecking order theory has been developed as an alternative to traditional theory. It states that firms will prefer retained earnings to any other source of finance, and then will choose debt, and last of all the issue of new equity shares.

The order of preference will be:

- Retained earnings
- Straight debt
- Convertible debt
- Preference shares
- Equity shares

2.3.1 Reasons for following pecking order

(a) It is easier to **use retained earnings** than go to the trouble of obtaining external finance and have to live up to the demands of external finance providers.

(b) There are **no issue costs** if retained earnings are used, and the issue costs of debt are lower than those of equity.

(c) Investors prefer **safer securities**, that is debt with its guaranteed income and priority on liquidation.

(d) Some managers believe that debt issues have a better **signalling effect** than equity issues because the market believes that managers are better informed about shares' true worth than the market itself. Their view is the market will interpret debt issues as a sign of confidence, that businesses are confident of making sufficient profits to fulfil their obligations on debt and that they believe that the shares are **undervalued**.

By contrast, the market will interpret equity issues as a measure of last resort, that managers believe that equity is currently **overvalued** and hence are trying to achieve high proceeds while they can.

However, an issue of debt may **imply a similar lack of confidence** to an **issue of equity**; managers may issue debt when they believe that the **cost of debt** is **low** due to the market underestimating the risk of default and hence undervaluing the risk premium in the cost of debt. If the market recognises this lack of confidence, it is likely to respond by raising the cost of debt.

The main consequence in this situation will to be **reinforce a preference** for **using retained earnings first**. However, debt (particularly less risky, secured debt) will be the next source as the market feels more confident about valuing it than more risky debt or equity.

2.3.2 Consequences of pecking order theory

(a) Businesses will try to match **investment opportunities** with **internal finance** provided this does not mean excessive changes in dividend payout ratios.

(b) If it is **not possible** to **match investment opportunities** with **internal finance**, surplus internal funds will be invested; if there is a deficiency of internal funds, external finance will be issued in the pecking order, starting with straight debt.

(c) Establishing an **ideal debt-equity mix** will be problematic, since internal equity funds will be the first source of finance that businesses choose, and external equity funds the last.

2.3.3 Limitations of pecking order theory

(a) It fails to take into account **taxation, financial distress, agency costs** or how the **investment opportunities** that are available may influence the choice of finance.

(b) Pecking order theory is an explanation of what businesses **actually** do, rather than what they **should** do.

Studies suggest that the businesses that are most likely to follow pecking order theory are those that are **operating profitably** in markets where **growth prospects** are **poor**. There will thus be limited opportunities to invest funds, and these businesses will be content to rely on retained earnings for the limited resources that they need.

2.4 Behavourial theories

A number of studies have suggested that businesses pursue rules of thumb or behaviour patterns:

(a) The **herd theory** states that businesses will stick closely to the industry average capital structure. Of course, the average may hide wide variations that are acceptable to different companies. However, there is evidence to suggest that companies that are significantly more highly geared than the industry average will have difficulty obtaining further debt finance.

(b) **Benchmarking** occurs, where businesses identify a leader in their market and adopt a similar capital structure. However, the capital structure that is appropriate for the market leader with the investment opportunities that it faces may not be appropriate for the less successful businesses in that industry.

(c) **Past experience** may be an important influence. The argument is that managers are aware of the advantages and disadvantages of both equity and debt, and choose the source of finance that experience suggests will cause them few or no problems.

3 Traditional theory of gearing

> **FAST FORWARD**
>
> Both traditional and MM theories agree that:
> - The optimal level of financial gearing will be that at which the WACC is minimised
> - The cost of equity increases as financial gearing increases
>
> Under the **traditional theory of cost of capital**, the cost declines initially and then rises as gearing increases. The **optimal capital structure** will be the point at which WACC is lowest, at a level somewhere between 0% and 100% gearing.

3.1 Assumptions of gearing theories

There are two main theories about the effect of changes in gearing on the weighted average cost of capital (WACC) and share values. These are the **'traditional' view**, and the **net operating income approach** (Modigliani and Miller).

The assumptions on which these theories are based are as follows:

(a) The company **pays out** all its **earnings** as **dividends**.

(b) The **gearing** of the company can be **changed immediately** by issuing debt to repurchase shares, or by issuing shares to repurchase debt. There are no transaction costs for issues.

(c) The **earnings** of the company are **expected to remain constant in perpetuity** and all investors share the same expectations about these future earnings.

(d) **Business risk** is also **constant**, regardless of how the company invests its funds.

(e) **Taxation**, for the time being, is **ignored**.

3.2 The traditional view of WACC

The **traditional view** is as follows:

(a) As the **level of gearing increases** the **cost of debt** remains **unchanged** up to a certain level of gearing. Beyond this level, the cost of debt will increase.

(b) The **cost of equity** rises as the level of **gearing increases**.

(c) The **weighted average cost of capital** does **not remain constant**, but rather falls initially as the proportion of debt capital increases, and then begins to increase as the rising cost of equity (and possibly of debt) becomes more significant.

(d) The **optimum level of gearing** is where the **company's weighted average cost of capital is minimised**.

The traditional view about the cost of capital is illustrated in Figure 1. It shows that the weighted average cost of capital will be minimised at a particular level of gearing P.

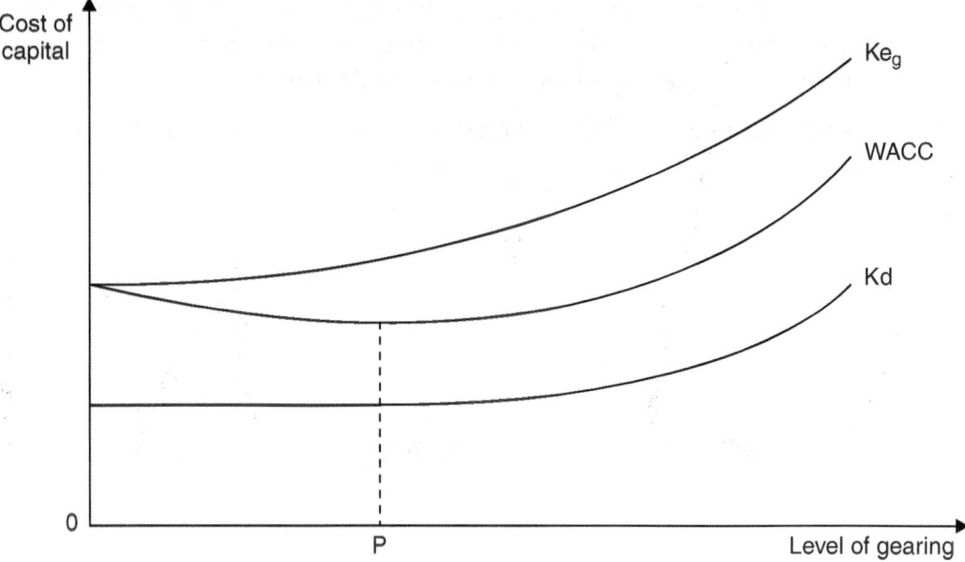

Figure 1

Ke_g is the cost of equity in the geared company
Kd is the cost of debt
WACC is the weighted average cost of capital

The traditional view is that the weighted average cost of capital, when plotted against the level of gearing, is saucer shaped. The optimum capital structure is where the weighted average cost of capital is lowest, at point P.

3.3 Example: Traditional approach

Gearing plc has the following capital structure (no tax):

		Constant annual payments to investors £m	Market value £m
Equity	dividends	27	150
Debt	interest	3	30
		30	180

The current cost of equity is thus: $K_e = \dfrac{D_0}{P_0} = \dfrac{27}{150} = 18\%$

The current cost of debt is thus: $K_d = \dfrac{i}{P_0} = \dfrac{3}{30} = 10\%$

Thus the WACC is: $\dfrac{150}{180} \times 18\% + \dfrac{30}{180} \times 10\% = 16.67\%$

Note. That in the case of constant dividends and interest, the WACC can be computed as

$$\text{WACC} = \dfrac{\text{Total payments to investors}}{\text{Total MV}} = \dfrac{£30m}{£180m} = 16.67\%$$

Conversely, discounting the total payments to investors by the WACC in perpetuity can derive the total MV:

$$\text{Total MV} = \dfrac{\text{Total payments to investors}}{\text{WACC}} = \dfrac{£30m}{0.1667} = £180m$$

Current gearing level, equity:debt, is 150:30 or 5:1

Now suppose the gearing is to be increased to (1) 3:1 or (2) 3:2 by the repurchase of shares, funded by new debt. It is estimated that the cost of equity will rise to compensate for the increase gearing risk, by (1) 0.75% and (2) 3%, and that the cost of debt will rise, in the case of (2) only, by 0.5%.

What are the effects on WACC and total MV of each change?

New WACC under (1): $\dfrac{3}{4} \times 18.75\% + \dfrac{1}{4} \times 10\% = 16.56\%$

and, since total payments to investors will be unchanged,

total MV under (1) $= \dfrac{£30m}{0.1656} = £181.16m$

New WACC under (2): $\dfrac{3}{5} \times 21\% + \dfrac{2}{5} \times 10.5\% = 16.8\%$

Total MV under (2) $= \dfrac{£30m}{0.168} = £178.57m$

Method (1), with the lower increase in gearing, had a small associated increase in the cost of equity, and the WACC went down – the impact of more cheaper debt outweighed the effect of the increased cost of equity. This led to a rise in the total MV.

Under Method (2), with the percentage of total capital represented by debt more than doubling, there was a much higher increase in the cost of equity, accompanied by an increase in the cost of debt. Despite the much higher proportion of cheap debt, the WACC went up, and the total MV fell.

3.4 Costs of high gearing

There are a number of potential costs of high gearing which would appear to support the traditional approach; investors will be worried about these costs and as a result demand a higher cost of capital.

3.4.1 Bankruptcy costs

The market value of a company may be decreased by the **expected present value of bankruptcy costs**. Bankruptcy costs include **legal and liquidation costs** and the costs of making staff redundant. Also if assets have to be sold on liquidation, they may realise less than their market value in 'normal' times.

Market value may also be restricted by the fact that in a financially precarious situation, managers have to spend a lot of time keeping **creditors happy rather than pursuing profitable investments**. Other impacts include stakeholder problems; it may be difficult for the company to keep employees who are anxious about working for a company in financial distress, and to find suppliers who are willing to take the risk of not being paid. There can be a long-term and ultimately fatal drag on the company's market value.

3.4.2 Agency costs

Agency costs are the opportunity costs caused by restrictions placed by lenders. In previous chapters we discussed how shareholder and creditor interest may not coincide and covered the covenants lenders include in loan agreements to protect their own interests.

3.4.3 Tax exhaustion

We shall see under the alternative (Modigliani and Miller) view of cost capital, a company's value is increased by the **tax benefits** it obtains from paying tax-allowable interest rather than dividends which are not tax allowable. However, beyond a certain level of gearing paid the interest will be greater than the taxable profits available for offset, and the company will cease to derive benefits from the tax allowance on interest. The situation may also be complicated by the capital allowances the company claims, which themselves are a function of the level of investment.

3.4.4 Sustainability issues

Excessive debt leads to high interest payments, these payments divert resources away from sustainability (ESG) initiatives and other critical areas like innovation which may be crucial for the long-term health of a company.

Debt often comes with repayment deadlines. Companies may prioritise short-term financial goals over long-term sustainability efforts.

However, it is also true that over-reliance on equity can create sustainability issues as companies relying solely on equity may face funding gaps during market downturns, affecting their ability to invest in sustainable practices. Also, as discussed in Chapter 2, pressure to pay dividends can also hinder investments in sustainability. So, from a ESG / sustainability perspective there is an argument for having a balance of debt and equity finance and to utilise green finance where possible (see Chapter 2).

4 Modigliani Miller (MM) theory without taxation

> **FAST FORWARD**
>
> Modigliani and Miller stated that a company's **capital structure** would have **no impact** upon its WACC. **Ignoring corporate tax**, the rise in the cost of equity as gearing rises would offset exactly the benefits of an increasing proportion of low-cost debt capital, resulting in a constant WACC.

4.1 The net operating income (MM) view of WACC

The net operating income approach takes a different view of the effect of gearing on WACC. In their 1958 theory, Modigliani and Miller (MM) proposed that the total market value of a company, in the absence of tax, will be determined only by two factors:

- The **total earnings** of the company
- To **level of operating (business) risk** attached to those earnings

The total market value would be computed by discounting the total earnings at a rate that is appropriate to the level of operating risk. This rate would represent the WACC of the company.

Thus Modigliani and Miller concluded that **the capital structure of a company would have no effect on its overall value of WACC.**

Modigliani and Miller made various assumptions in arriving at this conclusion, including:

- A **perfect capital market**, in which investors have the same information, upon which they act rationally, to arrive at the same expectations about future earnings and risks
- No **tax or transaction costs**
- **Debt being risk-free** and freely available at the same cost to investors and companies alike

Modigliani and Miller justified their approach by the use of **arbitrage**.

4.2 Example: Arbitrage

Consider two companies, Ordinary plc and Levered plc, in the same risk class, which are identical in all respects except that Ordinary plc is financed entirely by equity whereas the capital structure of Levered plc includes £40,000 of debt at 8% interest. We will assume that the annual earnings of both companies (before interest) are the same, £20,000, and we will begin by considering the traditional view of the cost of capital, and suppose that the cost of equity in the unlevered company is 13½%, and in the levered company, it is higher at 14%.

The market valuation of each company, according to the traditional view, would be as follows:

	Ordinary plc £	Levered plc £
Annual earnings	20,000	20,000
Less interest	–	3,200
Available for equity (earnings = dividends)	20,000	16,800
Cost of equity	0.135	0.14
	£	£
Market value of equity	148,148	120,000
Market value of debt	–	40,000
Market value of company	148,148	160,000
Weighted average cost of capital (PBIT ÷ market value)	13.5%	12.5%
Gearing ratio	0%	25%

How would arbitrage work in this situation?

Solution

The two companies, identical in every respect except their gearing, are therefore assumed by the traditional view to have different market values. MM argue that this situation could not last for long because investors in Levered plc would soon see that they could get the same return for a smaller investment by investing in Ordinary plc. Exercising arbitrage, they would **sell their shares** in **Levered plc** and **buy shares** in **Ordinary plc**.

This sale would **drive up** the **price of Ordinary plc shares** (thereby lowering the cost of its equity capital) and **force down** the **price of Levered plc** shares (thereby raising the cost of its equity capital) until the total market value of each company is the same. Arbitrage would then cease.

Arbitrage would occur as follows. Suppose Mr Onepercent owns 1% of the equity in Levered plc. These would have a market value of (1% × £120,000) = £1,200. He would notice that Ordinary plc makes the same annual earnings as Levered plc (£20,000) but with a smaller investment (£148,148 compared to £160,000). He would therefore take the following steps:

(a) He would sell his shares in Levered plc for £1,200.

(b) He would borrow £400 at 8% interest. This amount is equivalent to 1% of the debt of Levered plc (£40,000 at 8%). In this way, Mr Onepercent would have substituted personal gearing for the corporate gearing of Levered plc. His assets would be as follows.

£	
1,200	from the sale of his shares
400	borrowed at 8%
1,600	which is 1 % of the value of Levered plc

His personal gearing ratio (400/1,600 = 25%) is the same as the gearing ratio of Levered plc, and so MM would argue that his financial risk is in no way changed by this process of arbitrage.

(c) He would then buy 1% of the equity of Ordinary plc for £148,148 × 1% = £1,481.48. To do this, he would use the borrowed £400 plus £1081.48 of his own money.

(d) His annual earnings from Ordinary plc would be as follows.

	£
1% of £20,000	200
Less the interest he must repay on his personal loan (8% of £400)	32
Net earnings	168

This is exactly the same as he would earn from keeping 1% of the equity of Levered plc (1% of £16,800) but he can earn this from a smaller net investment of £1,081.48 rather than £1,200.

(e) Alternatively, if he spends the entire £1,600 in purchasing shares of Ordinary plc, his annual earnings would be a dividend of:

$$\frac{1,600}{148,148} \times £20,000 = £216 \text{ less loan repayments of £32, leaving him with £184}$$

which is £16 more than he currently earns from his Levered plc investment.

Rational investors will continue to **substitute personal** gearing for **corporate gearing**, and **buy shares** in **Ordinary plc**, until the price of these shares has risen, the price of Levered plc shares has fallen, and the market values of the two companies are the same. At this point:

(a) The **cost of equity** in the company with the **higher gearing** (Levered plc) will be **higher** than the cost of equity in the other company.

(b) Both the **market values** and the **annual earnings** of the companies are the same, therefore the **weighted average costs of capital** must be the **same**, despite the difference in gearing.

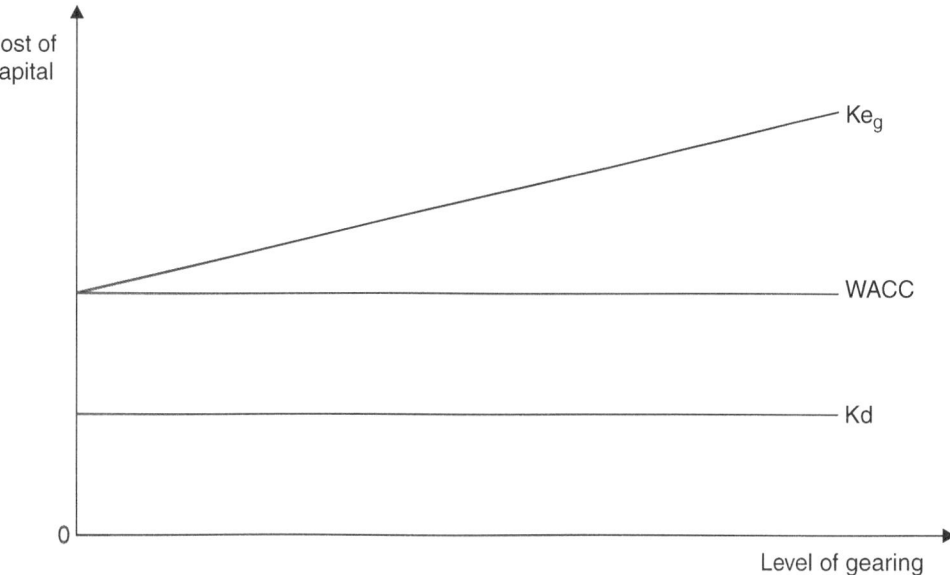

Figure 2

4.3 Implications of MM

If Modigliani and Miller's theory holds, it implies:

(a) The **cost of debt remains unchanged** as the **level of gearing increases**.
(b) The **cost of equity rises** in such a way as to **keep the weighted average cost of capital constant**.

This would be represented on a graph as shown in Figure 2.

The conclusion of the net operating income approach is that the **level of gearing** is a **matter of indifference** to an investor, because it does not affect the market value of the company, nor of an individual share.

4.4 The Modigliani Miller propositions, ignoring taxes

In setting out the proposition, we shall ignore tax relief on the interest charged on debt capital. The following symbols will be used:

MV_u = the market value of an ungeared (all equity) company

D = the market value of the debt capital in a geared company which is similar in every respect to the ungeared company (same profits before interest and same business risk) except for its capital structure. The debt capital is assumed, for simplicity, to be irredeemable.

E = the market value of the equity in the geared company

Ke_u = the cost of equity in an ungeared company

Ke_g = the cost of equity in the geared company

Kd = the cost of debt capital

The total market value of the geared company V_g is then equal to (E + D).

4.4.1 The total market value of a company and the WACC (ignoring taxation)

MM suggested that the total market value of any company is independent of its capital structure, and is given by discounting its expected return at the appropriate rate. The value of a geared company is therefore as follows:

$MV_g = MV_u$

LEARNING OUTCOME 2 THE INVESTMENT DECISION

$$MV_g = \frac{\text{Profit before interest}}{\text{WACC } (= K_e)}$$

$$MV_u = MV_g = \frac{\text{Earnings in an ungeared company}}{K_{e_u}}$$

Note that since WACC is unaltered by gearing, WACC = Ke under this theory.

4.4.2 The cost of equity in a geared company (ignoring taxation)

MM went on to argue that **the expected return on a share in a geared company** equals the expected cost of equity in a similar but ungeared company, plus a premium related to **financial risk**.

The **premium for financial risk** can be calculated as the debt/equity ratio multiplied by the difference between the cost of equity for an ungeared company and the risk-free cost of debt capital.

Formula to learn

$$Ke_g = Ke_u + \left((Ke_u - K_d)\frac{D}{E}\right)$$

Note the following points:

(a) The part of the formula to the right of the plus sign is the **value** of the **premium** for financial risk.

(b) The formula requires the **debt ratio** (debt:equity) to be used rather than the more common debt: (debt + equity).

(c) **Market** values are **used**, not book values.

4.5 Example: MM, ignoring taxation (1)

The cost of equity in Minehead plc, an all equity company, is 15%. The WACC is therefore also 15%.

Another company, Dunster plc, is identical in every respect to the first, except that it is geared, with a debt:equity ratio of 1:4. The cost of debt capital is 5% and this is a risk-free cost of debt. What is Dunster plc's WACC?

Solution

$Ke_g = 15\% + ((15 - 5)\% \times ¼) = 17.5\%$.

	Weighting	Cost	Product
Equity	80%	17.5%	14%
Debt	20%	5.0%	1%
		WACC =	15%

The WACC in the geared company is the same as in the ungeared company.

4.6 Example: MM, ignoring taxation (2)

Loesch plc is an all equity company and its cost of equity is 12%.

Berelco plc is similar in all respects to Loesch plc, except that it is a geared company, financed by £1,000,000 of 3% debentures (current market price £50 per cent) and 1,000,000 ordinary shares (current market price £1.50 ex div).

What is Berelco's cost of equity and weighted average cost of capital?

Solution

$$Kd = 3\% \times \frac{100}{50} = 6\%$$

$$Ke_g = 12\% + \left((12\% - 6\%) \times \frac{500}{1,500}\right) = 14\%$$

	Market value £'000		Cost		£'000
Equity	1,500	×	0.14	=	210
Debt	500	×	0.06	=	30
	2,000				240

$$WACC = \frac{240}{2,000} = 0.12 = 12\%$$

This is the same as Loesch plc's WACC. As gearing is introduced, the cost of equity rises, but in such a way that the WACC does not change.

5 Modigliani Miller theory adjusted for taxation

FAST FORWARD

With taxation, the tax relief available on debt will, according to MM, cause the WACC to fall, right up perhaps to a 100% level of gearing. This suggests that companies should gear to as high a level as possible.

5.1 Impact of tax relief

So far, our analysis of MM theory has ignored the **tax relief on debt interest**, which makes debt capital cheaper to a company, and therefore reduces the weighted average cost of capital where a company has debt in its capital structure.

MM modified their theory to admit that **tax relief** on **interest payments** does **lower the weighted average cost of capital**. They claimed that the weighted average cost of capital will continue to fall, up to very high levels of gearing.

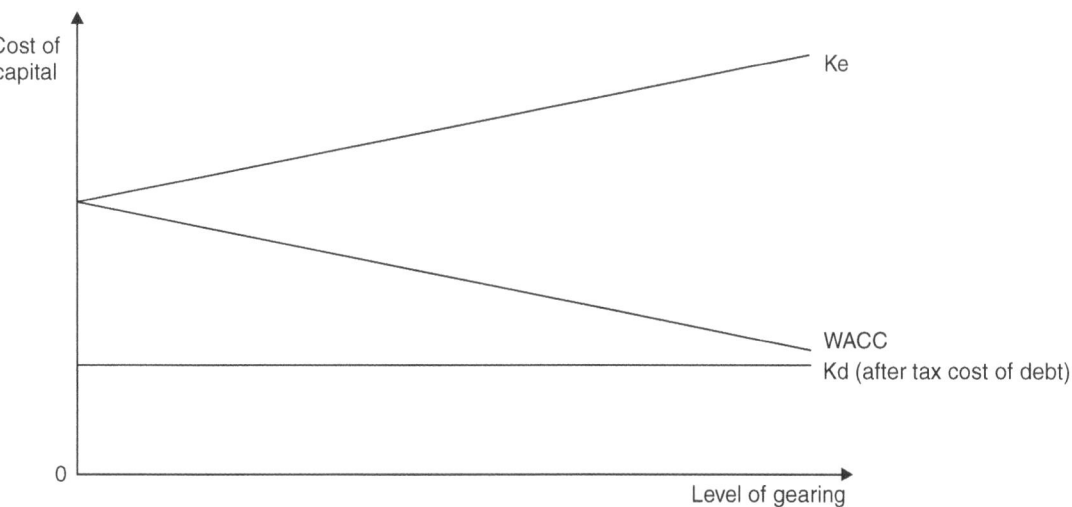

Figure 3

5.2 The adjustment to the MM cost of equity formula to allow for taxes

The formula for the cost of equity in a geared company becomes:

$$Ke_g = Ke_u + (1-t)\left[(Ke_u - Kd) \times \frac{D}{E}\right]$$

where t is the corporation tax rate and Kd is the pre-tax (gross) cost of debt capital.

The financial risk premium is adjusted by a factor of $(1-t)$.

From this formula we can derive the following formula.

Exam formula

$$WACC = Ke_u\left[1 - \frac{Dt}{E+D}\right]$$

where WACC is the weighted average cost of capital of a geared company
Ke_u is the cost of equity and the WACC of a similar ungeared company

Question — Cost of capital

Apply the formula given above to find the cost of equity and WACC for Berelco plc (using the information given above). The corporation tax rate is 30%.

Answer

Berelco plc's cost of equity would be:

$$12\% + (1 - 0.30) \times \left[(12-6)\% \times \frac{500}{1,500}\right] = 13.4\%$$

and its WACC would be:

$$12\%\left[1 - \frac{500 \times 0.30}{1,500 + 500}\right] = 12\% \times 0.925 = 11.1\%$$

This is below Loesch plc's WACC of 12%

The WACC in a geared company will be lower than the WACC in an ungeared company ($WACC_u = Ke_u$) by a measurable amount. WACC will fall as gearing increases.

$$WACC_g = WACC_u \times \frac{MV_u}{MV_g}$$

where $MV_g = E + D$

5.3 Is there an optimum level of gearing?

MM argued that since WACC falls as gearing rises, and the value of a company should rise as its WACC falls, the value of a geared company will always be greater than its ungeared counterpart, but only by the amount of the **debt-associated tax saving** of the geared company, assuming a permanent change in gearing.

Formula to learn

> $MV_g = MV_u + Dt$
>
> where MV_g is the value of the similar geared company.

However, the positive tax effects of debt finance will be exhausted where there is insufficient tax liability to use the tax relief which is available. This is known as **tax shield exhaustion**.

5.4 Example: MM, with taxes

Notnil plc and Newbegin plc are companies in the same industry. They have the same business risk and operating characteristics, but Notnil is a geared company whereas Newbegin is all equity financed. Notnil plc earns three times as much profit before interest as Newbegin plc. Both companies pursue a policy of paying out all their earnings each year as dividends.

The market value of each company is currently as follows:

			Notnil plc £m		Newbegin plc £m
Equity	(10m shares)		36	(20m shares)	15
Debt	(£12m of 12% loan stock)		14		—
			50		15

The annual profit before interest of Notnil is £3,000,000 and that of Newbegin is £1,000,000. The rate of corporation tax is 30%. It is thought that the current market value per ordinary share in Newbegin plc is at the equilibrium level, and that the market value of Notnil's debt capital is also at its equilibrium level. There is some doubt, however, about whether the value of Notnil's shares is at its equilibrium level.

Apply the MM formula to establish the equilibrium price of Notnil's shares.

Solution

$MV_g = MV_u + Dt$

MV_u = the market value of an ungeared company. Since Notnil's earnings (before interest) are three times the size of Newbegin's, V_u is three times the value of Newbegin's equity:

$3 \times £15,000,000 = £45,000,000$

$Dt = £14,000,000 \times 30\% = £4,200,000$

$MV_g = £45,000,000 + £4,200,000 = £49,200,000$

Since the market value of debt in Notnil plc is £14,000,000, it follows that the market value of Notnil's equity should be £49,200,000 − £14,000,000 = £35,200,000.

Value per share = $\dfrac{£35,200,000}{10,000,000}$ = £3.52 per share

Since the current share price is £3.60 per share, MM would argue that the shares in Notnil are currently over-valued by the market, but only by £800,000 in total or 8p per share.

Now let us relate the MM company valuation formula to the process of arbitrage.

5.5 Example: MM and arbitrage

Lenox plc and Groves plc are two companies operating in the same industry. They have the same business risk, and are identical in most other respects. The annual earnings before interest and tax are £40,000 for each company. The only differences between the companies are in their financial structures and their market values. Details of these are given below.

LEARNING OUTCOME 2 THE INVESTMENT DECISION

Lenox plc

	£
Ordinary shares of £1	30,000
Share premium account	10,000
Retained earnings	110,000
Shareholders' funds	150,000
12% loan stock (newly issued)	100,000
	250,000

Lenox's ordinary shares have a market value of 600 pence, and the 12% loan stock is trading at £100.

Groves plc

	£
Ordinary shares of £1	50,000
Share premium account	16,000
Retained earnings	100,000
Shareholders' funds	166,000

Groves' shares have a market value of 400 pence. Corporation tax is at 30%. Suppose that you are the owner of 1% of the equity of Lenox plc. If you agreed with the propositions of Modigliani and Miller, would you retain your shares in Lenox or could you improve your financial position? Ignore personal taxes.

Solution

A difficulty with this problem is the need to allow for tax relief on corporate debt, when working out how an investor should gear himself up so as to achieve personal gearing which is the same as the geared company. Check the solution carefully on this point.

Let us assume that the shares of Groves, the ungeared company, are correctly valued by the market at 400 pence. We would then predict that the total market value of Lenox, the geared company, should be ($MV_u + Dt$).

	£
Market value of Groves shares (50,000 × £4)	200,000
Market value of Lenox debt multiplied by tax rate (100,000 × 30%)	30,000
Correct market value of Lenox plc	230,000

Actual market value of Lenox

	£
Market value of Lenox shares (30,000 × £6)	180,000
Market value of Lenox debt capital	100,000
	280,000

We can conclude that Lenox plc is over-valued by the market and so an investor in Lenox shares can improve his or her financial position by:

(a) Selling all their shares in Lenox
(b) Gearing, by personal borrowing, so as to achieve the same personal gearing as Lenox
(c) Buying shares in Groves

This action will increase the investor's income without any change in the investor's business or financial risk. This process of arbitrage should continue until the equilibrium of $MV_g = MV_u + Dt$ is restored.

1% of the equity of Lenox has a current market value of 1% × £180,000 = £1,800

	£
Sell 1% holding of shares in Lenox to receive	1,800
Borrow, through personal borrowing*, an amount equal to 1% of the market value of Lenox's debt capital, adjusted to allow for the tax relief that Lenox gets on the debt interest (1% × £100,000 × 0.70)	700
	2,500

(* The rate of interest on personal borrowing is assumed to be the same as the market rate of interest on corporate debt, which is 12%.)

The investor should now invest £2,500 in the equity of Groves plc, and can buy £2,500 ÷ £200,000 = 1.25% of Groves' shares. The investor's income will now be higher than before, but because personal gearing has been substituted for corporate gearing, there is no change in the investor's financial risk.

Question — MM theory

The cost of equity in an ungeared company is 18%. The cost of risk free debt capital is 8%.

(a) What is the cost of equity in a similar geared company, according to MM, which is 75% equity financed and 25% debt financed, assuming corporation tax at a rate of 30%?

(b) What is the WACC of the geared company, allowing for taxation?

Answer

(a) $Ke_g = 18\% + (1-0.30)\left[(18-8)\% \times \dfrac{25}{75}\right] = 20.3\%$

(b) $WACC_g = 18\%\left[1 - \dfrac{0.30 \times 25}{25 + 75}\right]$

   $= 18\% \times 0.925 = 16.7\%$

5.6 Impact of personal taxes

Miller amended the taxation analysis to take account of the impact of personal taxes. The key point is that personal tax rates on debt income should be significantly higher than those for equity income.

(a) Once corporation tax is introduced firms will wish to **replace equity finance** with **debt finance**. To achieve this some equity holders will have to replace their equity holdings with debt holdings. Equity holders who are not subject to income taxes will be indifferent about doing this; however equity holders who are subject to **income taxes** will have to be persuaded to switch to debt by the offer of higher interest on debt. Firms can afford to give higher interest rates because they are making gains from the tax shield on debt.

(b) As more debt is issued, **interest rates** will have to **rise** further to persuade investors in higher income tax bands to switch to debt. As we have already seen, ultimately **the gain** made on the **tax shield** will be **cancelled out** by the **higher interest payments** made on debt. After this point firms have no reason to issue further debt, and therefore an equilibrium debt-equity ratio will have been established.

The main implication of this analysis is that for the economy as a whole there is an **equilibrium level of debt**. This depends on the **rate of corporation tax**, the rate of **personal tax**, and the **amount of funds** available. Once this equilibrium level has been achieved, there will be no point in issuing more debt, since the effect of the tax shield will equal the interest levels needed to persuade investors to take up the debt. Debt ratios in a number of major economies appear to have been relatively stable despite changes in corporation tax rates, since these have been accompanied by changes in personal tax rates.

As dividends and capital gains are taxed significantly in the UK, mostly the personal tax costs of gearing would not exceed the corporation tax benefits and hence **equilibrium is unlikely** in the UK.

5.7 Empirical testing and conclusion

It might be imagined that empirical testing should have been carried out by now either to prove or to disprove MM theory. Given, however, that MM accept that the weighted average cost of capital declines after allowing for tax, and that traditional theorists argue in favour of a flattish bottom to the weighted average cost of capital curve, it is very difficult to prove that one theory is preferable to the other.

5.8 Criticisms of Modigliani Miller theory

MM theory has been criticised on various grounds.

(a) The **risks for the investor** may **differ** between **personal gearing** and **corporate gearing**.

(b) The **cost of borrowing** for an **individual** is likely to be **higher** than the **cost of borrowing** for a **company**. MM assume that the cost is the same for personal and corporate borrowers.

(c) **Transaction** costs will **restrict** the arbitrage process.

Further weaknesses in the MM theory are as follows.

(a) In practice, it may be impossible to **identify** firms with **identical business risk** and operating characteristics.

(b) **Some earnings** may be **retained** and so the simplifying assumption of paying out all earnings as dividends would not apply.

(c) **Investors** are **assumed to act rationally** which may not be the case in practice.

MM also acknowledge that when the level of **gearing** gets **high**, the **cost of debt** will **rise**. They argue, however, that this does not affect the weighted average cost of capital because the cost of equity falls at the same time as risk seeking investors are attracted to buying shares in the company.

We have also seen that when a company's gearing reaches very high levels, it may be perceived as being in danger of insolvency, and its market value will be very low (instead of being very high, as MM would predict). MM ignored the possibility of **bankruptcy**, and so their theory may not be valid at very high levels of gearing.

Even if the Modigliani and Miller formulae do hold, in practice gearing is still a financing decision and thus subject to all the practical financing issues such as ability to obtain debt.

6 The adjusted present value method

> **FAST FORWARD**
>
> The **APV** method suggests that it is possible to calculate an **adjusted** cost of capital for use in project appraisal, as well as indicating how the net present value of a project can be increased or decreased by project financing effects.
>
> - Evaluate the project as if it was all equity financed
> - Make adjustments to allow for the effects of the financing method

6.1 NPV and APV

We have seen that a company's gearing level has implications for both the value of its equity shares and its WACC. The viability of an investment project will depend partly on how the investment is financed, and how the method of finance affects gearing.

The net present value method of investment appraisal is to **discount** the **cash flows** of a project at a **cost of capital**. This cost of capital might be the WACC, but it could also be another cost of capital, perhaps one which allows for the risk characteristics of the individual project (as we shall see later).

6.2 Carrying out an APV calculation

An alternative method of carrying out project appraisal is to use the **adjusted present value (APV) method**. The APV method involves three stages.

Step 1 Calculate the cost of equity of an equivalent ungeared company.

Step 2 Calculate the NPV of the project as if it was all equity-financed using the ungeared cost of equity calculated in Step 1 as the discount rate. This gives the base case NPV.

Step 3 Establish the effect of using debt finance on the project.

6.2.1 Example: APV method with debt in perpetuity

A company is considering a project that would cost £100,000 to be financed 50% by equity (cost 21.6%) and 50% by debt (pre-tax cost 12%). The financing method would maintain the company's WACC unchanged. The cash flows from the project would be £36,000 a year in perpetuity, before interest charges. Corporation tax is at 30%.

Appraise the project:

(a) Using the NPV method
(b) Using the APV method

Solution

(a) We can use the **NPV method** because the company's WACC will be unchanged.

	Cost %	Weighting		Product %
Equity	21.6	0.5		10.8
Debt (70% of 12%)	8.4	0.5		4.2
			WACC	15.0

Annual cash flows in perpetuity from the project are as follows.

	£
Before tax	36,000
Less tax (30%)	10,800
After tax	25,200

NPV of project = −£100,000 + (25,200 ÷ 0.15)
= −£100,000 + £168,000
= + £68,000

Note that the tax relief that will be obtained on debt interest is taken account of **in the WACC *not* in the project cash flows**.

Since £100,000 of new investment is being created, the value of the company will increase by £100,000 + £68,000 = £168,000, of which 50% must be debt capital.

LEARNING OUTCOME 2 THE INVESTMENT DECISION

The company must raise 50% × £168,000 = £84,000 of 12% debt capital, and (the balance) £16,000 of equity. The NPV of the project will raise the value of this equity from £16,000 to £84,000 thus leaving the gearing ratio at 50:50.

(b) The **APV approach** to this example is as follows.

Step 1 First, we need to know the **cost of equity in an equivalent ungeared company**. The MM formula we can use to establish this is as follows:

Formula to learn

Cost of ordinary (equity) share capital in a geared firm (with tax):

$$Ke_g = Ke_u + [Ke_u - Kd]\frac{D(1-t)}{E}$$

Remember Kd is the **pre-tax** cost of debt.

$$21.6\% = Ke_u + \left[(Ke_u - 12\%) \times \frac{50 \times 0.7}{50}\right]$$

$21.6\% = Ke_u + 0.70Ke_u - 8.4\%$
$1.70Ke_u = 30\%$
$Ke_u = 17.647\%$

Step 2 Next, we calculate the **NPV of the project as if it were all equity financed**. The cost of equity would be 17.647%

$$NPV = \frac{£25,200}{0.17647} - £100,000 = +£42,800$$

Step 3 Next, we can use an MM formula for the relationship between the value of geared and ungeared companies, to establish **the effect of gearing on the value of the project**. £84,000 will be financed by debt.

MVg (APV) = MVu + Dt
= + £42,800 + (£84,000 × 0.30 = £25,200)
= £68,000

The value Dt (value of debt × corporate tax rate) represents the **present value of the tax shield on debt interest,** that is the present value of the savings arising from tax relief on debt interest.

This can be proved as follows.

Annual interest charge = 12% of £84,000 = £10,080   Tax saving (30% × £10,080)
                                                        = £3,024.00

Cost of debt (pre-tax) = 12%

PV of tax savings in perpetuity = $\frac{£3,024}{0.12}$ (by coincidence only this equals the project net of tax cash flows)

= £25,200

Dt = £84,000 × 0.30 = £25,200 is a quicker way of deriving the same value. Note, however, this only works where the interest is payable in **perpetuity**. If not the PV of the tax shield, will need to be computed by the 'long hand' method, above using an appropriate annuity factor.

6.3 APV with limited tax shield

6.3.1 Example: APV with limited tax shield

Suppose in the example above the cash flows only lasted for five years, and corporation tax was payable one year in arrears. Calculate the present value of the tax shield.

Solution

The tax saving will now only last for Years 2 to 6. (Remember interest will be paid in Years 1 to 5, but the tax benefits will be felt a year in arrears.)

PV of tax savings = 3,024 × Annuity factor Years 2 to 6
= 3,024 × (Annuity factors Years 1 to 6 – Annuity factor Year 1)
= 3,024 × (4.111 – 0.893)
= £9,731

6.4 APV and changes in gearing

However, the APV method can also be adapted to allow for financing which **changes the gearing structure** and the WACC. In this respect, it is superior to the NPV method.

6.4.1 Example: APV and changes in gearing

Suppose, for example, that in the previous example, the **entire project were to be financed by debt**. The APV of the project would be calculated as follows:

Step 1 Ke_u = 17.647% as above

Step 2 The NPV of project if all equity financed is:

$$\frac{£25,200}{0.17647} - £100,000 = +£42,800 \text{ (as before)}$$

Step 3 The adjustment to allow for the method of financing is the present value of the tax relief on debt interest in perpetuity.

Dt = £100,000 × 0.30 = £30,000
APV = £42,800 + £30,000 = +£72,800

The project would increase the value of equity by £72,800

Question
APV

A project costing £100,000 is to be financed by £60,000 of irredeemable 12% debentures and £40,000 of new equity. The project will yield an annual after-tax cash flow of £21,000 in perpetuity. If it were all equity financed, an appropriate cost of capital would be 15%. The corporation tax rate is 30%. What is the project's APV?

Answer

	£
NPV if all equity financed: £21,000/0.15 – £100,000	40,000
PV of the tax shield: £60,000 × 12% × 30%/0.12	18,000
APV	58,000

6.5 Discounting tax relief at the risk-free rate

Often in exams you will be given the risk-free rate of return. As tax relief is allowed by the government and is almost certain, there is an argument for saying that **all tax relief** should be discounted at the **risk-free rate**. However, there is the opposing argument that the **risk of the tax relief** is the same as the **risk of the debt** to which it relates, and therefore the tax relief should be discounted at the cost of debt. The risk-free rate would also not be used if the company was unlikely to be in a taxpaying position for some years.

In the exam we suggest that you make clear the reasons for choosing the discount rate that you have chosen to discount the tax relief, and add a comment that an alternative rate might be used.

6.6 Issue costs

The costs of issuing the finance needed for the project may also be brought into APV calculations.

6.6.1 Example: Issue costs

Edted Ltd is about to start a project with an initial investment of £20 million, which will generate cash flow over four years. The project will be financed with a £10 million 10-year bank loan and a rights issue. Issue costs are 5% of the amount raised.

Calculate the issue costs that will be used in the APV calculation.

Solution

Issue costs will not equal 5% of £10 million (20 million – £10 million). The £10 million will be the figure left after the issue costs have been paid. Therefore £10 million must be 95%, not 100% of the amount raised, and the

issue costs = 5/95 × £10 million = £526,316

In the above example, the issue costs do not need to be discounted as they are assumed to be paid at Time 0. The complication comes if issue costs are allowable for tax purposes.

6.6.2 Example: The tax implications of issue costs

Assume in the example above that issue costs are allowable for tax purposes. The corporation tax is assumed to be 30% payable one year in arrears and the risk-free rate of return is assumed to be 8%.

Calculate the tax effect of the issuing costs to be included in the APV calculation.

Solution

Tax effect = Tax rate × Issue costs × Discount rate
 = 0.3 × 526,316 × 0.926
 = £146,211

6.7 Spare debt capacity

Projects may yield other incremental benefits, for example increased borrowing or debt capacity. These benefits should be included in the APV calculations, even if the debt capacity is utilised elsewhere.

6.7.1 Example: Spare debt capacity

Continuing with the Edted example, suppose the project increased the borrowing capacity of the company by £6 million, at the risk-free rate of return of 8%. Calculate the effect on the APV calculation.

Solution

Remember that we are concerned with the incremental benefit which is the **tax shield effect** of the increased debt finance.

Present value of tax shield effect = Increased debt capacity × Interest rate × Tax rate × Discount factor Years 2 to 5

= £6 million × 8% × 30% × 3.067
= £441,648

6.8 Subsidy

You may face a situation where a company can obtain finance at a lower interest rate than its normal cost of borrowing. In this situation you have to include in the APV calculation the tax shield effect of the cheaper finance and the effect of the saving in interest.

6.8.1 Example: Subsidy

Gordonbear Ltd is about to start a project requiring £6 million of initial investment. The company normally borrows at 12% but a government loan will be available to finance all of the project at 10%. The risk-free rate of interest is 6%.

Corporation tax is payable at 30% one year in arrears. The project is scheduled to last for four years.

Calculate the effect on the APV calculation if Gordonbear finances the project by means of the government loan.

Solution

(a) The tax shield is as follows.

We assume that the loan is for the duration of the project (four years) only.

Annual interest = £6 million × 10%
= £600,000

Tax relief = £600,000 × 0.3
= £180,000

This needs to be discounted over Years 2 to 5 (remember the one-year time lag). We do not however use the 10% to discount the loan and the tax effect; instead we assume that the government loan is risk-free and the tax effect is also risk-free. Hence, we use the 6% factor in discounting.

NPV tax relief = £180,000 × Discount factor Years 2 to 5
= £180,000 × 3.269
= £588,420

(b) We also need to take into account the benefits of **being able** to pay a **lower interest rate**.

Benefits = £6 million × (12% − 10%) × 6% Discount factor Years 1 to 4
= £6 million × 2% × 3.465
= £415,800

(c) Total effect = £588,420 + £415,800 = £1,004,220

6.9 Advantages of APV

(a) APV can be used to **evaluate** all the **effects of financing** a product including:

    (i) Tax shield
    (ii) Changing capital structure
    (iii) Any other relevant cost

(b) When using APV you do not have to adjust the WACC using assumptions of perpetual risk-free debt.

6.10 Disadvantages of APV

The main difficulties with the APV technique are:

(a) **Establishing** a **suitable cost of equity**, for the initial DCF computation as if the project were all-equity financed, and also establishing the all-equity β

(b) **Identifying all the costs** associated with the method of financing

(c) **Choosing the correct discount rates** used to discount the costs

7 Adjusted cost of capital

> **FAST FORWARD**
>
> The **adjusted cost of capital** reflects the expected rate of return available on equivalent assets, adjusted for the financing side-effects of the project.

7.1 Allowing for tax shield

One way of allowing for the effects of a tax shield is to calculate a new cost of capital. This can be done using the formula we saw earlier.

$$\text{WACC} = \text{Ke}_u \left[1 - \frac{Dt}{E+D} \right]$$

7.2 Adjusted cost of capital

Alternatively, the APV approach can be combined with the ideas of Modigliani and Miller to produce an adjusted cost of capital.

First of all, we can distinguish the opportunity cost of capital and the adjusted cost of capital.

(a) The **opportunity cost of capital** (r) is the expected rate of return available in capital markets on assets of equivalent risk. This depends on the risk of the project cash flows, and should be used if there are no significant side-effects arising from the method of financing.

(b) The **adjusted cost of capital** (r*) is an adjusted opportunity cost which reflects the financing side-effects of the project. A firm should accept projects which have a positive net present value (NPV) at the adjusted cost of capital r*.

7.3 Formula for adjusted cost of capital

The following is the formula for the adjusted cost of capital (r*) suggested by the work of Modigliani and Miller.

Formula to learn

$r^* = r(1 - T^*L)$, or $K_{adj} = K_{eu}(1 - T^*L)$

where T^* is the net tax saving, expressed in pounds, of £1 of future debt interest payments

L is the marginal contribution of the project to the debt capacity of the firm, expressed as a proportion of the **present value of the project** equivalent to $\frac{D}{D+E}$

7.4 Example: MM formula

Project X, requiring an investment of £1,000,000, adds £300,000 to a firm's debt capacity. The project leads to a constant annual saving of £350,000 indefinitely. The opportunity cost of capital is 20%. Assume that the tax shield on interest payments is T* = 0.30 (30 per cent). What is the adjusted cost of capital?

Solution

First we compute the APV of the project:

Base case NPV = $\frac{£350,000 \times 0.7}{0.2} - £1m = £225,000$

PV of tax shield = 0.3 × 300,000 = 90,000

APV = 225,000 + 90,000 = £315,000

Next we use this to compute L

D = 300,000

E = £700,000 + £315,000 = £1,015,000

D + E = £1,315,000

So L = $\frac{300}{1,315}$

Finally we apply the MM formula:

$r^* = 0.2 \left[1 - 0.3 \left(\frac{300}{1,315} \right) \right] = \mathbf{18.63\%}$

In what circumstances may the MM formula be used? The MM formula works exactly for any project which is expected to generate a level cash flow in perpetuity and to support permanent debt. The formula also works as a reasonable approximation for projects with limited lives or irregular cash flow streams.

LEARNING OUTCOME 2 THE INVESTMENT DECISION

8 CAPM and MM combined – geared betas

FAST FORWARD

When an investment has differing business and finance risks from the existing business, **geared betas** may be used to obtain an appropriate required return.

Geared betas are calculated by:

- Ungearing industry beta
- Converting ungeared beta back into a geared beta that reflects the company's own gearing ratio

8.1 Beta rules and the effects of gearing

The gearing of a company will affect the risk of its equity. If a company is geared and its **financial risk is therefore higher** than the risk of an all-equity company, then the β value of the geared company's equity will be higher than the β value of a similar ungeared company's equity.

The CAPM is consistent with the propositions of Modigliani and Miller. MM argue that as gearing rises, the cost of equity rises to compensate shareholders for the extra financial risk of investing in a geared company. This financial risk is an aspect of systematic risk, and ought to be reflected in a company's beta factor.

8.2 Geared betas and ungeared betas

The connection between MM theory and the CAPM means that it is possible to establish a mathematical relationship between the β value of an ungeared company and the β value of a similar, but geared, company. The β value of a geared company will be higher than the β value of a company identical in every respect except that it is all-equity financed. This is because of the extra financial risk. The mathematical relationship between the 'ungeared' and 'geared' betas is as follows.

Exam formula

$$\beta_a = \beta_e \frac{E}{E + D(1-t)} + \beta_d \frac{D(1-t)}{E + D(1-t)}$$

where β_a is the beta factor of an ungeared company: the ungeared beta
β_e is the beta factor of equity in a similar, but geared company: the geared beta
β_d is the beta factor of debt in the geared company
D is the market value of the debt capital in the geared company
E is the market value of the equity capital in the geared company
t is the rate of corporate tax

Debt is often assumed to be risk-free and its beta (β_d) is then taken as zero, in which case the formula above reduces to the following form.

Exam formula

$$\beta_a = \beta_e \times \frac{E}{E + D(1-t)}$$

Rearranging the formula, we have

$$\beta_e = \beta_a \frac{E + D(1-t)}{E} = \beta_a \left[1 + \frac{D(1-t)}{E} \right] = \beta_a + \beta_a \frac{D(1-t)}{E}$$

Formula to learn

$$\beta_e = \beta_a \frac{E + D(1-t)}{E}$$

8.3 Example: CAPM (1)

Two companies are identical in every respect except for their capital structure. Their market values are in equilibrium, as follows:

	Geared plc £'000	Ungeared plc £'000
Annual profit before interest and tax	1,000	1,000
Less interest (4,000 × 8%)	320	0
	680	1,000
Less tax at 30%	204	300
Profit after tax = dividends	476	700
Market value of equity	3,900	6,600
Market value of debt	4,180	0
Total market value of company	8,080	6,600

The total value of Geared plc is higher than the total value of Ungeared plc, which is consistent with MM's proposition that

Valuation of geared company = Valuation of ungeared company + Dt

All profits after tax are paid out as dividends, and so there is no dividend growth. The beta value of Ungeared plc has been calculated as 1.0. The debt capital of Geared plc can be regarded as risk-free.

Calculate:

(a) The cost of equity in Geared plc
(b) The market return R_m
(c) The beta value of Geared plc

Solution

(a) Since its market value (MV) is in equilibrium, the cost of equity in Geared plc can be calculated as:

$$\frac{d}{MV} = \frac{476}{3,900} = 12.20\%$$

(b) The beta value of Ungeared plc is 1.0, which means that the expected returns from Ungeared plc are exactly the same as the market returns, and $R_m = 700/6,600 = 10.6\%$

(c) $\beta_e = \beta_a \dfrac{E + D(1-t)}{E}$

$= 1.0 \times \dfrac{3,900 + (4,180 \times 0.70)}{3,900} = 1.75$

The beta of Geared plc, as we should expect, is higher than the beta of Ungeared plc.

8.4 Using the geared and ungeared betas to establish a discount rate for the appraisal of major projects

If a company plans to invest in a project which involves diversification into a new business, the investment will involve a different level of systematic risk from that applying to the company's existing business. A discount rate should be calculated which is specific to the project, and which takes account of both the project's systematic risk and the company's gearing level.

LEARNING OUTCOME 2 THE INVESTMENT DECISION

A discount rate can be found using the CAPM.

Step 1 Get an estimate of the systematic risk characteristics of the project's operating cash flows by obtaining published beta values for companies in the industry into which the company is planning to diversify.

Step 2 Adjust these beta values to allow for the company's capital gearing level. This adjustment is done in two stages.

Step 2A Convert the beta values of other companies in the industry to ungeared betas, using the formula:

$$\beta_a = \beta_e \left(\frac{E}{E + D(1-t)} \right)$$

Step 2B Having obtained an ungeared beta value βa, convert it back to a geared beta β_e, which reflects the company's own gearing ratio, using the formula:

$$\beta_e = \beta_a \frac{E + D(1-t)}{E}$$

Step 3 Having estimated a project-specific geared beta, use the CAPM to estimate:

Step 3A A project-specific cost of equity, and

Step 3B A project-specific cost of capital, based on a weighting of this cost of equity and the cost of the company's debt capital

8.5 Example: CAPM (2)

A company's debt:equity ratio, by market values, is 2:5. The corporate debt, which is assumed to be risk-free, yields 11% before tax. The beta value of the company's equity is currently 1.1. The average returns on stock market equity are 16%.

The company is now proposing to invest in a project which would involve diversification into a new industry, and the following information is available about this industry.

(a) Average beta coefficient of equity capital = 1.59
(b) Average debt:equity ratio in the industry = 1:2 (by market value)

The rate of corporation tax is 30%. What would be a suitable cost of capital to apply to the project?

Solution

Step 1 The beta value for the industry is 1.59.

Step 2A Convert the geared beta value for the industry to an ungeared beta for the industry.

$$\beta_a = 1.59 \left(\frac{2}{2 + (1(1-0.30))} \right) = 1.18$$

Step 2B Convert this ungeared industry beta back into a geared beta, which reflects the company's own gearing level of 2:5.

$$\beta_e = 1.18 \left(\frac{5 + (2(1-0.30))}{5} \right) = 1.51$$

Step 3A This is a project-specific beta for the firm's equity capital, and so using the CAPM, we can estimate the project-specific cost of equity as:

$K e_g$ = 11% + 1.51(16% − 11%) = 18.55%

Step 3B The project will presumably be financed in a gearing ratio of 2:5 debt to equity, and so the project-specific cost of capital ought to be:

$$[\frac{5}{7} \times 18.55\%] + [\frac{2}{7} \times 70\% \times 11\%] = 15.45\%$$

Question — Ungeared and geared betas

Two companies are identical in every respect except for their capital structure. XY plc has a debt: equity ratio of 1:3, and its equity has a β value of 1.20. PQ plc has a debt:equity ratio of 2:3. Corporation tax is at 30%. Estimate a β value for PQ plc's equity.

Answer

Estimate an ungeared beta from XY plc data.

$$\beta_a = 1.20 \frac{3}{3 + (1(1-0.30))} = 0.973$$

Estimate a geared beta for PQ plc using this ungeared beta.

$$\beta_e = 0.973 \frac{3 + (2(1-0.30))}{3} = 1.427.$$

8.6 Weaknesses in the formula

The problems with using the geared and ungeared beta formula for calculating a firm's equity beta from data about other firms are as follows:

(a) It is **difficult** to **identify other firms** with **identical operating characteristics**.

(b) **Estimates of beta values** from **share price information** are not **wholly accurate**. They are based on statistical analysis of historical data, and as the previous example shows, estimates using one firm's data will differ from estimates using another firm's data.

(c) There may be **differences in beta values** between firms caused by:

    (i) Different cost structures (eg, the ratio of fixed costs to variable costs)
    (ii) Size differences between firms
    (iii) Debt capital not being risk-free

(d) If the firm for which an equity beta is being estimated has opportunities for growth that are recognised by investors, and which will affect its equity beta, **estimates** of the **equity beta** based on other firms' data will be **inaccurate**, because the opportunities for growth will not be allowed for.

Perhaps the most significant simplifying assumption is that to link **MM theory** to the CAPM, it must be assumed that the **cost of debt** is a **risk-free rate of return**. This could obviously be unrealistic. Companies may default on interest payments or capital repayments on their loans. It has been estimated that corporate debt has a beta value of 0.2 or 0.3.

The consequence of making the assumption that debt is risk-free is that the formulae tend to **overstate** the financial risk in a geared company and to **understate** the business risk in geared and ungeared companies by a compensating amount. In other words, βa will be slightly higher and βe will be slightly lower than the formulae suggest.

LEARNING OUTCOME 2 THE INVESTMENT DECISION

8.7 Use of different techniques

The diagram below summarises when to use different techniques, the table when to use different formulae.

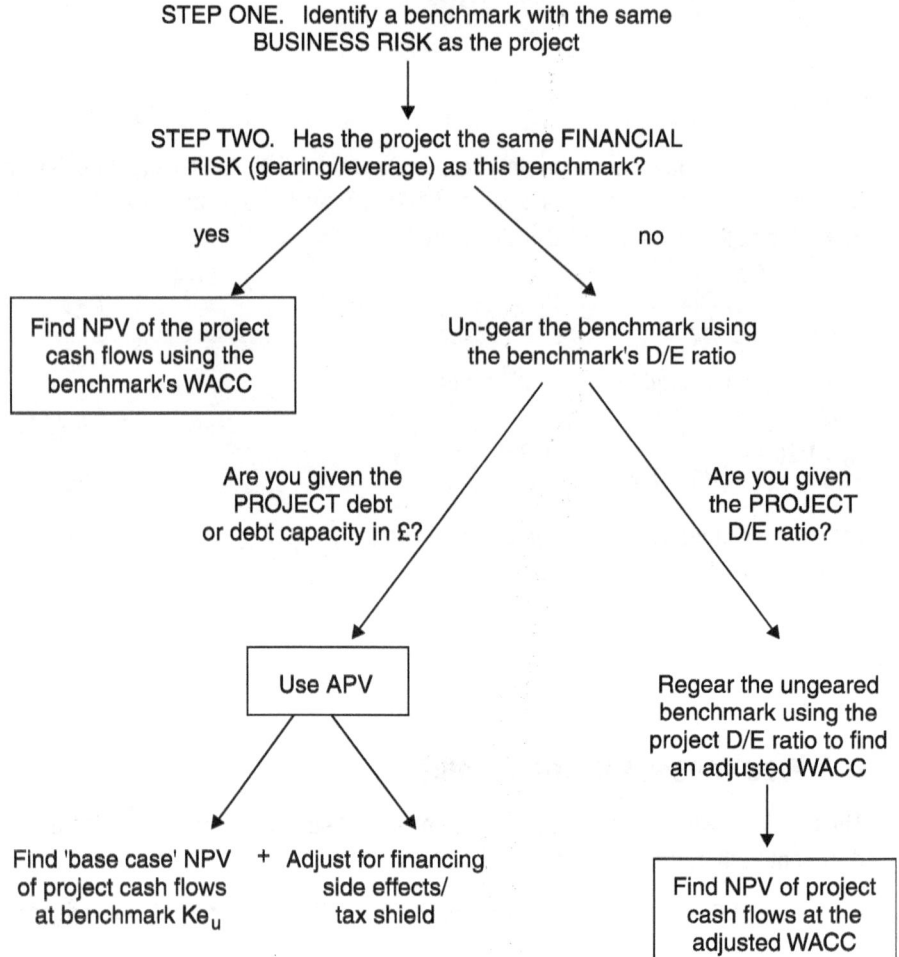

When to use which formula?

Formula		Purpose
1 Cost of equity Ke/Ke_g	$Ke = \dfrac{D_1}{P_0} + g$ $Ke = r_f + [r_m - r_f]\beta$	For calculating the existing cost of equity, which is then used in formula 2
2 WACC	$Ke_g \dfrac{E}{E+D} + Kd(1-t)\dfrac{D}{E+D}$	For appraising investments in the same business where gearing does not change
3 WACC	$Ke_u\left(1 - \dfrac{Dt}{E+D}\right)$	Shows the impact of introducing debt into your own capital structure or to strip out the impact of debt from a comparative company to identify its ungeared cost of equity (Ke_u) This is used to calculate WACC or used in APV (formula 6).
4 Asset beta β_a	$\beta_e \dfrac{E}{E+D(1-t)} +$ $\beta_d \dfrac{D(1-t)}{E+D(1-t)}$	To strip out the impact of debt from a comparative company to identify its ungeared cost of equity (Ke_u) used in formula 3 or 6.
5 Equity beta β_e	$\beta_a \dfrac{E+D(1-t)}{E}$	If β_d is zero, used to regear ungeared beta according to debt-equity mix of company. Used in conjunction with formula 1.
6 APV	PV of project (discounted at Ke_u) + PV of tax saved (discounted at Kd/risk-free rate).	To appraise projects which change gearing.
7 Valuing a share P_0	$\dfrac{D_1}{Ke - g}$	To value a target company. Ke from formula 1.
8 Cost of debt Kd	If irredeemable $\dfrac{i}{P_0}(1-t)$ If redeemable use IRR or $r_f + [r_m - r_f]\beta_d$	For calculating the existing cost of debt, which is then used in formula 2.

LEARNING OUTCOME 2 THE INVESTMENT DECISION

Chapter Roundup

- **Financial gearing** or **leverage** is the increased variability of earnings resulting from having debt in the capital structure.
- **Static trade-off theory** states that the debt-equity choice of finance decision will be determined by where a company is in relation to its ideal structure.
- **Pecking order theory** states that firms will prefer to use retained earnings, then debt, then equity to minimise issue costs, respond to investor preferences and send positive messages to the stock market.
- Both traditional and MM theories agree that:
    - The optimal level of financial gearing will be that at which the WACC is minimised
    - The cost of equity increases as financial gearing increases
- Under the **traditional theory of cost of capital**, the cost declines initially and then rises as gearing increases. The **optimal capital structure** will be the point at which WACC is lowest, at a level somewhere between 0% and 100% gearing.
- Modigliani and Miller stated that a company's **capital structure** would have **no impact** upon its WACC. **Ignoring corporate tax**, the rise in the cost of equity as gearing rises would offset exactly the benefits of an increasing proportion of low-cost debt capital, resulting in a constant WACC.
- **With taxation**, the tax relief available on debt will, according to MM, cause the WACC to fall, right up perhaps to a 100% level of gearing. This suggests that companies should gear to as high a level as possible.
- The **APV** method suggests that it is possible to calculate an **adjusted** cost of capital for use in project appraisal, as well as indicating how the net present value of a project can be increased or decreased by project financing effects.
    - Evaluate the project as if it was all equity financed
    - Make adjustments to allow for the effects of the financing method
- The **adjusted cost of capital** reflects the expected rate of return available on equivalent assets, adjusted for the financing side-effects of the project.
- When an investment has differing business and finance risks from the existing business, **geared betas** may be used to obtain an appropriate required return.
- Geared betas are calculated by:
    - Ungearing industry beta
    - Converting ungeared beta back into a geared beta that reflects the company's own gearing ratio

Quick Quiz

1. Explain the significance of lines 1 to 3 and point 4 in the diagram below illustrating the traditional view of the WACC.

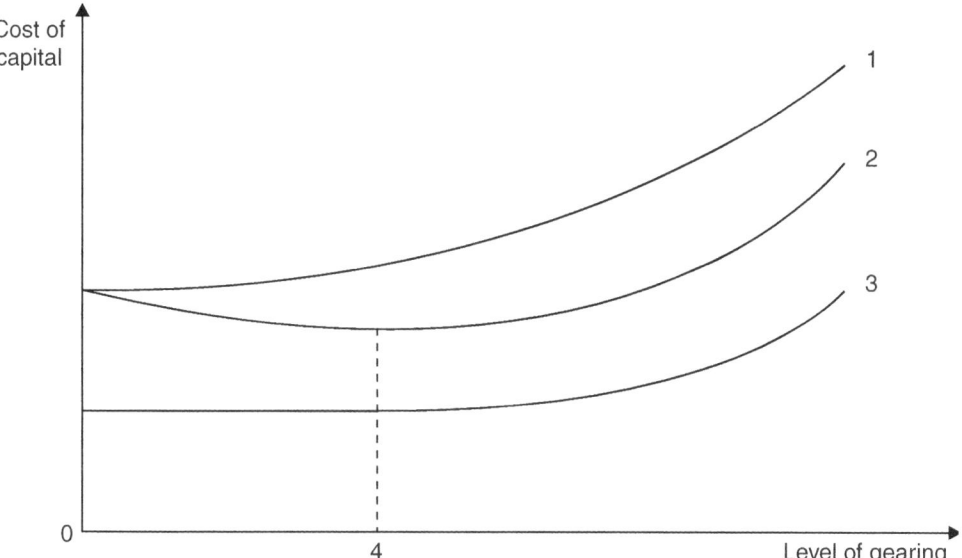

2. What method of project appraisal involves making adjustments for the method of financing used?

3. What are the main difficulties with the technique identified in quick quiz question 2 above?

4. Identify r*, r, T*, L in the following MM formula for the adjusted cost of capital.

   r* = r (1 – T* L)

5. What are the main problems of using geared and ungeared betas to calculate a firm's equity beta?

6. Assuming debt is risk-free β_a = ?

7. When using the adjusted present value, you discount all costs associated with a method of financing at the weighted average cost of capital.

   ☐ True
   ☐ False

Answers to Quick Quiz

1. Line 1 is the cost of equity in the geared company
   Line 2 is the weighted average cost of capital
   Line 3 is the cost of debt
   Point 4 is the optimal level of gearing

2. The APV method

3. (a) Establishing a suitable cost of equity as if the project was all equity financed
   (b) Identifying all costs associated with the method of financing
   (c) Choosing the correct discount rate

4. r is the opportunity cost of capital

   r* is the adjusted cost of capital reflecting financing side-effects

   T* is the net tax saving, in pounds, of £1 of future debt interest payments

   L is the marginal contribution of the project in the debt capacity of the firm, expressed as a proportion of the project's present value.

5. (a) It is difficult to identify other firms with identical operating characteristics
   (b) Estimates of beta values from share price information are not wholly accurate
   (c) There may be firm-specific causes of differences in beta values
   (d) The market may recognise opportunities for future growth for some firms but not others

6. $\beta_a = \beta_e \times \dfrac{E}{E + D(1-t)}$

7. False. The costs should be discounted at whatever the appropriate discount rate is for that cost.

End of chapter questions

1. Hair Co.Ltd (AIA May 2014)

Hair Co. Ltd. is a Chinese company that manufactures a range of hair products in China. The market value of debt of the company is ¥300m and the market value of equity is ¥900m. (For information, the currency in China is the Chinese Yuan Renminbi – ¥). The debt yield before tax is 8% and the debt is risk free. The geared (equity) beta for Hair Co. Ltd. is 0.9. The directors of Hair Co. Ltd. are considering a project in the restaurant industry in China as they think it may be good to diversify into a different industry sector.

The average debt:equity ratio in the restaurant sector is 1:2 and the average geared (equity) beta is 1.6. The return on the market is estimated to be 12% and the corporation tax rate is 25%.

Required

(a) Calculate the current cost of capital for Hair Co. Ltd. **(4 marks)**

(b) Calculate an appropriate cost of capital for appraising the project in the restaurant industry assuming that Hair Co. Ltd. wishes to maintain its current debt:equity ratio. **(10 marks)**

(c) The directors of Hair Co. Ltd. believe that it will be satisfactory for the company to appraise the project using the current cost of capital. You are required to critically evaluate why this is not appropriate for appraising the construction project. **(6 marks)**

(Total 20 marks)

2. Ashten plc (AIA May 2013)

Ashten plc is a food manufacturer and is financed by both debt and equity. The current market value of debt is £200m and the current market value of equity is £800m. The debt is risk free and the yield on the debt is 7% before tax. The equity (geared) beta for Ashten plc is 0.8. The company would like to diversify its activities and is considering undertaking a project in the construction sector. The directors of Ashten plc have been able to ascertain that the average debt:equity ratio in the construction industry is 1:3 and the average equity (geared) beta is 1.4. The corporation tax rate is 20%. The return on the market is estimated to be 15%.

Required

(a) Calculate Ashten plc's current cost of capital. **(4 marks)**

(b) Calculate an appropriate cost of capital for appraising the construction project assuming that Ashten plc wishes to maintain its current debt:equity ratio. **(10 marks)**

(c) Advise the directors of Ashten plc why it is not appropriate to use the current cost of capital for appraising the construction project. **(6 marks)**

(Total 20 marks)

3. Box Packaging Company (AIA May 2012)

Box Packaging Company is a Malaysian company that specialises in providing packaging to a wide range of international companies. The company has a significant loan for which there are three key covenants specified as follows:

(i) Interest cover must be not less than 3.0 times.
(ii) The maximum ratio of net debt to profit* is 3.25 times.
(iii) Net assets must exceed MYR350m.

*The covenant defines 'profit' in this ratio as profit before interest and before depreciation and amortisation.

LEARNING OUTCOME 2 THE INVESTMENT DECISION

The profits of the company have been relatively stable in the recent past, but the directors of the company are unsure whether they will remain as stable in the future. The gearing ratios of two competitor companies are as follows:

Company name	Industry	Gearing ratio (defined as the ratio of net debt to net assets)
The Giant Crate Company	Packaging	58%
The Recycled Container Company	Packaging	55%

The following information has been provided:

BOX PACKAGING COMPANY
SUMMARY OF THE CONSOLIDATED STATEMENT OF COMPREHENSIVE INCOME
FOR THE YEAR ENDED 30 APRIL

	Note	2011 MYRm	2012 MYRm
Revenue		1,960	1,995
Cost of sales		(1,423)	(1,480)
Gross profit		537	515
Operating expenses	1	(431)	(440)
Operating profit		106	75
Finance costs – interest payable		(16)	(24)
Profit before taxation		90	51
Taxation		(21)	(7)
Profit after tax		69	44

BOX PACKAGING COMPANY
EXTRACTS FROM THE CONSOLIDATED STATEMENT OF FINANCIAL POSITION AS AT 31 DECEMBER

	Note	2011 MYRm	2012 MYRm
ASSETS & LIABILITIES			
Total assets		1,634	1,671
Total liabilities		1,152	1,253
Net assets	2	482	418

Note 1: Depreciation and amortisation included within operating expenses amount to MYR68m in 2011 and MYR74m in 2012.

Note 2: Net debt calculated as according to the bank covenants amounts to MYR225m in 2011 and MYR286m in 2012.

Required

The board of directors have asked you to prepare a report that evaluates the current position of the company in respect of its capital structure and advises the board of directors as to whether it should make changes to the capital structure. The directors have asked that in preparing the report you should: (1) include any calculations that you consider appropriate, (2) advise of any further information that would be helpful, and (3) advise of any assumptions you have made. **(20 marks)**

4. Starscape plc (AIA November 2004 – amended)

Starscape plc is a company that normally builds luxury houses to customers' specifications. The current level of orders is low so the company is considering a speculative project for the building of commercial premises.

Details of the project are as follows.

- Initial investment in land of £3 million payable at the commencement of building
- Annual costs of £0.5 million for five years while building
- Forecast net rental income of £2.5 million per year for the foreseeable future commencing at the end of year six.

Notes

(a) The company's equity cost of capital is estimated at 17% and its weighted average cost of capital at 13%.

(b) There are no tenants for the property at the moment. It is planned to rent the accommodation on completion of the building.

(c) The company has no previous experience of speculative building.

(d) The project will be financed with a loan at 9% costing 2% of the gross proceeds in issuing expenses.

(e) Ignore any tax implications.

Required

(i) Calculate the net present value of the project using the company's weighted average cost of capital. **(6 marks)**

(ii) Discuss any doubts you may have concerning the use of weighted average cost of capital for the evaluation of the project. **(7 marks)**

(iii) Calculate the adjusted net present value of the project. **(7 marks)**

(Total 20 marks)

LEARNING OUTCOME 2 THE INVESTMENT DECISION

Appraisal of overseas investment decisions

Topic list	Syllabus reference
1 The international capital structure decision	LO2
2 Political risk and blocked funds	LO2
3 Taxation in the multinational environment	LO2
4 Litigation risks	LO2
5 Cultural risks	LO2

Introduction

In this chapter, we look at the factors that need to be considered when making overseas investment decisions. We look at the factors that might influence how these investments are financed and consider how other factors, such as overseas taxation arrangements, may complicate the treatment of tax in investment appraisal. We also look at the risks of investing overseas, including political risk, litigation risk and cultural risks.

LEARNING OUTCOME 2 THE INVESTMENT DECISION

1 The international capital structure decision

FAST FORWARD

The methods of financing overseas subsidiaries will depend on the **length of investment period** envisaged, also the **local finance costs, taxation systems** and **restrictions on dividend remittances**.

1.1 International investment appraisal

In Chapter 8, we looked at different appraisal techniques for evaluating investments using methods including the net present value (NPV) method. Section 7 of Chapter 8 focused on the special considerations needed for using the NPV method for international investment appraisals. To recap, these include:

- Predicting future exchange rates using **purchasing power parity theory**
- Comparing the project's NPV with those of similar host country projects
- Measuring the cash flows in terms of the **currency of the host country**
- Evaluating whether the cash flow remitted justifies the cash invested from the home country
- Differing national rates of inflation
- Different tax systems
- Difficulty in estimating terminal values

1.1.1 Implications of financing an overseas subsidiary

There are differences in the methods of financing used by parent companies and those used by foreign subsidiaries. The parent company itself is more likely than companies which have no foreign interests to raise finance in a foreign currency, or in its home currency from foreign sources.

The **need to finance a foreign subsidiary** raises the following questions:

(a) How much **equity capital** should the parent company put into the subsidiary?

(b) Should the subsidiary be allowed to **retain a large proportion** of its profits, to build up its equity reserves, or not?

(c) Should the parent company hold **100% of the equity** of the subsidiary, or should it try to create a minority shareholding, perhaps by floating the subsidiary on the country's domestic stock exchange?

(d) Should the subsidiary be encouraged to **borrow** as much **long-term debt** as it can, for example by raising large bank loans? If so, should the loans be in the domestic currency of the subsidiary's country, or should it try to raise a foreign currency loan?

(e) Should the subsidiary be encouraged to minimise its working capital investment by relying heavily on trade credit?

The **method of financing** a subsidiary will give some indication of the **nature and length of time** of the investment that the parent company is prepared to make. A sizeable equity investment (or long-term loans from the parent company to the subsidiary) would indicate a long-term investment by the parent company.

1.1.2 Factors influencing the choice of finance for an overseas subsidiary

(a) The **local finance costs**, and any subsidies which may be available

(b) **Taxation systems** of the countries in which the subsidiary is operating. Different tax rates can favour borrowing in high tax regimes, and no borrowing elsewhere

(c) Any restrictions on dividend remittances

(d) The possibility of flexibility in repayments which may arise from the parent/subsidiary relationship

Tax-saving opportunities may be maximised by **structuring the group** and its subsidiaries in such a way as to **take the best advantage** of the different local tax systems.

Because subsidiaries may be operating with a guarantee from the parent company, different gearing structures may be possible. Thus, a subsidiary may be able to operate with a higher level of debt that would be acceptable for the group as a whole.

Parent companies should also consider the following factors:

(a) **Reduced systematic risk.** There may be a small incremental reduction in systematic risk from investing abroad due to the segmentation of capital markets.

(b) **Access to capital.** Obtaining capital from foreign markets may increase liquidity, lower costs and make it easier to maintain optimum gearing.

(c) **Agency costs.** These may be higher due to political risk, market imperfections and complexity, leading to a higher cost of capital.

1.1.3 Dealing with currency risk on an overseas investment

To reduce the currency risk of an overseas investment, a company might **finance** it with **funds** in the **same currency** as the investment. The advantages of borrowing in the same currency as an investment are as follows:

(a) Assets and liabilities in the same currency can be **matched**, thus avoiding exchange losses on conversion in the group's annual accounts.

(b) **Revenues** in the foreign currency can be used to **repay borrowings** in the same currency, thus reducing losses due to fluctuating exchange rates.

2 Political risk and blocked funds

> **FAST FORWARD**
>
> Multinationals can take various measures to combat the risks of political **interference** or **turbulence** including agreements with governments, insurance, and location elsewhere of key parts of the production process.
>
> Multinationals can **counter exchange controls** by management charges or royalties.

2.1 Political risks for multinationals

Key term

> **Political risk** is the risk that political action will affect the position and value of a company.

When a multinational company invests in another country, by setting up a subsidiary, it may face a **political risk** of action by that country's government which restricts the multinational's freedom.

If a government tries to prevent the exploitation of its country by multinationals, it may take various measures.

(a) Import **quotas** could be used to limit the quantities of goods that a subsidiary can buy from its parent company and import for resale in its domestic markets.

(b) Import **tariffs** could make imports (such as from parent companies) more expensive and domestically produced goods therefore more competitive.

(c) Legal standards of safety or quality (**non-tariff barriers**) could be imposed on imported goods to prevent multinationals from selling goods through a subsidiary which have been banned as dangerous in other countries.

(d) **Exchange control regulations** could be applied (see below).

(e) A government could **restrict** the ability of foreign companies to buy domestic companies, especially those that operate in politically sensitive industries such as defence contracting, communications, energy supply and so on.

(f) A government could **nationalise** foreign-owned companies and their assets (with or without compensation to the parent company).

(g) A government could insist on a **minimum shareholding** in companies by residents. This would force a multinational to offer some of the equity in a subsidiary to investors in the country where the subsidiary operates.

2.2 Assessment of political risk

There are a large number of factors that can be taken into account when assessing political risk, for example:

- Government stability
- Political and business ethics
- Economic stability/inflation
- Degree of international indebtedness
- Financial infrastructure
- Level of import restrictions
- Remittance restrictions
- Assets seized
- Existence of special taxes and regulations on overseas investors, or investment incentives

In addition **micro factors**, factors only affecting the company or the industry in which it invests, may be more significant than macro factors, particularly in companies such as hi-tech organisations.

Measurement is often by **subjective weighting** of these factors. Macro analysis may involve use of measures such as those developed by Euromoney or the Economist Intelligence Unit. Micro analysis may be more problematic; specially tailored consultancy reports may be needed, also visits to the country or drawing on the experience of those who know the country

2.3 Dealing with political risks

There are various strategies that multinational companies can adopt to limit the effects of political risk.

2.3.1 Negotiations with host government

The aim of these negotiations is generally to obtain a **concession agreement**. This would cover matters such as the transfer of capital, remittances and products, access to local finance, government intervention and taxation, and transfer pricing.

2.3.2 Insurance

In the UK the Export Credits Guarantee Department (ECGD), operating under the name UK Export Finance, provides **protection against various threats** including nationalisation, currency conversion problems, war and revolution.

2.3.3 Production strategies

It may be necessary to strike a balance between **contracting out to local sources** (thus losing control) and **producing directly** (which increases the investment and hence increases the potential loss). Alternatively, it may be better to locate key parts of the production process or the distribution channels abroad. Control of patents is another possibility, since these can be enforced internationally.

2.3.4 Contacts with markets

Multinationals may have **contacts with customers** which interventionist governments cannot obtain.

2.3.5 Financial management

If a multinational obtains funds in local investment markets, these may be on terms that are **less favourable** than on markets abroad, but would mean that local institutions suffered if the local government intervened. However governments often do limit the ability of multinationals to obtain funds locally.

Alternatively guarantees can be obtained from the government for the investment that can be enforced by the multinational if the government takes action.

2.3.6 Management structure

Possible methods include **joint ventures** or **ceding control** to local investors and obtaining profits by a management contract.

If governments do intervene, multinationals may have to make use of the advantages they hold or threaten withdrawal. The threat of expropriation may be reduced by negotiation or legal threats.

2.4 Blocked funds

Exchange controls block the flow of foreign exchange into and out of a country, usually to defend the local currency or to protect reserves of foreign currencies. Exchange controls are generally more restrictive in developing and less developed countries although some still exist in developed countries. Typically, a government might enforce regulations:

(a) **Rationing the supply of foreign exchange**. Anyone wishing to make payments abroad in a foreign currency will be restricted by the limited supply, which stops them from buying as much as they want from abroad.

(b) **Restricting the types of transaction** for which payments abroad are allowed, for example by suspending or banning the payment of dividends to foreign shareholders, such as parent companies in multinationals, who will then have the problem of **blocked funds**.

2.5 Dealing with blocked funds

Ways of overcoming blocked funds include the following:

(a) The parent company could **sell goods or services** to the subsidiary and obtain payment. The amount of this payment will depend on the volume of sales and also on the transfer price for the sales.

(b) A parent company which grants a subsidiary the right to make goods protected by patents can charge a **royalty** on any goods that the subsidiary sells. The size of any royalty can be adjusted to suit the wishes of the parent company's management.

(c) If the parent company makes a **loan** to a subsidiary, it can set the interest rate high or low, thereby affecting the profits of both companies. A high rate of interest on a loan, for example, would improve the parent company's profits to the detriment of the subsidiary's profits.

(d) **Management charges** may be levied by the parent company for costs incurred in the management of international operations.

3 Taxation in the multinational environment

FAST FORWARD

Taxation, in particular, **double tax agreements**, may significantly affect returns from overseas investments.

3.1 Tax risks

International companies investing or trading abroad may risk a large tax burden:

(a) Through suffering local taxes that are **particularly heavy** on foreign investors

(b) Through **tariffs and customs charges**

(c) Through having the same profits taxed twice, once in the **country in which they are earned**, the other in the **company's country of residence**

(d) As we have seen, through using a **vehicle to invest abroad** that is subject to a **higher tax liability** (in other words in many regimes, using a subsidiary rather than a branch, as a subsidiary will be subject to a withholding tax on profits. This was explained in section 6.3 of chapter 1)

3.2 Double taxation relief

In order to prevent the same income being taxed twice **(double taxation)**, most countries give **double taxation relief**, a tax credit for taxes on income paid to the host country.

For example, suppose that the tax rate on profits in the Federal West Asian Republic is 20% and the UK corporation tax is 30%, and there is a double taxation agreement between the two countries. A subsidiary of a UK firm operating in the Federal West Asian Republic earns the equivalent of £1 million in profit, and therefore pays £200,000 in tax on profits. When the profits are remitted to the UK, the UK parent can claim a credit of £200,000 against the full UK tax charge of £300,000, and hence will only pay £100,000 to the UK tax authorities, and therefore only pays £300,000 in total.

Foreign tax credits are also available for withholding taxes on sums paid to other countries as dividends, interest, royalties and in other forms.

3.3 Tax havens

Tax havens are used by some multinationals as a means of deferring tax on funds prior to their repatriation or reinvestment. A tax haven is likely to have the following characteristics:

(a) Tax on foreign investment or sales income earned by resident companies, and withholding tax on dividends paid to the parent, should be low.

(b) There should be a stable government and a stable currency.

(c) There should be adequate financial services support facilities.

Pure tax havens impose a nil or low rate of tax. **Hybrid tax havens** offer specific tax incentives.

Examples of tax havens include the Channel Islands, Cayman Islands, Bermuda and the Bahamas.

3.3.1 Benefits of tax havens

(a) If a **tax haven holding company is used**, and all remittances to the home country are made from this company, the **income is pooled and treated** as if it all comes from this single source. This can allow the total of foreign tax paid to be offset against the total UK tax

liability of the tax haven holding company. This result is often that foreign tax credits are more **effectively used**.

(b) Capital gains may be **tax free**.

(c) There may be a **reduction in withholding tax** on dividends if they are paid by the tax haven holding company.

(d) It is often more **tax efficient** to channel cash from cash-rich subsidiaries to those requiring finance via a tax haven, rather than via the parent company.

(e) The company's affairs may be less transparent, as most tax havens have tough privacy laws and often bank secrecy arrangements.

3.3.2 Drawbacks of tax havens

(a) There may be **risks to post-tax earnings levels** as governments seek to close tax loopholes affecting tax havens.

(b) There are some **annual and incorporation costs** involved in registering in a tax haven.

(c) A political climate that is becoming more unfavourable to tax avoidance, and scandals involving companies registered in tax havens, may mean that there is a degree of **risk to reputation** involved in using them.

Overseas investment appraisal was considered in Chapter 8 of this Learning & Practice Workbook.

Question — International investment

Flagwaver plc is considering whether to establish a subsidiary in the USA, at a cost of $2,400,000. This would be represented by non-current assets of $2,000,000 and working capital of $400,000. The subsidiary would produce a product which would achieve annual sales of $1,600,000 and incur cash expenditures of $1,000,000 a year.

The company has a planning horizon of four years, at the end of which it expects the realisable value of the subsidiary's non-current assets to be $800,000.

It is the company's policy to remit the maximum funds possible to the parent company at the end of each year.

Tax is payable at the rate of 35% in the USA and is payable one year in arrears. A double taxation treaty exists between the UK and the USA and so no UK taxation is expected to arise.

Tax allowable depreciation is at a rate of 25% on a straight line basis on all non-current assets.

Because of the fluctuations in the exchange rate between the US dollar and sterling, the company would protect itself against the risk by raising a eurodollar loan to finance the investment. The company's cost of capital for the project is 16%.

Calculate the NPV of the project.

Answer

The annual writing down allowance (WDA) is 25% of US$2,000,000 = $500,000, from which the annual tax saving would be (at 35%) $175,000.

Year	Investment $m	Contribution $m	Tax on contribution $m	Tax saving on WDA & tax on realisable value $m	Net cash flow $m	Discount factor 16%	Present value $m
0	(2.4)				(2.400)	1.000	(2.400)
1		0.6		0.175	0.775	0.862	0.668
2		0.6	(0.21)	0.175	0.565	0.743	0.420
3		0.6	(0.21)	0.175	0.565	0.641	0.362
4	1.2*	0.6	(0.21)	0.175	1.765	0.552	0.974
5			(0.21)	(0.28)**	(0.490)	0.476	(0.233)
							(0.209)

*   Non-current assets realisable value $800,000 plus working capital $400,000

** It is assumed that tax would be payable on the realisable value of the non-current assets, since the tax written down value of the assets would be zero. 35% of $800,000 is $280,000.

The NPV is negative and so the project would not be viable at a discount rate of 16%.

4 Litigation risks

FAST FORWARD

Litigation risks can be reduced by keeping abreast of changes, acting as a good corporate citizen and lobbying.

4.1 Legal impacts

Companies may face government legislation or action in any jurisdiction that extend over its whole range of activities. Important areas may include the following:

(a) **Export and import controls** for political, environmental, or health and safety reasons. Such controls may not be overt but instead take the form of bureaucratic procedures designed to discourage international trade or protect home producers.

(b) **Favourable trade status** for particular countries, eg EU membership, former Commonwealth countries.

(c) **Monopolies and mergers legislation**, which may be interpreted not only within a country but also across nations. Thus the acquisition of a company in Country A, by Company B, which both sell in Country C may be seen as a monopolistic restraint of trade.

(d) **Law of ownership.** Especially in developing countries, there may be legislation requiring local majority ownership of a firm or its subsidiary in that country, for example.

(e) **Acceptance of international trademark, copyright and patent conventions**. Not all countries recognise such international conventions.

(f) Determination of minimum **technical standards** that the goods must meet eg noise levels, contents and so on.

(g) **Standardisation measures** such as packaging sizes.

(h) **Pricing regulations**, including credit (eg some countries require importers to deposit payment in advance and may require the price to be no lower than those of domestic competitors).

(i) **Restrictions on promotional messages**, methods and media.

(j) **Product liability**. Different countries have different rules regarding product liability (ie the manufacturer's/retailer's responsibility for defects in the product sold and/or injury caused). US juries are notoriously generous in this respect.

Bear in mind that organisations may also face legal risks from lack of legislation (or lack of enforcement of legislation) designed to protect them.

4.2 Dealing with legal risks

4.2.1 Consequences of non-compliance

Businesses that fail to comply with the law run the risk of **legal penalties** and accompanying **bad publicity**. Companies may also be forced into legal action to counter claims of allegedly bad practice that is not actually illegal; even a victory in such an action cannot prevent much bad publicity.

The issues of legal standards and costs have very significant implications for companies that trade internationally. Companies that meet a strict set of standards in one country may face accusations of **hypocrisy** if their practices are laxer elsewhere. Ultimately higher costs of compliance, as well as costs of labour may mean that companies **relocate** to countries where costs and regulatory burdens are lower.

4.2.2 The legislative process

Policy in many areas only changes slowly over time. Industries and organisations must however be alert for **likely changes in policy**.

Businesses also need to consider the impact of changes in how powers are **devolved** outside central government. In America state legislatures have been described as 'the forum for the ideas of the nation'. Directly elected mayors also wield considerable power in major cities.

4.2.3 Good citizenship

One aspect of minimising problems from governmental intervention is social and commercial good citizenship, **complying with best practice** and being responsive to **ethical concerns**. Often what is considered good practice at present is likely to acquire some regulatory force in the future. In addition, compliance with voluntary codes, particularly those relating to best practice or relations with consumers, can be **marketed positively**.

4.2.4 Other steps

Companies may wish to take all possible steps to avoid the bad publicity resulting from a court action. This includes implementing systems to make sure that the company **keeps abreast** of **changes in the law**, and staff are kept fully informed. Internal procedures may be designed to minimise the risks from legal action, for example **human resource policies** that minimise the chances of the company suffering an adverse judgement in a case brought by a disgruntled ex-employee. Contracts may be drawn up requiring **binding arbitration** in the case of disputes.

Of course compliance with legislation may involve **extra costs**, including the extra procedures and investment necessary to conform to safety standards, staff training costs and legal costs. However, these costs may also act as a **significant barrier to entry**, benefiting companies that are already in the industry.

5 Cultural risks

FAST FORWARD

Cultural risks affect the products and services produced and the way organisations are managed and staffed. Businesses should take cultural issues into account when deciding where to sell abroad, and how much to **centralise** activities.

5.1 Challenges of different cultures

Where a business trades with, or invests in, a foreign country additional uncertainty is introduced by the existence of different customs, laws and language. Communication between parties can be hindered, and potential deals put into jeopardy by ignorance of the expected manner in which such transactions should be conducted.

Case Study

Assumptions about particular cultures can also be dangerous. *Accountancy* magazine ran a series of articles some years ago about the major cultural issues involved in dealing with different countries. Its article on Greece suggested that 'unorthodox' methods might be required to be successful there:

'The concept of a bribe is one that is well understood in Greece.'

Unsurprisingly the magazine received a number of complaints about this article.

The following areas may be particularly important:

(a) The **cultures and practices of customers** and consumers in individual markets

(b) The **media and distribution systems** in overseas markets

(c) The **different ways of doing business** (eg it is reputed that Japanese companies are concerned to avoid excessive legalism) in overseas markets

(d) The degree to which **national cultural differences matter** for the product concerned (a great deal for some consumer products, eg washing machines where some countries prefer front-loading machines and others prefer top-loading machines, but less so for products such as gas turbines)

(e) The degree to which a firm can use its own **'national culture'** as a selling point

5.2 Dealing with cultural risk

5.2.1 Deciding which markets to enter

Making the right choices about which markets to enter is a key element in dealing with cultural risk. When deciding what types of country it should enter (in terms of environmental factors, economic development, language used, cultural similarities and so on), the major criteria for this decision should be as follows:

(a) **Market attractiveness**. This concerns such indicators as GNP/head and forecast demand.

(b) **Competitive advantage**. This is principally dependent on prior experience in similar markets, language and cultural understanding.

(c) **Risk**. This involves an analysis of political stability, the possibility of government intervention and similar external influences.

Some products are extremely sensitive to the **environmental differences**, which bring about the need for adaptation; others are not at all sensitive to these differences, in which case standardisation is possible.

Environmentally sensitive	Environmentally insensitive
Adaptation necessary	Standardisation possible
• Fashion clothes	• Industrial and agricultural products
• Convenience foods	• World market products, eg jeans

5.2.2 Use of control systems

Local conditions and the scale of operations will influence the organisation structure of companies trading internationally. Conglomerates with widely differing product groups may organise globally by product, with each operating division having its own geographic structure suited to its own needs.

Companies with more integrated operations may prefer their top-level structure to be broken down **geographically** with product management conducted locally.

Very large and complex companies may be organised as a **heterarchy,** an organic structure with significant local control.

(a) **Some headquarters functions are diffused geographically**. For example, R&D might be in the UK, marketing in the US. Some central functions might be split up: many firms are experimenting with having several centres for R&D.

(b) **Subsidiary managers have a strategic role for the corporation as a whole** (eg through bargaining and coalition forming).

(c) **Co-ordination is achieved through corporate culture and shared values** rather than a formal hierarchy. Employees with long experience might have worked in a number of different product divisions.

(d) **Alliances** can be formed with other company parts and other firms, perhaps in joint ventures or consortia.

5.3 Management of human resources

The balance between local and expatriate staff must be managed. There are a number of influences:

- The availability of technical skills such as financial management
- The need for control
- The importance of product and company experience
- The need to provide promotion opportunities
- Costs associated with expatriates such as travel and higher salaries
- Cultural factors

For an international company, which has to think globally as well as act locally, there are a number of problems:

- Do you employ mainly **expatriate staff** to control local operations?
- Do you employ **local managers**, with the possible loss of central control?
- Is there such a thing as the **global manager**, equally at home in different cultures?

Expatriate staff are sometimes favoured over local staff.

(a) Poor **educational opportunities** in the market may require the import of skilled technicians and managers. For example, expatriates have been needed in many western firms' operations in Russia and Eastern Europe, simply because they understand the importance of profit.

(b) Some senior managers believe that a business run by expatriates is easier to **control** than one run by local staff.

(c) Expatriates might be better able than locals to **communicate** with the corporate centre.

(d) The expatriate may **know more about the firm** overall, which is especially important if he or she is fronting a sales office.

The use of expatriates in overseas markets has certain disadvantages.

(a) They **cost** more (eg subsidised housing, school fees).

(b) **Culture shock**. The expatriate may fail to adjust to the culture (eg by associating only with other expatriates). This is likely to lead to poor management effectiveness, especially if the business requires personal contact.

(c) A substantial training programme might be needed.

   (i) **Basic facts** about the country will be given with basic language training, and some briefings about cultural differences.

   (ii) **Immersion training** involves detailed language and cultural training and simulation of field social and business experiences. This is necessary to obtain an intellectual understanding and practical awareness of the culture.

Employing local managers raises the following issues:

(a) A **glass ceiling** might exist in some companies. Talented local managers may not make it to board level if, most members of the board are drawn from one country.

(b) In some cases, it may be hard for locals to **assimilate** into the **corporate culture**, and this might led to communication problems.

(c) Locals will **have greater knowledge of the country**, but may find it difficult to understand the wider corporate picture.

The following issues may also be important:

(a) **Recruitment and training**. In countries with low levels of literacy, more effort might need to be spent on basic training.

(b) **Career management**. Can overseas staff realistically expect promotion to the firm's highest levels if they do well?

(c) **Appraisal schemes**. These can be a minefield at the best of times, and the possibilities for communications failure are endless. For example, in some cultures, an appraisal is a two way discussion whereas in others arguing back might be considered a sign of insubordination.

(d) Problems associated with the **status of women**.

(e) **Communications**. Human Resources Management tries to mobilise employees' commitment to the goals of the organisation. In far-flung global firms, the normal panoply of staff newsletters and team briefings may be hard to institute but are vital. Time differences also make communication difficult.

Chapter Roundup

- The methods of financing overseas subsidiaries will depend on the **length of investment period** envisaged, also the **local finance costs**, **taxation systems** and **restrictions on dividend remittances**.

- Multinationals can take various measures to combat the risks of political **interference** or **turbulence** including agreements with governments, insurance, and location elsewhere of key parts of the production process.

- Multinationals can **counter exchange controls** by management charges or royalties.

- Taxation, in particular, **double tax agreements**, may significantly affect returns from overseas investments.

- **Litigation risks** can be reduced by keeping abreast of changes, acting as a good corporate citizen and lobbying.

- **Cultural risks** affect the products and services produced and the way organisations are managed and staffed. Businesses should take cultural issues into account when deciding where to sell abroad, and how much to **centralise** activities.

Quick Quiz

1. Give three reasons why a multinational might establish an overseas subsidiary.
2. Give three factors that might influence the choice of finance for an overseas subsidiary.
3. By what methods do governments impose exchange controls?
4. Give four examples of ways companies can overcome exchange controls.
5. Forward integration would involve acquiring final production and distribution facilities in other countries.

    ☐ True

    ☐ False

6. What principal characteristics is a tax haven most likely to have?
7. Why might a firm looking to establish an overseas presence choose to set up a branch rather than a subsidiary?
8. What are the main differences between a contractual joint venture and a joint-equity venture?

LEARNING OUTCOME 2 THE INVESTMENT DECISION

Answers to Quick Quiz

1 Any three of:
   (a) Location of markets
   (b) Need for a sales organisation
   (c) Opportunity to produce goods more cheaply
   (d) Need to avoid import controls
   (e) Need to obtain access for raw materials
   (f) Availability of grants and tax concessions

2 Any three of:
   (a) Local finance costs
   (b) Taxation systems
   (c) Restrictions on dividend remittances
   (d) Flexibility in repayments

3 (a) Rationing the supply of foreign exchange
   (b) Restricting the types of transaction for which payments abroad are allowed

4 (a) Selling goods or services to subsidiary
   (b) Charging a royalty on goods sold by subsidiary
   (c) Interest rate manipulation
   (d) Management charges

5 True

6 (a) Tax on foreign investment or sales income earned by resident companies, and withholding tax on dividends paid to parent should be low
   (b) Stable government and stable currency
   (c) Adequate financial service support facilities

7 (a) More favourable tax (not subject to withholding tax)
   (b) Fewer legal formalities

8 A contractual joint venture is for a fixed period, duties and responsibilities are defined in a contract
   A joint-equity venture involves investment, is of no fixed duration and continually evolves.

12: APPRAISAL OF OVERSEAS INVESTMENT DECISIONS

End of chapter question

Kiwi Knitwear (AIA November 2012)

Kiwi Knitwear manufactures clothing. The company is based in New Zealand and it specialises in making woollen jumpers. It purchases the wool for the jumpers from sheep farmers in New Zealand. The company has had a sales enquiry from a very large department store group based in the UK. The UK department store group would like Kiwi Knitwear to manufacture woollen coats for sale in its shops in the UK. This would be a new venture for Kiwi Knitwear as the manufacture of coats requires completely different machinery to the manufacture of jumpers. The directors of Kiwi Knitwear are interested in the new venture as they have thought it would be useful to cease being wholly dependent on the jumper market. However, they are concerned that they may make the wrong decision and invest in a new business area that may not be successful.

The directors of Kiwi Knitwear have gathered the following information about this potential new venture:

1. The UK department store has indicated that it would agree to sign an initial three-year contract. Under this contract it would purchase 7,500 coats in the first year, 10,000 coats in the second year and 10,000 coats in the third year. It would pay Kiwi Knitwear in UK sterling and the price it would pay is £85 per coat. The payments for the coats would be made at the end of each year.

2. The UK department store recognises that Kiwi Knitwear could not begin manufacturing the coats immediately. Therefore, the three-year contract would commence in one year's time. This would give Kiwi Knitwear a period of one year during which it can find suitable factory premises. It would rent the premises for the three-year period of the contract. The directors of Kiwi Knitwear have estimated that the rent it would have to pay would be New Zealand dollars (NZ$)170,000 per year, payable at the end of each year.

3. The machinery required to manufacture the coats would cost NZ$225,000. This machinery would have to be paid for in one year's time. Assume that there is no market for selling the machine on to another company at the end of the project.

4. Kiwi Knitwear has estimated that the wool and other materials required to manufacture each coat would cost NZ$24 per coat. The suppliers of materials would be paid at the end of each year. In the year before the contract starts Kiwi Knitwear would employ two new managers to set up the venture. These managers would each be paid NZ$85,000 per year. The two managers would remain with the company for the additional three years whilst the contract was running. In addition, there would be further staffing costs incurred in the factory during the period of the three-year contract that would total NZ$800,000 per year.

5. The directors of Kiwi Knitwear have visited the UK to have a series of discussions with the UK department store group. This visit has just been paid for and cost NZ$5,000. If the venture were to go ahead then there would need to be visits to the UK at the start of each year of the three-year contract and it has been estimated this would incur hotel and travel costs of NZ$3,000 per visit.

6. The delivery of the coats to the UK would cost Kiwi Knitwear NZ$4 per coat, payable at the end of each year.

7. Kiwi Knitwear pays tax in New Zealand at a rate of 15%. Tax is payable one year in arrears. If the net cashflow for any year is negative then you should assume that zero tax will be paid on this cashflow, and that the negative cashflow will be used to reduce the next available positive cashflow when calculating tax on that positive cashflow.

8. The current exchange rate is NZ$1 = £0.4973. It has been estimated that the rate of inflation in New Zealand is expected to be 2.5% per year for the foreseeable future and the rate of inflation in the UK is expected to be 1.5% per year for the foreseeable future.

9. The company has a cost of capital of 9%.

LEARNING OUTCOME 2 THE INVESTMENT DECISION

Required

(a) Prepare calculations to evaluate whether it is worthwhile for Kiwi Knitwear to enter into the contract and, on the basis of these calculations, advise the directors whether the contract should be entered into. State any assumptions you have made in your calculations. **(16 marks)**

(b) The directors of Kiwi Knitwear recognise that there will be risks attached to the new venture should they decide to enter into the contract. You are required to advise the directors of what the principal risks might be in respect of the new venture. **(12 marks)**

(c) The directors of Kiwi Knitwear have heard that a real options approach to the appraisal of capital investments may be an appropriate technique to use in some situations. You are required to advise the directors what a real options approach is and whether it could be helpful to adopt a real options approach in respect of this potential new venture. **(12 marks)**

(Total 40 marks)

Valuation and corporate change

Valuation of companies

Topic list	Syllabus reference
1 Reasons for share valuations	LO3
2 Asset valuation bases	LO3
3 Earnings valuation bases	LO3
4 Cash flow valuation methods	LO3
5 Dividend bases	LO3
6 Other valuation bases	LO3
7 Valuation of debt	LO3

Introduction

Our main interest in this chapter is with methods of valuing the entire equity in a company, perhaps for the purpose of making a takeover bid, rather than with the value of small blocks of shares which an investor might choose to buy or sell on the stock market.

The main themes in this chapter that you need to understand are **how** to use each method, **when** they're used and their **problems**.

Free cash flows (Section 4) are relevant to investment appraisal as well.

The final section of this chapter looks at how to value debt instruments.

LEARNING OUTCOME 3 VALUATION AND CORPORATE CHANGE

1 Reasons for share valuations

> **FAST FORWARD**
>
> There are a number of different ways of **putting a value on a business**, or on shares in an unquoted company. It is best to use **several methods** of valuation, and to compare the values they produce.

1.1 When valuations are required

Given quoted share prices on the Stock Exchange, why devise techniques for estimating the value of a share? A share valuation will be necessary:

(a) For **quoted companies**, when there is a takeover bid and the offer price is an estimated 'fair value' in excess of the current market price of the shares

(b) For unquoted companies, when:

    (i) The company wishes to 'go public' and must fix an issue price for its shares
    (ii) There is a scheme of merger
    (iii) Shares are sold
    (iv) Shares need to be valued for the purposes of taxation
    (v) Shares are pledged as collateral for a loan

(c) For **subsidiary companies**, when the group's holding company is negotiating the sale of the subsidiary to a management buyout team or to an external buyer

Key term

> A **takeover** is the acquisition by a company of a controlling interest in the voting share capital of another company, usually achieved by the purchase of a majority of the voting shares.

Valuing **unquoted companies** presents some special considerations, for example:

(a) **It may not be sensible to use P/E ratios** of a quoted company for comparative purposes because the market value of a quoted company is likely to include a premium to reflect the marketability of its shares.

(b) A small unquoted company may be highly sensitive to the **loss of key employees** which may follow a merger or buyout. An arrangement to tie key employees in to the enterprise could be costly.

1.2 Common bases for valuing shares

- Asset based
- Earning based – P/E multiples, earning yield, ARR
- Cash flow based – DCF
- Dividends based
- Other – super profits, earn out arrangements

No one basis is 'correct'. The best possible valuation is market value, although this needs a willing buyer or seller.

1.3 Factors influencing share valuations

Companies or shareholdings can have different values depending on the circumstances of the purchase or sale.

- Size of holding
- Reactions of other shareholders
- Reasons for sale
- Liquidity
- Takeover scenarios

Exam focus point

> In an exam question as well as in practice, it is unlikely that one method would be used in isolation. Several valuations might be made, each using a different technique or different assumptions. The valuations could then be compared, and a final price reached as a compromise between the different values.

In addition, buying a company will give rise to a **premium for control**. The amount of the premium is often between 15% and 25%.

2 Asset valuation bases

FAST FORWARD

> The **net assets valuation** method can be used as one of many valuation methods, or to provide a lower limit for the value of a company. By itself it is unlikely to produce the most realistic value.

2.1 The net assets method of share valuation

Using this method of valuation

$$\text{Value of shares in class} = \frac{\text{Net tangible assets attributable to that class}}{\text{No of shares in class}}$$

Intangible assets (including goodwill) should be excluded, unless they have a market value (for example, patents and copyrights, which could be sold).

(a) **Goodwill**, if shown in the accounts, is unlikely to be shown at a true figure for purposes of valuation, and the value of goodwill should be reflected in another method of valuation (for example, the earnings basis, the dividend yield basis or the super-profits method).

(b) **Development expenditure**, if shown in the accounts, would also have a value which is related to future profits rather than to the worth of the company's physical assets.

2.2 Example: Net assets method of share valuation

The summary statement of financial position of Cactus Ltd is as follows:

	£	£	£
Non-current assets			
Land and buildings			160,000
Plant, property and equipment			80,000
Motor vehicles			20,000
			260,000
Goodwill			20,000
Current assets			
Inventories		80,000	
Receivables		60,000	
Short-term investments		15,000	
Cash and cash equivalents		5,000	
		160,000	
Current liabilities			
Payables	60,000		
Taxation	20,000		
Proposed ordinary dividend	20,000		
		(100,000)	
			60,000
			340,000
12% debentures			(60,000)
Deferred taxation			(10,000)
			270,000

LEARNING OUTCOME 3 VALUATION AND CORPORATE CHANGE

	£
Ordinary shares of £1	80,000
Reserves	140,000
	220,000
4.9% preference shares of £1	50,000
	270,000

What is the value of an ordinary share using the net assets basis of valuation?

Solution

If the figures given for asset values are not questioned, the valuation would be as follows:

	£	£
Total value of net assets		340,000
Less intangible asset (goodwill)		20,000
Total value of tangible assets (net)		320,000
Less: preference shares	50,000	
debentures	60,000	
deferred taxation	10,000	
		120,000
Net asset value of equity		200,000
Number of ordinary shares		80,000
Value per share		£2.50

2.3 Choice of valuation bases

The difficulty in an asset valuation method is establishing the **asset values** to use. Values ought to be realistic. The figure attached to an individual asset may vary considerably depending on whether it is valued on a **going concern** or a **break-up** basis.

Possibilities include:

- **Historic basis** – unlikely to give a realistic value
- **Replacement basis** – if the asset is to be used on an on-going basis
- **Realisable basis** – if the asset is to be sold, or the business as a whole broken up

The following list should give you some idea of the factors that must be considered:

(a) Do the assets need **professional valuation**? If so, how much will this cost?

(b) Have the **liabilities** been accurately quantified, for example deferred taxation? Are there any contingent liabilities? Will any balancing tax charges arise on disposal?

(c) How have the **current assets** been valued? Are all debtors collectable? Is all inventory realisable? Can all the assets be physically located and brought into a saleable condition? This may be difficult in certain circumstances where the assets are situated abroad.

(d) Can any **hidden liabilities** be accurately assessed? Would there be redundancy payments and closure costs?

(e) Is there an **available market** in which the assets can be realised (on a break-up basis)? If so, do the statement of financial position values truly reflect these break-up values?

(f) Are there any **prior charges** on the assets?

(g) Does the business have a regular **revaluation and replacement** policy? What are the bases of the valuation? As a broad rule, valuations will be more useful the better they estimate the **future cash flows** that are derived from the asset.

(h) Are there factors that might indicate that the **going concern valuation** of the business **as a whole is significantly higher** than the valuation of the individual assets?

(i) What shareholdings are being sold? If a minority interest is being disposed of, realisable value is of limited relevance as the assets will not be sold.

2.4 Use of net asset basis

The net assets basis of valuation might be used in the following circumstances.

(a) **As a measure of the 'security' in a share value**. A share might be valued using an earnings basis (discussed next), and this valuation might be:

    (i) **Higher than the net asset value per share** (If the company went into liquidation, the investor could not expect to receive the full value of his shares when the underlying assets were realised.)

    (ii) **Lower than the net asset value per share** (If the company went into liquidation, the investor might expect to receive the full value of his shares and perhaps much more, when the underlying assets were realised.)

The **asset backing** for shares thus provides a measure of the possible loss if the company fails to make the expected earnings or dividend payments. It is often thought to be a good thing to acquire a company with valuable tangible assets, especially freehold property which might be expected to increase in value over time.

(b) **As a measure of comparison in a scheme of merger**

For example, if Company A, which has a low asset backing, is planning a merger with Company B, which has a high asset backing, the shareholders of B might consider that their shares' value ought to reflect this. It might therefore be agreed that a something should be added to the value of the Company B shares to allow for this difference in asset backing.

(c) **As a 'floor value'**

This is for a business that is up for sale – shareholders will be reluctant to sell for less than the NAV. However, if the sale is essential for cash flow purposes or to realign with corporate strategy, even the asset value may not be realised.

3 Earnings valuation bases

FAST FORWARD

P/E ratios are used when a large block of shares, or a whole business, is being valued. This method can be problematic when quoted companies' P/E ratios are used to value unquoted companies.

3.1 The P/E ratio (earnings) method of valuation

This is a common method of valuing a controlling interest in a company, where the owner can decide on dividend and retentions policy. The P/E ratio relates earnings per share to a share's value.

Since P/E ratio = $\dfrac{\text{Market value}}{\text{EPS}}$

then market value per share = EPS × P/E ratio

The P/E ratio produce an **earnings-based** valuation of shares. This is done by deciding a suitable P/E ratio and multiplying this by the EPS for the shares which are being valued.

Market valuation or capitalisation = P/E ratio × earnings per share

The EPS could be a historical EPS or a prospective future EPS. For a given EPS figure, a higher P/E ratio will result in a higher price.

3.2 Significance of high P/E ratio

A high P/E ratio may indicate:

(a) **Expectations that the EPS will grow rapidly**

A **high price is being paid for future profit prospects.** Many small but successful and fast-growing companies are valued on the stock market on a high P/E ratio. Some stocks (for example, those of some software companies in the late 2010s) have reached high valuations before making any profits at all, on the strength of expected future earnings.

(b) **Security of earnings**

A well-established low-risk company would be valued on a higher P/E ratio than a similar company whose earnings are subject to greater uncertainty.

(c) **Status**

If a quoted company (the predator) made a share-for-share takeover bid for an unquoted company (the target), it would normally expect its own shares to be valued on a higher P/E ratio than the target company's shares. A quoted company ought to be a lower-risk company; but in addition, there is an advantage in having shares which are quoted on a stock market: the shares can be readily sold. **The P/E ratio of an unquoted company's shares might be around 50% to 60% of the P/E ratio of a similar public company with a full Stock Exchange listing** (and perhaps 70% of that of a company whose shares are traded on the AIM).

3.3 Problems with using P/E ratios

However using the price-earnings ratios of quoted companies to value unquoted companies may be problematic.

- Finding a quoted company with a **similar range of activities** may be difficult. Quoted companies are often **diversified**.
- A **single year's P/E ratio** may not be a good basis, if earnings are volatile, or the quoted company's share price is at an abnormal level, due for example to the expectation of a takeover bid.
- If a P/E ratio trend is used, then **historical data** will be being used to value how the unquoted company will do **in the future**.
- The quoted company may have a **different capital structure** to the unquoted company.

3.4 Guidelines for a P/E ratio-based valuation

When a company is thinking of acquiring an **unquoted** company in a takeover, the final offer price will be agreed by **negotiation**, but a list of some of the factors affecting the valuer's choice of P/E ratio is given below.

(a) General **economic** and **financial** conditions.

(b) The type of **industry** and the prospects of that industry. Use of current P/E ratios may give an unrealistically low valuation if these ratios are being affected by a lack of confidence throughout the industry.

(c) The **size** of the undertaking and its **status** within its industry. If an unquoted company's earnings are growing annually and are currently around £300,000 or so, then it could probably get a quote in its own right on the Alternative Investment Market, and a higher P/E ratio should therefore be used when valuing its shares.

(d) **Marketability**. The market in shares which do not have a Stock Exchange quotation is always a restricted one and a higher yield is therefore required.

> **Exam focus point**
>
> For examination purposes, you should normally **take a figure around one half to two thirds** of the industry average when valuing an unquoted company.

(e) The **diversity** of shareholdings and the **financial status** of any principal shareholders.

(f) The **reliability** of profit estimates and the past profit record. Use of profits and P/E ratios over time may give a more reliable valuation, especially if they are being compared with industry levels over that time.

(g) **Asset backing** and **liquidity**.

(h) The **nature of the assets**, for example whether some of the non-current assets are of a highly specialised nature, and so have only a small break-up value.

(i) **Gearing**. A relatively high gearing ratio will generally mean greater financial risk for ordinary shareholders and call for a higher rate of return on equity.

(j) The extent to which the business is dependent on the **technical skills** of one or more individuals.

(k) The predator may need to be particularly careful when valuing an unlisted company of using a P/E ratio of a '**similar**' **listed company**. The predator should obtain reasonable evidence that the listed company does have the same risk and growth characteristics, and has similar policies on significant areas such as directors' remuneration.

3.4.1 Use of predator's P/E ratio

A predator company may sometimes use their higher P/E ratio to value a target company. This assumes that the predator **can improve the target's business**, which is a dangerous assumption to make. It would be better to use an adjusted industry P/E ratio, or some other method.

3.4.2 Forecast growth in earnings

When one company is thinking about taking over another, it should look at the target company's **forecast earnings**, not just its historical results.

Forecasts of **earnings growth** should only be used if:

- There are good reasons to believe that earnings growth will be achieved
- A reasonable estimate of growth can be made
- Forecasts supplied by the target company's directors are made in good faith and using reasonable assumptions and fair accounting policies

Question — Valuations

Flycatcher Ltd wishes to make a takeover bid for the shares of an unquoted company, Mayfly Ltd. The earnings of Mayfly Ltd over the past five years have been as follows.

20X0	£50,000	20X3	£71,000
20X1	£72,000	20X4	£75,000
20X2	£68,000		

LEARNING OUTCOME 3 VALUATION AND CORPORATE CHANGE

The average P/E ratio of quoted companies in the industry in which Mayfly Ltd operates is 10. Quoted companies which are similar in many respects to Mayfly Ltd are:

(a) Bumblebee plc, which has a P/E ratio of 15, but is a company with very good growth prospects
(b) Wasp plc, which has had a poor profit record for several years, and has a P/E ratio of 7

What would be a suitable range of valuations for the shares of Mayfly Ltd?

Answer

(a) **Earnings**. Average earnings over the last five years have been £67,200, and over the last four years £71,500. There might appear to be some growth prospects, but estimates of future earnings are uncertain.

A low estimate of earnings in 20X5 would be, perhaps, £71,500.

A high estimate of earnings might be £75,000 or more. This solution will use the most recent earnings figure of £75,000 as the high estimate.

(b) **P/E ratio**. A P/E ratio of 15 (Bumblebee's) would be much too high for Mayfly Ltd, because the growth of Mayfly Ltd earnings is not as certain, and Mayfly Ltd is an unquoted company.

On the other hand, Mayfly Ltd's expectations of earnings are probably better than those of Wasp plc. A suitable P/E ratio might be based on the industry's average, 10; but since Mayfly is an unquoted company and therefore more risky, a lower P/E ratio might be more appropriate: perhaps 60% to 70% of 10 = 6 or 7, or conceivably even as low as 50% of 10 = 5.

The valuation of Mayfly Ltd's shares might therefore range between:

high P/E ratio and high earnings: 7 × £75,000 = £525,000; and

low P/E ratio and low earnings: 5 × £71,500 = £357,500.

3.5 Example: Earnings method of valuation

Spider plc is considering the takeover of an unquoted company, Fly Ltd. Spider's shares are quoted on the Stock Exchange at a price of £3.20 and since the most recent published EPS of the company is 20p, the company's P/E ratio is 16. Fly Ltd is a company with 100,000 shares and current earnings of £50,000, 50p per share. How might Spider plc decide on an offer price?

Solution

The decision about the offer price is likely to be preceded by the estimation of a 'reasonable' P/E ratio in the light of the particular circumstances.

(a) If Fly Ltd is in the **same industry** as Spider plc, its P/E ratio ought to be lower, because of its lower status as an unquoted company.

(b) If Fly Ltd is in a **different industry**, a suitable P/E ratio might be based on the P/E ratio that is typical for quoted companies in that industry.

(c) If Fly Ltd is thought to be **growing fast**, so that its EPS will rise rapidly in the years to come, the P/E ratio that should be used for the share valuation will be higher than if only small EPS growth is expected.

(d) If the acquisition of Fly Ltd would **contribute substantially to Spider's own profitability and growth**, or to any other strategic objective that Spider has, then Spider should be willing to offer a higher P/E ratio valuation, in order to secure acceptance of the offer by Fly's shareholders.

Of course, the P/E ratio on which Spider bases its offer will probably be lower than the P/E ratio that Fly's shareholders think their shares ought to be valued on. Some haggling over the price might be necessary.

Spider might decide that Fly's shares ought to be valued on a P/E ratio of 60% × 16 = 9.6, that is, at 9.6 × 50p = £4.80 each.

Fly's shareholders might reject this offer, and suggest a valuation based on a P/E ratio of, say, 12.5, that is, 12.5 × 50p = £6.25.

Spider's management might then come back with a revised offer, say valuation on a P/E ratio of 10.5, that is, 10.5 × 50p = £5.25.

The haggling will go on until the negotiations either break down or succeed in arriving at an agreed price.

3.6 The earnings yield valuation method

FAST FORWARD

Other earnings' methods include the **earnings yield valuation method** and the **accounting rate of return method**.

Earnings yield (EY) = $\dfrac{\text{EPS}}{\text{Market price per share}} \times 100\%$

This method is effectively a variation on the P/E method (the EY being the inverse of the P/E ratio), using an appropriate earnings yield effectively as a discount rate to value the earnings:

Market value = $\dfrac{\text{Earnings}}{\text{EY}}$

Exactly the same guidelines apply to this method as for the P/E method. Note that where **high growth** is envisaged, **the EY will be low,** as current earnings will be low relative to a market price that has built in future earnings growth.

3.7 The accounting rate of return (ARR) method of share valuation

This method considers the **accounting rate of return** which will be required from the company whose shares are to be valued. It is therefore distinct from the P/E ratio method, which is concerned with the **market** rate of return required.

The following formula should be used:

Value of business = $\dfrac{\text{Estimated future profits}}{\text{Required return on capital employed}}$

For a takeover bid valuation, it will often be necessary to adjust the profits figure to allow for **expected changes** after the takeover. Those arising in an examination question might include:

(a) New levels of **directors' remuneration**

(b) New levels of **interest charges** (perhaps because the predator company will be able to replace existing loans with new loans at a lower rate of interest, or because the previous owners had lent the company money at non-commercial rates)

(c) A charge for **notional rent** where it is intended to sell existing properties or where the rate of return used is based on the results of similar companies that do not own their own properties

(d) The effects of **product rationalisation** and improved management

Note that such an adjustment can also apply to earnings used in a P/E valuation approach.

3.7.1 Example: ARR method of share valuation

Sara Ltd is considering acquiring Hall Ltd. At present Hall Ltd is earning, on average, £480,000 after tax. The directors of Sara Ltd feel that after reorganisation, this figure could be increased to £600,000. All the companies in the Sara group are expected to yield a post-tax accounting return of 15% on capital employed. What should Hall Ltd be valued at?

Solution

$$\text{Valuation} = \frac{£600,000}{15\%} = £4,000,000$$

This figure is the maximum that Sara should be prepared to pay. The first offer would probably be much lower.

An ARR valuation might be used in a takeover when the acquiring company is trying to assess the **maximum amount it can afford to pay**. This is because it is a measure of management efficiency and the rate used can be selected to reflect (among other things) the return which the acquiring company thinks should be obtainable after any post-acquisition reorganisation has been completed.

3.8 Earnings growth model

This method assumes that earnings re-invested in the business earn only the required rate of return, that there are no positive net present value methods available.

Under the earnings growth model

$$P_0 \text{ (ex-div)} = \frac{E_1}{K_e}$$

where P_0 (ex-div) = price/value at time 0, excluding any dividend at time 0
 E_1 = earnings at time 1
 K_e = cost of equity (equals investor required return)

4 Cash flow valuation methods

> **FAST FORWARD**
>
> Cash flow **DCF valuation** may be used to value a company. **Free cash flows** are a development of the DCF method.

4.1 The discounted future cash flows method of share valuation

This method of share valuation may be appropriate when one company intends to buy the assets of another company and to make further investments in order to improve cash flows in the future.

4.2 Example: Discounted future cash flows method of share valuation

Diversification Ltd wishes to make a bid for Tadpole Ltd. Tadpole Ltd makes after-tax profits of £40,000 a year. Diversification Ltd believes that if further money is spent on additional investments, the after-tax cash flows (ignoring the purchase consideration) could be as follows:

Year	Cash flow (net of tax) £
0	(100,000)
1	(80,000)
2	60,000
3	100,000
4	150,000
5	150,000

The after-tax cost of capital of Diversification Ltd is 15% and the company expects all its investments to pay back, in discounted terms, within five years. What is the maximum price that the company should be willing to pay for the shares of Tadpole Ltd?

Solution

The maximum price is one which would make the return from the total investment exactly 15% over five years, so that the NPV at 15% would be 0.

Year	Cash flows ignoring purchase consideration £	Discount factor (from tables) 15%	Present value £
0	(100,000)	1.000	(100,000)
1	(80,000)	0.870	(69,600)
2	60,000	0.756	45,360
3	100,000	0.658	65,800
4	150,000	0.572	85,800
5	150,000	0.497	74,550
Maximum purchase price			101,910

4.3 Selection of an appropriate cost of capital

In the above example, Diversification used its own cost of capital to discount the cash flows of Tadpole Ltd. There are a number of reasons why this may not be appropriate. The use of a current weighted average cost of capital (WACC) to appraise new investment is covered elsewhere in this Learning & Practice Workbook:

(a) The **business risk** of the new investment may not match that of the investing company – if Tadpole is in a completely different line of business from Diversification, its cash flows are likely to be subject to differing degrees of risk, and this should be taken into account when valuing them.

(b) The **method of finance** of the new investment may not match the current debt/equity mix of the investing company, which may have an effect on the cost of capital to be used.

4.4 Free cash flow

Under NPV

Valuation of a new company = Cash subscribed/paid for investment + NPV of proposed activities

The **present value** of future **free cash flows model** focuses on the strategic need of companies to reinvest in new plant to maintain or increase current operating cash flows. This investment expenditure does not generally equal the depreciation charge in the accounts. Free cash flow takes into account this difference. In the free cash flow model:

Free cash flow to companies

= Revenues
− Operating costs (**excluding** interest)
+ Depreciation
− Lease obligations
− Working capital increases
− Taxes
− Replacement capital expenditure

You may see slightly different versions of the model.

If the cash flows are **discounted over time**, **free cash flows** to the **company** should be **discounted** using the company's **weighted average cost of capital**; **free cash flows** to **equity** should be **discounted** using **the cost of equity**. The different costs of capital are discussed further in Chapter 6.

LEARNING OUTCOME 3 VALUATION AND CORPORATE CHANGE

Using this model, the value of the company is the sum of **future discounted cash flows**.

Exam focus point: Students often forget to deduct replacement capital expenditure in free cash flow calculations.

Free cash flow to equity is calculated after also taking into account changes in debt:

- = Revenues
- − Operating costs
- + Depreciation
- − Lease obligations
- − Working capital increases
- − Taxes
- − Replacement capital expenditure
- + New debt
- − Debt repayments

4.4.1 Features of free cash flow

The **advantage** of including strategic value as well as existing project value in the definition of free cash flow is that **strategic value** can often be a significant element of **company value**.

Possible disadvantages are that free cashflows may **fluctuate significantly** and will depend considerably on the company's **capital replacement policy**.

Free cash flows can also be used as an element in ratio calculations. For example, the dividend cover ratio can be adjusted to take account of free cash flow:

$$\text{Dividend cover} = \frac{\text{Free cash flow}}{\text{Dividends paid}}$$

Thus emphasising the importance of having cash available to pay dividends.

Free cash flow is also an important element in shareholder value analysis.

4.5 Example: Free cash flow

The following financial data relates to Louie plc for the year ended 31 December 20X7.

	£'000
Profit before tax	200
Tax charge (30% tax rate)	(60)
Profit after tax	140

(i) The depreciation charge for the year was £50,000. During the year Louie spent £150,000 replacing its fleet of trucks and £1,500,000 on a new building which will be used to produce a new product range from April 20X8.

(ii) The change in working capital (inventory, receivables and payables) was a decrease of £90,000.

(iii) During the year Louie repaid £250,000 debentures and took out a long-term loan for £600,000.

The interest charge for the year was £60,000.

Required

Calculate the cash flows:

(a) To the company
(b) To equity

Solution

	£'000
Profit before tax	200
Depreciation	50
Interest (1 – Tax rate)	42
Working capital decrease	90
Tax	(60)
Replacement capital expenditure	(150)
Free cash flows to company (a)	172
New debt	600
Debt repayments	(250)
Free cash flows to equity (b)	522

Notes

- As we are given profit before tax, after-tax interest has to be added back.
- Capital expenditure for purposes of expansion is ignored in this calculation.

Question — Free cash flows

The following data has been included in the accounts of Dewie plc for the year ended 30 June 20X8.

	£'000
Profit before interest and tax	400
Interest	(80)
Tax charge	(90)
Profit after tax	230

(a) The depreciation charge for the year was £120,000. During the year Dewie spent £500,000 on non-current assets, including £240,000 on replacing its existing fleet of lorries and £110,000 on general expenditure reflecting its sales growth. Other expenditure related to new shops to be opened in autumn 20X8.

(b) The change in working capital, was an increase of £70,000.

(c) During the year Dewie repaid a £500,000 bank loan and issued £600,000 debentures. The company also paid £40,000 to a leasing company.

(d) The tax rate is 30%.

Required

Calculate the cash flows to equity.

Answer

	£'000
Profit before interest and tax	400
Depreciation	120
Working capital increase	(70)
Tax (90 + Tax charge on interest (80 × 0.3))	(114)
Replacement capital expenditure	(350)
Leases	(40)
New debt	600
Debt repayments	(500)
Free cash flows to equity	46

Note that the interest allowance on tax paid has to be adjusted for, and is adjusted differently in the example and the question. In the example we start with profit before tax, and so interest net of tax is added back. In the question we start with profit before interest and tax. As we are not adding back interest, here the tax charge has to be adjusted.

4.6 Shareholder value analysis

FAST FORWARD

Shareholder value analysis focuses on the key decisions affecting value and risk.

Key term

Shareholder value analysis is an approach to financial management which focuses on the creation of economic value for shareholders, as measured by share price performance and flow of dividends.

Shareholder value analysis (SVA) was developed during the 1980s from the work of Rappaport and focuses on value creation using the net present value (NPV) approach. Thus SVA assumes that **the value of a business is the net present value of its future cash flows, discounted at the appropriate cost of capital**. Many leading companies (including, for example, Pepsi, Quaker and Disney) have used SVA as a way of linking management strategy and decisions to the creation of value for shareholders.

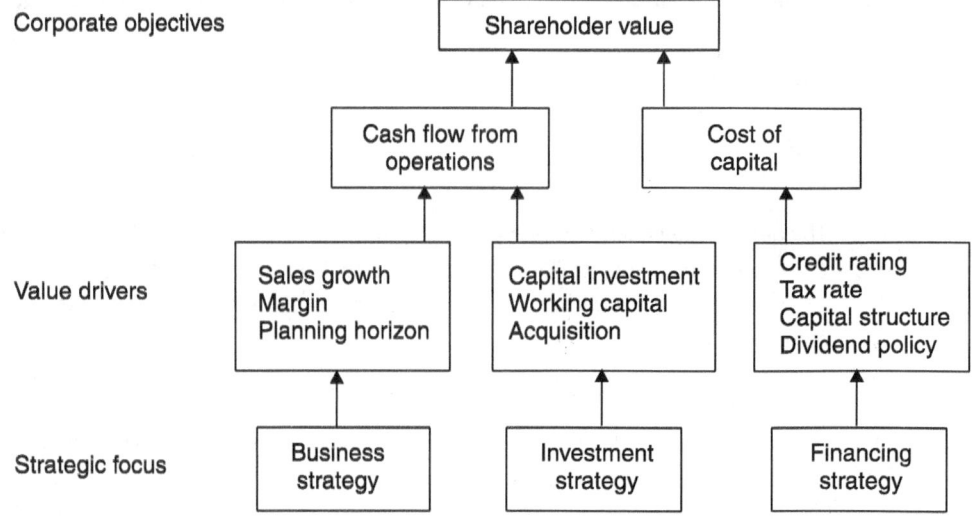

SVA takes the following approach:

(a) Key decisions with implications for cash flow and risk are specified. These may be **strategic, operational, related to investment** or **financial**.

(b) **Value drivers** are identified as the factors having the greatest impact on shareholder value, and management attention is focused on the decisions which influence the value drivers.

Value drivers are identified as being fundamental to the determination of value.

- Sales growth rate
- Operating profit margin
- Tax rate
- Non-current asset capital investment
- Working capital investment
- The planning horizon
- The required rate of return

The model assumes a constant percentage rate of sales growth and a constant operating profit margin. Tax is assumed to be a constant percentage of operating profit. Finally, fixed and working capital investments are assumed to be a constant percentage of changes in sales.

4.6.1 Calculating shareholder value

Using the free cash flows, **corporate value** is then computed using a rate reflecting the company's **risk**. Watch out for details of the discount rate to use in questions. If you are not told what rate to use to discount free cash flows, the WACC should **not** be used if interest is included in the calculation of free cash flow. After tax cost of equity (ungeared) may be appropriate if debt is assumed to be risk-free.

Corporate value = PV of free cash flows + current value of marketable securities and other non-operating investments

Shareholder value can then be computed as **corporate value – debt**.

4.6.2 Advantages of SVA

This approach is:

- **Inclusive of the cost of capital** and **risk**
- **Not sensitive** to the choice of **accounting policies**
- Relatively **simple to apply**
- **Consistent with the concept of share valuation by DCF**
- A spur to management awareness of the **key long-term value variables** (drivers)

SVA should lead to the establishment of a value management system aimed at maximising long-term shareholder value added. The system should include strategic assessment, long-term planning, operational planning, performance measurement and management, and incentive compensation.

4.6.3 Disadvantages of SVA

The drawbacks of SVA include the following:

(a) The **constant percentage assumptions** may be **unrealistic**.

(b) The **input data** may **not** be **easily available** from current systems, particularly to outsiders. It may not be easy to test whether the assumptions on which the forecasts are based are realistic.

(c) It may be **misused in target setting** – giving managers a 12-month target cash flow may discourage longer-term profitable investment. On the other hand a longer-term target may be very difficult to set because of uncertainties over future cash flows.

(d) Other models have been suggested with different value drivers; Copeland, Koller and Murrin suggested that there are three value drivers, **return on invested capital, cash flow** and **economic profit or economic value added**.

4.7 Economic value added

FAST FORWARD

Economic value added is based on after-tax cash flows, less a charge for **capital consumed.**

Economic value added (EVA®) is closely associated with shareholder value analysis and gives the economic value or profit added per year. It can be used as a means of **measuring managerial performance,** by assessing the net present value of revenues (profits) less resources used (capital employed). It is **not** a measure of share valuation.

Economic value added = NOPAT – (cost of capital × capital employed)

where NOPAT = net operating profit after tax adjusted for non-cash expenses (see below)

(cost of capital × capital employed) = imputed charge for the capital consumed, the cost of capital being the weighted average cost of capital for the firm's **target capital structure**

Adjustments may be needed to the profit figures in the accounts to arrive at NOPAT.

(a) **Interest** and **tax relief on interest** should be excluded from NOPAT, as they are taken into account in the imputed capital charge.

(b) **Investing cash flows** should be excluded from NOPAT **but** added to **capital employed**. These include **goodwill, research and development** and **advertising**, and other expenditure designed to build the business up over the next few years. The amount added to capital employed should be a figure that reflects the expenditure that has affected profit this year, say the research and development charge for the last four years, or goodwill that has previously been written off.

(c) **Lease charges** should be excluded from NOPAT but added in as part of capital employed.

(d) In theory, accounting **depreciation** should be added to the profit figures, and economic depreciation subtracted from profit figures to arrive at NOPAT. Economic depreciation is a charge for the fall in asset value due to wear or tear and obsolescence. In practice, the depreciation figure in the accounts is often used as an approximation for economic depreciation, so no adjustment is necessary.

4.7.1 Benefits of economic value added

(a) **Net present value**

Economic value added focuses on the **long-term net present value of a company**. Managerial performance will be improved by investing in positive NPV projects, not investing in negative NPV projects and lowering the cost of capital.

(b) **Financing**

By including a financing element, the **cost of capital** is emphasised, and hence managers must have regard for **careful investment** and **control of working capital**. If managers choose negative NPV projects, the imputed capital charge will ultimately be greater than earnings.

(c) **Cash flows**

The adjustments within the model mean that economic value added should be based on **cash flows** rather than accounting data and hence it may be **less distorted** by the **accounting policies** chosen.

(d) **Clarity of measure**

Economic value added is a **monetary figure** rather than a ratio, and one that can be easily **linked to financial objectives**.

4.7.2 Drawbacks of economic value added

(a) **Failure to measure short-term position**

Economic value added does **not measure NPV** in the short-term. Projects with good long-term NPV, but large initial cash investments or poor initial returns, may be rejected by managers who are being judged on their **short-term performance**.

(b) **Use of historical accounts**

Economic value added is based on historical accounts which may be of **limited use** as a guide to the future. Also, in practice the influences of accounting policies on the starting profit figure may not be completely negated by the adjustments made to it in the economic value added model.

(c) **Other value drivers**

Other value drivers such as non-capitalised goodwill may be important despite being **excluded from the accounts**.

(d) **Adjustments**

Making the necessary adjustments can be **problematic** as sometimes a large number of adjustments are required.

(e) **Cost of capital**

The cost of capital used is calculated by the **capital asset pricing model,** and is therefore based upon the **assumptions** of that model such as **no change in risk**.

(f) **Inter-company comparisons**

Companies which are **larger in size** may have larger economic value added figures for this reason. **Allowance for relative size** must be made when inter-company comparisons are performed.

4.7.3 Example: Economic value added

The following data relates to Growler plc.

Extracts from income statement

	20X7 £m	20X8 £m
Revenue	550	650
Pre-tax accounting profit	120	145
Taxation	35	45
Profit after tax	85	100
Dividends	25	30
Retained earnings	60	70

Extracts from statement of financial position

	20X7 £m	20X8 £m
Non-current assets	195	265
Net current assets	210	275
	405	540
Financed by:		
Shareholders' funds	310	380
Medium- and long-term bank loans	95	160
	405	540

Pre-tax accounting profit is taken after deducting the economic depreciation of the company's non-current assets (also the depreciation used for tax purposes).

Other relevant information

(a) Economic depreciation was £50 million in 20X7 and £55 million in 20X8.
(b) Interest was £8 million in 20X7 and £10 million in 20X8.
(c) Other non-cash expenses were £18 million in 20X7 and £22 million in 20X8.
(d) The tax rate in 20X7 and 20X8 was 30%.
(e) Growler had non-capitalised leases valued at £15 million in each year 20X6-20X8.
(f) The company's pre-tax cost of debt was estimated as 9% in 20X7 and 10% in 20X8.
(g) The company's cost of equity was estimated as 15% in 20X7 and 17% in 20X8.
(h) The target capital structure is 80% equity, 20% debt.
(i) In the statement of financial position total assets less current liabilities at the end of 20X6 was £315 million.

Required

Estimate the EVA™ for Growler plc for 20X7 and 20X8.

Solution

Net operating profit after tax

Net operating profit after tax is arrived at after making a number of adjustments.

	20X7 £m	20X8 £m
Profit after tax	85	100
Add: non-cash expenses	18	22
interest after tax charge (1 – 0.3)	5.6	7
NOPAT	108.6	129

Capital employed

Capital employed is the start of year figure

20X7 Capital employed = Capital employed at end of 20X6 + Leases
= 315 + 15
= £330 million

20X8 Capital employed = Book value of shareholders' funds + Bank loans + Leases
= 310 + 95 + 15
= £420 million

Weighted average cost of capital

20X7 Cost of capital = $(0.8 \times 15\%) + (0.2 \times (9\%(1 – 0.3)))$
= 13.26%

20X8 Cost of capital = $(0.8 \times 17\%) + (0.2 \times (10\%(1 – 0.3)))$
= 15%

Economic value added

20X7 EVA™ = $108.6 – (0.1326 \times 330)$
= £64.84 million

20X8 EVA™ = $129 – (0.15 \times 420)$
= £66 million

Question — Economic Value Added

The following data relates to Tigger plc.

Extracts from statement of comprehensive income

	20X8 £m	20X9 £m
Revenue	825	985
Pre-tax accounting profit	240	300
Taxation	70	90
Profit after tax	170	210
Dividends	40	50
Retained earnings	130	160

13: VALUATION OF COMPANIES

Extracts from statement of financial position

	20X8 £m	20X9 £m
Non-current assets	305	420
Net current assets	270	330
	575	750
Financed by:		
Shareholders' funds	470	630
Medium- and long-term bank loans	105	120
	575	750

Other relevant information

(a) Economic depreciation was £70 million in 20X8 and £80 million in 20X9. Accounting depreciation, which has been deducted from pre-tax operating profits, was £80 million in 20X8 and £90 million in 20X9.

(b) Interest expenses were £10 million in 20X8 and £12 million in 20X9.

(c) Other non-cash expenses were £25 million in 20X8 and £28 million in 20X9. There were no tax consequences of these expenses.

(d) The tax rate in 20X8 and 20X9 was 30%.

(e) Tigger had non-capitalised operating leases valued at £25 million in each year 20X7 – 20X9.

(f) The average research and development charge per annum for the period 20X4 – 20X7 was £10 million. Tigger charged £12 million to research and development in 20X8 and 20X9. Industry research suggests that companies benefit from research and development expenditure for approximately four years subsequent to the year of expenditure.

(g) Tigger's pre-tax cost of debt was estimated as 7% in 20X8 and 8% in 20X9.

(h) Tigger's cost of equity was estimated as 12% in 20X8 and 14% in 20X9.

(i) The target capital structure is 70% equity, 30% debt.

(j) Balance sheet long-term capital employed at the end of 20X7 was £415 million.

Required

Estimate the EVA™ for Tigger plc for 20X8 and 20X9.

Answer

Net operating profit after tax

Net operating profit after tax is arrived at after making a number of adjustments.

	20X8 £m	20X9 £m
Profit after tax	170	210
Add: non-cash expenses	25	28
research and development	12	12
accounting depreciation	80	90
Less economic depreciation	(70)	(80)
Add interest after tax charge (1 – 0.3)	7	8.4
NOPAT	224	268.4

LEARNING OUTCOME 3 VALUATION AND CORPORATE CHANGE

Capital employed

Capital employed is on start of year figures

20X8 Capital employed = Capital employed at end of 20X7 + Leases + R and D
= 415 + 25 + 40
= £480 million

20X9 Capital employed = Book value of shareholders' funds + Bank loans + Leases + R and D
= 470 + 105 + 25 + 42
= £642 million

Weighted average cost of capital

20X8 Cost of capital = $(0.7 \times 12\%) + (0.3 \times (7\%(1 - 0.3)))$
= 9.87%

20X9 Cost of capital = $(0.7 \times 14\%) + (0.3 \times (8\%(1 - 0.3)))$
= 11.48%

Economic value added

20X8 EVA™ = $224 - (0.0987 \times 480)$
= £176.62 million

20X9 EVA™ = $268.4 - (0.1148 \times 642)$
= £194.70 million

Question — Economic value added

The most recent published results for V plc are shown below.

	£m
20XX profit before tax	13.6
Summary consolidated statement of financial position at 31 December 20XX	
Non-current assets	35.9
Current assets	137.2
Less current liabilities	(95.7)
Net current assets	41.5
Total assets less current liabilities	77.4
Borrowings	(15.0)
Deferred tax provisions	(7.6)
Net assets	54.8
Capital and reserves	54.8

An analyst working for a stockbroker has taken these published results, made the adjustments shown below, and has reported his conclusion that 'the management of V plc is destroying value'.

Analyst's adjustments to profit before tax

		£m
Profit before tax		13.6
Adjustments		
Add:	Interest paid (net)	1.6
	R&D (research and development)	2.1
	Advertising	2.3
	Amortisation of goodwill	1.3
Less:	Taxation paid	(4.8)
Adjusted profit		16.1

13: VALUATION OF COMPANIES

Analyst's adjustments to summary consolidated statement of financial position at 31 December 20XX

		£m	
Capital and reserves		54.8	
Adjustments			
Add:	Borrowings	15.0	
	Deferred tax provisions	7.6	
	R&D	17.4	Last 7 years' expenditure
	Advertising	10.5	Last 5 years' expenditure
	Goodwill	40.7	Written off against reserves on acquisitions in previous years
Adjusted capital employed		146.0	
Required return		17.5	12% cost of capital
Adjusted profit		16.1	
Value destroyed		1.4	

The chair of V plc has obtained a copy of the analyst's report.

Explain, as accountant of V plc, in a report to your chair, the principles of the approach taken by the analyst. Comment on the treatment of the specific adjustments to R&D, advertising, interest and borrowings and goodwill.

Answer

REPORT

To: Chair
From: Management accountant   Date: XX.XX.XX
Subject: **Destroying value in V plc**

This report considers the recent report by the analyst of X Stockbrokers on our 20XX results. It will explain the principles of the approach taken by the analyst and will provide a commentary on the treatment of the specific adjustments made to our reported profit figure and statement of financial position.

1 **Principles of the approach taken: economic value added**

1.1 A management team is required by an **organisation's shareholders** to **maximise the value of their investment** in the organisation and a plethora of performance indicators is used to assess whether or not the management team is fulfilling this duty.

1.2 The majority of these **performance measures** are based on the information contained in the organisation's published accounts. These indicators can be easily **manipulated** and often provide **misleading** information. Earnings per share, for example, is reduced by capital-building investments in research and development and in marketing.

1.3 The **financial statements** themselves **do not provide a clear picture of whether or not shareholder value is being created or destroyed**.

(a) The statement of consolidated income, for example, indicates the quantity but not the quality of earnings.

(b) It **ignores the cost of equity financing** and only takes into account the costs of debt financing, thereby penalising organisations such as ourselves which choose a mix of debt and equity finance.

(c) Neither does the **cashflow statement** provide particularly appropriate information. Cashflows can be large and positive if an organisation underspends on maintenance and undertakes little capital investment in an attempt to increase short-term profits at the expense of long-term success.

1.4 The analyst has therefore adopted an approach known as **economic value added** to evaluate our performance.

(a) This approach hinges on the calculation of **economic profit,** which requires **several adjustments** to be made to traditionally-reported accounting profits.

(b) These adjustments are made to **avoid the immediate write-off of value-building expenditure** such as research and development or the purchase of goodwill. They are intended to produce a figure for capital employed which is a more accurate reflection of the base upon which shareholders expect their returns to accrue and to provide a profit after tax figure which is a more realistic measure of the actual cash yield generated for shareholders from recurring business activities.

It is not very surprising that if management are assessed using performance measures calculated using traditional accounting policies, they are unwilling to invest in or spend money on activities which immediately reduce current year's profit.

2 The treatment of specific items

2.1 Research and development

The analyst has added back expenditure of £2.1 million to the 20XX profit figure on the grounds that the **expenditure is providing a base for future**. Similarly, the research and development expenditure over the last seven years of £17.4 million has been added back to the capital employed figure on the basis that we are continuing to benefit from the expenditure. A depreciation charge should probably be made against this capitalised value, however, to reflect any fall in its value.

2.2 Advertising

The analyst has added back advertising expenditure of £2.3 million to the 20XX profit figure on the assumption that the **expenditure has supported sales, raised customer awareness and/or increased brand image/loyalty**, all of which could produce significant cashflows in the future and hence are for the **long-term benefit of the organisation**. The advertising expenditure over the last five years of £10.5 million has been added back to the capital employed figure (in much the same way as the research and development expenditure) to reflect the fact that the costs will provide for future growth. Again, an amortisation charge should be made if brand values are being eroded, possibly by competition.

2.3 Interest and borrowings

Because our profits are being earned using both debt and equity finance, the **published profit figure is overstated since it takes no account of the cost of the equity finance**. The analyst has therefore added back the cost of the debt finance to the 20XX profit figure and the borrowings figure to the capital employed. This produces a profit figure before the cost of borrowing which can be compared with a figure representing the total long-term finance in our organisation.

2.4 Goodwill

The analyst has added back goodwill amortisation of £1.3 million to the 20XX profit figure. Goodwill is the difference between the price paid for a business acquisition and the current cost valuation of that acquisition's net assets. On the assumption that a realistic price was paid, the **goodwill purchased should provide benefits in the future**, not just in the year of purchase. The goodwill of £40.7 million, which has been written off against reserves on acquisitions in previous years, has been added back to the capital employed figure so as to provide a more realistic base upon which we must earn a return. Again, the goodwill capitalised should be regularly reviewed and amortised to reflect any reductions in its value.

I hope this information has been of use. If I can be of any further assistance please do not hesitate to contact me.

Signed: Management accountant

4.8 Market value added

FAST FORWARD

Market value added compares the **amount invested** with the increase in market value of shares resulting from the investment.

Market value added (MVA) is the difference between:

(a) The **contribution** put into the business by investors (the purchase price of their shares **and** the re-investment of profits that would otherwise have been distributed)

(b) The increase in the **current market value of their shares** resulting from the contribution.

The MVA figure tends to correspond closely to the difference between the market value of equity and the book value of equity. To assess whether market value added is reasonable, assessment is needed of what Economic value added will be for several years into the future; this assessment may not be easy to make. Market value added also does not adjust for size differences for comparisons.

4.9 Drawbacks of cash flow methods

Whichever method is used, cash flow methods suffer from the following general drawbacks:

(a) As we have seen above, selection of an **appropriate cost of capital** may prove difficult.

(b) **Estimating future cash flows**, particularly of companies that are being acquired, may be **very difficult**.

(c) Cash flows are most appropriate for valuing **controlling interests**, which might have a significant influence on whether expected cash flows are attained.

5 Dividend bases

FAST FORWARD

Dividend yield and valuation methods are more relevant to small shareholdings. **Earnings valuation methods** may be preferable if dividends are irregular.

5.1 The dividend yield method of share valuation

The **dividend yield method** of share valuation is suitable for the valuation of **small shareholdings in unquoted companies**. It is based on the principle that small shareholders are mainly interested in **dividends**, since they cannot control decisions affecting the company's profits and earnings. A suitable offer price would therefore be one which compensates them for the future dividends they will be giving up if they sell their shares.

This approach is similar to that of the earnings yield methods – a 'suitable', dividend yield is applied as a discount rate to the expected level of dividend:

$$\text{Dividend yield} = \frac{\text{Dividend per share}}{\text{Market price per share}} \times 100\% \text{ and thus}$$

$$\text{Market price} = \frac{\text{Dividend}}{\text{Dividend yield}}$$

This method has the same problems as those of the earning based methods – the determination of a **'suitable' dividend yield**, and the appropriate level of sustainable dividend to use. Again, note that the dividend yield will be lower the higher the level of growth envisaged in the market price.

LEARNING OUTCOME 3 VALUATION AND CORPORATE CHANGE

5.2 Using the dividend valuation model

The dividend yield approach is in fact a crude approximation to the application of the dividend valuation model (DVM).

Knowledge brought forward from earlier studies

Formulae to learn

- The **dividend valuation model assumes that** the value of a share will be the discounted present value of all **future expected dividends on the share, discounted at the shareholders' cost of capital**.
- When the company is expected to pay **constant dividends** every year into the future, 'in perpetuity' the following formula applies. Ke is the shareholders' cost of capital (the required rate of return).

    Ordinary (equity) share, paying a constant annual dividend D in perpetuity, where P_0 is the ex-div value:

    $$P_0 = \frac{D}{Ke}$$

- When the company is expected to pay a dividend which increases at a constant rate g, every year into the future, the following **dividend growth model** may be used.

    $$P_0 = \frac{D_1}{Ke - g} = \frac{D_0(1+g)}{Ke - g}$$

    where D_0 = is the dividend in the current year (year 0)
    and so $D_0(1 + g)$ = the expected future dividend in year 1 (D_1)

Knowledge brought forward from earlier studies (continued)

Formula to learn

The growth rate for dividends, g can be obtained by the formula

g = rb

where r = accounting ROCE (constant forever)
and   b = proportion of earnings retained (constant forever)

Alternatively g can be found by using the formula

$$g = \sqrt[n]{\frac{\text{latest dividend x}}{\text{earliest dividend x - n}}} - 1$$

This model simply assumes that the past is a good guide for the future.

Shares may be valued using the DVM using estimates of future growth rates and the required return by shareholders (possibly using the dividend yield of a similar company, with its expected growth adjusted out and taking account of differences in size, status etc).

5.3 Assumptions in the dividend valuation models

(a) The **dividends** from **projects** for which the **funds** are **required** will be of the **same risk** type or quality as **dividends** from **existing operations**. D_0 should not vary from the trend of dividends.

(b) There would be **no increase** in the **cost of capital**, for any other reason than (a) above, from a new issue of shares.

(c) All shareholders have **perfect information** about the **company's future**, there is no **delay** in obtaining this information and all **shareholders interpret** it in the **same way**.

(d) **Taxation** can be **ignored**.

(e) **Other influences** on share prices are ignored.

(f) All shareholders have the same **marginal cost of capital**.

(g) There would be **no issue expenses** for new shares.

5.4 Problems of the dividend valuation models

(a) Companies that have a stated policy of **not paying** a **dividend** do not have zero values. The model fails to take into account different shareholder preferences for dividends v capital growth.

(b) There may **not** be **enough projects** in the future with sufficient NPVs to maintain the dividend stream. The models also assume that dividends either show **no growth** or **constant growth**.

(c) The model has difficulties coping with **rapid growth rates**, when the growth rate exceeds the discount rate.

(d) The model may be a **better means** of **valuing shares**, rather than companies in takeover situations, since if the company changes hands, the dividend policy might also change.

6 Other valuation bases

FAST FORWARD

The super-profits method uses **excess profits** to **value goodwill**. **Earn-out arrangements** are where the buyer of a business agrees to pay the seller an additional amount of consideration if the acquired company achieves a certain level of profitability.

6.1 The super-profits method of share valuation

This method starts by applying a 'fair return' to the net tangible assets and comparing the result with the expected profits. Any excess of profits **(the super-profits)** is used to calculate goodwill. The goodwill is normally taken as a fixed number of years super-profits. The goodwill is then added to the value of the target company's tangible assets to arrive at a value for the business.

6.2 Example: Super-profits method of share valuation

Light Ltd has net tangible assets of £120,000 and present earnings of £20,000. Doppler Ltd wants to take over Light Ltd and considers that a fair return for this type of industry is 12%, and decides to value Light Ltd taking goodwill at three years' super-profits.

	£
Actual profits	20,000
Less fair return on net tangible assets: 12% × £120,000	14,400
Super-profits	5,600
Goodwill: 3 × £5,600	16,800
Value of Light Ltd: £120,000 + £16,800	136,800

The principal drawbacks to this valuation method are as follows:

(a) The rate of return required is chosen subjectively.

(b) The number of years purchase of super-profits is arbitrary. In the example above, goodwill was valued at three years of super-profits, but it could have been, for example, two years or four years of super-profits.

6.3 Earn-out arrangements

Earn-out arrangements are where the buyer of a business agrees to pay the seller an additional amount of consideration if the acquired company achieves a certain level of performance.

For example, the consideration may be structured as follows:

(a) An **initial amount payable** at the time of acquisition

(b) A **guaranteed minimum amount of deferred consideration**, payable in, say, three years' time

(c) An **additional amount of deferred consideration**, payable if a specified target performance is achieved over the next three years, say profits exceeding a certain amount

The **total of the initial and guaranteed deferred consideration** amounts may be **based** upon an **assets based approach to valuation**, or on an earnings basis, using, for example, the average level of expected profits over a given future period.

This method would only be appropriate if the acquired company was to be run independently of the buyer's company, at least for the period upon which the contingent consideration is based. If the acquired business were to be immediately integrated within the buyer's, it would be difficult to identify separately the relevant sales or profits.

Under these types of arrangement, then, the overall valuation of the business will have a **variable element**. The buyer will need to estimate the minimum, maximum and expected total amounts they may have to pay, with corresponding probabilities, relating to the likelihood of the business reaching the specified targets. In particular, they will have to ensure that they could, if necessary, afford to pay the maximum amount, regardless of how unlikely that is to arise.

Question — Valuation methods

Profed Ltd provides a tuition service to professional students. This includes courses of lectures provided on their own premises and provision of study material for home study. Most of the lecturers are qualified professionals with many years' experience in both their profession and tuition. Study materials are written and word processed in-house, but sent out to an external printers.

The business was started 15 years ago, and now employs around 40 full-time lecturers, 10 authors and 20 support staff. Freelance lecturers and authors are employed from time to time in times of peak demand.

The shareholders of Profed Ltd mainly comprise the original founders of the business who would now like to realise their investment. In order to arrive at an estimate of what they believe the business is worth, they have identified a long-established quoted company, City Tutors plc, who have a similar business, although they also publish texts for external sale to universities, colleges etc.

Summary financial statistics for the two companies for the most recent financial year are as follows:

	Profed Ltd	City Tutors Ltd
Issued shares (million)	4	10
Net asset values (£m)	7.2	15
Earnings per share (pence)	35	20
Dividend per share (pence)	20	18
Debt: equity ratio	1:7	1:65
Share price (pence)		362
Expected rate of growth in earnings/dividends	9% pa	7.5%

13: VALUATION OF COMPANIES

Notes

1. The net assets of Profed Ltd are the net book values of tangible non-current assets plus net working capital. However:

   - A recent valuation of the buildings was £1.5m above book value
   - Inventories include past editions of textbooks which have a realisable value of £100,000 below their cost
   - Due to a dispute with one of their clients, an additional allowance for bad debts of £750,000 could prudently be made

2. Growth rates should be assumed to be constant per annum; Profed's earnings growth rate estimate was provided by the marketing manager, based on expected growth in sales adjusted by normal profit margins. City Tutors' growth rates were gleaned from press reports.

3. Profed uses a discount rate of 15% to appraise its investments, and has done for many years.

You are required to:

(a) Compute a range of valuations for the business of Profed Ltd, using the information available and stating any assumptions made.

(b) Comment upon the strengths and weaknesses of the methods you used in (a) and their suitability for valuing Profed Ltd.

Answer

(a) The information provided allows us to value Profed on three bases: net assets, P/E ratio and dividend valuation.

All three will be computed, even though their validity may be questioned in part (b) of the answer.

Assets based

	£'000
Net assets at book value	7,200
Add increased valuation of buildings	1,500
Less decreased value of inventories and receivables	(850)
Net asset of equity	7,850
Value per share	£1.96

P/E ratio

	Profed Ltd	City Tutors Ltd
Issued shares (million)	4	10
Share price (pence)		362
Market value (£m)		36.2
Earnings per shares (pence)	35	20
P/E ratio (share price ÷ EPS)		18.1

The P/E for a similar quoted company is 18.1. This will take account of factors such as marketability of shares, status of company, growth potential that will differ from those for Profed. Profed's growth rate has been estimated as higher than that of City Tutors, possibly because it is a younger, developing company, although the basis for the estimate may be questionable.

All other things being equal, the P/E ratio for an unquoted company should be taken as between one half to two thirds of that of an equivalent quoted company. Being generous, in view of the possible higher growth prospects of Profed, we might estimate an appropriate P/E ratio of around 12, assuming Profed is to remain a private company.

This will value Profed at 12 × £0.35 = £4.20 per share, a total valuation of £16.8m.

Dividend valuation model

The dividend valuation method gives the share price as:

$$\frac{\text{next year's dividend}}{\text{cost of equity} - \text{growth rate}}$$

which assumes dividends being paid into perpetuity, and growth at a constant rate.

For Profed, next year's dividend = £0.20 × 1.09 = £0.218 per share

While we are given a discount rate of 15% as being traditionally used by the directors of Profed for investment appraisal, there appears to be no rational basis for this. We can instead use the information for City Courses to estimate a cost of equity for Profed. This is assuming the business risks to be similar, and ignoring the small difference in their gearing ratio.

Again, from the DVM, cost of equity = $\frac{\text{next year's dividend}}{\text{market price}}$ + growth rate

For City Tutors Ltd, cost of equity = $\frac{£0.18 \times 1.075}{£3.62}$ + 0.075 = 12.84%

Using, say, 13% as a cost of equity for Profed:

Share price = $\frac{£0.218}{0.13 - 0.09}$ = £5.45

valuing the whole of the share capital at £21.8 million

Range for valuation

The three methods used have thus come up with a range of value of Profed Ltd as follows:

	Value per share	Total valuation
	£	£m
Net assets	1.96	7.9
P/E ratio	4.20	16.8
Dividend valuation	5.45	21.8

(b) **Comment on relative merits of the methods used, and their suitability**

Asset based valuation

Valuing a company on the **basis of its asset values** alone is rarely appropriate if it is to be sold on a going-concern basis. Exceptions would include property investment companies and investment trusts, the market values of the assets of which will bear a close relationship to their earning capacities.

Profed Ltd is typical of a lot of service companies, a large part of whose value lies in the **skill, knowledge and reputation of its personnel**. This is not reflected in the net asset values, and renders this method quite inappropriate. A potential purchaser of Profed Ltd will generally value its intangible assets such as knowledge, expertise, customer/supplier relationships, brands etc more highly than those that can be measured in accounting terms.

Knowledge of the net asset value (NAV) of a company will, however, be important as a floor value for a company in financial difficulties or subject to a takeover bid – shareholders will be reluctant to sell for less than the net asset value even if future prospects are poor.

P/E ratio valuation

The P/E ratio measures the **multiple of the current year's earnings** that is reflected in the **market price of a share**. It is thus a method that reflects the earnings potential of a company from a market point of view. Provided the marketing is efficient, it is likely to give the most meaningful basis for valuation.

One of the first things to say is that the market price of a share at any point in time is determined by supply and demand forces prevalent during small transactions, and will be dependent upon a lot of factors in addition to a realistic appraisal of future prospects. A downturn in the market, economies and political changes can all affect the day-to-day price of a share, and thus its prevalent P/E ratio. It is not known whether the share price given for City Tutors was taken on one particular day, or was some sort of average over a period. The latter would perhaps give a sounder basis from which to compute an applicable P/E ratio.

Even if the P/E ratio of City Tutors can be taken to be **indicative of its true worth**, using it as a basis to value a smaller, unquoted company in the same industry can be problematic.

The status and marketability of shares in a quoted company have tangible effects on value but these are difficult to measures.

The P/E ratio will also be affected by **growth prospects** – the higher the growth expected, the higher the ratio. The growth rate incorporated by the shareholders of City Tutors is probably based on a more rational approach than that used by Profed Ltd.

If the growth prospects of Profed as would be perceived by the market did not coincide with those of **Profed management**, it is difficult to see how the P/E ratio should be adjusted for relative levels of growth.

In the valuation in (a) a crude adjustment has been made to City Tutors' P/E ratio to arrive at a ratio to use to value Profed's earnings. This can result in a very inaccurate result if account has not been taken of all the differences involved.

Dividend based valuation

The dividend valuation model (DVM) is a **cash flow based approach**, which valued the dividends that the shareholders expect to receive from the company by discounting them at their required rate of return. It is perhaps more appropriate for valuing a minority shareholding where the holder has no influence over the level of dividends to be paid than for valuing a whole company, where the total cash flows will be greater relevance.

The practical problems with the dividend valuation model lie mainly in its **assumptions**. Even accepting that the required 'perfect capital market' assumptions may be satisfied to some extent, in reality, the formula used in (a) assumes constant growth rates and constant required rates of return in perpetuity.

Determination of an **appropriate cost of equity** is particularly difficult for a unquoted company, and the use of an 'equivalent' quoted company's data carried the same drawbacks as discussed above. Similar problems arise in estimating future growth rates, and the results from the model are highly sensitive to changes in both these inputs.

It is also highly dependent upon the **current year's dividend** being a **representative base** from which to start.

The dividend valuation model valuation provided in (a) results in a higher valuation than that under the P/E ratio approach. Reasons for this may be:

- The **share price** for City Tutors may be **currently depressed** below its normal level, resulting in an inappropriately low P/E ratio

- The **adjustment** to get to an **appropriate P/E ratio** for Profed may have been too harsh, particularly in light of its apparently better growth prospects
- The **cost of equity used** in the dividend valuation model was that of City Tutors. The validity of this will largely depend upon the relative levels of risk of the two companies. Although they both operate the same type of business, the fact that City Tutors sells its material externally means it is perhaps less reliant on a fixed customer base
- Even if business risks and gearing risk may be thought to be comparable a prospective buyer of Profed may consider investment in a **younger, unquoted company** to carry **greater personal risk**. His required return may thus be higher than that envisaged in the dividend valuation model, reducing the valuation.

Exam focus point

Remember when answering valuation questions that you are trying to find a fair reflection of the valuation of the company. This is not just a matter of carrying out calculations mechanically; it also means seeing (and discussing) the factors that impact significantly upon valuation, yet which may not be fairly reflected in your calculations.

7 The valuation of debt

FAST FORWARD

For irredeemable debt

Market price, ex interest $(P_0) = \dfrac{i}{K_d}$

$= \dfrac{i(1-t) \text{ with tax}}{K_{d_{net}}}$

For redeemable debt, the market value is **the discounted present value of future interest receivable**, up to the year of redemption, plus the **discounted present value of the redemption payment**.

7.1 Debt calculations – a few notes

(a) Debt is always quoted in **£100 nominal units**, or blocks; always use £100 nominal values as the basis to your calculations.

(b) Debt can be quoted in **%** or as a **value**, eg 97% or £97. Both mean that £100 nominal value of debt is worth £97 market value.

(c) Interest on debt is stated as a **percentage** of **nominal value**. This is known as the coupon rate. It is **not** the same as the redemption yield on debt or the cost of debt.

(d) The examiner sometimes quotes an **interest yield**, defined as coupon/market price.

(e) Always use **ex-interest prices** in any calculations.

7.2 The value of debentures

The same valuation principle as applied to the valuation of shares can be applied to the valuation of debentures and other loan stock. However, the future income from fixed interest debentures is predictable, which should make the process of valuation more straightforward.

(a) For **irredeemable debentures** or loan stock, where the company will go on paying interest every year in perpetuity, without ever having to redeem the loan (ignoring taxation).

Formula to learn

$$P_0 = \frac{i}{K_d}$$

where P_0 is the market price of the stock ex interest, that is, excluding any interest payment that might soon be due

  i is the annual interest payment on the stock

  K_d is the return required by the loan stock investors

With taxation, we have the following:

Formula to learn

Irredeemable (undated) debt, paying annual after tax interest $i(1-t)$ in perpetuity, where P_0 is the ex-interest value:

$$P_0 = \frac{i(1-t)}{Kd_{net}}$$

(b) For **redeemable debentures** or loan stock, the market value is the discounted present value of future interest receivable, up to the year of redemption, **plus** the discounted present value of the redemption payment.

Question — Value of debentures

A company has issued some 9% debentures, which are now redeemable at par in three years' time. Investors now require an interest yield of 10%. What will be the current market value of £100 of debentures?

Answer

Year		Cash flow £	Discount factor 10%	Present value £
1	Interest	9	0.909	8.18
2	Interest	9	0.826	7.43
3	Interest	9	0.751	6.76
3	Redemption value	100	0.751	75.10
				97.47

£100 of debentures will have a market value of £97.47.

You may be given a more complicated example.

7.3 Example: Valuation of debt

Furry plc has in issue 12% debenture stock with par value £100,000 and redemption value £110,000, with interest payable quarterly. The redemption yield on the bond is 8% annually and 2% quarterly. The debenture is redeemable on 30 June 20X4 and it is now 31 December 20X0.

Required

Calculate the market value of the debenture stock.

Solution

You need to use the redemption yield as the discount rate, and remember to use an annuity factor for the interest. We are discounting over 14 periods using the quarterly discount rate (8%/4).

Period		Cash flow £	Discount factor 2%	Present value £
1–14	Interest	3,000	12.11	36,330
14	Redemption	110,000	0.758	83,380
				119,710

Market value is £119,710.

7.4 Covenants

Issuing loan stock often entails certain obligations for the borrower over and above repaying the bond. These obligations are called **covenants**.

(a) **Positive covenants** require a borrower to do something, for example:

   (i) Provide the bank with its annual financial statements
   (ii) Submit certificates that the company is keeping to the loan agreement
   (iii) Provide management accounts

(b) **Negative or restrictive covenants** are promises by a borrower not to do something, eg the company pledges not to borrow more money until the current loan is repaid, **acquire or dispose** of certain types of assets or make certain investments.

(c) **Quantitative covenants** set limitations on the borrower's financial position. For example, the company might agree that its total borrowings shall not exceed 100% of shareholders' funds, or that **dividends** should not rise above a certain level.

There may be **a bonding covenant** in place which provides a mechanism for enforcing the covenant, including the appointment of an auditor and/or trustee.

Covenants clearly restrict the decisions companies can take, and may mean that the company cannot pursue potentially lucrative (although risky) opportunities.

7.5 Convertible loan stock

> **FAST FORWARD**
>
> **Convertible securities** give investors the opportunity to turn their stock into shares at a later date if they wish and, because of this, they usually carry a lower rate of interest than a similar non-convertible security.
>
> For the companies issuing them, convertibles may be viewed as a **delayed form of equity** that does not immediately affect EPS.

Convertible securities are fixed return securities that may be **converted**, on pre-determined dates and at the option of the holder, into ordinary shares of the company at a predetermined rate. Once converted they cannot be converted back into the original fixed return security. For example, the conversion terms of convertible stock might be that on 1 April 20X0, £2 of stock can be converted into one ordinary share, whereas on 1 April 20X1, the conversion price will be £2.20 of stock for one ordinary share.

The current market value of ordinary shares into which a unit of stock may be converted is known as the **conversion value**. The conversion value will be below the value of the stock at the date of issue, but will be expected to increase as the date for conversion approaches on the assumption that a company's shares ought to increase in market value over time. The difference between the issue value of the stock and the conversion value as at the date of issue is the implicit **conversion premium**.

7.6 Example: Convertible loan stock

The 10% convertible loan stock of Starchwhite plc is quoted at £142 per £100 nominal. The earliest date for conversion is in four years' time, at the rate of 30 ordinary shares per £100 nominal loan stock. The share price is currently £4.15. Annual interest on the stock has just been paid.

(a) What is the average annual growth rate in the share price that is required for the stockholders to achieve an overall rate of return of 12% a year compound over the next four years, including the proceeds of conversion?

(b) What is the implicit conversion premium on the stock?

Solution

(a)

Year	Investment £	Interest £	Discount 12%	Present value £
0	(142)		1.000	(142.00)
1		10	0.893	8.93
2		10	0.797	7.97
3		10	0.712	7.12
4		10	0.636	6.36
				(111.62)

The value of 30 shares on conversion at the end of Year 4 must have a present value of at least £111.62, to provide investors with a 12% return.

The money value at the end of Year 4 needs to be £111.62 ÷ 0.636 = £175.50.

The current market value of 30 shares is (× £4.15) £124.50.

The growth factor in the share price over four years needs to be:

$$\frac{175.50}{124.50} = 1.4096$$

If the annual rate of growth in the share price, expressed as a proportion, is g, then:

$(1 + g)^4$ = 1.4096
$1 + g$ = 1.0896
g = 0.0896, say 0.09

Conclusion. The rate of growth in the share price needs to be 9% a year (compound).

(b) The conversion premium can be expressed as an amount per share or as a percentage of the current conversion value.

(i) As an amount per share $\quad \frac{£142 - £(30 \times 4.15)}{30} = £0.583$ per share

(ii) As a % of conversion value $\quad \frac{£0.583}{£4.15} \times 100\% = 14\%$

7.7 The issue price of convertible loan stock

A company will aim to issue loan stock with the greatest **possible conversion premium** as this will mean that, for the amount of capital raised, it will, on conversion, have to issue the lowest number of new ordinary shares. The premium that will be accepted by potential investors will depend on the company's growth potential and so on prospects for a sizeable increase in the share price.

Convertible loan stock issued at **par** normally has a **lower coupon rate of interest** than **straight debentures**. This lower yield is the price the investor has to pay for the conversion rights. It is, of course, also one of the reasons why the issue of convertible stock is attractive to a company.

7.8 The market price of convertible loan stock

When convertible loan stock is traded on a stock market, its **minimum market price** will be the price of straight debentures with the same coupon rate of interest. If the market value falls to this minimum, it follows that the market attaches no value to the conversion rights.

The actual market price of convertible stock will depend on:

- The price of straight debt
- The current conversion value
- The length of time before conversion may take place
- The market's expectation as to future equity returns and the associated risk

If the conversion value rises above the straight debt value then the price of convertible stock will normally reflect this increase.

Most companies issuing convertible stocks expect them to be converted. They view the stock as **delayed equity**. They are often used either because the company's ordinary share price is considered to be particularly depressed at the time of issue or because the issue of equity shares would result in an immediate and significant drop in earnings per share.

7.9 Warrants (or subscription rights)

FAST FORWARD

> Share **warrants** give their holder the right to apply for new shares at a specified exercise price in the future. They might be issued as an 'add-on' to a new issue of loan notes.

Key term

> A **warrant** is a right given by a company to an investor, allowing him to buy new shares at a future date or dates at a fixed, pre-determined price (the **exercise price**).

Warrants are usually issued as **part of a package** with unsecured loan stock: an investor who buys stock will also acquire a certain number of warrants. The purpose of warrants is to make the loan stock more attractive. Once issued, warrants are **detachable from the stock** and can be sold and bought separately before or during the 'exercise period' (the period during which the right to use the warrants to subscribe for shares is allowed). The market value of warrants will depend on expectations of actual share prices in the future.

During the exercise period, the price of a warrant should not fall below the higher of:

- Nil, and
- The 'theoretical value', which equals:

(Current share price − Exercise price) × Number of shares obtainable from each warrant

If, for example, a warrant entitles the holder to purchase two ordinary shares at a price of £3 each, when the current market price of the shares is £3.40, the minimum market value ('theoretical value') of a warrant would be (£3.40 − £3) × 2 = 80p.

If the price fell below the theoretical value during the exercise period, then arbitrage would be possible. For example, suppose the share price is £2.80 and the warrant exercise price is £2.20. The warrants are priced at 50p with each entitled to one share. Ignoring transactions costs, investors could make an instant gain of 10p per share by buying the warrant, exercising it and then selling the share.

For a company with good growth prospects, the warrant will usually be quoted at a premium above the minimum prior to the exercise period. This premium is known as the **warrant conversion premium**. It is sometimes expressed as a percentage of the current share price.

7.10 Example: Warrant conversion premium

An investor holds some warrants which can be used to subscribe for ordinary shares on a one for one basis at an exercise price of £2.50 at a specified future date. The current share price is £2.25 and the warrants are quoted at 50p. What is the warrant conversion premium?

Solution

The easiest way of finding the premium is to deduct the current share price from the cost of acquiring a share using the warrant, treating the warrant as if it were currently exercisable.

	£
Cost of warrant	0.50
Exercise price	2.50
	3.00
Current share price	2.25
Premium	0.75

7.11 Attractions of warrants to the investor

(a) **Low initial outlay**

   The investor only has to spend 50p per share as opposed to £2.25. This means that he could buy 4½ times as many warrants as shares or, alternatively, he could invest the remaining £1.75 in other, less risky investments.

(b) **Lower downside potential**

   The maximum loss per share is 50p instead of £2.25. Of course the risk of the loss of 50p is much greater than the risk of losing £2.25. The share price of £2.25 is below the exercise price. If it remained at this level until the beginning of the exercise period, the warrants would become worthless as it would not be worthwhile exercising them.

(c) **High potential returns**

   See below.

   In the short run, the warrant price and share price normally move fairly closely in line with each other. **In the longer term** the price of the warrant and hence the premium will depend on:

   - The **length of time before** the warrants may be **exercised**
   - The **current price** of the shares compared with the exercise price, and
   - The **future prospects** of the company

   As the exercise period approaches, any premium will reduce. Towards the end of the exercise period the premium will disappear because, if there were a premium, it would be cheaper to buy the shares directly rather than via the warrant.

LEARNING OUTCOME 3 VALUATION AND CORPORATE CHANGE

Chapter Roundup

- There are a number of different ways of **putting a value on a business**, or on shares in an unquoted company. It is best to use **several methods** of valuation, and to compare the values they produce.

- The **net assets valuation** method can be used as one of many valuation methods, or to provide a lower limit for the value of a company. By itself it is unlikely to produce the most realistic value.

- **P/E ratios** are used when a large block of shares, or a whole business, is being valued. This method can be problematic when quoted companies' P/E ratios are used to value unquoted companies.

- Other earnings methods include the **earnings yield valuation method** and the **accounting rate of return method**.

- Cash flow **DCF valuation** may be used to value a company. **Free cash flows** are a development of the DCF method.

- **Shareholder value analysis** focuses on the key decisions affecting value and risk.

- **Economic value added** is based on after-tax cash flows, less a charge for **capital consumed**.

- **Market value added** compares the **amount invested** with the increase in market value of shares resulting from the investment.

- **Dividend yield and valuation methods** are more relevant to small shareholdings. **Earnings valuation methods** may be preferable if dividends are irregular.

- The super-profits method uses **excess profits** to **value goodwill**. **Earn-out arrangements** are where the buyer of a business agrees to pay the seller an additional amount of consideration if the acquired company achieves a certain level of profitability.

- For irredeemable debt

    Market price, ex interest (P_0) $= \dfrac{I}{K_d}$

    $= \dfrac{i(1-t) \text{ with tax}}{K_{d_{net}}}$

- For redeemable debt, the market value is the **discounted present value of future interest receivable**, up to the year of redemption, plus the **discounted present value of the redemption payment**.

- **Convertible securities** give investors the opportunity to turn their stock into shares at a later date if they wish and, because of this, they usually carry a lower rate of interest than a similar non-convertible security.

- For the companies issuing them, convertibles may be viewed as a **delayed form of equity** that does not immediately affect EPS.

- Share **warrants** give their holder the right to apply for new shares at a specified exercise price in the future. They might be issued as an 'add-on' to a new issue of loan notes.

Quick Quiz

1. Give four circumstances in which the shares of an unquoted company might need to be valued.
2. How is the P/E ratio related to EPS?
3. What is meant by 'multiples' in the context of share valuation?
4. Value = Estimated future profits/Required return on capital employed. What is the name of this valuation model?
5. Suggest two circumstances in which net assets might be used as the basis for valuation of a company.
6. **Fill in the blanks**

    In a free cash flow model free cash flow to equity = _____

    − _____

    + _____

    − _____

    − _____

    − _____

    − _____

    + _____

7. Give five examples of value drivers in the shareholder value analysis model.
8. **Fill in the blank**

    An _____ is where the buyer of a business agrees to pay the seller an additional amount of consideration if the acquired company achieves a certain level of performance.
9. Interest yield = _____ .
10. Cum interest prices should always be used in calculations involving debt. True/False?
11. **Fill in the blanks**

    For redeemable debentures Market value = _____ + _____
12. What is the theoretical value of the price of a warrant?

Answers to Quick Quiz

1. (a) Setting an issue price if the company is floating its shares
   (b) When shares are sold
   (c) For tax purposes
   (d) When shares are pledged as collateral for a loan

2. P/E ratio = Share price/EPS.

3. The P/E ratio: the multiple of earnings at which a company's shares are traded.

4. Accounting rate of return method.

5. (a) As a measure of asset backing
   (b) For comparison, in a scheme of merger

6. Free cash flow to equity =

   Revenues
   − Operating costs
   + Depreciation
   − Working capital increases
   − Taxes
   − Replacement capital expenditure
   − Debt repayments and lease obligations
   + New debt

7. Any five of:
   (a) Sales growth rate
   (b) Operating profit margin
   (c) Tax rate
   (d) Fixed capital investment
   (e) Working capital investment
   (f) The planning horizon
   (g) The required rate of return

8. Earn-out arrangement

9. Interest yield = $\dfrac{\text{Coupon rate}}{\text{Market rate}}$

10. False. Ex interest prices should be used.

11. Market value

    = Discounted present value of future interest receivable up to year of redemption
    + Discounted present value of redemption payment

12. (Current share price − Exercise price) × Number of shares obtainable from each warrant

End of chapter questions

1. Mr Li (AIA May 2013)

Mr Li bought 10% of the shares of a company two years ago. The other 90% of the shares in this company are owned by Mr Chang who established the business ten years ago. The company is unquoted and Mr Li now wishes to sell his shares. Mr Chang would like to buy the shares as he wishes to return to a position where he owns all the equity. Therefore, they are trying to negotiate a value for the 10% shareholding.

The company is based in Hong Kong and the following information has been provided about the company:

(i) The net assets total HK$2,100,000 on the most recent statement of financial position.

(ii) The net assets include land and buildings totalling HK$350,000. However, the land and buildings have recently been valued at HK$570,000.

(iii) The trade receivables have a value of HK$200,000 on the most recent statement of financial position. However, a major customer has just gone out of business and it is unlikely they will pay any of their debt, which represents HK$40,000 of the total HK$200,000.

(iv) Last year the profit after tax was HK$478,000 and this year the profit after tax was HK$565,000.

(v) Mr Chang decides on the level of dividends that will be paid. Last year a total dividend of HK$221,500 was paid and this year the total dividend was HK$226,000. Mr Chang received 90% of the total dividend and Mr Li received 10% of the total dividend.

(vi) The company sells office stationery. The P/E ratios and costs of equity of two listed companies that also sell office stationery are as follows:

Company	P/E ratio	Cost of equity
Office Stuff	5	8%
Officeware	8	7%

Required

(a) Calculate the value of Mr Li's shareholding based on: (1) net assets, (2) earnings and (3) dividend yield approaches. State any assumptions you have made in your calculations. **(12 marks)**

(b) Advise Mr Li as to what value he might achieve for his shareholding. **(8 marks)**

(Total 20 marks)

2. Mr Smith (AIA May 2012)

Mr Smith is aged 45 and has worked as a human resources manager for a large electricity company for the last 16 years. Prior to this he had worked in human resources for other companies. He has recently inherited approximately £500,000. This is a substantial sum of money and he is considering using the inheritance to change his lifestyle. He has become aware that a shop based in his home city may be available for purchase as the current owner is close to retirement. The shop sells sports equipment and sports clothing. Mr Smith enjoys playing and watching sport and considers this may be a good opportunity to run his own business.

Mr Smith has approached the current owner of the sports shop and ascertained the following information:

1. The shop premises are owned rather than rented. The historical cost of the shop premises is £100,000. The shop premises were recently valued at £220,000. The shop is in the centre of the city. A new and substantial shopping centre is being built on the outskirts of the city.

2. The stock held in the shop was valued two months ago at £50,000. Some of the equipment and clothing is last season's stock, and this would need to be sold at a discount. The owner has estimated that the total discount would amount to approximately £5,000.

LEARNING OUTCOME 3 VALUATION AND CORPORATE CHANGE

3. As well as selling to retail customers who must pay cash when they buy any goods, the shop has started to sell sports equipment to a local sports centre. The sports centre is permitted three months' credit and currently owes £3,500. The current owner has thought about selling items over the internet but has not made any progress on this.

4. The current owner has lost interest in running the business in recent years and, as a consequence, both turnover and profit have been falling. This has had a negative effect upon the reputation of the business. Turnover over the last 12 months was £420,000 and the profit after tax was £51,000. In the year prior to this the turnover of the business was £480,000 and the profit after tax was £61,000.

5. The fixtures and fittings of the shop have a net book value of £25,000. The fixtures and fittings do look out of date and the shop needs some renovation and modernising.

6. The owner of the shop has built up a good credit record with suppliers. Trade payables relating to sports equipment and clothing currently amount to £8,000.

7. The business has cash of £5,500.

8. The owner of the shop did not like borrowing and, therefore, the business does not have a bank overdraft or any borrowings.

9. The business is set up as a limited company and the owner holds 95% of the share capital. The remaining 5% is held by his wife. No dividends have ever been paid.

10. The P/E ratios of two listed companies that sell sports equipment and clothing are as follows:

Company name	P/E ratio	Notes
Sports City	6	This is a national company that sells a very wide range of sports equipment and clothing through shops.
Sporting Success	10	This is a national company that sells a very wide range of sports equipment and clothing through both shops and the internet.

Required

(a) Prepare calculations valuing the business on the basis of: (1) assets and (2) earnings. You must clearly state any assumptions that you have made in preparing the calculations. **(8 marks)**

(b) Advise Mr Smith on what further information he should gather and what other significant issues he should consider before deciding whether to purchase the business. You must explain why this further information is important. **(12 marks)**

(Total 20 marks)

Mergers and acquisitions

Topic list	Syllabus reference
1 Mergers and takeovers (acquisitions)	LO3
2 The conduct of a takeover	LO3
3 Payment methods	LO3
4 The position of shareholders in a merger/takeover	LO3
5 Regulation of takeovers	LO3
6 Post-acquisition integration	LO3

Introduction

In this chapter, we are concerned with the issues of **business combinations** and **restructuring** from the point of view of financial management and financial strategy. It is often in such circumstances that the **valuations** discussed earlier are needed. Don't forget also the wider strategic issues as you may need to bring these into discussions.

The section to spend most time on is Section 4, as this includes calculations which you might be asked to do, so work carefully through the examples we have provided.

LEARNING OUTCOME 3 VALUATION AND CORPORATE CHANGE

1 Mergers and takeovers (acquisitions)

> **FAST FORWARD**
>
> **Takeovers** often target companies that are good **strategic fits** with the acquiring companies, often to acquire a new product range or to develop a presence in a new market. **Mergers** have been more common in industries with low growth and returns.

1.1 Definition of mergers and takeovers

Key terms

> **Takeover** is the **purchase** by a company of a controlling interest in the voting share capital of another company.
>
> **Merger** is a business combination that results in the creation of a new reporting entity formed from the combining parties, in which the shareholders of the combining entities come together in a partnership for the mutual sharing of the risks and benefits of the combined entity, and in which no party to the combination in substance obtains control over any other, or is otherwise seen to be dominant, whether by virtue of the proportion of its shareholders' rights in the combined entity, the influence of its directors or otherwise (Financial Reporting Council).
>
> A **reverse takeover** occurs when a smaller company takes over a larger one, so that a predator company may have to increase its voting equity by over 100% to complete the takeover.

The distinction between mergers and takeovers (acquisitions) is not always clear, for example when a large company 'merges' with another smaller company. The methods used for mergers are often the same as the methods used to make takeovers. In practice, the number of genuine mergers is small relative to the number of takeovers.

Exam focus point

> Business amalgamations (mergers and takeovers) will be a key topic for exam questions.

1.2 The reasons for mergers and takeovers

When two or more companies join together, there should be a **'synergistic'** effect. Synergy is when a group after a takeover achieves combined results that reflect a better rate of return than was being achieved by the same resources used in two separate operations before the takeover.

The aim of a merger or acquisition should be to make profits **in the long term** as well as in the short term.

(a) **Acquisitions** may provide a means of entering a market at a lower cost than would be incurred if the company tried to develop its own resources, or a means of acquiring the business of a competitor. Acquisitions or mergers which might reduce or eliminate competition in a market may be prohibited in the UK by the Competition and Markets Authority.

(b) **Mergers**, especially in the UK, have tended to be more common in industries with a history of little growth and low returns. Highly profitable companies tend to seek acquisitions rather than mergers.

Reasons for mergers and acquisitions	
Operating economies	Through, for example, the elimination of duplicate and competing facilities and economies of scale
Management acquisition	Obtaining an aggressive quality management team to ensure continued growth
Diversification	Spreading risk
Asset backing	Companies in risky industry with high earnings:asset ratios acquiring companies with substantial asset backing

14: MERGERS AND ACQUISITIONS

Reasons for mergers and acquisitions	
Quality of earnings	Acquisition of companies with less variable earnings
Finance and liquidity	Improvement of liquidity and finance-raising ability through acquisition of companies with greater financial stability
Cost	Acquisition may be a cheaper method than internal expansion
Tax factors	Exceptionally a cash-financial takeover may be tax efficient way of transferring cash out of corporate sector
Defensive merger	Merging to prevent other competitors obtaining an advantage
Economic efficiency	Reciprocal buying and selling arrangements, cross-subsidisation

1.2.1 A strategic approach to takeovers

Strategic opportunities	
Where you are	**How to get to where you want to be**
Growing steadily but in a mature market with limited growth prospects	Acquire a company in a younger market with a higher growth rate
Marketing an incomplete product range, or having the potential to sell other products or services to your existing customers	Acquire a company with a complementary product range
Operating at maximum productive capacity	Acquire a company making similar products operating substantially below capacity
Under-utilising management resources	Acquire a company into which your talents can extend
Needing more control of suppliers or customers	Acquire a company which is, or gives access to, a significant customer or supplier
Lacking key clients in a targeted sector	Acquire a company with the right customer profile
Preparing for flotation but needing to improve your statement of financial position	Acquire a suitable company which will enhance earnings per share
Needing to increase market share	Acquire an important competitor
Needing to widen your capability	Acquire a company with the key talents and/or technology

A strategic approach to takeovers would imply that acquisitions are only made after a full analysis of the underlying strengths of the acquirer company, and identification of candidates' **'strategic fit' with its existing activities**. Possible strategic reasons for a takeover are matched with suggested ways of achieving the aim in the list above from a publication of 3i (Investors in Industry), which specialises in offering advice on takeovers.

1.3 Factors in a takeover decision

Several factors will need to be considered before deciding to try to take over a target business. These include the following.

1.3.1 Price factors

(a) What would the **cost** of acquisition be?

(b) Would the acquisition be **worth** the price?

(c) Alternatively, factors (a) and (b) above could be expressed in terms of:

What is the **highest price** that it would be worth paying to acquire the business?

The value of a business could be assessed in terms of:

- Its earnings
- Its assets
- Its prospects for sales and earnings growth
- How it would contribute to the strategy of the 'predator' company
- The **savings** brought about by combination as compared with the companies' separate requirements and expenditure added together

The valuation of companies was covered in the previous chapter of this Learning & Practice Workbook.

1.3.2 Other factors

(a) Would the takeover be regarded as **desirable** by the predator company's shareholders and (in the case of quoted companies) the stock market in general?

(b) Are the owners of the target company **amenable** to a takeover bid? Or would they be likely to adopt defensive tactics to resist a bid?

(c) What form would the **purchase consideration** take? An acquisition is accomplished by buying the shares of a target company. The purchase consideration might be cash, in which case the purchasing company will need adequate surplus cash or borrowing capabilities. The purchasing company might alternatively issue new shares (or loan stock) and exchange them for shares in the company taken over.

(d) How would the takeover be **reflected in the published accounts** of the predator company?

(e) Would there be any **other potential problems** arising from the proposed takeover, such as future dividend policy and service contracts for key personnel?

2 The conduct of a takeover

> **FAST FORWARD**
>
> A takeover may be **resisted** by the target company, if its directors believe that the terms are poor or there are no obvious advantages. Possible **defensive tactics** include issuing a forecast of attractive future profits, lobbying or finding a white knight (a company that would make a welcome takeover bid).

2.1 Will the bidding company's shareholders approve of a takeover?

When a company is planning a takeover bid for another company, its board of directors should give some thought to **how its own shareholders might react** to the bid. A company does not have to ask its shareholders for their approval of every takeover.

(a) When a large takeover is planned by a listed company involving **the issue of a substantial number of new shares by the predator company** (to pay for the takeover), Stock Exchange rules may require the company to obtain the formal approval of its shareholders to the takeover bid at a general meeting.

(b) If shareholders, and the stock market in general, think the takeover is not a good one the **market value of the company's shares is likely to fall**. The company's directors have a responsibility to protect their shareholders' interests, and are accountable to them at the annual general meeting of the company.

A takeover bid might seem **unattractive** to shareholders of the bidding company because:

(a) It might **reduce** the **EPS** of their company.

(b) The target company is in a **risky industry**, or is in danger of going into liquidation.

(c) It might **reduce** the **net asset backing** per share of the company, because the target company will probably be bought at a price which is well in excess of its net asset value.

(d) Frequently the **share price** of the predator company falls.

2.2 Will a takeover bid be resisted by the target company?

Quite often, a takeover bid will be resisted. Resistance comes from the target company's board of directors, who adopt defensive tactics, and ultimately the target company's shareholders, who can refuse to sell their shares to the bidding company. Grounds for refusal may include:

(a) A basic unwillingness to sell

(b) A belief that the predator has under-bid

(c) The after-tax personal value of the offer being unattractive

(d) If the consideration is the shares of the predator, these shares being unattractive in terms of value, beta, dividend policy

Resistance can be overcome by **offering a higher price**.

(a) In cases where an **unquoted** company is the target company, if resistance to a takeover cannot be overcome, the takeover will not take place, and negotiations would simply break down.

(b) Where the target company is a **quoted company**, the situation is different. The target company will have many shareholders, some of whom will want to accept the offer for their shares, and some of whom will not. In addition, the target company's board of directors might resist a takeover, even though their shareholders might want to accept the offer.

Because there are likely to be major **differences of opinion** about whether to accept a takeover bid or not, the Stock Exchange has issued formal rules for the conduct of takeover bids, in the City Code on Takeovers and Mergers.

> **Exam focus point**
>
> **Detailed knowledge** of the City Code will not be tested in your examination, but you should be aware of its **implications**.

2.3 Contesting an offer

The directors of a target company must **act in the interests of their shareholders, employees and creditors**. They may decide to contest an offer on several grounds.

(a) The offer may be unacceptable because the **terms are poor**. Rejection of the offer may lead to an improved bid.

(b) The merger or takeover may have **no obvious advantage**.

(c) Employees may be **strongly opposed** to the bid.

(d) The **founder members** of the business may **oppose** the bid, and appeal to the loyalty of other shareholders.

When a company receives a takeover bid which the board of directors considers unwelcome, the directors must act quickly to fight off the bid.

2.4 Defensive tactics

The steps that might be taken to **thwart a bid** or **make it seem less attractive** includes the following:

(a) Issuing a **forecast** of **attractive future profits** and dividends to persuade shareholders that to sell their shares would be unwise, that the offer price is too low, and that it would be better for them to retain their shares to benefit from future profits, dividends and capital growth. (Such profit and dividend forecasts can be included in 'defence documents' circulated to shareholders, and in press releases)

(b) Refer the merger to the Competition and Markets Authority for investigation (see later in the chapter)

(c) Launching an **advertising campaign** against the takeover bid (one technique is to attack the accounts of the predator company)

(d) Finding a **'white knight'**, a company which will make a welcome takeover bid

(e) **Making a counter-bid** for the predator company (this can only be done if the companies are of reasonably similar size)

(f) Arranging a **management buyout**

(g) Introducing a 'poison-pill' **anti-takeover device** (for example, allowing all shareholders apart from the acquirer to buy shares at a bargain price, or threatening that the entire management team will resign on takeover, leaving the target company without any managers)

2.5 Costs of contested takeover bids

Takeover bids, when contested, can be very expensive, involving:

- Costs of professional services, eg merchant bank and public relations agency
- Advertising costs
- Underwriting costs
- Interest costs
- Possible capital loss on buying/selling the target company's shares

2.6 Gaining the consent of the target company shareholders

A takeover bid will only succeed if the predator company can persuade enough shareholders in the target company to sell their shares. Shareholders will only do this if they are dissatisfied with the performance of their company and its shares, or they are attracted by a high offer and the chance to make a good capital gain.

2.7 Services of a merchant bank and stockbroker

During the acquisition process, a company may be assisted by its merchant bank and stockbroker, or by one financial institution fulfilling both roles.

3 Payment methods

> **FAST FORWARD**
>
> Payment can be in the form of **cash**, a **share exchange** or **convertible loan stock**. The choice will depend on available cash, desired levels of gearing, shareholders' taxation position and changes in control.

3.1 Methods of payment

The terms of a takeover will involve a purchase of the shares of the target company for **cash** or for **'paper'** (shares, or possibly loan stock). A purchase of a target company's shares with shares of the predator company is referred to as a **share exchange**.

3.2 Cash purchases

If the purchase consideration is in **cash**, the shareholders of the target company will simply be bought out. For example, suppose that there are two companies.

	Big Ltd	Small Ltd
Net assets (book value)	£1,500,000	£200,000
Number of shares	100,000	10,000
Earnings	£2,000,000	£40,000

Big Ltd negotiates a takeover of Small Ltd for £400,000 in cash.

As a result, Big Ltd will end up with:

(a) Net assets (book value) of

£1,500,000 + £200,000 − £400,000 cash = £1,300,000

(b) 100,000 shares (no change)

(c) Expected earnings of £2,040,000, minus the loss of interest (net of tax) which would have been obtained from the investment of the £400,000 in cash which was given up to acquire Small Ltd

3.3 Purchases by share exchange

One company can acquire another company by **issuing shares** to pay for the acquisition. The new shares might be issued:

(a) **In exchange** for shares in the target company. Thus, if A plc acquires B Ltd, A plc might issue shares which it gives to B Ltd's shareholders in exchange for their shares.

The B Ltd shareholders therefore become new shareholders of A plc. This is a takeover for a 'paper' consideration. Paper offers will often be accompanied by a **cash alternative**.

(b) **To raise cash** on the stock market, which will then be used to buy the target company's shares. To the target company shareholders, this is a cash bid.

Sometimes, a company might acquire another in a share exchange, but the shares are then **sold immediately** on a stock market to raise cash for the seller.

Whatever the detailed arrangements of a takeover with paper, the end result will be an **increase in the issued share capital of the predator company**.

3.4 Use of convertible loan stock

Alternative forms of paper consideration, including debentures, loan stock and preference shares, are not so commonly used, due to

- **Difficulties** in **establishing a rate of return** that will be attractive to target shareholders
- The **effects** on the **gearing levels** of the acquiring company
- The **change** in the **structure** of the target shareholders' portfolios
- The **securities** being potentially **less marketable**, and possibly lacking voting rights

Issuing **convertible loan stock** will overcome some of these drawbacks, by offering the target shareholders the option of partaking in the future profits of the company if they wish.

Key term

> **Convertible loan stock** is a loan which gives the holder the right to convert to other securities, normally ordinary shares, at a predetermined price/rate and time.

3.5 The choice between a cash offer and a paper offer

The choice between cash and paper offers (or a combination of both) will depend on how the different methods are viewed by the company and its existing shareholders, and on the attitudes of the shareholders of the target company. The factors that the directors of the bidding company must consider include the following.

Company and its existing shareholders	
Dilution of EPS	Fall in EPS attributable to existing shareholders may occur if purchase consideration is in equity shares
Cost to the company	Use of loan stock to back cash offer will attract tax relief on interest and have lower cost than equity. Convertible loan stock can have lower coupon rate than ordinary stock
Gearing	Highly geared company may not be able to issue further loan stock to obtain cash for cash offer
Control	Control could change considerably if large number of new shares issued
Authorised share capital increase	May be required if consideration is in form of shares. This will involve calling a general meeting to pass the necessary resolution
Borrowing limits increase	General meeting resolution also required if borrowing limits have to change

Shareholders in target company	
Taxation	If consideration is cash, many investors may suffer immediate liability to tax on capital gain
Income	If consideration is not cash, arrangement must mean existing income is maintained, or be compensated by suitable capital gain or reasonable growth expectations
Future investments	Shareholders who want to retain stake in target business may prefer shares
Share price	If consideration is shares, recipients will want to be sure that the shares retain their values

3.6 Mezzanine finance and takeover bids

When the purchase consideration in a takeover bid is cash, the cash must be obtained somehow by the bidding company, in order to pay for the shares that it buys. Occasionally, the company will have sufficient cash in hand to pay for the target company's shares. More frequently, the cash will have to be raised, possibly from existing shareholders, by means of **a rights issue** or, more probably, by **borrowing from banks** or other financial institutions.

When cash for a takeover is raised by borrowing, the loans would normally be **medium-term** and **secured**.

However, there have been many takeover bids, with a cash purchase option for the target company's shareholders, where the bidding company has arranged loans that:

(a) Are **short-to-medium term**

(b) Are **unsecured** (that is, 'junior' debt, low in the priority list for repayment in the event of liquidation of the borrower)

(c) Because they are unsecured, attract a **much higher rate of interest** than secured debt (typically 4% or 5% above SONIA)

(d) Often, give the lender the **option to exchange** the loan for shares after the takeover

This type of borrowing is called **mezzanine finance** (because it lies between equity and debt financing) – a form of finance which is also often used in **management buyouts** (which are discussed later in Chapter 15.

3.7 Earn-out arrangements

The purchase consideration may not all be paid at the time of acquisition. Part of it may be deferred, payable upon the target company reaching certain performance targets.

4 The position of shareholders in a merger/takeover

> **FAST FORWARD**
>
> Shareholders of both the companies involved in a merger will be sensitive to the effect of the merger on **share prices** and **earnings per share**.

4.1 The market values of the companies' shares during a takeover bid

Market share prices can be very important during a takeover bid. Suppose that Velvet plc decides to make a takeover bid for the shares of Noggin plc. Noggin plc shares are currently quoted on the market at £2 each. Velvet shares are quoted at £4.50 and Velvet offers one of its shares for every two shares in Noggin, thus making an offer at current market values worth £2.25 per share in Noggin. This is only the value of the bid so long as Velvet's shares remain valued at £4.50. If their value falls, the bid will become less attractive.

This is why companies that make takeover bids with a share exchange offer are always concerned that the market value of their shares should not fall during the takeover negotiations, before the target company's shareholders have decided whether to accept the bid.

4.2 EPS before and after a takeover

If one company acquires another by issuing shares, its EPS will go up or down according to the P/E ratio at which the target company has been bought.

(a) If the **target company's shares** are **bought** at a **higher P/E** ratio than the predator company's shares, the predator company's shareholders will suffer a **fall in EPS**.

(b) If the target company's shares are valued at a lower **P/E ratio**, the **predator company's shareholders** will benefit from a **rise in EPS**.

4.3 Example: Mergers and takeovers (1)

Giant plc takes over Tiddler Ltd by offering two shares in Giant for one share in Tiddler. Details about each company are as follows:

	Giant plc	Tiddler Ltd
Number of shares	2,800,000	100,000
Market value per share	£4	–
Annual earnings	£560,000	£50,000
EPS	20p	50p
P/E ratio	20	

By offering two shares in Giant worth £4 each for one share in Tiddler, the valuation placed on each Tiddler share is £8, and with Tiddler's EPS of 50p, this implies that Tiddler would be acquired on a P/E ratio of 16. This is lower than the P/E ratio of Giant, which is 20.

If the acquisition produces no synergy, and there is no growth in the earnings of either Giant or its new subsidiary Tiddler, then the EPS of Giant would still be higher than before, because Tiddler was bought on a lower P/E ratio.

The combined group's results would be as follows:

	Giant group
Number of shares (2,800,000 + 200,000)	3,000,000
Annual earnings (560,000 + 50,000)	610,000
EPS	20.33p

If the P/E ratio is still 20, the market value per share would be £4.07 (70.33 × 20), which is 7p more than the pre-takeover price.

The process of buying a company with a higher EPS in order to boost your own EPS is known as bootstrapping. Whether the stock market is fooled by this process is debatable. The P/E ratio is likely to fall after the takeover in the absence of synergistic or other gains.

4.4 Example: Mergers and takeovers (2)

Redwood plc agrees to acquire the shares of Hawthorn Ltd in a share exchange arrangement. The agreed P/E ratio for Hawthorn's shares is 15.

	Redwood plc	Hawthorn Ltd
Number of shares	3,000,000	100,000
Market price per share	£2	–
Earnings	£600,000	£120,000
P/E ratio	10	

The EPS of Hawthorn Ltd is £1.20, and so the agreed price per share will be £1.20 × 15 = £18. In a share exchange agreement, Redwood would have to issue nine new shares (valued at £2 each) to acquire each share in Hawthorn, and so a total of 900,000 new shares must be issued to complete the takeover.

After the takeover, the enlarged company would have 3,900,000 shares in issue and, assuming no earnings growth, total earnings of £720,000. This would give an EPS of:

$$\frac{£720,000}{3,900,000} = 18.5p$$

The pre-takeover EPS of Redwood was 20p, and so the EPS would fall. This is because Hawthorn has been bought on a higher P/E ratio (15 compared with Redwood's 10).

4.5 Buying companies on a higher P/E ratio, but with profit growth

Buying companies on a higher P/E ratio will result in a fall in EPS unless there is profit growth to offset this fall. For example, suppose that Starving plc acquires Bigmeal plc, by offering two shares in Starving for three shares in Bigmeal. Details of each company are as follows:

	Starving plc	Bigmeal plc
Number of shares	5,000,000	3,000,000
Value per share	£6	£4
Annual earnings		
Current	£2,000,000	£600,000
Next year	£2,200,000	£950,000
EPS	40p	20p
P/E ratio	15	20

Starving plc is acquiring Bigmeal plc on a higher P/E ratio, and it is only the profit growth in the acquired subsidiary that gives the enlarged Starving group its growth in EPS.

	Starving group
Number of shares (5,000,000 + 3,000,000 × 2/3)	7,000,000
Earnings	
If no profit growth (2,000,000 + 600,000) £2,600,000	EPS would have been 37.24p
With profit growth (2,200,000 + 950,000) £3,150,000	EPS will be 45p

If an acquisition strategy involves buying companies on a higher P/E ratio, it is therefore essential for continuing EPS growth that the acquired companies offer prospects of strong profit growth.

4.6 Further points to consider: Net assets per share and the quality of earnings

You might think that dilution of earnings must be avoided at all cost. However, there are three cases where a dilution of earnings might be accepted on an acquisition if there were other advantages to be gained.

(a) **Earnings growth** may hide the dilution in EPS as above.

(b) A company might be willing to accept earnings dilution if the **quality of the acquired company's earnings** is superior to that of the acquiring company.

(c) A trading company with high earnings, but with few assets, may want to increase its assets base by acquiring a company which is strong in assets but weak in earnings so that assets and earnings get more into line with each other. In this case, **dilution in earnings is compensated for by an increase in net asset backing**.

Question — Effect of acquisition

Intangible plc has an issued capital of 2,000,000 £1 ordinary shares. Net assets (excluding goodwill) are £2,500,000 and annual earnings average £1,500,000. The company is valued by the stock market on a P/E ratio of 8. Tangible Ltd has an issued capital of 1,000,000 ordinary shares. Net assets (excluding goodwill) are £3,500,000 and annual earnings average £400,000. The shareholders of Tangible Ltd accept an all-equity offer from Intangible plc valuing each share in Tangible Ltd at £4. Calculate Intangible plc's earnings and assets per share before and after the acquisition of Tangible Ltd.

Answer

(a) Before the acquisition of Tangible Ltd, the position is as follows:

$$\text{Earnings per share (EPS)} = \frac{£1,500,000}{2,000,000} = 75\text{p}$$

$$\text{Assets per share (APS)} = \frac{£2,500,000}{2,000,000} = £1.25$$

(b) Tangible Ltd's EPS figure is 40p (£400,000 ÷ 1,000,000), and the company is being bought on a multiple of 10 at £4 per share. As the takeover consideration is being satisfied by shares, Intangible plc's earnings will be diluted because Intangible plc is valuing Tangible Ltd on a higher multiple of earnings than itself. Intangible plc will have to issue 666,667 (4,000,000/6) shares valued at £6 each (earnings of 75p per share at a multiple of 8) to satisfy the £4,000,000 consideration. The results for Intangible plc will be as follows.

$$\text{EPS} = \frac{£1,900,000}{2,666,667} = 71.25\text{p} \text{ (3.75p lower than the previous 75p)}$$

$$\text{APS} = \frac{£6,000,000}{2,666,667} = £2.25 \text{ (£1 higher than the previous £1.25)}$$

If Intangible plc is still valued on the stock market on a P/E ratio of 8, the share price should fall by approximately 30p (8 × 3.75p, the fall in EPS) but because the asset backing $\left(\dfrac{\text{Net assets exc goodwill}}{\text{Shares}}\right)$ has been increased substantially the company will probably now be valued on a higher P/E ratio than 8.

The shareholders in Tangible Ltd would receive 666,667 shares in Intangible plc in exchange for their current 1,000,000 shares, that is, two shares in Intangible for every three shares currently held.

(a) Earnings

	£
Three shares in Tangible earn (3 × 40p)	1.200
Two shares in Intangible will earn (2 × 71.25p)	1.425
Increase in earnings, per three shares held in Tangible	0.225

(b) Assets

	£
Three shares in Tangible have an asset backing of (3 × £3.5)	10.50
Two shares in Intangible will have an asset backing of (2 × £2.25)	4.50
Loss in asset backing, per three shares held in Tangible	6.00

The shareholders in Tangible Ltd would be trading asset backing for an increase in earnings.

4.7 Valuation using post-merger dividends or cash flows

An alternative method to using the P/E ratios, is to consider the dividends or cash flows of the merged company. Reliable cash flow estimates should take into account the effects of the merger such as economies of scale and greater combined power.

4.7.1 Dividend method

The steps are as follows:

Step 1 Estimate the initial dividends of the combined company and the dividend growth rate

Step 2 Estimate the **new cost of capital**; if the cost of the two old companies differs significantly, some sort of weighted average method will be required

Step 3 Calculate the **value of the combined company** using the dividend valuation model

Step 4 Compare the **value of the combined company** with the **pre-merger value** of the acquiror. The excess is the value of the target

In practice, the level of dividends and dividend cover expected by shareholders in both companies may create difficulties before the merger or takeover is agreed.

4.7.2 Cash flow method

The steps here are as follows:

Step 1 Estimate the **cash flows of the combined company**, including the acquired's, the acquiror's and the additional cash flows arising from the beneficial effects of the merger

Step 2 Estimate the **new cost of capital** as above

Step 3 Calculate the **net present value** of the combined cash flows

Step 4 Compare the **value of the combined cash flows** with the acquiror's cash flows if no merger took place. The excess is the value of the target

14: MERGERS AND ACQUISITIONS

5 Regulation of takeovers

FAST FORWARD

Directors of companies of any size must treat all shareholders **fairly** and give them **sufficient information** about the takeover. Larger mergers will be of interest to the competition authorities.

5.1 The City Code on Takeovers and Mergers and UK legislation

Takeover regulation in the UK goes back to 1968 when a **voluntary code**, the **City Code on Takeovers and Mergers** (known as the City Code), was introduced. Since then the Code, a set of general principles and rules governing takeovers and mergers of UK companies, has been frequently amended.

Mergers and acquisitions in the UK are also regulated by legislation through the **Companies Acts**, the **Financial Services and Markets Act 2000** (the FSMA) and the insider dealing provisions of the **Criminal Justice Act 1993**.

In continental Europe, takeover regulation was put in place in the late 1980s based largely on voluntary codes following the UK City Code. However, these were soon replaced by legislation in the mid-1990s.

5.2 The City Code: General principles

The City Code is divided into general principles and detailed rules which must be observed by persons involved in a merger or takeover transaction. The key requirements of the City Code include the following:

(1) **All the shareholders of the target company must be treated similarly**

'All holders of the securities of an offeree company of the same class must be afforded equivalent treatment; moreover, if a person **acquires control** of a company, the other holders of securities must be protected.'

In other words, a company making a takeover bid cannot offer one set of purchase terms to some shareholders in the target company, and a different set of terms to other shareholders holding shares of the same class in that company.

An offer must be made for **all** other shares if the % shareholding rises above **30%**, at not less than the highest price paid by the bidding company in last year.

(2) **Sufficient time and information to be given for a properly informed decision**

'The holders of the securities of an offeree company must have sufficient time and information to enable them to reach a properly informed decision on the bid; where it advises the holders of securities, the board of the offeree company must give its views on the effects of the implementation of the bid on employment, conditions of employment and the locations of the company's places of business.'

To reinforce this a bid timetable is set – details are provided in the following section but **detailed knowledge of this timetable is not required**.

(3) **The directors of the offeree company must act in the interest of the company as a whole**

'The board of an offeree company must act in the interests of the company as a whole and must not deny the holders of securities the opportunity to decide on the merits of the bid.'

The board may not use poison pills to frustrate a takeover bid without shareholder approval.

5.3 The Competition and Markets Authority

A UK company might have to consider whether its proposed takeover would be drawn to the attention of the Competition and Markets Authority (formerly called the Competition Commission and the Monopolies and Mergers Commission).

351

If a transaction is referred to the Competition and Markets Authority and the Authority finds that it results in a substantial lessening of competition in the defined market, it will specify action to remedy or prevent the adverse effects identified, or it may decide that the merger does not take place (or, in the case of a completed merger, is reversed).

Any person aggrieved by a decision of the Competition and Markets Authority in connection with a reference or possible reference may apply to the Competition Appeal Tribunal for a review of that decision.

A number of tests may be used to decide whether there has been a **substantial lessening** of **competition** (SLC). These normally include:

(a) **The revenue test**

No investigation will normally be conducted if the target's revenue is less than £70 million.

(b) **The share of supply test**

An investigation will not normally be conducted unless, following the merger, the combined entity supplies 25%. The 25% share will be assessed by the Authority.

(c) **The SLC test**

Even if the thresholds in (a) and (b) above are met, the Competition and Markets Authority will only be involved if there has been an SLC in the market.

6 Post-acquisition integration

FAST FORWARD

Many takeovers fail to achieve their full potential because of lack of attention paid to **post-acquisition integration**. A clear programme should be in place, designed to re-define objectives and strategy, and take appropriate care of the human element.

6.1 Problems of integration

Failures of takeovers often result from **inadequate integration** of the companies after the takeover has taken place. There is a tendency for senior management to devote their energies to the next acquisition rather than to the newly-acquired firm. The particular approach adopted will depend upon the **culture** of the organisation as well as the **nature** of the company acquired and **how it fits** into the amalgamated organisation (eg horizontally, vertically, or as part of a diversified conglomerate).

6.2 Drucker's Golden Rules

Drucker has suggested Five Golden Rules for the process of post-acquisition integration.

Rule 1	There should be a 'common core of unity' shared by the acquiror and acquiree. The ties should involve overlapping characteristics such as shared technology and markets, and not just financial links.
Rule 2	The acquiror should ask 'What can we offer them?' as well as 'What's in it for us?'
Rule 3	The acquiror should treat the products, markets and customers of the acquired company with respect, and not disparagingly.
Rule 4	The acquiror should provide top management with relevant skills for the acquired company within a year.
Rule 5	Cross-company promotions of staff should occur within one year.

6.3 Service contracts for key personnel

When the target company employs certain key personnel, on whom the success of the company has been based, the predator company might want to ensure that these key people do not leave as soon as the takeover occurs. To do this, it might be necessary to insist as a condition of the offer that the key people should agree to sign **service contracts**, tying them to the company for a certain time (perhaps three years). Service contracts would have to be attractive to the employees concerned, perhaps through offering a high salary or other benefits such as share options in the predator company. Where key personnel are shareholders, they might be bound not to sell shares for a period.

6.4 Merging systems

The degree to which the information, control and reporting systems of the two companies involved in a takeover are merged will depend to some extent upon the **degree of integration** envisaged. There are two extremes of integration.

(a) **Complete absorption of the target firm**

This is where the cultures, operational procedures and organisational structures of the two firms are to be fused together. This approach is most suitable where significant cost reductions are expected to be achieved through economies of scale, and/or combining marketing and distribution effort can enhance revenues.

(b) **The preservation approach**

This is where the target company is to become an independent subsidiary of the holding company. This would be most beneficial for the merger of companies with very different products, markets and cultures.

6.5 Failure of mergers and takeovers

The aim of any takeover will be to **generate value for the acquiring shareholders**. Where this does not happen, there may be a number of reasons, including **a strategic plan that fails to produce the benefits expected,** or **over-optimism** about future market conditions, operating synergies and the amount of time and money required to make the merger work.

A recurring reason for failure is **poor integration management**, in particular:

(a) **Inflexibility** in the application of integration plans drawn up prior to the event. Once the takeover has happened, management must be prepared to adapt plans in the light of changed circumstances or inaccurate prior information.

(b) **Poor man management**, with lack of communication of goals and future prospects of employees. There may be a failure to recognise and deal with the uncertainty and anxiety invariably felt by them.

A survey carried out through the interviewing of senior executives of the UK's top 100 companies covering 50 deals, revealed some common factors contributing to the failure of mergers.

- Cultural differences and poor attitude of target management
- Little or no post-acquisition planning
- Lack of knowledge of industry or target company
- Poor management and poor practices in target company
- Little or no experience of acquisitions

6.6 Corporate mentoring

Key term

> Mentoring: A long-term relationship in which a more experienced person acts as a **teacher**, counsellor, role model, supporter and encourager, to foster the individual's personal and career development.

Corporate mentoring can be a useful technique in improving the chances of successful integration of an acquisition. While many of the post-acquisition challenges relate to the integration of systems and structures, the people challenges are often the most challenging and long lasting. Purchasers often fail to carry out a full management audit of the acquisition target, and fail to consider the human resource issues which impact on the ultimate success of the acquisition.

As discussed in section 6.3, a key objective post acquisition is the retention of key personnel. Members of staff who receive support from a mentor are more likely in the short term to feel valued and appreciated by the organisation. This will also continue into the longer term where mentoring forms part of the organisation's succession plan. Mentoring will help drive the commitment and performance of individuals if they are able to request support relating to areas of personal interest. When staff members feel valued and are given support in areas of personal interest they are more likely to want to work harder which should improve organisational performance. Greater levels of staff commitment and loyalty resulting from mentoring schemes will also help reduce high levels of staff turnover.

Conqueror syndrome is a common post-acquisition issue. Employees of the acquired company are made to feel inferior, especially if their company was bought because it was not doing well. Corporate mentoring provides a safe environment where people can discuss their fears and concerns, stereotypes and assumptions about the two organisations can therefore be challenged in a safe environment.

In a typical acquisition situation, cross-organisational communication can diminish, partly because of a lack of trust but also because it takes time to build new informal networks. Well-designed and managed corporate mentoring schemes can improve workplace culture and engagement, they help to build trust and create an informal communication network. This is increasingly important as companies become more reliant on the quality and effectiveness of their internal, informal social networks. Getting people from the two organisations physically together post acquisition can be difficult, however E-mentoring between the organisations can create an instant communication network enabling relationships to be developed immediately.

6.7 The impact of mergers and takeovers on stakeholders

FAST FORWARD

> Don't forget that **managers**, **employees** and **financial institutions** are key stakeholders in mergers as well as shareholders.

The following comments are based upon extensive empirical research:

(a) **Acquiring company shareholders**

At least half of mergers studied have shown a decline in profitability compared with industry averages. Returns to equity can often be poor relative to the market in the early years, particularly for equity-financed bids and first time players. Costs of mergers frequently outweigh the gains.

(b) **Target company shareholders**

In the majority of cases, it is the target shareholders who benefit the greatest from a takeover. Bidding companies invariably have to offer a significant premium over the market price prevailing prior to the bid in order to achieve the purchase.

(c) **Acquiring company management**

The management of the newly enlarged organisation will often enjoy increased status and influence, as well as increased salary and benefits.

(d) **Target company management**

While some key personnel may be kept on for some time after the takeover, a significant number of managers will find themselves out of a job. However, a 'golden handshake' and the prospect of equally remunerative employment elsewhere may lessen the blow of this somewhat.

(e) **Other employees**

Commonly the economy of scale cost savings anticipated in a merger will be largely achieved by the loss of jobs, as duplicated service operations are eliminated and loss-making divisions closed down. However, in some instances, the increased competitive strength of the newly enlarged enterprise can led to expansion of operations and the need for an increased workforce.

(f) **Financial institutions**

These are perhaps the outright winners. The more complex the deal, the longer the battle, and the more legal and financial problems encountered, the greater their fee income, regardless of the end result.

Question — Mega mergers

There have been a number of proposed and actual mega mergers throughout the world over recent years in sectors such as financial services, oil, pharmaceuticals and automobiles.

(a) What are the main reasons for these mergers?

(b) What are the main problems arising from these mergers? Comment from the point of view of the companies concerned.

Answer

There are a variety of factors that have contributed to the recent rise in mega mergers.

(a) (i) The increasing level of **deregulation** in the financial markets has made it easier to organise the finance for large deals.

(ii) The increasing trend towards **globalisation** of both operations and financing has made the concept of the 'mega company' more attractive.

(iii) There is some evidence that there has been a trend towards getting bigger becoming a **defence** against being taken over, as the number of key players in the different market sectors has gradually declined.

(iv) In some sectors, for example vehicle manufacturing, there is a trend towards bigger companies, as the market becomes **increasingly concentrated** in the hands of a declining number of large producers.

(v) Large corporations see the opportunity for achieving **significant economies of scale** and thereby becoming more competitive. These economies are no longer primarily in the field of operations, but rather in the overhead areas such as head office costs, research and IT.

(vi) In some sectors, takeover activity is still driven through the opportunity to achieve **operating economies**.

(vii) Sometimes, a merger may be the **quickest and cheapest way of achieving the growth in earnings** that is demanded by investors, and the increasing size of leading companies means that some of these mergers will fall into the 'mega merger' category.

(b) (i) The creation of very large companies may lead to unforeseen **diseconomies of scale**. For example, there may be problems of communication and control within the organisation which mean that large and costly new IT solutions are required that were not originally envisaged.

(ii) There is an increasing climate of **job uncertainty** within the companies concerned as staff anticipate possible redundancies as part of a post-merger rationalisation. This may translate into a reduced level of commitment to the new organisation, a higher level of staff turnover with a loss of key staff, and a corresponding decline in performance.

(iii) The **cultures** of the two organisations may be so different as to make integration very difficult. This is less important where a small company is taken over by a large one since in this situation there will be a greater expectation of change. In the mega merger, change will be required by all staff within both companies, and if the cultural divergence is too great, this may be difficult to achieve successfully. If such integration is not achieved, then the merger is less likely to succeed operationally and financially.

(iv) Very large organisations may lose their **flexibility** and ability to provide a good quality of local **customer service**, as managers become increasingly distanced from their customers. This in turn may mean that they lose some of their competitive advantage.

Chapter Roundup

- **Takeovers** often target companies that are good **strategic fits** with the acquiring companies, often to acquire a new product range or to develop a presence in a new market. **Mergers** have been more common in industries with low growth and returns.
- A takeover may be **resisted** by the target company, if its directors believe that the terms are poor or there are no obvious advantages. Possible **defensive tactics** include issuing a forecast of attractive future profits, lobbying or finding a white knight (a company that would make a welcome takeover bid).
- Payment can be in the form of **cash**, a **share exchange** or **convertible loan stock**. The choice will depend on available cash, desired levels of gearing, shareholders' taxation position and changes in control.
- Shareholders of both the companies involved in a merger will be sensitive to the effect of the merger on **share prices** and **earnings per share**.
- Directors of companies of any size must treat all shareholders **fairly** and give them **sufficient information** about the takeover. Larger mergers will be of interest to the competition authorities.
- Many takeovers fail to achieve their full potential because of lack of attention paid to **post-acquisition integration**. A clear programme should be in place, designed to re-define objectives and strategy, and take appropriate care of the human element.
- Don't forget that **managers**, **employees** and **financial institutions** are key stakeholders in mergers as well as shareholders.

Quick Quiz

1. What is the name for 'the acquisition by a company of a controlling interest in the voting share capital of another company?
2. What is meant by a 'white knight'?
3. What is a 'poison pill' in the context of takeovers and mergers?
4. A smaller company takes over a larger one, so that the smaller company must increase its voting equity by over 100% to complete the takeover. What is this process called?
5. What is the name of the arrangement where part of the purchase consideration is only paid when the target company reaches certain performance targets?
6. What are Drucker's five golden rules for post-acquisition integration?
7. What is the five step post-integration sequence suggested by Jones?
8. If the target company's shares are valued at a lower P/E ratio, the predator company's shareholders will suffer a fall in EPS.

    ☐ True

    ☐ False

Answers to Quick Quiz

1. A takeover
2. A company which will make a welcome takeover bid
3. An anti-takeover device
4. A reverse takeover
5. An earn-out arrangement
6. (1) Common sense of unity shared by acquiror and acquiree
   (2) Acquiror should ask 'what can we offer them'?
   (3) Acquiror should treat products, markets and customers of acquired company with respect
   (4) Acquiring company should provide top management with relevant skills for managing acquired company within one year
   (5) Cross-company promotions of staff within one year
7. (1) Establish initial reporting relationships
   (2) Achieve rapid control of key factors
   (3) Resource audit
   (4) Redefine corporate objectives and develop strategic plans
   (5) Revise organisational structure
8. False. The predator company's shareholders will benefit from a rise in earnings per share.

End of chapter question

JG plc (AIA November 2009)

JG plc is a company listed on the UK Stock Exchange. It was floated three years ago and sells health foods and snacks through a chain of city centre shops. It has done well since its launch and it has already made significant inroads into the market share of the UK's largest chain of health food shops, namely Smith and Brown plc. It has achieved this by mainly undercutting its rival's prices. This has forced Smith and Brown to reduce its prices and has had a significant impact on its profitability. Smith and Brown has a market capitalisation which is currently three times higher than that of JG and operates twice the number of shops. JG plc has seen its share price fall significantly recently as a result of the economic difficulties. Smith and Brown has also suffered a similar fall in its share price. The management of JG fear the possibility of a hostile takeover bid from Smith and Brown. The share price is actually currently slightly below its issue price and in spite of this its dividend yield is still less than 1%.

Required

Discuss the steps that might be taken by JG plc to thwart any possible bid by Smith and Brown. Your discussion should cover the situation before a bid has been made and after a bid has been made. How might the payment method used by Smith and Brown (cash, shares or securities) influence the difficulties of such a defence?

(20 marks)

Corporate reorganisation

Topic list	Syllabus reference
1 Divestments	LO3
2 Management buy-outs (MBOs) and buy-ins	LO3
3 Going private	LO3

Introduction

In this chapter we discuss other means of corporate re-shaping, many of which arise when companies are in difficulties or seeking to change their focus. Again, the strategic issues covered earlier may be significant.

1 Divestments

FAST FORWARD

Divestments (reductions in ownership stakes) can take a number of forms.

Mergers and takeovers are not inevitably good strategy for a business. In some circumstances, strategies of internal growth, no growth or even some form of **divestment** might be preferable.

Key term

A **divestment** is a proportional or complete reduction in ownership stake in an organisation.

1.1 Demergers

FAST FORWARD

A **demerger** is the splitting up of corporate bodies into two or more separate bodies, to ensure share prices reflect the true value of underlying operations.

Key term

A **demerger** is the opposite of a merger. It is the **splitting up of a corporate body into two or more separate and independent bodies**.

For example, the ABC Group plc might demerge by splitting into two independently operating companies AB plc and C plc. Existing shareholders are given a stake in each of the new separate companies.

Demerging, in its strictest sense, stops short of selling out, but is an attempt to ensure that share prices reflect the true value of the underlying operations.

1.1.1 Advantages of demergers

(a) The main advantage of a demerger is its **greater operational efficiency and the greater opportunity to realise value**. A two-division company with one loss-making division and one profit-making, fast-growing division may be better off splitting the two divisions. The profitable division may acquire a valuation well in excess of its contribution to the merged company.

(b) Even if both divisions are profit making, a demerger may still have benefits. Management can focus on **creating value for both companies individually and implementing a suitable financial structure** for each company. The full value of each company may then become appropriate.

(c) Shareholders will continue to own both companies, which means that the **diversification of their portfolio** will **remain unchanged**.

1.1.2 Disadvantages of demergers

(a) **Economies of scale** may be **lost**, where the demerged parts of the business had operations in common to which economies of scale applied.

(b) The **smaller companies** which result from the demerger will have **lower turnover**, profits and status than the group before the demerger.

(c) There may be **higher overhead** costs as a percentage of turnover, resulting from (b).

(d) The **ability** to raise **extra finance**, especially debt finance, to support new investments and expansion may be reduced.

(e) **Vulnerability to takeover** may be **increased**.

1.2 Sell-offs

FAST FORWARD

A **sell-off** is the sale of part of a company to a third party, generally for cash.

Key term

A **sell-off** is a form of **divestment** involving the sale of part of a company to a third party, usually another company. Generally, cash will be received in exchange.

1.2.1 Reasons for sell-offs

(a) As part of its strategic planning, it has decided to **restructure**, concentrating management effort on particular parts of the business. Control problems may be reduced if peripheral activities are sold off.

(b) It wishes to sell off a part of its business which **makes losses**, and so to improve the company's future reported consolidated profit performance. This may be in the form of a management buy-out (MBO) – see below.

(c) In order to **protect the rest of the business from takeover**, it may choose to sell a part of the business which is particularly attractive to a buyer.

(d) The company may be **short of cash**.

(e) A **subsidiary** with **high risk** in its operating cash flows could be sold, so as to reduce the business risk of the group as a whole.

(f) A **subsidiary** could be sold at a **profit**. Some companies have specialised in taking over large groups of companies, and then selling off parts of the newly-acquired groups, so that the proceeds of sales more than pay for the original takeovers.

1.2.2 Liquidations

The extreme form of a sell-off is where the entire business is sold off in a **liquidation**. In a voluntary dissolution, the shareholders might decide to close the whole business, sell off all the assets and distribute net funds raised to shareholders.

1.3 Spin-offs

FAST FORWARD

A **spin-off** is the creation of a new company, where the shareholders of the original company own the shares.

Key term

In a **spin-off**, a new company is created whose shares are owned by the shareholders of the original company which is making the distribution of assets.

In a spin-off:

(a) There is **no change** in the **ownership of assets**, as the shareholders own the same proportion of shares in the new company as they did in the old company.

(b) Assets of the part of the business to be separated off are transferred into the new company, which will usually have different management from the old company.

(c) In more complex cases, a spin-off may involve the original company being split into a number of separate companies.

For a number of possible reasons such as those set out below, a spin-off appears generally to meet with favour from stock market investors:

(a) The change may make a **merger** or takeover of some part of the business **easier** in the future, or may protect parts of the business from predators.

(b) There may be **improved efficiency** and more streamlined management within the new structure.

(c) It may be easier to see the value of the **separated parts** of the business now that they are no longer hidden within a conglomerate.

(d) The **requirements** of **regulatory agencies** might be met more easily within the new structure, for example if the agency is able to exercise price control over a particular part of the business which was previously hidden within the conglomerate structure.

(e) After the spin-off, shareholders have the opportunity to **adjust** the **proportions** of their **holdings** between the different companies created.

2 Management buy-outs (MBOs) and buy-ins

FAST FORWARD

A **management buy-out** is the purchase of all or part of the business by its managers. Management buy-outs can be the best way of maintaining links with a subsidiary, and can ensure the co-operation of management if a disposal is inevitable.

The main complication with **management buy-outs** is obtaining the consent of all parties involved. Venture capital may be an important source of financial backing.

Key term

A **management buy-out** is the purchase of all or part of a business from its owners by its managers.

For example, the directors of a subsidiary company in a group might buy the company from the holding company, with the intention of running it as proprietors of a separate business entity.

- **To the managers,** the buy-out would be a method of setting up in business for themselves.
- **To the group**, the buy-out would be a method of **divestment**, selling off the subsidiary as a going concern.

2.1 The parties to a buy-out

There are usually three parties to a management buy-out:

(a) A **management team** wanting to make a buy-out. This team ought to have the skills and ability to convince financial backers that it is worth supporting.

(b) **Directors** of a group of companies, who make the divestment decision.

(c) **Financial backers** of the buy-out team, who will usually want an equity stake in the bought-out business, because of the **venture capital risk** they are taking. Often, several financial backers provide the venture capital for a single buy-out.

The management team making the buy-out would probably have the aims of setting up in business themselves, being owners rather than mere employees; or avoiding redundancy, when the subsidiary is threatened with closure.

2.2 Reasons for a management buy-out

A large organisation's board of directors may agree to a management buy-out of a subsidiary for any of a number of different reasons.

(a) The **subsidiary** may be **peripheral** to the group's mainstream activities, and no longer fit in with the group's overall strategy.

(b) The **group may** wish to **sell off a loss-making subsidiary**, and a management team may think that it can restore the subsidiary's fortunes.

(c) The parent company may need to **raise cash quickly**.

(d) The subsidiary may be part of a **group** that has just been **taken over** and the new parent company may wish to sell off parts of the group it has just acquired.

(e) The **best offer price** might come from a **small management group** wanting to arrange a buy-out.

(f) When a group has taken the decision to sell a subsidiary, it will probably get better co-operation from the management and employees of the subsidiary if the sale is a management buy-out.

(g) The sale can be arranged more quickly than a **sale** to an **external party**.

(h) The selling organisation is more likely to be able to maintain beneficial links with a segment sold to management rather than to an **external party**.

A private company's shareholders might agree to sell out to a management team because they need cash, they want to retire, or the business is not profitable enough for them.

To help convince a bank or other institution that it can run the business successfully, the management team should prepare a **business plan** and estimates of sales, costs, profits and cash flows, in reasonable detail.

2.3 The role of the venture capitalist

Knowledge brought forward from earlier studies

Venture capital

- **Venture capital** is risk capital, normally provided in return for an equity stake.
- Examples of **venture capital organisations** in the UK are 3i and the various venture capital subsidiaries of the clearing banks.
- Venture capital **may be provided to fund** business start-ups, business development, MBOs and the purchase of shares from one of the owners of the business.
- Venture capital can also be provided through **venture capital funds**, which is a pool of finance provided by a variety of investors, which will then be applied to MBOs or expansion projects.
- Venture capitalists will normally require an **equity stake** in the company and may wish to have a **representative on the board** to look after its interests.
- A number of clearly defined **exit routes** will be sought by the venture capitalists in order to ensure the easy realisation of their investment when required.

Venture capitalists are far more inclined to fund MBOs, management buy-ins (MBI) and corporate expansion projects than the more risky and relatively costly early stage investments such as start-ups. The minimum investment considered will normally be around £100,000, with average investment of £1m-£2m.

While the return required on venture capital for the high-risk, early stage investments may be as high as 80%, where the funding is for a well established business with sound management, it is more commonly around the 25-30% mark. While this may be achieved by the successful investments, of course there will be many more that fail, and the overall returns on venture capital funds averages out at around 10-15%.

For MBOs and MBIs the venture capitalist will not necessarily provide the majority of the finance – a £50m buy-out may be funded by, say, £15m venture capital, £20m debt finance and £15m mezzanine debt, discussed earlier.

Venture capital funds may require:

- A 20-30% shareholding
- Special rights to appoint a number of directors
- The company to seek their prior approval for new issues or acquisitions

2.3.1 Exit strategies

Venture capitalists generally like to have a predetermined **target exit date,** the point at which they can recoup some or all of their investment in an MBO.

At the outset, they will wish to establish various **exit routes**, the possibilities including:

(a) The sale of shares to the public or to institutional investors following a **flotation** of the company's shares on a recognised stock exchange, or on the equivalent of the UK's Alternative Investment Market (AIM)

(b) The **sale** of the company to another firm

(c) The **repurchase** of the venture capitalist's shares by the company or its owners

(d) The sales of the venture capitalist's shares to an **institution** such as an investment trust

2.4 The appraisal of proposed buy-outs

2.4.1 How likely is a management buy-out to succeed?

Management-owned companies seem to achieve better performance probably because of:

- A **favourable buy-out price** having been achieved
- **Personal motivation and determination**
- **Quicker decision making** and so **more flexibility**
- **Keener decisions** and action on pricing and debt collection
- **Savings in overheads**, eg in contributions to a large head office

However, many management buy-outs, once they occur, begin with some redundancies to cut running costs.

2.4.2 How should an institutional investor evaluate a buy-out?

An institutional investor (such as a venture capitalist) should evaluate a buy-out before deciding whether or not to finance. Aspects of any buy-out that ought to be checked are as follows:

(a) Does the management team have the **full range of management skills** that are needed (for example a technical expert and a finance director)? Does it have the right blend of experience? Does it have the commitment?

(b) **Why** is the **company for sale**? The possible reasons for buy-outs have already been listed. If the reason is that the parent company wants to get rid of a loss-making subsidiary, what evidence is there to suggest that the company can be made profitable after a buy-out?

(c) What are the **projected profits and cash flows** of the business? The prospective returns must justify the risks involved.

(d) What is **being bought**? The buy-out team might be buying the shares of the company, or only selected assets of the company. Are the assets that are being acquired sufficient for the task? Will more assets have to be bought? When will the existing assets need replacing? How much extra finance would be needed for these asset purchases? Can the company be operated profitably?

(e) What is the **price**? Is the price right or is it too high?

(f) What **financial contribution** can be made by members of the management team themselves?

(g) What are the **exit routes** and when might they be taken?

2.5 The financial arrangements in a typical buy-out

Typically, the **buy-out team** will have a **minority** of the equity in the bought-out company, with the **various financial backers** holding a **majority** of the shares between them. A buy-out might have several financial backers, each providing finance in exchange for some equity.

Investors of venture capital usually want the **managers to be financially committed**. Individual managers could borrow personally from a bank, say £20,000 to £50,000.

The suppliers of equity finance might insist on investing part of their capital in the form of **redeemable convertible preference shares**. These often have voting rights should the preference dividend fall in arrears, giving increased influence over the company's affairs. They are issued in a redeemable form to give some hope of taking out part of the investment if it does not develop satisfactorily, and in convertible form for the opposite reason: to allow an increased stake in the equity of a successful company.

2.6 Problems with buy-outs

A common problem with management buy-outs is that the managers have little or no experience in **financial management** or **financial accounting**.

Other problems are:

(a) Tax and legal complications

(b) Difficulties in deciding on a fair price to be paid

(c) Convincing employees of the need to change working practices

(d) Inadequate cash flow to finance the maintenance and replacement of tangible non-current assets

(e) The maintenance of previous employees' pension rights

(f) Accepting the board representation requirement that many sources of funds will insist upon

(g) The loss of key employees if the company moves geographically, or wage rates are decreased too far, or employment conditions are unacceptable in other ways

(h) Maintaining continuity of relationships with suppliers and customers

2.6.1 Example: MBO

Arga is a listed company specialising in the development and sale of beauty products. Arga owns a number of beauty brands, each owned and managed by a separate business unit. Arga is seeking to sell Beauty One, one of these business units.

Beauty One owns a beauty product brand that is aimed at the younger end of the market. The management team of Beauty One is young and dynamic like the brand and has become frustrated by the constraints

LEARNING OUTCOME 3 VALUATION AND CORPORATE CHANGE

imposed on it by Arga in managing the brand and developing the business; it believes that Beauty One has huge growth potential.

The management team of Beauty One has decided to purchase the business from Arga under a management buy-out (MBO). Arga has accepted this proposal as Beauty One has not proved to be a good 'fit' with the rest of the business and has agreed on the selling price.

The MBO team has been in initial discussions with a venture capitalist and a bank which are interested in helping to finance the acquisition.

What factors are most likely to affect the success of the MBO?

Solution

The following factors are most likely to affect the success of the MBO:

1. The ability of the management team to take over the head office functions successfully – this will be important as the young dynamic team are unlikely to possess all the necessary skills to perform the head office functions and may need to outsource some.

2. Securing sufficient funding from the venture capitalist and the bank – this will be vital to the success. They are currently at the discussion stage, so it will be important that the management team secures the support of the proposed financers.

3. The ability of the management team to develop the brand and achieve the expected growth – growth is likely to be a condition set by the VC. Developing the brand and achieving growth will be important to ensure that B generates sufficient CF to operate effectively.

2.7 Buy-ins

Key term

> 'Buy-in' is when a team of **outside managers**, as opposed to managers who are already running the business, mount a takeover bid and then run the business themselves.

A management buy-in might occur when a business venture is running into trouble, and a group of outside managers see an opportunity to take over the business and restore its profitability.

Alternatively, research suggests that buy-ins often occur when the major shareholder of a small family company wishes to retire.

Many features are common to management buy-outs and buy-ins, including **financing**.

Buy-ins work best for companies where the existing managers are being replaced by managers of **much better quality**. However, managers who come in from outside may take **time** to get used to the company, and may encounter **opposition** from employees if they seek to introduce significant changes.

3 Going private

FAST FORWARD

> A company **goes private** when a small group of individuals buys all the company's shares. Going private may **decrease costs** and make the company **less vulnerable** to hostile takeover bids.

3.1 Procedures for going private

A public company **'goes private'** when a **small group of individuals**, possibly including existing shareholders and/or managers and with or without support from a financial institution, **buys all of the company's shares.** This form of restructuring is relatively common in the USA and may involve the shares in the company ceasing to be listed on a stock exchange. It is often referred to as a 'private equity buy-in'.

3.2 Advantages of going private

(a) The **costs of meeting listing requirement**s can be saved.

(b) The **company is protected** from **volatility** in share prices which financial problems may create.

(c) The company will be **less vulnerable** to hostile takeover bids.

(d) Management can **concentrate** on the **long-term needs** of the business rather than the short-term expectations of shareholders.

(e) Shareholders are likely to be **closer to management** in a private company, reducing costs arising from the separation of ownership and control (the 'agency problem').

3.3 Disadvantages of going private

The main disadvantage with going private is it may mean that the company loses its ability to have its share publicly traded. If a share cannot be **traded** it may **lose some of its value**. However, one reason for seeking private company status is that the company has had difficulties as a quoted company, and have the prices of its shares may be low anyway.

3.3.1 Example: Reorganisation strategies

Mr Giblin and Mr Connolly incorporated a new company PXP five years ago.

PXP has grown extremely quickly and Mr Giblin and Mr Connolly still own 100% of the share capital in the company. They now feel that the company needs an injection of funds to enable it to grow further. Mr Giblin and Mr Connolly want to keep a controlling interest in their company and they feel that the company's growth prospects would be damaged by disposing of any part of it.

Which two of the following corporate reorganisation strategies could Mr Giblin and Mr Connolly consider?

- Spin off
- Initial public offering (IPO)
- Private equity buy-in
- Management buy-ou
- Sell off of the whole company to a competitor

Solution

To meet their stated objectives, Mr Giblin and Mr Connolly could consider an IPO or a private equity buy in. Both options would allow the owners of PXP to raise additional finance while still retaining control of the business. A spin off is not appropriate as it would not generate any cash. An MBO would split the business up or take control away from Mr Giblin and Mr Connolly. A sell off would also result in the owners losing control and would therefore not be appropriate.

LEARNING OUTCOME 3 VALUATION AND CORPORATE CHANGE

Chapter Roundup

- **Divestments** (reductions in ownership stakes) can take a number of forms.
- A **demerger** is the splitting up of corporate bodies into two or more separate bodies, to ensure share prices reflect the true value of underlying operations.
- A **sell-off** is the sale of part of a company to a third party, generally for cash.
- A **spin-off** is the creation of a new company, where the shareholders of the original company own the shares.
- A **management buy-out** is the purchase of all or part of the business by its managers. Management buy-outs can be the best way of maintaining links with a subsidiary, and can ensure the co-operation of management if a disposal is inevitable.
- The main complication with **management buy-outs** is obtaining the consent of all parties involved. Venture capital may be an important source of financial backing.
- A company **goes private** when a small group of individuals buys all the company's shares. Going private may **decrease costs** and make the company **less vulnerable** to hostile takeover bids.

Quick Quiz

1   **Fill in the blank**

    A _____ is a splitting up of a corporate body into two independent bodies.

2   **Fill in the blank**

    A _____ involves the sale of part of a company to a third party.

3   **Fill in the blank**

    In a _____, a new company is created whose shares are owned by the shareholders of the old company.

4   Name three factors that an institutional investor will consider when deciding whether to invest in a management buy-out.

5   Give four examples of possible exit strategies for a venture capitalist.

6   What is a management buy-in?

7   Give five advantages of a public company going private.

Answers to Quick Quiz

1. Demerger

2. Sell-off

3. Spin-off

4. Any three of:
   - (a) Management skills
   - (b) Reason why company is for sale
   - (c) Projected profits and cash flows of the business
   - (d) What is being bought
   - (e) Price
   - (f) Financial contribution made by the management team
   - (g) Exit routes

5.
   - (a) Sale of shares to public or institutional investors following a flotation
   - (b) Sale of shares to another company
   - (c) Sale to company itself or its owners
   - (d) Sale to institution management

6. A buy-in is when a team of outside managers mount a takeover bid and run the business.

7.
   - (a) Saving of costs of legal formalities
   - (b) Protection from volatility in share prices
   - (c) Less vulnerability to hostile takeover
   - (d) More concentration on long-term needs of business
   - (e) Closer relationships with shareholders

LEARNING OUTCOME 3 VALUATION AND CORPORATE CHANGE

End of chapter questions

Endeavour plc (AIA November 2013)

Three senior managers of Endeavour plc are considering purchasing the company through a management buy-out. Endeavour plc designs and sells accounting software. The company was established 15 years ago by Mr Grey who owns all of the shares. Mr Grey is now approaching retirement. The company was very successful initially, but its profits have declined over the last 3 years. The three managers all work in the sales department and are convinced they can stop the profit decline. They are very keen to go ahead with the management buy-out as they would like to manage the company according to their own ideas. Many of the employees have worked for the company since it was established and they have a great respect for Mr Grey.

The following information has been provided:

ENDEAVOUR PLC
SUMMARY OF THE CONSOLIDATED STATEMENT OF COMPREHENSIVE INCOME FOR THE FINANCIAL YEAR ENDED 30 OCTOBER

	2011 £'000	2012 £'000	2013 £'000
Revenue	3,194	3,056	2,885
Operating profit	1,051	1,020	971
Finance income	20	25	26
Finance costs	(195)	(197)	(204)
Profit before taxation	876	848	793
Taxation	(161)	(154)	(142)
Profit for the year	715	694	651

The total dividends paid to Mr Grey over the last three years were the same amount of £450,000 per year.

ENDEAVOUR PLC
EXTRACTS FROM THE STATEMENT OF FINANCIAL POSITION AS AT 30 OCTOBER 2013

	2013 £'000
ASSETS & LIABILITIES	
Non-current assets	
Property, plant & equipment	2,143
Intangible assets	1,629
	3,772
Current assets	
Inventories	516
Trade and other receivables	1,243
Cash and short term deposits	1,135
	2,894
Total assets	6,666

	2013 £'000
Current liabilities	
Unsecured bank loans	(473)
Trade and other payables	(578)
Current tax liabilities	(101)
	(1,152)
Non-current liabilities	
Corporate bonds	(1,037)
Provisions	(965)
	(2,002)
Total liabilities	(3,154)
Net assets/(liabilities)	3,512

The property, plant and equipment figure includes property that is showing on the statement of financial position at £1,432,000. However, it has a current market value of £2,763,000.

The intangible assets relate to the brand names of some of the software products.

The inventories include some older stocks of software products totalling £115,000. New software has been introduced that makes these products obsolete.

Two other listed accounting software companies that are competitors of Endeavour plc have current price-earnings (P-E) ratios of 14 and 16 respectively. Endeavour plc is not listed on a stock exchange.

In recent years Mr Grey has appraised investments using a discount rate of 6%.

Required

The three managers who are considering the management buy-out have asked you to prepare a report. In the report the managers require you to:

(1) Prepare calculations that provide three alternative values for Endeavour plc,
(2) Advise on any issues that they should be aware of in respect of the valuations, and
(3) Advise on any likely problems that they may encounter should the management buy-out proceed.

(20 marks)

LEARNING OUTCOME 3 VALUATION AND CORPORATE CHANGE

International finance and interest rate risk

Foreign currency risk

Topic list	Syllabus reference
1 Exchange rates	LO4
2 Risk and foreign exchange	LO4
3 Managing transaction exposure	LO4
4 Forward exchange rates and contracts	LO4
5 Hedging using the money markets	LO4
6 Choosing between a forward contract and a money market hedge	LO4
7 Futures	LO4
8 Deciding how to hedge with currency futures	LO4
9 Choosing between forward contracts and futures contracts	LO4
10 Hedging economic and translation exposure	LO4

Introduction

Previously we looked at various techniques for the management of risk, in particular **foreign exchange (currency risk)** and **interest risk**. In this chapter, we are particularly concerned with risks related to exchange rate fluctuations.

The first section contains some very important basic concepts so make sure you're happy with how foreign exchange rates are quoted. The simpler techniques covered in Section 3 may be useful discussion points. Forward exchange rate calculations are straightforward, but you need to use a step-by-step approach to tackle money markets and futures. Don't feel overwhelmed by the terminology in the futures section; it should become clearer once you go through the calculations, so you may want to go back to it after you've gone through the approach.

LEARNING OUTCOME 4 INTERNATIONAL FINANCE AND INTEREST RATE RISK

1 Exchange rates

FAST FORWARD

Currencies are quoted at Term currency X units:Base currency 1 unit.

The **spot rate** is the rate at which currencies are currently quoted on the foreign exchange markets. The **forward rate** is the rate at which currencies will be exchanged on a set future date.

1.1 Exchange rates

Key terms

An **exchange rate** is the rate at which one country's currency can be traded in exchange for another country's currency.

The **spot rate** is the exchange or interest rate currently offered on a particular currency or security.

The **spot rate** is the rate of exchange in currency for **immediate delivery**.

The **forward rate** is an exchange rate set for currencies to be exchanged at a future date.

Every traded currency in fact has many exchange rates. There is an exchange rate with every other traded currency on the foreign exchange markets. Foreign exchange dealers make their profit by buying currency for less than they sell it, and so there are really two exchange rates, a selling rate and a buying rate.

1.2 Foreign exchange demand

If an importer has to pay a foreign supplier in a foreign currency, he might ask his bank to sell him the required amount of the currency. For example, suppose that a bank's customer, a UK trading company, has imported goods for which it must now pay US$10,000.

(a) The company will ask the bank to sell it US$10,000. If the company is buying currency, the bank is selling it.

(b) When the bank agrees to sell US$10,000 to the company, it will tell the company what the spot rate of exchange will be for the transaction. If the bank's selling rate (known as the **'offer'**, or **'ask'** price) is, say $1.2987 for the currency, the bank will charge the company:

$$\frac{\$10,000}{1.2987} = £7,700$$

Similarly, if an exporter is paid, say, US$10,000 by a customer in the USA, he may wish to exchange the dollars to obtain sterling. He will therefore ask his bank to buy the dollars from him. Since the exporter is selling currency to the bank, the bank is buying the currency.

If the bank quotes a buying rate (known as the **bid** price) of, say $1.3075, for the currency the bank will pay the exporter:

$$\frac{\$10,000}{1.3075} = £7,648$$

A bank expects to make a profit from selling and buying currency, and it does so by offering a rate for selling a currency which is different from the rate for buying the currency.

If a bank were to buy a quantity of foreign currency from a customer, and then were to re-sell it to another customer, it would charge the second customer more (in sterling) for the currency than it would pay the first customer. The difference would be profit. For example, the figures used for illustration in the previous paragraphs show a bank selling some US dollars for £7,700 and buying the same quantity of dollars for £7,648, at selling and buying rates that might be in use at the same time. The bank would make a profit of £52.

Question — Sterling receipts

Calculate how much sterling exporters would receive or how much sterling importers would pay, ignoring the bank's commission, in each of the following situations, if they were to exchange currency and sterling at the spot rate.

(a) A UK exporter receives a payment from a Danish customer of 150,000 kroners.
(b) A UK importer buys goods from a Japanese supplier and pays 1 million yen.

Spot rates are as follows:

	Bank sells (offer)	Bank buys (bid)
Danish Kr/£	9.4340	9.5380
Japan Y/£	203.650	205.781

Answer

(a) The bank is being asked to buy the Danish kroners and will give the exporter:

$$\frac{150{,}000}{9.5380} = £15{,}726.57 \text{ in exchange}$$

(b) The bank is being asked to sell the yen to the importer and will charge for the currency:

$$\frac{1{,}000{,}000}{203.650} = £4{,}910.39$$

1.3 The foreign exchange (FX) markets

Banks buy currency from customers and sell currency to customers – typically, **exporting and importing firms**. Banks may buy currency from the **government** or sell currency to the government – this is how a government builds up its official reserves. Banks also buy and sell currency **between themselves**. Consider what is actually happening when currencies are bought and sold: essentially, bank deposits denominated in one currency are being exchanged for bank deposits denominated in another currency.

International trade involves foreign currency, for either the buyer, the seller, or both (for example, a Saudi Arabian firm might sell goods to a UK buyer and invoice for the goods in US dollars). As a consequence, it is quite likely that exporters might want to sell foreign currency earnings to a bank in exchange for domestic currency, and that importers might want to buy foreign currency from a bank in order to pay a foreign supplier.

Since most foreign exchange rates are not fixed but are allowed to vary, rates are continually changing and each bank will offer new rates for new customer enquiries according to how its dealers judge the market situation.

Although exchange rates in the market are influenced by the forces as exercised through the actions of the central bank of supply and demand, a **government's policy on the exchange rate** for its currency can have an important effect on how the exchange rate is determined. In the case of the common European currency, the **euro**, the actions of the **European central bank** influence its exchange rate.

1.4 Direct and indirect currency quotes

Key terms

A **direct quote** is the amount of domestic currency which is equal to one foreign currency unit.

An **indirect quote** is the amount of foreign currency which is equal to one domestic currency unit.

In the UK indirect quotes are invariably used but, in most countries, direct quotes are more common.

Currencies may be quoted in either direction. For example, the US dollar and Euro might be quoted as €/$ = 0.9100 or $/€ = 1.0989. In other words 0.9100€ = $1 and 1.0989$ = €1. One rate is simply the reciprocal of the other.

Key term

If a currency is quoted at $1.2900:£, the $ is the **term currency** (the **reference currency**), the £ is the **base currency**.

1.4.1 Buying low and selling high

When considering the prices banks are using, remember that the bank will **sell the term/reference currency low**, and **buy the term/reference currency high**. For example, if a UK bank is buying and selling dollars, the selling (offer) price may be $1.2900, the buying (bid) price may be $1.3100.

The examination will not be confined to the activities of UK companies. Exchange rates given in the examination could be as quoted in foreign countries. Because of these complications you should always double-check which rate you are using when choosing between the bid or offer rate. One sure method is to recognise that the bank **makes money** out of the transaction and will therefore offer you the worse of the two possible rates!

A simple example may help. If you come back to the United Kingdom from a holiday in America with spare dollars, and you are told the spread of $/£ rates is 1.2900 – 1.3100, will you have to pay the bank $1.29 or $1.31 to obtain £1? Answer: you will have to pay the higher price, $1.31.

1.5 Spread

The price of foreign currency (the exchange rate) is normally quoted in terms of the local currency. The closing (end-of-day) exchange rates are shown in the *Financial Times*. Some of the rates for a particular date are shown below.

The difference between the bid price and the offer price, covering dealers' costs and profit, is called the **spread**.

Suppose the closing spot rate between sterling and the US dollar was £1 = $1.2767 – $1.2771 on a particular day in question. A dealer will offer $1.2767 in exchange for £1. A dealer will give £1 for every $1.2767 received. The **mid-point** between these two rates is £1 = $1.2769.

If the one month forward rate is **lower** than the spot rate, say $1.2765, we can say that the one month forward $/£ price is at a **premium** to the spot rate. If it is higher, it is at a **discount** to the spot rate. The one month forward price is at a discount of $1.2777 minus $1.2769 = 0.08 cents on the spot price.

(a) This premium is sometimes called the **swap rate.** The fact that there is a premium reflects the fact that interest rates in sterling are higher than interest rates in US dollars for deposits over the next month. For a one month forward transaction, less dollars will be paid per pound than the spot price.

(b) If the forward rate was higher than the spot rate, we would say it was at a **discount** to the spot rate.

We should bear in mind that **the forward rate may be higher or lower than the spot rate turns out to be at the relevant future date**. The forward rate is the rate agreed **now** for the delivery of currency at a future date.

1.6 Foreknowledge of foreign currency receipts and payments: transaction exposure

Much international trade involves credit. An importer will take credit often for several months and sometimes longer, and an exporter will grant credit. One consequence of taking and granting credit is that international traders will know in advance about the receipts and payments arising from their trade. They will know:

- What foreign currency they will receive or pay
- When the receipt or payment will occur
- How much of the currency will be received or paid

The great danger to profit margins is in the **movement in exchange rates**. The risk faces (i) exporters who invoice in a foreign currency and (ii) importers who pay in a foreign currency.

2 Risk and foreign exchange

> **FAST FORWARD**
>
> **Currency risk** occurs in three forms: **transaction exposure** (short-term), **economic exposure** (effect on present value of longer term cash flows) and **translation exposure** (book gains or losses).

2.1 Risk and risk management

Risk management describes the policies which a firm may adopt and the techniques it may use to manage the risks it faces. **Exposure** means being open to or vulnerable to risk. If entrepreneurship is about risk, why should businesses want to 'manage' risk? Broadly, there are two reasons why risk management makes good business sense:

(a) First, a business may wish to reduce **risks** to which it is exposed to acceptable levels. What is an acceptable level of risk may depend upon various factors, including the scale of operations of the business and the degree to which its proprietors or shareholders are risk-averse.

(b) Second, a business may wish to avoid **particular kinds of risks**. For example, a business may be averse to taking risks with exchange rates. The reasons may include the fact that the risks are simply **too great** for the business to bear, for example if exchange rate movements could easily bankrupt the business.

2.2 Reducing risk exposure

There are basically two ways in which exposure to risk may be reduced:

(a) **Pooling of risks**

This method underlies insurance, in which risks which may be unacceptable to individual policyholders are aggregated or 'pooled' by being taken on by the insurance company. Pooling of risk also underlies the diversification of a portfolio of investments.

(b) **Hedging of risks**

In the case of hedging, different parties come to an agreement which cancels one of the parties' risks against the other's. The different parties may be subject to similar but opposite risks which they wish to hedge. Alternatively, one party may wish to hedge a risk while the other party may be a speculator.

2.3 Bearing risk exposure

For any particular kind of risk faced by a business someone somewhere will generally be prepared to accept that risk. Some may be happy to bear the risk because they **already bear an opposing risk** which would cancel out its effect. Others may be prepared to take on the risk if there is the prospect of them **making a profit**.

2.4 Currency risk

The following different types of currency risk may be distinguished:

2.4.1 Transaction risk

This is the risk of adverse exchange rate movements occurring in the course of **normal international trading transactions**. This arises when the prices of imports or exports are fixed in foreign currency terms and there is movement in the exchange rate between the date when the price is agreed and the date when the cash is paid or received in settlement.

2.4.2 Translation risk

This is the risk that the organisation will make exchange losses when the accounting results of its foreign branches or subsidiaries are translated into the home currency. Translation losses are not cashflow losses but instead result from restating the book value of a foreign subsidiary's assets at the exchange rate on the reporting date. This can impact on a company's gearing ratio and its ability to comply with loan covenants based on book values.

2.4.3 Economic risk

This refers to the effect of exchange rate movements on the **international competitiveness** of a company. For example, a UK company might use raw materials which are priced in US dollars, but export its products mainly within the EU. A depreciation of sterling against the dollar or an appreciation of sterling against other EU currencies will both erode the competitiveness of the company. Economic exposure can be difficult to avoid, although **diversification of the supplier and customer base** across different countries will reduce this kind of exposure to risk.

3 Managing transaction exposure

> **FAST FORWARD**
>
> Basic methods of hedging risk include **matching receipts and payments**, **invoicing in own currency**, and **leading and lagging** the times that cash is received and paid.

3.1 Transaction risk

We shall now look at the various means by which a business can manage its exposure to currency, or exchange rate, risk. We are principally concerned here with the risk that has a direct effect on immediate cash flows – transaction risk. This risk is illustrated in the following question.

Exam focus point

You could be presented with different types of currencies in the exam, therefore a number of different currencies will be used throughout this text. The currencies used may relate to fictitious countries and may not reflect real life rates.

Question: Changes in exchange rates

Bulldog Ltd, a UK company, buys goods from Redland which cost 100,000 Reds (the local currency). The goods are re-sold in the UK for £32,000. At the time of the import purchase the exchange rate for Reds against sterling is 3.5650 – 3.5800.

Required

(a) What is the expected profit on the re-sale?

(b) What would the actual profit be if the spot rate at the time when the currency is received has moved to:

    (i)   3.0800 – 3.0950
    (ii)   4.0650 – 4.0800?

Ignore bank commission charges.

Answer

(a) Bulldog must buy Reds to pay the supplier, and so the bank is selling Reds. The expected profit is as follows.

	£
Revenue from re-sale of goods	32,000.00
Less cost of 100,000 Reds in sterling (÷ 3.5650)	28,050.49
Expected profit	3,949.51

(b) (i) If the actual spot rate for Bulldog to buy and the bank to sell the Reds is 3.0800, the result is as follows.

	£
Revenue from re-sale	32,000.00
Less cost (100,000 ÷ 3.0800)	32,467.53
Loss	(467.53)

(ii) If the actual spot rate for Bulldog to buy and the bank to sell the Reds is 4.0650, the result is as follows.

	£
Revenue from re-sale	32,000.00
Less cost (100,000 ÷ 4.0650)	24,600.25
Profit	7,399.75

This variation in the final sterling cost of the goods (and thus the profit) illustrated the concept of transaction risk.

3.2 Direct risk reduction methods

The **forward exchange contract** is perhaps the most important method of obtaining cover against risks, where a firm decides that it does not wish to speculate on foreign exchange. This is discussed later in the chapter. However, there are **other methods of reducing risk** which we shall consider first.

3.3 Invoice in home currency

One way of avoiding exchange risk is for an **exporter** to **invoice his foreign customer in his domestic currency**, or for an **importer** to **arrange with his foreign supplier to be invoiced in his domestic currency**. However, although either the exporter or the importer can avoid any exchange risk in this way, only one of them can deal in his domestic currency. The other must accept the exchange risk, since there will be a period of time elapsing between agreeing a contract and paying for the goods (unless payment is made with the order).

If a UK exporter is able to quote and invoice an overseas buyer in sterling, then the foreign exchange risk is **in effect transferred** to the **overseas buyer**. An **alternative method** of achieving the same result is to negotiate contracts expressed in the **foreign currency** but specifying a **fixed rate of exchange** as a condition of the contract.

There are certain advantages in invoicing in a foreign currency which might persuade an exporter to take on the exchange risk. One of the most important is the possible marketing advantage by proposing to invoice in the buyer's own currency, when there is competition for the sales contract. The exporter may also be able to **offset payments** to his own suppliers in a particular foreign currency against **receipts** in that currency. In addition, by arranging to sell goods to customers in a foreign currency, a UK exporter might be able to **obtain a loan** in that currency at a **lower rate of interest** than in the UK, and at the same time obtain cover against exchange risks by arranging to repay the loan out of the proceeds from the sales in that currency.

3.4 Matching receipts and payments

A company can reduce or eliminate its foreign exchange transaction exposure by **matching** receipts and payments. Wherever possible, a company that expects to make payments and have receipts in the same foreign currency should plan to **offset its payments against its receipts in the currency**. Since the company will be setting off foreign currency receipts against foreign currency payments, it does not matter whether the currency strengthens or weakens against the company's 'domestic' currency because there will be no purchase or sale of the currency.

The process of matching is made simpler by having **foreign currency accounts** with a bank. UK residents are allowed to have bank accounts in any foreign currency. Receipts of foreign currency can be credited to the account pending subsequent payments in the currency. (Alternatively, a company might invest its foreign currency income in the country of the currency – for example it might have a bank deposit account abroad – and make payments with these overseas assets/deposits.)

Since a company is unlikely to have exactly the same amount of receipts in a currency as it makes payments, it will still be exposed to the extent of the surplus of income, and so the company may wish to avoid exposure on this surplus by arranging **forward exchange cover**.

Offsetting (matching payments against receipts) will be **cheaper than arranging a forward contract** to buy currency and another forward contract to sell the currency, provided that receipts occur before payments, and the time difference between receipts and payments in the currency is not too long. Any differences between the amounts receivable and the amounts payable in a given currency should be covered by a forward exchange contract to buy/sell the amount of the difference.

Exam focus point

> Don't forget the possibility of netting receipts and payments in the same currency. In currency risk questions the examiner quite often tests situations where the hedging required can be simplified by netting receipts and payments in the same currency.

3.5 Matching assets and liabilities

A company which expects to receive a substantial amount of income in a foreign currency will be concerned that this currency may weaken. It can hedge against this possibility by borrowing in the foreign currency and using the foreign receipts to repay the loan. For example, US dollar receivables can be hedged by taking out a US dollar overdraft. In the same way, US dollar trade payables can be matched against a US dollar bank account which is used to pay the creditors.

A company which has a long-term foreign investment, for example an overseas subsidiary, will similarly try to **match its foreign assets** (property, plant etc) by a **long-term loan in the foreign currency**.

3.6 Leads and lags

Companies might try to use:

- **Lead payments** (payments in advance)
- **Lagged payments** (delaying payments beyond their due date)

in order to take advantage of foreign exchange rate movements. With a lead payment, paying in advance of the due date, there is a finance cost to consider. This is the interest cost on the money used to make the payment, but early settlement discounts may be available.

3.7 Bilateral netting

Unlike matching, netting is not technically a method of managing exchange risk. However, it is conveniently dealt with at this stage. The objective is simply to save transactions costs by netting off inter-company balances before arranging payment. Many **multinational groups** of companies engage in **intra-group trading**. Where related companies located in different countries trade with one another, there is likely to be inter-company indebtedness denominated in different currencies.

Key term

> **Netting** is a process in which credit balances are netted off against debit balances so that only the reduced net amounts remain due to be paid by actual currency flows.

In the case of **bilateral netting**, only two companies are involved. The lower balance is netted off against the higher balance and the difference is the amount remaining to be paid.

3.7.1 Example: Bilateral netting

A and B are respectively UK and US based subsidiaries of a Swiss based holding company. At 31 March 20X5, A owed B SFr300,000 and B owed A SFr220,000. Bilateral netting can reduce the value of the intercompany debts: the two intercompany balances are set against each other, leaving a net debt owed by A to B of SFr 80,000 (SFr300,000 − 220,000).

3.8 Multilateral netting

As you will have guessed, **multilateral netting** is a more complex procedure in which the debts of more than two group companies are netted off against each other. There are different ways of arranging multilateral netting. The arrangement might be co-ordinated by the company's own central treasury or alternatively by the company's bankers.

The **common currency** in which netting is to be effected needs to be decided upon, as does the method of establishing the exchange rates to use for netting purposes. So that it is possible to agree the outstanding amounts in time but with minimum risk of exchange rate fluctuations in the meantime, this may involve using the exchange rates applying a few days before the date at which payment is to be made.

Netting has the following advantages:

(a) **Foreign exchange purchase** costs, including commission and the spread between selling and buying rates, and money transmission costs are **reduced**.

(b) There is **less loss in interest** from having money in transit.

Local laws and regulations need to be considered before netting is used, as netting is restricted by some countries. In some countries, bilateral netting is permitted but multilateral netting is prohibited; in other cases, all payments can be combined into a single payment which is made on a 'gross settlements' basis.

3.8.1 Example: Multilateral netting

A group of companies controlled from the USA has subsidiaries in the UK, South Africa and Denmark. Below, these subsidiaries are referred to as UK, SA and DE respectively. At 30 June 20X5, inter-company indebtedness is as follows:

Debtor	Creditor	Amount
UK	SA	1,200,000 South African rand (R)
UK	DE	480,000 Danish kroners (Kr)
DE	SA	800,000 South African rand
SA	UK	£74,000 British sterling
SA	DE	375,000 Danish kroners

It is the company's policy to net off inter-company balances to the greatest extent possible. The central treasury department is to use the following exchange rates for this purpose.

US$1 equals R 6.1260/£0.6800/Kr 5.8800.

You are required to calculate the net payments to be made between the subsidiaries after netting off of inter-company balances.

Solution

The first step is to convert the balances into US dollars as a common currency.

Debtor	Creditor	Amount in US dollars
UK	SA	1,200,000 ÷ 6.1260 = $195,886
UK	DE	480,000 ÷ 5.8800 = $81,633
DE	SA	800,000 ÷ 6.1260 = $130,591
SA	UK	£74,000 ÷ 0.6800 = $108,824
SA	DE	375,000 ÷ 5.880 = $63,776

Receiving subsidiaries	Paying subsidiaries			Total
	UK $	SA $	DE $	$
UK		108,824		108,824
SA	195,886		130,591	326,477
DE	81,633	63,776	–	145,409
Total payments	(277,519)	(172,600)	(130,591)	580,710
Total receipts	108,824	326,477	145,409	
Net receipt/(payment)	(168,695)	153,877	14,818	

The UK subsidiary should pay $153,877 to the South African subsidiary and $14,818 to the Danish subsidiary. By using multilateral netting the company only has to pay the bank for two transactions not five, and therefore will reduce the bank charges it incurs.

> **Exam focus point**: Don't forget in the exam to consider netting between all the companies in a group.

4 Forward exchange rates and contracts

FAST FORWARD

A **forward contract** specifies in advance the rate at which a specified quantity of currency will be bought and sold.

4.1 Forward exchange rates

As you will already appreciate, a forward exchange rate might be higher or lower than the spot rate. If it is higher, the quoted currency will be cheaper forward than spot. For example, if in the case of Swiss francs against sterling (i) the spot rate is 2.1560 – 2.1660 and (ii) the three months forward rate is 2.2070 – 2.2220:

(a) A bank would sell 2,000 Swiss francs:

　(i)　At the spot rate, now, for £927.64 = $\left(\dfrac{2,000}{2.1560}\right)$

　(ii)　In three months' time, under a forward contract, for £906.21 = $\left(\dfrac{2,000}{2.2070}\right)$

(b) A bank would buy 2,000 Swiss francs

　(i)　At the spot rate, now, for £923.36 = $\left(\dfrac{2,000}{2.1660}\right)$

　(ii)　In three months' time, under a forward contract, for £900.09 = $\left(\dfrac{2,000}{2.2220}\right)$

In both cases, the quoted currency (Swiss franc) would be worth less against sterling in a forward contract than at the current spot rate. This is because it is quoted forward 'at a discount', against sterling.

If the forward rate is thus higher than the spot rate, then it is 'at a discount' to the spot rate.

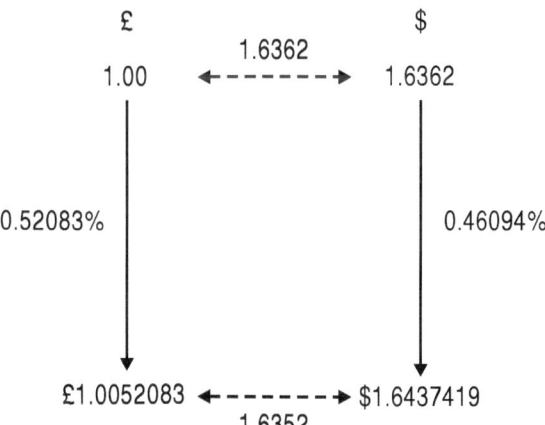

The forward rate can be calculated today without making any estimates of future exchange rates. **Future exchange rates** depend largely on future events and will often turn out to be very different from the forward rate. However, the forward rate is probably an **unbiased predictor of the expected value of the future exchange rate**, based on the information available today. It is also likely that the spot rate will move in the direction indicated by the forward rate.

LEARNING OUTCOME 4 INTERNATIONAL FINANCE AND INTEREST RATE RISK

4.1.1 The rule for adding or subtracting discounts and premiums

Forward rates as adjustments to spot rates	
Forward rate cheaper	Quoted at discount
Forward rate more expensive	Quoted at premium

A **discount** is therefore **added** to the spot rate, and a **premium** is therefore **subtracted** from the spot rate. (The mnemonic **ADDIS** may help you to remember that we ADD Discounts and so subtract premiums.) The longer the duration of a forward contract, the larger will be the quoted premium or discount.

4.2 Interest rate parity

FAST FORWARD

The principle of **interest rate parity** links the currency and money markets and explains differences between the **forward and spot rates**.

The difference between **spot and forward rates reflects differences in interest rates**. If this were not so, then investors holding the currency with the lower interest rates would switch to the other currency for (say) three months, ensuring that they would not lose on returning to the original currency by fixing the exchange rate in advance at the forward rate. If enough investors acted in this way (known as **arbitrage**), forces of supply and demand would lead to a change in the forward rate to prevent such risk-free profit making.

The principle of **interest rate parity** (not to be confused with purchasing power parity) links the foreign exchange markets and the international money markets. The principle can be stated as follows.

Formula to learn

$$\frac{i_f - i_{uk}}{1 + i_{uk}} = \frac{\text{Forward rate}}{\text{Spot rate}} - 1$$

This equation links the spot and forward rates to the difference between the interest rates:

where i_f is the foreign currency interest rate on a deposit for a certain time period
       i_{uk} is the home currency interest rate on a deposit for the same time period

4.3 Example: Interest rate parity

Exchange rates between two currencies, the £ and the Southland dollar (S$) are listed in the financial press as follows.

Spot rates	4.7250	£/$S
	0.21164	$S/£
90 day rates	4.7506	£/$S
	0.21050	$S/£

The money market interest rate for 90 day deposits in £s is 7.5% annualised. What is implied about interest rates in Southland?

Assume a 365 day year.

Note. In practice, foreign currency interest rates are often calculated on an alternative **360-day basis**, one month being treated as 30 days.

Solution

Today, $S1.000 buys £4.7250.

£4.7250 could be placed on deposit for 90 days to earn interest of £(4.7250 × 0.075 × 90/365) = £0.0874, thus growing to £(4.7250 + 0.0874) = £4.8124.

This is then worth $S1.0130 at the 90 day exchange rate.

This tells us that the annualised expected interest rate on 90-day deposits in Southland is 0.013 × 365/90 = 5.3%.

Alternatively, we can reach the same answer as follows:

UK interest rate on 90 day deposit = i_{uk} = 7.5% × 90/365 = 1.85%

Southland interest rate on 90 day deposit = i_f

90-day forward exchange rate = 0.21050

Spot exchange rate = 0.21164

$$\frac{i_f - 0.0185}{1 + 0.0185} = \frac{0.21050}{0.21164} - 1$$

i_f = 0.013, or 1.3%

Annualised, this is 0.013 × 365/90 = 5.3%

4.4 Use of interest rate parity to forecast future exchange rates

As seen above, the **interest rate parity** formula links the forward exchange rate with interest rates in a fairly exact relationship, because risk-free gains are possible if the rates are out of alignment. We have previously noted that the forward rate tends to be an unbiased predictor of the future exchange rate. So does this mean that future exchange rates can be predicted using interest rate parity, in the same way as **purchasing power parity** can be used?

The simple answer is 'yes', but of course the prediction is subject to very large inaccuracies, because events which arise in the future can cause large currency swings in the opposite direction to that predicted by interest rate parity. In general, interest rate parity is regarded as less accurate than purchasing power parity for predicting future exchange rates.

> **Exam focus point**
>
> Exam papers in recent years have favoured the purchasing power parity method over the interest rate parity method in predicting future exchange rates.

Formally, interest rate parity is expressed in the following equation.

$$\frac{S_t - S_0}{S_0} = \frac{i_f - i_{uk}}{1 + i_{uk}} \quad \text{or} \quad S_t = S_0 \times \frac{1 + i_f}{1 + i_{uk}}$$

where S_0 is the current foreign currency spot exchange rate (at time 0)
 S_t is the expected spot rate at time t
 i_f is the expected interest in the foreign country to time t (expressed as a decimal)
 i_{uk} is the expected interest in the home country to time t (expressed as a decimal)

4.4.1 Example: Interest rate parity

A Canadian company is expecting to receive Kuwaiti dinars in one year's time. The spot rate is Canadian dollar/dinar 5.4670. The company could borrow in dinars at 9% or in dollars at 14%. There is no forward rate for one year's time. Predict what the exchange rate is likely to be in one year.

Solution

Using interest rate parity, dollar is the numerator and dinar is the denominator. So the expected future exchange rate dollar/dinar is given by:

$$5.4670 \times \frac{1.14}{1.09} = 5.7178$$

This prediction is subject to great inaccuracy, but note that the company could 'lock into' this exchange rate, working a money market hedge by borrowing today in dinars at 9%, converting the cash to dollars at spot and repaying some of its 14% dollar overdraft. When the dinar cash is received from the customer, the dinar loan is repaid.

4.5 Use of interest rate parity to compute the effective cost of foreign currency loans

As we have seen, loans in some currencies are cheaper than in others. However, when the likely strengthening of the exchange rate is taken into consideration, the cost of apparently cheap foreign loans becomes a lot more expensive. This is illustrated in the following example.

4.5.1 Example: Effective cost of foreign currency loans

Cato, a Polish company, needs a one year loan of about 50 million zlotys. It can borrow in zlotys at 10.80% pa but is considering taking out a sterling loan which would cost only 6.56% pa. The current spot exchange rate is zloty/£ 5.1503. The company decides to borrow £10 million at 6.56% per annum. Converting at the spot rate, this will provide zloty51.503 million. Interest will be paid at the end of one year along with the repayment of the loan principal.

Assuming the exchange rate moves in line with interest rate parity, you are required to show the zloty values of the interest paid and the repayment of the loan principal. Compute the effective interest rate paid on the loan.

Solution

By interest rate parity, the zloty will have weakened in one year to:

$$5.1503 \times \frac{1.1080}{1.0656} = 5.3552$$

Time		£'000	Exchange rate	Zloty '000
Now	Borrows	10,000	5.1503	51,503
In 1 year	6.56% interest	(656)		
	Repayment	(10,000)	5.3552	(57,065)
		(10,656)		

The effective interest rate paid is $\frac{57,065}{51,503} - 1 = 10.80\%$, the same as it would have paid in £.

Exam focus point

In an exam situation, it may be possible to pick up loans at cheaper interest rates in other currencies.

The term 'Fisher effect' is sometimes used in looking at the relationship between interest rates and expected rates of inflation. The rate of interest can be seen as made up of two parts: the real required rate of return plus a premium for inflation.

Then:

(1 + nominal rate of interest) = (1 + real rate of interest) × (1 + expected rate of inflation)

Countries with **relatively high rates of inflation will generally** have **high nominal rates of interest**, partly because high interest rates are a mechanism for reducing inflation and partly because of the Fisher effect: higher nominal interest rates serve to allow investors to obtain a high enough real rate of return where inflation is relatively high.

According to the international Fisher effect, interest rate differentials between countries provide an unbiased predictor of future changes in spot exchange rates. The currencies of countries with relatively high interest rates are expected to depreciate against currencies with lower interest rates, because the higher interest rates are considered necessary to compensate for the anticipated currency depreciation.

16: FOREIGN EXCHANGE RISK

Given free movement of capital internationally, this idea suggests that the real rate of return in different countries will equalise as a result of adjustments to spot exchange rates.

The Fisher effect can be expressed as:

Formula to learn

$$\frac{1+r_f}{1+r_h} = \frac{1+i_f}{1+i_h}$$

where r_f is the nominal interest rate in the foreign country
 r_h is the nominal interest rate in the home country
 i_f is the inflation rate in the foreign country
 i_h is the inflation rate in the home country

4.6 Forward exchange contracts

Forward exchange contracts hedge against transaction exposure by allowing the importer or exporter to arrange for a bank to sell or buy a quantity of foreign currency at a future date, at a **rate of exchange determined** when the **forward contract is made**. The trader will know in advance either how much local currency he will receive (if he is selling foreign currency to the bank) or how much local currency he must pay (if he is buying foreign currency from the bank).

Forward contracts are very popular with small companies. The current spot price is irrelevant to the outcome of a forward contract.

Key term

A **forward exchange contract** is:

(a) An immediately firm and binding contract, eg between a bank and its customer
(b) For the purchase or sale of a specified quantity of a stated foreign currency
(c) At a rate of exchange fixed at the time the contract is made
(d) For performance (delivery of the currency and payment for it) at a future time which is agreed when making the contract. (This future time will be either a specified date, or any time between two specified dates)

4.7 Example: Forward exchange contracts

A UK importer knows on 1 April that he must pay a foreign seller 26,500 Swiss francs in one month's time, on 1 May. He can arrange a forward exchange contract with his bank on 1 April, whereby the bank undertakes to sell the importer 26,500 Swiss francs on 1 May, at a fixed rate of say 2.6400 to the £.

The UK importer can be certain that whatever the spot rate is between Swiss francs and sterling on 1 May, he will have to pay on that date, at this forward rate:

$$\frac{26,500}{2.6400} = £10,037.88$$

(a) If the spot rate is **lower than 2.6400**, the importer would have successfully protected himself against a weakening of sterling, and would have avoided paying more sterling to obtain the Swiss francs.

(b) If the spot rate is **higher than 2.6400**, sterling's value against the Swiss franc would mean that the importer would pay more under the forward exchange contract than he would have had to pay if he had obtained the francs at the spot rate on 1 May. He cannot avoid this extra cost, because a forward contract is binding.

Exam focus point

You will need to remember that option forward exchange contracts are different from **currency options**.

4.8 Option forward exchange contracts

Option forward contracts are forward exchange contracts where the customer has the option to call for performance of the contract:

- At any date **from the contract** being made up to a specified date in the future or
- At any date **between two dates** both in the future

Performance must take place at some time: it cannot be avoided altogether.

Option forward contracts are normally used to cover whole months straddling the likely payment date, where the customer is not sure of the exact date on which he will want to buy or sell currency. (The purpose of an option forward contract is to avoid having to renew a forward exchange contract and extend it by a few days, because extending a forward contract can be expensive.)

4.8.1 Example: Option forward exchange contract

A company is expecting to receive 32 billion South Korean won at some time between three and six months from now. The spot and forward rates for won/£ are:

Spot	1,703 – 1,708
Three months forward	1,717 – 1,724
Six months forward	1,725 – 1,732

The company covers the receipt with an option forward contract, to be fulfilled at any time between three and six months from now. What rate will apply to the contract?

Solution

The relevant rates for selling won to the bank are 1,724 and 1,732. Of these, the worse rate is 1,732, which will give fewer pounds than the rate of 1,724. The contract will be agreed at an exchange rate of won/£1,732.

4.9 What happens if a customer cannot satisfy a forward contract?

A customer might be unable to satisfy a forward contract for any one of a number of reasons.

(a) An **importer** might find that:

　(i)　His supplier **fails to deliver the goods** as specified, so the importer will not accept the goods delivered and will not agree to pay for them

　(ii)　The **supplier sends fewer goods** than expected, perhaps because of supply shortages, and so the importer has less to pay for

　(iii)　The supplier is **late with the delivery**, and so the importer does not have to pay for the goods until later than expected

(b) An **exporter** might find the same types of situation, but in reverse, so that he does not receive any payment at all, or he receives more or less than originally expected, or he receives the expected amount, but only after some delay.

If a customer cannot satisfy a forward exchange contract, the bank will make the customer fulfil the contract.

(a) If the customer has arranged for the bank to buy currency but then cannot deliver the currency for the bank to buy, the bank will:

　(i)　**Sell currency** to the **customer** at the **spot rate** (when the contract falls due for performance)
　(ii)　**Buy** the **currency back**, under the terms of the **forward exchange contract**

(b) If the customer has contracted for the bank to sell him currency, the bank will:

　(i)　**Sell** the customer **the specified amount of currency** at the **forward exchange rate**
　(ii)　**Buy back** the **unwanted currency** at the **spot rate**

Thus, the bank arranges for the customer to perform his part of the forward exchange contract by either selling or buying the 'missing' currency at the spot rate. These arrangements are known as **closing out** a forward exchange contract.

5 Hedging using the money markets

> **FAST FORWARD**
>
> **Money market hedging** involves borrowing in one currency, converting the money borrowed into another currency and putting the money on deposit until the time the transaction is completed, hoping to take advantage of favourable interest rate movements.

5.1 Money market hedges

Because of the close relationship between forward exchange rates and the interest rates in the two currencies, it is possible to 'manufacture' a forward rate by using the spot exchange rate and money market lending or borrowing. This technique is known as a **money market hedge** or **synthetic forward**.

5.2 Setting up a money market hedge for a foreign currency payment

Suppose a British company needs to **pay** a Swiss creditor in Swiss francs in three months' time. It does not have enough cash to pay now, but will have sufficient in three months' time. Instead of negotiating a forward contract, the company could:

Step 1 Borrow the appropriate amount in pounds now

Step 2 Convert the pounds to francs immediately

Step 3 Put the francs on deposit in a Swiss franc bank account

Step 4 When the time comes to pay the company:

(a) Pays the creditor out of the franc bank account
(b) Repays the pound loan account

The effect is exactly the same as using a forward contract, and will usually cost almost exactly the same amount. If the results from a money market hedge were very different from a forward hedge, speculators could make money without taking a risk. Therefore market forces ensure that the two hedges produce very similar results.

5.3 Example: Money market hedge (1)

A UK company owes a Danish creditor Kr3,500,000 in three months' time. The spot exchange rate is Kr/£ 7.5509 – 7.5548. The company can borrow in Sterling for three months at 8.60% per annum and can deposit kroners for three months at 10% per annum. What is the cost in pounds with a money market hedge and what effective forward rate would this represent?

Solution

The interest rates for three months are 2.15% to borrow in pounds and 2.5% to deposit in kroners. The company needs to deposit enough kroners now so that the total including interest will be Kr3,500,000 in three months' time. This means depositing:

Kr3,500,000/(1 + 0.025) = Kr3,414,634.

These kroners will cost £452,215 (spot rate 7.5509). The company must borrow this amount and, with three months' interest of 2.15%, will have to repay:

£452,215 × (1 + 0.0215) = £461,938.

Thus, in three months, the Danish creditor will be paid out of the Danish bank account and the company will effectively be paying £461,938 to satisfy this debt. The effective forward rate which the company has 'manufactured' is 3,500,000/461,938 = 7.5768. This effective forward rate shows the kroner at a discount to the pound because the kroner interest rate is higher than the sterling rate.

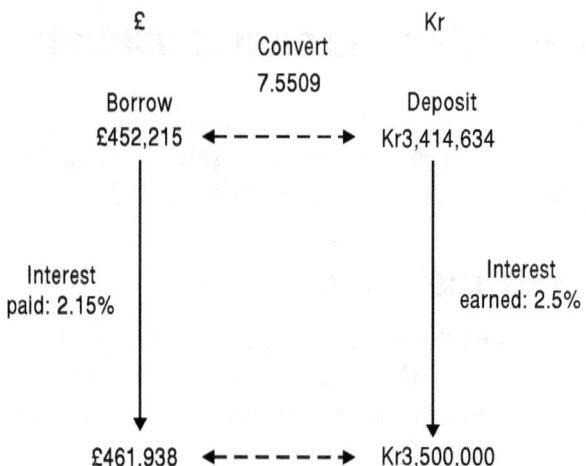

5.4 Setting up a money market hedge for a foreign currency receipt

A similar technique can be used to cover a foreign currency **receipt** from a debtor. To manufacture a forward exchange rate, follow the steps below:

Step 1 Borrow an appropriate amount in the foreign currency today

Step 2 Convert it immediately to home currency

Step 3 Place it on deposit in the home currency

Step 4 When the debtor's cash is received:
  (a) Repay the foreign currency loan
  (b) Take the cash from the home currency deposit account

> **Exam focus point**: Variations on these money market hedges are possible.

5.5 Example: Money market hedge (2)

A UK company is owed SFr 2,500,000 in three months' time by a Swiss company. The spot exchange rate is SFr/£ 2.2498 – 2.2510. The company can deposit in Sterling for three months at 8.00% per annum and can borrow Swiss Francs for three months at 7.00% per annum. What is the receipt in pounds with a money market hedge and what effective forward rate would this represent?

Solution

The interest rates for three months are 2.00% to deposit in pounds and 1.75% to borrow in Swiss francs. The company needs to borrow SFr2,500,000/1.0175 = SFr 2,457,003 today. These Swiss francs will be converted to £ at 2,457,003/2.2510 = £1,091,516. The company must deposit this amount and, with three months' interest of 2.00%, will have earned

£1,091,516 × (1 + 0.02) = £1,113,346

Thus, in three months, the loan will be paid out of the proceeds from the debtor and the company will receive £1,113,346. The effective forward rate which the company has 'manufactured' is

2,500,000/1,113,346 = 2.2455. This effective forward rate shows the Swiss franc at a premium to the pound because the Swiss franc interest rate is lower than the sterling rate.

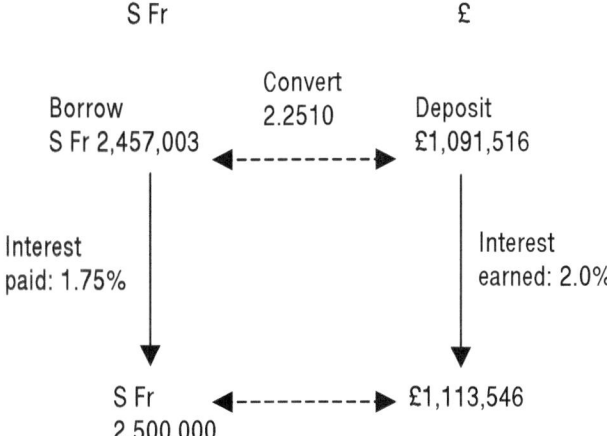

6 Choosing between a forward contract and a money market hedge

FAST FORWARD

The choice between forward and money markets is generally made on the basis of which method is **cheaper**, with other factors being of limited significance.

6.1 Choosing the hedging method

When a company expects to receive or pay a sum of foreign currency in the next few months, it can choose between using the **forward exchange market** and the **money market** to hedge against the foreign exchange risk. Other methods may also be possible, such as **making lead payments**. The cheapest method available is the one that ought to be chosen.

6.2 Example: Choosing the cheapest method

Trumpton plc has bought goods from a US supplier, and must pay $4,000,000 for them in three months' time. The company's finance director wishes to hedge against the foreign exchange risk, and the three methods which the company usually considers are:

- Using **forward exchange contracts**
- Using **money market borrowing or lending**
- Making **lead payments**

The following annual interest rates and exchange rates are currently available.

	US dollar		Sterling	
	Deposit rate	Borrowing rate	Deposit rate	Borrowing rate
	%	%	%	%
1 month	7	10.25	10.75	14.00
3 months	7	10.75	11.00	14.25

	$/£ exchange rate ($ = £1)
Spot	1.8625 – 1.8635
1 month forward	0.60c – 0.58c pm
3 months forward	1.80c – 1.75c pm

Which is the cheapest method for Trumpton plc? Ignore commission costs (the bank charges for arranging a forward contract or a loan).

Solution

The three choices must be compared on a similar basis, which means working out the cost of each to Trumpton either now or in three months' time. In the following paragraphs, the cost to Trumpton now will be determined.

Choice 1: the forward exchange market

Trumpton must buy dollars in order to pay the US supplier. The exchange rate in a forward exchange contract to buy $4,000,000 in three months time (bank sells) is:

	$
Spot rate	1.8625
Less 3 months premium	0.0180
Forward rate	1.8445

The cost of the $4,000,000 to Trumpton in three months' time will be:

$$\frac{\$4,000,000}{1.8445} = £2,168,609.38$$

This is the cost in **three months**. To work out the cost now, we could say that by deferring payment for three months, the company is:

- Saving having to borrow money now at 14.25% a year to make the payment now, or
- Avoiding the loss of interest on cash on deposit, earning 11% a year

The choice between (a) and (b) depends on whether Trumpton plc needs to borrow to make any current payment (a) or is cash rich (b). Here, assumption (a) is selected, but (b) might in fact apply.

At an annual interest rate of 14.25% the rate for three months is 14.25/4 = 3.5625%. The 'present cost' of £2,168,609.38 in three months' time is:

$$\frac{£2,168,609.38}{1.035625} = £2,094,010.26$$

Choice 2: the money markets

Using the money markets involves

(a) **Borrowing in the foreign currency**, if the company will eventually receive the currency.

(b) **Lending in the foreign currency**, if the company will eventually pay the currency. Here, Trumpton will pay $4,000,000 and so it would lend US dollars (i.e. putting money on deposit).

It would lend enough US dollars for three months, so that the principal repaid in three months' time plus interest will amount to the payment due of $4,000,000.

(a) Since the US dollar deposit rate is 7%, the rate for three months is approximately 7/4 = 1.75%.

(b) To earn $4,000,000 in three months' time at 1.75% interest, Trumpton would have to lend now:

$$\frac{\$4,000,000}{1.0175} = \$3,931,203.93$$

These dollars would have to be purchased now at the spot rate of (bank sells) $1.8625. The cost would be:

$$\frac{\$3,931,203.93}{1.8625} = £2,110,713.52$$

By lending US dollars for three months, Trumpton is matching eventual receipts and payments in US dollars, and so has hedged against foreign exchange risk.

Choice 3: lead payments

Lead payments should be considered when the currency of payment is expected to strengthen over time, and is quoted forward at a premium on the foreign exchange market. Here, the cost of a lead payment (paying $4,000,000 now) would be $4,000,000 ÷ 1.8625 = £2,147,651.01.

Summary

	£
Forward exchange contract	2,094,010.26 (cheapest)
Currency lending	2,110,713.52
Lead payment	2,147,651.01

Exam focus point

Although you will need to spend time on the more complex techniques which we shall now move on to discuss, don't forget forward and money market hedging. The examiner regards these methods as important, and has commented in the past that candidates often do not spend enough time on them.

7 Futures

FAST FORWARD

A future is a standard contract to buy or sell a **specific amount** at a **particular price** on a **stipulated future date**.

Key terms

Derivative is a financial security whose value is derived partly from the value and characteristics of an underlying security. Option contracts, financial futures and swaps are types of derivative.

Future is a standardised contract to **buy** or **sell** a specific amount of a commodity, currency or financial instrument at a **particular price** on a **stipulated future date**.

Financial future is a futures contract which is based on a financial instrument, rather than a physical commodity. There are financial futures for interest rates, currencies and stock market indices.

Currency future is a futures contract to buy or sell a currency.

7.1 What is a future?

A future represents a **commitment** to an **additional transaction** in the future that limits the risk of existing commitments.

7.2 Example: Futures

1 January

(a) On 1 January the price (the spot price) of a consignment of cocoa beans is $1,000.

(b) You have already agreed to buy a consignment of cocoa beans for $1,200 on 28 February.

(c) You buy a three-month cocoa futures contract at $1,100 that expires on 31 March. This means you are committing to buying an additional consignment of cocoa beans, not at today's spot price, but at the **futures price** of $1,100. $1,100 represents what the market thinks the spot price will be on 31 March.

28 February

(a) You buy the consignment of cocoa beans at $1,200.

(b) You are still committed to buying the consignment at $1,100 on 31 March, but that will mean that you have two consignments of cocoa beans rather than just the one you need. You therefore sell the futures contract you bought on 1 January to eliminate this additional commitment. The futures contract is now priced at $1,233, as the market now believes that $1,233 will be the spot price on 31 March.

(c) Because you have sold the contract for more than the purchase price, you have made a gain on the futures contract of 1,233 − 1,100 = $133. This can be set against the purchase you made.

Net cost = 1,200 − 133 = $1,067

7.3 The development of futures contracts

Futures are derivatives which have their origins in the markets for commodities such as wheat, coffee, sugar, meat, oil, base metals and precious metals.

(a) The prices of all of these commodities **fluctuate seasonally** and are also subject to large changes because of unpredictable events such as storms, drought, wars and political unrest.

(b) To avoid the uncertainty arising from large swings in prices, buyers and sellers of these commodities would **agree quantities** and **prices in advance**. This encouraged investment in production and benefited buyers and sellers alike by enabling them to plan in advance.

Originally the buyer and seller would agree a forward price for settlement by actual delivery of an agreed amount of the commodity on an agreed date. As a protection against defaulting on the deal, both parties would put down a deposit.

However, the commodity futures markets developed rapidly when the contracts were **standardised** in terms of **delivery date** and **quantity**. This enabled the futures contracts to be traded purely on the basis of price, like shares on a stock exchange. The London International Financial Futures and Options Exchange (LIFFE) was set up in 1982.

7.4 Difference between forward contracts and futures contracts

The key difference between a forward contract and a futures contract is as follows:

(a) A forward contract is negotiated **'over the counter'** between a buyer and a seller. For example, a currency forward contract is negotiated between a bank and its customer and a commodity forward contract is negotiated between a producer and a buyer. This means that the contract can be **tailored** to the customer's exact requirements. Three things must be negotiated: quantity to be delivered, delivery date and price.

(b) A futures contract is **bought and sold** on a **futures exchange**, which operates like a stock exchange. In order to make a futures contract tradeable it must be **standardised** as to quantity and delivery date. The only factor which is traded is the price. The prices of futures contracts change continuously and are quoted by the futures exchange and in the financial press like share prices or currency prices.

The standardisation of contract sizes means that amounts required must be **rounded** to the **nearest whole number of contracts**. For example, a requirement to buy 950,000 Euros must be dealt with on the futures market by buying eight contracts (€950,000/€125,000 = 7.6, which is eight contracts to the nearest whole number). This introduces some inaccuracies when transactions are being hedged.

However, it is the **standardisation** of **delivery dates** which results in the biggest difference between the way that futures contracts and forward contracts are used. Whereas most forward contracts are settled by delivery of the actual currency or commodity, it is very unlikely that the person who buys euro futures or cotton futures will need the commodity at exactly the same time as the standardised date when the futures contract is settled. For this reason the vast majority of futures contracts are not settled by delivery but by 'closing out'.

7.5 Currency futures

Currency futures – our main concern in this chapter – are not nearly as common as forward contracts, and their market is much smaller. On the currency futures markets, currencies such as the pound, euro, yen and Swiss franc all priced in US dollars. There is no contract for the US dollar itself.

We shall discuss the main elements of futures transactions in the rest of this section in the context of currency futures.

7.6 The contract size

Key term

> The **contract size** is the fixed minimum quantity of commodity which can be bought or sold using a futures contract.

Dealing in this amount is referred to as buying or selling one contract. In general, dealing on futures markets must be in a whole number of contracts.

7.7 The contract price

Key term

> The **contract price** is the price at which the futures contract can be bought or sold.

The contract price is the figure which is traded on the futures exchange on the date the company **originally purchases** the futures contract. It is **always in US dollars**. It changes continuously and is the basis for computing gains or losses.

7.8 The settlement date

Key term

> The **settlement date** (or delivery date, or expiry date) is the date when trading on a particular futures contract stops and all accounts are settled.

The settlement dates for all currency futures are at the end of March, June, September and December. The period for which a currency contract is traded before the settlement date is normally a maximum of nine months. This means that for each currency there will be three contracts being traded at any time, each to a different settlement date. For example from April to June, the currency futures being traded will be the June contract, the September contract and the December contract.

7.9 Long and short positions

POSITIONS	
Buyer of futures contract	Long position
Seller of futures contract	Short position

7.10 The tick size

Key term

> One **tick** (or the **tick size**) is the smallest measured movement in the contract price. For currency futures this is a movement in the fourth decimal place.

The value of one tick = contract size × tick size. A movement in the price of the Swiss franc contract from $/SFr 0.5800 to 0.5801 is a one-tick movement. The **value of a tick** is the gain or loss which is made if there is one tick price movement. This value depends on the contract size. Examples of tick values and contract sizes are shown in the following table.

Currency future	Contract size	Tick	Value of one tick
Swiss franc	SFr 125,000	$0.0001 per SFr	$12.50
Japanese yen	Y 12.5 million	$0.0001 per Y100	$12.50
Sterling	£62,500	$0.0001 per £	$6.25
Euro	€125,000	$0.0001 per €	$12.50

Market traders will compute gains or losses on their futures positions by reference to the number of ticks by which the contract price has moved. For instance, the futures market gain in buying and then selling eight Swiss Franc futures contracts could have been computed as follows.

Bought at	0.5800
Sold at	0.6000
Gain	0.0200 = 200 ticks.

8 contracts × 200 ticks × $12.50 = $20,000.

7.11 The initial margin

Key term

> When futures contracts are bought or sold, a **deposit** known as the **initial margin** must be advanced.

The size of this margin depends on the actual contract but might typically amount to about 5% of the value of contracts dealt in. This deposit is refunded when the contract is closed out.

The objective of the initial margin is to cover any possible losses made from the first day's trading. Thereafter, any variations in the contract price are covered by a **variation** margin. Profits are advanced to the trader's account but losses must be covered by advancing further collateral. This process is known as **marking to market**.

7.12 Basis

Key term

> A future's price may be different from the spot price, and this difference is the **basis**.
>
> **Basis** = spot price − futures price

(Some books show it the other way round, so that the basis is the amount by which the futures price exceeds the spot price.)

The basis will move towards zero at the delivery date. If it did not, **arbitrage profits** would be possible. If, for example, the basis was negative at the delivery date, profits could be earned by selling futures contracts (at the higher price) and simultaneously buying in the cash market (at the lower price) goods – gold, pork bellies, dollars or whatever – for delivery to the futures buyers.

7.13 Hedge efficiency

Hedgers who need to buy or sell the underlying currency or commodity do not use the margin to trade more than they otherwise would and can use the futures markets quite safely provided they understand how the system operates. The only risk to hedgers is that the futures market does not always provide a perfect hedge. This can result from two causes.

(a) The first reason is that amounts must be **rounded to a whole number of contracts**, causing inaccuracies.

(b) The second reason is **basis risk** – the risk that the futures contract price may move by a different amount from the price of the underlying currency or commodity. The actions of speculators may increase basis risk. A measure of **hedge efficiency** compares the profit made on the futures market with the loss made on the cash or commodity market, or *vice versa*.

7.14 Closing out futures contracts

Closing out a futures contract means **entering** into a **second futures contract** which **reverses** the effect of the first one. We saw above that this is necessary to avoid taking more than you need. If, on 1 July, a company buys eight euro contracts, it closes out by selling eight euro contracts at a later date, say 31 July. The effect is that the company now has no liability to buy or sell any euro, but it will have made a gain or loss resulting from the difference in price between 1 July and 31 July.

7.14.1 Example: Closing out

On 1 July the price of Swiss franc futures with a 30 September settlement date is $/SFr 0.5800 (ie US$0.5800 = SFr 1). By 31 July the price of these futures contracts has moved to $/SFr 0.6000. Your company buys eight Swiss franc futures contracts on 1 July and sells eight Swiss franc futures contracts on 31 July. Each Swiss franc futures contract has a standard size of SFr 125,000. What gain or loss has been made?

Solution

Swiss franc futures contracts with a standard settlement date of 30 September are called 'Swiss franc September contracts'. **On 1 July**, when you buy eight Swiss franc September contracts at $/SFr 0.5800, you have contracted to buy SFr 125,000 × 8 = SFr 1,000,000 on 30 September, paying a price in US$ of 0.5800 × 1,000,000 = $580,000. Like a forward contract, this is a binding obligation. **On 31 July**, when you sell eight Swiss franc contracts, you incur a second obligation. This is to sell SFr 1,000,000 on 30 September, receiving the price of US$ 0.6000 × 1,000,000 = $600,000. Combining the two transactions, the Swiss francs cancel out, leaving you with a profit in dollars of $20,000.

Closing out of futures contracts is a technique used both by hedgers and speculators. In the above example, a speculator with no particular interest in Swiss francs could have made a profit by buying futures contracts on 1 July and selling them on 31 July. Over 90% of contracts are closed out before delivery on the trading markets.

8 Deciding how to hedge with currency futures

> **FAST FORWARD**
>
> **Currency futures** are contracts for the sale or purchase at a set future date of a set quantity of currency. A step-by-step approach can be used to deal with complications.
>
> | Transaction on future date | | Now | | On future date | |
> |---|---|---|---|---|---|
> | Receive | currency | Sell | currency futures | Buy | currency futures |
> | Pay | currency | Buy | currency futures | Sell | currency futures |
> | Receive | $ | Buy | currency futures | Sell | currency futures |
> | Pay | $ | Sell | currency futures | Buy | currency futures |

8.1 Setting up a futures hedge

In the preceding section we showed how futures contracts are traded and how they can be used for speculation or for hedging by the technique of 'closing out'. In this section we discuss the factors a treasurer must consider when deciding how to set up a currency futures hedge.

When deciding to use futures to hedge currency risk, you need to consider the following things when **setting up** the hedge:

- Which settlement date?
- What type of contract?
- How many contracts?

8.2 Which contract settlement date?

Currency futures are traded for a period of about nine months before the settlement date is reached. This means that at any time there will be a choice of three settlement dates to choose from. To hedge currency receipts and payments a futures contract must have a **settlement date after the date that the actual currency is needed**. Usually the best hedge is achieved by selecting the contract which matures **next after** the actual cash is needed.

> **Exam focus point**
>
> The point that the settlement date of the future must be **after** the company needs the currency is very important, but it is one that students often get wrong in exams.

8.2.1 Example: Which settlement date?

For example, in July, suppose the following figures are quoted:

Sterling futures: contract size £62,500: price in $ per £

	12 July price
Sep	1.5552
Dec	1.5556
Mar	1.5564

Your company, based in Britain, will receive US$2,000,000 on 13 December. How should you hedge the receipt using futures?

Solution

The receipt of dollars is hedged by buying sterling futures now (12 July) and selling sterling futures on 13 December. The September contract will be no use because it expires on 30 September. Either of the other two contracts can be used. It is usual to choose the contract which expires next after 13 December. This is the December contract which expires on 31 December.

Assuming the December contract is chosen, the receipt of $2,000,000 converts, using the futures contract price, to £2,000,000/1.5556 = £1,285,678. The contract size is £62,500. The number of contracts to be bought is £1,285,678/£62,500 = 20.57, rounded to 21 contracts.

Summary. On 12 July, buy 21 December sterling contracts at $/£ 1.5556. On 13 December, sell 21 December sterling contracts.

8.3 Which type of contract?

One of the limitations of currency futures is that currencies can only be bought or sold for US dollars.

The basic rules are given below.

(a) If you need to **buy** a currency on a future date with US dollars, take the following action:

- **Step 1** Buy the **appropriate currency futures** contracts now
- **Step 2** Close out by **selling** the **same number of futures** contracts on the date that you buy the actual currency

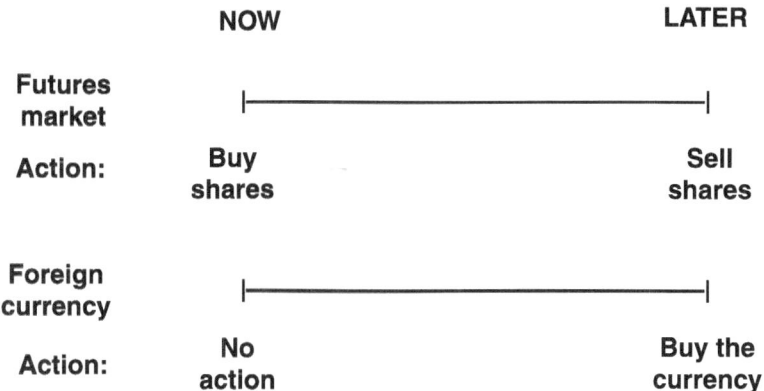

This was the procedure we used in the examples involving Swiss francs in the previous section.

(b) If you need to **sell** a currency on a future date for US$, take the following steps:

Step 1   Sell the **appropriate currency futures** contracts now

Step 2   Close out by **buying** the **same number** of **futures** contracts on the date that you sell the actual currency

8.3.1 Example: Which type of contract?

Natterjack Inc, an American company, will receive a dividend of three million Swiss francs in 70 days' time. What action should it take on the futures market to hedge currency risk?

Solution

In 70 days, the Swiss francs will need to be sold for dollars. The company should **sell** Swiss franc futures now and buy them in 70 days when it sells the actual Swiss francs. The contract size is SFr125,000, so 24 contracts should be sold.

8.4 Non-US companies

If companies are not based in the United States but wish to hedge the receipt or payment of US dollars, they must re-state their requirements in a format which shows whether their **own currency** needs to be bought or sold.

8.4.1 Example: Non-US companies (1)

Starburst plc, a British company, expects a large receipt of US dollars in six months' time. How can it hedge this receipt on the futures market?

Solution

The company cannot sell US dollar futures. They do not exist. Instead it must restate its requirements as a need to buy pounds with dollars in six months' time. It must therefore **buy sterling futures** now and sell them in six months.

8.4.2 Example: Non-US companies (2)

Geheim AG, a German company, needs to pay US dollars to an American supplier in 90 days. How can it hedge the transaction using currency futures?

Solution

In 90 days the company will need to sell euros for US dollars. It should sell euro futures now and buy them in 90 days.

8.5 Transactions not involving US dollars

If a company wishes to buy or sell a currency with another currency, neither of which are US dollars, it needs to deal in more than one type of contract. This complication makes the use of the currency futures markets much more complex than the use of forward markets and contributes to their relative lack of popularity.

8.5.1 Example: Transactions not involving US dollars

Great Eastern plc, a British company, has purchased steel from Japan and needs to pay for this in 90 days' time. How can it hedge the cost of the purchase by using currency futures?

Solution

The company needs to buy Japanese yen. On the futures market, it can hedge this by buying Japanese yen futures. On the futures market yen are bought with US dollars. The company therefore needs to **sell sterling futures** (to get dollars) and **buy yen futures** (with dollars). In 90 days it will close out by buying sterling futures and selling yen futures.

8.6 How many contracts?

We have already made the point that futures can only be bought or sold as a whole number of contracts. When hedging, there is no necessary advantage in rounding **up** because futures trading can produce a loss as regularly as a profit. The problem which has not yet been covered is **how many contracts to use when the receipt or payment is in US dollars**. The method normally used is to convert to the other currency using the exchange rate implicit in the futures contract (ie today's contract price) and then divide by the futures contract size. You should always round to the nearest number of contracts.

8.6.1 Example: How many contracts? (1)

Great Eastern plc, a British company, has purchased steel worth Y100 million from Japan and needs to pay for this in 90 days' time. How can it hedge the cost of the purchase by using currency futures? On IMM the Japanese yen future is trading at $0.8106 per 100 yen and the Sterling future is trading at $1.6250 per pound. The size of the Japanese yen futures contract is Y12.5 million.

Solution

The company must buy yen futures and sell sterling futures. The number of yen futures to buy is:

100/12.5 = 8.

8 contracts represent $\dfrac{8 \times 12{,}500{,}000 \times \$0.8106}{100}$ = $810,600.

$810,600, converted at the sterling futures price, gives £810,600/1.6250 = £498,831. The sterling contract size is £62,500. The company should sell £498,831/£62,500 = 7.98 contracts, rounded to eight contracts.

Summary. Today, buy eight yen contracts and sell eight sterling contracts. In 90 days, close out by selling eight yen contracts and buying eight sterling contracts.

8.6.2 Example: How many contracts? (2)

Starburst plc, a British company, expects to receive 5 million US dollars in six months' time. How can it hedge this receipt on the futures market? The current spot rate is $/£ 1.5320 and the sterling futures contract is trading at $/£ 1.5275. The sterling futures contract size is £62,500.

Solution

Using the futures contract price, $5 million = £5,000,000/1.5275 = £3,273,322.

Number of contracts to be used = £3,273,322/£62,500 = 52.37, rounded to 52.

The company should buy 52 sterling contracts now and sell 52 contracts in six months.

8.7 Dealing with a futures question

A number of possible stages are involved:

Step 1 The setup process

This may involve the following steps.

(a) **Choose which contract**

You must choose an expiry date after the underlying exposure.

(b) **Choose type of contract**

A €125,000 contract will be used to buy or sell €. If the company owes €, it will wish to buy € so will **buy € futures**. However, a UK company receiving $ will wish to sell $ or buy £. As the contract size is quoted in £, £62,500, the company will **buy £ futures**.

(c) **Choose number of contracts**

You need to divide the amount being hedged by the size of contract, rounding to the nearest whole contract.

You may also need to calculate how much of the currency of the future is needed. You do this by using today's price for the futures contract to convert the amount being hedged into the currency of the futures contract, and then divide by the size of the futures contract.

(d) **Calculate tick size**

Tick size = Minimum price movement × standard contract size

Remember that the minimum price has to be calculated to the **fourth** decimal place, for example $0.0001 per £.

Step 2 **Estimate the closing futures price**

You may be given this in the question or you may have to estimate it using basis, the difference between the spot and futures prices. A common assumption to make is that basis declines evenly to zero over the life of the futures contract.

Step 3 **Hedge outcome**

(a) **Calculate futures market outcome**

This will be

Tick movement × tick value × number of contracts

(b) **Calculate net outcome**

Spot market payment or receipt converted at the closing spot rate

+ Futures market profit/(loss)

The currency used for this calculation will be the opposite to the currency of the receipt/payment being hedged. Ultimately, therefore, unless a dollar receipt or payment is being hedged, the value of the futures profit or loss will also have to be converted using the **closing spot rate**.

The gain or loss on the future will accrue during the contract. In exam questions you will take this gain or loss at the end of the contract at the prevailing closing spot rate.

(c) **Calculate hedge efficiency**

$$\frac{\text{Spot market profit}}{\text{Futures market loss}}$$

Where

Spot market profit = (Payment or receipt being hedged × (Closing rate − opening rate))

or $\dfrac{\text{Futures market profit}}{\text{Spot market loss}}$

8.8 Example: Futures contract

A US company buys goods worth €720,000 from a German company payable in 30 days. The US company wants to hedge against the € strengthening against the dollar.

Current spot is 0.9215 – 0.9221 $/€ and the € futures rate is 0.9245 $/€. The standard size of a three-month € futures contract is €125,000. In 30 days' time the spot is 0.9345 – 0.9351 $/€.

Evaluate the hedge.

Solution

Step 1 Setup

(a) **Which contract?**

We assume that the three month contract is the best available.

(b) **Type of contract**

We need to buy € or sell $. As the futures contract is in €, we need to buy futures.

(c) **Number of contracts**

$\dfrac{720,000}{125,000}$ = 5.76, say 6 contracts

(d) **Tick size**

Minimum price movement × contract size = 0.0001 × 125,000 = $12.50

Step 2 **Closing futures price**

The basis now is 0.9245 – 0.9221 = 24 ticks.

(0.9221 is used rather than 0.9215 because the company has to pay the bank 0.9221 dollars to obtain each € it needs – remember the bank always has the advantage.) The basis in 3 months' time is expected to be zero.

If basis reduces evenly over the life of the contract, in one month's time basis will be ²/₃ × 24 ticks = 16 ticks.

0.9351 + 16 ticks = 0.9367

(It would also be legitimate to calculate basis using the average of current spot, 0.9218.)

Step 3 Hedge outcome

(a) **Outcome in futures market**

Opening futures price	0.9245	Buy at low price
Closing futures price	0.9367	Sell at high price
Movement in ticks	122 ticks	Profit

Futures profit/loss   122 × $12.50 × 6 contracts = $9,150

(b) **Net outcome**

	$
Spot market payment (720,000 × 0.9351$/€)	673,272
Futures market profit	(9,150)
	664,122

(c) **Hedge efficiency**

$$\frac{9{,}150}{720{,}000 \times (0.9351 - 0.9221)} \times 100\% = 97.8\%$$

Remember the following table.

Transaction on future date		Now		On future date	
Receive	currency	Sell	currency futures	Buy	currency futures
Pay	currency	Buy	currency futures	Sell	currency futures
Receive	$	Buy	currency futures	Sell	currency futures
Pay	$	Sell	currency futures	Buy	currency futures

9 Choosing between forward contracts and futures contracts

FAST FORWARD

> The choice between the **forward** and **futures** market will depend on **availability, flexibility** and **transaction costs** as well as outcomes.

9.1 Forward and futures contracts

A futures market hedge attempts to achieve the same result as a forward contract, that is to fix the exchange rate in advance for a future foreign currency payment or receipt. As we have seen, hedge inefficiencies mean that a futures contract can only fix the exchange rate subject to a margin of error. It is useful at this stage to consider the advantages and disadvantages of futures hedges over forward contracts and then to work some examples which compare the two.

Forward contracts are agreed 'over the counter' between a bank and its customer. Futures contracts are standardised and traded on futures exchanges. This results in the following advantages and disadvantages.

9.2 Advantages of futures over forward contracts

(a) **Transaction** costs should be **lower**.

(b) The **exact date** of **receipt** or **payment** of the currency does **not have to be known**, because the futures contract does not have to be closed out until the actual cash receipt or payment is made. In other words, the futures hedge gives the equivalent of an 'option forward' contract, limited only by the expiry date of the contract.

9.3 Disadvantages of futures compared with forward contracts

(a) The **contracts cannot be tailored** to the user's exact requirements.

(b) **Hedge inefficiencies** are **caused** by having to deal in a whole number of contracts and by basis risk.

(c) **Only a limited number of currencies** are the subject of futures contracts (although the number of currencies is growing, especially with the rapid development of Asian economies).

(d) The **procedure for converting** between two currencies neither of which is the US dollar is twice as complex for futures as for a forward contract.

In general, the disadvantages of futures mean that the market is much smaller than the currency forward market.

Question — Futures

Allbrit plc, a company based in the UK, imports and exports to the USA. On 1 May it signs three agreements, all of which are to be settled on 31 October:

(a) A sale to a US customer of goods for $205,500
(b) A sale to another US customer for £550,000
(c) A purchase from a US supplier for $875,000

On 1 June the $/£ spot rate is 1.5500 – 1.5520 and the October forward rate is at a premium of 4.00 – 3.95 cents per pound. Sterling futures contracts are trading at the following prices:

Sterling futures (IMM) Contract size £62,500

Contract settlement date	Contract price $ per £
Jun	1.5370
Sep	1.5180
Dec	1.4970

Required

(a) Compute the net amount receivable or payable in pounds if the transactions are covered on the forward market.

(b) Show how a futures hedge could be set up.

(c) Compute the result of the futures hedge if, by 31 October, the spot market price for dollars has moved to 1.5800 – 1.5820 and the sterling futures price has moved to 1.5650.

(d) Calculate the efficiency of the futures hedge.

Answer

(a) Before covering any transactions with forward or futures contracts, match receipts against payments. The sterling receipt does not need to be hedged. The dollar receipt can be matched against the payment giving a net payment of $669,500 on 31 October.

The appropriate spot rate for buying dollars on 1 May (bank sells low) is 1.5500. The forward rate for October is **spot – premium** = 1.5500 – 0.0400 = 1.5100.

Using a forward contract, the sterling cost of the dollar payment will be 669,500/1.5100 = £443,377. The net cash received on October 31 will therefore be £550,000 – 443,377 = £106,623.

(b) **Setup**

(i) **Which contract**

December contracts

(ii) **Type of contract**

Sell sterling futures in May, we sell the sterling in order to buy the $ that we need

(iii) **Number of contracts**

Here we need to convert the dollar payment to £ as contracts are in £.

Using December futures price

$$\frac{669{,}500}{1.4970} = £447{,}228$$

$$\text{No of contracts} = \frac{447{,}228}{62{,}500}$$

$$= 7.16 \text{ contracts, round to } 7$$

(iv) **Tick size**

$0.0001 \times 62{,}500 = \$6.25$

(v) **Closing futures price**

1.5650 given in question

(c) **Result of futures hedge**

(i) **Outcome in futures market**

Opening futures price	1.4970	Sell
Closing futures price	1.5650	Buy
Movement in ticks	680	Loss

Value of tick movement $680 \times 6.25 \times 7 = \$29{,}750$

(ii) **Net outcome**

	$
Spot market payment	(669,500)
Futures market loss	(29,750)
	(699,250)
Translated at closing rate	1.5800
The bank sells low hence we use the rate of 1.5800	£442,563

(d) **Hedge efficiency**

$$\frac{\frac{669{,}500}{1.5800} - \frac{669{,}500}{1.5500}}{29{,}750 \div 1.5800} \times 100\% = 43.5\%$$

Alternatively we can gauge the success of the hedge by comparing the outcome in the futures market, £442,563 against the forward payment of £443,377.

9.4 Comparison of hedging methods

	Forward	**Money Market**	**Futures**
Tailored	✓	✓	✗
Secondary market to 'unwind' hedge	✗	✓	✓
Transaction cost	Via spread	Via spreads on interest and spot rate	Brokerage fees
Complexity	Low	Medium	High
Management costs	Low	Medium	High
Volume/popularity	Small/medium companies	Banks	Growing especially for companies with high exposure

Exam focus point

Remember hedging questions are not just about calculations, and you should always earn at least a couple of marks (more depending on question requirements) for mentioning relevant factors from this table.

10 Hedging economic and translation exposure

FAST FORWARD

Economic exposure can be hedged by **matching assets and liabilities** and **diversification**.

Translation exposure, the risk of apparent losses appearing when accounting results are translated, probably does not need to be hedged.

10.1 Economic exposure

Key term

Economic exposure is the risk that longer-term exchange rate movements might reduce the international competitiveness of a company. It is the risk that the present value of a company's future cash flows might be reduced by adverse exchange rate movements.

Sometimes economic exposure is defined as transaction exposure + real operating exposure, where real operating exposure is the risk to the present value of future cash flows as defined above.

Suppose a UK company invests in setting up a subsidiary in Eastern Europe. The currency of the Eastern European country depreciates continuously over a five-year period. The cash flows remitted back to the UK are worth less in sterling terms each year, causing a reduction in the value of the investment project.

Another UK company buys raw materials that are priced in US dollars. It converts these materials into finished products that it exports mainly to Spain. Over a period of several years, the pound depreciates against the dollar but strengthens against the euro. The sterling value of the company's income declines while the sterling cost of its materials increases, resulting in a drop in the value of the company's cash flows.

The value of a company depends on the **present value** of its **expected future cash flows**. If there are fears that a company is exposed to the sort of exchange rate movements described above, this may reduce the company's value. Protecting against economic exposure is therefore necessary to protect the company's share price.

A company need not even engage in any foreign activities to be subject to **economic exposure**. For example, if a company trades only in the UK but the pound strengthens appreciably against other world currencies, it may find that it loses UK sales to a foreign competitor who can now afford to charge cheaper sterling prices.

As well as trends in exchange rates, one-off events such as a major stock market crash or major economic events such as the UK's referendum vote in favour of exit from the European Union in June 2016 may administer a 'shock' to exchange rate levels. The value of sterling fell to its lowest in 31 years following the vote.

10.2 Economic exposure and inflation

None of these examples are as simple as they seem, however, because of the compensating actions of economic forces. For example, if the exchange rate of an Eastern European country depreciates significantly, it is probably because of its high inflation rate.

So if the Eastern European subsidiary of a UK company **increases its prices** in line with inflation, its cash flows in the local currency will increase each year. However under purchasing power parity the currency will depreciate. The cash flows will therefore be converted at the depreciating exchange rate to produce a fairly constant sterling value of cash flows. Alternatively, if the subsidiary does not increase its prices, it may increase its sales volume by selling at more competitive prices.

Thus the effects of economic exposure may be mitigated or minimised by changes in prices, which mean the real exchange rate changes little if at all. However, there may be timing differences involved and if exchange rate movements are very large, the business might suffer for a while before compensating economic forces take effect.

10.3 Economic exposure complications

In practice, a company is unlikely to face a simple situation where changes in exchange rates are exactly countered by changes in inflation for a number of reasons:

(a) Purchasing power parity may not hold and real exchange rates therefore will change.

(b) The rate of price changes won't be uniform throughout the economy, and the goods that the company is concerned with may face very different price movements to those that would be suggested by exchange rate movements under purchasing power parity. Some prices may not change at all.

(c) Tax charges will be on nominal cash flows, not real cash flows.

10.4 Hedging economic exposure

Various actions can reduce unexpected economic exposure; expected changes in the exchange rate should be incorporated into projections of cash flow, using the **forward rate** as an **unbiased predictor of the future spot rate**. It can be difficult to hedge against economic exposure in the next twelve months or so; only in the longer term, where sales prices and resource costs can change, and strategy developed, can steps be taken.

10.4.1 Diversifying operations world-wide

On the principle that countries which confine themselves to one country suffer from economic exposure, international diversification is a method of reducing economic exposure. Companies may look to diversify any or all of **sales, production, raw material supplies and finance sources**. Often the decisions required will need to be taken quickly, so flexibility is important, together with an awareness of what the **most likely possible scenarios** are. However, managers need to consider whether the costs involved mean that changes such as opening new production facilities should only be made if they are expected to bring **long-term benefits**.

10.4.2 Market and promotional management

Having taken the decision to diversify, the company must then carefully decide in which markets to operate. This decision will **link in** with **strategic objectives**, and weigh the economic exposure against the earnings that the market is reckoned to be able to generate. The choice of markets and the risk of exchange rate changes will in turn determine money and resources spent in promoting the company's products in each market.

10.4.3 Product management

High levels of economic exposure may mean high-risk product decisions, particularly the decision to **launch new products**, are not **taken**.

10.4.4 Pricing

Again pricing strategy must respond to the risk of fluctuations in exchange rates, but this must also tie in with other objectives; reducing prices may maintain market share but may result in a reduction in distributable profits. Changing prices to combat exchange rate movements may also cause complications in the company's own local markets, particularly if competitors respond.

10.4.5 Production management

As indicated above, levels of economic exposure may influence **supply** and **location of production** decisions. Complications will be changing the **mix of inputs**; this may reduce economic exposure but there may be costs involved in becoming more flexible. Also it will be much easier to shift production to countries with falling exchange rates and lower relative production costs if the company already has facilities in these places and it is feasible to shift production to them. Opening new production facilities in different countries is likely to be in response to expectations that the cost advantages of producing in the new countries will be maintained over the long-term

10.4.6 Other strategies

Possible strategies include **improving domestic efficiency** or seeking government support to **subsidise exporting**.

10.5 Translation exposure

Key term

> **Translation exposure** is the risk that the organisation will make **exchange losses** when the **accounting results** of its foreign branches or subsidiaries are **translated** into the **home currency**.

Translation losses can result, for example, from restating the book value of a foreign subsidiary's assets at the exchange rate on the reporting date. Such losses will not have an impact on the firm's cash flow unless the assets are sold.

There are opposing arguments as to whether translation exposure is important. The arguments centre on whether the reporting of a translation gain or loss will affect the company's share price. There is a powerful argument that, to the extent that cash flows are not affected, translation exposure can be ignored. On the other hand, those who believe that accounting results are an important determinant of share price argue that translation losses should be reduced to a minimum.

The argument can be perhaps resolved by saying that it is important to consider potential losses arising from changes to the **economic value** of assets whereas changes to their **book values** are unimportant if there is no change to the economic value.

Chapter Roundup

- Currencies are quoted at Term currency X units:Base currency 1 unit.

- The **spot rate** is the rate at which currencies are currently quoted on the foreign exchange markets. The **forward rate** is the rate at which currencies will be exchanged on a set future date.

- **Currency risk** occurs in three forms: **transaction exposure** (short-term), **economic exposure** (effect on present value of longer term cash flows) and **translation exposure** (book gains or losses).

- Basic methods of hedging risk include **matching receipts and payments**, **invoicing in own currency**, and **leading and lagging** the times that cash is received and paid.

- A **forward contract** specifies in advance the rate at which a specified quantity of currency will be bought and sold.

- The principle of **interest rate parity** links the currency and money markets and explains differences between the **forward and spot rates**.

- **Money market hedging** involves borrowing in one currency, converting the money borrowed into another currency and putting the money on deposit until the time the transaction is completed, hoping to take advantage of favourable interest rate movements.

- The choice between forward and money markets is generally made on the basis of which method is **cheaper**, with other factors being of limited significance.

- A **future** is a standard contract to **buy or sell a specific amount** at a **particular price** on a **stipulated future date**.

- **Currency futures** are contracts for the sale or purchase at a set future date of a set quantity of currency. A step-by-step approach can be used to deal with complications.

Transaction on future date		Now		On future date	
Receive	currency	Sell	currency futures	Buy	currency futures
Pay	currency	Buy	currency futures	Sell	currency futures
Receive	$	Buy	currency futures	Sell	currency futures
Pay	$	Sell	currency futures	Buy	currency futures

- The choice between the **forward** and **futures** market will depend on **availability, flexibility** and **transaction costs** as well as outcomes.

- **Economic exposure** can be hedged by **matching assets and liabilities** and **diversification**.

- **Translation exposure,** the risk of apparent losses appearing when accounting results are translated, probably does not need to be hedged.

Quick Quiz

1. Identify the three types of currency risk.
2. Define a 'forward exchange rate'.
3. The principle of purchasing power parity must always hold.

   ☐ True

   ☐ False

4. What is the difference between a direct quote and an indirect quote for a currency?
5. **Fill in the blanks**

   (a) Forward rate higher than spot rate is quoted at a _____

   (b) Forward rate lower than spot rate is quoted at a _____
6. What steps can be taken in money markets to cover a foreign currency receipt in the future from a debtor?
7. What is meant by closing out a futures contract?
8. Complete the following table.

Transaction on future date		Now		On future date	
Receive	currency		currency futures		currency futures
Pay	currency		currency futures		currency futures
Receive	$		currency futures		currency futures
Pay	$		currency futures		currency futures

Answers to Quick Quiz

1. (a) Transaction risk
   (b) Translation risk
   (c) Economic risk

2. An exchange rate set for the exchange of currencies at some future date

3. False. In reality commodity prices do differ significantly in different countries.

4. A direct quote is the amount of domestic currency which is equal to one foreign currency unit.
   An indirect quote is the amount of foreign currency that is equal to one domestic currency unit.

5. (a) Discount
   (b) Premium

6. (a) Borrow an appropriate amount in the foreign currency today
   (b) Convert it immediately to home currency
   (c) Place on deposit home currency
   (d) When the debtor's cash is received, repay the foreign currency loan and take the cash from the home currency deposit account

7. Entering a second futures contract that reverses the effect of the first one

8.

Transaction on future date		Now		On future date	
Receive	currency	Sell	currency futures	Buy	currency futures
Pay	currency	Buy	currency futures	Sell	currency futures
Receive	$	Buy	currency futures	Sell	currency futures
Pay	$	Sell	currency futures	Buy	currency futures

LEARNING OUTCOME 4 INTERNATIONAL FINANCE AND INTEREST RATE RISK

End of chapter questions

1 Eye plc (AIA November 2012)

Eye plc is a UK company that manufactures glass for windows. It has received a large order for glass from a construction company based in the USA. The US company requires invoicing in $ and the value of the order has been agreed at $322,000. You should assume that today's date is 1 November 2012 and that the US company is due to pay the $322,000 in three months on 1 February 2013. The spot rate on 1 November 2012 is 1.5731 – 1.5754 $/£. The company wishes to hedge the exchange rate risk using futures contracts. Futures contracts are available on the Chicago Mercantile Exchange on 1 November 2012 as follows:

GBP/USD futures:

Settlement date	Price
December 2012	1.5683
March 2013	1.5624

The contract size for these futures is £62,500 and the tick size $0.0001.

Eye plc is also exporting to another country (assume this country is called Bithland). This country has a floating exchange rate system, but it is more difficult to hedge against foreign exchange risk in respect of this country. The country has a developing economy that has grown rapidly in the last five years. This growth has largely been due to substantial deposits of minerals and raw materials including copper, iron, gold and zinc. This has increased the level of exports substantially and has attracted overseas investment. However, the economy has not been well managed. The balance of payments is in deficit and the rate of inflation is relatively high. There has been political instability in the past, although the current government is quite popular.

Required

(a) Prepare calculations that evaluate the outcome of the hedge for Eye plc assuming that on 1 February 2013 the spot rate is 1.5446 – 1.5571 and the price for March 2013 futures contracts is 1.5402. **(8 marks)**

(b) Eye plc are concerned about their exposure to exchange rate risk in respect of exports to Bithland. Using the information provided about Bithland in the question, you are required to advise Eye plc on how the different factors may influence the future exchange rate for Bithland. **(12 marks)**

(Total 20 marks)

2 ZXY International plc (AIA November 2007)

ZXY International plc is a UK-based company which imports and exports consumable goods.

The details of transactions for settlement in three months' time are as follows:

	Receipts	Payments
Belgium	€900,000	€800,000
Netherlands	€200,000	€600,000
USA	US$460,000	US$350,000
Malaysia	RM246,000	RM144,000

Foreign Exchange Rates

	Euro/£	US$/£	RM/£
Spot	1.6227 – 1.6259	1.4267 – 1.4291	5.4213 – 5.4321
3 months forward	1.6177 – 1.6209	1.4196 – 1.4221	Not available

Annual Interest Rates (valid for three months)

	Borrowing	Investing
UK	6.00%	4.00%
Belgium	4.75%	2.50%
Netherlands	4.75%	2.50%
USA	4.00%	2.00%
Malaysia	N/A	3.00%

Required

(a) Devise a foreign exchange hedging strategy that is designed to maximise ZXY International's net cash inflows in respect of the above overseas transactions at the end of three months. Use forward contracts or money market hedges as appropriate. **(14 marks)**

(b) Money market hedges make certain assumptions which may cause misleading decisions to be made. Discuss this and suggest how this problem might be overcome. **(6 marks)**

(Total 20 marks)

LEARNING OUTCOME 4 INTERNATIONAL FINANCE AND INTEREST RATE RISK

Foreign exchange risk: options

Topic list	Syllabus reference
1 The nature of options	LO4
2 Currency options	LO4
3 Traded currency options – some complications	LO4
4 A graphical approach to options	LO4
5 Collars and other option combinations	LO4
6 Theory of the valuation of options	LO4
7 Applications of options theory	LO4

Introduction

Options can take various forms and are important as a form of hedging instrument. The chapter opens with a general introduction to options, including **share options**. Your syllabus requires a working knowledge of options, especially currency options and interest rate options. **Currency options**, the main subject of this chapter, provide a flexible method of hedging currency transactions exposure in the same sorts of situation where forward contracts, money market hedges or futures were used in the last chapter. Again a step-by-step approach will be helpful.

The syllabus also requires a general understanding of how options can be **valued**. This is dealt with at the end of this chapter. Numerical questions will **not** be set on the Black Scholes option pricing model.

LEARNING OUTCOME 4 INTERNATIONAL FINANCE AND INTEREST RATE RISK

1 The nature of options

> **FAST FORWARD**
>
> Options give the **right** but **not the obligation** to buy or sell an asset.

1.1 The nature of an option

Key term

> An **option** is an agreement giving the **right but not the obligation** to buy or to sell a specific quantity of something (eg shares in a company, a foreign currency or a commodity) at a known or determinable price within a stated period.

The key to options of all types is that they give the holder a **right** but not an **obligation**. For example, the holder of share options at a £2 exercise price has a right to buy the shares at £2 but need not exercise this right if it is not to his or her advantage. If the market price of the shares has fallen to £1.80 then the option will not be exercised. **Options offer a choice** between:

(a) **Exercising** your right to buy or sell at a pre-determined price (known as the **exercise price**, or **strike price**), and

(b) Not exercising this right: allowing the option to lapse, sometimes known as **abandoning** the option – an option which is not used is either discarded or, possibly, sold to somebody else who might find it valuable, if the rules allow this

It is this element of **choice** which is the **distinction between options and futures** or forward contracts.

2 Currency options

> **FAST FORWARD**
>
> **Currency options** protect against adverse exchange rate movements while allowing the investor to take advantage of favourable exchange rate movements. They are particularly useful in situations where the cash flow is not certain to occur (eg when tendering for overseas contracts).

2.1 Currency options as hedging mechanism

Forward exchange contracts and currency futures contracts are contracts to buy or sell a given quantity of foreign exchange, which must be carried out because they are binding contracts. Some exporters might be uncertain about the amount of currency they will earn in several months time, and so would be unable to enter forward exchange contracts or futures contracts without the risk of contracting to sell more or less currency to their bank than they will actually earn when the time comes. An alternative method of obtaining foreign exchange cover which overcomes much of the problem is the **foreign currency option**.

Key term

> A **currency option** is an agreement involving a right, but not an obligation, to buy or to sell a certain amount of currency at a stated rate of exchange (the **exercise price**) at some time in the future.

As with other types of option, **buying** a currency option involves **paying a non-refundable premium upfront**, which is the most the buyer of the option can lose. **Selling** (or 'writing') options, unless covered by other transactions, is risky because the seller ('writer') bears the whole of the cost of the variation and can face potentially unlimited losses. It is very rare for companies (other than specialist traders) to sell options.

2.2 Currency option terminology

Some terminology relating to traded options was explained in the previous section of the chapter in the context of options to buy and sell shares. Much of the same terminology applies to currency options.

(a) **Call options** give the buyer of the option the right to buy the underlying currency at a **fixed rate of exchange** (and the seller of the option would be required to sell the underlying currency at that rate).

(b) **Put options** give the buyer of the option the right to sell the underlying currency at a **fixed rate of exchange** (and the seller of the option would be required to buy the underlying currency at that rate).

(c) The **exercise price** may be the same as the current spot rate, or it may be more favourable or less favourable to the option holder than the current spot rate. Options are **at the money**, **in the money** or **out of the money** accordingly.

(d) **Over the counter (OTC)** or **negotiated currency options** are tailor-made options available from a bank, suited to the company's specific needs. **Traded options** or **exchange-traded** options are standardised options, available from an options exchange in certain currencies only.

2.3 Currency option quotations

A company wishing to purchase an option to buy or sell sterling might use currency options traded on the important Philadelphia Stock Exchange. The schedule of prices for £/$ options is set out in tables such as the one shown below.

Philadelphia SE £/$ options £31,250 (cents per pound)

Strike price	Calls Aug	Calls Sep	Calls Oct	Puts Aug	Puts Sep	Puts Oct
1.5750	2.58	3.13	–	–	0.67	–
1.5800	2.14	2.77	3.24	–	0.81	1.32
1.5900	1.23	2.17	2.64	0.05	1.06	1.71
1.6000	0.50	1.61	2.16	0.32	1.50	2.18
1.6100	0.15	1.16	1.71	0.93	2.05	2.69
1.6200	–	0.81	1.33	1.79	2.65	3.30

Note the following points.

(a) The contract size is £31,250.

(b) If a firm wished to have the **option to buy pounds** (selling dollars) in September, it can buy a **call option on sterling**. To have the option to buy pounds at an exchange rate of $1.5800/£, it would need to pay a premium of 2.77 cents per pound (check for yourself in the table). For a higher exchange rate, the premium is lower, since the higher exchange rate is less favourable to the buyer of the option: more dollars are needed to buy the same number of pounds.

(c) A **put option** here is the **option to sell sterling** in exchange for dollars. Note that a put option with a strike price of 1.6000 $/£ exercisable in September is, at 1.50 cents per pound, cheaper than a September put option exercisable at 1.6100 $/£, which is available at a premium of 2.05 cents per pound. The premium on put options is higher for the higher exchange rate since the purchaser will receive more dollars for each pound sold than with the lower exchange rate.

(d) Note that a call option with a strike price of 1.6000 $/£ exercisable in September will **cost more** than an option with the same strike price which is exercisable in August. This difference reflects the fact that for the September option there is a **longer period** until the exercise date and consequently the likelihood of it being beneficial to exercise the option is increased (ie it is more likely to be 'in the money' at the exercise date). The difference also reflects the market's view of the direction in which the exchange rate is likely to move between the two dates.

LEARNING OUTCOME 4 INTERNATIONAL FINANCE AND INTEREST RATE RISK

2.4 Using currency options

The main purpose of currency options is to **reduce exposure** to **adverse currency movements**, while allowing the holder to profit from favourable currency movements. They are particularly useful for companies in the following situations.

(a) Where there is **uncertainty** about **foreign currency receipts** or **payments**, either in timing or amount. Should the foreign exchange transaction not materialise, the option can be sold on the market (if it has any value) or exercised if this would make a profit.

(b) To **support the tender** for an **overseas contract**, priced in a foreign currency (see example below).

(c) To **allow the publication of price lists** for its goods in a foreign currency.

(d) To **protect the import or export** of price-sensitive goods. If there is a favourable movement in exchange rates, options allow the importer/exporter to profit from the favourable change (unlike forward exchange contracts, when the importer/exporter is **tied** to a **fixed rate of exchange** by the binding contract). This means that the gains can be passed on in the prices to the importer's or exporter's customers.

In both situations (b) and (c), the company would not know whether it had won any export sales or would have any foreign currency income at the time that it announces its selling prices. It cannot make a forward exchange contract to sell foreign currency without becoming exposed in the currency.

2.5 Example: Using currency options

Tartan plc has been invited to tender for a contract in Blueland with the bid priced in Blues (the local currency). Tartan thinks that the contract would cost £1,850,000. Because of the fierce competition for the bid, Tartan is prepared to price the contract at £2,000,000, and since the exchange rate is currently B2.8 = £1, it puts in a bid of B5,600,000. The contract will not be awarded until after six months.

What can happen to Tartan with the contract? There are two 'worst possible' outcomes.

(a) Tartan plc decides to **hedge against the currency risk**, and on the assumption that it will be awarded the contract in six months' time, it enters into a **forward exchange contract** to sell B5,600,000 in six months' time at a rate of B2.8 = £1.

As it turns out, the company fails to win the contract and so it must buy B5,600,000 spot to meet its obligation under the forward contract. The exchange rate has changed, say, to B2.5 = £1.

	£
At the outset:	
Tartan sells B5,600,000 forward at B2.8 to £1	2,000,000
Six months later:	
Tartan buys B5,600,000 spot to cover the hedge, at B2.5 to £1	(2,240,000)
Loss	(240,000)

(b) Alternatively, Tartan plc might decide not to make a forward exchange contract at all, but to wait and see what happens. As it turns out, Tartan is awarded the contract six months later, but by this time, the value of the Blue has fallen, say, to B3.2 = £1.

	£
Tartan wins the contract for B5,600,000, which has a sterling value of (B3.2 = £1)	1,750,000
Cost of the contract	(1,850,000)
Loss	(100,000)

(c) A **currency option** would, for a fixed cost, **eliminate these risks** for Tartan plc. When it makes its tender for the contract, Tartan might purchase an over-the-counter currency option to sell B5,600,000 in six months' time at B2.8 to £1, at a cost of £40,000.

The worst possible outcome for Tartan plc is now a loss of £40,000.

(i) If the company **fails to win the contract**, Tartan will abandon the option (unless the exchange rate has moved in Tartan's favour and the Blue has weakened against sterling so that the company can make a profit by buying B5,600,000 at the spot rate and selling it at B2.8 = £1).

(ii) If the company **wins the contract** and the exchange rate of the Blue has weakened against sterling, Tartan will **exercise the option** and sell the Blues at 2.80.

	£	£
Proceeds from selling B5,600,000		2,000,000
Cost of contract	1,850,000	
Cost of currency option	40,000	
		1,890,000
Net profit		110,000

(d) If the Blue has **strengthened against sterling**, Tartan will **abandon the option**. For example, if Tartan wins the contract and the exchange rate has moved to B2.5 = £1, Tartan will sell the B5,600,000 at this rate to earn £2,240,000, and will incur costs, including the abandoned currency option, of £1,890,000.

	£	£
Proceeds from selling B5,600,000		2,240,000
Cost of contract	1,850,000	
Cost of currency option	40,000	
		1,890,000
Net profit		350,000

2.6 Comparison of currency options with forward contracts and futures contracts

In the last chapter, we saw that a hedge using a currency future will produce approximately the same result as a currency forward contract, subject to hedge inefficiencies. When comparing currency options with forward or futures contracts we usually find the following.

(a) If the currency movement is adverse, the option will be exercised, but the hedge will not normally be quite as good as that of the forward or futures contract; this is because of the **premium cost of the option**.

(b) If the currency movement is favourable, the option will not be exercised, and the result will normally be better than that of the forward or futures contract; this is because the option allows the holder to **profit from the improved exchange rate**.

These points are illustrated by the next series of examples.

2.7 Example: Currency options (1)

Crabtree plc is expecting to receive 20 million South African rands (R) in one month's time. The current spot rate is R/£ 19.3383 – 19.3582. Compare the results of the following actions.

(a) The receipt is hedged using a forward contract at the rate 19.3048.

(b) The receipt is hedged by buying an over-the-counter (OTC) option from the bank, exercise price R/£ 19.3000, premium cost 12 pence per 100 schillings.

(c) The receipt is not hedged.

In each case compute the results if, in one month, the exchange rate moves to:

(a) 21.0000
(b) 17.6000

Solution

The target receipt at today's spot rate is 20,000,000/19.3582 = £1,033,154.

(a) The receipt using a forward contract is fixed with certainty at 20,000,000/19.3048 = £1,036,012. This applies to both exchange rate scenarios.

(b) The cost of the option is 20,000,000/100 × 12/100 = £24,000. This must be paid at the start of the contract.

The results under the two scenarios are as follows:

Scenario	(a)	(b)
Exchange rate	21.0000	17.6000
Exercise price	19.3000	19.3000
Exercise option?	YES	NO
Exchange rate used	19.3000	17.6000
	£	£
Pounds received	1,036,269	1,136,364
Less option premium	24,000	24,000
Net receipt	1,012,269	1,112,364

(c) The results of not hedging under the two scenarios are as follows:

Scenario	(a)	(b)
Exchange rate	21.0000	17.6000
Pounds received	£952,381	£1,136,364

Summary. The option gives a result between that of the forward contract and no hedge.

- If the South African rand weakens to 21.0000, the best result would have been obtained using the forward market (£1,036,012).

- If it strengthens to 17.6000, the best course of action would have been to take no hedge (£1,136,364).

- In both cases the option gives the second best result, being £24,000 below the best because of its premium cost.

2.8 Example: Currency options (2)

In **Example: Currency options (1)**, by how much would the exchange rate have moved if the forward and option contracts gave the same result? Comment on your answer.

Solution

The forward contract gives a receipt of £1,036,012 whatever the movement in exchange rate. If the option is to give a net receipt of £1,036,012, it must give a gross amount (before deducting the premium) of £1,036,012 + £24,000 = £1,060,012. This implies that the exchange rate has moved to 20,000,000/1,060,012 = 18.8700 rands to the pound.

The option will not be exercised at this exchange rate. It is allowed to lapse, giving an exchange gain which just covers the premium cost. The option becomes advantageous over a forward contract if the exchange rate strengthens beyond 18.8700 rands to the pound.

2.9 Example: Currency options (3)

Prices (premiums) on 1 June for Sterling traded currency options on the Philadelphia Stock Exchange are shown in the following table.

Sterling £31,250 contracts (cents per £)

Exercise price	Calls		Puts	
$/£	September	December	September	December
1.5000	5.55	7.95	0.42	1.95
1.5500	2.75	3.85	4.15	6.30
1.6000	0.25	1.00	9.40	11.20

Prices are quoted in cents per £. On the same date, the September sterling futures contract (contract size £62,500) is trading at $/£ 1.5390 and the current spot exchange rate is $1.5404 – $1.5425. Stark Inc, a US company, is due to receive sterling £3.75 million from a debtor in four months' time at the end of September. The treasurer decides to hedge this receipt using either September £ traded options or September £ futures.

Required

Compute the results of using

(a) Futures
(b) Options hedges

(illustrating the results with all three possible option exercise prices) if by the end of September the spot exchange rate moves to (i) 1.4800; (ii) 1.5700; (iii) 1.6200. Assume that the futures price moves by the same amount as the spot rate and that by the end of September the options contracts are on the last day before expiry.

Solution

The target receipt is 3,750,000 × 1.5404* = $5,776,500.

*The American company gets the lower number of dollars for selling sterling.

A receipt of £3.75 million will represent 3,750,000/62,500 = 60 futures contracts or 3,750,000/31,250 = 120 option contracts. The value of a one-tick movement will be $6.25 on the futures contract (and $3.125 on the options contract, although this figure will not be needed in the calculation).

(a) If we make the assumption that the futures price moves by the same amount as the spot rate, there will be no basis risk and the future will give a perfect hedge.

On 1 June, 60 sterling futures contracts are sold for $1.5390 (a price which is $0.0014 below the spot rate). The results of this hedge are as follows.

Scenario	(i)	(ii)	(iii)
Spot rate, 30 Sept	1.4800	1.5700	1.6200
Sell 60 at	1.5390	1.5390	1.5390
Buy 60 at (spot – 0.0014)	1.4786	1.5686	1.6186
Gain/(loss) in ticks	604	(296)	(796)
	$	$	$
Value of gain/(loss)	226,500	(111,000)	(298,500)
£3.75 million sold at spot for	5,550,000	5,887,500	6,075,000
Total net receipt	5,776,500	5,776,500	5,776,500

LEARNING OUTCOME 4 INTERNATIONAL FINANCE AND INTEREST RATE RISK

(b) Using options, the treasurer will purchase 120 September **put** options. The premium cost will vary with the exercise price as follows.

Exercise price	Cost $
1.5000	120 × 0.42/100 × 31,250 = $15,750
1.5500	120 × 4.15/100 × 31,250 = $155,625
1.6000	120 × 9.40/100 × 31,250 = $352,500

Scenario 1

Spot rate moves to 1.4800.

In all cases, exercise the option and sell £3.75 million at the exercise price.

Exercise price $/£	Cash received $	Premium cost $	Net $	
1.5000	5,625,000	(15,750)	5,609,250	
1.5500	5,812,500	(155,625)	5,656,875	← Best result
1.6000	6,000,000	(352,500)	5,647,500	

Scenario 2

Spot rate moves to 1.5700.

Exercise price	Exercise option?	Exchange rate used	Cash received $	Premium cost $	Net $	
1.5000	No	1.57	5,887,500	(15,750)	5,871,750	← Best result
1.5500	No	1.57	5,887,500	(155,625)	5,731,875	
1.6000	Yes	1.60	6,000,000	(352,500)	5,647,500	

Scenario 3

Spot rate moves to 1.6200.

In all cases, abandon the option.

Cash received = $6,075,000

Exercise price $/£	Cash received $	Premium cost $	Net $	
1.5000	6,075,000	(15,750)	6,059,250	← Best result
1.5500	6,075,000	(155,625)	5,919,375	
1.6000	6,075,000	(352,500)	5,722,500	

Summary. The futures hedge achieves the target exactly. The options give a range of possible results around the target. As in the previous example when the option is exercised, it does not give as good a result as the future. However, when the option is allowed to lapse because of a favourable movement in the exchange rate, it allows the company to make a gain over target.

> **Exam focus point**
>
> Make sure you appreciate the differences between how futures and options work. The examiner has complained regularly that many students don't.

2.10 Deciding on the exercise price

It is possible to do a **simple computation** to predict the best exercise price under each scenario. If the pound strengthens, as in scenarios (ii) and (iii), the options are not needed, so, with the benefit of hindsight, the best option is the one with the cheapest premium (just as the best car insurance is the cheapest, provided you don't need to use it!) In this case it is the 1.50 exercise price.

However, if the pound weakens the **options** will be **exercised**. The best exercise price will be the one which gives the highest net $ per £ when the premium is deducted. For this purpose, the premium must be expressed as $ per £ (ie divide the quoted premium by 100).

Best option if exercised

Exercise price	Premium	Net	
$/£	$/£	$/£	
1.5000	(0.0042)	1.4958	
1.5500	(0.0415)	1.5085	← Best result
1.6000	(0.0940)	1.5060	

Thus, in scenario (i), the best option is the 1.5500 exercise price.

3 Traded currency options – some complications

FAST FORWARD

Surplus cash may, but need not be, covered on the forward market.

Currency options are often **closed out** rather than **expire**.

Transaction on future date		Now		On future date	
Receive	currency	Buy	currency put	Sell	currency
Pay	currency	Buy	currency call	Buy	currency
Receive	$	Buy	currency call	Buy	currency
Pay	$	Buy	currency put	Sell	currency

3.1 Using traded options

The last example showed how traded options can be used as a hedge to reduce currency losses while allowing the possibility of exchange gains if there are favourable exchange rate movements. As with futures, a number of complications are encountered when using traded options. The most important of these complications are:

- Choosing the correct type of option (call or put)
- Choosing the strike price and the number of contracts to be used
- Surplus cash when the number of contracts is rounded
- Closing out when traded options still have time to run
- Use of collars to reduce the option premium cost

3.2 Choosing the correct type of option

In the previous example the American company needed to sell pounds sterling. It therefore purchased options to sell pounds, which are sterling put options. Note that the vast majority of options examples which we consider are concerned with **hedgers** who **purchase** options in order to reduce risk.

So, given that we are normally going to **purchase** options, should we **purchase puts or calls**? With OTC options there is usually no problem in making this decision. If, for example, we may need to buy US dollars at some stage in the future, we can hedge by purchasing a US dollar call option. With traded options, however, we run into the same problem as with futures. Only a limited number of currencies are available and there is no US dollar option as such. We have to **rephrase the company's requirements**, as we did with futures.

LEARNING OUTCOME 4 INTERNATIONAL FINANCE AND INTEREST RATE RISK

(a) A UK company wishing to sell US dollars in the future can hedge by purchasing £ sterling call options (ie options to buy sterling with dollars).

(b) Similarly, a German company which needs to buy US dollars can hedge by purchasing euro put options.

Transaction on future date		Now		On future date	
Receive	currency	Buy	currency put	Sell	currency
Pay	currency	Buy	currency call	Buy	currency
Receive	$	Buy	currency call	Buy	currency
Pay	$	Buy	currency put	Sell	currency

3.3 Choosing the exercise price and the number of contracts to be used

When the American company wished to sell £3.75 million, the computation of the number of contracts (with a contract size of £31,250) was easy (£3,750,000/£31,250 = 120 option contracts). A problem arises when a non-US company wishes to buy or sell US dollars using traded options. The amount of US dollars must first be converted into the home currency. For this purpose the best exchange rate to use is the **exercise price**, which means that the number of contracts may vary according to which exercise price is chosen. The following example demonstrates this problem.

3.3.1 Example: Choosing the exercise price and the number of options to be used

A British company needs to hedge the receipt of US$ 10 million from an American customer at the end of June. The spot rate is (US$/£) 1.4461 – 1.4492 and the 30 June forward rate is 1.4050 – 1.4101. The following currency options are available.

Sterling £31,250 contracts (cents per £)

Exercise price $/£	Calls June	Puts June
1.4000	5.74	7.89
1.4250	3.40	9.06
1.4500	1.94	11.52
1.4750	0.89	14.69

The company needs to purchase sterling call options. If the exercise price chosen is 1.4000, the value of $10 million is £7,142,857, which is 228.57 contracts. If the exercise price of 1.4750 is used, the $10 million becomes £6,779,661, which is 216.95 contracts. Under such circumstances it sometimes becomes too lengthy (in exam-style questions) to test out the results of all possible exercise prices in detail. It may be better to choose one exercise price to demonstrate how the option works.

There are various ways of choosing an exercise price and an appropriate number of contracts and in the end the choice is subjective. However the following method is suggested for exam questions. The company wants to pay as little as possible for its pounds. Assuming the options are to be exercised, it can find this cheapest figure by **adding together** the **exercise prices and the premiums**, as in the example in the previous section.

Exercise price $/£	Premium $/£	Total $/£	
1.4000	0.0574	1.4574	← Best (cheapest cost per £)
1.4250	0.0340	1.4590	
1.4500	0.0194	1.4694	
1.4750	0.0089	1.4839	

The cheapest total cost per pound is $1.4574 resulting from an exercise price of 1.4000. At this exercise price, the receipt of $10 million converts to £7,142,857 which, with a contract size of £31,250, represents 228.57 contracts, rounded to 229.

As stated above, many alternatives are available for choosing an exercise price. Some might choose the 1.4750 exercise price, simply because it has the **cheapest premium**. This would be the best option if the **dollar strengthens** and the option is abandoned. Others might choose the **exercise price nearest the spot rate**, and still others might choose the **exercise price nearest the June forward rate**. In the end there is no right answer, because the future is unknown.

3.4 Surplus cash when the number of contracts is rounded

Assume that a UK company chooses to hedge the receipt of $10 million by purchasing 229 June £ call option contracts, exercise price 1.4000 $/£ at a premium of 5.74 cents per £. Demonstrate the result if the spot rate on June 30 is (i) 1.5500; (ii) 1.3500.

The premium cost is 229 × $0.0574 × 31,250 = $410,769. This must be purchased at today's spot $/£ rate, which is 1.4461, giving a cost of £284,053.

Scenario (i)

The option will be exercised and £31,250 × 229 = £7,156,250 will be purchased with 7,156,250 × 1.4000 = $10,018,750. The customer provides $10,000,000, but $18,750 has to be purchased at the June 30 spot rate of 1.5500 $/£, giving an additional cost of £12,097. (Note that this additional amount **could** have been covered on the forward market, but that this would have created an exchange loss under Scenario (ii) when the option is abandoned. We therefore assume that forward cover is not taken.)

The total sterling amount received from the sale of $10 million is:

	£
Option premium paid	(284,053)
£ purchased by exercising option	7,156,250
Purchase of surplus $ on 30 June	(12,097)
Net £ received	6,860,100

Note. An approximate result can be obtained by converting $10,000,000 at 1.4574 (the sum of the exercise price and the option premium) giving £6,861,534. However, this method ignores the fact that the premium is paid in advance and that surplus $ must be purchased at the end.

Scenario (ii)

The option is abandoned. $10,000,000 is converted at the spot rate 1.3500, giving £7,407,407. After subtracting the option premium of £284,053, the net receipt is £7,123,354.

Exam focus point

The position with options is equivalent to the position with futures; the expiry date of the option must be **on or after** the date of the key event. Thus if you were told that a company was receiving a payment on 10 September and you were given a choice of using June, September or December options:

- You **would** most likely choose **September** as that expires the soonest after 10 September (on 30 September)

- You **could** choose **December**

- You **would not** choose **June** (as June options expire before 10 September, the date on which you will receive the payment)

3.5 Closing out when traded options still have time to run

The above example assumes that the traded option is at its expiry date when the decision needs to be made between exercising or abandoning. In practice, most traded options are **closed out**, like futures contracts, because the date when the cash is required does not match the option expiry date.

Suppose that the company in the above example was due to receive $10 million on 10 June. Then June option contracts would still be used, but on 10 June the decision that needs to be made is whether to **close out** the option, to **exercise it** or to allow it to **lapse**. Closing out will be more beneficial than exercising or allowing to lapse if the option still has a positive time value.

3.6 Dealing with an options question

Because of the complications, it is best to use a similar method to the method we used for futures to assess the impact of options.

Step 1   Set up the hedge

(a) Choose contract date
(b) Decide whether put or call option required
(c) Decide which strike price applies
(d) How many contracts
(e) Tick size
(f) The premium may need to be converted using the spot rate

Step 2   Ascertain closing prices

If you are not given the price to use in the option calculation in Step 3 (b) below, you may have to work it out using basis (see Chapter 16), or you may have to assume that it is the same as the closing spot price.

Step 3   Calculate outcome of hedge

You may have to calculate the outcome under more than one closing spot rate.

(a) Outcome in options market. This will include deciding whether to exercise the option
(b) Net outcome

3.7 Example: Dealing with an options question

A UK company owes a US supplier $2,000,000 payable in July. The spot rate is 1.5350-1.5370 $/£ and the UK company is concerned that the $ might strengthen.

The details on the Philadelphia Stock Exchange for $/£ £31,250 options (cents per £1) are as follows:

Strike price	Calls			Puts		
	June	July	August	June	July	August
1.4750	6.34	6.37	6.54	0.07	0.19	0.50
1.5000	3.86	4.22	4.59	0.08	0.53	1.03
1.5250	1.58	2.50	2.97	0.18	1.25	1.89

Show how traded $/£ currency options can be used to hedge the risk at 1.5250. Calculate the sterling cost of the transaction if the spot rate in July is:

(a) $1.4600 – $1.4620
(b) $1.6100 – $1.6120

Solution

Step 1 Set up the hedge

(a) Which date contract?   July

(b) Put or call?   Put, we need to put (sell) pounds in order to generate the dollars we need

(c) Which strike price?   1.5250

(d) How many contracts

$$\frac{2{,}000{,}000 \div 1.525}{31{,}250} \approx 42 \text{ contracts}$$

(e) Tick size = 31,250 × 0.0001 = $3.125

(f) Premium = $\frac{1.25}{100} \times 31{,}250 \times 42$

= $16,406 @ 1.5350
= £10,688

We need to pay for the option in $ now. Therefore the bank sells low at 1.5350.

Step 2 Closing prices

Case (a) $1.4600
Case (b) $1.6100

Step 3 Outcome

	Case (a) $1.4600	Case (b) $1.6100
(a) Options market outcomes		
Strike price put (sell at)	1.5250	1.5250
Closing price (buy at)	1.4600	1.6100
Exercise?	Yes	No
If exercised, tick movement	650	–
Outcome of options position	650 × 42 × $3.125 = $85,313	–
(b) Net outcome	$	$
Spot market payment	(2,000,000)	(2,000,000)
Option market	85,313	–
	(1,914,687)	(2,000,000)
	£	£
Translated at closing spot rate 1.46/1.61	(1,311,429)	(1,242,236)
Premium (remember premium has to be added in separately as translated at the **opening** spot rate)	(10,688)	(10,688)
	(1,322,117)	(1,252,924)

3.8 The drawbacks of currency options

The major drawbacks of currency options are as follows.

(a) The **cost is about 5%** of the **total amount** of **foreign exchange covered**, although the exact amount depends on the expected volatility of the exchange rate.

(b) **Options** must be **paid for as soon** as they are bought.

(c) **Tailor-made options lack negotiability**.

(d) Traded options are **not available** in every currency.

4 A graphical approach to options

FAST FORWARD

Options can be illustrated **graphically** by plotting price of underlying instrument against profit.

4.1 Illustrating options graphically

A **graphical approach** to options may help you to understand options more fully.

4.2 Graphical illustration of currency options

The graphical approach can also be used to illustrate **currency options**. Suppose that a UK-based company expects to receive an amount of export income in dollars ($) in three months' time. Figure 1 illustrates the profit/loss profile of different strategies.

(a) Selling dollars and buying sterling in the forward market **eliminates all uncertainty**. The outcome is represented by a horizontal line.

(b) Relying on the spot market results in a **net gain or loss** compared with the forward market if the spot exchange rate in three months' time turns out to be below or above $X per pound respectively.

(c) If a call option is used, it will not be exercised if the exchange rate is less than $X per pound. A currency call option reduces the potential gain compared with the spot market strategy (b) by the amount of the premium on the option, but has the advantage that potential losses are contained as they will not exceed the value of the premium.

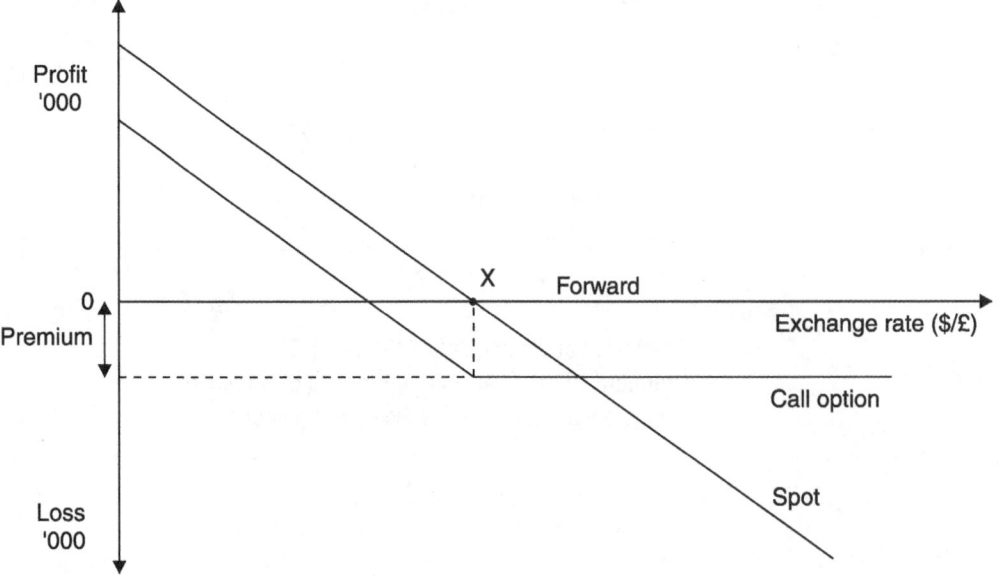

Figure 1 Currency call option, forward and spot markets: profit/loss profile

5 Collars and other option combinations

FAST FORWARD

Various combinations of options are possible. **Collars** are an important example:

- Fear currency will **strengthen**; purchase call, sell put
- Fear currency will **weaken**; sell call, purchase put

5.1 Collars

Speculators and hedgers have devised many combinations of purchasing and writing options. One of the most important combinations for hedgers is the **collar**. This is illustrated in the following paragraphs, after which other possible combinations will be described in outline.

5.2 How to construct a collar

One of the main problems with purchasing an option is that the premium cost **reduces the value of the hedge** and tends to wipe out any potential gains that might be made. A collar is an attempt to reduce the premium cost. It is achieved by simultaneously purchasing and writing options. The premium income from the sale of an option offsets the premium paid for the purchase of the other. It's just a way of reducing the cost of using an option. **A collar can work in one of two ways**. We can:

- Purchase a call option and simultaneously sell a put option
- Purchase a put option and simultaneously sell a call option

As we shall see, the advantage of the reduced premium cost is balanced by the fact that we allow a limit to be imposed on our potential gains. The techniques can be illustrated using over-the-counter currency options.

Using traded options, a number of different collars can be created. The put and call should have the **same expiry date** and the **same number of contracts** but a range of exercise prices is possible.

5.3 Collar if currency is expected to strengthen

If we need to buy a currency at some future date and we fear that it may strengthen, we can:

- **Purchase a call option** from a bank (to protect us in case the currency strengthens)
- At the same time, **sell a put option** to the bank (in order to get some money to offset against the cost of our call option)

Both options should be for the same amount of currency.

The premium which we receive for writing the put option will be offset against the premium cost of the call option, lowering our initial outlay substantially without reducing the protection against a strengthening currency. However, as a result of this strategy, we will place a limit on the gains we can make if the currency weakens.

Exam focus point

You need to have an understanding of caps, floors and collars but numeric questions will not be set.

5.3.1 Example: Collar if the currency is expected to strengthen

Suppose we will need to purchase Swiss francs with US dollars in one month's time and the current spot rate is $0.6100 per SFr. We can protect ourselves by purchasing a Swiss franc call option (exercise price, say, $0.6200 per SFr) and then get some money back by selling a Swiss franc put option (exercise price, say, $0.6000 per SFr). In a collar of this type, the exercise price of the call option needs to be a higher figure than that of the put option. Why is this?

Our objective is to place a **ceiling** on the **maximum cost** for the currency (in this case $0.6200 to be paid for every SFr purchased). This maximum cost is determined by the **call** option we have purchased.

However, if the exchange rate weakens below $0.6000 per SFr, the bank will exercise its put option. Since we wrote the put option, the bank has the right to sell us SFr for $0.6000.

In other words we will be forced to buy SFr for $0.6000. The **put** option determines the **minimum cost** we must pay for the currency. Consequently, the exercise price for the call option will need to be a larger figure than the exercise price for the put option.

In summary, the collar can be achieved by purchasing a Swiss franc call option at an exercise price of $0.6200 per SFr and selling a Swiss franc put option at an exercise price of $0.6000 per SFr.

Question — Exchange rate movements

Show what happens if the exchange rate moves to (i) 0.6300 $/SFr; (ii) 0.5900 $/SFr; (iii) What happens if it remains at 0.6100 $/SFr?

Answer

(a) If the SFr strengthens to $0.6300 we will exercise our call option to buy at $0.6200. The bank will not exercise its put option. The SFr are therefore bought at $0.6200.

(b) If the SFr weakens to $0.5900 we will not want to exercise our call option, but the bank will exercise the right to sell SFr to us at the agreed price of $0.6000. We will therefore be forced to purchase SFr at $0.6000. The overall effect of the collar is that we have a maximum cost of $0.6200 per SFr and a minimum cost of $0.6000. The premium cost must be added to these figures, but this will be small because the proceeds from selling the put option are offset against the cost of the call option.

(c) If the spot rate stays between the two exercise prices of $0.6000 and $0.6200 then neither of the options will be exercised and the Swiss francs are simply bought at the spot rate. So if the spot rate stays at $0.6100, the SFr will be bought at $0.6100.

5.4 Collar if the currency is expected to weaken

If we need to sell a currency at some future date and we fear that it may weaken, we can **purchase a put option** and simultaneously **sell a call option** for the same amount of currency. The premium which we receive for selling the call option will offset our premium cost of the put option. The exercise price for the put option will need to be a lower figure than the exercise price for the call option.

For example, if we need to sell SFr for US$, we might **purchase a Swiss franc put option at an exercise price of $0.6000 per SFr and sell a Swiss franc call option at an exercise price of $0.6200 per SFr**. The profile of this collar will be the same as that in the diagram above, except that our company exercises the put option and the bank exercises the call option. The result is that we can sell Swiss francs for at least $0.6000 but no more than $0.6200.

5.5 Example: Collar using over-the-counter options

Blackberry Inc, a US company, needs to pay £300,000 to a British supplier in six months' time. The current spot rate is 1.5000 $/£. The company purchases an OTC sterling call option on £300,000 at an exercise price of 1.5100 $/£. The premium cost is 2.5 cents per pound. At the same time the company writes a put option on £300,000 for the bank at an exercise price of 1.4700 $/£, earning a premium of 1.2 cents per pound.

Show the results of the hedge assuming that the spot rate moves to (i) 1.5500; (ii) 1.5300; (iii) 1.4800; (iv) 1.4500; (v) 1.4300.

Solution

At today's spot rate of 1.5000 $/£, the 'target cost' of £300,000 is $450,000. The cost of the call option is 300,000 × $0.025 = $7,500. The premium received from the put option sold is 300,000 × $0.012 = $3,600. The net cost of the collar is $7,500 − $3,600 = $3,900.

Scenario	(i)	(ii)	(iii)	(iv)	(v)
Spot rate $/£	1.5500	1.5300	1.4800	1.4500	1.4300
Does the company exercise its $1.5100 call?	Yes	Yes	No	No	No
Does the bank exercise its $1.4700 put?	No	No	No	Yes	Yes
Exchange rate obtained by the company $/£:	1.5100	1.5100	1.4800	1.4700	1.4700
	$	$	$	$	$
Cost of £300,000	453,000	453,000	444,000	441,000	441,000
Add: premium cost	3,900	3,900	3,900	3,900	3,900
Total cost	456,900	456,900	447,900	444,900	444,900
	Maximum				Minimum

The company has used the collar to fix a maximum cost of $456,900 but must accept a minimum cost of $444,900.

5.6 Collars on the same strike price

Philadelphia SE £ sterling options (contract size £31,250, premium in cents per £)

Strike price	.... Calls			.... Puts		
	May	Jun	Jul	May	Jun	Jul
1.6200	1.78	2.34	2.75	0.28	0.93	1.46
1.6300	1.09	1.75	2.23	0.59	1.33	1.90
1.6400	0.59	1.26	1.75	1.10	1.85	2.42

If collars are made from puts and calls on the same strike price, and if the markets are in equilibrium, the result should be identical to that of a future. This can be seen by investigating the figures in the table of sterling options given above and comparing the result with the futures price on the same day, which was 1.6341 $/£. There are three possible collars, as seen in the table below.

Collar	(iv)	(v)	(vi)
Buy put	1.6200	1.6300	1.6400
Sell call	1.6200	1.6300	1.6400
	Cents per £	Cents per £	Cents per £
Premium cost of put	(0.93)	(1.33)	(1.85)
Premium received from call	2.34	1.75	1.26
Net premium received/(paid)	1.41	0.42	(0.59)
	$	$	$
£1 sold for	1.6200	1.6300	1.6400
Net premium in $	0.0141	0.0042	(0.0059)
Total $ per £	1.6341	1.6342	1.6341

LEARNING OUTCOME 4 INTERNATIONAL FINANCE AND INTEREST RATE RISK

All three collars give $ per £ equal to the futures price of 1.6341 (subject to small differences). In other words, buying a put and selling a call on the same strike price is the same as selling a future. In the same way, buying a call and selling a put on the same strike price is the same as buying a future.

There are several other possible combinations which give the same results. For example:

- **Buying a future** and **buying a put** is the same as **buying a call**
- **Selling a future** and **buying a call** is the same as **buying a put**

If these relationships were not true, speculators could make gains without incurring extra risk.

6 Theory of the valuation of options

FAST FORWARD

The **value** of an option depends on:
- The current price of the asset
- The exercise price
- The volatility (standard deviation) of the asset value
- The time period to expiry
- The risk-free rate of interest

6.1 Value of options

Earlier we stated that the value of an option is made up of:

- 'Intrinsic value'
- 'Time value'

The **intrinsic value** of an option depends upon:

- Share price
- Exercise price

The **time value** of an option is affected by:

- Time period to expiry
- Volatility of the underlying security
- General level of interest rates

In this section we will use a share call option to illustrate how the factors listed affect the option's value. We will then describe in outline the Black-Scholes model for valuing options.

6.2 Time to expiry

The value of all options will increase with the length of the expiry period, because in this period the underlying security has time to rise and create a gain for the option holder. If the underlying security falls in value, the option holder makes no loss other than the initial premium cost.

6.3 Volatility of the underlying security

Options on volatile securities will be more valuable than options on securities whose prices do not change much. This is because volatile securities will either show large increases or large decreases in value. The holder of a call option will gain a lot from a large increase in the value of the security but will lose nothing if it falls in value. The following example illustrates this point.

6.4 The general level of interest rates

The intrinsic value of an in-the-money call option is equal to the share price minus the exercise price. If the option has time to run before expiry, the exercise price will not have to be paid until the option is exercised.

(a) The option's value will therefore depend on the current share price minus the **present value of the exercise price**.

(b) If interest rates increase, this present value will decrease and **the value of the call option will increase**.

7 Applications of options theory

> **FAST FORWARD**
>
> Many decision making situations can be analysed as examples of **options** including convertible loan stock, share values and real options.

7.1 Uses of option theory

Options theory is relevant to financial decisions beyond the areas of financial instruments such as traded options, currency options and interest rate options. The following examples should give some idea of the range of possible applications:

(a) **Convertible loan stock** provides a combination of a conventional loan with a call option.
If the option is exercised, the loan is exchanged for a specified number of shares in the company.

(b) **Share warrants** provide the holder with an option to purchase shares from the company at a specified exercise price during a specified time period.

(c) **Insurance** more generally is a form of put option which is exercised when an insurance claim is made.

(d) **Share purchase** at the prevailing market price can be seen as equivalent to the purchase of a call option combined with the sale of a put option, while putting the remaining amount on deposit at a risk-free rate of return over the option period.

(e) **Real options** as discussed in Chapter 8.

Chapter Roundup

- Options give the **right** but **not the obligation** to buy or sell an asset.
- A **call option** is a right to buy the underlying instrument.
- A **put option** is the right to sell the underlying instrument.
- **Currency options** protect against adverse exchange rate movements while allowing the investor to take advantage of favourable exchange rate movements. They are particularly useful in situations where the cash flow is not certain to occur (eg when tendering for overseas contracts).
- Surplus cash may, but need not be, covered on the forward market.
- Currency options are often **closed out** rather than **expire**.

Transaction on future date		Now		On future date	
Receive	currency	Buy	currency put	Sell	currency
Pay	currency	Buy	currency call	Buy	currency
Receive	$	Buy	currency call	Buy	currency
Pay	$	Buy	currency put	Sell	currency

- Options can be illustrated **graphically** by plotting price of underlying instrument against profit.
- Various combinations of options are possible. **Collars** are an important example:
    - Fear currency will **strengthen**; purchase call, sell put
    - Fear currency will **weaken**; sell call, purchase put
- The **value** of an option depends on:
    - The current price of the asset
    - The exercise price
    - The volatility (standard deviation) of the asset value
    - The time period to expiry
    - The risk-free rate of interest

Quick Quiz

1   Complete the following table to illustrate hedging with options.

Transaction on future date		Now		On future date	
Receive	currency				
Pay	currency				
Receive	$				
Pay	$				

2   Complete the following grid with the words 'above' or 'below'.

	Call option	*Put option*
In the money (exercised)	Exercise price _____ security price	Exercise price _____ security price
Out of the money (not exercised)	Exercise price _____ security price	Exercise price _____ security price

3   **Fill in the blanks**

   The intrinsic value of a call option is the higher of

   (i)   _____ price minus _____ price and

   (ii)   Zero

4   The intrinsic value of a put option is the higher of

   (i)   _____ price minus _____ price and

   (ii)   Zero

5   How can a speculator construct a collar?

Answers to Quick Quiz

1

Transaction on future date		Now		On future date	
Receive	currency	Buy	currency put	Sell	currency
Pay	currency	Buy	currency call	Buy	currency
Receive	$	Buy	currency call	Buy	currency
Pay	$	Buy	currency put	Sell	currency

2

	Call option	*Put option*
In the money (exercised)	Exercise price **below** security price	Exercise price **above** security price
Out of the money (not exercised)	Exercise price **above** security price	Exercise price **below** security price

3   The intrinsic value of a call option is the higher of:

(i) Share price minus exercise price and
(ii) Zero

4   The intrinsic value of a put option is the higher of:

(i) Exercise price minus share price and
(ii) Zero

5   By simultaneously purchasing and writing options

17: FOREIGN EXCHANGE RISK: OPTIONS

End of chapter question

Methods of hedging (AIA November 2006)

You are the treasurer for a public relations company based in Hong Kong and you have extracted the following information from a financial daily newspaper. You wish to use it to decide how to hedge the exposure caused by the potential receipt of 2,000,000 Japanese Yen (¥) in three months' time (assume that it is now the end of June).

The spot rate is ¥16.249 – 16.251 to the Hong Kong $ (HK$).

The forward rate for 3 months is ¥16.155 – 16.157 to the HK$.

Currency Options for HK$/¥ are quoted as follows.

Strike Price	Calls			Puts		
July 31	August	September	October	August	September	October
15.90	–	3.40	–	0.22	0.90	1.60
16.00	2.02	–	–	0.38	1.00	2.00
16.10	1.70	–	–	0.52	1.66	–
16.20	1.06	–	–	0.92	2.14	–

The contract size is HK$31,250 and the premiums quoted are HKcents* per HK$.

(*100 HKcents to the HK$).

Three months interest rates are as follows:

Hong Kong   3.75% pa
Japan   1.5% pa

You think that you can borrow in Hong Kong at 2% over the above rate and deposit at 2% below. In Japan you could borrow at 1% over the above rate and deposit at 0.75% below.

Required

(a) Evaluate three different methods your company could use to hedge the potential exposure using the above data. **(12 marks)**

(b) If you had doubts that the ¥ 2,000,000 would be paid to you might it influence the choice of hedging method used? Explain your answer. **(8 marks)**

(Total 20 marks)

LEARNING OUTCOME 4 INTERNATIONAL FINANCE AND INTEREST RATE RISK

Interest rate risk

18

Topic list	Syllabus reference
1 Interest rates	LO4
2 Interest rate risk	LO4
3 Interest rate futures	LO4
4 Interest rate options	LO4
5 Hedging strategy alternatives: Examples	LO4

Introduction

Here we consider **interest rate risk** and some of the financial instruments which are now available for managing financial risks, including **'derivatives'** such as **options**. The risk of interest rate changes is however less significant in most cases than the risk of currency fluctuations which, in some circumstances, can fairly easily wipe out profits entirely if it is not hedged.

As before take your time with the examples and the proformas.

LEARNING OUTCOME 4 INTERNATIONAL FINANCE AND INTEREST RATE RISK

1 Interest rates

> **FAST FORWARD**
>
> The interest rates available are dependent on **risk, profit requirements** and **duration** and **size** of loan.

1.1 Types of interest rate

The interest rates in the UK financial markets which are most commonly quoted are as follows.

(a) The clearing banks' **base rates**. Banks will lend money to small companies and individual customers at certain margins above their base rate. The base rate is set independently by each clearing bank, although in practice, an increase in the base rate of one bank will be followed by similar changes by other banks.

(b) The inter-bank lending rate on the London inter-bank money market (**SONIA**). For large loans to big companies, banks will set interest rates at a margin above SONIA rather than at a margin above base rate.

(c) The **Treasury bill rate**. This is the rate at which the Bank of England sells Treasury bills to the discount market. It is an average rate, since discount houses tender for bills and tender prices vary.

(d) The **yield on long-dated gilt-edged securities** (20 years to maturity). Gilt-edged securities are securities issued by the government.

Key term

> **SONIA**, or the Sterling Overnight Index Average, is the average of the interest rates that banks in the UK pay to borrow sterling overnight from other financial institutions and other institutional investors.

1.2 Why are there so many different interest rates?

There are several reasons why interest rates differ in different markets and market segments.

1.2.1 Risk

Higher risk borrowers must pay higher rates on their borrowing, to compensate lenders for the greater risk involved (see below on **default risk**).

1.2.2 The need to make a profit on re-lending

Financial intermediaries make their profits from re-lending at a higher rate of interest than the cost of their borrowing.

1.2.3 The duration of the lending

Normally, long-term loans will earn a higher yield than short-term loans.

(a) The investor must be compensated for tying up his money in the asset for a **longer period of time**. In other words, if the government were to make two issues of 9% Treasury Stock on the same date, one with a term of five years and one with a term of 20 years (and if there were no expectations of changes in interest rates in the future) then the **liquidity preference** of investors would make them prefer the five-year stock.

The only way to overcome the liquidity preference of investors is to compensate them for the loss of liquidity; in other words, to offer a higher rate of interest on longer-dated stock.

(b) There is a **greater risk** in lending long term than in lending short term. To compensate investors for this risk, they might require a higher yield on longer-dated investments.

18: INTEREST RATE RISK

1.2.4 The size of the loan

Deposits above a certain amount with a bank or building society might attract higher rates of interest than smaller deposits.

1.2.5 International interest rates

The level of interest rates varies from country to country. The reasons for these variations are:

(a) Differing rates of inflation from country to country
(b) Government policies on interest rates and foreign currency exchange rates

1.2.6 Different types of financial asset

Different types of financial asset attract different rates of interest. This is largely because of the competition for deposits between different types of financial institution.

1.3 Term structure of interest rates – the yield curve

Knowledge brought forward from previous studies

The term structure of interest rates: the yield curve

- Interest rates depend on the term to maturity of the asset. For example, Treasury Stock might be short-dated, medium-dated, or long-dated depending on when the stock is to be redeemed and the investor repaid.

- The term structure of interest rates refers to the way in which the yield on a security varies according to the term of the borrowing, as shown by the yield curve.

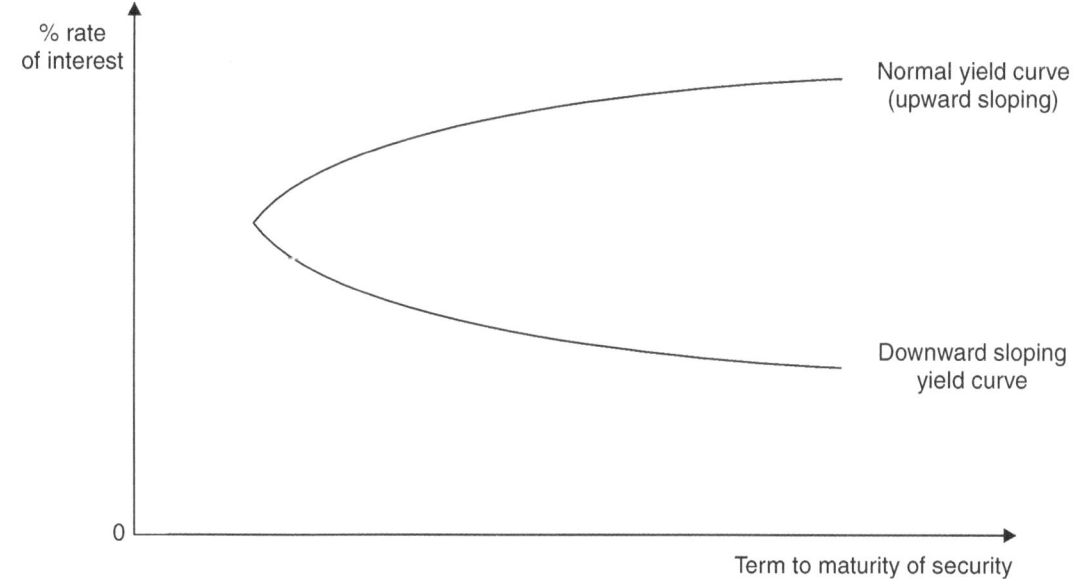

Yield curves

- The reasons why, in theory, the yield curve will normally be upward sloping, so that long-term financial assets offer a higher yield than short-term assets, are as follows.

    – The investor must be compensated for tying up his money in the asset for a longer period of time. The only way to overcome this liquidity preference of investors is to compensate them for the loss of liquidity; in other words, to offer a higher rate of interest on longer-dated stock.

LEARNING OUTCOME 4 INTERNATIONAL FINANCE AND INTEREST RATE RISK

> **Knowledge brought forward from previous studies**
>
> - There is a greater risk in lending long-term than in lending short-term. To compensate investors for this risk, they might require a higher yield on longer-dated investments.
> - A yield curve might slope downwards, with short-term rates higher than longer term rates for the following reasons.
>   - **Expectations.** When interest rates are expected to fall, short-term rates might be higher than long-term rates, and the yield curve would be downward sloping.
>   - **Government policy.** A policy of keeping interest rates relatively high might therefore have the effect of forcing short-term interest rates higher than long-term rates.
>   - **The market segmentation theory.** The slope of the yield curve will reflect conditions in different segments of the market. This theory holds that the major investors are confined to a particular segment of the market and will not switch segment even if the forecast of likely future interests rates change.

1.4 The reverse yield gap

Because debt involves lower risk than equity investment, we might expect yields on debt to be lower than yields on shares. In fact, the opposite applies from time to time, so that the yields on shares are lower than on low-risk debt: this situation is known as a **reverse yield gap**. A reverse yield gap can occur because shareholders may be willing to accept lower returns on their investment in the short term, in anticipation that they will make capital gains in the future.

2 Interest rate risk

FAST FORWARD

Factors influencing **interest rate risk** include the following.
- Fixed rate **versus** floating rate debt
- The term of the loan

2.1 Managing a debt portfolio

Corporate treasurers will be responsible for managing the company's **debt portfolio**, that is, in deciding how a company should obtain its short-term funds so as to:

(a) Be able to **repay debts** as they mature

(b) Minimise **any inherent risks**, notably invested foreign exchange risk, in the debts the company owes and is owed

Where the magnitude of the risk is **immaterial** in comparison with the company's overall cash flows, one option is to **do nothing** and to accept the effects of any movement in interest rates which occur.

Exam focus point

Bear in mind this possibility – the decision **not** to take action to reduce interest rate risk – when answering questions in the exam.

2.2 Risks from interest rate movements

2.2.1 Fixed rate versus floating rate debt

A company can get caught paying **higher interest rates** by having fixed rather than floating rate debt, or floating rather than fixed rate debt, as market interest rates change.

2.2.2 Currency of debt

This is also a foreign currency exposure. A company can face higher costs if it borrows in a currency for which exchange rates move adversely against the company's domestic currency. The treasurer should seek to **match the currency of the loan** with the **currency of the underlying operations/assets** that generate revenue to pay interest/repay the loans.

2.2.3 Term of loan

A company can be exposed by having to **repay a loan earlier** than it can afford to, resulting in a need to re-borrow, perhaps at a higher rate of interest.

2.2.4 Term loan or overdraft facility

A company might prefer to **pay for borrowings only when it needs the money** as with an overdraft facility: the bank will charge a commitment fee for such a facility. Alternatively, a term loan might be preferred, but this will cost interest even if it is not needed in full for the whole term.

2.3 Analysis of interest rate risk

Some of the interest rate risks to which a firm is exposed may **cancel each other out**, where there are both assets and liabilities with which there is exposure to interest rate changes. If interest rates rise, more interest will be payable on loans and other liabilities, but this will be compensated for by higher interest received on assets such as money market deposits.

The effect of interest rate changes depends upon whether interest rates for the assets and liabilities are floating or fixed:

(a) **Floating** interest rates, of course, change according to general market conditions.

(b) With **fixed** interest rates, the interest on the asset or liability will only be repriced at the date of maturity in the light of prevailing market conditions. If a fixed interest rate liability matures at the same time as a fixed rate asset, then the interest rate risks arising from the repricing of the two instruments will cancel each other out.

2.3.1 Gap analysis of interest rate risk

The degree to which a firm is exposed to interest rate risk can be identified by using the method of **gap analysis**. Gap analysis is based on the principle of **grouping together** assets and liabilities which are sensitive to interest rate changes according to their maturity dates. Two different types of 'gap' may occur:

1   **A negative gap**

    A negative gap occurs when a firm has a larger amount of interest-sensitive liabilities maturing at a certain time or in a certain period than it has interest-sensitive assets maturing at the same time. The difference between the two amounts indicates the net exposure.

2   **A positive gap**

    There is a positive gap if the amount of interest-sensitive assets maturing in a particular time exceeds the amount of interest-sensitive liabilities maturing at the same time.

With a **negative** gap, the company faces exposure if interest rates **rise** by the time of maturity. With a **positive** gap, the company will lose out if interest rates **fall** by maturity. The company's interest rate hedge should be based on the size of the gap.

Methods of reducing interest rate risk include:

- Forward rate agreements (FRAs)
- Pooling
- Interest rate futures
- Interest rate options (or interest rate guarantees)
- Interest rate swaps (covered in Chapter 19)

In the remainder of this section, we look at FRAs, before considering interest rate futures and options.

Exam focus point

> In the exam, and throughout this text, you will encounter interest rates that do not reflect the current rate of interest. This should not concern you, illustrative rates are used to ensure that you are comfortable with the hedging techniques examinable.

2.4 Forward rate agreements (FRAs)

FAST FORWARD

> **Forward rate agreements** hedge risk by **fixing the interest rate** on future borrowing.

A company can enter into a FRA with a bank that **fixes the rate of interest** for borrowing at a certain time in the future. If the actual interest rate proves to be higher than the rate agreed, the bank pays the company the difference. If the actual interest rate is lower than the rate agreed, the company pays the bank the difference.

One **limitation** of FRAs is that they are usually only available on loans of at least £500,000. They are also likely to be **difficult to obtain for periods of over one year**.

An **advantage** of FRAs is that, for the period of the FRA at least, they **protect the borrower** from adverse market interest rate movements to levels above the rate negotiated for the FRA. With a normal variable rate loan (for example, linked to a bank's base rate or to SONIA) the borrower is exposed to the risk of such adverse market movements. On the other hand, the borrower will similarly not benefit from the effects of favourable market interest rate movements.

The **interest rates** which banks will be willing to set for FRAs will reflect their current expectations of interest rate movements. If it is expected that interest rates are going to rise during the term for which the FRA is being negotiated, the bank is likely to seek a higher fixed rate of interest than the variable rate of interest which is current at the time of negotiating the FRA.

2.5 FRA terminology

The terminology is as follows:

(a) 5.75-5.70 means that you can fix a borrowing rate at 5.75%
(b) A '3-6' forward rate agreement is one that starts in three months and lasts for three months
(c) A basis point is 0.01%

2.6 Example: Forward rate agreement

It is 30 June. Lynn plc will need a £10 million six-month fixed rate loan from 1 October. Lynn wants to hedge using an FRA. The relevant FRA rate is 6% on 30 June.

(a) State what FRA is required.

(b) What is the result of the FRA and the effective loan rate if the six-month FRA benchmark rate has moved to

(i) 5%
(ii) 9%

Solution

(a) The Forward Rate Agreement required is '3-9'.

(b) (i) At 5% because interest rates have fallen, Lynn plc will pay the bank:

	£
FRA payment £10 million × (6% – 5%) × $^6/_{12}$	(50,000)
Payment on underlying loan 5% × £10 million × $^6/_{12}$	(250,000)
Net payment on loan	(300,000)
Effective interest rate on loan	6%

(ii) At 9% because interest rates have risen, the bank will pay Lynn plc:

	£
FRA receipt £10 million × (9% – 6%) × $^6/_{12}$	150,000
Payment on underlying loan at market rate 9% × £10 million × $^6/_{12}$	(450,000)
Net payment on loan	(300,000)
Effective interest rate on loan	6%

2.7 Pooling of subsidiaries' cash balances

> **FAST FORWARD**
>
> **Pooling** can help avoid paying higher interest rates on borrowing and can make management of interest rate risk easier.

If an organisation, for example a group of companies, has a large number of different bank accounts with the same bank, it can ask the bank to pool balances when considering interest and overdraft limits.

2.7.1 Benefits of pooling

(a) **Netting surpluses and deficits**

For the parent company, the main benefit of pooling cash balances is that **surpluses** can **be netted off** against deficits, thus reducing the amount of interest payable. Because borrowing rates are higher than deposit rates, it is better to use surplus cash to **reduce borrowing** than to put it on deposit. A central treasury could lend funds to subsidiaries at better rates than they would be able to borrow.

Unfortunately when cash balances are in different currencies this tactic does not necessarily work. If the **forward rates** are **not in equilibrium** with the interest rates, then there may be opportunities for making gains by keeping cash in other currencies.

(b) **Greater control**

Pooling balances means that it is easier for a central treasury department to exercise control over funds, and use its **expertise** to ensure risks are managed and opportunities exploited effectively.

(c) **Greater investment opportunities**

Better rates may be available for pooled funds, and the central treasury function that holds the pooled funds may have **access to markets** such as offshore markets that are not available to local operations.

(d) **Elimination of exchange risk**

Another benefit to the parent company of pooling all resources in the home currency is that **currency exchange risk** is **eliminated** for the net surplus.

LEARNING OUTCOME 4 INTERNATIONAL FINANCE AND INTEREST RATE RISK

2.7.2 Drawbacks of pooling of subsidiaries' cash balances

(a) **Need for cash**

Operating subsidiaries need **cash balances** as part of their working capital in order to make payments. If these payments are higher than expected, there may be insufficient cash in the subsidiaries. Local managers may try to ensure that they have the maximum amount of cash possible to make the payments, leading to disharmony within the group.

(b) **Local decision-making**

Local managers may feel **demotivated** if the responsibility for investing funds is taken away from them. They may not therefore provide **full co-operation** to the centralised department.

(c) **Transaction costs**

Transferring cash surpluses to the parent company and then back to the subsidiary again when required incurs **unnecessary transaction costs**, which can be relatively high compared with any interest saving, particularly when interest rates are low.

(d) **Matching**

Good currency risk management will attempt to **minimise risk** by **matching receipts and payments**, and assets and liabilities, in the same currency. Pooling might conflict with this principle.

2.8 Example: Cash pooling

Two group companies K and L have accounts with the same bank. During September 20X4, K has an overdraft of £120,000 and L has a credit balance of £200,000. The bank charges interest on the group's overdraft balances at a rate of 0.8% per month and pays interest of 0.5% per month on credit balances. Calculate how much interest would be gained by adopting cash pooling for 20X4.

Solution

	£
Without cash pooling	
Interest charged (120,000 × 0.008)	(960)
Interest receivable (200,000 × 0.005)	1,000
Net interest receivable	40
With cash pooling	
The net balance is (200,000 – 120,000)	£80,000
Interest receivable (80,000 × 0.005)	£400
The net gain is (400 – 40) per month	£360

3 Interest rate futures

FAST FORWARD

Interest rate futures can be used to hedge against interest rate changes between the current date and the date at which the interest rate on the lending or borrowing is set. Borrowers **sell futures** to hedge against **interest rate rises**; lenders **buy futures** to hedge against **interest rate falls**.

3.1 Futures contracts

Most LIFFE (London International Financial Futures and Options Exchange) futures contracts involve interest rates (**interest rate futures**), and these offer a means of hedging against the risk of interest rate movements. Such contracts are effectively a gamble on whether interest rates will rise or fall. Like other futures contracts, interest rate futures offer a way in which **speculators can 'bet'** on market movements just as they offer others who are more risk-averse a way of **hedging risks**.

Interest rate futures are similar in effect to FRAs, except that the terms, amounts and periods are **standardised**. For example, a company can contract to buy (or sell) £100,000 of a notional 30-year Treasury bond bearing an 8% coupon, in say, six-months' time, at an agreed price. The basic principles behind such a decision are:

(a) The futures price is likely to vary with changes in interest rates, and this acts as a **hedge** against adverse interest rate movements. We shall see how this works in a later example.

(b) The outlay to buy futures is much less than for buying the financial instrument itself, and so a company can hedge large exposures of cash with a relatively **small initial employment of cash**.

3.1.1 Nature of contracts

The **standardised nature** of interest rate futures is a limitation on their use by the corporate treasurer as a means of hedging, because they **cannot always be matched** with specific interest rate exposures. However, their use is growing. Futures contracts are frequently used by banks and other financial institutions as a means of hedging their portfolios: such institutions are often not concerned with achieving an exact match with their underlying exposure.

3.1.2 Entitlement with contracts

With interest rate futures what we **buy** is the entitlement to **interest receipts** and what we **sell** is the promise to make **interest payments**. So when a lender buys one three-month sterling contract he has the right to receive interest for three months in pounds. When a borrower sells a three-month sterling contract he incurs an obligation to make interest payments for three months.

(a) **Borrowers** will wish to hedge against an interest rate rise by **selling futures now** and **buying futures** on the day that the interest rate is fixed.

(b) **Lenders** will wish to hedge against the possibility of falling interest rates by **buying futures now** and **selling futures** on the date that the actual lending starts.

3.1.3 Other factors to consider

(a) Most of the interest rate futures we shall encounter are for short term interest rates. **Short-term interest rate futures** contracts normally represent interest receivable or payable on notional lending or borrowing **for a three-month period** beginning on a standard future date. The contract size depends on the currency in which the lending or borrowing takes place. For example, the three-month sterling interest rate futures March contract represents the interest on notional lending or borrowing of £500,000 for three months, starting at the end of March. £500,000 is the contract size.

(b) As with all futures, a **whole number of contracts** must be dealt with. Note that the notional **period of lending or borrowing starts** when the **contract expires**, at the **end of March**.

(c) On LIFFE, futures contracts are available with **maturity dates** at the end of March, June, September and December. The three-month eurodollar interest rate futures contract is for notional lending or borrowing in US dollars. The contract size is $1 million.

3.2 Pricing futures contracts

The **pricing** of an interest rate futures contract is determined by the three-month interest rate r% contracted for and is calculated as (100 − r). For example, if three-month eurodollar time deposit interest rates are 8%, a three-month eurodollar futures contract will be priced at 92 (100 − 8). If interest rates are 11%, the contract price will be 89 (100 − 11). This decrease in price, or value, of the contract, reflects the reduced attractiveness of a fixed rate deposit in time of rising interest rates.

Note that the interest rate must be stated as a **percentage**, not a decimal. If, over the next week, the futures price **increases** to 92.20, this implies that interest rates at the end of March are now expected to be **lower** at 7.8% (because 100 – 7.8 = 92.20).

The investor can close out his position by selling one three-month sterling interest rate futures March contract at 92.20. This means that he is notionally contracting to borrow £500,000 for three months at 7.8%. A gain has therefore been made by notionally borrowing £500,000 at 7.8% and lending it at 8%. The value of the gain is 0.2% × 3/12 × £500,000 = £250. The gain on closing out can be calculated directly from the prices at which the future was bought and sold:

Sell at	92.20
Buy at	92.00
Gain	0.20

0.2% × 3/12 × £500,000 = £250.

Interest rate futures are not all priced in the same way.

(a) Prices of **short-term interest rate futures**, which, as already indicated, reflect the interest rates on the underlying financial instrument, are quoted at a **discount to a par value of 100**. For example, a price of 93.40 indicates that the underlying money market deposit is being traded at a rate of 6.6% (100 – 93.40).

(b) Pricing for **long-term bond futures** is as a **percentage of par value**, similarly to the pricing of bonds themselves.

3.3 Tick sizes

A **tick** (or **basis point of price**) has a known, measurable value. Here are some examples:

(a) In the case of three-month eurodollar futures, the amount of the underlying instrument is a three-month deposit of $1,000,000. As a tick is 0.01% (or one-hundredth of one per cent), the value of a tick is $25 (0.01% × $1,000,000 × 3/12).

(b) In the case of long gilt futures, the underlying instrument is £100,000 of notional gilts. As a tick is 0.01%, the value of one tick is (0.01% × £100,000) = £10.

(c) In the use of Short-Term Interest Rate (STIR) futures (short sterling), the underlying instrument is £500,000 of notional bonds so the tick value (taking into account the life of the future) is 500,000 × 0.01 % × 3/12 = £12.50.

3.4 Basis risk

The concept of hedge efficiency was introduced earlier. There are two reasons why it is often not possible to achieve a perfect (100%) hedge with futures, as follows:

(a) The fact that futures are available only in certain standard sizes means that the contracts may not fit exactly the company's needs.

(b) There is also **basis risk,** arising from the fact that the price of the futures contract may not move as expected in relation to the value of the instrument which is being hedged. There are two main reasons for basis risk.

   (i) **Cash flow requirements** may differ, altering the relative values of the underlying financial instrument and the derivative futures contract.

   (ii) The **financial instrument** which the firm is seeking to hedge may be different from the financial instrument which underlies the futures contract.

If a firm takes a position in the futures contract with a view to closing out the contract before its maturity, there is still likely to be basis, and the firm can only **estimate what effect** this will **have on the hedge**. **'Basis risk'** refers to the problem that the **basis may result in an imperfect hedge**. The basis will be **zero** at the **maturity date of the contract**.

The basis risk can be calculated as the difference between the futures price and the current price (**'cash market' price**) of the underlying security.

3.4.1 Example: Basis and basis risk

To give an example, if three-month SONIA (Sterling Over Night Indexed Average) is 7% and the September price of the three-month sterling future is 92.70 now (at the end of March, say) then the basis is:

SONIA (100–7)   93.00
Futures   92.70
                   0.30% or 30 basis points

Exam focus point

> In the exam, you might be given other price information and have to calculate the closing futures price from it.

3.4.2 Example: Calculating closing futures price and basis

Tigs plc has a $10 million loan with a six-monthly rollover which is next due on 1 July.

On 1 May SONIA is 8%.

The appropriate futures contract on LIFFE is the short eurodollar three month interest rate contract. The standard size of these contracts is US$1 million and contracts expire at the end of the relevant month. Prices are quoted at (100-annual yield) in basis points as follows:

July 91.46   August 91.25   September 91.15

On 1 July the interest rate on the eurodollar loan had risen to 12%.

Calculate the closing futures price assuming basis declines uniformly.

Solution

Here, we are not told the closing futures price and the contract expires before the end of three months.

We therefore need to estimate what the futures price might be at 1 July, and we do so using the July price details, since a 3 month contract from 1 May runs to 31 July.

Therefore

Opening basis 91.46 – (100 – 8% = 92.00) = 54 ticks.

We assume the gap between the futures price and spot narrows uniformly over the three month period to reach 0 ticks by 31 July. Therefore closing basis = 54 × $1/3$ = 18 ticks.

Closing futures price (100 – 12% = 88.00) – 0.18 = 87.82.

3.5 Example: Futures price movements (1)

June 3-month euro futures fell in price on a particular day from 96.84 to 96.76. Privet plc has purchased June futures, having a 'long' position on five contracts ie they have bought now to sell later. Calculate the change in value of the contracts on the day concerned, given the value of one tick is 25 euros (size 0.01%).

Solution

The fall in price represents 8 ticks (96.84 – 96.76 = 0.08 and the tick size is 0.01%). The value of one tick is 25 euros. Each contract has fallen in value by 25 × 8 = 200 euros. Privet plc has bought five contracts and so the day's price movement represents for the company a loss on the contracts of 200 × 5 = 1,000 euros.

3.6 Example: Futures price movements (2)

September long gilts sterling futures fell in price on a particular day from 96.10 to 95.96. Privet plc has sold September futures, having a 'short' position of 15 contracts. Calculate the change in value of the contract on the day concerned given that the tick size is 0.01%.

Solution

The fall in price represents 14 ticks (96.10 – 95.96 and the tick size of 0.01%). The value of one tick for long gilts sterling futures is £10. Each contract has fallen in value by £10 × 14 = £140. For Privet plc, which has sold 15 contracts, the day's price movement represents a profit of £140 × 15 = £2,100, (ie it will cost them less to purchase the contracts they need to buy to match the contracts they have sold).

3.7 Maturity mismatch

Maturity mismatch occurs if the actual period of lending or borrowing does not match the notional period of the futures contract (three months). The number of futures contracts used has to be adjusted accordingly. Since fixed interest is involved, the number of contracts is adjusted in proportion to the time period of the actual loan or deposit compared with three months. For example, if the period of borrowing is **six months** the number of contracts is **doubled**. This leads to the following formula.

$$\text{Number of futures contracts} = \frac{\text{Amount of actual loan or deposit} \times \text{length of loan}}{\text{Futures contract size} \times 3 \text{ months}}$$

Exam focus point

Remember that it is the **length** of the loan that determines how many future contracts are needed. The period between today's date and the start of the loan is **not** relevant; we are hedging over the **life** of the loan.

3.7.1 Example: Maturity mismatch

On 5 June, a corporate treasurer decides to hedge a short-term loan of 17 million Swiss francs which will be required for two months from 4 October to 3 December. Three month Euro Swiss franc futures, December contract, are trading at 98.15. The contract size is SFr1 million. Show the action taken.

Solution

$$\text{Number of futures contracts} = \frac{\text{SFr 17 million} \times 2 \text{ months}}{\text{SFr 1 million} \times 3 \text{ months}}$$

= 11.33 contracts, rounded to 11.

Question — *Interest rate futures*

The following futures price movements were observed during a week in October.

Contract	Price at start of week	Price at end of week
December short sterling	90.40	91.02
December Japanese government bond	93.80	94.25

Hawthorn plc has the following positions in these contracts.

(a) A short position (seller) of ten December short sterling contracts (tick value = £12.50, size 0.01%)

(b) A long position of eight December Japanese government bonds contracts (tick value = Y10,000, size = 0.01%)

Required

Calculate the profit or loss to the company on the contracts.

Answer

Short sterling

Increase in price (91.02 – 90.40 = 0.62)	62 ticks
Value per tick	£12.50
Increase in value of one contract (62 × £12.50)	£775

The company is a seller of ten contracts and would lose £7,750 (£775 × 10)

Japanese government bonds

Increase in price (94.25 – 93.80 = 0.45)	45 ticks
Value per tick	Y10,000
Increase in value of one contract (45 × Y10,000)	Y450,000

The company is a buyer of eight contracts and would gain Y3,600,000 (Y450,000 × 8)

3.8 Example: Interest rate hedge using futures

Yew plc has taken a six-month $10,000,000 dollar loan with interest payable of 8%, the loan being due for rollover on 31 March. At 1 January, the company treasurer considers that interest rates are likely to rise in the near future. The futures price is 91 representing a yield of 9%. Given a standard contract size of $1,000,000 the company **sells** a dollar three-month contract to hedge against interest on the three-month loan required at 31 March (to **sell** a contract is to commit the seller to take a deposit). At 31 March the spot interest rate is 11% and the futures price had fallen to 88.5. Demonstrate how futures can be used to hedge against interest rate movements.

Solution

The following steps should be taken.

Setup

(a) What contract?: 3 month contract

(b) What type?: sell (as rates expected to rise)

(c) How many contracts?: $\frac{\text{Exposure}}{\text{Contract size}} \times \frac{\text{Loan period}}{\text{Length of contract}} = \frac{10m}{1m} \times \frac{6}{3} = 20$ contracts

(d) Tick size (min price movement as % × $^3/_{12}$) × contract size: $^{0.01}/_{100} \times {^3/_{12}} \times 1m = \$25$

Closing price

Opening basis –
Closing basis –
Closing futures price 88.5

LEARNING OUTCOME 4 INTERNATIONAL FINANCE AND INTEREST RATE RISK

Outcome

(a) Futures outcome

At opening rate: 91 sell
At closing rate: 88.5 buy
Tick movement: $^{91-88.5}/_{0.01}$ = 250 ticks
Futures outcome: 20 × $25 × 250 = $125,000

(b) Net outcome

	$
Payment in spot market $10m × 11% × 6/12	(550,000)
Receipt in futures market	125,000
Net payments	(425,000)

(c) Hedge efficiency: $\dfrac{125{,}000}{(\$10m \times 6/12 \times (11-8)\%)} \times 100\% = 83.3\%$

3.9 Hedge ratio

The **hedge ratio** is the ratio of the amount of the futures contracts bought or sold to the amount of the underlying financial instrument being hedged. For example, if a company is exposed to interest rate risk on a loan of £210,000 and it takes a position in futures contracts for £200,000, the hedge ratio is:

$\dfrac{200{,}000}{210{,}000} = 95.2\%$

The **optimal hedge ratio** is given by the formula:

$$p \dfrac{\sigma_i}{\sigma_f}$$

where p = the coefficient of correlation between the change in price of the underlying instrument and the change in price of the futures contract, each measured over the period of the hedge

σ_i = the standard deviation of the change in the price of the underlying instrument

σ_f = the standard deviation of the change in the price of the futures contract

As you can probably appreciate, establishing values for the variables p, σ_i and σ_f is more of a problem than calculating the optimal hedge ratio using the formula.

3.9.1 Example: Optimal hedge ratio

Melbury plc wishes to hedge the interest rate risk on a 1 year floating rate loan of £2,000,000. The futures price is more volatile than the price of the debt, such that σ_i = 0.08 and σ_f = 0.10. p = 0.6. What is the optimal hedge ratio?

Solution

Optimal hedge ratio = $p \dfrac{\sigma_i}{\sigma_f} = 0.6 \times \dfrac{0.08}{0.10} = 0.48$

It follows that Melbury plc should take a position in interest rate futures for:

2,000,000 × 0.48 = £960,000

3.9.2 Hedging lending

In the language of interest rate futures, lending equals buying. The treasurer hedges against the possibility of falling interest rates by buying futures now and selling futures on the date that the actual lending starts. The calculation proceeds in a similar way to the example above.

3.10 Example: Hedging by a lender

Beech plc will have a surplus of 2 million US dollars for three months starting in August. The cash will be placed on fixed interest deposit, for which the current rate of interest is 5% pa. How can the deposit income be hedged using futures contracts? The September three-month eurodollar futures contract is currently trading at 94.00.

Solution

The target interest to be earned is $2 million $\times$ 5% $\times$ $^3/_{12}$ = $25,000. To hedge lending, buy two three-month eurodollar September futures contracts now and sell two contracts in August.

Suppose that by August, interest rates have fallen by 1%. The $2 million is deposited at 4% for three months, yielding $20,000, a shortfall on target of $5,000. If the futures market has also moved by 1%, the contract price will have risen to 95.00, giving a gain of 100 ticks. The gain from selling two contracts at the higher price is 2 $\times$ 100 ticks $\times$ $25 = $5,000. This compensates for the shortfall in actual interest.

4 Interest rate options

> **FAST FORWARD**
>
> **Interest rate options** allow an organisation to limit its exposure to adverse interest rate movements, while allowing it to take advantage of favourable interest rate movements.
>
> **Borrowers** can set a **maximum** on the interest they have to pay by buying **put** options.
>
> **Lenders** can set a **minimum** on the interest they receive by buying **call** options.

4.1 Interest rate options and interest rate guarantees

> **Key term**
>
> An **interest rate option** grants the buyer of it the right, but **not the obligation**, to deal at an agreed interest rate (strike rate) at a future maturity date. On the date of expiry of the option, the buyer must decide whether or not to exercise the right.

Clearly, a buyer of an **option to borrow** will **not wish to exercise** it if the **market interest rate** is now **below** that specified in the option agreement. Conversely, an **option to lend** will not be worth exercising if **market rates** have **risen above** the rate specified in the option by the time the option has expired.

> **Key term**
>
> An **interest rate guarantee (IRG)** refers to an interest rate option which hedges the interest rate for a single period of up to one year. It is an otion on an FRA.

Tailor-made **'over-the-counter' interest rate options** can be purchased from major banks, with specific values, periods of maturity, denominated currencies and rates of agreed interest. The cost of the option is the 'premium'. Interest rate options offer more flexibility than and are more expensive than FRAs.

4.2 Interest rate caps, collars and floors

> **FAST FORWARD**
>
> **Caps** set a ceiling to the interest rate; a **floor** sets a lower limit. A **collar** is the simultaneous purchase of a cap and sale of a floor.

LEARNING OUTCOME 4 INTERNATIONAL FINANCE AND INTEREST RATE RISK

Various **cap** and **collar** agreements are possible.

Key terms

(a) An interest rate **cap** is an option which sets an interest rate ceiling.

(b) A **floor** is an option which sets a lower limit to interest rates.

(c) Using a **'collar'** arrangement, the borrower can buy an interest rate cap (buying a put option) and at the same time sell an interest rate floor (selling a call option). This limits the cost for the company as it receives a premium for the option it has sold.

The cost of a collar is lower than for buying an option alone. However, the borrowing company forgoes the benefit of movements in interest rates **below the floor limit** in exchange for this cost reduction and an investing company forgoes the benefit of **movements in interest rates above the cap level**. A **zero cost collar** can even be negotiated sometimes, if the **premium paid** for buying the cap **equals** the **premium received** for selling the floor.

Exam focus point

You need to have an understanding of caps, floors and collars but numeric questions will not be set.

4.3 Example: Collar

Suppose you create a borrowing collar: Buy put (cap) (say at 6%), sell call (floor) (say at 4%)

The put option maximises the interest you pay. If interest rates are above 6%, you can exercise the put option and fix the interest you pay at 6%. If rates are lower than 6% you can pay interest at that lower rate down to 4%. Below 4% the holder of the call option can exercise his option and force you to pay interest at 4%, rather than a lower rate.

4.4 Interest rates caps, collars and floors illustrated graphically

In the example shown in Figure 1, a company has a loan at SONIA (Sterling Over Night Indexed Average). Suppose that for an annual cost of 1% of principal, it can buy a cap at 8%. When SONIA is between 6% and 8%, the vertical distance between the two lines on the graph represents the cost of the cap. The cap begins to pay off when SONIA rises above 8%, with a break-even point where SONIA is 9%.

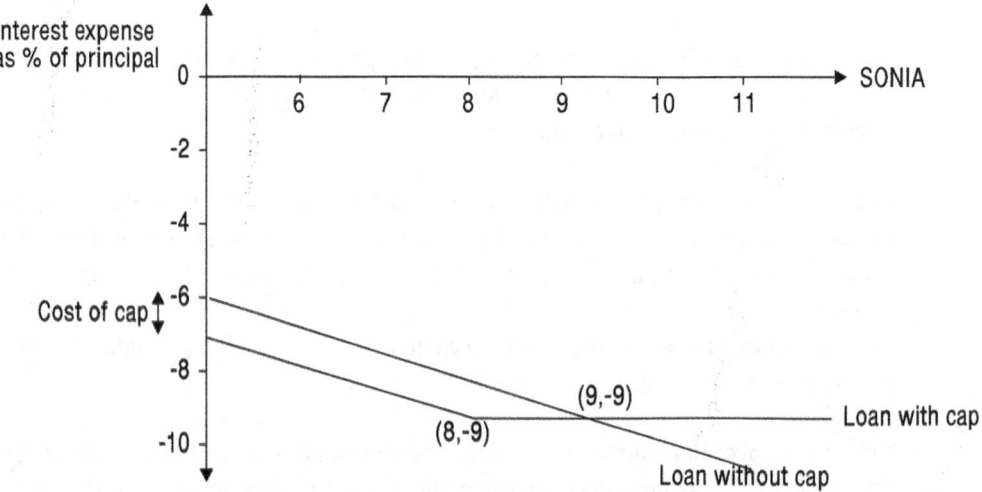

Figure 1 Loan with Interest rate cap

Part or all of the cost of the cap may be set off by agreeing to an interest rate floor, thus making a collar. In the case of a **zero cost collar**, the cost of the cap is fully offset by the proceeds of the floor.

Figure 2 illustrates the profit/loss profile for a zero cost collar. This might be achieved by combining a floor with the arrangement illustrated in Figure 1. The interest expense cannot exceed 8% and cannot be less than 5%. Between 5% and 8%, the interest expense matches SONIA.

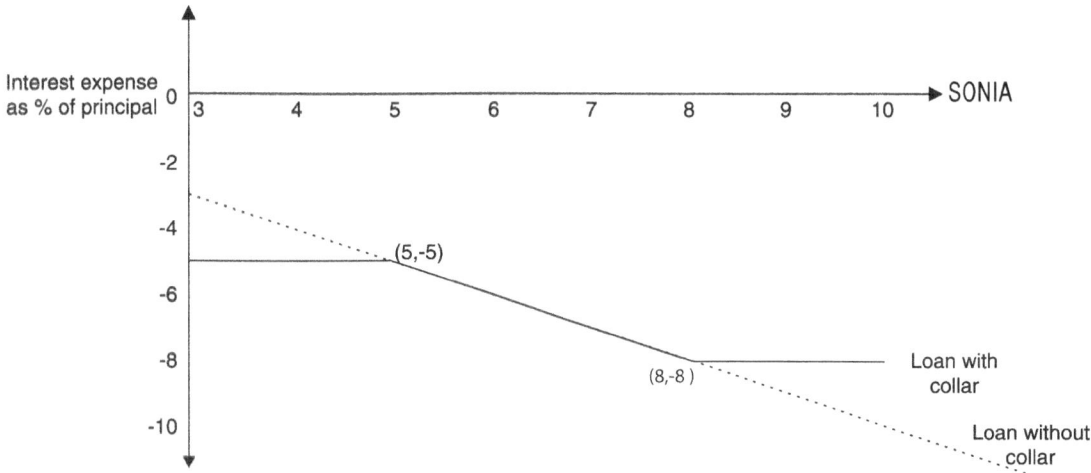

Figure 2 Loan with interest rate collar

4.5 Traded interest rate options

Exchange-traded interest rate options are available as **options on interest rate futures,** which give the holder the right to buy (call option) or sell (put option) one futures contract on or before the expiry of the option at a specified price. The best way to understand the pricing of interest rate options is to look at a schedule of prices.

UK long gilt futures options (LIFFE) £100,000 100ths of 100%

Strike price	Calls			Puts		
	Nov	Dec	Jan	Nov	Dec	Jan
11,350	0.87	1.27	1.34	0.29	0.69	1.06
11,400	0.58	0.99	1.10	0.50	0.91	1.32
11,450	0.36	0.76	0.88	0.77	1.18	1.60

Note the following.

(a) The **contract size** is £100,000.

(b) The **strike price** is the price that will be **paid for the futures contract** (if the option is exercised) as a percentage of the face value.

(c) The numbers under each month represent the **premium** that must be paid for the options.

(d) The market is predicting that **interest rates will rise**, since put options are more expensive than calls.

This schedule shows that an investor could pay 1.34/100 × £100,000 = £1,340 to purchase the right to buy a sterling futures contract in January at a price of £113.50 per £100 stock.

If, say, in December, January sterling futures are priced **below** £113.50 (reflecting an interest rate **rise**), the option will not be exercised. In calculating any gain from the option, the premium cost must also be taken into account.

If the futures price moves **higher,** as it is likely to if interest rates **fall,** the option will be exercised. The profit for each contract is:

(Current futures price – 113.50 – 1.34)

4.6 Using traded interest rate options for hedging

To use traded interest rate options for hedging, follow exactly the same principles as for traded currency options, noting the following specific points.

(a) If a company needs to **hedge borrowing** at some future date, it should **purchase put options**. Instead of selling futures now and buying futures later, it **purchases** an option to **sell futures** and only exercises the option if interest rates have risen causing a fall in the price of the futures contract.

(b) Similarly, if a company needs to **lend money**, it should **purchase call options**.

4.7 Example: Traded options

Panda Ltd wishes to borrow £4 million fixed rate in June for nine months and wishes to protect itself against rates rising above 6.75%. It is 11 May and the spot rate is currently 6%. The data is as follows.

SHORT STERLING OPTIONS (STIR)
£500,000 points of 100%

Strike price	Calls			Puts		
	June	Sept	Dec	June	Sept	Dec
9325	0.16	0.03	0.03	0.14	0.92	1.62
9350	0.05	0.01	0.01	0.28	1.15	1.85
9375	0.01	0.01	0.01	0.49	1.39	2.10

Tick size is half of one basis point.

Panda negotiates the loan with the bank on 12 June (when the £4m loan rate is fixed for the full nine months) and closes out the hedge.

What will be the outcome of the hedge and the effective loan rate if prices on 12 June have moved to:

Closing prices

	Case 1	Case 2
Spot price	7.4%	5.1%
Futures price	92.31	94.75

Solution

The following method should be used.

Step 1 Setup

(a) Which contract?   June
(b) What type?   As paying interest put
(c) Strike price   93.25 (100 – 6.75)
(d) How many? $£4m/£0.5m \times 9/3 = 24$ contracts
(e) Tick size   £500,000 × 0.0005% × 3/12 = £6.25
(f) Premium   At 93.25 (6.75%) June Puts = 0.14 = 14 ticks

Contracts × premium in ticks × tick value = 24 × 14 × 12.50 = £4,200

Step 2 Closing prices

	Case 1	Case 2
Spot price	7.4%	5.1%
Futures price	92.31	94.75

Step 3 Outcome

		Case 1	Case 2
(a)	Options market outcome		
	Strike price right to sell (Put) at	93.25	93.25
	Closing price buy at	92.31	94.75
	Exercise?	Yes	No
	If exercised, tick movement	188	–
	Outcome of options position	188 × 6.25 × 24 = £28,200	–
(b)	Net position	£	£
	Spot £4m × 9/12 × 7.4/5.1%	222,000	153,000
	Option	(28,200)	–
	Option premium	4,200	4,200
	Net outcome	198,000	157,200
(c)	Effective interest rate	$\frac{198{,}000}{4{,}000{,}000} \times \frac{12}{9} = 6.6\%$	$\frac{157{,}200}{4{,}000{,}000} \times \frac{12}{9} = 5.24\%$

Exam focus point

In the example of Panda you are told the maximum interest rate the company wishes to pay, and given two closing situations in one of which the option would be exercised, and in the other one it would not.

In the exam the situation may not be as clear. There may be a choice of different strike prices, and you may not have time to calculate the results of different closing prices for all possible strike prices.

Ideally in this situation you want to choose a strike price that illustrates different possibilities (will mean that the option is exercised in one of the closing price outcomes given in the question but not the other for example). One possible way of deciding on the strike price is to choose an option that is as near as possible to today's Spot/SONIA rate (if for example spot is 6%, choose 100 – 6 = 9400, a strike price of 9400 for example.

4.8 Traded caps, floors and collars

4.8.1 Traded caps

Say you are a borrower and have bought a put option (a right to sell the future). The exercise price is 93.00, reflecting an interest rate of 7%.

Interest rate rises

- If the interest rate you have to pay **rises to 8%**, the price of the future will fall to 92.00
- You will buy the future at 92.00 and exercise your right to sell it at 93.00
- The profit you make on buying and then selling the future can be set against the 8% interest you have to pay, to give an **effective interest rate of 7%**

Interest rate falls

- If the interest rate **falls to 6%**, you don't exercise the option, therefore don't worry about buying and selling the future, and just pay interest at 6%

4.8.2 Traded floors

In order to set a floor if you are investing/lending, you have to buy a call option – a right to buy a future. Say the exercise price is 95.00, corresponding to an interest rate of 5%.

Interest rate falls

- If the interest rate **falls to 4%**, the price of the future will rise to 96.00
- You will only receive interest at 4%
- However you will exercise your option to buy the future at 95.00 and then you will sell it on at 96.00
- The profit you make on the future will be added to the 4% interest you receive to give an effective net interest rate of 5%

Interest rate rises

- If the interest rate **rises to 6%**, you will not exercise the option, and you will receive interest at 6%

4.8.3 Traded collars

With collars, if you're a borrower, you are buying a put and selling a call. Say the exercise price is 96.00, corresponding to an interest rate of 4%.

- Buying a put as above
- Selling a call means that you are selling someone else the right to buy a future from you

Interest rate falls

- If the interest rate **falls to 3%**, the price of the future will rise to 97.00
- You will pay interest at 3%
- However the holder of the call option will wish to exercise the option to buy the future at 96.00
- You therefore have to buy the future yourself at 97.00 and sell it to the option holder at 96.00, thus incurring a loss
- The loss you incur will be added to the 3% interest you have to pay to give an effective net interest rate of 4%
- If interest rates **fall further**, you will pay a lower interest rate but incur a larger loss on the option, netting out always at an interest rate of 4%

Interest rate rises

- If the interest rate rises above 4%, the option holder will not exercise the option
- You will pay interest at more than 4%, but be able to offset against this a profit on selling the future, to give an effective interest rate of 4%

5 Hedging strategy alternatives: Examples

FAST FORWARD

If you have to discuss which instrument should be used to hedge interest rate risk, consider **cost, flexibility, expectations** and **ability to benefit** from favourable interest rate movements.

5.1 Hedging instruments

Different hedging instruments often offer alternative ways of managing risk in a specific situation. In this section, after initial discussion of three possible hedging methods, we work through an example in which different ways in which a company can hedge interest rate risk are evaluated, covering both interest rate futures and interest rate options (interest rate guarantees).

5.2 Example: Hedging alternatives

It is 31 December. Octavo plc needs to borrow £6 million in three months' time for a period of six months. For the type of loan finance which Octavo would use, the rate of interest is currently 13% per year and the Corporate Treasurer is unwilling to pay a higher rate.

The treasurer is concerned about possible future fluctuations in interest rates, and is considering the following possibilities:

(a) Forward rate agreements (FRAs)
(b) Interest rate futures
(c) Interest rate guarantees or short-term interest rate caps

Required

Explain briefly how each of these three alternatives might be useful to Octavo plc.

Solution

Forward rate agreements (FRAs)

Entering into a FRA with a bank will allow the treasurer of Octavo plc effectively **to lock in an interest rate** for the six months of the loan. This agreement is independent of the loan itself, upon which the prevailing rate will be paid. If the FRA were negotiated to be at a rate of 13%, and the actual interest rate paid on the loan were higher than this, the bank will pay the difference between the rate paid and 13% to Octavo plc. Conversely, if the interest paid by Octavo turned out to be lower than 13%, they would have to pay the difference to the bank. Thus the cost of Octavo will be 13%.

Interest rate futures

Interest rate futures have the same effect as FRAs, in effectively **locking in an interest rate**, but they are standardised in terms of size, duration and terms. They can be **traded on an exchange** (such as LIFFE in London), and they will generally be **closed out before the maturity date**, yielding a profit or loss that is offset against the loss or profit on the money transaction that is being hedged. So, for example, as Octavo is concerned about rises in interest rates, the treasurer can sell future contracts now; if that rate does rise, their value will fall, and they can then be bought at a lower price, yielding a profit which will compensate for the increase in Octavo's loan interest cost. If interest rates fall, the lower interest cost of the loan will be offset by a loss on their futures contracts.

Interest rate guarantees

Interest rate guarantees is an option on an FRA and gives Octavo the opportunity to **benefit from favourable interest rate movements** as well as protecting them for their effects on adverse movements. They give the holder the **right** but not the **obligation** to use the FRA rate at a future maturity date. This means that if interest rates rise, the treasurer would exercise the option, and 'lock in' to the predetermined borrowing rate. If, however, interest rates fall, then the option would simply lapse, and Octavo would feel the benefit of lower interest rates.

5.3 Example: Hedging with futures

The Corporate Treasurer of Octavo decides on 31 December to hedge the interest rate risk on the £6 million to be borrowed in three months' time for six months by using interest rate futures. Her expectation is that interest rates will increase from 13% by 2% over the next three months.

The current price of March sterling three months' time deposit futures is 87.25. The standard contract size is £500,000, while the minimum price movement is one tick, the value of which is 0.01% per year of the contract size.

LEARNING OUTCOME 4 INTERNATIONAL FINANCE AND INTEREST RATE RISK

Set out calculations of the effect of using the futures market to hedge against movements in the interest rate and estimate the hedge efficiency:

(a) If interest rates increase from 13% by 2% and the futures market price moves by 2%
(b) If interest rates increase from 13% by 2% and the futures market price moves by 1.75%
(c) If interest rates fall from 13% by 1.5% and the futures market price moves by 1.25%

The time value of money, taxation and margin requirements can be ignored.

Solution

Hedge using the futures market

	(a)	(b)	(c)
Setup			
Which contract?	March		
What type?	Sell		
How many contracts?	$\dfrac{\text{Exposure}}{\text{Contract size}} \times \dfrac{\text{Loan period}}{\text{Length of contract}}$		
	$= \dfrac{£6,000,000}{£500,000} \times \dfrac{6}{3}$		
	= 24 contracts		
Tick size	$0.01\% \times 500,000 \times {}^3/_{12} = £12.50$		
Closing prices	(87.25 − 2) 85.25	(87.25 − 1.75) 85.50	(87.25 + 1.25) 88.50
Outcome			
(a) Futures outcome			
At opening rate	87.25	87.25	87.25
At closing rate	85.25	85.50	88.50
Tick movement	200 ticks profit	175 ticks profit	125 ticks loss
Futures outcome	200 × £12.50 × 24 = £60,000 profit	175 × £12.50 × 24 = £52,500 profit	125 × £12.50 × 24 = £37,500 loss
	£	£	£
(b) Net outcome			
Payment in spot market £6 million × 6/12 × 15% ((a) and (b))/11.5% (c)	(450,000)	(450,000)	(345,000)
Receipt in futures market	60,000	52,500	(37,500)
Net payment	(390,000)	(397,500)	(382,500)
	(a)	(b)	(c)
(c) Hedge efficiency	$\dfrac{60,000}{60,000^*} = 100\%$	$\dfrac{52,500}{60,000} = 87.5\%$	$\dfrac{45,000}{37,500} = 120\%$

* 60,000 = £6m × 6/12 × (15 − 13)%
** 45,000 = £6m × 6/12 × (13 − 11.5)%

5.4 Example: Hedging with IRGs

We now extend the example to look at an alternative hedging method.

Required

Calculate, for the situations above, whether the total cost of the loan after hedging would have been lower with the futures hedge chosen by the treasurer or with an interest rate guarantee which she could have purchased at 13% for a premium of 0.25% of the size of the loan to be guaranteed.

Again, the time value of money, taxation and margin requirements are to be ignored.

Solution

Futures hedge costs

(a) Interest £6m × 15% × 6/12 = £450,000
Less gain £60,000 = **£390,000**

(b) Interest (as in (a)) £450,000
Less gain £52,500 = **£397,500**

(c) Interest £6m × 11.5% × 6/12 = £345,000
Add loss £37,500 = **£382,500**

IRG hedge costs

The premium for the guarantee is:

£6m × 0.25% = £15,000.

The guarantee would be used in cases (a) and (b) when interest rates increase.

Then, total cost limiting interest rates to 13% is:

£6m × 13% × 6/12 = £390,000
Plus premium £15,000 equals **£405,000**

This costs more than the futures contracts hedge in cases (a) and (b).

In case (c), the guarantee is not used.

Interest costs at 11.5% are:

£6m × 11.5% × 6/12 = £345,000
Plus £15,000 premium = **£360,000**

This costs less than the futures hedge, reflecting the fact that declining to take up the interest rate option in the case of the guarantee has allowed the company to take advantage of the lower interest rates in the cash market.

> **Exam focus point**
>
> When considering interest rate or currency risk hedging, don't discuss every possible technique that you can recall. Marks will only be awarded for techniques that are **appropriate** to the circumstances described in the question.

LEARNING OUTCOME 4 INTERNATIONAL FINANCE AND INTEREST RATE RISK

Chapter Roundup

- The interest rates available are dependent on **risk, profit requirements** and **duration** and **size** of loan.
- Factors influencing **interest rate risk** include the following.
    - Fixed rate versus floating rate debt
    - The term of the loan
- **Forward rate agreements** hedge risk by **fixing the interest rate** on future borrowing.
- **Pooling** can help avoid paying higher interest rates on borrowing and can make management of interest rate risk easier.
- **Interest rate futures** can be used to hedge against interest rate changes between the current date and the date at which the interest rate on the lending or borrowing is set. Borrowers **sell futures** to hedge against **interest rate rises**; lenders **buy futures** to hedge against **interest rate falls**.
- **Interest rate options** allow an organisation to limit its exposure to adverse interest rate movements, while allowing it to take advantage of favourable interest rate movements.
- **Borrowers** can set a **maximum** on the interest they have to pay by buying **put** options.
- **Lenders** can set a **minimum** on the interest they receive by buying **call** options.
- **Caps** set a ceiling to the interest rate; a **floor** sets a lower limit. A **collar** is the simultaneous purchase of a cap and sale of a floor.
- If you have to discuss which instrument should be used to hedge interest rate risk, consider **cost**, **flexibility**, **expectations** and **ability to benefit** from favourable interest rate movements.

Quick Quiz

1. Identify three aspects of a debt in which a company may be exposed to risk from interest rate movements. (Example: Fixed rate **versus** floating rate debt.)

2. What name is given to the degree or percentage to which risk exposure is covered?

3. **Fill in the blanks**

    With a **collar**, the borrower buys (1) _____ and at the same time sells (2) _____ .

4. What is SONIA?

5.
    Managing a debt portfolio
    ```
         ?           ?           ?
        ---         ---         ---
        MIX         MIX         MIX
    ```

6. What is basis risk?

7. Number of futures contracts = $\dfrac{?}{?}$

8. If a company wishes to hedge borrowing at a future date, it should purchase _____ options, if it wishes to hedge lending, it should purchase _____ options.

Answers to Quick Quiz

1. Here are four aspects:

   (a) Fixed rate **versus** floating rate debt
   (b) Debt in different currencies
   (c) Different terms of loan
   (d) Term loan or overdraft facility

2. Hedge efficiency

3. (1) An interest rate cap
   (2) An interest rate floor

4. The rate of interest that applies to wholesale money market lending between London banks

5.
   Managing a debt portfolio
   - Maturity MIX
   - Currency MIX
   - Fixed and floating rate debt MIX

6. The risk that the price of the futures contract may not move as expected in relation to the value of the instrument being hedged.

7. Number of futures contracts = $\dfrac{\text{Amount of loan or deposit} \times \text{Time period of loan}}{\text{Futures contract size} \times \text{Length of futures contract}}$

8. If a company wishes to hedge borrowing at a future date, it should purchase **put** options, if it wishes to hedge lending, it should purchase **call** options.

LEARNING OUTCOME 4 INTERNATIONAL FINANCE AND INTEREST RATE RISK

End of chapter question

1. Regent plc (AIA May 2013)

Regent plc wants to raise a £20m floating rate loan at the beginning of September 2013 for a period of three months. The company is expecting to borrow at a rate of 7%, but it is worried that the interest rate may rise between now and the beginning of September. Therefore, the company wishes to hedge the interest rate risk using interest rate futures.

Currently, three month sterling futures are quoted as follows:

June	93.34
September	93.29
December	93.21

The futures contracts have a notional value of £500,000. The tick size is 0.01 and the tick value is £12.50.

The reason Regent plc wants to raise the £20m loan is because it is expanding operations overseas. The directors are considering establishing a subsidiary in country Z. 20 years ago the economy of country Z was considered under-developed. However, there has been significant economic growth since then. Some of this success in economic development has been attributed to the stable political situation and there has been only one change of government during the period. The current government has been keen to encourage business development in all areas. The government has managed to keep government debt at low levels in recent years. Twenty years ago the inflation rate was 11% but this has fallen steadily and is currently 3%. The exchange rate for the currency of country Z has fluctuated by relatively small amounts when compared to the US$ over the 20-year period. The stock exchange in country Z is still very small, but the banking sector has grown considerably.

Required

(a) Assume that at the beginning of September 2013 interest rates have risen and the company is borrowing at a rate of 8.25% and that the price of three month September sterling futures contracts has moved to 92.13. You are required to prepare calculations that evaluate the outcome of the interest rate hedge for the company in the above scenario. **(10 marks)**

(b) Advise the directors of Regent plc of the possible level of political risk that may exist in country Z.
(10 marks)

(Total 20 marks)

Swaps

Topic list	Syllabus reference
1 Interest rate swaps	LO4

Introduction

In this chapter, we conclude our discussion of risk management by focusing on **swaps**. Again, work through the examples we show but make sure also you understand **why** swaps are used – a question on swaps is virtually certain to contain a discussion element.

LEARNING OUTCOME 4 INTERNATIONAL FINANCE AND INTEREST RATE RISK

1 Interest rate swaps

> **FAST FORWARD**
>
> **Interest rate swaps** are where two parties agree to exchange interest rate payments.
>
> Interest rate swaps can act as a means of **switching** from paying one type of interest to another, raising **less expensive loans** and **securing better** deposit **rates**.
>
> A **fixed to floating rate currency swap** is a combination of a currency and interest rate swap.

Key term

> **Interest rate swap** is an agreement whereby the parties to the agreement exchange interest rate commitments.

1.1 Swap procedures

Interest rate swaps involve two parties agreeing to exchange interest payments with each other over an agreed period. In practice, however, the major players in the swaps market are banks and many other types of institution can become involved, for example national and local governments and international institutions.

In the simplest form of interest rate swap, Party A agrees to pay the interest on Party B's loan, while party B reciprocates by paying the interest on A's loan. If the swap is to make sense, **the two parties must swap interest which has different characteristics**. Assuming that the interest swapped is in the same currency, the most common motivation for the swap is to switch from paying floating rate interest to fixed interest or *vice versa*. This type of swap is known as a '**plain vanilla**' or **generic** swap.

1.2 Why bother to swap?

Obvious questions to ask are:

- Why do the companies bother swapping interest payments with each other?
- Why don't they just terminate their original loan and take out a new one?

The answer is that **transaction costs** may be too high. Terminating an original loan early may involve a significant termination fee and taking out a new loan will involve issue costs. Arranging a swap can be significantly cheaper, even if a banker is used as an intermediary. Because the banker is simply acting as an agent on the swap arrangement and has to bear no default risk, the arrangement fee can be kept low.

1.3 Advantages of interest rate swaps in a single currency

(a) They enable a **switch** from **floating rate** to **fixed rate interest**, or *vice versa*, for use as a hedge against interest rate risk.

(b) The **arrangement costs** are **often significantly less** than terminating an existing loan and taking out a new one.

(c) They can be used to make **interest rate savings**, either out of the counterparty or out of the loan markets, by using the principle of comparative advantage.

(d) They are available for **longer periods** than the short-term methods of hedging risk (FRAs, futures, options) that we have considered in earlier chapters.

(e) They are **flexible** and can be easily reversed.

(f) They can be a means of **accessing a type of finance** that would **not be available directly**.

Like all financial instruments, swaps can be used for speculation as well as hedging. In cases receiving much publicity, some local authority treasurers in the UK have engaged in such speculation with disastrous results.

1.4 Example: Interest rate swaps (1)

Company A has borrowed £10 million at a fixed interest rate of 9% per annum. Company B has also borrowed £10 million but pays interest at SONIA + 1%. SONIA is currently 8% per annum. The directors of Company A feel that interest rates are going to fall and would prefer to be paying floating rate interest. The feeling at Company B is that interest rate risk could be removed if they were paying fixed interest and that this would facilitate cash planning. The two companies agree to swap interest payments. A pays SONIA + 1% to B and B pays 9% to A. No loan principals are swapped and both parties retain the obligation to repay their original loans. A summary of the arrangements can be shown as follows.

	Company A		*Company B*
Interest paid on original loan	(9%)		(SONIA + 1%)
A pays to B	(SONIA + 1%)	→	SONIA + 1%
B pays to A	9%	←	(9%)
Net payment after swap	(SONIA + 1%)		(9%)

Both parties have achieved their objective of switching the nature of their interest payments and, if SONIA stays at 8%, neither party gains or loses. However, if SONIA falls, A gains at the expense of B and the reverse happens if SONIA rises.

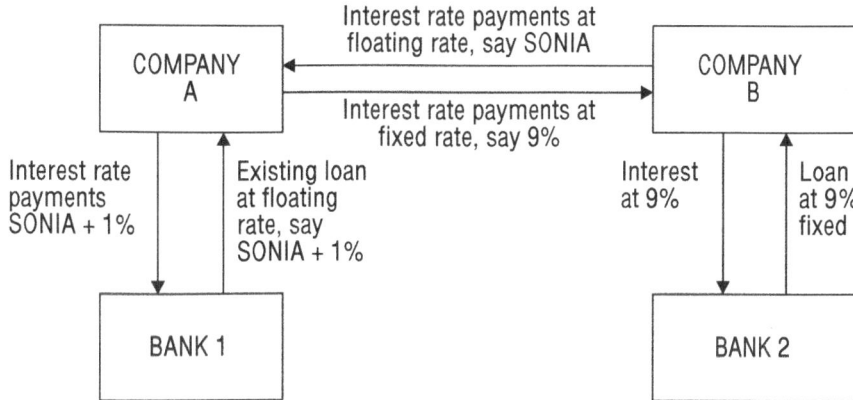

Figure 1 Interest rate swap

1.5 Interest rate swap complications

Most interest rate swap deals are more complex than the simple arrangement illustrated above. It is unlikely that both parties will have loans outstanding of exactly the same amount or that they will want to arrange an exact swap of each others' interest payments. In practice, a notional amount of loan principal is agreed and interest payments made to each other are negotiated. This can result in one party making a **gain out of the other** or, in some cases, both parties making a gain out of the loan markets. The following example illustrates a situation where both parties gain.

1.6 Example: Interest rate swaps (2)

Goodcredit plc has been given a high credit rating. It can borrow at a fixed rate of 11%, or at a variable interest rate equal to SONIA, which also happens to be 11% at the moment. It would like to borrow at a variable rate. Secondtier plc is a company with a lower credit rating, which can borrow at a fixed rate of 12.5% or at a variable rate of SONIA plus 0.5%. It would like to borrow at a fixed rate.

LEARNING OUTCOME 4 INTERNATIONAL FINANCE AND INTEREST RATE RISK

	Goodcredit	**Secondtier**	**Sum total**
Company wants	Variable	Fixed	
Would pay (no swap)	(SONIA)	(12.5%)	(SONIA + 12.5%)
Could pay	(11%)	(SONIA + 0.5%)	(SONIA + 11.5%)
Potential gain			1%
Split evenly	0.5%	0.5%	
Expected outcome	(SONIA – 0.5%)	(12%)	(SONIA + 11.5%)
Swap terms			
Could pay	(11%)	(SONIA + 0.5%)	(SONIA + 11.5%)
Swap floating	(SONIA + 0.5%)	SONIA + 0.5%	
Swap fixed	12%	(12%)	
Net paid	(SONIA – 0.5%)	(12%)	(SONIA + 11.5%)
Would pay	(SONIA)	(12.5%)	(SONIA + 12.5%)
Gain	0.5%	0.5%	1%

The results of the swap are that Goodcredit ends up paying variable rate interest, but at a lower cost than it could get from a bank, and Secondtier ends up paying fixed rate interest, also at a lower cost than it could get from investors or a bank.

If both parties ended up paying interest at a lower rate than was obtainable from the bank, where did this gain come from? To answer this question, set out a table of the rates at which both companies could borrow from the bank.

	Goodcredit	Secondtier	Difference
Can borrow at fixed rate	11%	12.5%	1.5%
Can borrow at floating rate	SONIA	SONIA + 0.5%	0.5%
Difference between differences			1%

Goodcredit has a **better credit rating** than Secondtier in both types of loan market, but **its advantage** is **comparatively higher** in the fixed interest market. The 1% differential between Goodcredit's advantage in the two types of loan may represent a market imperfection or there may be a good reason for it. Whatever the reason, it represents a potential gain which can be made out of a swap arrangement.

Assume that the gain is split equally between Goodcredit and Secondtier, 0.5% each. Then Goodcredit will be targeting a floating rate loan of SONIA less 0.5% (0.5% less than that at which it can borrow from the bank). Similarly, Secondtier will be targeting a fixed interest loan of 12.5% – 0.5% = 12%. These are precisely the rates which are obtained by the swap arrangement illustrated above. Note that for the swap to give a gain to both parties:

(a) Each company must borrow in the loan market in which it has **comparative advantage**. Goodcredit has the greatest advantage when it borrows fixed interest. Secondtier has the least disadvantage when it borrows floating rate.

(b) The parties must actually **want** interest of the opposite type to that in which they have comparative advantage. Goodcredit wants floating and Secondtier wants fixed.

Once the target interest rate for each company has been established, there is an infinite number of swap arrangements which will produce the same net result. The example illustrated above is only one of them.

Question — Swaps

We illustrated above one way in which the swap could work. Swap fixed 12%, swap floating (SONIA + 0.5%). Suggest an alternative arrangement for the swap by entering swap interest payments into this *pro-forma* to move from the original interest paid to the desired result.

	Goodcredit	Secondtier
Could pay	(11%)	(SONIA + 0.5%)
Swap floating		
Swap fixed		
Net interest cost	(SONIA – 0.5%)	(12%)

Answer

Enter any figure into any slot of the pro-forma and the other figures must automatically balance out. Here is one of many possible solutions.

	Goodcredit	Secondtier
Could pay	(11%)	(SONIA + 0.5%)
Swap floating	(SONIA – 0.5%)	SONIA – 0.5%
Swap fixed	11%	(11%)
Net interest cost	(SONIA – 0.5%)	(12%)

Other types of interest rate swaps	
Basis swap	Swap between two different types of floating rate debt in the same currency
Zero coupon swap	Swap between floating rate debt and a single payment of fixed interest at maturity
Amortising swap	Swap where notional principal decreases over its life for matching with loan with similar characteristics
Forward swap	A swap transacted today to commence on an agreed future date
Callable swap	A swap giving the payer of fixed interest the right but not the obligation to terminate the swap
Puttable swap	Swap giving the receiver of fixed interest the right to terminate the swap

1.7 Termination of swaps

The ability to terminate a swap is an important aspect of the liquidity of the market.

(a) Termination takes place by both parties agreeing a **settlement interest rate**, generally the current market rate for swaps of an appropriate type and time period to maturity.

(b) The **settlement fee** is the difference between the swap fixed interest rate and the settlement rate, discounted to maturity at the settlement rate.

1.8 Example: Termination of interest rate swap

Pauline plc entered a four year £10 million interest rate swap with McGee Bank in which Pauline pays 7% fixed interest and receives SONIA. After one year, the market rate for a three year sterling swap has fallen to 5% against SONIA. Pauline wishes to terminate the swap arrangement. What amount should Pauline pay on settlement? (Assume annual interest payment.)

Solution

Excess interest = 7% – 5% = 2% per year for three years.

2% × £10 million = £200,000

Discounted for three years at 5% = £544,650

Chapter Roundup

- **Interest rate swaps** are where two parties agree to exchange interest rate payments.
- Interest rate swaps can act as a means of **switching** from paying one type of interest to another, raising **less expensive loans** and **securing better** deposit **rates**.
- A **fixed to floating rate currency swap** is a combination of a currency and interest rate swap.

Quick Quiz

1. What happens if one party to a swap arrangement defaults on the arrangements to pay interest?
2. What is a generic swap?
3. What is a fixed to floating currency swap?
4. Give three uses of an interest rate swap.
5. What are the two conditions needed for an interest rate swap to be successful?
6. How are swaps terminated?
7. How can the parties to a swap counter possible market risk?

Answers to Quick Quiz

1. The original party is liable to the lender

2. A switch from paying floating rate interest to fixed rate interest or *vice versa*

3. A fixed to floating rate currency swap is a combination of a straight currency swap and an interest rate swap.

4. Any three of:

    (a) Switching from paying one type of interest to another
    (b) Raising less expensive loans
    (c) Securing better deposit rates
    (d) Acting as a cost-effective method of managing interest rate risk
    (e) Avoiding charges for early termination of loans
    (f) Accessing a type of finance that could not be accessed directly

5. (a) Each company must borrow in the loan market in which it has comparative advantage.

    (b) The parties must actually want interest of the opposite type to that in which they have comparative advantage.

6. Both parties agree a settlement interest rate, generally the current market rate for swaps of an appropriate type and time period to maturity.

7. Use a clause maintaining the value of notional debt

End of chapter question

Mesha plc (AIA May 2008)

The abbreviated statement of financial position for Mesha plc at the end of 2006 is as follows.

	£ million
Non-current assets	55
Current assets	15
Total assets	70
20,000,000 ordinary shares at £1 each	20
Debenture 12% 2009 (redeemable 31.12.2009)	50
Capital employed	**70**

The debenture was issued several years ago when interest rates were a lot higher than currently. Current redemption yields on a debenture of the same risk class as Mesha are 6%.

Mesha is considering the possibility of buying the debt back on the open market. It currently does not have the cash to redeem the debt and would like to borrow in order to refinance the debt. It can either borrow at a fixed rate of interest of 6% per annum or at a variable rate of SONIA + 1% per annum. The Finance Director of Mesha favours borrowing at the variable rate because he feels that interest rates are likely to fall even further.

Mesha's bank has offered to arrange a swap deal for the company with another of its customers, a company called Ahsem. Ahsem has an inferior credit rating to Mesha and can only borrow at a fixed rate of 7.7% and a variable rate of SONIA + 1.7%. Ahsem has decided to borrow at a fixed rate in order to diversify its debt portfolio.

Required

(a) Calculate the likely amount that Mesha would have to borrow in order to fully redeem its debenture. Ignore transaction costs and assume that the interest on the debenture is paid annually at the end of each year. **(4 marks)**

(b) On the assumption that Mesha and Ahsem share the benefits of the swap deal equally show, with suitable calculations, how a swap would work in this case. **(10 marks)**

(c) Mesha have asked you to look into alternative sources of funds to repurchase its debenture. Discuss the main criteria you would use in deciding the most suitable source of finance for the company. **(6 marks)**

(Total 20 marks)

Working capital management

Management of working capital

Topic list	Syllabus reference
1 Working capital and its management	LO5
2 Working capital and cash flow	LO5

Introduction

In the following chapters, we consider functions of the financial manager relating to the **management of working capital** in general terms.

1 Working capital and its management

1.1 Importance of working capital management

FAST FORWARD

The amount tied up in **working capital** is equal to the value of raw materials, work-in-progress, finished inventories and receivables less payables. The size of this net figure has a direct effect on the **liquidity** of an organisation.

Key term

> **Net working capital** of a business is its current assets less its current liabilities.

Key current assets and liabilities	
Current assets	**Current liabilities**
Cash	Amounts payable to trade creditors
Stock of raw materials	Taxation payable
Work in progress	Dividend payments due
Finished goods	Short-term loans
Amounts receivable from debtors	Long-term loans maturing within one year
Marketable securities	

Every business needs adequate **liquid resources** to maintain day-to-day cash flow. It needs enough to pay wages, salaries and creditors if it is to keep its workforce and ensure its supplies.

Maintaining adequate working capital is **not just important** in the **short term**. Adequate liquidity is needed to ensure the survival of the business in the long term. Even a profitable company may fail without adequate cash flow to meet its liabilities.

On the other hand, an excessively conservative approach to working capital management resulting in high levels of cash holdings will harm profits because the opportunity to make a return on the assets tied up as cash will have been missed.

Exam focus point

Some aspect of working capital management is likely to be included in every exam.

Key term

> **Working capital cycle** is the period of time which elapses between the point at which cash begins to be expended on the production of a product and the collection of cash from a purchaser.

The connection between investment in working capital and cash flow may be illustrated by means of the **working capital cycle** (also called the **cash cycle, operating cycle** or **trading cycle**).

The working capital cycle in a manufacturing business equals:

- The average time that raw materials remain in inventory
- **Less** the period of credit taken from suppliers
- **Plus** the time taken to produce the goods
- **Plus** the time taken by customers to pay for the goods

If the turnover periods for inventories and receivables lengthen, or the payment period to creditors shortens, then the operating cycle will lengthen and the investment in working capital will increase.

1.2 Example: Working capital cycle

Wines Ltd buys raw materials from suppliers that allow Wines 2.5 months' credit. The raw materials remain in stock for one month, and it takes Wines two months to produce the goods. The goods are sold within a couple of days of production being completed and customers take on average 1.5 months to pay.

Required

Calculate Wines's working capital cycle.

Solution

We can ignore the time finished goods are in inventory as it is no more than a couple of days.

	Months
The average time that raw materials remain in inventory	1.0
Less the time taken to pay suppliers	(2.5)
The time taken to produce the goods	2.0
The time taken by customers to pay for the goods	1.5
	2.0

The company's working capital cycle is two months. This can be illustrated diagrammatically as follows.

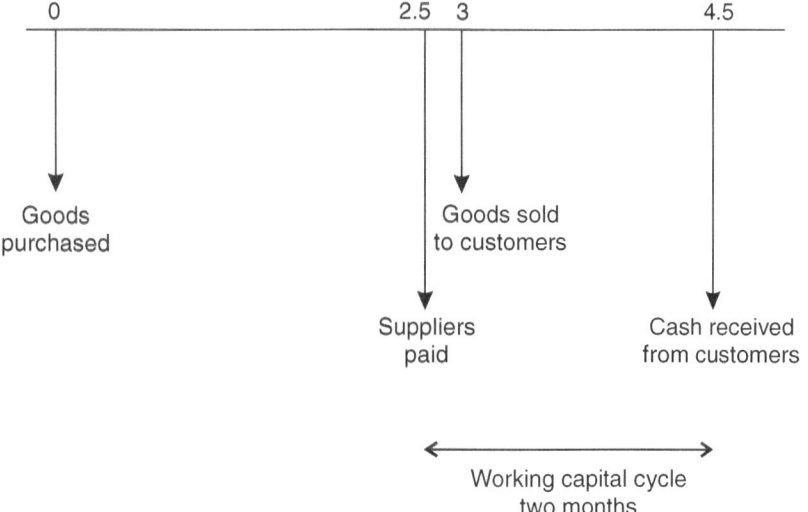

The working capital cycle is the period between the suppliers being paid and the cash being received from the customers.

1.3 Working capital (liquidity) ratios

FAST FORWARD

Liquidity ratios may help to indicate whether a company is **over-capitalised**, with excessive working capital, or if a business is likely to fail. A business which is trying to do too much too quickly with too little long-term capital is **overtrading**.

1.3.1 The current ratio and the quick ratio

The **current ratio** is the standard test of liquidity.

Key term

$$\text{Current ratio} = \frac{\text{Current assets}}{\text{Current liabilities}}$$

A company should have enough current assets that give a promise of 'cash to come' to meet its commitments to pay its current liabilities. Obviously, a ratio in **excess of 1** should be expected.

In practice, a ratio comfortably in excess of 1 should be expected, but what is 'comfortable' varies between different types of businesses.

1.3.2 The quick ratio

Key term

> **Quick ratio** or **acid test ratio** = $\dfrac{\text{Current assets less inventories}}{\text{Current liabilities}}$

Companies are not able to convert all their current assets into cash very quickly. In some businesses, where inventory turnover is slow, most stocks are not very liquid assets, because the cash cycle is so long. For these reasons, we calculate an additional liquidity ratio, known as the quick ratio or acid test ratio.

This ratio should ideally be at least 1 for companies with a slow inventory turnover. For companies with a fast inventory turnover, a quick ratio can be less than 1 without suggesting that the company is in cash flow difficulties.

1.3.3 The receivables' payment period

Key term

> **Receivables' days** or **receivables' payment period** = $\dfrac{\text{Trade receivables}}{\text{Credit sales turnover}} \times 365 \text{ days}$

This is a rough measure of the average length of time it takes for a company's debtors to pay what they owe.

The trade debtors are not the **total** figure for receivables in the statement of financial position, which includes prepayments and non-trade receivables. The trade debtors figure will be itemised in an analysis of the total debtors, in a note to the accounts.

The estimate of receivable days is only approximate.

(a) The **year end value** of receivables might be **abnormally high** or low compared with the 'normal' level the company usually has. This may apply especially to smaller companies, where the size of year-end receivables may largely depend on whether a few or even a single large debtor pay just before or just after the year-end.

(b) Revenue in the statement of comprehensive income excludes sales tax (value added tax (VAT)), but the receivables' figure in the statement of financial position includes VAT. We are not strictly comparing like with like.

1.3.4 The stock turnover period

Key terms

> **Inventory turnover** = $\dfrac{\text{Cost of sales}}{\text{Average inventory}}$
>
> The inventory turnover period can also be calculated:
>
> **Inventory turnover period (Finished goods)** = $\dfrac{\text{Average inventory}}{\text{Cost of sales}} \times 365 \text{ days}$
>
> **Raw materials inventory holding period** = $\dfrac{\text{Average raw materials inventory}}{\text{Annual purchases}} \times 365 \text{ days}$
>
> **Average production (work-in-progress) period** = $\dfrac{\text{Average WIP} \times \text{Degree of WIP completion} \times 365 \text{ days}}{\text{Cost of sales}}$

These indicate the average number of days for which items of inventory are held for. As with the average debt collection period, these are only approximate figures, but ones which should be reliable enough for finding changes over time. Average inventory can be replaced by end-of-year inventory in order to compare changes in inventory turnover over the year.

A lengthening inventory turnover period indicates:

(a) A **slowdown** in **trading**, or

(b) A **build-up** in **inventory levels**, perhaps suggesting that the investment in inventories is becoming excessive

If we add together the inventory days and the receivable days, this should give us an indication of how soon inventory is convertible into cash, thereby giving a further indication of the **company's liquidity**.

1.3.5 The payables payment period

Key term

> **Payables payment period** = $\dfrac{\text{Average trade payables}}{\text{Purchases or Cost of sales}} \times 365$ days
>
> or **Payables turnover period**

The payables payment period often helps to assess a company's liquidity; an increase in paybles days is often a sign of lack of long-term finance or poor management of current assets, resulting in the use of extended credit from suppliers, increased bank overdraft and so on.

All the ratios calculated above will **vary by industry**; hence **comparisons** of ratios calculated with other similar companies in the same industry are important.

You may need to use the periods to calculate the operating cycle.

	Days
Raw materials inventory holding period	X
Payables payment period	(X)
Average production period	X
Inventory turnover period (finished goods)	X
Receivables payment period	X
Operating cycle	X

1.4 The need for funds for investment in current assets

These liquidity ratios are a guide to the risk of cash flow problems and insolvency. If a company suddenly finds that it is **unable to renew** its **short-term liabilities** (for example, if the bank suspends its overdraft facilities, there will be a **danger of insolvency** unless the company is able to turn enough of its current assets into cash quickly).

Current liabilities are often a cheap method of finance (trade creditors do not usually carry an interest cost). Companies may therefore consider that, in the interest of higher profits, it is worth accepting some risk of insolvency by increasing current liabilities, taking the maximum credit possible from suppliers.

1.5 Working capital needs of different types of business

Different industries have different optimum working capital profiles, reflecting their methods of doing business and what they are selling.

(a) Businesses with a lot of **cash sales** and few credit sales should have **minimal debtors**.

(b) Businesses that exist solely to trade will only have **finished goods in stock**, whereas **manufacturers** will have **raw materials** and **work in progress** as well. Also some finished goods, notably foodstuffs, have to be sold within a few days because of their perishable nature.

(c) **Large companies** may be able to use their strength as customers to obtain **extended credit periods** from their suppliers. By contrast small companies, particularly those that have recently commenced trading, may be required to pay their suppliers immediately.

(d) Some businesses will be receiving **most of their monies** at **certain times** of the year, while incurring expenses throughout the year. Examples include travel agents who will have peaks reflecting demand for holidays during the summer and at Christmas.

1.6 Over-capitalisation and working capital

If there are excessive inventories, receivables and cash, and very few payables, there will be an over-investment by the company in current assets. Working capital will be excessive and the company will be in this respect over-capitalised.

Indicators of over-capitalisation	
Sales/working capital	Low compared with previous years or, similar companies
Liquidity ratios	Current ratio > 2:1 Quick ratio > 1:1
High receivables payment / inventory turnover periods / Low payables payment period	Long turnover periods for inventory and receivables or short credit period from suppliers may be unnecessary

Overcapitalisation can be unsustainable. The inability to generate adequate returns on invested capital can lead to **investor dissatisfaction** and potential **withdrawal of investment**, threatening the company's long-term viability. Additionally, having too much capital tied up in long-term assets can **reduce a company's financial flexibility**. It may struggle to adapt to market changes or seize new opportunities quickly.

1.6.1 Overtrading

In contrast with over-capitalisation, overtrading happens when a business tries to **do too much too quickly** with **too little long-term capital**, so that it is trying to support too large a volume of trade with the capital resources at its disposal.

Symptoms of overtrading are as follows:

(a) There is a **rapid increase** in **turnover**.

(b) There is a **rapid increase** in the **volume of current assets** and possibly also non-current assets. **Inventory turnover** and **receivables turnover** might slow down, in which case the rate of increase in inventories and receivables would be even greater than the rate of increase in sales.

(c) There is only a **small increase** in **proprietors' capital** (perhaps through retained profits). Most of the increase in assets is financed by credit, especially:

  (i) **Trade payables** – the payment period to creditors is likely to lengthen

  (ii) A **bank overdraft**, which often reaches or even exceeds the limit of the facilities agreed by the bank

(d) Some **debt ratios** and **liquidity ratios** alter dramatically.

  (i) The **proportion** of **total assets** financed by proprietors' capital falls, and the proportion financed by credit rises.

  (ii) The **current ratio** and the **quick ratio** fall.

  (iii) The business might have a **liquid deficit**, that is, an excess of current liabilities over current assets.

  (iv) The rate of revenue to working capital will increase as revenue increases rapidly.

Exam focus point

> This list of signs is important; you must be aware of why businesses run into financial difficulties. In the exam you might be expected to diagnose overtrading from information given about a company.

Even if an overtrading business operates at a profit, it will potentially suffer from the following issues:

(i) **Liquidity Issues:** Businesses may struggle to pay their debts on time, leading to a **loss of creditworthiness**, strained relationships with suppliers, and potential legal action.

(ii) **Increased Financial Risk:** The **reliance on short-term financing**, such as overdrafts and trade credit, increases financial risk. High levels of short-term debt can lead to **higher interest costs and financial distress**, especially if the business cannot convert assets into cash quickly enough.

(iii) **Operational Inefficiencies:** Rapid expansion without adequate capital can lead to operational inefficiencies. Inventory management may become challenging, leading to **stockouts or excess inventory**, both of which can harm profitability.

(iv) **Sustainability Concerns**: Overtrading is not sustainable in the long term. The **continuous strain on financial resources** can lead to business failure, as the company might not be able to sustain its operations or growth without adequate capital.

1.7 Example: Overtrading

Great Ambition appoints a new managing director who has great plans to expand the company. He wants to increase revenue by 100% within two years, and to do this he employs extra sales staff. He recognises that customers do not want to have to wait for deliveries, and so he decides that the company must build up its inventory levels. There is a substantial increase in the company's inventory. These are held in additional warehouse space which is now rented. The company also buys new cars for its extra sales representatives.

The managing director's policies are immediately successful in boosting sales, which double in just over one year. Inventory levels are now much higher, but the company takes longer credit from its suppliers, even though some suppliers have expressed their annoyance at the length of time they must wait for payment. Credit terms for debtors are unchanged, and so the volume of debtors, like the volume of sales, rises by 100%.

In spite of taking longer credit, the company still needs to increase its overdraft facilities with the bank, which are raised from a limit of $40,000 to one of $80,000. The company is profitable, and retains some profits in the business, but profit margins have fallen. **Gross profit margins** are lower because some prices have been reduced to obtain extra sales. **Net profit margins** are lower because overhead costs are higher. These include sales representatives' wages, car expenses and depreciation on cars, warehouse rent and additional losses from having to write off out-of-date and slow-moving inventory items.

The statement of financial position of the company might change over time from (A) to (B).

	Statement of financial position (A)			Statement of financial position (B)		
	$	$	$	$	$	$
Non-current assets			160,000			210,000
Current assets						
Inventory		60,000			150,000	
Receivables		64,000			135,000	
Cash and cash equivalents		1,000			–	
		125,000			285,000	
Current liabilities						
Bank	25,000			80,000		
Payables	50,000			200,000		
		75,000			280,000	
			50,000			5,000

LEARNING OUTCOME 5 WORKING CAPITAL MANAGEMENT

	Statement of financial position (A)	Statement of financial position (B)
	$ $ $	$ $ $
	210,000	215,000
Share capital	10,000	10,000
Retained earnings	200,000	205,000
	210,000	215,000
Sales	$1,000,000	$2,000,000
Gross profit	$200,000	$300,000
Net profit	$50,000	$20,000

In situation (B), the company has **reached** its **overdraft** limit and has **four times** as many **creditors** as in situation (A) but with only **twice the sales turnover**. **Inventory levels** are much **higher**, and **inventory turnover** is **lower**.

The company is overtrading. If it had to pay its next trade creditor, or salaries and wages, before it received any income, it could not do so without the bank allowing it to exceed its overdraft limit. The company is profitable, although profit margins have fallen, and it ought to expect a prosperous future. But if it does not sort out its cash flow and liquidity, it will not survive to enjoy future profits.

Suitable solutions to the problem would be measures to reduce the degree of overtrading.

(a) **New capital** from the shareholders could be injected.

(b) **Better control** could be applied to inventories and receivables. The company could **abandon ambitious plans** for increased sales and more non-current asset purchases until the business has had time to consolidate its position, and build up its capital base with retained profits.

A business seeking to increase its turnover too rapidly without an adequate capital base is not the only **cause of overtrading**. **Other causes** are as follows:

(a) When a business repays a loan, it often replaces the old loan with a new one. However, a business might **repay a loan without replacing it**, with the consequence that it has **less long-term capital** to finance its current level of operations.

(b) A business might be profitable, but in a period of **inflation**, its **retained profits** might be **insufficient** to pay for **replacement** non-current assets and inventories, which now cost more because of inflation.

1.8 Maturity matching of assets and finance

Maturity matching, or asset-liability matching, involves aligning the maturities of assets and the financing used to purchase them. This helps in managing financial risks associated with interest rate fluctuations and refinancing. It ensures that long-term assets are financed with long-term funds, and short-term assets are financed with short-term funds.

Maturity matching **contributes to the sustainability** of a business by promoting **prudent financial management**. It prevents scenarios where the company might face a liquidity crunch due to a mismatch between asset and liability maturities. This practice ensures that a company's obligations are met without undue stress on its liquidity and financial stability.

1.9 Example: Maturity matching

A company planning to purchase new machinery worth $600,000. The machinery is expected to have a useful life of 8 years. To ensure financial sustainability, the company should ideally finance this purchase with a long-term loan or equity that matches the 8-year life span of the machinery, rather than using short-term financing options like a one-year bank loan or overdraft.

Scenario 1: Mismatched Financing

The company decides to finance the machinery with a one-year bank loan. After one year, the loan needs to be repaid or refinanced. If the company cannot secure a new loan or if interest rates have increased, it may face financial difficulties, impacting its liquidity and operational stability.

Scenario 2: Matched Financing

The company finances the machinery with an 8-year loan. The loan's repayment schedule aligns with the expected cash flows generated by the machinery over its useful life. This reduces the pressure on the company's cash flow and ensures that the business can manage its financial obligations without undue stress.

1.10 The working capital requirement

Computing the working capital requirement is a matter of calculating the value of current assets less current liabilities, perhaps by taking averages over a one-year period.

The level of investment in working capital may be described as aggressive, conservative or moderate in approach. The approach will reflect the attitude of owners and managers.

1.11 Example: Working capital requirements

The following data relate to Corn Ltd, a manufacturing company.

Revenue for the year	$1,500,000
Costs as percentages of sales	%
Direct materials	30
Direct labour	25
Variable overheads	10
Fixed overheads	15
Selling and distribution	5

On average:

(a) Debtors take 2.5 months before payment

(b) Raw materials are in inventory for three months

(c) Work-in-progress represents two months worth of half produced goods

(d) Finished goods represents one month's production

(e) Credit is taken as follows:

(i)	Direct materials	2 months
(ii)	Direct labour	1 week
(iii)	Variable overheads	1 month
(iv)	Fixed overheads	1 month
(v)	Selling and distribution	0.5 months

Work-in-progress and finished goods are valued at material, labour and variable expense cost.

Compute the working capital requirement of Corn Ltd assuming the labour force is paid for 50 working weeks a year.

Solution

(a) The annual costs incurred will be as follows:

		$
Direct materials	30% of $1,500,000	450,000
Direct labour	25% of $1,500,000	375,000
Variable overheads	10% of $1,500,000	150,000
Fixed overheads	15% of $1,500,000	225,000
Selling and distribution	5% of $1,500,000	75,000

LEARNING OUTCOME 5 WORKING CAPITAL MANAGEMENT

(b) The average value of current assets will be as follows:

			$	$
Raw materials	3/12 × $450,000			112,500
Work-in-progress				
Materials (50% complete)	1/12 × $450,000		37,500	
Labour (50% complete)	1/12 × $375,000		31,250	
Variable overheads (50% complete)	1/12 × $150,000		12,500	
				81,250
Finished goods				
Materials	1/12 × $450,000		37,500	
Labour	1/12 × $375,000		31,250	
Variable overheads	1/12 × $150,000		12,500	
				81,250
Receivables	2.5/12 × $1,500,000			312,500
				587,500

(c) Average value of current liabilities will be as follows:

Materials	2/12 × $450,000	75,000	
Labour	1/50 × $375,000	7,500	
Variable overheads	1/12 × $150,000	12,500	
Fixed overheads	1/12 × $225,000	18,750	
Selling and distribution	0.5/12 × $75,000	3,125	
			116,875

(d) Working capital required is ($(587,500 – 116,875)) = **470,625**

It has been assumed that all the direct materials are allocated to work-in-progress when production starts.

Exam focus point

In the exam you may be asked to calculate the working capital requirement in £ using the method described above. Alternatively, you may be asked to calculate the requirement in terms of time, in which case the answer would be the length of the **working capital cycle** (see earlier in this chapter).

1.12 Predicting business failure

Investors will wish to know whether additional funds could be lent to the company with reasonable safety, and whether the company would fail without additional funds.

One method of predicting business failure is the use of **liquidity ratios** (the current ratio and the quick ratio). A company with a current ratio well below 2:1 or a quick ratio well below 1:1 might be considered illiquid and in danger of failure, although as previously noted the value of these ratios depends upon the nature of the business being considered.

2 Working capital and cash flow

FAST FORWARD

Cash budgeting is an important part of short-term planning, but there will always be unforeseen changes which can affect the pattern and quantities of cash flows.

2.1 Cash flow planning

Since a company must have adequate cash inflows to survive, management should plan and control cash flows as well as profitability. **Cash budgeting** is an important element in short-term cash flow planning. If a budget reveals that a short-term cash shortage can be expected, steps will be taken to meet the problem (perhaps by arranging a bigger bank overdraft facility).

Cash budgets and cash flow forecasts on their own do not give full protection against a cash shortage and enforced liquidation of the business by creditors. There may be **unexpected changes** in cash flow patterns.

Question
Changes to cash flow

Give examples of unforeseen changes which may affect cash flow patterns.

Answer

Your list probably included some of the following:

(a) A change in the **general economic environment**. An economic recession will cause a slump in trade.

(b) A **new product**, launched by a competitor, which takes business away from a company's traditional and established product lines.

(c) **New cost-saving product technology**, which forces the company to invest in the new technology to remain competitive.

(d) **Moves by competitors** which have to be countered (for, example a price reduction or a sales promotion).

(e) **Changes in consumer preferences**, resulting in a fall in demand.

(f) **Government action** against certain trade practices or against trade with a country that a company has dealings with.

(g) **Strikes** or other industrial action.

(h) **Natural disasters**, such as floods or fire damage, which curtail an organisation's activities.

2.2 Strategic fund management

Strategic fund management is an extension of cash flow planning, which takes into consideration the ability of a business to overcome unforeseen problems with cash flows. It recognises that the assets of a business can be divided into three categories:

(a) Assets which are needed to carry out the 'core' activities of the business.

(b) **Assets** which are **not essential** for carrying out the main activities of the business, and which could be **sold off** at **fairly short notice**. These assets will consist mainly of short-term marketable investments.

(c) **Assets** which are **not essential** for carrying out the main activities of the business, and which could be sold off to raise cash, although it would probably take **time to arrange** the sale, and the amount of **cash obtainable** from the sale might be **uncertain**. These assets would include:

   (i) Long-term investments (for example, substantial shareholdings in other companies)

   (ii) Subsidiary companies engaged in 'peripheral' activities, which might be sold off to another company or in a management buyout

   (iii) Land and buildings

LEARNING OUTCOME 5 WORKING CAPITAL MANAGEMENT

If an unexpected event takes place which threatens a company's cash position, the company could meet the threat by:

(a) **Working capital management** to improve cash flows by reducing inventories and receivables, taking more credit, or negotiating a higher bank overdraft facility

(b) **Changes to dividend policy**

(c) Arranging to **sell off non-essential assets**

> **Exam focus point**
>
> Look out when you read through the remaining chapters of this text for ways of improving working capital management, as this is a popular topic in the exam.

Chapter Roundup

- The amount tied up in **working capital** is equal to the value of raw materials, work-in-progress, finished inventories and receivables less payables. The size of this net figure has a direct effect on the **liquidity** of an organisation.

- **Liquidity ratios** may help to indicate whether a company is **over-capitalised**, with excessive working capital, or if a business is likely to fail. A business which is trying to do too much too quickly with too little long-term capital is **overtrading**.

- Cash budgeting is an important part of short-term planning, but there will always be unforeseen changes which can affect the pattern and quantities of cash flows.

LEARNING OUTCOME 5 WORKING CAPITAL MANAGEMENT

Quick Quiz

1. Which of the following is the most likely to be a symptom of overtrading?

    A Static levels of inventory turnover
    B Rapid increase in profits
    C Increase in the level of the current ratio
    D Rapid increase in sales

2. The operating cycle is:

    A The time [_____]
    Less B The time [_____]
    Plus C The time [_____]
    Plus D The time [_____]

    Fill in the blanks

3. **Fill in the blanks** with the following.

    Current liabilities; current assets; inventories; 2; 1.

    Quick ratio = _____ less _____ (This should be at least _____.)
    _____

4. Which of the following describes **overcapitalisation** and which describes **overtrading**?

    A A company with excessive investment in working capital
    B A company trying to support too large a volume of trade with the capital resources at its disposal

5. Which of the following statements best defines the current ratio?

    A The ratio of current assets to current liabilities.
       For the majority of businesses it should be at least 2.

    B The ratio of current assets to current liabilities.
       For the majority of businesses it should be at least 1.

    C The ratio of current assets excluding inventory to current liabilities.
       For the majority of businesses it should be at least 1.

    D The ratio of current assets excluding inventory to current liabilities.
       For the majority of businesses it should be at least 2.

6. The receivables payment period is a calculation of the time taken to pay by all debtors.

    ☐ True
    ☐ False

7. What are the two most likely reasons for a lengthening inventory turnover period?

8. What is the working capital requirement of a company with the following average figures over a year?

	£
Inventory	3,750
Trade receivables	1,500
Cash and cash equivalents	500
Trade payables	1,800

Answers to Quick Quiz

1. D   Rapid increase in sales

2. A   The time raw materials remain in inventory
   B   The time period of credit taken from suppliers
   C   The time taken to produce goods
   D   The time taken by customers to pay for goods

3. Quick ratio = $\dfrac{\text{Current assets less inventories}}{\text{Current liabilities}}$ (This should be at least 1)

4. A   Overcapitalisation
   B   Overtrading

5. A   Current assets to current liabilities: 2

6. False; the calculation normally only includes trade receivables.

7. (a)   A slowdown in trading
   (b)   A build-up of inventory levels

8. Working capital requirement = current assets less current liabilities

   = 3,750 + 1,500 + 500 − 1,800
   = £3,950

LEARNING OUTCOME 5 WORKING CAPITAL MANAGEMENT

End of chapter questions

1. Mr Lee (AIA November 2012)

Mr Lee owns two companies in Malaysia. He bought these companies a number of years ago, but he has not taken any role in managing the companies. Instead he has always employed managers to run the two companies on his behalf. He is concerned about the management of working capital in the companies and has extracted the following data from the latest sets of accounts of each company:

	Company A MYR000	Company B MYR000
Inventories	42	190
Trade receivables	0	760
Other receivables	180	40
Cash and cash equivalents	150	35
Current assets	**372**	**1,025**
Interest bearing loans and borrowings	50	325
Trade payables	385	245
Other payables	75	35
Current tax liabilities	20	15
Current liabilities	**530**	**620**
Revenue	5,100	4,600
Cost of sales	3,980	3,090

Company A is a supermarket business. Company B manufactures fashion clothing that it then sells to clothing retail businesses.

The accounts were both prepared for the year ending 31 October 2012.

Required

Mr Lee has asked you to prepare a report advising him whether he should be concerned about the working capital positions of the two companies. The report should: (1) include any calculations that you consider appropriate, (2) advise Mr Lee of any further information that would be helpful, and (3) advise of any assumptions you have made. **(20 marks)**

2. X plc (AIA November 2009)

Shown below is the Statement of Financial Position for X plc as at 31 October 2008:

	€m	€m	€m
Non-current assets			320
Current assets			
Inventory		170	
Trade receivables		128	
Cash		2	
		300	
Current liabilities			
Bank Overdraft	50		
Trade Payables	100		
Dividend Payable	50	200	100
			420

	€m	€m	€m
Share Capital			20
Retained Profits			400
			420
Turnover			2,000
Gross Margin			400
Net Margin			100
Dividend			50
Retained Profit			50

You may assume that the figures given for inventory, trade receivables and trade payables shown in the financial statement represent the annual averages for the financial year.

The Statement of Financial Position for X plc as at 31 October 2009 has not been produced but you are given the following data for the financial year:

The company embarked upon a very ambitious programme of expansion which saw the Turnover more than doubled to €4,350 million.

In order to achieve the increase in turnover the company had to reduce the 2008 average percentage gross margin achieved in the last financial year by a half.

The company's overheads had increased by 25% as a result of additional staff wages and other costs.

The inventory had been increased considerably so that the present inventory turnover period had increased from 38.78 days to 45.03 days.

The company had also needed to extend the period of credit allowed in order to attract new customers. As a result the company's receivables' payment period had increased from its previous 23.36 days to 40.02 days.

Because of a shortage of cash the company had also extended its payables payment period from its previous 22.8 days to 50.07 days. As a result many of the company's suppliers were beginning to threaten withdrawal of supplies.

Non current assets had been increased by €80 million to cope with the additional production (ignore depreciation). All the additional investment and costs had been funded out of the company's bank overdraft, which was now up to its limit.

The company had decided to pay the same dividend as in the previous year.

Required

(a) Using the data above produce the Statement of Financial Position for X plc as at 31 October 2009 (Ignore tax and depreciation and round your figures to the nearest € million). **(12 marks)**

(b) The company's accountants have warned that the company is 'showing symptoms of overtrading' and heading for significant financial difficulties if action is not taken very quickly. Explain just what this means and suggest possible solutions to the problems. **(8 marks)**

(Total 20 marks)

LEARNING OUTCOME 5 WORKING CAPITAL MANAGEMENT

The management of receivables and payables

Topic list	Syllabus reference
1 Total credit	LO5
2 The management of receivables	LO5
3 Using debtor information	LO5
4 Foreign trade and debt management	LO5
5 The management of payables and short-term finance	LO5

Introduction

This chapter deals with specific techniques in the management of receivables, payables and short-term finance. These include overall credit control policies (should the business offer credit – if so how much and to whom), and ensuring amounts owed are not excessive.

While working through this chapter, try not to think of receivables and payables in isolation; they are part of working capital, each element of which will have knock-on effects when there is a change in another. For example, an increase in the credit period taken by debtors will reduce the amount of cash available to pay creditors and invest in inventory.

LEARNING OUTCOME 5 WORKING CAPITAL MANAGEMENT

1 Total credit

FAST FORWARD

Offering credit has a cost: the value of the interest charged on an overdraft to fund the period of credit, or the interest lost on the cash not received and deposited in the bank. An increase in profit from extra sales resulting from offering credit could offset this cost.

Finding a **total level of credit** which can be offered is a matter of finding the least costly balance between enticing customers, whose use of credit entails considerable costs, and refusing opportunities for profitable sales. First, it helps to see what debtors (receivables), which often account for 30% of the total assets of a business, actually represent.

1.1 Measuring total receivables

Debtors control can be measured using the **receivables turnover** ratio. This can be calculated as an annual figure. It represents the length of the credit period taken by customers.

Key term

$$\text{Receivables turnover} = \frac{\text{Total receivables} \times 365}{\text{Sales in 365 days}}$$

For example, in 20X4 X plc made sales of £700,000 and at 31 December 20X4, receivables stood at £90,000. The comparable figures for 20X3 were £600,000 (annual sales) and £70,000 (receivables at 31.12.X3).

	20X4		20X3	
Receivables turnover	$\frac{£90,000 \times 365}{£700,000}$ = 47 days		$\frac{£70,000 \times 365}{£600,000}$ = 43 days	

In 20X4, the company is taking longer to collect its debts.

1.2 Effect on profit of extending credit

The main cost of offering credit is the interest expense. How can we assess the effect on profit?

Let us assume that the Zygo Company sells widgets for £1,000, which enables it to earn a profit, after all other expenses except interest, of £100 (ie a 10% margin).

(a) Aibee buys a widget for £1,000 on 1 January 20X1, but does not pay until 31 December 20X1. Zygo relies on overdraft finance, which costs it 10% pa. The effect is:

	£
Net profit on sale of widget	100
Overdraft cost £1,000 × 10% pa	(100)
Actual profit after 12 months' credit	Nil

In other words, the entire profit margin has been wiped out in 12 months.

(b) If Aibee had paid after six months, the effect would be:

	£
Net profit	100
Overdraft cost £1,000 × 10% pa × 6/12 months	(50)
	50

Half the profit has been wiped out. (**Tutorial note.** The interest cost might be worked out in a more complex way to give a more accurate figure.)

(c) If the cost of borrowing had been 18%, then the profit would have been absorbed before seven months had elapsed. If the net profit were 5% and borrowing costs were 15%, the interest expense would exceed the net profit after four months.

A second general point is the relation of **total credit to bad debts**. Burt Edwards argues that there is a law of 10-to-1: 'Experience in different industries shows that the annual interest expense of borrowings to support overdue debts, ie those in excess of agreed payment terms, is at least ten times the total lost in bad debts'. This is not a 'law', but has been observed to be the case over a variety of UK businesses.

Question — Cost of debtors

Winterson Tools Ltd has an average level of debtors of £2m at any time representing 60 days outstanding. (Their terms are thirty days.) The firm borrows money at 10% a year. The managing director is proud of the credit control: 'I only had to write off £10,000 in bad debts last year,' she says proudly. Is she right to be proud?

Answer

At the moment, Winterson Tools Ltd is paying 10% × £1m (ie $^{30}/_{60}$ days × £2m) = £100,000 in interest caused by customers taking the extra month to pay.

The level of total credit can then have a significant effect on **profitability**. That said, if credit considerations are included in pricing calculations, extending credit can, in fact, increase profitability. If offering credit generates extra sales, then those extra sales will have additional repercussions on:

(a) The amount of inventory maintained in the warehouse, to ensure that the extra demand must be satisfied

(b) The amount of money the company owes to its creditors (as it will be increasing its supply of raw materials)

2 The management of receivables

Several factors should be considered by management when a policy for **credit control** is formulated. These include:

(a) The administrative costs of **debt collection**

(b) The procedures for **controlling credit** to individual customers and for debt collection

(c) The amount of **extra capital required** to finance an extension of total credit – there might be an increase in receivables, inventories and payables, and the net increase in working capital must be financed

(d) The cost of the **additional finance** required for any increase in the volume of receivables (or the savings from a reduction in debtors) – this cost might be bank overdraft interest, or the cost of long-term funds (such as loan stock or equity)

(e) Any **savings or additional expenses** in operating the credit policy (for example, the extra work involved in pursuing slow payers)

(f) The **ways** in which the credit policy could be **implemented** – for example:

   (i) Credit could be eased by giving debtors a longer period in which to settle their accounts – the cost would be the resulting increase in receivables

   (ii) A discount could be offered for early payment – the cost would be the amount of the discounts taken

(g) The **effects of easing credit**, which might be to encourage a higher proportion of bad debts, and an increase in sales volume. Provided that the extra gross contribution from the increase in sales exceeds the increase in fixed cost expenses, bad debts, discounts and the finance cost of an increase in working capital, a policy to relax credit terms would be profitable

2.1 Assessing creditworthiness

FAST FORWARD

In managing **receivables**, the **creditworthiness** of customers needs to be assessed. The risks and costs of a customer defaulting will need to be balanced against the profitability of the business provided by that customer.

Credit control involves the initial investigation of potential credit customers and the continuing control of outstanding accounts. The main points to note are as follows:

(a) New customers should give two **good references**, including one from a bank, before being granted credit.

(b) **Credit ratings** might be **checked** through a credit rating agency.

(c) A **new customer's credit limit** should be **fixed** at a **low level** and only increased if his payment record subsequently warrants it.

(d) For large value customers, a **file** should be **maintained** of any available financial information about the customer. This file should be reviewed regularly. Information is available from:

　(i) An analysis of the company's annual report and accounts

　(ii) Online company databases, (eg Duedil) contain accounting information on UK registered businesses

(e) The **Department for Business, Energy and Industrial Strategy** and UK Export Finance (the Export Credits Guarantee Department) will both be able to advise on overseas companies.

(f) **Press comments** may give information about what a company is currently doing (as opposed to the historical results in published accounts which only show what the company has done in the past).

(g) The company could send a member of staff to **visit** the company concerned, to get a first-hand impression of the company and its prospects. This would be advisable in the case of a prospective major customer.

(h) **Aged lists of debts** should be produced and reviewed at regular intervals. Credit control monitoring should be an integral part of monitoring total working capital.

(i) The **credit limit** for an existing customer should be periodically **reviewed**, but it should only be raised if the customer's credit standing is good.

(j) Procedures should be in place to ensure that **further orders** are **not accepted** from nor goods sent to a customer who is in difficulties. If a customer has exceeded his credit limit, or has not paid debts despite several reminders, or is otherwise known to be in difficulties, sales staff and warehouse staff must be notified immediately (and not, for example, at the end of the week, by which time more goods might have been supplied).

An organisation might devise a **credit-rating system** for new individual customers that is based on characteristics of the customer (such as whether the customer is a home owner, and the customer's age and occupation). Points would be awarded according to the characteristics of the customer, and the amount of credit that is offered would depend on his or her credit score.

The overall **debt collection policy** of the firm should be such that the administrative costs and other costs incurred in debt collection do not exceed the benefits from incurring those costs. Beyond a certain level of spending, however, additional expenditure on debt collection would not have enough effect on bad debts or on the average collection period to justify the extra administrative costs.

Collecting debts is a two-stage process.

(a) Having agreed credit terms with a customer, a business should issue an invoice and expect to receive payment when it is due. **Issuing invoices** and **receiving payments** is the task of sales ledger staff. They should ensure that:

(i) The **customer is fully aware** of the terms.
(ii) The **invoice is correctly drawn up** and issued promptly.
(iii) They are aware of any **potential quirks** in the customer's system.
(iv) **Queries are resolved quickly**.
(v) **Monthly statements** are **issued promptly**.

(b) If payments become overdue, they should be 'chased'. Procedures for pursuing overdue debts must be established, for example:

(i) **Instituting reminders or final demands**

These should be sent to a named individual, asking for repayment. A second or third reminder may be required, followed by a final demand stating clearly the action that will be taken. The aim is to goad customers into action, perhaps by threatening not to sell any more goods on credit until the debt is cleared.

(ii) **Chasing payment by telephone**

The telephone is of greater nuisance value than a letter, and the greater immediacy can encourage a response. It can however be time-consuming, in particular because of problems in getting through to the right person.

(iii) **Making a personal approach**

Personal visits can be very time-consuming and tend only to be made to important customers who are worth the effort.

(iv) **Notifying debt collection section**

This means not giving further credit to the customer until he has paid the due amounts.

(v) **Handing over debt collection to specialist debt collection section**

Certain, generally larger, organisations may have a section to collect debts under the supervision of the credit manager.

(vi) **Instituting legal action to recover the debt**

Premature legal action may unnecessarily antagonise important customers.

(vii) **Hiring external debt collection agency to recover debt**

Again this may upset customers.

2.2 Extension of credit

To determine whether it would be profitable to extend the level of total credit, it is necessary to assess:

- The **extra sales** that a **more generous credit policy** would stimulate
- The **profitability** of the **extra sales**
- The **extra length** of the **average debt collection period**
- The **required rate of return** on the investment in additional receivables

2.3 Example: Debtor management (1)

Russian Beard Ltd is considering a change of credit policy which will result in an increase in the average collection period from one to two months. The relaxation in credit is expected to produce an increase in sales in each year amounting to 25% of the current sales volume.

Selling price per unit	£10
Variable cost per unit	£8.50
Current annual sales	£2,400,000

The required rate of return on investments is 20%. Assume that the 25% increase in sales would result in additional inventories of £100,000 and additional payables of £20,000.

Advise the company on whether or not to extend the credit period offered to customers, if:

(a) All customers take the longer credit of two months

(b) Existing customers do not change their payment habits, and only the new customers take a full two months credit

Solution

The change in credit policy is justifiable if the rate of return on the additional investment in working capital would exceed 20%.

Extra profit	
Contribution/sales ratio	15%
Increase in sales revenue	£600,000
Increase in contribution and profit	£90,000

(a) *Extra investment, if all debtors take two months' credit*

	£
Average receivables after the sales increase (2/12 × £3,000,000)	500,000
Less current average receivables (1/12 × £2,400,000)	200,000
Increase in receivables	300,000
Increase in inventories	100,000
	400,000
Less increase in payables	20,000
Net increase in working capital investment	380,000

Return on extra investment $\dfrac{£90,000}{£380,000} = 23.7\%$

(b) *Extra investment, if only the new debtors take two months' credit*

	£
Increase in receivables (2/12 of £600,000)	100,000
Increase in inventories	100,000
	200,000
Less increase in payables	20,000
Net increase in working capital investment	180,000

Return on extra investment $\dfrac{£90,000}{£180,000} = 50\%$

In both case (a) and case (b) the new credit policy appears to be worthwhile.

2.4 Settlement discounts

FAST FORWARD

Settlement discounts may be employed to shorten average credit periods, and to reduce the investment in receivables and therefore **interest costs**. The benefit in interest cost saved should exceed the cost of the discounts allowed.

To see whether the offer of a **settlement discount** (for early payment) is financially worthwhile we must compare the cost of the discount with the benefit of a reduced investment in receivables.

Varying the discount allowed for early payment of debts affects the **average collection period** and affects the **volume of demand** (and possibly, therefore, indirectly affects bad debt losses). We shall begin with examples where the offer of a discount for early payment does not affect the volume of demand.

2.5 Example: Debtor management (2)

Lowe and Price Ltd has annual credit sales of £12,000,000, and three months are allowed for payment. The company decides to offer a 2% discount for payments made within ten days of the invoice being sent, and to reduce the maximum time allowed for payment to two months. It is estimated that 50% of customers will take the discount. If the company requires a 20% return on investments, what will be the effect of the discount? Assume that the volume of sales will be unaffected by the discount.

Solution

Our approach is to calculate:

(a) The profits forgone by offering the discount
(b) The interest charges saved or incurred as a result of the changes in the cash flows of the company

Thus:

(a) The volume of receivables, if the company policy remains unchanged, would be:

$3/12 \times £12,000,000 = £3,000,000$.

(b) If the policy is changed the volume of receivables would be:

$(\frac{10}{365} \times 50\% \times £12,000,000) + (\frac{2}{12} \times 50\% \times £12,000,000)$ = £164,384 + £1,000,000

= £1,164,384

(c) There will be a reduction in receivables of £1,835,616.

(d) Since the company can invest at 20% a year, the value of a reduction in receivables (a source of funds) is 20% of £1,835,616 each year in perpetuity, that is, £367,123 a year.

(e) *Summary*

	£
Value of reduction in receivables each year	367,123
Less discounts allowed each year (2% × 50% × £12,000,000)	120,000
Net benefit of new discount policy each year	247,123

An extension of the payment period allowed to receivables may be introduced in order to increase sales volume.

Question — Extension of credit

Enticement Ltd currently expects sales of £50,000 a month. Variable costs of sales are £40,000 a month (all payable in the month of sale). It is estimated that if the credit period allowed to debtors were to be increased from 30 days to 60 days, sales volume would increase by 20%. All customers would be expected to take advantage of the extended credit. If the cost of capital is 12½% a year (or approximately 1% a month), is the extension of the credit period justifiable in financial terms?

LEARNING OUTCOME 5 WORKING CAPITAL MANAGEMENT

Answer

	£
Current receivables (1 month)	50,000
Debtors after implementing the proposal (2 months)	120,000
Increase in receivables	70,000
Financing cost (× 12½%)	8,750
Annual contribution from additional sales	
(12 months × 20% × £10,000)	24,000
Annual net benefit from extending credit period	15,250

The percentage cost of an early settlement discount to the company giving it can be estimated by the formula:

Formula to learn

$$\left(\frac{100}{100-d}\right)^{\frac{365}{t}} - 1\%$$

where d is the discount offered (5% = 5, etc)
       t is the reduction in the payment period in days that is necessary to obtain the early payment discount

2.6 Bad debt risk

Different credit policies are likely to have differing levels of bad debt risk. The higher turnover resulting from easier credit terms should be sufficiently profitable to exceed the cost of:

- Bad debts, and
- The additional investment necessary to achieve the higher sales

2.7 Example: Debtor management (3)

Grabbit Quick Ltd achieves current annual sales of £1,800,000. The cost of sales is 80% of this amount, but bad debts average 1% of total sales, and the annual profit is as follows.

	£
Sales	1,800,000
Less cost of sales	1,440,000
	360,000
Less bad debts	18,000
Profit	342,000

The current debt collection period is one month, and the management consider that if credit terms were eased (Option A), the effects would be as follows.

	Present policy	Option A
Additional sales (%)	–	25%
Average collection period	1 month	2 months
Bad debts (% of sales)	1%	3%

The company requires a 20% return on its investments. The costs of sales are 75% variable and 25% fixed. Assume there would be no increase in fixed costs from the extra turnover; and that there would be no increase in average inventories or payables. Which is the preferable policy, Option A or the present one?

Solution

The increase in profit before the cost of additional finance for Option A can be found as follows:

(a)
	£
Increase in contribution from additional sales	
25% × £1,800,000 × 40%*	180,000
Less increase in bad debts	
(3% × £2,250,000) − £18,000	49,500
Increase in annual profit	130,500

* The C/S ratio is 100% − (75% × 80%) = 40%

(b)
	£
Proposed investment in receivables	
£2,250,000 × 1/6	375,000
Less current investment in receivables	
£1,800,000 × 1/12	150,000
Additional investment required	225,000
Cost of additional finance at 20%	£45,000

(c) As the increase in profit exceeds the cost of additional finance, Option A should be adopted.

2.8 Credit insurance

Companies might be able to obtain credit insurance against certain approved debts going bad through a specialist credit insurance firm. A company cannot insure against all its bad debt losses, but may be able to insure against losses above the normal level.

When a company arranges **credit insurance**, it must submit specific proposals for credit to the insurance company, stating the name of each customer to which it wants to give credit and the amount of credit it wants to give. The insurance company will accept, amend or refuse these proposals, depending on its assessment of each of these customers.

2.9 Factoring

FAST FORWARD

> Some companies use **factoring** and **invoice discounting** to help short-term liquidity or to reduce administration costs. **Insurance**, particularly of overseas debts, can also help reduce the risk of bad debts.

A **factor** is defined as 'a doer or transactor of business for another', but a factoring organisation specialises in trade debts, and manages the debts owed to a client (a business customer) on the client's behalf.

Key term

> **Factoring** is an arrangement to have debts collected by a factor company, which advances a proportion of the money it is due to collect.

The **main aspects of factoring** include the following:

(a) **Administration** of the client's invoicing, sales accounting and debt collection service.

(b) **Credit protection** for the client's debts, whereby the factor takes over the risk of loss from bad debts and so 'insures' the client against such losses. This is known as a **non-recourse** service.

However, if a **non-recourse** service is provided the factor, not the firm, will decide what action to take against non-payers.

(c) Making **payments** to the client **in advance** of collecting the debts. This is sometimes referred to as 'factor finance' because the factor is providing cash to the client against outstanding debts.

2.10 Benefits of factoring

The **benefits of factoring** for a business customer include the following:

(a) The business can **pay** its **suppliers promptly**, and so be able to take advantage of any early payment discounts that are available.

(b) **Optimum inventory levels** can be **maintained**, because the business will have enough cash to pay for the stocks it needs.

(c) **Growth** can be **financed** through **sales** rather than by injecting fresh external capital.

(d) The business gets **finance linked** to its **volume of sales**. In contrast, overdraft limits tend to be determined by historical balance sheets.

(e) The **managers** of the business **do not** have to **spend** their **time** on the problems of **slow paying debtors**.

(f) The business does **not incur** the **costs** of **running** its own **sales ledger department**, and can use the **expertise** of receivables management that the factor has.

An important **disadvantage** is that debtors will be making payments direct to the factor, which is likely to present a negative picture of the firm's **attitude to customer relations**. It may also indicate that the firm is in need of rapid cash, raising questions about its **financial stability**.

2.11 Example: Factoring

A company makes annual credit sales of £1,500,000. Credit terms are 30 days, but its debt administration has been poor and the average collection period has been 45 days with 0.5% of sales resulting in bad debts which are written off.

A factor would take on the task of debt administration and credit checking, at an annual fee of 2.5% of credit sales. The company would save £30,000 a year in administration costs. The payment period would be 30 days.

The factor would also provide an advance of 80% of invoiced debts at an interest rate of 14% (3% over the current base rate). The company can obtain an overdraft facility to finance its receivables at a rate of 2.5% over base rate.

Should the factor's services be accepted? Assume a constant monthly turnover.

Solution

It is assumed that the factor would advance an amount equal to 80% of the invoiced debts, and the balance 30 days later.

(a) The current situation is as follows, using the company's debt collection staff and a bank overdraft to finance all debts.

Credit sales £1,500,000 pa
Average credit period 45 days

The annual cost is as follows.

	£
$\frac{45}{365} \times £1,500,000 \times 13.5\% \ (11\% + 2.5\%)$	24,966
Bad debts: 0.5% × £1,500,000	7,500
Administration costs	30,000
Total cost	62,466

(b) **The cost of the factor.** 80% of credit sales financed by the factor would be 80% of £1,500,000 = £1,200,000. For a consistent comparison, we must assume that 20% of credit sales would be financed by a bank overdraft. The average credit period would be only 30 days. The annual cost would be as follows:

		£
Factor's finance	$\frac{30}{365} \times £1,200,000 \times 14\%$	13,808
Overdraft	$\frac{30}{365} \times £300,000 \times 13.5\%$	3,329
		17,137
Cost of factor's services: 2.5% × £1,500,000		37,500
Cost of the factor		54,637

(c) **Conclusion.** The factor is cheaper. In this case, the factor's fees exactly equal the savings in bad debts (£7,500) and administration costs (£30,000). The factor is then cheaper overall because it will be more efficient at collecting debts. The advance of 80% of debts is not needed, however, if the company has sufficient overdraft facility because the factor's finance charge of 14% is higher than the company's overdraft rate of 13.5%.

An **alternative way** of carrying out the calculation is to consider the changes in costs that using a factor will mean.

			£
Effect of reduction in collection period	$\frac{45-30}{365}$	× £1,500,000 × 13.5%	8,322
Extra interest cost of factor finance	$\frac{30}{365}$	× £1,200,000 × (14 – 13.5)%	(493)
Cost of factor's services: 2.5% × £1,500,000			(37,500)
Savings in bad debts 0.5% × £1,500,000			7,500
Savings in company's administration costs			30,000
Net benefit of using factor			7,829

Check: £62,466 – £54,637 = £7,829

> **Exam focus point**
>
> Points to look out for in questions about factoring are who bears the risk of bad debts, and company administration costs that may be saved by using a factor. The examiner has commented that calculations of the cost of factoring have often been poor.

2.12 Invoice discounting

> **Key term**
>
> **Invoice discounting** is the purchase (by the provider of the discounting service) of trade debts at a discount. Invoice discounting enables the company from which the debts are purchased to raise working capital.

Invoice discounting is related to factoring and many factors will provide an invoice discounting service. It is the purchase of a selection of invoices, at a discount. The invoice discounter does not take over the administration of the client's sales ledger.

A client should only want to have some invoices discounted when he has a temporary cash shortage, and so invoice discounting tends to consist of one-off deals. **Confidential invoice discounting** is an arrangement whereby a debt is confidentially assigned to the factor, and the client's customer will only become aware of the arrangement if he does not pay his debt to the client.

If a client needs to generate cash, he can approach a factor or invoice discounter, who will offer to purchase selected invoices and advance up to 75% of their value. At the end of each month, the factor will pay over the balance of the purchase price, less charges, on the invoices that have been settled in the month.

2.13 The impact of technology on Factoring and Invoice discounting

Technology is dramatically transforming factoring and invoice discounting, making these financial services more efficient, accessible, and secure. **Advanced digital platforms** and fintech solutions **streamline the entire** process, from invoice submission to funds disbursement. AI and **machine learning algorithms assess credit risk** more accurately and swiftly, allowing for better risk management and faster approval times.

Blockchain technology ensures the authenticity and transparency of transactions, reducing the risk of fraud and errors. Additionally, automation simplifies the tracking of invoices and payments, reducing administrative burden and improving cash flow management for businesses.

These technological advancements enable companies to access working capital more quickly and at lower costs, providing greater financial flexibility. By utilising these innovations, factoring and invoice discounting services can offer more competitive rates, enhance customer experiences, and support the financial stability and growth of businesses.

3 Using debtor information

> **FAST FORWARD**
>
> Regular monitoring of receivables is very important. Individual debtors can be assessed using a **customer history analysis** and a **credit rating system**. The overall level of receivables can be monitored using an **aged receivables listing** and **credit utilisation report**, as well as reports on the level of bad debts.

3.1 Payment record of individual debtors

Debtors' payment records must be **monitored** continually. This depends on successful sales ledger administration.

(a) **Invoices** must be posted at the right time.

(b) **Receipts** should be posted when they arrive, and allocated specifically to the invoices to which they relate.

(c) Any **queries** (eg customers debiting their own credit balance with a debit note as 'notification' to the supplier) need to be dealt with quickly.

(d) Orders should **always** be **vetted against credit limits**: this indicates the importance of prompt updating, as above.

(e) A **customer history analysis** can be prepared: this is like a statement, but with:
　(i)　Total annual sales, on a rolling 12-month basis
　(ii)　Outstanding amounts owed
　(iii)　Days sales outstanding at each month end

The advantage of this is that trends in the account can be monitored, as can also the ageing of the debtor balance.

Account Name:							
Number:							
Credit Limit:							
Month	Total debt at month end	Current	1 - 30 days	31 - 60 days	61 - 90 days	91 days and over	Sales in past 12 months	Days sales outstanding
January								
February								
March								

With this information it should be possible to develop in-house credit ratings.

3.2 In-house credit ratings

Credit monitoring can be simplified by a system of **in-house credit ratings**. For example, a company could have five credit-risk categories for its customers. These credit categories or ratings could be used to decide either individual credit limits for customers within that category or the frequency of the credit review. Guidelines could be provided to help credit controllers decide into which category a customer belongs.

Over time, the payment habits of a customer can be assessed, and the customer's credit rating (and credit limits) can be set accordingly. Any deterioration in a customer's payment record could raise concerns about the customer's creditworthiness.

3.3 Example: Categorisation of credit customers

A company categorises its credit customers into the following four groups:

1. Prompt payers
2. Those who pay within 30 days of the due date
3. Those who pay between 40 and 60 days of the due date
4. Those who pay over 60 days late

The recent payment record of a regular customer, Victor, is as follows:

Invoice number	Date of invoice	Date payable	Payment received	Days overdue
3257	7 March	7 April	28 April	21
3816	26 June	26 July	1 September	37
3942	19 July	19 August	1 September	13
4185	3 September	3 October	5 November	33
				104

Average days overdue = 26 days (104 ÷ 4)

Victor would be rated in credit category 2 by the company. A review of the payment record suggests that Victor delays payment until around the end of the month following the due date. This is quite typical business practice, and although Victor is not a good payer, there is a discernible payment pattern that could persuade the company to treat Victor as an average credit risk.

A **credit taken ratio** can be used to monitor the credit limits of customers. This compares the amount currently owed by a customer with the annual sales turnover in his account.

3.4 Example: Credit taken ratio

A company has two debtors, Able and Baker. Each customer owes £20,000. Annual sales to Able are about £200,000, and annual sales to Baker are about £100,000.

The credit taken ratio is 10% for Able (20,000 ÷ 200,000 × 100%) and 20% for Baker. Baker could be regarded as a higher credit risk. The company might wish to keep the credit-taken ratio for customers below a certain limit. If this limit were 20%, a request from Baker for further credit would be refused until the outstanding debts are settled. The company would be willing, however, to consider a request from Able for more credit.

3.5 Credit reviews

A **customer's payment record** and the **receivables aged analysis** should be examined regularly, as a matter of course. Breaches of the credit limit, or attempted breaches of it, should be brought immediately to the attention of the credit controller.

Otherwise, the credit controller will not have the time to examine **each** customer's account thoroughly every month. The credit controller's efforts will be expended on customers thought to be higher risk, or where there are other special factors (a debt that has gone bad). The credit situation will be reviewed more frequently, and a decision taken as to whether the credit should be extended. Illustrative internal weightings, review periods and credit offered are indicated below.

Rating	Payment record	Financial indicators	Frequency of credit reviews	Credit limit (as % of customer's annual purchases)
A Very high risk	Accounts over-due by 60 + days	Low profits Poor liquidity Highly indebted		Cash only (payment with order)
B High risk	Accounts over-due by 30 – 60 days	Deteriorating profitability, liquidity, or gearing	Monthly	Reduce to 10% of annual purchases
C Average risk	Accounts over-due up to 30 days	Stable position	Quarterly	15% of annual purchases
D Below average risk	Accounts paid on time	Stable or improving position	Six-monthly	25% of annual purchases
E Low risk	Accounts paid early Public sector customers	Strong financial position, or public sector ownership	Annually	For negotiation with the customer

HEATH LIMITED						
AGE ANALYSIS OF DEBTORS AS AT 31.1.X2						
Account number	Customer name	Balance	Up to 30 days	Up to 60 days	Up to 90 days	Over 90 days
B004	Brilliant Ltd	804.95	649.90	121.00	0.00	34.05
E008	Easimat Ltd	272.10	192.90	72.40	6.80	0.00
H002	Hampstead Ltd	1,818.42	0.00	0.00	724.24	1,094.18
M024	Martlesham Ltd	284.45	192.21	92.24	0.00	0.00
N030	Nyfen Ltd	1,217.54	1,008.24	124.50	0.00	84.80
T002	Todmorden College	914.50	842.00	0.00	72.50	0.00
T004	Tricorn Ltd	94.80	0.00	0.00	0.00	94.80
V010	Volux Ltd	997.06	413.66	342.15	241.25	0.00
Y020	Yardsley Smith & Co	341.77	321.17	20.60	0.00	0.00
Totals		6,745.59	3,620.08	772.89	1,044.79	1,307.83
Percentage		100%	53.6%	11.5%	15.5%	19.4%

3.6 Receivables age analysis

An **aged receivables listing** will probably look very much like the schedule illustrated below. The analysis splits up the total balance on the account of each customer across different columns according to the dates of the transactions which make up the total balance. Thus, the amount of an invoice which was raised 14 days ago will form part of the figure in the column headed 'up to 30 days', while an invoice which was raised 36 days ago will form part of the figure in the column headed 'up to 60 days'. (In the schedule below, 'up to 60 days' is used as shorthand for 'more than 30 days but less than 60 days'.)

The age analysis of receivables may be used to help decide what action to take about older debts. Going down each column in turn starting from the column furthest to the right and working across, we can see that there are some rather old debts which ought to be investigated.

A number of **refinements** can be suggested to the aged receivables listing to make it easier to use.

(a) A report can be printed in which **overdue accounts** are seen first: this highlights attention on these items.

(b) It can help to aggregate data by **class of customer**. In this case, a report would be printed containing, for debtors aggregated into regions, type of customer, industry sectors etc:

 (i) Sales revenue
 (ii) Outstanding amount owed, broken down into age
 (iii) Days' sales outstanding

(c) There is no reason why this should not apply to individual receivable accounts as below. You could also include the date of the last transaction on the account (eg last invoice, last payment).

Account number	Customer name	Balance	Up to 30 days	Up to 60 days	Up to 90 days	Over 90 days	Sales revenue in last 12 months	Days sales outstanding
B004	Brilliant Ltd	804.95	649.90	121.00	0.00	34.05	6,789.00	43

We can see from the age analysis of Heath Ltd's debtors given earlier that the relatively high proportion of debts over 90 days (19.4%) is largely due to the debts of Hampstead Ltd. Other customers with debts of this age are Brilliant Ltd, Nyfen Ltd and Tricorn Ltd.

3.7 Debtors' ageing and liquidity

Also of interest to the credit controller is the **total** percentage figure calculated at the bottom of each column. In practice, the credit controller will be concerned to look at this figure first of all, in order to keep the ageing figures consistent. Why might a credit controller be worried by an increase in the ageing? If the credit controller knows the customers are going to pay, should it matter?

The answer is that any reduction in the inflow caused by an overall increase in the receivables period affects the company's ability to pay its debts and increases its use of overdraft finance: unauthorised overdrafts carry a hefty fee as well as interest.

Additional ratios which might be useful in receivables management, in addition to days' sales outstanding, are as follows.

(a) **Overdues as a percentage of total debt.** For example, assume that if Heath Ltd (Paragraph 3.6) offers credit on 30-day terms. Brilliant Ltd's debt could be analysed as:

$$\frac{£121.00 + £34.05}{£804.95} = 19.3\% \text{ overdue}$$

(b) **If debts are disputed**, it is helpful to see what a proportion these are of the total receivables and the total overdue. If, of Heath's total receivables of £6,745.59, an amount of £973.06 related to disputed items, the ratio of disputed debts to total outstanding would be:

$$\frac{£973.06}{£6,745.59} = 14.4\%$$

As a percentage of total items **over** 30 days old:

$$\frac{£973.06}{£6,745.59 - £3,620.08} = 31\%$$

An increasing disputes ratio can indicate:

(i) Invoicing problems
(ii) Operational problems

3.8 Debtor quality and liquidity

The **quality** of debtors has an important impact on a firm's overall liquidity. Debtor quality is determined by their age and risk.

Some **industries** have a higher level of risk than others, in other words, there is a higher probability that customers will fail to pay. Some markets are riskier than others, which is why export credit insurance premiums are higher for some countries than others. Selling goods to a country with possible payment difficulties is riskier than selling them in the home market.

3.8.1 Policing total credit

The total amount of credit offered, as well as individual accounts, should be policed to ensure that the senior management policy with regard to the total credit limits is maintained. A **credit utilisation report** can indicate the extent to which total limits are being utilised. An example is given below.

Customer	Limit £'000	Utilisation £'000	%
Alpha	100	90	90
Beta	50	35	70
Gamma	35	21	60
Delta	250	125	50
	435	271	
		62.2%	

This might also contain other information, such as days' sales outstanding and so on.

Reviewed in aggregate, this can reveal the following:

(a) The **number of customers** who might **want more credit**

(b) The **extent** to which the **company is exposed to debtors**

(c) The **'tightness'** of the policy (It might be possible to increase profitable sales by offering credit. On the other hand, perhaps the firm offers credit too easily.)

It is possible to design credit utilisation reports to highlight other trends:

(a) The **degree of exposure** to **different countries**

(b) The **degree of exposure** to **different industries** (Some countries or industries may be worthy of more credit; others may be too risky.)

Credit utilisation can also be analysed by industry within country or by country within industry. It is also useful to relate credit utilisation to total sales.

4 Foreign trade and debt management

FAST FORWARD

Exporters have to address the problems of larger inventories and receivables, and an increased risk of bad debts owing to the transportation time and additional paperwork involved in sending goods abroad.

Foreign debts raise the following special problems:

(a) When goods are sold abroad, the customer might ask for credit. Exports take time to arrange, and there might be complex paperwork. Transporting the goods can be slow, if they are sent by sea. These **delays** in **foreign trade** mean that exporters often build up large investments in inventories and receivables. These working capital investments have to be financed somehow.

(b) The **risk of bad debts** can be **greater** with foreign trade than with domestic trade. If a foreign debtor refuses to pay a debt, the exporter must pursue the debt in the debtor's own country, where procedures will be subject to the laws of that country.

There are several measures available to exporters to overcome these problems.

4.1 Reducing the investment in foreign debtors

A company can reduce its investment in foreign receivables by insisting on **earlier payment** for goods. Another approach is for an exporter to arrange for a bank to give **cash for a foreign debt**, sooner than the exporter would receive payment in the normal course of events. There are several ways in which this might be done.

(a) **Advances against collections**. Where the exporter asks his bank to handle the collection of payment (of a bill of exchange or a cheque) on his behalf, the bank may be prepared to make an advance to the exporter against the collection. The amount of the advance might be 80% to 90% of the value of the collection.

(b) **Negotiation of bills or cheques.** This is similar to an advance against collection, but would be used where the bill or cheque is payable outside the exporter's country (for example, in the foreign buyer's country).

(c) **Documentary credits.** These are described below.

4.2 Reducing the bad debt risk

Methods of minimising bad debt risks are broadly similar to those for domestic trade. An exporting company should vet the creditworthiness of each customer, and grant credit terms accordingly.

4.3 Export factoring

The functions performed by an **overseas factor** or **export factor** are essentially the same as with the factoring of domestic trade debts, which was described earlier in this chapter.

The charges levied by an overseas factor may turn out to be cheaper than using alternative methods such as letters of credit, which are discussed below.

4.4 Documentary credits

Documentary credits provide a method of payment in international trade, which gives the exporter a secure risk-free method of obtaining payment.

The buyer (a foreign buyer, or a UK importer) and the seller (a UK exporter or a foreign supplier) first of all agree a contract for the sale of the goods, which provides for payment through a documentary credit.

The **buyer** then requests a bank in his country to issue a **letter of credit** in favour of the exporter. The issuing bank, by issuing its letter of credit, guarantees payment to the beneficiary.

A documentary credit arrangement must be made between the exporter, the buyer and participating banks **before the export sale takes place**. Documentary credits are slow to arrange, and administratively cumbersome; however, they might be considered essential where the risk of non-payment is high.

One form of trade credit is Bills of Exchange which are dealt with more fully in Section 5.4 below.

4.5 Export credit insurance

Key term

> **Export credit insurance** is insurance against the risk of non-payment by foreign customers for export debts.

You might be wondering why export credit insurance should be necessary, when exporters can pursue **non-paying customers** through the courts in order to obtain payment. The answer is that:

(a) If a credit customer defaults on payment, the task of pursuing the case through the courts will be lengthy, and it might be a long time before payment is eventually obtained.

(b) There are various reasons why non-payment might happen. (Export credit insurance provides insurance against non-payment for a variety of risks in addition to the buyer's failure to pay on time.)

Not all exporters take out export credit insurance because premiums are very high and the benefits are sometimes not fully appreciated. If they do, they will obtain an insurance policy from a private insurance company that deals in export credit insurance.

4.6 Overseas debtors; general policies

There are also a number of general credit control policies that can be particularly important when dealing with overseas customers.

(a) Prior to the sale, the customer's **credit rating** should be **checked**, and the terms of the contract specified. One key term may be demanding the use of an **irrevocable letter of credit** as a term of release of goods. The terms of the **remittance** and the bank to be used should be specified.

(b) The **paperwork** relating to the sales should be carefully completed and checked, in particular the shipping and delivery documentation.

(c) Goods should only be released if payment has been made, or is sufficiently certain, either because of the customer's **previous record** or because the customer has issued a **promissory note**.

(d) Receipts should be **rapidly processed** and late **payments chased**.

5 The management of payables and short-term finance

FAST FORWARD

> Effective management of **trade payables** involves seeking satisfactory credit terms from suppliers, getting credit extended during periods of cash shortage, and maintaining good relations with suppliers.

Exam focus point

> It may seem an obvious point, but take care not to confuse receivables (debtors) and creditors (payables), as many students do under exam pressure.

5.1 Management of trade payables

The management of trade payables involves:

- Attempting to obtain **satisfactory credit** from suppliers
- Attempting to **extend credit** during periods of cash shortage
- Maintaining **good relations** with regular and important suppliers

If a supplier offers a discount for the early payment of debts, the evaluation of the decision whether or not to **accept the discount** is similar to the **evaluation of the decision** whether or not to **offer a discount**. One problem is the mirror image of the other. The methods of evaluating the offer of a discount to customers were described earlier.

5.2 Sources of short-term finance

Taking trade credit from suppliers is one way in which a company can obtain some **short-term finance**, in addition to its longer-term sources. Short-term finance can also be obtained:

(a) With a **bank overdraft**

(b) By **raising finance** from a bank or other organisation against the **security of trade payables**, for example through factoring or invoice discounting (both described earlier in this chapter)

(c) For larger companies, by issuing **short-term debt instruments**, such as a 'commercial paper'

5.2.1 Trade credit

Taking credit from suppliers is a normal feature of business. Nearly every company has some trade creditors waiting for payment. Trade credit is a source of short-term finance because it helps to keep working capital down. It is usually a cheap source of finance, since suppliers rarely charge interest.

LEARNING OUTCOME 5 WORKING CAPITAL MANAGEMENT

However, trade credit **will** have a cost, whenever a company is offered a discount for early payment, but opts instead to take longer credit.

5.2.2 Trade credit and the cost of lost early payment discounts

Trade credit from suppliers is a major source of finance. It is particularly important to small and fast growing firms. The costs of making maximum use of trade credit include the loss of suppliers' goodwill, and the loss of any available cash discounts for the early payment of debts.

The cost of lost cash discounts can be estimated by the formula:

$$\left(\frac{100}{100-d}\right)^{\frac{365}{t}} - 1\%$$

where d is the % discount, d = 5 for 5%

t is the reduction in the payment period in days which would be necessary to obtain the early payment discount, final date to obtain discount – final date for payment

This is the same formula that was used for receivables.

5.3 Example: Trade credit

X Ltd has been offered credit terms from its major supplier of 2/10, net 45. That is, a cash discount of 2% will be given if payment is made within ten days of the invoice, and payments must be made within 45 days of the invoice. The company has the choice of paying 98p per £1 on day 10 (to pay before day 10 would be unnecessary), or to invest the 98p for an additional 35 days and eventually pay the supplier £1 per £1. The decision as to whether the discount should be accepted depends on the opportunity cost of investing 98p for 35 days. What should the company do?

Solution

If the company refuses the cash discount, and pays in full after 45 days, the implied cost in interest per annum would be approximately:

$$\left(\frac{100}{100-2}\right)^{\frac{365}{35}} - 1 = 23.5\%$$

Suppose that X Ltd can invest cash to obtain an annual return of 25%, and that there is an invoice from the supplier for £1,000. The two alternatives are as follows.

	Refuse discount £	Accept discount £
Payment to supplier	1,000.0	980
Return from investing £980 between day 10 and day 45: $£980 \times \frac{35}{365} \times 25\%$	23.5	
Net cost	976.5	980

It is cheaper to refuse the discount because the investment rate of return on cash retained, in this example, exceeds the saving from the discount.

Although a company may delay payment beyond the final due date, thereby obtaining even longer credit from its suppliers, such a policy would generally be inadvisable. Unacceptable delays in payment will **worsen the company's credit rating**, and additional credit may become difficult to obtain.

5.4 Bills of exchange

Bills of exchange are a form of trade credit. When A sells goods to B, the settlement of the debt might be arranged by means of a **bill of exchange** (called a **trade bill** as B is a trader).

Step 1   A draws bill on B

> B will pay certain sum of money on certain date

Step 2   B accepts the bill by signing it, acknowledging B's debt to A and giving a promise to pay

> B will pay certain sum of money on certain date.
> Signed: B

Step 3   After term of bill expired, B pays A

B = £££ ⇒ A

5.4.1 Trade bills and obtaining finance against the security of debtors

When a company obtains payment from its customers through **trade bills**, it can arrange to obtain finance from its bank against the security of the bill.

If A Ltd sells goods to B Ltd for £50,000, the terms of payment might be agreed so that A Ltd draws a 90 day bill of exchange on B Ltd for £50,000, which B Ltd 'accepts'. A Ltd can then ask its bank to discount the bill, and A Ltd will receive payment (less discount) now from the bank instead of in 90 days from B Ltd. After 90 days, B Ltd must pay the bank or other holder of the bill.

The rate of discount on the bill, which is the cost to A Ltd of discounting, will depend on the **'quality'** of the bill. A **higher discount** applies to **trade bills** (bills drawn on and accepted by companies such as B Ltd) than to **bank bills** (bills drawn on and accepted by a bank). A lower discount is called a 'finer' discount.

5.4.2 Acceptance credits

Acceptance credits (also known as **bank bills**) are a source of finance from banks for large companies, which are an alternative to bank overdrafts. Acceptance credits have much in common with bills of exchange, but they are different.

(a) A bank and a large corporate customer **agree a facility** which allows the customer to **draw bills** on the bank, which the bank will accept. The bills are normally payable after 60 or 90 days, but might have a term as long as 180 days. They can be denominated in sterling or in a foreign currency.

(b) The **accepted bills** are then **sold** (discounted) by the bank in the discount market on behalf of the customer, and the money obtained from the sale, minus the bank's acceptance commission, is made available to the customer. Because of the bank's standing and reputation, bills accepted by it can be sold in the market at a low rate of discount.

(c) When a bill matures, the **company** will **pay the bank** the **value** of the bill and the bank will use the money in turn to pay the bill holder.

Acceptance credits are attractive to customers for the following reasons.

(a) They provide companies with **alternative finance** to a bank overdraft, with the money being obtained from a source outside the bank (the purchaser of the discounted bills).

(b) The amount of credit is promised to the customer for a **stated period of time**.

(c) There may be a **cost advantage** to the customer, because the rate of discount on bank bills in the discount market might be lower than the interest rate on a bank loan, or overdraft, which is related to the bank base rate or SONIA. The reason for this is mainly that the interest rate on a discounted bill is fixed for the life of the bill (typically 90 days). Overdraft rates are going up, it would be more costly to maintain an overdraft than to have an acceptance credit facility.

(d) The company can **assess** the **cost of its credit facility** with **more certainty**, because costs are fixed over the life of a bill.

5.5 Assessment of creditors

How long a company takes to pay its trade creditors is measured by the payables turnover.

Key term

> **Payables turnover** or **Payables payment period** = $\dfrac{\text{Average payables}}{\text{Purchases}} \times 365$ days
>
> Cost of sales may be used as an alternative to purchases.

The payables turnover ratio often helps to assess a company's liquidity. An increase in payable days is often a sign of **lack** of **long-term finance** or **poor management** of **current assets**.

Chapter Roundup

- Offering credit has a cost: the value of the interest charged on an overdraft to fund the period of credit, or the interest lost on the cash not received and deposited in the bank. An increase in profit from extra sales resulting from offering credit could offset this cost.

- In managing **receivables**, the **creditworthiness** of customers needs to be assessed. The risks and costs of a customer defaulting will need to be balanced against the profitability of the business provided by that customer.

- **Settlement discounts** may be employed to shorten average credit periods, and to reduce the investment in receivables and therefore **interest costs**. The benefit in interest cost saved should exceed the cost of the discounts allowed.

- Some companies use **factoring** and **invoice discounting** to help short-term liquidity or to reduce administration costs. **Insurance**, particularly of overseas debts, can also help reduce the risk of bad debts.

- Regular monitoring of receivables is very important. Individual debtors can be assessed using a **customer history analysis** and a **credit rating system**. The overall level of receivables can be monitored using an **aged receivables listing** and **credit utilisation report**, as well as reports on the level of bad debts.

- Exporters have to address the problems of larger inventories and receivables, and an increased risk of bad debts owing to the transportation time and additional paperwork involved in sending goods abroad.

- Effective management of **trade payables** involves seeking satisfactory credit terms from suppliers, getting credit extended during periods of cash shortage, and maintaining good relations with suppliers.

Quick Quiz

1. How can we calculate the number of days' sales represented by receivables?

2. List typical column headings that you would expect to see in an aged analysis of receivables.

3. What service involves collecting debts of a business and advancing a proportion of the money it is due to collect?

4. What service involves advancing a proportion of a selection of invoices, without administration of the sales ledger of the business?

5. Cost of lost discount = $1 - \left(\dfrac{100}{(100-d)}\right)^{\frac{365}{t}}$ %. What do d and t represent?

6. Which of the following does not determine the amount of credit offered by a supplier?

    A   The credit terms the supplier obtains from its own suppliers
    B   The ease with which the buyer can go elsewhere
    C   The supplier's total risk exposure
    D   The number of purchases made by the buyer each year

7. If a customer decided to pass up the chance of a cash discount of 1% in return for reducing her average payment period from 70 to 30 days, what would be the implied cost in interest per annum?

    A   9.13%
    B   9.6%
    C   12.17%
    D   12.29%

8. Which of the following is a **disadvantage** to a company of using a factor for its receivables?

    A   It is easier to finance growth through sales
    B   Managers spend less time on slow paying debtors
    C   Debtors pay direct to the factor
    D   It is easier to pay suppliers promptly to obtain discounts

Answers to Quick Quiz

1. $\dfrac{\text{Total receivables}}{\text{Annual sales}} \times 365 = \text{Days' sales}$

2.
   - Account number
   - Customer name
   - Total balance
   - Up to 30 days
   - Up to 60 days
   - Up to 90 days
   - Over 90 days

3. Factoring

4. Invoice discounting

5. d is the percentage discount given, t is the reduction in payment to obtain the discount (in days).

6. D   The number of purchases. (Although the amount of annual purchases may well be a factor.)

7. B $\text{Cost} = 1 - \left(\dfrac{100}{100-d}\right)^{\frac{365}{t}} \%$

   $\phantom{\text{Cost}} = 1 - \left(\dfrac{100}{100-1}\right)^{\frac{365}{40}}$

   $\phantom{\text{Cost}} = 9.6\%$

8. C   This may present a negative picture of the company to customers.

LEARNING OUTCOME 5 WORKING CAPITAL MANAGEMENT

End of chapter question

Ng Fan (AIA November 2008)

Ng Fan manufactures and exports all its output to USA and Europe. Below is shown the latest Income Statement and Balance Sheet for the company:

Income Statement – Year Ended 30 June 2008

	HK$
Turnover	3,000,000
Gross Profit	551,000
Overdraft Interest	(27,367)
Bad Debts	(32,900)
Administration Costs	(340,000)
Net Profit	150,733

Balance Sheet as at 30 June 2008

	HK$	HK$
Non Current Assets		4,375,340
Current Assets		
Inventories	102,988	
Accounts Receivable	369,863	472,851
Current Liabilities		
Accounts payable	150,887	
Bank Overdraft*	321,964	(472,851)
		4,375,340
Financed by:		
Ordinary Shares		3,000,000
Retained Earnings		1,375,340
		4,375,340

*The bank overdraft has an annual interest rate of 8.5%.

The company has been investigating the possibility of employing a Factor to take over the management of all its Accounts Receivable. Typical services and costs offered by Factors are as follows:

Debt administration and credit checking at an annual fee of 1.5% of sales

Immediate advance of 80% of invoiced amounts at an interest rate of 9% with the remainder payable in 30 days

Overseas credit covered by a comprehensive insurance policy. This would cost 65 cents per HK$100 insured and cover 90% of the risk of non-payment for exports

You have been asked to show how the company's profit would be affected by the use of a Factor's services.

Required

(a) Calculate a revised Income Statement and Balance Sheet to show the effect of using the Factor's services with the following assumptions:

Turnover and gross profit would be unaffected.

There would be a saving of HK$100,000 in administrative costs as a result.

Assume a constant monthly turnover, a 365 day year and make all calculations to the nearest HK$.

(12 marks)

(b) The Finance Department of Ng Fan have complained that they seem to spend a disproportionate amount of their time controlling the company's working capital. They appreciate the vital importance of optimising the levels of working capital employed but feel that their job would be so much easier if management would plan ahead a little more.

Discuss what is meant by the optimisation of working capital levels and explain why appropriate planning can make this easier and more effective. **(8 marks)**

(Total 20 marks)

The management of inventories and cash

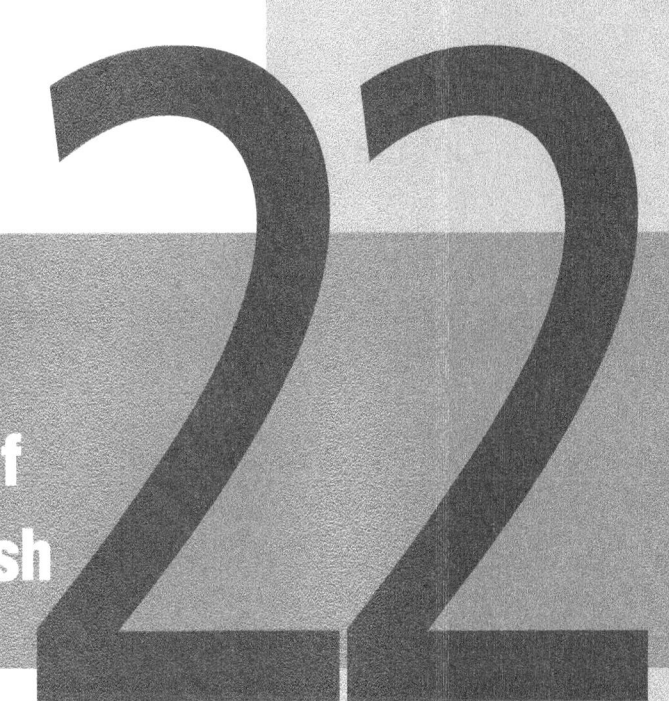

Topic list	Syllabus reference
1 The management of inventories	LO5
2 The management of cash	LO5
3 Treasury management	LO5

Introduction

This chapter concludes our study of working capital management methods by considering how inventory and cash are managed.

1 The management of inventories

FAST FORWARD

An **economic order quantity** can be calculated as a guide to minimising costs in managing **inventory** levels. **Bulk discounts** can however mean that a different order quantity minimises inventory costs.

Almost every company carries inventories of some sort, even if they are only stocks of consumables such as stationery. For a manufacturing business, inventories, in the form of **raw materials**, **work in progress** and **finished goods**, may amount to a substantial proportion of the total assets of the business.

Some businesses attempt to control inventories on a scientific basis by balancing the costs of stock shortages against those of stockholding. The 'scientific' control of stocks may be analysed into three parts.

(a) The **economic order quantity (EOQ) model** can be used to decide the optimum order size for inventories which will minimise the costs of ordering inventories plus inventory holding costs.

(b) If **discounts for bulk purchases** are available, it may be cheaper to buy inventories in large order sizes so as to obtain the discounts.

(c) Uncertainty in the demand for inventories and/or the supply lead time may lead a company to decide to hold **buffer stocks** in order to reduce or eliminate the risk of 'stock-outs' (running out of stock).

Stock costs	
Holding costs	The cost of capital Warehousing and handling costs Deterioration Obsolescence Insurance Pilferage
Procuring costs	Ordering costs Delivery costs
Shortage costs	Contribution from lost sales Extra cost of emergency stock Cost of lost production and sales in a stock-out
Cost of inventory	Relevant particularly when calculating discounts

1.1 The basic EOQ formula

Key term

The **economic order quantity (EOQ)** is the optimal ordering quantity for an item of inventory which will minimise costs.

Let D = usage in units for one period (the demand)
 P = purchase price per item
 C_o = cost of placing one order   relevant costs only
 C_H = holding cost per unit of inventory for one period
 Q = reorder quantity

Assume that demand is constant, the lead time is constant or zero and purchase costs per unit are constant (ie no bulk discounts).

22: THE MANAGEMENT OF INVENTORIES AND CASH

The total annual cost of having inventory is:

(a) Holding costs + ordering costs

$$\frac{Q \times C_H}{2} + \frac{C_o \times D}{Q}$$

The more orders are made each year the higher the ordering costs, but the lower the holding costs (as less inventory is held).

(b) The objective is to minimise $T = \frac{Q \times C_H}{2} + \frac{C_o \times D}{Q}$

The order quantity, EOQ, which will minimise these total costs is:

Exam formula

$$EOQ = \sqrt{\frac{2C_oD}{C_H}}$$

Exam focus point

The EOQ formula will be given on the exam formulae sheet but you do need to be confident in using it.

1.2 Example: Economic order quantity

The demand for a commodity is 40,000 units a year, at a steady rate. It costs £20 to place an order, and 40p to hold a unit for a year. Find the order size to minimise inventory costs, the number of orders placed each year, and the length of the inventory cycle.

Solution

$$Q = \sqrt{\frac{2C_oD}{C_H}} = \sqrt{\frac{2 \times 20 \times 40,000}{0.4}} = 2,000 \text{ units.}$$

This means that there will be

$$\frac{40,000}{2,000} = 20 \text{ orders placed each year.}$$

The inventory cycle is therefore

$$\frac{52 \text{ weeks}}{20 \text{ orders}} = 2.6 \text{ weeks.}$$

Total costs will be $(20 \times £20) + (\frac{2,000}{2} \times 40p) = £800$ a year.

1.3 Uncertainties in demand and lead times: a re-order level system

FAST FORWARD

Uncertainties in demand and lead times taken to fulfil orders mean that inventory will be ordered once it reaches a re-order level (maximum usage × maximum lead time).

Key term

Reorder level = maximum usage × maximum lead time.

The re-order level is the measure of inventory at which a replenishment order should be made.

(a) If an order is placed **too late**, the organisation may run out of stock, resulting in a loss of sales and/or a loss of production.

(b) If an order is placed **too soon**, the organisation will hold too much inventory, and inventory holding costs will be excessive.

Use of a re-order level builds in a measure of safety inventory and minimises the risk of the organisation running out of stock, a **stock-out**. This is particularly important when the volume of demand or the supply lead time are uncertain.

The **average annual** cost of such a safety inventory would be:

Quantity of safety inventory (in units) × Inventory holding cost per unit per annum

The diagram below shows how the inventory levels might fluctuate with this system. Points marked 'X' show the re-order level at which a new order is placed. The number of units ordered each time is the EOQ. Actual inventory levels sometimes fall below the safety inventory level, and sometimes the re-supply arrives before inventories have fallen to the safety level. On average, however, extra stockholding will approximate the safety inventory. The size of the safety stock will depend on whether stock-outs are allowed.

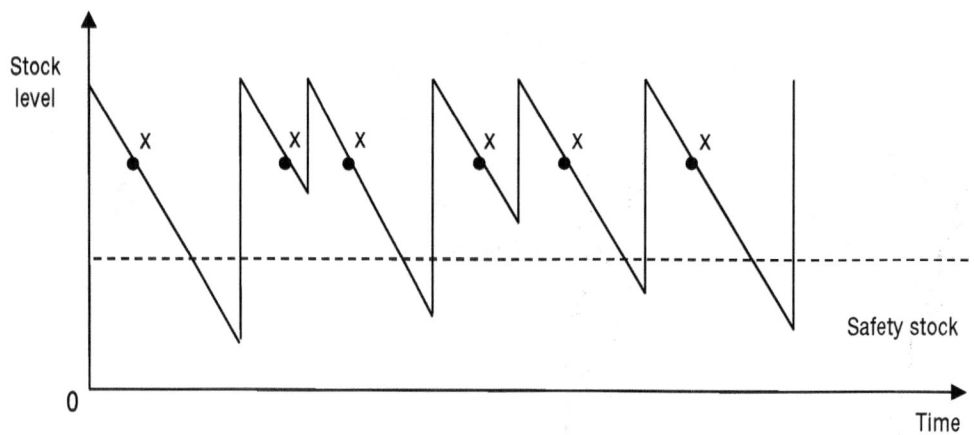

1.4 Maximum and minimum inventory levels

Key term

Maximum **inventory level** = reorder level + reorder quantity – (minimum usage × minimum lead time)

The maximum level acts as a warning signal to management that inventories are reaching a potentially wasteful level.

Key term

Minimum **inventory level** or **buffer safety inventory** = reorder level – (average usage × average lead time)

The minimum level acts as a warning to management that inventories are approaching a dangerously low level and that stockouts are possible.

Key term

$$\text{Average stock} = \text{Minimum level} + \frac{\text{reorder level}}{2}$$

This formula assumes that inventory levels fluctuate evenly between the minimum (or safety) inventory level and the highest possible inventory level (the amount of inventory immediately after an order is received, safety inventory and reorder quantity).

This approach assumes that a business wants to minimise the risk of stock-outs at all costs. In the modern manufacturing environment stock-outs can have a disastrous effect on the production process.

If, however, you are given a question where the risk of stock-outs is assumed to be worth taking, and the costs of stock-outs are quantified, the re-order level may not be calculated in the way described above. For **each possible re-order level**, and therefore each **possible level** of buffer stock, **calculate**:

- The **costs of holding buffer inventory** per annum
- The **costs of stock-outs** (Cost of one stock-out × expected number of stock-outs per order × number of orders per year)

The expected number of stock-outs per order reflects the various levels by which demand during the lead time could exceed the re-order level.

1.5 Example: Possibility of stock-outs (1)

If re-order level is 4 units, but there was a probability of 0.2 that demand during the lead time would be 5 units, and 0.05 that demand during the lead time would be 6 units, then

Expected number of stock-outs = $((5 - 4) \times 0.2) + ((6 - 4) \times 0.05) = 0.3$.

1.5.1 Demand normally distributed

Alternatively, you may be told that demand is normally distributed. If this is the case you need to know:

- Average weekly demand
- Standard deviation of demand
- Lead time
- Acceptable risk levels

Re-order level = (Average weekly demand × lead time) + $x\sigma$

where x = number of standard deviations that correspond to the chance business wishes to have of avoiding stock-outs

σ = standard deviation of demand

1.6 Example: Possibility of stock-outs (2)

Average weekly demand is 200 units, the standard deviation of demand (σ) is 40 units and demand is normally distributed. Lead time for orders is one week. What re-order levels should the business set if it wishes to have

(a) A 90% chance
(b) A 95% chance
(c) A 99% chance

of avoiding running out of stock? The relevant values from normal distribution tables are respectively:

(a) 1.28
(b) 1.65
(c) 2.33

LEARNING OUTCOME 5 WORKING CAPITAL MANAGEMENT

Solution

Re-order level = (Average weekly demand × lead time) + xσ

(a) Re-order level = (200 × 1) + (1.28 × 40)
= 251.2 units

(b) Re-order level = 200 + (1.65 × 40)
= 266 units

(c) Re-order level = 200 + (2.33 × 40)
= 293.2 units

1.7 The effect of discounts

The solution obtained from using the simple EOQ formula may need to be modified if bulk discounts (also called quantity discounts) are available. To decide mathematically whether it would be worthwhile taking a discount and ordering larger quantities, it is necessary to minimise:

Total purchasing costs + Ordering costs + Stockholding costs.

The total cost will be minimised:

- At the pre-discount EOQ level, so that a discount is not worthwhile, or
- At the minimum order size necessary to earn the discount

1.8 Example: Bulk discounts

The annual demand for an item of inventory is 45 units. The item costs £200 a unit to purchase, the holding cost for one unit for one year is 15% of the unit cost and ordering costs are £300 an order. The supplier offers a 3% discount for orders of 60 units or more, and a discount of 5% for orders of 90 units or more. What is the cost-minimising order size?

Solution

(a) The EOQ ignoring discounts is:

$$\sqrt{\frac{2 \times 300 \times 45}{15\% \text{ of } 200}} = 30 \text{ units}$$

	£
Purchases (no discount) 45 × £200	9,000
Holding costs ($^{30}/_2$) 15 units × £30	450
Ordering costs 1.5 orders × £300	450
Total annual costs	9,900

(b) With a discount of 3% and an order quantity of 60 units costs are as follows.

	£
Purchases £9,000 × 97%	8,730
Holding costs 30 units × 15% of 97% of £200	873
Ordering costs 0.75 orders × £300	225
Total annual costs	9,828

(c) With a discount of 5% and an order quantity of 90 units costs are as follows.

	£
Purchases £9,000 × 95%	8,550.0
Holding costs 45 units × 15% of 95% of £200	1,282.5
Ordering costs 0.5 orders × £300	150.0
Total annual costs	9,982.5

The cheapest option is to order 60 units at a time.

Question Bulk orders

Question: Bulk orders

A company uses an item of inventory as follows.

Purchase price:	£96 per unit
Annual demand:	4,000 units
Ordering cost:	£300
Annual holding cost:	10% of purchase price
Economic order quantity:	500 units

Should the company order 1,000 units at a time in order to secure an 8% discount?

Answer

The total annual cost at the economic order quantity of 500 units is as follows.

	£
Purchases 4,000 × £96	384,000
Ordering costs £300 × (4,000/500)	2,400
Holding costs £96 × 10% × (500/2)	2,400
	388,800

The total annual cost at an order quantity of 1,000 units would be as follows.

	£
Purchases £384,000 × 92%	353,280
Ordering costs £300 × (4,000/1,000)	1,200
Holding costs £96 × 92% × 10% × (1,000/2)	4,416
	358,896

The company should order the item 1,000 units at a time, saving £(388,800 − 358,896) = £29,904 a year.

1.9 Just-in-time (JIT) procurement

Some manufacturing companies have sought to reduce their inventories of raw materials and components to as low a level as possible. **Just-in-time procurement** and **stockless production** are terms which describe a policy of obtaining goods from suppliers at the latest possible time (ie when they are needed) and so avoiding the need to carry any materials or components stock.

Introducing JIT might bring the following potential benefits:

- Reduction in stockholding costs
- Reduced manufacturing lead times
- Improved labour productivity
- Reduced scrap/rework/warranty cost

Reduced inventory levels mean that a lower level of investment in working capital will be required.

JIT will not be appropriate in some cases. For example, a restaurant might find it preferable to use the traditional economic order quantity approach for staple non-perishable food stocks but adopt JIT for perishable and 'exotic' items. In a hospital, a stock-out could quite literally be fatal and so JIT would be quite unsuitable.

> **Exam focus point**
>
> You may be required to evaluate the benefits of introducing a JIT arrangement, given certain assumptions about the costs and benefits.

1.10 Artificial intelligence

Artificial Intelligence (AI) is revolutionising inventory management by enhancing efficiency, accuracy, and responsiveness. AI-powered systems utilise advanced algorithms and machine learning to forecast demand with greater precision, reducing the risks of overstocking and stockouts. These systems analyse vast amounts of data, including historical sales, market trends, and external factors like weather or economic conditions, to predict inventory needs.

AI facilitates real-time inventory tracking and automated reordering processes, ensuring optimal stock levels are maintained without manual intervention. By integrating AI into inventory management, businesses can significantly reduce costs, improve customer satisfaction through timely availability of products, and increase overall operational efficiency. The adoption of AI technologies enables companies to respond swiftly to market changes, maintain leaner inventories, and ultimately enhance their competitive advantage in the marketplace.

1.11 Inventory ratios

> **Key terms**
>
> $$\text{Inventory days} = \frac{\text{Average inventory}}{\text{Cost of sales}} \times 365 \text{ days}$$
>
> $$\text{Inventory turnover} = \frac{\text{Cost of sales}}{\text{Average inventory}}$$

The optimum period of **inventory days** will vary industry by industry, and may vary for different lines held by the same firm.

A high inventory days or low inventory turnover figure may arise for various reasons. It may be that the firm is being excessively **prudent** in its stockholding policies, or it may be due to **obsolete** or **slow-moving** stock.

An excessively low figure for **inventory days** or **high turnover** figure may also give cause for concern. It may indicate **supply difficulties**, and that there is a significant chance that the company will run out of stock and hence lose sales.

2 The management of cash

2.1 Why organisations hold cash

The economist John Maynard Keynes identified three reasons for holding cash:

(a) First, a business needs cash to meet its **regular commitments** of paying its creditors, its employees' wages, its taxes, its annual dividends to shareholders and so on. This reason for holding cash is what Keynes called the **transactions motive**.

(b) Keynes identified the **precautionary motive** as a second motive for holding cash. This means that there is a need to maintain a 'buffer' of cash for **unforeseen contingencies**. In the context of a business, this buffer may be provided by an **overdraft facility**, which has the advantage that it will cost nothing until it is actually used.

(c) Keynes identified a third motive for holding cash – the **speculative motive**. Some businesses hold surplus cash as a speculative asset in the hope that interest rates will rise. However, many businesses would regard large long-term holdings of cash as not prudent.

How much cash should a company keep on hand or 'on short call' at a bank? The more cash which is on hand, the easier it will be for the company to meet its bills as they fall due and to take advantage of discounts.

However, holding cash or near equivalents to cash has a cost – the **loss of earning** which would otherwise have been obtained by using the funds in another way. The financial manager must try to balance liquidity with profitability.

2.2 Cash flow problems

Cash flow problems can arise in various ways:

(a) **Making losses**

If a business is continually making losses, it will eventually have cash flow problems. If the loss is due to a large depreciation charge, the cash flow troubles might only begin when the business needs to replace non-current assets.

(b) **Inflation**

In a period of inflation, a business needs **ever-increasing amounts** of cash just to replace used-up and worn-out assets. A business can be making a profit in historical cost accounting terms, but still not be receiving enough cash to buy the replacement assets it needs.

(c) **Growth**

When a business is growing, it needs to **acquire more non-current assets**, and to **support higher amounts of inventories and receivables**. These additional assets must be paid for somehow (or financed by creditors).

(d) **Seasonal business**

When a business has seasonal or cyclical sales, it may have cash flow difficulties at certain times of the year, when:

(i) Cash inflows are low, but

(ii) Cash outflows are high, perhaps because the business is building up its stocks for the next period of high sales

(e) **One-off items of expenditure**

A single non-recurring item of expenditure may create a cash flow problem. Examples include the repayment of loan capital on maturity of the debt or the purchase of an exceptionally expensive item, such as a freehold property.

2.3 Methods of easing cash shortages

FAST FORWARD

Cash shortages can be eased by postponing capital expenditure, leasing assets, selling assets, taking longer to pay creditors and pressing debtors for earlier payment.

The steps that are usually taken by a company when a need for cash arises, and when it cannot obtain resources from any other source such as a loan or an increased overdraft, are as follows:

(a) **Postponing capital expenditure**

Some new non-current assets might be needed for the development and growth of the business, but some capital expenditures might be postponable without serious consequences. If a company's policy is to replace company cars every two years, but the company is facing a cash shortage, it might decide to replace cars every three years.

(b) **Leasing assets**

A company could choose to lease an asset rather than buying it outright. Leasing avoids the need to find the cash to acquire an asset.

(c) **Accelerating cash inflows which would otherwise be expected in a later period**

One way would be to press debtors for earlier payment. Often, this policy will result in a loss of goodwill and problems with customers. It might be possible to encourage debtors to pay more quickly by offering discounts for earlier payment.

(d) **Reversing past investment decisions by selling assets previously acquired**

Some assets are less crucial to a business than others. If cash flow problems are severe, the option of selling investments or property might have to be considered.

(e) **Negotiating a reduction in cash outflows, to postpone or reduce payments**

There are several ways in which this could be done.

(i) **Longer credit** might be taken from suppliers. Such an extension of credit would have to be negotiated carefully: there would be a risk of having further supplies refused.

(ii) **Loan repayments** could be rescheduled by agreement with a bank.

(iii) A **deferral** of the payment of **corporation tax** might be agreed with the tax authorities who will charge interest on the outstanding amount of tax.

(iv) **Dividend payments** could be **reduced**. Dividend payments are discretionary cash outflows, although a company's directors might be constrained by shareholders' expectations, so that they feel obliged to pay dividends even when there is a cash shortage.

2.4 Deviations from expected cash flows

Cash budgets, whether prepared on an annual, monthly, weekly or even a daily basis, can only be estimates of cash flows. Even the best estimates will not be exactly correct, so deviations from the cash budget are inevitable.

A cash budget model could be constructed, using a PC and a spreadsheet package, and the **sensitivity** of cash flow forecasts to changes in estimates of sales, costs and so on could be analysed. By planning for different eventualities, management should be able to prepare **contingency measures** in advance and also **appreciate** the **key factors** in the cash budget.

A knowledge of the **probability distribution** of possible outcomes for the cash position will allow a **more accurate estimate** to be made of the minimum cash balances, or the borrowing power necessary, to provide a satisfactory margin of safety. Unforeseen deficits can be hard to finance at short notice, and advance planning is desirable.

2.5 Float

The term **float** is sometimes used to describe the amount of money tied up between **the time when a payment is initiated** (for example, when a debtor pays by cheque), and **the time when the funds become available for use** in the recipient's bank account. This is less relevant for businesses who receive most of their payments electronically. However for small businesses and sole traders who receive payment by cheque, the float is an important factor in cash flow.

There are three reasons why there might be a lengthy float:

(a) **Transmission delay**

When payment is sent through the post, it will take a day or longer for the payment to reach the payee.

(b) **Delay in banking the payments received**

The payee, on receipt of a cheque or cash, might **delay presenting** the **cheque** or the cash to his bank. The length of this (lodgement) delay will depend on administrative procedures in the payee's organisation.

(c) **The time needed for a bank to clear a cheque**

A payment is not available for use in the payee's bank account until the **cheque** has been **cleared**. This will usually take two or three days for cheques payable in the UK. For cheques payable abroad, the delay is much longer.

There are several measures that could be taken to reduce the float:

(a) The payee should ensure that the lodgement delay is kept to a minimum. **Cheques** received should be presented to the bank on the day of receipt.

(b) The payee might, in some local cases, arrange to **collect cheques** from the payer's premises.

(c) The payer might be asked to pay through his own branch of a bank, using the **bank giro system**.

(d) **BACS** (Bankers' Automated Clearing Services Ltd) is a banking system which provides for the computerised transfer of funds between banks. In addition, BACS is available to **corporate customers** of banks for **making payments**.

(e) For regular payments, **standing orders** or **direct debits** might be used.

(f) **CHAPS** (Clearing House Automated Payments System) is a computerised system for banks to make **same-day clearances** (that is, immediate payment) between each other.

(g) The Faster Payments service is provided by many banks in the UK which enables payments to be made and cleared within a few hours.

2.6 Inefficient cash management

A lengthy float suggests inefficient cash management. But there are other types of delay in receiving payment from debtors, which might also suggest inefficient cash management.

(a) There is the delay created by the **length of credit** given to customers. There is often a 'normal' credit period for an industry, and companies might be unable to grant less time for payment than this.

(b) There are avoidable delays caused by **poor administration** (in addition to lodgement delay), such as:

   (i) **Failure to notify** the **invoicing department** that goods have been despatched, so that invoices are not sent promptly

   (ii) **Cheques from debtors** being **made out incorrectly**, to the wrong company perhaps, because invoices do not contain clear instructions

2.7 Example: Cash management

Ryan Coates owns a chain of seven clothes shops in the London area. Takings at each shop are remitted once a week on Thursday evening to the head office, and are then banked at the start of business on Friday morning. As business is expanding, Ryan Coates has hired an accountant to help him. The accountant gave him the following advice.

> 'Turnover at the seven shops totalled £1,950,000 last year, at a constant daily rate, but you were paying bank overdraft charges at a rate of 11%. You could have reduced your overdraft costs by banking the shop takings each day, except for Saturday's takings. Saturday takings could have been banked on Mondays.'

Comment on the significance of this statement, stating your assumptions. The shops are closed on Sundays.

Solution

(a) A bank overdraft rate of 11% a year is approximately 11/365 = 0.03% a day.

(b) Annual takings of £1,950,000 would be an average of £1,950,000/312 = £6,250 a day for the seven shops in total, on the assumption that they opened for a 52 week year of six days a week (312 days).

(c) Using the approximate overdraft cost of 0.03% a day, the cost of holding £6,250 for one day instead of banking it is 0.03% × £6,250 = £1.875.

(d) Banking all takings up to Thursday evening of each week on Friday morning involves an unnecessary delay in paying cash into the bank. The cost of this delay would be **either** the opportunity cost of investment capital for the business **or** the cost of avoidable bank overdraft charges.

It is assumed here that the overdraft cost is higher and is therefore more appropriate to use. It is also assumed that, for interest purposes, funds are credited when banked.

Takings on	Could be banked on	Number of days delay incurred by Friday banking
Monday	Tuesday	3
Tuesday	Wednesday	2
Wednesday	Thursday	1
Thursday	Friday	0
Friday	Saturday	6
Saturday	Monday	4
		16

In one week, the total number of days' delay incurred by Friday banking is 16. At a cost of £1.875 a day, the weekly cost of Friday banking was £1.875 × 16 = £30.00, and the annual cost of Friday banking was £30.00 × 52 = £1,560.

(e) **Conclusion.** The company could have saved about £1,560 a year in bank overdraft charges last year. If the overdraft rate remains at 11% and turnover continues to increase, the saving from daily banking would be even higher next year.

2.8 Baumol model approach to cash management

FAST FORWARD

Optimal **cash** holding levels can be calculated from formal models, such as the **Baumol model** and the **Miller-Orr model**.

A number of different cash management models indicate the **optimum amount of cash** that a company should hold. One such model is based on the idea that deciding on optimum cash balances is like deciding on optimum stock levels. This is known as either the Baumol model or inventory approach.

We can distinguish two types of cost which are involved in obtaining cash:

(a) The **fixed cost** represented, for example, by the issue cost of equity finance or the cost of negotiating an overdraft

(b) The **variable cost** (opportunity cost) of keeping the money in the form of cash

The inventory approach uses an equation of the same form as the EOQ formula for stock management which we looked at earlier. The average total cost incurred for period in holding a certain average level of cash (C) is:

$$\frac{Qi}{2} + \frac{FS}{Q}$$

where S = the amount of cash to be used in each time period
F = the fixed cost of obtaining new funds
i = the interest cost of holding cash or near cash equivalents
Q = the total amount to be raised to provide for S

Similarly to the EOQ, C is minimised when:

$$Q = \sqrt{\frac{2FS}{i}}$$

2.8.1 Example: Baumol approach to cash management

Finder Ltd faces a fixed cost of £4,000 to obtain new funds. There is a requirement for £24,000 of cash over each period of one year for the foreseeable future. The interest cost of new funds is 12% per annum; the interest rate earned on short-term securities is 9% per annum. How much finance should Finder Ltd raise at a time?

Solution

The cost of holding cash is 12% – 9% = 3%

The optimum level of Q (the 'reorder quantity') is:

$$\sqrt{\frac{2 \times 4,000 \times 24,000}{0.03}} = £80,000$$

The optimum amount of new funds to raise is £80,000. This amount is raised every 80,000 ÷ 24,000 = 3^{1}/$_{3}$ years.

2.9 Drawbacks of the Baumol approach

The inventory approach illustrated above has the following drawbacks.

(a) In reality, it is unlikely to be **possible** to **predict amounts required** over future periods with much certainty.

(b) No **buffer stock** of cash is allowed for. There may be costs associated with running out of cash.

(c) There may be other **normal costs** of holding cash which increase with the average amount held.

2.10 The Miller-Orr model

In an attempt to produce a more realistic approach to cash management, various models more complicated than the inventory approach have been developed. One of these, the **Miller-Orr model**, manages to achieve a reasonable degree of realism while not being too elaborate.

We can begin looking at the Miller-Orr model by asking what will happen if there is no attempt to manage cash balances. Clearly, the cash balance is likely to 'meander' upwards or downwards. The Miller-Orr model imposes limits to this meandering.

If the cash balance reaches an **upper limit** (point A in Figure 2) the firm **buys sufficient securities** to return the cash balance to a normal level (called the 'return point'). When the cash balance reaches a lower limit (point B in Figure 2), the firm sells securities to bring the balance back to the return point.

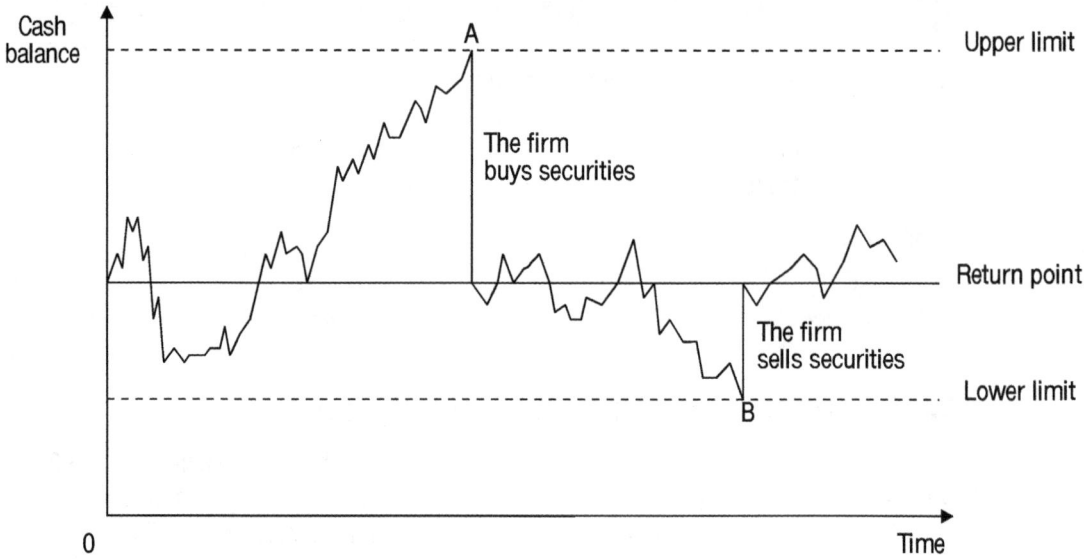

Figure 2 Miller-Orr model

How are the upper and lower limits and the return point set? Miller and Orr showed that the answer to this question depends on the **variance of cash flows**, **transaction costs** and **interest rates**. If the day-to-day variability of cash flows is high or the transaction cost in buying or selling securities is high, then wider limits should be set. If interest rates are high, the limits should be closer together.

To keep the interest costs of holding cash down, the return point is set at one-third of the distance (or 'spread') between the lower and the upper limit.

Exam formula provided

Return point = Lower limit + $\frac{1}{3}$ × spread

The formula for the spread is:

$$\text{Spread} = 3\left(\frac{3}{4} \times \frac{\text{transaction cost} \times \text{variance of cash flows}}{\text{interest rate}}\right)^{\frac{1}{3}}$$

Exam focus point

> The Miller-Orr formulae for return point and spread are included in the formulae sheet provided with the examination paper.

To use the Miller-Orr model, it is necessary to follow the steps below.

Step 1 Set the **lower limit** for the **cash balance**. This may be zero, or it may be set at some minimum safety margin above zero.

Step 2 **Estimate** the **variance** of **cash flows**, for example from sample observations over a 100-day period.

Step 3 **Note the interest rate** and the **transaction cost** for each sale or purchase of securities (the latter is assumed to be fixed).

Step 4 **Compute the upper limit** and the **return point** from the model and implement the limits strategy.

You may be given the information to help you through the early steps, as in the question below.

Question — Miller-Orr model

The following data applies to a company.

Step 1 The minimum cash balance is £8,000.

Step 2 The variance of daily cash flows is 4,000,000, equivalent to a standard deviation of £2,000 per day.

Step 3 The transaction cost for buying or selling securities is £50. The interest rate is 0.025 per cent per day.

You are required to formulate a decision rule using the Miller-Orr model.

Answer

Step 4 The spread between the upper and the lower cash balance limits is calculated as follows.

$$\text{Spread} = 3\left(\frac{3}{4} \times \frac{\text{transaction cost} \times \text{variance of cash flows}}{\text{interest rate}}\right)^{\frac{1}{3}}$$

$$= 3\left(\frac{3}{4} \times \frac{50 \times 4{,}000{,}000}{0.00025}\right)^{\frac{1}{3}} = 3(6 \times 10)^{\frac{1}{3}} = 3 \times 8434.33$$

$$= £25{,}303, \text{ say } £25{,}300$$

The upper limit and return point are now calculated.

Upper limit = lower limit + £25,300 = £8,000 + £25,300 = £33,300
Return point = lower limit + $\frac{1}{3}$ × spread = £8,000 + $\frac{1}{3}$ × £25,300 = £16,433, say £16,400

The decision rule is as follows. If the cash balance reaches £33,300, buy £16,900 (= 33,300 – 16,400) in marketable securities. If the cash balance falls to £8,000, sell £8,400 of marketable securities for cash.

The **usefulness of the Miller-Orr model** is limited by the assumptions on which it is based. In practice, cash inflows and outflows are unlikely to be entirely **unpredictable** as the model assumes, for example, for a retailer, seasonal factors are likely to affect cash inflows.

LEARNING OUTCOME 5   WORKING CAPITAL MANAGEMENT

However, the Miller-Orr model may save management time which might otherwise be spent in responding to those cash inflows and outflows which cannot be predicted.

2.11 Applying probabilities in cash management problems

Probabilities can be applied to cash management problems.

2.12 Example: Probabilities in cash management

Sinkos Wim Ltd has an overdraft facility of £100,000, and currently has an overdraft balance at the bank of £34,000. The company maintains a cash float of £10,000 for transactions and precautionary purposes. It is unclear whether a long awaited economic recovery will take place, and the company has prepared cash budgets as set out below for the next three months using two different assumptions about economic events. The cash flow in Months 2 and 3 depend on the cash flows in the previous month.

Estimated net cash flows

	Month 1		Month 2		Month 3
Probability	Cash flow £'000	Probability	Cash flow £'000	Probability	Cash flow £'000
		0.8	25	0.5	30
0.7	(40)			0.5	20
		0.2	10	0.5	10
				0.5	0
		0.8	0	0.5	(10)
0.3	(60)			0.5	(20)
		0.2	(10)	0.5	(40)
				0.5	(50)

If the company intends to maintain a cash float of £10,000 at the end of each month, what is the probability that this will be possible at the end of each of Months 1, 2 and 3 given the current overdraft limit?

Solution

The opening balance at the beginning of Month 1 is £10,000.

	Month 1				Month 2				Month 3		
Prob.	Cash flow £'000	Clos. bal. £'000	Over-draft £'000	Prob.	Cash flow £'000	Clos. bal. £'000	Over-draft £'000	Prob.	Cash flow £'000	Clos. bal. £'000	Over-draft £'000
								0.28	30	10	19
				0.56	25	10	49	0.28	20	10	29
0.7	(40)	10	74								
								0.07	10	10	54
				0.14	10	10	64	0.07	0	10	64
								0.12	(10)	6	100
				0.24	0	10	94	0.12	(20)	(4)	100
0.3	(60)	10	94								
								0.03	(40)	(34)	100
				0.06	(10)	6	100	0.03	(50)	(44)	100

The probabilities that the cash float of £10,000 can be maintained at the end of each month are as follows.

Month 1:   0.7 + 0.3 = 1.0
Month 2:   0.56 + 0.14 + 0.24 = 0.94
Month 3:   0.28 + 0.28 + 0.07 + 0.07 = 0.7

Question — Cash shortage

Using the figures in the above example, state the probabilities that the company completely runs out of cash at the end of each month.

Answer

Under none of the projected outcomes for Months 1 and 2 does the company run out of cash.

For Month 3, the probability of the company running out of cash is:

0.12 + 0.03 + 0.03 = 0.18

2.13 Investing surplus cash

FAST FORWARD

Temporary surpluses of cash can be invested in a variety of financial instruments. Longer-term surpluses should be returned to shareholders if there is a lack of investment opportunities.

Companies and other organisations sometimes have a **surplus of cash** and become 'cash rich'. A cash surplus is likely to be **temporary**, but while it exists the company should invest or deposit the cash bearing the following considerations in mind.

(a) **Liquidity** – money should be available to take advantage of favourable short-term interest rates on bank deposits, or to grasp a strategic opportunity, for example paying cash to take over another company

(b) **Profitability** – the company should seek to obtain a **good return** for the **risk** incurred

(c) **Safety** – the company should **avoid** the risk of a **capital loss**

Other factors that organisations need to consider include:

(a) Whether to invest at **fixed or floating rates**. Floating rate investments are likely to be chosen if interest rates are expected to rise.

(b) **Term to maturity**. The terms chosen will be affected by the business's desire for **liquidity** and **expectations** about future rates of interest; if there are major uncertainties about future interest rate levels it will be better to choose short-term investments. There may also be **penalties** for **early liquidation**.

(c) How easy it will be to **realise** the investment.

(d) Whether a **minimum amount** has to be invested in certain investments.

(e) Whether to invest on **international markets**.

If a company has no plans to grow or to invest, then surplus cash not required for transactions or precautionary purposes should normally be **returned** to **shareholders**.

Surplus cash may be returned to shareholders by:

(a) Increasing the usual level of the annual **dividends** which are paid

(b) Making a one-off **special dividend payment** (for example, Kingfisher made such a payment for the year ended 31 January 2015.

(c) Using the money to **buy back its own shares** from some of its shareholders. This will reduce the total number of shares in issue, and should therefore raise the level of **earnings per share**

If surplus cash is to be invested on a regular basis, organisations should have investment guidelines in place covering the following issues:

(a) Surplus funds can only be invested in **specified types of investment** (eg no equity shares).

(b) All investments must be **convertible into cash** within a set number of days.

(c) Investments should be **ranked**: surplus funds to be invested in higher risk instruments only when a sufficiency has been invested in lower risk items (so that there is always a cushion of safety).

(d) If a firm invests in certain financial instruments, a **credit rating** should be obtained. Credit rating agencies, such as Moody's, Fitch and Standard and Poor's, issue gradings according to risk.

2.13.1 Short-term investments

Temporary cash surpluses are likely to be:

(a) **Deposited** with a **bank** or similar financial institution

(b) Invested in **short-term debt instruments.** (Debt instruments are debt securities which can be traded)

(c) Invested in **longer-term debt instruments**, which can be sold on the stock market when the company eventually needs the cash

(d) Invested in **shares of listed companies**, which can be sold on the stock market when the company eventually needs the cash

2.13.2 Short-term deposits

Cash can of course be put into a **bank deposit** to **earn interest**. The rate of interest obtainable depends on the size of the deposit, and varies from bank to bank.

There are other types of deposit:

(a) **Money market lending**

There is a very large money market in the UK for inter-bank lending. The interest rates in the market are related to the Sterling Overnight Index Average (SONIA).

(b) **Local authority deposits**

Local authorities often need **short-term cash**, and investors can deposit funds with them for periods ranging from overnight up to one year or more.

(c) **Finance house deposits**

These are **time deposits** with finance houses (usually subsidiaries of banks).

2.13.3 Short-term debt instruments

There are a number of **short-term debt instruments** which an investor can re-sell before the debt matures and is repaid. These debt instruments include **certificates of deposit** (CDs) and **Treasury bills**.

2.13.4 Certificates of deposit (CDs)

A **CD** is a security that is issued by a bank, acknowledging that a certain amount of money has been deposited with it for a certain period of time (usually, a short term). The CD is issued to the **depositor**, and attracts a **stated amount of interest**. The **depositor** will be another bank or a large commercial organisation.

CDs are negotiable and traded on the CD market (a money market), so if a CD holder wishes to obtain immediate cash, he can sell the CD on the market at any time. This second-hand market in CDs makes them attractive, flexible investments for organisations with excess cash.

2.13.5 Treasury bills

Treasury bills are issued weekly by the government to finance short-term cash deficiencies in the government's expenditure programme. They are **IOUs** issued by the government, giving a promise to pay a certain amount to their holder on maturity. Treasury bills have a term of **91 days to maturity**, after which the holder is paid the full value of the bill.

3 Treasury management

FAST FORWARD

> A large organisation will have a **treasury department** to manage liquidity, short-term investment, borrowings, foreign exchange risk and other, specialised, areas such as forward contracts and futures etc.

Key term

> **Treasury management** can be defined as: 'The corporate handing of all financial matters, the generation of external and internal funds for business, the management of currencies and cash flows, and the complex strategies, policies and procedures of corporate finance.' (Association of Corporate Treasurers)

Large companies rely heavily on the financial and currency markets. These markets are volatile, with interest rates and foreign exchange rates changing continually and by significant amounts. To manage cash (funds) and currency efficiently, many large companies have set up a separate treasury department.

A treasury department, even in a large organisation, is likely to be quite small, with perhaps a staff of three to six qualified accountants, bankers or corporate treasurers working under the treasurer.

3.1 Centralisation of the treasury department

The following are advantages of having a specialist **centralised treasury department**:

(a) **Centralised liquidity management**

   (i) Avoids having a mix of cash surpluses and overdrafts in different localised bank accounts
   (ii) Facilitates bulk cash flows, so that lower bank charges can be negotiated

(b) Larger volumes of cash are available to invest, giving better **short-term investment opportunities** (for example money markets, high-interest accounts and CDs).

(c) Any **borrowing** can be **arranged in bulk**, at lower interest rates than for smaller borrowings, and perhaps on the eurocurrency or eurobond markets.

(d) **Foreign exchange risk management** is likely to be improved in a group of companies. A central treasury department can **match foreign currency income** earned by one subsidiary with **expenditure** in the same currency by another subsidiary. In this way, the risk of losses on adverse exchange rate movements can be avoided without the expense of forward exchange contracts or other hedging methods.

(e) A specialist treasury department can employ **experts** with knowledge of dealing in forward contracts, futures, options, eurocurrency markets, swaps and so on. Localised departments could not have such expertise.

(f) The centralised pool of **funds required for precautionary purposes** will be **smaller** than the sum of separate precautionary balances which would need to be held under decentralised treasury arrangements.

(g) Through having a separate **profit centre**, attention will be focused on the contribution to group profit performance that can be achieved by good cash, funding, investment and foreign currency management.

Possible advantages of **decentralised** cash management are as follows:

(a) Sources of finance can be **diversified** and can match **local assets**.

(b) **Greater autonomy** can be given to **subsidiaries** and divisions because of the closer relationships they will have with the decentralised cash management function.

(c) A decentralised treasury function may be **more responsive** to the needs of individual operating units.

(d) Since cash balances will not be aggregated at group level, there will be **more limited opportunities** to invest such balances on a short-term basis.

Chapter Roundup

- An **economic order quantity** can be calculated as a guide to minimising costs in managing **inventory** levels. **Bulk discounts** can however mean that a different order quantity minimises inventory costs.

- **Uncertainties** in demand and lead times taken to fulfil orders mean that inventory will be ordered once it reaches a re-order level (maximum usage × maximum lead time).

- **Cash shortages** can be eased by postponing capital expenditure, selling assets, taking longer to pay creditors and pressing debtors for earlier payment.

- Optimal **cash** holding levels can be calculated from formal models, such as the **inventory approach** and the **Miller-Orr model**.

- **Temporary surpluses** of cash can be invested in a variety of financial instruments. Longer-term surpluses should be returned to shareholders if there is a lack of investment opportunities.

- A large organisation will have a **treasury department** to manage liquidity, short-term investment, borrowings, foreign exchange risk and other, specialised, areas such as forward contracts and futures etc.

LEARNING OUTCOME 5 WORKING CAPITAL MANAGEMENT

Quick Quiz

1 The basic EOQ formula for inventory indicates whether bulk discounts should be taken advantage of

   ☐ True

   ☐ False

2 Identify the potential benefits of JIT manufacturing.

3 Possible reasons for a lengthy float are:

   (a) .... delay

   (b) .... delay

   (c) .... delay

4 In the Miller-Orr cash management model

   Return point = Lower limit + ... × spread

5 Why might a treasurer choose **not** to 'hedge' against the risk of a foreign exchange movement?

6 PB Ltd uses 2,500 units of component X per year. The company has calculated that the cost of placing and processing a purchase order for component X is £185, and the cost of holding one unit of component X for a year is £25.

   What is the economic order quantity (EOQ) for component X, and assuming a 52-week year, what is the average frequency at which purchase orders should be placed?

7 The economic order quantity model can be used to determine:

Order quantity	Buffer inventory	Re-order level
Yes/No	Yes/No	Yes/No

8 Which of the following is most likely to reduce a firm's working capital?

   A   Adopting the Miller-Orr model of cash management
   B   Lengthening the period of credit given to debtors
   C   Buying new machinery
   D   Adopting just-in-time procurement and lean manufacturing

Answers to Quick Quiz

1. False. It may be necessary to modify the formula to take account of bulk discounts.

2. (a) Reduction in stockholding costs
   (b) Reduced manufacturing lead times
   (c) Improved labour productivity
   (d) Reduced scrap/warranty/rework/costs
   (e) Price reductions on purchased materials
   (f) Reduction in the number of accounting transactions

3. (a) Transmission delay
   (b) Lodgement delay
   (c) Clearance delay

4. One third

5. Because they think it likely that a profit will be made in refraining from hedging the risk.

6. $EOQ = \sqrt{\dfrac{2C_o D}{C_h}}$

   Economic order quantity $= \sqrt{\dfrac{2 \times 185 \times 2{,}500}{25}}$

   $= 192$ units

   Frequency of ordering $= \dfrac{192}{2{,}500} \times 52$ weeks

   $= 4$ weeks

7. The EOQ model finds order quantity only, not buffer stock and re-order level.

8. D The aim of using these methods is to minimise stockholdings. The impact of using the Miller-Orr model will depend on how the firm was managing cash before (A). Giving more credit to debtors will increase working capital (B). New machinery is not part of working capital (C); the impact, if any, on working capital will depend on how the purchase is financed.

LEARNING OUTCOME 5 WORKING CAPITAL MANAGEMENT

End of chapter question

Whitlow Engineering (AIA November 2005)

Whitlow Engineering has just announced a disappointing set of financial results. It has explained to its shareholders that the failure to meet its profit targets was, in part, due to reduced orders but was mainly due to the following:

- A large write off due to, largely unexplained, inventory losses;
- High levels of bad debts;
- Customers taking much longer to pay;
- High interest payments due to the increased use of the company's overdraft facility.

A major investor has threatened to withdraw support from the company if it does not install the necessary financial controls to avoid reoccurrences of the above problems.

Required

(a) Discuss the nature and operation of the controls referred to above by the major investor.

(10 marks)

(b) Briefly explain why planning is such an important aspect of operating such controls. **(10 marks)**

(Total 20 marks)

Answers to end of chapter questions

ANSWERS TO END OF CHAPTER QUESTIONS

Chapter 1 – EarthCare

This question tests the candidate's ability to appraise financial and non-financial objectives in the context of a business whose aim is not to maximise shareholder wealth (LO1)

EarthCare is not a typical company in respect of it how it is organised, or its ethical position. Therefore, it might be expected that its objectives will bear little or no resemblance to the prime objective usually cited of maximising shareholder wealth. However, before this can be concluded we need to assess whether this is correct.

Any company must have sufficient financial funds to survive. Therefore, although there are no explicit financial objectives stated for EarthCare it must have at a minimum the aim of having sufficient funds to continue. A typical company would also have this aim, but it would also have to meet more than this financial objective if it is to maximise shareholder wealth. Therefore, other financial objectives could include having target goals for profit levels and earnings per share. It is likely that EarthCare will also want to ensure profit is at least acceptable as that will enable it to continue operating. It is less likely to be concerned about earnings per share as a co-operative is worker-owned and not shareholder-owned.

EarthCare has a clear focus on a number of non-financial objectives that it deems of great importance. Other companies will also have non-financial objectives and these will not necessarily undermine its prime objective of maximising shareholder wealth. It is explained below how this can also be the case for EarthCare.

Selling organic, vegetarian food to customers may limit the range of foodstuffs that EarthCare can offer, but it may also imply it understands its target audience well. It might also be that a high level of trust has been engendered that leads to significant customer loyalty with the promotion of healthy eating adding to this trust.

Ensuring a fair price is paid to suppliers may imply that this will reduce profit (and this would have a negative impact on shareholder wealth in other companies). However, sourcing locally may imply lower delivery costs and fresher food leading to less wastage of perishable items. Ethically-minded customers may also be happy to accept that they pay a slight premium on the price as this fits with their social conscience. It is unlikely the large supermarket chains can premium price in this way.

The policy on employee training and the non-hierarchical structure may have a positive impact on profit. First, as EarthCare invests in caring for employees it is creating better motivated and multi-skilled staff. Second, paying all employees the same will reduce the overall wages bill compared to a company with a hierarchical structure.

EarthCare's efforts to minimise its impacts on the environment can also be positive for its financial position. Energy use for both electricity and company vehicles is kept as low as possible and this adds to profitability. Waste is recycled; however, it is less certain whether this will impact on profitability.

There is some evidence that the non-financial objectives pursued by EarthCare are good for profit too. This evidence is that the company has existed for a reasonably long period to date (30 years) and that it has steadily grown over that period. The sector it operates in is very competitive with large supermarket chains dominating the food retail market.

Therefore, although EarthCare does not pursue shareholder wealth it is possible that the non-financial objectives it follows lead to enhanced profits and in firms that are not co-operatives this would generally improve shareholder wealth. Consequently, the financial and non-financial objectives of EarthCare do have some connection to the objective of maximising the market value of the company's shares.

ANSWERS TO END OF CHAPTER QUESTIONS

Chapter 2

1. Mrs Johnson

This question tests the candidate's ability to:

(i) **Evaluate financing options (IO1)**

Report

To: Mrs Johnson
Subject: Evaluation of financing options
From: XXXX
Date: XXXX

The funding options you are considering are debt (bank loan) or equity (your friend purchasing a proportion of the shares). It is usual for companies to be financed by a mix of both debt and equity. However, when setting up a business it can be difficult to acquire finance and start-ups often have to take whatever funding is available. Therefore, you have a choice to make and there are advantages and disadvantages to both sources of finance.

Should you choose the bank loan then there is a fixed interest commitment that must be met each month. You must be confident that you can make these monthly interest payments. Your business is new and for the initial two years profits are projected to be small. You need to calculate the affordability of the interest on a monthly basis relative to the profit per month for all five years and include this in your business plan. You should remember that profitability is not the only aspect related to interest affordability as cashflow is important too. Therefore, your business plan should include cashflow projections too.

A further consideration regarding the affordability of the interest is that profits might fluctuate month by month. This is especially so given the product. It might be that a significant proportion of the schoolbags are likely to be sold just before the start of the school year. Therefore, at that time profits will be high relative to other times in the year. This volatility in respect of profits might mean you can afford the interest at some points in the year and not at others. Including interest payments on the business plan will assist you ascertaining affordability.

The loan option requires you to provide security and you can provide this based on your own house as security. You need to be aware that if you do not continually meet the terms of the loan agreement that this puts your house at risk. That is, the bank can require you to sell the house should you get into difficulties. You must think carefully whether you are willing to accept this risk as it has significant ramifications for you personally.

The debt interest is tax allowable. You are anticipating profits and, therefore, you can offset the interest against your taxable profits. This makes the cost of the debt (ie the interest) effectively cheaper than the interest rate charged by the bank, as you will have a tax saving.

If you decide to fund the business using equity then your friend will acquire a part of your business. This means you do not own all of the business. You need to decide whether you are willing to give up a part of the business. Additionally, you need to know what proportion of the business you will be giving up for two reasons. First, if you retain more than 50% of the equity then you still retain the majority of the equity. Second, you need to know that the amount of money you are receiving for the amount of equity you are selling is appropriate and fair. It is particularly difficult valuing a start-up business, and you should be aware that an exact valuation is not possible.

The friend may require having input into the business and its strategy in return for providing the equity funding. You need to know if this is the case. The friend has significant business experience and their input could be potentially useful as you do not have business experience. However, you should be aware that a professional business relationship is different to a friendship. To be useful in assisting in running the business your friend may need to be critical. You have to understand this might affect your current relationship.

Whilst interest is paid on borrowings; dividends are paid to shareholders. However, a key difference between interest and dividends is that there is no obligation for a business to pay dividends. Therefore, in the early years of the business you could choose not to pay dividends and retain cash to grow the business. This may be helpful as the profits in the early years of a business can be very difficult to forecast. However, it would be a good idea to talk to your friend about this as they may be expecting returns in the form of dividends from the outset.

Normally, the cost of equity is more costly than the cost of debt. That is, shareholders normally require a higher return because they are in a riskier position than a lender of funding. Shareholders have no security and are last to receive any funds (should there be any) if a company ceases to trade. Further, dividends are not tax allowable. As an experienced business person your friend is very likely to be aware of the risk attached to their potential investment. However, I would recommend you discuss the risk as it could be very difficult for you (and your friend) should the business fail and the friend lose their investment.

A provider of share capital in a new position will normally want to have planned an exit route. That is, they will want to know how they can sell their shares and recover their investment (plus an additional amount) after, say, five years. For example, it could be that a business is planning it will have grown to a point where a trade sale is feasible. You need to know whether your friend has any such expectation.

2. Bryden Ltd

This question tests the candidate's ability to evaluate alternative sources of finance (LO1)

Report

To: Mr and Mrs Bryden
Subject: Financing options
From: XXXX
Date: XXXX

There are two financing options that you are considering for funding the expansion of the business. The first is to borrow and the second is to bring in a businesswoman as a shareholder. There are merits and demerits to both methods and it is not always evident whether one method is better than another.

It is important to recognise that whichever method you choose the expansion will have an impact upon you as the current owners and managers of the business. You will be responsible for developing three further sales outlets. This will be aided by your current reputation. However, you will not be able to rely on reputation alone and will need to spend time and effort developing the new outlets. If you do not do this then the new businesses may not thrive, which in turn may then negatively impact on your current reputation. As you initially established the business because of your great interest in gardening then you need to be clear that you do want to expand the business.

You forecast that the £750,000 will enable you to increase profit by £90,000. The 2013 profit was £224,000 and this was a year where you had not successfully predicted plant trends. Had you predicted trends successfully then the profit would have been approximately £320,000 (£224,000/70%). Therefore, assuming this 2013 profit is representative your overall profit would be approximately £410,000.

If you choose to raise debt then there will be interest of £67,500 per year (£750,000 x 9%) to pay, whereas raising equity from the businesswoman incurs no interest charge. The potential effect on your income statement will be:

	Debt £'000	Equity £'000
Operating profit	410	410
Finance costs – interest payable	(67.5)	(0)
Profit before taxation	342.5	410
Taxation	(68.5)	(82)
Profit after tax	274	328

Both options result in increased profits after tax. The appearance is that the equity option is better as the profit after tax figure is greater. However, you should bear in mind that the businesswoman will want to have a return on her investment. She may want this return in the form of dividends. The return the businesswoman requires is unknown but as she is in a riskier position than debt holders she would normally require a higher return. It is also the case that the debt interest is tax allowable which further reduces the cost of the debt. Debt does bring with it a fixed commitment to pay the interest (and eventually the principal). The profit calculations above suggest the interest is easily affordable. If the operating profit is re-calculated on the basis of having not successfully anticipated the trend then it falls by 30% to £287,000 and the interest remains easily affordable even factoring that cashflows accrue unevenly during the year.

It is likely debtholders will want some form of security. This can be provided as you own the land for your business. This land has a current value of £950,000 and you wish to borrow £750,000. Therefore, it should be sufficiently valuable. You will need to accept that should the business get into difficulties then the debtholders may acquire the land in the event you cannot repay them. This is not the case should you raise the finance via the businesswoman.

The businesswoman may bring to the company expertise that you do not have. You established the business as you were keen gardeners, but no information has been provided about your business knowledge. As she has been successful in business this indicates she has significant skills that you can draw on. Therefore, it would be worthwhile establishing whether she would wish to participate actively in the business and whether the skills are additional to yours. Debtholders do not normally provide any input, other than capital, into the business.

A potential downside to bringing in an external equity holder is that some aspects of their participation may possibly be problematic. The businesswoman will have a 50% stake in the business and may wish to have a say in the strategy of the business and her view may not coincide with yours. She may also wish to exit the business at some point and this entails selling her equity stake. This can occur in different ways, but it could impinge greatly on you and particularly if you are not wanting to exit the business at the same time. Debtholders have no equity stake in the business and do not participate in the decision making. There is no information given as to the maturity of the debt, but there will be a point in the future when the debt needs repaying. This is not the same as equity exit strategies, but will need to be planned for.

ANSWERS TO END OF CHAPTER QUESTIONS

Chapter 3 - Crowther Systems plc

This question tests the candidate's ability to evaluate and explain the impact of the financial environment on an organisation. (Syllabus reference LO1).

(a) The Financial markets can be subdivided into:

- The Money Markets
- The Capital Markets
- The Foreign Exchange Markets
- The Financial Derivatives Markets

Financial markets promote savings and investment by providing the facilities which enable the requirements of the suppliers of funds and the users of funds to be met.

(b) There is a basic mismatch between the requirements and attitudes of the personal and business sectors. For example, the personal sector:

- Mostly wish to invest relatively small sums of money
- Do not wish to take substantial risks
- Wish to maintain a reasonable level of liquidity

Whereas the business sector generally:

- Requires large amounts of money
- Do often take substantial risks
- Invest in undertakings which can tie up funds for considerable periods of time

Financial intermediaries successfully match the requirements of the two sectors by:

- Pooling the small amounts invested by the personal sector into large amounts which then lends on to the business sector
- Reducing the risks involved either by taking on the risks themselves (as with banks and deposit accounts) or offering investors the opportunity to diversify their risks (as with Unit Trusts etc)
- Borrowing for short periods and lending for long periods

(c) The Efficient Market Hypothesis argues that in an efficient market current market prices fully reflect available information. The degree of efficiency is seen as the extent and speed with which markets reflect new information. The EMH maintains that market efficiency may exist at three different levels:

- **Weak Form** – here current prices reflect all information contained in past price movements.
- **Semi-strong Form** – here current prices reflect all past price movements and all publicly available information.
- **Strong Form** – here current prices reflect all relevant information, even if not publicly available.

To support his case, the financial controller should argue for the Weak Form of the EMH. That is, the share price is static because it is reflecting the lack of past movements and is not reflecting all publicly available information about the future potential of the company.

ANSWERS TO END OF CHAPTER QUESTIONS

Chapter 4 – Strategic management

A **strategic plan** can be defined as 'a statement of long-term goals along with a definition of the strategies and policies which will ensure achievement of these goals'. A **strategy** can be defined as a 'course of action, including the specification of resources required to achieve a given objective'.

(i) **Mission.** For a manufacturing company part of its **mission** may be to produce products **technically superior** to the competition.

(ii) **Strategy.** To do this a strategy might be to spend 15% of gross revenues on **research and development**.

(iii) **Tactics.** Tactics would include **recruitment** from the best university courses.

(iv) **Operations.** Operational control would include participants feedback on all programmes attended and the integration of **training** needs with training programmes.

Strategic management

Strategic management is 'an integrated management approach drawing together all the elements involved in planning, integrating and controlling a business strategy'. The concerns of **corporate strategic decisions** are these.

(i) The **scope** of the organisation's activities, in other words the product and markets the organisation deals with

(ii) The organisation's **'fit' with the environment** and the relationships it has with stakeholder groups

(iii) Matching its **resource capability** with the environment

(iv) **Resource allocation** (between divisions or functions of the business, and directed towards different product-market areas)

(v) The organisation's **long-term direction**

(vi) **Change**

(vii) **Value systems**

The implementation of a strategic management approach involves a three-stage process of **strategic analysis** of the organisation's current situation and the environment, **strategic choice** (the generation and evaluation of alternative strategic options) and **implementation** of the chosen strategy. Many strategic decisions are one-off, non-programmable decisions.

Operational management

The concerns of **operational management** are quite different.

(i) Its **scope is restricted** to the particular task in hand.

(ii) **Internal.** Operational management is generally more **internally focused** – although day to day relationships with customers are an operational concern.

(iii) **Implementation.** Operations managers have to work with the resource allocation decisions set by the strategy. Their concern is the most **efficient** use of these resources.

(iv) **Time scale.** Operations management is generally **shorter-term** than strategic management.

(v) **Routine.** Operational decisions are often more **routine** than strategic decisions and are more likely to be programmed.

There are some cases when short-term decisions are of strategic importance, for example if the survival of the organisation is at stake. Moreover, poor performance at operational level can make or break a strategy.

# Chapter 5

1. Ben Hawk

This question tests the candidate's ability to advise on raising additional finance (LO1).

Report

To: Ben Hawk
Subject: Advice on financing expansion using borrowings
From: XXXX
Date: XXXX

You are considering borrowing additional monies to fund an expansion into Europe. Should you decide to approach a bank for this borrowing they will have a number of queries as they need to establish that you will have the ability to pay the interest on the loan and can repay the capital as it becomes due. You have provided some relevant information on which I can base this advice. However, further information is needed as indicated below.

To repay the loan requires the agency to have sufficient profits. The profits have been increasing over the fifteen years and this track record of profitability will provide some confidence to the bank in making their lending decision. However, as the loan amount, interest cost and profit figures of the agency are not provided I cannot state whether you have sufficient profits (current and projected from the expansion) to provide the bank with the necessary confidence to lend the monies.

The bank may look at the industry average for gearing levels as a guide as to whether the agency borrowing levels are appropriate. At present the agency has gearing of 40% and this is slightly below the industry average of 42%. However, as the loan is likely to result in a doubling of current borrowings this suggests that the new gearing level will significantly exceed the industry average. This may be a cause for concern for the bank.

In respect of profitability the bank will also consider the stability of profits. It is known that the profits are dependent upon the strength of the economy. Should the economy decline your agency will become less profitable as clients reduce their advertising and marketing spend. It would be helpful to know more specifically how changes in the economy may affect your business as the bank will want to be reassured that you can afford the loan interest even in difficult years.

There is a further issue in respect of those years when the economy is weak. The agency's reputation is partly dependent upon the staff it employs. The industry you operate in is a service business and you need to retain the high calibre staff if you are not to lose clients. If the agency is in a position where it is struggling to meet interest and capital commitments (ie it is in some financial distress) then staff may choose to move to competitors to achieve greater job security. Therefore, the bank will need reassurance in this respect too.

The bank is highly likely to require security on any loan it provides. The agency owns the London premises and these are a possible source of security. However, it is not known whether any loan is secured on the premises. Nor is the current value of the premises known and how this compares to the potential borrowing. The bank will apply a loan to value ratio and will not allow the agency to borrow against the full value of the premises.

The bank will need to assess whether you have the requisite skills to expand the business successfully. It will be deemed positive that you have had significant prior advertising experience in a wide range of roles before setting up your own agency. It will also be seen as positive that you have successfully (and profitably) run your own business over a reasonably long period of time (fifteen years). However, the bank will want to know if you have experience in the European market as this may differ from the UK market.

ANSWERS TO END OF CHAPTER QUESTIONS

The bank will be keen to see that you have entrepreneurial drive and ambition as this increases the likelihood that you will be successful in the expansion. They will want to know why you are choosing to finance the acquisition using all debt. Is this an issue connected to the possible loss of control should equity be issued or is it that risk is then transferred to the bank? The bank will want to ensure that you are willing to accept the risk associated with the expansion and, therefore, the latter reason will not be acceptable.

2. Southern Drive plc

(a) **Before the Upgrading**

$$\text{Degree of operating gearing} = \frac{\text{Contribution}}{\text{Profit before interest and tax}}$$

$$= \frac{3,144 - 244}{1,128}$$

$$= 2.57$$

$$\text{Financial Gearing} = \frac{\text{Debt}}{\text{Debt} + \text{Equity}}$$

$$= \frac{1,390}{1,390 + 3,686}$$

$$= 27.4\%$$

Earnings per Share = 693,000/6,000,000

= 11.6p

After Upgrading

STATEMENT OF COMPREHENSIVE INCOME

	£'000	£'000
Revenue		9,488
Cost of Sales		4,698
Gross Profit		4,790
Variable Operating Expenses	224	
Fixed Operating Expenses	1,982	2,206
Profit before Interest and Tax		2,584
Interest		364
Profit before tax		2,220
Tax		556
Profit after tax		1,664

STATEMENT OF FINANCIAL POSITION

	£'000
Net Assets	7,076
Long-Term Debt	(3,390)
	3,686
Capital and Reserves	3,686

$$\text{Degree of operating gearing} = \frac{4,566}{2584}$$

$$= 1.77$$

Financial gearing $= \dfrac{3{,}390}{3{,}390+3{,}686}$

$= 47.9\%$

Earnings per share $= 1{,}664/6{,}000{,}000$

$= 27.73\text{p}$

The upgrading will lead to a fall in the company's degree of operating gearing, and increases in its financial gearing and earnings per share.

The changes in the financial gearing and the earnings per share are understandable. However, where a company takes on higher fixed costs, as Southern Drive has done, then you might expect a higher degree of operating gearing. This would lead to a higher sensitivity of earnings levels to changes in revenue. However, in this case the reductions in operating costs have more than compensated for the increase in fixed costs at the level chosen (ie an increase of 15%) Had the fixed costs increased more, or the savings in variable costs been less, then the degree of operating gearing would have increased.

(b) **Fall in Revenue of 20%**

	£'000	£'000
Turnover		6,600
Cost of Sales		3,268
Gross Profit		3,332
Variable Operating Expenses	156	
Fixed Operating Expenses	1,982	2,138
Profit before Interest and Tax		1,194
Interest		364
Profit before tax		830
Tax		208
Profit after tax		622

Earnings per Share = 622/6,000,000
= 10.37p

At this level of revenue the degree of operating gearing and financial gearing is proportionally higher than before the upgrading (2.66 compared to 2.57). This had led to a higher proportionate fall in earnings per share than the fall in revenue. The fall in revenue from £9,488,000 to £6,600,000 is just over 30%. While the fall in earnings per share (27.73p to 10.37p) is 63%. As a result the risks to shareholders have substantially increased.

(c) Business risk (sometimes referred to as the asset beta) is caused mainly by business cyclicity. That is because some companies are more affected by business and economic cycles than others. For example, supermarket chains tend to be less affected than do banks.

Operating gearing has the effect of magnifying the effect of cyclicity on a company's asset beta. This can be seen in the answer to part (b) above.

The equity beta is made up of asset beta (business risk) and financial risk (financial gearing). So, by definition a company with higher financial gearing should have a higher equity beta.

A higher equity beta will, as illustrated by the capital asset pricing model, have a higher equity cost of capital.

ANSWERS TO END OF CHAPTER QUESTIONS

Chapter 6

1. Fragrance plc

This question tests the candidate's ability to:

(i) **Calculate cost of capital for a company (LO1)**

(ii) **Advise on raising finance and how it may impact upon cost of capital including demonstrating understanding of beta factors and diversification (LO1)**

(a) Total market value of equity = 20m shares × £1.36 = £27.2m

$$\text{Growth rate of dividends} = \sqrt[3]{\frac{1.138m}{1.088m}} - 1 = 0.015 = 1.5\%$$

$$ke = \frac{D_0 \times (1+g)}{P_0} + g$$

$$ke = \frac{1.138m \times (1+0.015)}{27.2m} + 0.015 = 5.75\%$$

The cost of the irredeemable debt is:

$$kd = \frac{i}{P_0}(1-t)$$

$$kd = \frac{25m \times 6\% \times (1-22\%)}{30m} = 3.9\%$$

The market value of equity = £27.2m
The market value of debt is £30m
Total market value is £27.2m + £30m = £57.2m

The WACC is:

$$\left(\frac{27.2m}{57.2m} \times 5.75\%\right) + \left(\frac{30m}{57.2m} \times 3.9\%\right) = 4.78$$

(b) Report

To:	Directors – Fragrance plc
Subject:	Possible impact of raising £20m debt on cost of capital
From:	XXXX
Date:	XXXX

It is likely that there will be an impact on the cost of capital for the company should the company decide to go ahead with its diversification strategy. However, it is difficult to know exactly what the size of the impact will be or whether it will increase or decrease the cost of capital.

The size of the finance, £20m, is substantial in the context of the current position of the company. That is, the company is currently financed by debt and equity with a combined market value of £57.2m. Therefore, the additional £20m would potentially increase this by approximately 35% to £77.2m. This would alter the gearing level from a current debt: equity ratio of 110% to a ratio of 184%. This is a relatively high level of gearing and it may result in shareholders (and possibly debtholders too) requiring a higher rate of return as compensation for the greatly increased financial risk. If this were to occur then it would lead to an increase in the overall cost of capital.

The use of debt can also have an impact on the cost of capital. Debt is a cheaper source of finance than equity both because it carries less risk and because the interest on debt is tax-deductible.

ANSWERS TO END OF CHAPTER QUESTIONS

Therefore, potentially, the introduction of more debt could have the effect of lowering the cost of capital.

The use to which the debt will be put can also have an impact. The strategy is to diversify and this should lower the risk of the overall business. If the risk is lowered then the required returns of the providers of capital should reduce. This would reduce the overall cost of capital. The beta factor for Fragrance plc is 1.2 compared to the beta factor of the company manufacturing soaps and shampoos which is 0.85 and these relative beta factors imply that the risk of manufacturing soaps and shampoos is lower than the risk associated with luxury perfumes. Commonsense also suggests that the relative risk levels are as suggested as demand for soaps and shampoos is likely to remain relatively constant regardless of economic conditions unlike luxury perfumes. Therefore, this suggests that risk will be lowered through this strategy.

There are alternative ideas as to how capital structure impacts upon weighted average cost of capital. The principal theories are the traditional theory and Modigliani and Miller's theory. Depending on which theory is accepted then this suggests different outcomes should the finance be raised as suggested. However, it should be noted that neither theory has been fully proven.

2. Chan Wai Merchandising Company

This question aims to test the candidates' ability to:

Demonstrate an understanding of the relationship between capital structure and cost of capital (LO1)

(a) *Calculation of Cost of Equity*

$Ke = 3 + 1.2(13 - 3)$

$Ke = 15\%$

Calculation of cost of debt

Year	Cash Flow	Discount factor 3%	Present Value	Discount factor 6%	Present value
0	(105)	1	(105)	1	(105)
1	6	0.9709	5.825	0.9434	5.660
2	6	0.9426	5.656	0.8900	5.340
3	106	0.9151	97.001	0.8396	88.998
NPV			3.482		(5.002)

Redemption Yield (IRR) $= 3 + \dfrac{(3.482)}{(3.482 + 5.002)} \times 3$

$= 4.23\%$

Calculation of WACC

Market Value of Equity = HK$10,000,000

Market Value of Debt = HK$525,000

WACC $= 15 \times \dfrac{10m}{10.525m} + 4.23 \times \dfrac{0.525m}{10.525m}$

$= 14.46\%$

(b) According to Modigliani and Miller a company's cost of equity will increase as gearing increases (ignoring the effect of the tax shield). As a result of this it is unlikely that additional debt will in fact reduce CWM's weighted average cost of capital. This is because it is argued that the cost of equity will increase by an amount which will cancel out the cheaper cost of debt.

(c) Two aspects of the new investment would suggest that the use of the company's existing weighted average cost might not be sensible:

The new investment may have a significantly different level of business risk to its existing business. This could have the effect of changing the company's equity beta (and thus its equity cost of capital) significantly.

The fact that the new funds, if in fact debt, would have the effect of increasing the company's gearing significantly. This could add to the company's perceived financial risk and also have an effect on the company's cost of capital.

Chapter 7 – Henderson Logitech Ltd

(a)

	Earnings £'000	Total dividends £'000	Payout ratio %
2000	900	540	60
2001	950	570	60
2002	1,800	1,080	60
2003	3,600	2,160	60
2004	5,300	3,180	60

The company has adopted a policy of a stable payout ratio of 60% of earnings. Growth has been funded out of the remaining retained earnings plus borrowings.

It is questionable whether or not such a dividend policy would be acceptable for a listed company. The following considerations may apply:

- Such a policy might make the shares attractive to income seekers. For example, the 'Institutions' do demonstrate a preference for dividends over capital gains because of their liquidity requirements. They would have to be convinced, however, that the policy was sustainable and that gearing was not likely to become a concern.

- Continuing with the present policy might leave Henderson as a 'hostage to fortune'. The policy generates significant annual increases in dividend per share. If the company, for whatever reason, could not pay a dividend that was a significant increase on the previous one then this might be taken as a pessimistic signal by investors and thus adversely affect share price. Worse still, the company might be required to reduce the dividend in a particular year; a move which stands a very good chance of causing significant investor relations problems for the company.

- The issue of 450,000 new shares will certainly have a beneficial effect on the company's gearing. In theory it will open up the potential for access to more equity funding in the future through the medium of a rights issue. However, the large shareholding by non-family members could raise issues of control and even the spectre of take over bids.

- The company has expanded very rapidly over the last five years and this has enabled the generous dividend policy. Such growth is likely to be harder to sustain in the future. This might well lead to ever increasing reliance on debt funding if the present dividend policy was continued.

- While not necessarily an over influential factor the dividend policy of other companies in the same sector as Henderson's might be a factor. It would hardly be necessary for the company to adopt similar policies to its rivals (there is unlikely to be any one uniform policy it could copy). However, a policy that was significantly out of line with other companies in the sector could attract attention; which might not be of the desired kind.

- In conclusion, it must be said that it is probably unlikely that Henderson's would be advised to continue with their present dividend policy.

(b) The share price predicted by the Dividend Valuation Model would be as follows.

The present value of the dividends from the first three years would be:

Year	Expected Dividends £	Discount Factor 14%	Present Value £
1	7.63	0.8772	6.69
2	9.16	0.7695	7.05
3	10.99	0.6750	7.42
			21.16

After three years the present value of dividends to infinity would be:

$$\frac{10.99 \times 1.1}{0.14 - 0.10} \times 0.5921 = £178.95$$

Share price = 21.16 + 178.95 = £200 (say)

(c) It is probably unlikely that £200 would be suggested as the flotation price for the following reasons:

(i) It is open to considerable debate as to whether or not the 'market' uses the dividend valuation model to value shares.

(ii) If by any chance it did then it would be likely to substitute its own estimates for dividend growth rather than just accepting Henderson's projections.

(iii) Even if by chance the 'market' did value the shares at £200 it is unlikely that they would pay that amount. A discount would almost certainly be required in order to encourage a full take up of the share issue.

(iv) Having said that, a lot would depend upon the amount of interest and 'hype' generated by the issue. A price in excess of £200 might be generated if the issue caught the imagination of the general investing public.

Chapter 8

1. Mrs Grand

This question tests the candidate's ability to:

(i) **Calculate the net present value of a project including an overseas element (LO2)**

(ii) **Use purchasing power parity to calculate future exchange rates (LO4)**

(iii) **Evaluate the uncertainties associated with business planning (LO2)**

(iv) **Advise on the different objectives of stakeholders (LO1)**

(a) Purchasing power parity to calculate future exchange rates:

Year 1: $4.92 \times \frac{1.01}{1.015} = 4.90$

Year 2: $4.90 \times \frac{1.01}{1.015} = 4.88$

Year 3: $4.88 \times \frac{1.01}{1.015} = 4.86$

Year 4: $4.86 \times \frac{1.01}{1.015} = 4.84$

ANSWERS TO END OF CHAPTER QUESTIONS

	0 £	1 £	2 £	3 £	4 £	5 £
Sales numbers		2,100	2,400	2,500	2,800	
Selling price per handbag		130	130	130	130	
Total revenue		273,000	312,000	325,000	364,000	
Cost of handbags (see working)	-117,857	-135,246	-141,461	-159,091		
Rent	-45,000	-45,000	-45,000	-45,000		
Fixtures and fittings	-40,000				6,000	
Market research (ignore)						
Manager's salary		-30,000	-30,000	-30,000	-30,000	
Staff salaries		-32,000	-32,000	-32,000	-32,000	
Heat and light		-11,000	-11,000	-11,000	-11,000	
Advertising	-5,000	-5,000	-5,000	-5,000		
	-207,857	14,754	47,539	42,909	297,000	0
Tax at 20% one year in arrears						-38,869
Net cashflow	-207,857	14,754	47,539	42,909	297,000	-38,869
Discount factor 12%	1	0.893	0.797	0.712	0.636	0.567
Present value	-207,857	13,175	37,889	30,551	188,892	-22,039

Net present value 40,611

Working – handbag cost

	0	1	2	3
Number of handbags bought	2,100	2,400	2,500	2,800
Cost per handbag in MYR	275	275	275	275
Total cost in MYR	577,500	660,000	687,500	770,000
Exchange rate (working)	4.90	4.88	4.86	4.84
Cost of handbags in £	-117,857	-135,246	-141,461	-159,091

Net present value is positive – accept the project

(b) All businesses involve risk and uncertainty. As this is a new business venture then it is likely to have more risk and uncertainty than an established business, and it is important to be aware of the potential risks.

Mrs Grand has no experience of retail and this might present a risk. This risk is mitigated to some extent as she has extensive prior business experience and some of this experience will be transferable to the retail venture. Further, if a manager is employed that has relevant prior experience this will aid in reducing this risk.

It is stated that the handbags have just become fashionable. However, there is no discussion of the likelihood of the handbags remaining fashionable. The venture is covering a four year period; however, fashion changes on a season by season basis. The sales projections indicate increasing sales over the four-year period and it needs to be assessed whether this is too optimistic.

More generally many of the cashflows included in the calculations are subject to uncertainty. For example, salaries may have to increase over the period if staff are to be retained or heat and light may deviate from the estimated figures.

The handbags are being imported from Malaysia and are being paid for in MYR not sterling. Therefore, this exposes the business to exchange rate risk. Depending on how exchange rates move in the future this could either benefit the business or add an extra cost. Mrs Grand could potentially hedge this risk using an appropriate hedging instrument such as forward contracts.

There is no explanation given as to how the discount rate used in the project has been arrived at. It may be an inappropriate rate to use. It may have been an appropriate rate for previous business ventures but they might have had different risk levels compared to this project or they may have used particular sources of finance.

(c) The principal stakeholders will be: (1) the employees including the manager of the shop, (2) the Malaysian supplier, (3) customers, (4) government and (5) Mrs Grand as the business owner. There are no other shareholders mentioned and the company is too small to have a management team. Nor is there any mention of debtholders. These stakeholders will have different objectives.

The employees will want to ensure that they are remunerated appropriately according to their experience, skills and the effort they put in. Mrs Grand can ensure that she pays appropriate rates and provide appropriate benefits. However, they may also want to ensure they have longevity of employment, and in this case the business is only going to be running for a four year period which may be problematic.

The supplier will want to ensure that they are paid on time according to the agreement between the supplier and Mrs Grand. This is especially so as Mrs Grand is an overseas customer and it can be more difficult to ensure payment occurs on time or to enforce payment should it not occur. The supplier may also wish to develop a relationship with Mrs Grand. However, as is the case with the employees the business will only be operating for four years and a long-term relationship is not feasible.

Customers are an important stakeholder group as they are fundamental to the success of the business. The handbags are relatively expensive to buy and they will want to know that they are acquiring something that is of high quality and fashionable. That the shop will cease operating after four years may become problematic for customers as this date approaches as they will want to know that they are able to return goods that are of unsuitable quality.

Government has a variety of objectives. They will want to collect taxation, but will also want to be supportive of new businesses that provide employment and stimulate economic growth. However, as the business is in operation for four years only, then it will only meet these last two objectives in a minor way.

Mrs Grand will presumably want to maximise the wealth that results from her ownership of the business. It may also be that this business appeals because of its nature (she may want to be involved in the fashion industry). Mrs Grand is taking the risk of setting up the business and, therefore, will likely seek to gain from the rewards. If there are no other investors in the business then she will be able to extract any residual profits.

2. Mr Li

This question tests the candidate's ability to:

(i) **Calculate the net present value of an overseas project (LO2)**

(ii) **Use purchasing power parity to calculate future exchange rates (LO4)**

(iii) **Evaluate the uncertainties associated with business planning (LO2)**

ANSWERS TO END OF CHAPTER QUESTIONS

(iv) **Explore how working capital management is affected by the nature of the industry a business operates in (LO5)**

(a) Purchasing power parity to calculate future exchange rates:

Year 1: $12.82 \times \dfrac{1.02}{1.025} = 12.76$

Year 2: $12.76 \times \dfrac{1.02}{1.025} = 12.70$

Year 3: $12.70 \times \dfrac{1.02}{1.025} = 12.64$

Year 4: 12.64

NPV calculation	Year 0	Year 1	Year 2	Year 3	Year 4	Year 5
Sterling payments						
Total cost of purchasing coffee plus biscuits (see working)		−21,000	−25,000	−28,000	−28,000	
Initial payment	−40,000					
Advertising literature	−5,000	−5,000	−5,000	−5,000		
Total sterling payments (£)	−45,000	−26,000	−30,000	−33,000	−28,000	
Exchange rate (see working)	12.82	12.76	12.70	12.64	12.58	
Amount in HK$000	−576,900	−331,760	−381,000	−417,120	−352,240	
Turnover (see working)		1,950,000	2,250,000	2,600,000	2,600,000	
Less: franchise payment of 5% of turnover		−97,500	−112,500	−130,000	−130,000	
Rent		−500,000	500,000	−500,000	−500,000	
Staff costs		−1,150,000	−1,150,000	−1,150,000	−1,150,000	
Other costs		−8,000	−8,000	−8,000	−8,000	
NET FLOWS	−576,900	−137,260	98,500	394,880	459,760	
Tax paid at 15% one year in arrears		0	0	0	0	−35,847
NET FLOWS AFTER TAX	−576,900	−137,260	98,500	394,880	459,760	−35,847
Six times Year 4 pre-tax cashflow						2,758,560
CASHFLOWS	−576,900	−137,260	98,500	394,880	459,760	2,722,713
Discount factor 12%	1	0.893	0.797	0.712	0.636	0.567
PRESENT VALUE	−576,900	−122,573	78,505	281,155	292,407	1,543,778

NET PRESENT VALUE (HK$)   1,496,372

ANSWERS TO END OF CHAPTER QUESTIONS

PURCHASING COST WORKING

	Year 0	Year 1	Year 2	Year 3	Year 4	Year 5
Number of cups of coffee sold		90,000	100,000	120,000	120,000	
Purchase cost		0.10	0.10	0.10	0.10	
Coffee purchase cost (£)		9,000	10,000	12,000	12,000	
Number of biscuits sold		60,000	75,000	80,000	80,000	
Purchase cost		0.20	0.20	0.20	0.20	
Biscuits purchase cost (£)		12,000	15,000	16,000	16,000	
TOTAL COST OF PURCHASING COFFEE PLUS BISCUITS (£)		**21,000**	**25,000**	**28,000**	**28,000**	

TURNOVER WORKING

	Year 0	Year 1	Year 2	Year 3	Year 4	Year 5
Number of cups of coffee sold		90,000	100,000	120,000	120,000	
Average selling price		15	15	15	15	
Coffee turnover (HK$)		1,350,000	1,500,000	1,800,000	1,800,000	
Number of biscuits sold		60,000	75,000	80,000	80,000	
Average selling price		10	10	10	10	
Biscuits turnover (HK$)		600,000	750,000	800,000	800,000	
TOTAL TURNOVER (HK$)		**1,950,000**	**2,250,000**	**2,600,000**	**2,600,000**	

(b) To: Mr Li
Subject: Risks associated with the venture
From: XXXX
Date: XXXX

There are a number of risks that the bank may consider to be associated with this venture and that may affect their decision whether to lend monies for the venture.

The Coffee Company has only been in existence for three years. This is a relatively short time and this may not be a long enough period over which to assess whether the concept and brand will be successful. The number of franchisees is 65 and this is also relatively small which raises a similar question about the likelihood of the brand becoming successful. Additionally, the number of franchisees fell from 72 one year ago. It would be useful to know why these franchises have ceased as it may be that they were unable to establish themselves as viable coffee shops and this may be due to the concept not being sufficiently attractive to potential customers.

This risk is compounded by this being the first year that the company has franchised overseas. There is no evidence of The Coffee Company concept being transferable to countries outside the UK. This is an especial risk in respect of your venture as there have been no franchises set up in Hong Kong yet and, therefore, this would be a pilot case. The provision of advertising literature that is relevant to the UK is of concern as it may not be appropriate and, further, may be another indicator that insufficient consideration has gone into whether the concept can be viable overseas

The bank would be keen to know about the credentials of the wife and husband who set up The Coffee Company as this could be a significant determinant of its future success. The wife and husband do have prior business experience, and this experience is complementary (in accounting and sales). However, they do not have any direct experience in retail or coffee shop businesses and they do not run any coffee shops themselves. This may suggest that they have not the required in-depth knowledge of this specific business sector. Additionally, you have no experience of this area.

The initial training provided is important in helping to establish the business. Therefore, that The Coffee Company is only providing three days training instead of the usual five days training may present a risk. The ability to ask for further advice by email or telephone is useful, but may not compensate fully for losing two days of training.

The bank may also consider it a risk that you have had no guidance or assistance in finding suitable premises or in estimating future sales volumes. The bank may consider that you have insufficient expertise to have been able to make sound decisions in this respect. It may also be that the bank considers that this suggests that the quality of the support that is offered to franchisees is insufficient.

A number of payments have to be made in pounds sterling and this exposes the venture to exchange rate risk. Dependent on how exchange rates actually move in the future this may make the project more or less viable.

(c) Mr Li's current business is manufacturing bricks for the construction industry whereas the new venture is in respect of coffee shops. Therefore, they are very different industries and this affects the management of debtors, creditors and stocks.

In respect of debtors there are likely to be standard credit terms that apply to the construction industry. Therefore, Mr Li will have to wait for payment according to the relevant number of days credit for this industry. He will have to monitor payments and if payment is not received by this due date he will then have to take appropriate actions. This may commence with a reminder letter and may eventually end up in court action being taken. Bad debts may occur in some cases. In the coffee shop business credit is not offered as it is based on cash transactions. Therefore, receipt of payment is immediate and there is no requirement to have staff monitoring debtors and their payments.

In respect of creditors then when considering the construction industry Mr Li will normally have agreed standard credit terms with suppliers. He is unlikely to make payments in advance of the due date unless an adequate discount is being offered, and his cashflow permits this. If he chooses to make late payments then there may be penalties incurred. Further, this may damage his reputation. He does have the option to look at alternative suppliers should he feel that this is beneficial. This may be done because of concerns about product quality or the ability of the supplier to supply on time; but it may also be that Mr Li can obtain better credit terms by moving supplier. In the coffee shop business Mr Li can only obtain supplies from The Coffee Company. However, in other respects the position is similar with credit terms being known at the outset. A potential difference is that the relationship between Mr Li and The Coffee Company is such that there is a greater mutual dependence.

Fundamentally, the same principle will apply in respect of stock management in both types of business. Namely, Mr Li will want to keep stocks to a minimum (hence keeping stockholding costs to a minimum) whilst ensuring that stockouts do not occur as this can lead to a loss of goodwill and sales. Two potential differences may be noted however, if the different business types are considered. First, a construction customer may be willing to wait a little longer for goods than a coffee shop customer. That is, if a coffee shop customer wants a coffee and it is not available they will not return later to have that coffee. Thus, stockouts may be more critical in this type of business. Second, brick stocks are not perishable whereas some of the stocks in a coffee shop are (for example, milk). Hence, overstocking in the coffee shop may not only have a cost in respect of stockholding stocks but also in respect of stocks going past a sell by date and having to be discarded.

Chapter 9

1. Craxon

This question tests the candidate's ability to calculate the expected net present value of a project and to discuss risk and uncertainty. (LO2)

(a) **Calculation of expected NPV year**

Year	1	2	3	4
	$'000	$'000	$'000	$'000
Revenue	9,078	15,735	26,184	20,424
Variable cost	(4,770)	(8,400)	(14,160)	(11,460)
Contribution	4,308	7,335	12,024	8,964
Overhead	(880)	(968)	(1,065)	(1,172)
Cash flow before tax	3,428	6,367	10,959	7,792
Tax	(1,028)	(1,910)	(3,288)	(2,338)
Depreciation benefits	675	675	675	675
Cash flow after tax	3,075	5,132	8,346	6,129
Scrap value				1,000
Project cash flow	3,075	5,132	8,346	7,129
Discount at 11%	0.901	0.812	0.731	0.659
Present values	2,771	4,167	6,101	4,698

	$'000
PV of future cash flows	17,737
Initial investment	(10,000)
ENPV	7,737

The investment project has a positive ENPV of $7,737,000. This is a mean or average NPV which will result from the project being repeated many times. However, as the project is not being repeated, the NPVs associated with each future economic state must be calculated as it is one of these NPVs which is expected to occur. The decision by management on the financial acceptability of the project will be based on these NPVs and the risk associated with each one.

Workings

Mean or average selling price = $(24 \times 0.40) + (30 \times 0.45) + (40 \times 0.15) = \$29.1$ per unit

Year	1	2	3	4
Inflated selling price ($ per unit)	30.26	31.47	32.73	34.04
Sales volume (units/year)	300,000	500,000	800,000	600,000
Sales revenue ($'000/year)	9,078	15,735	26,184	20,424

Year	1	2	3	4
Inflated overhead ($'000/year)	880	968	1,065	1,172

Total tax-allowable depreciation = 10,000,000 − 1,000,000 = $9,000,000
Annual tax-allowable depreciation = 9,000,000/4 = $2,250,000 per year
Annual cash flow from tax-allowable depreciation = 2,250,000 × 0.3 = $675,000 per year

(b) Risk appetite or attitude is the amount of risk (or uncertainty) an organisation is willing to take on, or is prepared to accept, in pursuing its strategic objectives. Decision-makers may be risk seekers, risk neutral or risk averse.

A decision maker is risk neutral if they are concerned with what will be the most likely outcome. A risk-neutral decision maker will be concerned with the most likely outcome, using expected values.

However, not all decision-makers are risk neutral and will not base their decision-making on the most likely outcome as calculated by expected values, making this technique irrelevant for investment appraisal.

A risk seeker is a decision maker who is interested in trying to secure the best outcomes, no matter how small the chance that they may occur. Here a maximax approach may be used, this looks at the best possible results from each decision option and selects the option that gives the best possible result.

A risk-averse decision maker acts on the assumption that the worst outcome might occur. Here a maximin approach may be used which looks at the worst possible results from each decision option and selects the option that gives the best possible of these worst case scenario results. Alternatively, minimax regret may be appropriate, where a decision is chosen that minimises the impact of it turning out to be the wrong decision (ie minimises regret).

Expected values will not be relevant to risk seekers or risk-averse decision-makers.

(c) Sensitivity analysis assesses the extent to which the NPV of an investment project responds to changes in project variables. Sensitivity analysis will normally involve identifying key project variables and determining the percentage change in a project variable which results in a zero NPV. The critical project variables are identified as those to which the NPV is most sensitive, for example, ie those where the smallest percentage change in the variable results in a zero NPV. Sensitivity analysis is therefore concerned with calculating relative changes in project variables.

When discussing risk in the context of investment appraisal, it is important to note that, unlike uncertainty, risk can be quantified and measured. The probabilities of the occurrence of particular future outcomes can be assessed and used to evaluate the volatility of future cash flows, for example, by calculating their standard deviation. The probabilities of the future economic states in the assessment of the investment project of Craxon Co are an example of probability analysis and these probabilities can lead to an assessment of project risk.

Sensitivity analysis is usually studied in investment appraisal in relation to understanding how risk can be incorporated in the investment appraisal process. While sensitivity analysis can indicate the critical variables of an investment project, sensitivity analysis does not give any indication of the probability of a change in any critical variable. Selling price (or energy prices) may be a critical variable, for example, but sensitivity analysis is not able to say whether a change in selling price is likely to occur. In the appraisal of the investment project of Craxon Co, the probabilities of different selling prices arising from the related economic states have come from probability analysis, not from sensitivity analysis.

Sensitivity analysis will not therefore directly assist Craxon Co in assessing the risk of the investment project. However, it does provide useful information which helps management to gain a deeper understanding of the project and which focuses management attention on aspects of the investment project where problems may arise.

2. Samson Conglomerates

This question aims to test the candidates' ability to:

Demonstrate an understanding of Portfolio Theory and its application in the management of business risk (LO2).

(a) Calculation of Return and Standard Deviation

ACom Expected Return (40%)	BCom Expected Return (60%)	Return on ACom/BCom (R)	p	pR
4.8	9.0	13.8	0.2	2.76
6.0	12.0	18.0	0.6	10.80
7.2	15.0	22.2	0.2	4.44
				18.0

Portfolio Return (Rp) = 18.0%

Portfolio Standard Deviation

$$\sigma_p = \sqrt{[(1.90^2 \times 0.4^2) + (3.16^2 \times 0.6^2) + (2 \times 0.4 \times 0.6 \times 1 \times 1.90 \times 3.16)]}$$
$$= \sqrt{[0.58 + 3.59 + 2.88]}$$
$$= 2.66\%$$

(b) The appropriate theory in this case is Portfolio Theory. This basically argues that it is true that diversification is necessary to reduce risk. However it goes further than this to argue that the diversification must be of the correct kind. The most effective form of diversification is where the constituents of the portfolio are not perfectly positively correlated. Perfect negative correlation would be ideal, but this is extremely unlikely to ever happen. However anything less than perfect positive correlation will still contribute to some risk reduction in a portfolio.

In the case of the ACom/BCom portfolio then because the two companies are very similar it is likely that the correlation between the returns from the two companies could be almost perfectly positive as the managing director suspects.

In the case of DCom/ECom the correlation is likely to be much less because of the very dissimilar nature of the two companies.

(c) Advantages of diversification include:
- Less volatile cash flows
- Less possibility of corporate failure

Disadvantages of diversification include:
- Less opportunity to specialise in a limited set of skills – thus improving efficiency
- The requirement to recruit people with the very different skills and experience levels

Chapter 10

1. Core plc

This question tests the candidate's ability to:

(i) **Calculate the cost of capital for a firm both using CAPM and the dividend growth model (LO2)**

(ii) **Advise of the problems inherent in calculating a cost of capital using CAPM and the dividend growth model (LO2)**

(a) Growth rate of dividends = $\sqrt[3]{\frac{14.0}{12.1}} - 1 = 0.0498 = 4.98\%$

$$k_e = \frac{D_0 \times (1+g)}{P_0} + g$$

$$k_e = \frac{14.0 \times (1+0.0498)}{245} + 0.0498 = 10.98\%$$

The cost of the irredeemable debt is:

$$k_d = \frac{i}{P_0}(1-t)$$

$$k_d = \frac{450m \times 5.5\% \times (1-20\%)}{480m} = 4.125\%$$

The market value of equity = 160m × £2.45 = £392m

ANSWERS TO END OF CHAPTER QUESTIONS

The market value of debt is £480m
Total market value is £392m + £480m = £872m

The WACC is:

$$\left(\frac{392m}{872m} \times 10.98\%\right) + \left(\frac{480m}{872m} \times 4.125\%\right) = 7.2\%$$

(b) The cost of equity calculated using CAPM equation:

$Ke = rf + \beta(rm - rf)$

$Ke = 4\% + 1.15(8.5\% - 4\%) = 9.175\%$

The WACC is:

$$\left(\frac{392m}{872m} \times 9.175\%\right) + \left(\frac{480m}{872m} \times 4.125\%\right) = 6.4\%$$

(c) The fundamental rationale underlying the use of weighted average cost of capital (WACC) as a rate for appraising the acquisition is that it provides a figure for the required return of the providers of capital. However, this does not necessarily mean that the current WACC is appropriate for appraising the acquisition.

First, the directors need to note that the calculation of WACC is not an exact science. WACC comprises cost of equity and cost of debt, and cost of equity can be calculated in different ways – for example, using the dividend growth model or using the capital asset pricing model. Therefore, the existing weighted average cost of capital is not necessarily an accurate reflection of the required return of the providers of capital.

Second, the acquisition will affect the capital structure of Core plc and, in turn this will affect the WACC. We do not know Oxton plc's capital structure, but we do know that Core plc would be funding the acquisition through borrowing. This is likely to increase the required return of providers of share capital as it will increase the financial (gearing) risk of the firm post-acquisition. However, we can also note that the borrowings are likely to be at a cheaper rate than using equity (as debt is less risky than equity) and borrowing has a tax advantage being tax deductible. Therefore, the overall impact on WACC is unknown.

Third, Oxton plc has a higher equity beta than Core plc. The equity beta takes account of both business and financial risk, and in this case the two companies have similar gearing levels. Therefore, we can surmise that the operations of Oxton plc are riskier than those of Core plc. Consequently, if Core plc acquires Oxton plc then its overall risk increases. This will entail an increase in the WACC of Core plc as shareholders will require a higher return to compensate for the increased risk.

Fourth, shareholder and debtholder reaction to the acquisition more generally is not known. These providers of capital may not be wholly in favour of the acquisition and this may impact on required returns, ultimately affecting WACC. The directors of Core plc have had recent experience of this; however, this acquisition is not in a wholly unrelated area and may not be received with such a mixed reaction.

2. Hesco and Asarco

This question tests the candidate's ability to understand and explain the contribution of finance theory to the determination of the costs of equity capital (LO2).

(a) Both models attempt to 'second guess' the way in which investors determine the returns they require from an investment in a company.

The Capital Asset Pricing Model is based upon the premise that investors value shares based upon their likely price movements relative to the rest of the market. Return is related to risk and risk is measured, in this case, by the relative volatility of the share price. The beta factor is used to measure and represent the risk caused by this volatility. Dividends do not feature in the determination of an investor's required rate of return when this model is employed. It would, therefore, appear to be most applicable to situations where investors obtain all, or at least the majority of, their returns from share price growth.

The Dividend Valuation Model is based upon the premise that investors value their investments based upon predicted future income in the form of dividends. It would, therefore, appear to be most applicable to situations where investors obtain the majority of their return from dividends rather than share price growth.

(b) **Hesco**

Calculation of dividend per share

Dividend per share = 390 × 2.2% = 8.58p

Calculation of cost of capital using CAPM

$$Ke = Rf + \beta(Rm - Rf)$$
$$Ke = 5 + 0.83(13 - 5)$$
$$Ke = 11.64\%$$

Calculation of cost of capital using Dividend Valuation Model

$$Ke = \frac{D_1}{V_0} + G$$

$$= \frac{(8.58 \times 1.09)}{390} + .09$$

$$= 11.40\%$$

Asarco

Calculation of dividend per share

Dividend per share = 449 × 1.1% = 4.94p

Calculation of cost of capital using CAPM

$$Ke = Rf + \beta(Rm - Rf)$$
$$Ke = 5 + 0.90(13 - 5)$$
$$Ke = 12.20\%$$

Calculation of cost of capital using Dividend Valuation Model

$$Ke = \frac{D_1}{V_0} + G$$

$$= \frac{(4.94 \times 1.165)}{449} + .165$$

$$= 17.78\%$$

(c) The investors in Hesco have obtained their returns from a combination of both capital growth and dividends and therefore it seems sensible that both models may be applicable.

The investors in Asarco have obtained much more of their return from capital growth and thus it is likely that the dividend valuation model is not necessarily applicable to this company.

ANSWERS TO END OF CHAPTER QUESTIONS

Chapter 11

1. Hair Co. Ltd

This question tests the candidate's ability to:

(i) Calculate cost of capital for a company using CAPM (LO1 and LO2)

(ii) Calculate cost of capital to use in appraising an investment including understanding the effect of debt on beta factors (LO2)

(iii) Advise on raising finance and how it may impact upon cost of capital including demonstrating understanding of beta factors and diversification (LO2)

(a) Calculation of current cost of capital.

Current cost of equity

$8\% + 0.9(12\% - 8\%) = 11.6\%$

Current cost of capital

$$\left(\frac{900m}{1200m} \times 11.6\%\right) + \left(\frac{300m}{1200m} \times 8\% \times (1-25\%)\right) = 10.2\%$$

(b) Calculation of cost of capital for project

De-gear the equity beta for the project in the restaurant sector:

$$\text{Ungeared beta} = 1.6 \left\{ \frac{2}{2 + 1(1-25\%)} \right\} = 1.16$$

Re-gear the beta to reflect gearing in Hair Co. Ltd.:

$$\text{Geared beta} = 1.16 \left\{ \frac{900m + 300m(1-25\%)}{900m} \right\} = 1.45$$

The cost of equity for this project =

$8\% + 1.45(12\% - 8\%) = 13.8\%$

As the debt:equity ratio is being maintained then the cost of capital relevant to the project is:

$$\left(\frac{900m}{1200m} \times 13.8\%\right) + \left(\frac{300m}{1200m} \times 8\% \times (1-25\%)\right) = 11.85\%$$

(c) **Advising directors**

The current cost of capital for Hair Co. Ltd. reflects the required return of the providers of finance, and the return they require will be dependent upon the current level of risk they perceive is attached to the company as a business operating in the hair products industry, and with a particular debt-equity ratio. That is, the risk will depend upon the business risk of the company (related to the hair products industry in which it operates) and the financial risk of the company (dependent upon its gearing).

Hair Co. Ltd. plans to maintain the current debt:equity ratio. Therefore, financial risk will remain unchanged. However, the level of business risk for the restaurant sector is different to the level of business risk for hair products. Business risk in the restaurant sector is higher and this is reflected in a higher cost of equity (cost of equity for the project is 13.8% compared to cost of equity in respect of the current company of 11.6%).

2. Ashten plc

This question tests the candidate's ability to:

(i) Calculate cost of capital for a company using CAPM (LO2)

(ii) Calculate cost of capital to use in appraising an investment including understanding the effect of debt on beta factors (LO2)

(iii) Advise on raising finance and how it may impact upon cost of capital including demonstrating understanding of beta factors and diversification (LO2)

(a) **Calculation of current cost of capital**

Current cost of equity

7% + 0.8 (15% − 7%) = 13.4%

Current cost of capital

$$\left(\frac{800m}{1000m} \times 13.4\%\right) + \left(\frac{200m}{1000m} \times 7\% \times (1-20\%)\right) = 11.84\%$$

(b) **Calculation of cost of capital for project**

De-gear the equity beta for the project (construction industry):

$$\text{Ungeared beta} = 1.4 \left\{ \frac{3}{3 + 1(1-20\%)} \right\} = 1.1$$

Re-gear the beta to reflect gearing in Ashten plc:

$$\text{Geared beta} = 1.1 \left\{ \frac{800m + 200m(1-20\%)}{800m} \right\} = 1.32$$

The cost of equity for this project = 7% + 1.32(15% − 7%) = 17.56%

As the debt:equity ratio is being maintained then the cost of capital relevant to the project is:

$$\left(\frac{800m}{1000m} \times 17.56\%\right) + \left(\frac{200m}{1000m} \times 7\% \times (1-20\%)\right) = 15.17\%$$

(c) **Advising directors**

The current cost of capital reflects the required return of the providers of finance, and the return they require will depend upon the risk they perceive is attached to the company. The risk will depend upon the business risk of the company (principally related to the industry in which it operates) and the financial risk of the company (dependent upon its level of gearing).

The company intends maintaining its current level of gearing and, therefore, financial risk will remain unchanged. However, the level of business risk for construction is different to the level of business risk for food manufacturing. In the case of Ashten plc it can be seen that business risk is deemed higher for construction as the cost of equity for the project is 17.56% compared to cost of equity in respect of the current company (food manufacturing) of 13.4%.

3. Box Packaging Company

Report

To: Directors – Box Packaging Company
Subject: Capital Structure
From: XXXX
Date: XXXX

The current position of the company is that gearing levels based on ratio of net debt to net assets have altered over the last two years as follows:

2011: $\frac{225}{482} = 46.7\%$

2012: $\frac{286}{418} = 68.4\%$

These figures indicate that the gearing level has increased from 2011 to 2012. An increase in gearing level of itself is not always a cause for concern. However, the increase is substantial.

There is information concerning comparator companies, and this can be useful as a means of seeing whether the company lies outside industry norms. These figures indicate that Box Packaging Company has a gearing ratio that is higher than its competitors. However, it is not significantly higher. It may be helpful to know what the overall industry norm is to provide a further comparison.

There are three key covenants and the calculations for these over the last two years are as follows:

	2011	2012
Interest cover	$\frac{106}{16} = 6.6$ times	$\frac{75}{24} = 3.1$ times
Net debt to profit ratio	$\frac{225}{106+68} = 1.3$ times	$\frac{286}{75+74} = 1.9$ times
Net assets	MYR482m	MYR418m

In all cases the company's position in respect of the covenants has deteriorated.

The net debt to profit ratio must be a maximum of 3.25 times. Although this ratio has also deteriorated over the past year, from 1.3 times to 1.9 times, the company is not yet approaching a situation whereby it might breach the covenant.

The net assets figure has decreased from MYR482m to MYR418m. This figure must exceed MYR350m. Therefore, although it has declined the company is not yet approaching a situation whereby it might breach the covenant.

Interest cover must be not less than 3.0 times. In 2011 the cover greatly exceeded this at 6.6 times. However, in 2012 the company only just exceeded the required cover. Should this worsen then there is a great danger that this covenant will be breached.

Therefore, overall these figures indicate that the company needs to re-evaluate its capital structure. This is particularly so given that profits may not remain stable in the future. Should profits fall then the company may have issues in respect of breaking the covenant in respect of interest cover.

Additional information that would be helpful includes:

Does the company have projects which will require further finance in the near future? If it does then altering its capital structure may be appropriate as it could find it difficult to obtain financing in its current position.

What is the current reaction of the loan provider and of the overall market? The directors need to know whether there is a general concern from these perspectives as they do need to consider external views on the current capital structure and to address concerns sooner rather than later.

What are the alternatives to this capital structure and who will provide funding?

ANSWERS TO END OF CHAPTER QUESTIONS

4. Starscape plc

(i)

Year	Cash flow £m	Discount factor 13%	Present value £m
0	(3)	1	(3)
1–5	(0.5)	3.517	(1.76)
6–∞	2.5/0.13	0.480	9.23
Net present value			4.47

(ii) The problem focuses on the question of what figure should best be as for the discount factor. The following considerations apply here:

- Is WACC the appropriate figure to use? This project is arguably unlike anything else the company has ever undertaken – the investor's reaction might be difficult to gauge. Will they see the project as adding risk, in terms of potential losses, or as reducing risk, in terms of diversification?

- Will the company's WACC itself be changed by the use of more debt? It is difficult to say for sure.

- Could there actually be a case for the project to be discounted at 9%? Although the case is not strong.

(iii) Calculation of adjusted present value of project:

Base case net present value.

Year	Cash flow £m	Discount factor 17%	Present value £m
0	(3)	1	(3)
1–5	(0.5)	3.199	(1.60)
6–∞	2.5/0.17	0.390	5.74
Base Case net present value			1.14

Financial Side Effects are just the cost of raising the debt as follows:

Cost of raising loan $= \dfrac{£3m}{0.98} - £3m$

$= £61,224$

Adjusted Present Value $= £1.14m - £61,224$

$= £1,078,776$

Chapter 12- Kiwi Knitwear

This question tests the candidate's ability to:

(i) **Calculate future exchange rates using purchasing power parity (LO4)**

(ii) **Advise on risks associated with investment projects (LO2)**

(iii) **Advise on real options strategies (LO2)**

(a) Workings for exchange rate calculation – using purchasing power parity:

Year 1

Expected exchange rate $= 0.4973 \times \dfrac{(1 + 1.5\%)}{(1 + 2.5\%)} = 0.4924$

Year 2

Expected exchange rate $= 0.4924 \times \dfrac{(1 + 1.5\%)}{(1 + 2.5\%)} = 0.4876$

Year 3

$$\text{Expected exchange rate} = 0.4876 \times \frac{(1+1.5\%)}{(1+2.5\%)} = 0.4828$$

Year 4

$$\text{Expected exchange rate} = 0.4828 \times \frac{(1+1.5\%)}{(1+2.5\%)} = 0.4781$$

	Time					
	0	1	2	3	4	5
	£	£	£	£	£	
Number of coats sold			7,500	10,000	10,000	
Price received per coat (£)			85	85	85	
Total revenue in £	0	0	637,500	850,000	850,000	
Exchange rate	0.4973	0.4924	0.4876	0.4828	0.4781	
Total revenue in NZ$	0	0	1,307,424	1,760,563	1,777,871	
Factory rent			-170,000	-170,000	-170,000	
Machinery		-225,000				
Wool and other materials			-180,000	-240,000	-240,000	
Visit to UK (visit just made is a non-relevant cost)	0	-3,000	-3,000	-3,000		
Staffing – two managers		-170,000	-170,000	-170,000	-170,000	
Staffing – additional staff			-800,000	-800,000	-800,000	
Delivery			-30,000	-40,000	-40,000	
	0	-398,000	-45,576	337,563	357,871	
Tax at 15%		0	0	0	0	-37,779
Net cashflow	0	-398,000	-45,576	337,563	357,871	-37,779
Discount factor 9%	1.000	0.917	0.842	0.772	0.708	0.650
Present value	0	-364,966	-38,375	260,599	253,372	-24,556
Net present value (NZ$)	86,074					

NPV is positive:

Enter into contract – shareholder wealth increased

(b) The directors are correct to assert that the new venture will entail risks. Risks will be present for any potential new venture and companies need to be aware of these risks. It may be possible to hedge some of these risks or to implement relevant controls to limit their impact. However, uncertainty will still remain as it is not likely that all risks can be hedged. The principal risks are set out below.

The company will be moving into a new business area as it has not previously manufactured coats. This potentially brings with it the risk that the company may make mistakes in the set up and running of the manufacturing process. However, the company can mitigate this risk by ensuring that the two managers it recruits to set up and run the coat manufacturing have prior experience in this field. Additionally, the new venture is still within the clothing manufacturing area and the company does have prior experience of this.

The company will be exporting the coats to the UK and, therefore, it will be exposed to exchange rate risk. Purchasing power parity formula has been used to calculate future exchange rates, but this only provides an estimate of the future rates and these estimates may be incorrect. The company does have the possibility of eliminating some, or possibly all, of the exchange rate risk by using appropriate exchange rate hedging techniques such as forward exchange contracts. If the company does sign the contract then it would know well in advance what the future sterling cashflows are going to be and this would make hedging feasible.

The cashflows have been discounted at the company's cost of capital of 9%. However, this may alter in the future. If the company's risk alters by taking on this new venture then this would impact on the cost of capital. Similarly, if the company's gearing level alters in the years ahead then this can impact on the cost of capital. If the company becomes riskier then this would increase the cost of capital and reduce the net present value of the project.

Another principal source of risk is the future cashflow estimates. It can be very difficult to estimate future cashflows, even into the near future. The company cannot know for certain the future cost of materials, labour and the like. It may be possible to mitigate against some of this risk by entering into long-term agreements with suppliers. This would certainly be likely to be feasible in respect of the rental of the factory. However, it may be harder in respect of costs such as material and labour.

A further source of risk might relate to the contract with the UK company. Kiwi Knitwear would need to be certain that the contract is enforceable otherwise there is a risk that they invest in the new venture and partway through the contract the UK company reneges on the deal. Employing legal practitioners who are experienced in preparing this type of contract and who have experience of UK law can help to reduce this risk.

(c) Commonly the approach used to appraise a company project is to calculate a net present value and to accept the project if this value is positive or to reject it if the value is negative. However, this approach effectively assumes that decisions are made once and for all. The issue with this is that it does not reflect what actually the case in practice is. In practice managers react to projects as they progress; they do not simply start a project and then refuse to intervene thereafter. Fundamentally, options are concerned with the idea of choice. Real options are no different, and are concerned with the idea that managers have flexibility to intervene in projects as they progress.

Flexibility can be built into projects at the outset. For example, if a company is unsure whether future demand will grow for a new product it could choose to rent only a small factory at the beginning and then it may build a larger factory later, but only when demand is proven. This would be referred to as a growth option. Other types of real option exist such as follow-on options, options to switch and abandonment options.

In the case of Kiwi Knitwear then once the contract has been signed this implies that it cannot choose to abandon the project as it retains its commitment to supply the UK company. Therefore, there is no option to abandon should the project start to fail in some way.

However, the directors have been looking at expanding into new areas but have been concerned that they over-commit to an unsuitable area. In this sense they could view the project as a growth option. That is, they could view the investment in machinery as an initial investment. If the project is successful then they can decide to invest further amounts into more machinery and factory space. They can then build on this project to either increase the contract amounts with the UK customer or expand into other parts of the world.

Chapter 13

1. Mr Li

This question tests the candidates' ability to:

(i) **Calculate the value of a business (LO3)**

(ii) **Appraise alternative business valuation methods (LO3)**

(a) *Valuation on a net assets basis*

	HK$
Net assets as per statement of financial position	2,100,000
Adjustment for land and buildings valuation	220,000
Adjustment for trade receivables	(40,000)
Total valuation	**2,280,000**

Mr Li owns 10% of the shares and, therefore his value = 10% × 2,280,000 = **HK$228,000**.

Valuation on an earnings basis

The earnings of the business have risen from last year to this. The prior pattern of earnings is not known and, therefore, an average earnings figure is used = (478,000 + 565,000)/2 = HK$521,500.

P/E ratios are provided for two similar companies. The P/E ratios differ and as no further information is provided an average is used = (5 + 8)/2 = 6.5.

A further assumption is that the P/E ratio should be reduced by 40% to 3.9 to reflect that the company is unquoted.

Therefore, the total valuation = 3.9 × HK$521,500 = HK$2,033,850.

Mr Li owns 10% of the shares and, therefore his value = 10% × 2,033,850 = **HK$203,385**.

Valuation on dividend yield

The dividends have increased from HK$221,500 to HK$226,000. This is a growth rate of 2.03%.

Assuming this continues into the future then next year's dividend will be 226,000 × 1.0203 = HK$230,588.

The cost of equity in respect of the company is not known. Therefore, as an approximation take an average of the costs of equity for the two similar listed companies = (8% + 7%)/2 = 7.5%.

The total valuation = 230,588/(7.5% − 2.03%) = HK$4,215,503.

Mr Li owns 10% of the shares and, therefore his value = 10% × 4,215,503 = **HK$421,550**.

(b) The three valuations are:

Net assets based = **HK$228,000**
Earnings based = **HK$203,385**
Dividend yield based = **HK$421,550**

Therefore, the first two methods have produced valuations that are reasonably similar, whilst the third method results in a much higher valuation.

It is common that the valuations result in different results as they are very different methods and are based on a wide range of different assumptions. There is no one correct method, rather they provide a range of values that can be used as basis for commencing negotiations.

The highest valuation has been produced by the dividend yield method. This is particularly subjective as the valuation is dependent upon the dividend payment levels that have been selected. These levels may not reflect profitability – for example, a highly profitable company may have a policy of paying zero dividends which would result in a valuation of zero which is evidently incorrect.

That said, you will no doubt want to negotiate as high a price for your shares as possible. You may try to convince Mr Chang that the dividend yield is appropriate as a method but it is unlikely he will agree. The minimum you should accept is HK$228,000 as this represents the value of the net assets of the company. Therefore, it is likely you will have to compromise and accept a valuation within the range of HK$228,000 to HK$421,550. The outcome of the negotiation will be dependent upon how keen Mr Chang is to acquire the 10% stake.

2. Mr Smith

This question tests the candidate's ability to:

(i) **Prepare business valuations (LO3)**

(ii) **Appraise alternative business valuation methods (LO3)**

(a) *Valuation on an assets basis*

Based on the information provided the assets and liabilities of the business are:

	£	
Premises	220,000	Based on current valuation
Stocks	45,000	Deducting discount in respect of selling 'old' stock
Trade debtors	3,500	
Fixtures and fittings	25,000	Based on net book value as no current valuation is provided
Trade payables	(8,000)	
Cash	5,500	
Valuation	**£291,000**	

Valuation on an earnings basis

The earnings of the business have been in decline. When earnings fluctuate it is common to take an average of earnings. However, in this case it may be more appropriate to take the most recent earnings figure of £51,000.

P/E ratios are provided for two similar companies. The P/E ratios differ and the business appears to have a greater similarity to Sports City as it does not sell via the internet.

A further assumption is that the P/E ratio should be reduced by 40% to 3.6 to reflect that Sports City is listed and the business being valued is not.

Therefore, the valuation = 3.6 × £51,000 = £183,600

(b) There is a substantial amount of additional information that would be useful to gather and for different reasons, as well as other important factors to consider including:

Mr Smith has no prior experience of running a business. His previous experience is all in the human resource function and, latterly, within the context of a utility company. Therefore, he needs to consider what his motives are for wanting to run his own business. It is insufficient to just state that he enjoys playing and watching sport.

If Mr Smith wishes to set up a sports shop business then he could buy, or lease, different premises and become a competitor of the current business. As the current business is in decline then offering a superior service may be feasible. In this way Mr Smith does not acquire a business with a diminished reputation that he then has to rebuild.

The majority of the asset valuation derives from the value of the premises. Is it wise for Mr Smith to acquire these premises given that there is a new and substantial shopping centre being built on the outskirts of the city? Mr Smith needs to ascertain how likely it is that the new shopping centre may attract footfall away from the city centre location. He may decide it is better to lease premises in the new shopping centre and set up his own business rather than buying the existing business.

Conversely, as the current owner is losing interest then this may be advantageous to Mr Smith as he may be open to negotiation on the value of the business. The current owner is the majority shareholder and, therefore, negotiations are relatively uncomplicated.

The current owner has started to sell sports equipment to a local sports centre. It would be useful to know the level and trend of these sales. These sales may be a positive part of the business and could potentially be built upon.

Mr Smith should try to ascertain if the decline in turnover and profit is solely due to the current owner losing interest. It is possible that a part of the decline is also due to competition from the large stores (such as Sports City) and to internet based shopping (such as offered by Sporting Success). This information is important as Mr Smith needs to ensure he is not buying into a business that will be in decline regardless of how much effort he puts in.

Chapter 14 - JG plc

This question aims to test the candidates' ability to:

Discuss and evaluate the defence strategies of a company threatened with a hostile takeover (LO3)

Because of the recent falls in share price; the shareholders are likely to be more open to a cash offer for their shares than the offer of shares in Smith and Brown. So unless Smith and Brown has access to sufficient funds with which to finance their bid it does seem a little unlikely at the current time. So if a bid is thought to be a long-term, rather than a short-term, threat then JB might consider the following steps:

Publicise the company's long term plans for the improvement of turnover, profits and dividends.

Introduce a 'poison pill' as an anti-takeover device. This can take many forms but is a provision or clause in the company's constitution which would have the effect of making it less attractive as a takeover target. These very often take the form of 'shareholder rights plans' which give shareholders the rights to buy shares at a discount in the case of a takeover bid. This in turn has the effect of making the takeover more expensive for the bidder.

If a bid has been made then JB might consider the following measures:

- Lobbying the trading and competition authorities with a view to stopping the bid on the grounds of a possible monopoly situation arising as a result of a takeover. The success of this tactic would depend upon the number of other health food shops operating in city centres and their relative market shares.

- Attempting to convince existing shareholders that the offer is not enough and that they will better off if the company remains independent.

- Looking for potential weaknesses in the bidder's financial position and future plans. Advertising any such weaknesses would be the next step.

- Attempting to find a 'white knight' to make a counter offer. As it seems a possible motive for Smith and Brown would be to reduce competition then this might make JB's employees feel a little pessimistic about their future. If they could find another bidder that would be willing to allow them to continue competing against Smith and Brown then this might be a better alternative.

- A variation on the above alternative would be to take the company private. This might be achieved by means of a management buyout or some other means.

- Another possibility might be to make a counter offer for Smith and Brown. However this might be difficult given the relative sizes of the two organisations.

- Just contesting the bid may produce benefits. A contested bid can be very expensive in terms of the costs of professional services, advertising and underwriting and this might be enough to deter Smith and Brown from continuing with the bid.

Chapter 15 – Endeavour plc

This question tests the candidate's ability to:

(i) **Prepare calculations to value a business and advise on the difficulties inherent in these calculations (LO3)**

(ii) **Advise on the problems associated with a management buy-out (LO3)**

Report

To: Senior managers – Endeavour plc
Subject: Management buy-out
From: XXXX
Date: XXXX

In the management buy-out you would be purchasing the share capital of the company from the current owner, Mr Grey. There are a number of methods available for valuing a business, but these all provide a valuation that is imperfect. However, they are useful as they can aid in the process of negotiating the actual value that is eventually negotiated in respect of any buy-out. Further, it is important to be aware that a management buy-out will not always be successful and that you must be aware of possible difficulties.

Three valuations are set out below using three different approaches:

Valuation on an assets basis

The net assets of the company are £3,512,000 but adjustments need to be made to this figure as follows:

	£'000
Net assets	3,512
Property (£2,763,000 – £1,432,000)	1,331
Inventories	(115)
Valuation	**4,728**

The valuation that results is £4,728,000

The adjustments to make to this are for the property and inventories values as stated in the question to bring them to their current value. This assumes the other items on the statement of financial position are reflecting realisable values. In practice it can be difficult to determine realisable values.

The intangible assets figure may also require adjusting. More information is required to ascertain whether it is appropriate. However, you need to be aware that if you were to agree to pay £4,728,000 then a significant part of this sum would relate to the purchase of the brand names.

Valuation on an earnings basis

The earnings of the company have been declining.

One approach would be to value the company on the average earnings over the last three years.

This would give a valuation as follows:

(715,000 + 694,000 + 651,000)/3 = £686,667

The P-E ratios for two competitor companies in the same business average as follows:

(14 + 16)/2 = 15

We need to reduce this average P-E ratio to reflect that the shares in Endeavour plc are not listed and, hence, are not as marketable. If we reduce this by 40% then the adjusted P-E is 9.

Therefore, the valuation = £686,667 × 9 = £6,180,003

It is important to note that the adjustment required for the P-E ratio is highly debateable. Further, it is debateable as to whether average earnings should be used. If we use the latest earnings then we have the following:

Valuation = £651,000 × 9 = £5,859,000

ANSWERS TO END OF CHAPTER QUESTIONS

This may be more appropriate as you are purchasing the company in its current state, which is with declining profits. Ideally, a figure for estimated future earnings would be more useful because if you acquire the company then it is the future earnings you will be benefitting from.

As you would be acquiring the entire business then it is appropriate to consider an earnings-based valuation, as you will be acquiring the right to the future earnings.

Valuation on a dividends basis

The total dividends of the company have been provided for the last three years. These dividends have been constant. The cost of equity is assumed to be 6% based on the rate used by Mr Grey in his prior appraisals.

If the dividend valuation model is used then the valuation is:

$$\frac{D_0}{k_e}$$

$$= \frac{450,000}{6\%}$$

$$= £7,500,000$$

This has resulted in the highest valuation. However, there are two important problems associated with this calculation. This rate of 6% may not be appropriate, but no other alternative is given. If a different rate should apply then this could have a significant effect on the figure.

Further, as Mr Grey owns and controls all the equity, he determines the dividend paid. If you acquire the company then you can alter the dividend policy. Therefore, past dividend payments are not of real significance.

There are three key issues in respect of the management buy-out.

You all work in the sales department. This may be problematic as you may not have expertise across the range of business functions. Any funder of the buy-out would be concerned that there is no expertise in accounting or software development. So although you are convinced you can stop the profit decline, you need to convince providers of finance.

You are keen to manage the company according to your own ideas. This does not take into account that a provider of finance is likely to require board representation. This may curb your freedom and demotivate you.

Because many of the employees have worked for the company since it was established they have a great respect for Mr Grey. Therefore, there is a danger that employees leave at some point during or after the buy-out. They may consider it an appropriate time to move positions and this could leave significant knowledge and skills gaps in the company.

Chapter 16

1 Eye plc

This question tests the candidate's ability to:

(i) **Calculate the outcome of hedging using futures contracts (LO4)**

(ii) **Evaluate how a range of factors may impact upon an exchange rate (LO4)**

(a) The company requires March contracts with rate $1.5624

Number of contracts required = $\frac{\$322,000 / \$1.5624}{62,500} = £206,093 / £62,500 = 3.3$

(ie 3 contracts).

On 1 February:

Tick movement = $1.5624 - $1.5402/$0.0001 = 222 ticks
Tick value = £62,500 × $0.0001 = $6.25
Loss on futures = 3 contracts x $6.25 × 222 ticks = $4,162.50
Overall: receipt minus futures loss = $322,000 - $4,162.50 = $317,837.50
In sterling the overall receipt is $317,837.50/$1.5571 = £204,121

(b) There is a limited amount of information provided about Bithland. Therefore, it must be understood that there are limitations to the advice that can be given as to how the different factors may influence the future exchange rate.

The floating rate system certainly implies that exchange rates can move freely and fluctuations should be expected, although it is possible that in the future a government may choose to intervene to attempt to manage exchange rates. It is difficult for governments to manage exchange rates and the outcome of any intervention would be unknown. As there has been prior economic mismanagement then it may be that the government would struggle if it attempted to intervene.

The mineral deposits and raw materials have had a beneficial effect on exports levels and on overseas investment. If this positive impact continues in the future then this should result in relatively strong demand for the currency and, in turn, should lead to the currency appreciating. The extent to which the currency appreciates will depend upon the level of demand for the currency. More detailed information on anticipated export levels and overseas investment would be needed to make any further assessment of the possible impact.

The economy has been mismanaged and the balance of payments is in deficit. That the economy has been mismanaged may deter some overseas investors. Further, as the balance of payments is in deficit this normally results in a negative impact on confidence in the country. The resulting effect upon the currency is that the exchange rate would fall. This would be especially the case if the deficit is maintained over a long period of time.

The high inflation rate would, similarly, likely lead to a weakening of the exchange rate as implied by purchasing power parity.

Political instability has been a feature of Bithland and typically this lowers confidence in the country and reduces demand for the currency. This would then cause the currency to depreciate. However, the current government is popular and this may imply that a period of political stability could occur. Overall, we would need to know how the international community views the future political situation will be to make any assessment in this respect.

The economy of the country is stated to be developing and growing rapidly. This possibly implies that there is no overall consensus on how the country will develop in the future and whether it will develop successfully. This may imply that speculators will be watching to see how things develop. Speculation can result in unanticipated exchange rate movements and in either direction.

2 ZXY International plc

This question tests the candidate's ability to:

- **Evaluate the economic consequences of different strategies for the management of risk associated with international trades (LO4)**

(a) Any hedging strategy should be based on net receipts and payments:

	Receipts	Payments
Euro Zone		€300,000
USA	US$110,000	
Malaysia	RM102,000	

Forward Market Hedges

Euro Zone	$\dfrac{300{,}000}{1.6177}$	=	£185,448 Payment
USA	$\dfrac{110{,}000}{1.4221}$	=	£77,350 Receipt
Malaysia			Not available

Money Market Hedges

Euro Zone

Borrow £183,728 @ 6% for three months – total cost £186,484
Convert @ spot to €298,136
Invest @ 2.5% for three months to give €300,000 which will be used to make the payment

USA

Borrow US$108,910 @ 4% for three months to give $110,000
Convert to £76,208 @ spot
Invest @ 4% for three months to give £76,970

Malaysia

Not available

Comparison of the methods

	Forward Contracts	Money Market
Euro Zone	(185,448)	(186,484)
USA	77,350	76,970

On the basis of the above comparisons it may well be that the best hedging strategy for ZXY will be to make use of Forward Contracts for hedging its exposure in the Euro Zone and USA.

Neither Forward Contracts nor Money Market hedges are available for its Malaysian exposure and ZXY may well need to consider alternatives. These might include:

- Requesting payment in sterling
- Requesting payment in another currency which can be hedged (eg US$)
- Requesting payment in advance

The use of any of the above however, will depend upon the strength of the bargaining position of ZXY and the level of perceived risk involved.

(b) In both cases above the forward contracts give marginally the better outcome. However, there may be a case for contemplating the use of the alternative as follows.

In the case of the US$ receipt the assumption has been made that the sterling receipts could only be invested at 4% – it may well be well in excess of this. For example, the early receipt of the sterling may be used to pay off a debt at a much higher rate or possibly used in a project giving an even higher yield. It might be better to use, say, the company's cost of capital (as a compromise figure) when evaluating the money market option. A lot would depend upon circumstances and also management attitudes to risk. If for example, the US$ receipts did not materialise for whatever reason then it might be argued that the sterling receipts would be needed to pay off the US$ debt.

A similar argument could be put for the money market options on the two net payment cases. It just might be possible to get better rates of investment than those quoted – although again if they required jeopardising the potential availability of the cash when required to clear the payables then they might well be rejected.

Chapter 17 – Methods of hedging

(a) *Using a Forward Contract you will receive:*

$$\frac{2,000,000}{16.157} = HK\$123,785$$

Using Options you would receive:

You will have to buy either the September ¥15.90 Call option.

One contract will buy HK$31,250 for ¥496,875.

Number of contracts required:

$$\frac{2,000,000}{496,875} = 4.025$$

You could buy four contracts and hedge ¥12,500 forward.

4 contracts × HK$31,250	125,000
Sell ¥12,500 forward @16.157	774
	125,774
Less Option costs	
4 × HK$31,250 × 3.40 cents	(4,250)
Net proceeds	121,524

Using Money Market Hedge you would receive:

Borrow ¥1,987,578 (¥2,000,000/1.00625) at 2.5% for three months to give ¥2,000,000 to repay with Japanese receipt.

Convert at spot ¥1,987,578/16.251 to give HK$122,305.

This could be invested at 1.75% for three months to give HK$122,841.

So a forward contract would appear to be the best alternative.

(b) **Forward Contract**

If the ¥2,000,000 was not received and you had used a forward contract then the bank would still expect you to fulfil the contract. This would involve you in a loss equivalent to the difference between the bid and offer price of ¥2,000,000.

Currency Option

If a currency option was used and the ¥2,000,000 not received then the situation would be different from the forward contract. The option could be sold if it still had any value or left to lapse.

Money Market Hedge

With this alternative you would have to repay the Yen loan which might involve you in losses or gains depending upon how the ¥/HK$ exchange rate had moved in the meantime.

Overall the Currency Option might be the best under these circumstances but there are other aspects to be considered. These include the 'up front' cost of the option.

Chapter 18

1. Regent plc

This question tests the candidate's ability to:

(i) **Calculate the outcome of hedging using interest rate futures (LO4)**

(ii) **Assess political risk (LO4)**

(a) The increase in interest rates from 7% to 8.25% will cost Regent plc an additional £62,500 (£20 million × 3/12 × 1.25%).

Using interest rate futures Regent plc can offset this cost of £62,500 as follows:

The contract size is £500,000 and Regent plc will need 40 futures contracts to hedge its loan of £20m.

Regent plc will initially enter into an agreement to sell 40 September contracts at 93.29.

At the beginning of September, Regent plc will then enter into an agreement to buy 40 September contracts at 92.13.

Consequently, Regent plc will make a profit on its futures contracts calculated as follows:

Contracts entered into initially	93.29
Contracts entered into beginning of September	92.13
Difference	**1.16**

Therefore, the futures difference in number of ticks = 1.16/0.01 = 116 ticks.

Therefore, the total futures profit = 116 ticks × £12.50 × 40 contracts = £58,000.

Hence, although Regent plc has an additional interest cost of £62,500 this is largely offset by the profit on the futures contracts of £58,000.

(b) Assessing the level of political risk of a country is a difficult matter. Further, any assessment undertaken may become out of date as factors relevant to political risk may change over time for any given country. The information given allows some assessment of the political risk of country Z to be made, but it must be recognised that this will be a basic assessment as the information provided is relatively limited.

There has been economic growth occurring and over a relatively extended period of 20 years. This suggests the economic growth is sustainable, and, in turn, this suggests a relatively lower level of political risk as does the low level of government debt.

Government stability can be an indicator of the level political risk. In the case of country Z there has been only one change of government in the last 20 years and this stability suggests that there is limited political risk. This does assume that the government has been freely elected and is not imposed upon the country.

The exchange rate has remained stable and this is in comparison with the $ which is a major currency. This supports that the economy has been successful and, hence, suggests political risk is low.

The inflation rate has decreased from 11% to 3%. Thus, it has moved from a relatively high rate to a relatively low rate. Again, this is suggestive of low political risk.

All the above factors suggest that political risk is low. The information provided concerning the financial sector further supports this, for although the stock exchange is small, the banking sector has experienced considerable growth.

Chapter 19 – Mesha plc

This question tests the candidate's ability to evaluate and explain the management of interest rate exposure. (Syllabus reference LO4)

(a)
Year	Cash flow £m	6% discount factor	Present value £m
0	(X)	1	(X)
1	6	0.9434	5.66
2	6	0.8900	5.34
3	56	0.8396	47.02
Net present value			Nil

Current value = £58 million

(b)
	Fixed rate	Variable rate
Mesha	6.0	SONIA + 1.0
Ahsem	7.7	SONIA + 1.7
Difference	1.7	0.7

Spread differential = 1.7 – 0.7 = 1.0

Mesha would pay SONIA + 0.5%

Ahsem would pay 7.2% Fixed

This could be arranged as follows:

Mesha

Pays to Bank	6% fixed
Pays to Ahsem	SONIA + 1.2%
Receives from Ahsem	6.7% fixed
Pays net	SONIA + 0.5%

Ahsem:

Pays to Bank	SONIA + 1.7%
Pays to Mesha	6.7% fixed
Receives from Mesha	SONIA + 1.2%
Pays net	7.2% fixed

(c) Criteria to consider:

- **Cost of the finance** – debt is the cheapest but has more implications in terms of cash flows (interest payments) and risk (default) than equity
- **For the right time period** – presumably Mesha will be requiring long-term funds – but this may need planning in terms of future requirements
- **Security required** – debt usually requires security. Is this available within the company?
- Is there any financial risk involved? eg interest rate or currency rate risk
- Are there any conditions involved?
    - Debt often attracts restrictions imposed by the lender (eg restrictions on the payment of dividends)
    - Equity may have control and/or ownership implications

ANSWERS TO END OF CHAPTER QUESTIONS

Chapter 20

1. Mr Lee

This question tests the candidate's ability to advise on the working capital position of companies in differing industries (LO5)

Report

To: Mr Lee
Subject: Advice on working capital position of companies A and B
From: XXXX
Date: XXXX

I have set out below the advice on the working capital position of the two companies that you own. It is important to recognise that the two companies operate in very different business areas and this can have a significant impact upon both the working capital position of each company and how working capital should be managed in each company.

Relevant calculations that give some indication of the working capital position of each company are set out below and it can be seen that they do differ greatly from company to company:

	A		B	
Current ratio				
$\dfrac{\text{Current assets}}{\text{Current liabilities}}$	$\dfrac{372}{530}$	0.70	$\dfrac{1{,}025}{620}$	1.65
Quick ratio				
$\dfrac{\text{Current assets less inventories}}{\text{Current liabilities}}$	$\dfrac{330}{530}$	0.62	$\dfrac{835}{620}$	1.35
Receivables payment period				
$\dfrac{\text{Trade receivables}}{\text{Sales}}$	$\dfrac{0 \times 365 \text{ days}}{5{,}100}$	0 days	$\dfrac{760 \times 365 \text{ days}}{4{,}600}$	60.30 days
Stock turnover period				
$\dfrac{\text{Inventory}}{\text{Cost of sales}}$	$\dfrac{42 \times 365 \text{ days}}{3{,}980}$	3.85 days	$\dfrac{190 \times 365 \text{ days}}{3{,}090}$	22.44 days
Payable payment period				
$\dfrac{\text{Trade payables}}{\text{Cost of sales}}$	$\dfrac{385 \times 365 \text{ days}}{3{,}980}$	35.31 days	$\dfrac{245 \times 365 \text{ days}}{3{,}090}$	28.94 days
OPERATING CYCLE		−31.46 days		53.80 days

The current ratio measures the ability of a company to pay its short-term liabilities. Company A has a relatively low current ratio, this might be thought a cause for concern. However, the company is in the supermarket industry and it would be expected that the current assets figure may be relatively low. This is because inventories and trade receivables will be relatively low as explained below. The current ratio for company B appears somewhat low, but not to the same extent as company A. It is in a different industry to company A and we might expect it to have a higher current ratio. Again, there are some circumstances that may be impacting on this and these are explained below.

The quick ratio is the current ratio but adjusted by deducting inventories from the current assets figure. The quick ratio indicates how well the company might cope should it suddenly have to repay short-term liabilities. Typically, this might be expected to be a ratio of 1:1. For the supermarket company A it is well below this figure for the same reasons as the current ratio is well below the expected norm. For the fashion manufacturing company B the ratio is well above the expected norm. This indicates that inventories are relatively low and suggests that the company can cope well if it should suddenly have to repay short-term liabilities.

The receivables payment period indicates how long it takes for the company to receive monies due from trade debtors. In the case of company A this is zero. That company A has no trade debtors is to be expected. It is a supermarket company and it does not offer credit periods to customers. This is also one reason why the current assets figure is low. For company B the period is approximately 60 days. This may appear to be a long period, as it is normal for 30 days credit to be cited. This could suggest that the company is poor at getting monies in from trade debtors. However, another reason could be that the company is selling fashion items to retailers. Fashion is sold in two ranges; Spring/Summer range and Autumn/Winter range. The Autumn/Winter range will normally have gone to retailers shortly before the year end (31 October). Therefore, inventories will be low but trade debtors high.

If we look at the stock turnover period for company B then this is approximately 22 days and this is lower than expected as just explained. If we had looked at inventories two months previously they would have appeared very high. For company A the stock turnover period is even lower at approximately 4 days. This is to be expected in a supermarket company where a significant proportion of the stocks is perishable. Therefore, stockholding periods should be low.

The payables payment period indicates how long a company is taking to pay its trade creditors (suppliers). This would typically be 30 days and for both companies the figures are not too different from this expectation. Therefore, these seem appropriate for both company A and B.

The operating cycle measures how long it takes a company to receive cash in from its sales compared to when it pays cash out for its supplies. This is negative 31 days for company A. This indicates company A is receiving cash in from sales before it has paid its suppliers for these items. This is to be expected for a supermarket where sales are cash-based, the stockholding period is very short but suppliers must wait approximately 35 days for payment. In effect suppliers are financing a part of company A's business. For company B this period is positive 53 days. This is expected given the previous comments and indicates that company A must finance this period.

Overall, this suggests that there is no need for concern about the working capital position of either company based on the data provided. Additional data would be useful to help confirm if this is the case. If the full set of financial data were to be provided then discussions could be contextualised better. Further, if data from previous years was provided then a trend analysis would indicate if any ratios have improved or deteriorated over time. Finally, data from competitor companies in the same industries would enable me to give you an insight into whether company A or B are better or worse than competitors at managing working capital.

2. X plc

This question aims to test the candidates' ability to:

Evaluate working capital management strategies and the use of appropriate ratio analysis (LO5)

(a) *Preliminary calculations*

$$\text{Inventory Turnover Period} = \frac{\text{Average Inventory}}{\text{Cost of Sales}} \times 365$$

Therefore:

$$\text{Average Inventory} = \frac{\text{Inventory Turnover Period} \times \text{Cost of Sales}}{365}$$

$$= \frac{45.03 \times 3{,}915}{365}$$

$$= €483m$$

Receivables Payment Period $= \dfrac{\text{Average Receivables}}{\text{Turnover}} \times 365$

Therefore:

Average Receivables $= \dfrac{\text{Receivables Payment Period} \times \text{Turnover}}{365}$

$= \dfrac{40.02 \times 4{,}350}{365}$

= €477m

Payables Payment Period $= \dfrac{\text{Average payables}}{\text{Cost of Sales}} \times 365$

Therefore:

Average Payables $= \dfrac{\text{Payables Payment Period} \times \text{Cost of Sales}}{365}$

$= \dfrac{50.07 \times 3{,}915}{365}$

= €537m

Statement of Financial Position for X plc for the year ended 31 October 2009:

	€m	€m	€m
Non-current assets			400
Current assets			
Inventory		483	
Trade receivables		477	
Cash		–	
		960	
Current liabilities			
Bank Overdraft	343		
Trade Payables	537		
Dividend Payable	50	930	30
			430
Share Capital			20
Retained Profits			410
			430
Turnover			4,350
Gross Margin			435
Net Margin			60
Dividend			50
Retained Profit			10

(b) Overtrading is where a company tries to support too large a volume of trade with insufficient long term capital. The symptoms are often:

- Rapid increase in turnover without significant increases in long term capital
- Large increases in:
- Non-current assets
- Inventory
- Trade receivables
- Trade payables
- Short term funding such as overdrafts

X plc is suffering all these symptoms and needs to quickly find sources of long term funding so that it can:

- Reduce its overdraft which is at its limit
- Pay off the most urgent of its trade payables or it may lose its sources of supply

Such sources might include:

- Chasing for earlier payment of its trade receivables
- Finding suitable debt funding
- Increase its equity funding
- Make use of internal sources of funds by making use of leasing facilities or selling unused assets (if any)

Chapter 21 – Ng Fan

This question tests the candidate's ability to:

(i) **Evaluate the financial impact of factoring (LO5).**
(ii) **Explain the importance of effective working capital management (LO5).**

(a) Calculation of changes to Income Statement

		HK$
Factor's Finance	3 million × 80% × 30/365 × 9%	17,753
Overdraft Interest	3 million × 20% × 30/365 × 8.5%	4,192
Cost of Factor's services	3 million × 1.5%	45,000
Insurance Costs	3 million × 0.65 cents	19,500
Savings in bad debts	32,900 × 90%	29,610
Savings in Administration		100,000

Calculation of changes to Balance Sheet

	HK$
Savings in Administration Costs	55,000
Increase in income from reduction in bad debts	29,610
Savings in Overdraft interest	27,367
Interest paid to Factor	(17,753)
Insurance payments	(19,500)
Overdraft required (102,988 + 49,315 – 150,887)	(1,416)
Net cash increase	73,308

Income Statement – Year Ended 30 June 2008

	HK$
Turnover	3,000,000
Gross Profit	551,000
Factor Interest	(17,753)
Insurance	(19,500)
Bad Debts	(3,290)
Administration Costs	(285,000)
Net Profit	225,457

Balance Sheet as at 30 June 2008

	HK$	HK$
Non Current Assets		4,375,340
Current Assets		
Inventories	102,988	
Accounts Receivable	49,315	
Cash	73,308	225,611
Current Liabilities		
Accounts payable		(150,887)
		4,450,064
Financed by:		
Ordinary Shares		3,000,000
Retained Earnings		1,450,064
		4,450,064

(b) Planning is such an important aspect of effective working capital management because it usually involves some element of compromise.

Typical compromises include:

- High stock levels facilitate production and sales but tie up capital and increase the risks of losses
- The granting of long periods of credit enhance marketing efforts but can be expensive
- Large early payment discounts may encourage early payment but can be ineffective from a cost point of view
- The use of overdraft and other credit facilities can be extremely useful for production and selling purposes but can be prohibitively expensive

Careful planning is often required to ensure that the correct levels of stock, credit and cash are available at reasonable cost.

Chapter 22 – Whitlow Engineering

(a) The financial controls referred to by the major investor involve the management of working capital.

Working capital management includes the following aspects:

(i) Inventory management
(ii) Debtor management
(iii) Trade creditor management
(iv) Cash management

Effective inventory management can require the installation of some or all of the following:

(i) Stock control systems
(ii) Economic ordering
(iii) Just in Time Ordering (JIT)
(iv) Materials Resource Planning (MRP)
(v) Standardisation

Effective debtor control usually involves:

(i) Credit status checks
(ii) Credit control
(iii) Cash discounts

(iv) Debt collection procedures
(v) Credit insurance
(vi) Factoring
(vii) Invoice discounting
(viii) The use of banking instruments such as letters of credit

Effective cash control can require the use of:

(i) Cash budgets
(ii) Bank cash management services
(iii) Cash flow statements
(iv) Cash management models
(v) Float management

(b) Planning is such an important aspect of effective working capital management because it usually involves some element of compromise.

Typical compromises include:

(i) High inventory levels facilitate production and sales but tie up capital and increase the risks of losses
(ii) The granting of long periods of credit enhance marketing efforts but can be expensive
(iii) Large early payment discounts may encourage early payment but can be ineffective from a cost point of view
(iv) The use of overdraft and other credit facilities can be extremely useful for production and selling purposes but can be prohibitively expensive

Careful planning is often required to ensure that the correct levels of inventory, credit and cash are available at reasonable cost.

Practice Exam question bank

May 2018 (Adapted)

Question 1 — 36 mins

An important financial decision which every firm faces is the choice between debt and equity capital of its capital structure. However, how companies choose their capital structure remains a puzzle for both academics and practising managers.

Required

(a) Critically analyse the factors that may influence the choice of capital structure. **(14 marks)**

(b) Provide advice on two main methods/techniques which finance managers should employ to decide whether to borrow and, if so, how much borrowing to undertake. **(6 marks)**

(Total 20 marks)

Question 2 — 36 mins

The directors of Blackpool plc are currently considering what value to place on Golden Tulip Ltd, a company they are planning to take over in the near future. Negotiations between the senior management team of each business has begun. The most recent accounts of Golden Tulip Ltd are as follows:

SUMMARY OF THE STATEMENT OF INCOME FOR THE YEAR ENDED
31 DECEMBER 2017

	£
Revenue	2,500,000
Profit before interest and taxation	260,000
Interest charges	45,000
Profit before taxation	215,000
Corporation tax	70,000
Profit after taxation	145,000
Dividend proposed and paid	17,000
Profit for the year	128,000
Transfer to general reserve	20,000
Retained profit for the year	108,000

EXTRACTS FROM THE STATEMENT OF FINANCIAL POSITION AS AT 31 DECEMBER, 2017

	£	£
Fixed assets		
Freehold premises at cost	420,000	
Less accumulated depreciation	38,000	
		382,000
Motor van at cost	96,000	
Less accumulated depreciation	44,000	
		52,000
Plant & machinery at cost	209,000	
Less accumulated depreciation	64,000	
		145,000
Total Fixed assets		579,000
Current assets		
Stock	125,000	
Trade debtors	140,000	
		265,000
Total assets		844,000
Current liabilities		
Trade creditors	143,000	
Taxation	70,000	
Bank overdraft	53,000	
		(266,000)
Long-term liability		
13% loan: Barclays bank		(180,000)
Total liabilities		(446,000)
Total assets less total liabilities		398,000
Capital and reserves		
100,000 ordinary shares of £2.00 each		200,000
General reserve		90,000
Retained profit		108,000
		398,000

The following additional information is also available:

(1) The subsidiary has shown a stable level of sales and profits over the past five years.

(2) An independent valuer has estimated the current realisable values of the assets of the company as follows:

	£
Freehold premises at cost	485,000
Motor van at cost	40,000
Plant & Machinery at cost	125,000
Stock	135,000

For the trade debtors, the balance sheet value is considered to reflect the current realisable value.

(3) Bridgewater Ltd is listed on the Stock Exchange and is in the same line of business as Blackpool Ltd. Bridgewater Ltd has a price/earnings ratio of 10.

(4) The free cash flows of the business over the next 10 years are estimated as follows:

Year	
2018	£97,000
2019	£115,000
2020–2027	£130,000

Market analysts provide the following information about the risk of Blackpool plc's market returns: risk free rate is 7%; market return is 11% and the beta 1.25.

Required

As a financial advisor, you have been asked by the directors of Blackpool plc to prepare a report. Your report should include:

(a) Calculation of the value of Golden Tulip Ltd using the following methods: net assets liquidation basis; free cash flow basis; price/earnings ratio basis. **(10 marks)**

(b) Acquisition has become an important means for corporate growth, yet evidence suggests that over 75% of acquisitions fail to achieve the expected outcomes in terms of profitability. Assess the five reasons why acquisitions fail. **(10 marks)**

(Total 20 marks)

Question 3 — 36 mins

Shanghai Electronics of China currently exports around 20 per cent of its output, valued at 4,265 million RMB, to West Africa. With rising transport costs and the completion of the Economic Community of West African States (ECOWAS) single market, the company is considering establishing production facilities in one of the Economic Community member countries. While the Chinese parent company will no longer export finished products to West Africa, it expects to continue to export significant quantities of component parts to the three West African countries seeking to attract Shanghai Electronics. The export of component parts will depend upon the domestic (African) input which each of the three countries requires.

The government of each of the three countries has put together attractive packages to persuade Shanghai Electronics to locate their operations in their country. The packages essentially involve assistance with the costs of establishing operations and labour training.

Required

(a) Recommend three main methods available to pay for foreign investment and discuss two factors that will influence the choice of finance to use. **(10 marks)**

(b) Advise the management of Shanghai Electronics of the risks involved in investing overseas and how to deal with these risks. **(10 marks)**

(Total 20 marks)

November 2017 (Adapted)

Question 4 — 72 mins

The Board of Directors of the UK-based company, Lincoln Technology Products plc, is reviewing its investment plans for the next financial year. At its next meeting, the directors of Lincoln are expected to discuss two proposals produced by the technical and production directors below.

Project 1: New Haven Devices

The technical director of Lincoln has been contacted by the New Haven Devices, a US company, which is prepared to offer Lincoln an opportunity to manufacture a patented product under licence, for exclusive sale to the European Union market. The new product, named Super Wonder, will complement Lincoln's existing product range and no additional fixed manufacturing costs will be required before production can be recommended. Sales and service support are to be carried out by Lincoln's current staff. However, additional marketing expenses will be incurred to launch the product and to maintain its identity in the marketplace.

An initial cost of licensing fee of £100,000.00 will be payable to New Haven Devices. In addition, annual royalty of 4 per cent of sales value is payable for the first year, rising to 4.5 per cent thereafter. Licence fees are payable in US dollars.

Forecasts have been prepared for a three-year project as follows:

Year	2018	2019	2020
	£	£	£
Total value of stock for sale	320,000	470,000	540,000
Manufacturing costs	160,000	240,000	270,000
Additional marketing costs	100,000	120,000	130,000

In order to provide adequate customer service and delivery, New Haven Devices insists that a minimum of two months' sale should be held in inventory in 2018 and 2019.

Project 2: Hashimoto Ltd

Lincoln's sales director has been involved in extensive discussions with Hashimoto Ltd of Japan with a view of Lincoln taking over a role as the exclusive distributor for its products within the European Union. Hashimoto is prepared to offer a contract for a three-year period, but demands that Lincoln make a considerable investment to show its commitment to the success of the project as follows:

(i) Lincoln makes a minimum annual purchase commitment of 500 units at a price of £450 each, payable on delivery and in Japanese yen.

(ii) Lincoln invests in a properly equipped Service Workshop to support the product line. The estimated cost for such workshop is £75,000 now and annual operating costs of £25,000. If the contract terminates at the end of year 3, there will be no residual value in the equipment.

Forecasts for project 2 over the three-year period are as follows:

Year	2018	2019	2020
Sales (units)	400	900	1,400
	£	£	£
Sales price per unit	675	695	720
Advertising costs	30,000	50,000	75,000
Wages & salaries	20,000	35,000	63,000
Transport costs	5,000	14,000	33,000
Sundry expenses	15,000	23,000	18,000

The capital structure of Lincoln is as follows:

	%	cost per annum
Ordinary share capital	25	10.00%
Preference share capital	15	9.40%
Debenture stock	15	10.00%
Retained profit	45	8.00%
	100	

Required

The managing director of Lincoln has asked you, as a finance director, to evaluate the two proposals. Assume there is no shortage of investment funds.

(a) Estimate the cost of capital using the Weighted Average Cost of Capital from the various sources of capital above. **(2 marks)**

(b) Prepare calculations to evaluate and determine which of the two projects is worthwhile in pound sterling. **(20 marks)**

(c) Discuss the three types of foreign exchange risk that Lincoln might face and how the company might manage each type of foreign exchange risk. **(18 marks)**

(Total 40 marks)

Question 5   36 mins

Fast Lane Ltd is considering the acquisition of a car maintenance company to expand its automobile interests. Its chief executive has highlighted one possible target, Executive Car Maintenance Ltd. The most recent accounts of Executive Car Maintenance Ltd are as follows:

SUMMARY OF THE STATEMENT OF INCOME FOR THE YEAR ENDED 30 SEPTEMBER 2017

	£m
Sales	830.4
Profit before interest and taxation	120.8
Interest charges	(14.0)
Profit before taxation	106.8
Corporation tax	(23.4)
Profit after taxation	83.4
Dividend proposed and paid	(17.2)
Profit for the year	66.2
Transfer to general reserve	(10.0)
Retained profit for the year	56.2

EXTRACTS FROM THE STATEMENT OF FINANCIAL POSITION AS AT 30 SEPTEMBER 2017

	£m	£m
Fixed assets		
Freehold premises at cost		200.0
Less accumulated depreciation		(40.0)
		160.0
Motor van at cost	37.4	
Less accumulated depreciation	(3.0)	
		34.4
Machinery at cost	45.0	
Less accumulated depreciation	(2.0)	
		43.0
Total fixed assets		237.4
Current assets		
Stock	104.7	
Trade receivable	43.2	
Cash at bank	271.6	
		419.5
Total assets		656.9
Current liability		
Trade payables	(346.2)	

	£m	£m
Long-term liability		
12% loan: Barclays bank	(77.5)	
Total liabilities		(423.7)
Total assets less total liabilities		233.2
Capital and reserves		
£0.25 ordinary share	45.2	
General reserve	2.8	
Retained profit	185.2	
		233.2

The following additional information is also available:

(1) A professional surveyor has recently established the current realisable values of the assets of the company as follows:

	£m
Freehold premises	265.0
Motor van	25.0
Machinery	57.0
Stock	120.0

For the remaining assets, the balance sheet values were considered to reflect their current realisable values.

(2) Share capital comprises 180.9 million ordinary shares of 25 pence each. Following the publication of these results, the market price stands currently at £5.80 per share.

(3) The free cash flows of the business over the next 10 years are estimated as follows:

Year	£m
2017	67.0
2018	70.0
3-10	95.0

The cost of capital for the business is 10 per cent.

Required

As an Accounting Consultant, you have been asked by the directors of Fast Lane Ltd to prepare a report. Your report should include:

Calculation of the value of Executive Car Maintenance Ltd using the following methods:

(a) (i) Net assets liquidation basis
    (ii) Free cash flow basis
    (iii) Price/earnings basis
    (iv) Dividend yield basis (assume tax rate to 20%) **(9 marks)**

(b) Briefly evaluate the strengths and weaknesses of the share valuation methods used in (a) above. **(8 marks)**

(c) Advise the directors which share valuation method you consider to be most appropriate for your negotiation and why. **(3 marks)**

(Total 20 marks)

Question 6   36 mins

Spencer Trading Ltd deals in a wide range of household items in the UK. The managing director is particularly concerned with the company's liquidity position in recent months. The most recent accounts of the company are as follows:

SUMMARY OF THE STATEMENT OF INCOME FOR THE YEAR ENDED 30 SEPTEMBER 2017

	£	£
Sales		552,000
Opening stock	225,000	
Purchases	441,000	
	666,000	
Less closing stock	243,000	
Cost of sales		423,000
Profit before expenses		129,000
Interest & sundry expenses		135,000
Profit/(Loss) for the period		(6,000)

EXTRACTS FROM THE STATEMENT OF FINANCIAL POSITION AS AT 30 SEPTEMBER 2017

	£	£	£
Fixed assets			
Freehold premises			280,000
Motor vehicles net of depreciation			25,000
Fixtures net of depreciation			52,000
Total fixed assets			357,000
Current assets			
Stock		143,000	
Trade receivable		163,000	
		306,000	
Current liabilities			
Trade payables	(145,000)		
Bank overdraft	(140,000)		
		(285,000)	
			21,000
			378,000
Long-term liability			
Bank loan			(120,000)
Total assets less total liabilities			258,000
Capital and reserves			
£1 ordinary share			100,000
General reserve			158,000
			258,000

The receivables and payables were maintained at a constant level throughout the year.

Required

(a) Calculate the relevant ratios and evaluate the liquidity position of Spencer Ltd. **(4 marks)**

(b) Calculate the operating cash cycle of Spencer Ltd and indicate what steps can be taken to improve the operating cash cycle. **(8 marks)**

(c) Advise the directors as to the benefits and drawbacks of using a large overdraft to finance the activities of the company and suggest two suitable alternative ways of raising funds to finance the business working capital requirements.

(8 marks)

(Total 20 marks)

May 2015 (Adapted)

Question 7   72 mins

Gorforth plc is a UK company that manufactures tables. The tables are very modern in design and are sold to department stores in the UK. It is considering undertaking a project to manufacture a new range of tables based on traditional English furniture designs. It believes this traditional range will appeal to consumers in the USA as Americans have always been interested in the history of England. This interest has increased because of the popularity of English history television programmes that have been broadcast on American television networks in recent years.

The directors have no prior experience of the USA market for their product so six months ago the directors of Gorforth plc commissioned a marketing and branding company to undertake some research into this project at an agreed cost of £50,000. The marketing and branding company has suggested that Gorforth plc run a three year marketing campaign that employs an actor who has been in a recent English history television programme. It is estimated the campaign would cost $150,000 per year and this would be payable at the start of each year. The marketing and branding company has estimated that the sales Gorforth plc could anticipate for the three years are as follows:

	Year 1	Year 2	Year 3
Estimated number of tables sold	5,000	6,000	6,500
Estimated average selling price per table	$800	$800	$850

If the project goes ahead the tables will be made in the UK and then shipped to the USA. A new factory will need to be rented for the three year period and at a cost of £70,000 per year. The rent is payable in advance at the start of each year. The company will recruit 70 employees to work in the factory. The average salary of each employee will be £20,000 in year one and rising by 5% per year. Two managers will be seconded from the current factory to run this new operation. These managers are each paid £50,000 per year. Machinery will be leased for the three years at a cost of £50,000 payable at the end of Year 1, £60,000 payable at the end of Year 2 and £70,000 payable at the end of Year 3.

The average materials cost for each table is estimated to be £120. Other costs associated with running the factory are estimated to be £12,000 per year. Shipping costs to the USA are estimated to be £1,500 per 50 tables. Sales personnel will be employed for the three year period. These sales personnel will be people who are from the UK, but currently based in the USA. The directors of Gorforth plc believe this will be an advantage as the sales personnel will understand the requirements of both Gorforth plc and potential USA customers. The total cost of their salaries and associated expenses are estimated to be $300,000 per year. The directors of Gorforth plc will oversee the project.

The current spot rate is $1.75 to the £. It is expected that the exchange rate will change in the future, and it has been estimated that the inflation rate in the UK will be 2% per year and the inflation rate in the USA will be 1% per year.

Tax would be payable for the business 1 year in arrears and at a rate of 20%. If the net cashflow for any year is negative then you should assume that zero tax will be paid on this cashflow, and that the negative cashflow will be used to reduce the next available positive cashflow when calculating tax on that positive cashflow.

Gorforth plc believes it has a cost of capital of 11%. This figure is based on calculations the finance team made approximately five years ago. The capital structure of Gorforth plc has changed since then.

Required

(a) Prepare calculations to evaluate whether it is worthwhile for Gorforth plc to go ahead with the new venture. State any assumptions you have made in your calculations. **(18 marks)**

(b) Advise the directors of any potential risks that may be associated with this new venture.

(14 marks)

(c) Gorforth plc has just received an order from a company based in the USA for its current product range. The order value is $315,000 and the USA company has agreed to pay this amount on 1 July 2015. The finance director has decided to hedge the exchange rate risk using currency futures contracts. The spot rate is 1.6147 - 1.6168 $/£. Futures contracts are available today as follows:

GBP/USD futures:

Settlement date	Price
June	1.6188
September	1.6192

The contract size for these futures is £62,500 and the tick size $0.0001.

You are required to prepare calculations that evaluate the outcome of the hedge for Gorforth plc assuming that on 1 July 2015 the spot rate is 1.5672 – 1.5693 and the price for September futures contracts is 1.5697. **(8 marks)**

(Total 40 marks)

Question 8   36 mins

Strand plc is a quoted company. The current market value of each share is £2.82 and the company has 40 million shares in issue. Dividend payments in recent years have been as follows:

Total dividend	Amount
Just paid	£9.60m
Paid one year ago	£9.24m
Paid two years ago	£9.04m
Paid three years ago	£8.88m
Paid four years ago	£8.40m

The capital structure of the company also includes long-term debt. This debt has a market value of £60m and a book value of £50m. The interest rate on the debt is 7% and the debt is irredeemable. The company pays corporation tax at a rate of 20%.

The directors of Strand plc have been debating about the dividend policy of the company. Director A had wanted to pay a reduced dividend this year. He wanted to retain the cash to finance a project he thought would generate good returns for the company. Director B argued against cutting the dividend like this as he did not want the company to upset loyal shareholders. Director C also disagreed with the dividend cut on the grounds that Director A had not provided a convincing argument that this was a project with good prospects. Director D also disagreed with the dividend cut, but his argument was that shareholders might have complicated tax affairs and dramatic changes in dividend levels might make their tax affairs even more complicated.

PRACTICE EXAM QUESTION BANK

Required

(a) Calculate the weighted average cost of capital for Strand plc. You should use the dividend growth model to calculate the cost of equity. **(10 marks)**

(b) Explore the validity of the four directors' opinions concerning the dividend policy of the company. **(10 marks)**

(Total 20 marks)

Question 9 — 36 mins

Timepiece plc is a quoted company that manufactures watches. The company has been operating for 15 years and the watches it manufactures are not expensive for customers to purchase. It sells the watches to watch and jewellery shops, and in the last five years their watches have been very fashionable. The brand is particularly strong amongst customers aged 18-30 years, and the company has built on this through an innovative advertising campaign that emphasises the design appeal for younger people. A strength of the management team is that it is very creative and can apply this creativity both to watch design and to branding and advertising. The watch market is very competitive and competitors are always seeking to take market share. A concern for Timepiece plc is that the watches it designs will cease to be fashionable; further, the directors of Timepiece plc think that they are unlikely to gain much more market share within the 18-30 years age group even if the company is able to ensure new designs continue to have a strong appeal. A further concern of the directors is that the company has had some issues in respect of product reliability.

Timepiece plc is considering acquiring another watch manufacturing company, Diamond Watches. Diamond Watches manufactures more expensive watches that appeal to more wealthy customers who are as concerned about quality as design. Additionally, these customers tend to be in the age range 35-65 years. The company has advanced technical know-how in watch manufacture and this enables it to innovate in its manufacturing processes. This innovation helps ensure manufacturing is carried out very cost efficiently. Diamond Watches sells its watches through more upmarket watch and jewellery shops than Timepiece plc. Customer spending at these shops is less affected by changes in the overall economy as its customers are relatively affluent. The brand name of Diamond Watches is not especially strong and the management team has focused on ensuring the manufacturing processes are of high quality, rather than on marketing.

The directors of Timepiece plc have considered purchasing additional manufacturing facilities and extending their product range to cover segments of the watch market beyond the segment they operate in. However, watch manufacturing requires employing specialist staff and these are in short supply in the market place. Timepiece plc could give intensive training to non-specialist staff but this would require considerable effort by existing managers and would detract from their current roles for a period of time.

Timepiece plc has built up a substantial amount of cash in the company during the last five years due to the success it has enjoyed. The company currently has this cash on deposit, but as interest rates are currently very low the returns on the cash invested are small.

Required

Prepare a report advising the directors of Timepiece plc on reasons why they may wish to acquire Diamond Watches. **(20 marks)**

Question 10 — 36 mins

Mrs Smith and Mr Grace both have extensive experience of running companies. Mrs Smith has significant experience in accounting and finance, and Mr Grace has extensive experience in marketing and selling. They are thinking they will team up and are considering undertaking a management buy-in of Hope plc. Hope plc was set up twenty years ago and is a printing company. Hope plc is not listed on a stock exchange and the shares are owned by three members of the Hope family. None of these three family members take an active role in running the business. It is not known what level of dividends they have received in past years. The printing business is very competitive and in recent years the company has not been as successful as it once was. Two of the family shareholders are keen to sell their stake in the business; however, the third shareholder is not sure whether they wish to sell their stake.

The following information has been provided:

HOPE PLC
SUMMARY OF THE CONSOLIDATED INCOME STATEMENT FOR THE FINANCIAL YEAR ENDED 31 MARCH

	2013 £m	2014 £m	2015 £m
Revenue	5.1	4.9	4.6
Operating profit	1.1	0.9	0.8
Finance costs net of finance income	(0.2)	(0.3)	(0.3)
Profit before taxation	0.9	0.6	0.5
Taxation	(0.2)	(0.1)	(0.1)
Profit for the year	0.7	0.5	0.4

HOPE PLC
EXTRACTS FROM THE STATEMENT OF FINANCIAL POSITION AS AT 31 MARCH 2015

	2015 £m
ASSETS & LIABILITIES	
Non-current assets	
Property, plant & equipment	5.9
Intangible assets	0.3
	6.2
Current assets	
Inventories	0.3
Trade and other receivables	0.5
Cash and short term deposits	0.8
	1.6
Total assets	7.8
Current liabilities	
Unsecured bank loans	(0.5)
Trade and other payables	(0.7)
Current tax liabilities	(0.1)
	(1.3)
Non-current liabilities	
Corporate bonds	(3.5)
Provisions	(0.3)
	(3.8)
Total liabilities	(5.1)
Net assets/(liabilities)	2.7

The property, plant and equipment figure includes property that is showing on the statement of financial position at an amount of £1.7m, but has a current market value of £2.5m. The current market value is high because the area where it is situated has become very attractive to property developers.

Trade debtors and trade payables as at 31 March 2015 amounted to £0.4m and £0.5m respectively.

For the financial year ended 31 March 2015 the cost of sales figure was £2.1m.

Two other listed companies that are competitors of Hope plc in the printing industry have current price earnings (P-E) ratios of 12 and 10 respectively, and they have costs of equity of 8% and 9% respectively.

Required

Mrs Smith and Mr Grace need further information before they decide whether to progress with the management buy-in. Consequently, they have asked you to prepare a report. In the report they require you to:

(1) Calculate the value of Hope plc based on:

    (a) Net assets and
    (b) Earnings,

(2) Evaluate the working capital position of Hope plc, and

(3) Advise on any further information they might find useful for making the decision whether to progress. **(20 marks)**

November 2014 (Adapted)

Question 11   72 mins

Stark plc is a successful and profitable UK company that designs and manufactures electronic products such as televisions and mobile phones. The company is innovative and its products are highly advanced. Consequently, the company has made a number of significant technological breakthroughs in recent years. The company has just developed a new television and is trying to decide whether it should commence manufacturing and selling this new product. The cost of development has amounted to £10m in total. Because of the pace of new product development Stark plc believes that this design of television will be obsolete after three years and, for this reason, its sales forecast of the new television are as follows:

Year	Number of televisions sold
1	60,000
2	120,000
3	10,000

To manufacture the televisions the company would rent a factory in the UK for the three year period at a cost of £400,000 per year. 500 new employees would be recruited for the three year period and each employee would be paid £25,000 per year. The employee pay rate is relatively high as the company needs to employ staff who can learn advanced manufacturing techniques and can be highly productive. Ten managers who are already employed by Stark plc would be seconded to this project for the three years. The ten managers would not be replaced in their current jobs during their 3-year absence. In addition to managing the manufacturing operation, these managers would provide relevant training to all employees. These managers are paid an average of £40,000 per year each.

The material and component costs amount to £255 per television, and energy costs associated with running the factory are estimated to be £55,000 per year. The selling price of the televisions would not be constant and it is envisaged the selling price per television would be £490 in Year 1, £450 in Year 2 and £390 in Year 3. Marketing costs have been estimated at £150,000 for the first year and £90,000 for the second year; these marketing costs would be payable at the start of each year. There are no other selling costs associated with the new product.

Corporation tax is payable 1 year in arrears and at a rate of 20%. If the net cashflow for any year is negative then you should assume that the company has sufficient profits from other projects against which it can offset the negative cashflow.

The company has a cost of capital of 11%.

Required

(a) Prepare calculations to evaluate whether it is worthwhile manufacturing and selling the new television. State any assumptions you have made in your calculations. **(10 marks)**

(b) Advise the directors of Stark plc of any risks associated with this new project. **(10 marks)**

(c) One of the directors of Stark plc has suggested that the company should engage in foreign direct investment (FDI) and set up a subsidiary company in an overseas country. The director has argued that as the cost of labour is cheaper in the overseas country then the televisions should be manufactured by the subsidiary company. However, a concern is that the government of this overseas country may not be happy with Stark plc establishing the subsidiary. You are required to advise the directors of Stark plc on the arguments it could put forward to convince the government that it would be beneficial if Stark plc were to establish a subsidiary in its country. **(10 marks)**

(d) The managing director of Stark plc is also the founder of the company and owner of the majority of the shares. He set up the business with the objective of maximising profit as he believed that this would also maximise his personal wealth. One of his senior managers has suggested that if Stark plc were to also pursue a range of non-financial objectives then these could potentially have a positive effect on profit. You have been asked to write a report setting out what non-financial objectives the company could pursue for all its products and explaining why they might have a positive impact on the profit. **(10 marks)**

(Total 40 marks)

Question 12   36 mins

The directors of a recruitment company, Finance Jobs plc, are looking to expand the business. They have identified another recruitment company, People Ltd, which they may decide to acquire. Finance Jobs plc has all its offices in the City of London and specialises in working with banks and other financial organisations to recruit suitably qualified finance and accounting staff. The directors of Finance Jobs plc have all previously worked in major international banks and are highly entrepreneurial. This prior banking experience has been important as it helps them in understanding what type of staff the banks and other financial organisations will want to recruit, and it has also helped in developing networks of contacts to win new business from these banks and other financial organisations. The employees of Finance Jobs plc work within a demanding environment as the directors expect them to be dynamic in winning new business and to work very hard. In return for this significant commitment employees are very well paid and, if successful, can expect to receive substantial bonuses.

People Ltd, the potential target company, specialises in recruiting staff for charities and other not-for-profit organisations. It operates across the UK and recruits staff into all types of management positions (for example, marketing, human resources, legal, accounting, general management). This company was set up 15 years ago by Mary Storey, who had previously worked for a small charity. Mary had noted that charities were looking to recruit staff with specific skills and from particular backgrounds as they wanted to operate professionally. However, many charities did not have the time or expertise available for recruitment and, therefore, Mary saw an opportunity to establish People Ltd to assist the charities in this process. Mary does not like to charge the charities high fee levels and, because of this, tries to keep the costs of People Ltd as low as possible. Hence, the offices she rents are not of the highest quality and are typically situated outside the main city centre as rents are lower. Similarly, she does not pay her employees particularly high salaries; instead she recruits employees who are motivated to want to help charities rather than by money and she aims to create a very positive and supportive working atmosphere.

The following information has been provided concerning People Ltd:

PEOPLE LTD

SUMMARY OF THE CONSOLIDATED INCOME STATEMENT FOR THE FINANCIAL YEAR ENDED 30 SEPTEMBER 2014

	£
Revenue	560,000
Operating profit	108,000
Finance income	1,000
Finance costs	(4,000)
Profit before taxation	105,000
Taxation	(21,000)
Profit for the year	84,000

EXTRACT OF PEOPLE LTD

SUMMARY OF THE STATEMENT OF FINANCIAL POSITION AS AT 30 SEPTEMBER 2014

	£
ASSETS & LIABILITIES	
Non-current assets	
Office equipment	210,000
Intangible assets	–
	210,000
Current assets	
Trade and other receivables	75,000
Cash and short term deposits	30,000
	105,000
Total assets	315,000
Current liabilities	
Unsecured bank loans	(18,000)
Trade and other payables	(42,000)
Current tax liabilities	(20,000)
	(80,000)
Non-current liabilities	
Bank loans	(34,000)
Provisions	(–)
	(34,000)
Total liabilities	(114,000)
Net assets/(liabilities)	201,000

People Ltd is not listed and Mary owns all the share capital. Mary normally pays herself only a very small dividend as she prefers to retain any profit within the business. In each of the last three years Mary has paid a dividend to herself of £8,000 per year.

People Ltd owns no property as all offices are rented. The office equipment it owns is quite old and, although the office equipment is showing on the statement of financial position at £210,000, the current market value is only £132,000.

Mary often shows leniency to charities in paying their fees. Consequently, within the trade receivables figure there are fees due from three charities which Mary will reduce. In total the fees reduction for each of the three charities will amount to £3,000 per charity.

The P-E ratio of a listed recruitment company, Andover plc, is 12. Andover plc is an international recruitment firm that works in all industry sectors. Andover plc has a cost of equity of 9%.

Required

The directors of Finance Jobs plc have asked you to prepare a report. In the report the directors require you to:

(a) Calculate the value of People Ltd based on: (a) net assets, (b) earnings and (c) dividend yield approaches, and **(8 marks)**

(b) Advise on any likely problems that they may encounter in integrating the acquisition with their business. **(12 marks)**

(Total 20 marks)

Question 13   36 mins

Charlton plc is currently an all equity company with an equilibrium market value of £20m and a cost of equity of 11%. The company's chief executive officer (CEO) is considering repurchasing £7m of equity and replacing it with irredeemable debt. The irredeemable debt has a cost of 6%. Charlton plc's earnings before interest and tax are constant. All profits are paid out as dividends. The corporation tax rate is 25%. The CEO has asked the company's four directors for their views on this proposal to change capital structure.

Required

(a) Using the assumptions of Modigliani and Miller, calculate how the proposed change in capital structure will affect the market value of Charlton plc. **(3 marks)**

(b) Using the assumptions of Modigliani and Miller calculate how the proposed change in capital structure will affect the weighted average cost of capital of Charlton plc. **(5 marks)**

(c) The four directors of Charlton plc are debating whether the proposed change in capital structure is appropriate. They have different opinions and these are as follows:

Director 1: It is good to bring debt into the capital structure as the interest on the debt is tax-deductible.

Director 2: I am concerned that shareholders will be unhappy with this change and it may affect the return they require.

Director 3: I can see it may be good to have some borrowings, but what will happen if we borrow too much?

Director 4: It seems a good idea to introduce some borrowings. Also, if we need further capital in the future then I think that borrowing will be better than issuing equity. My reasoning is that it is more expensive and more difficult to obtain equity funding than debt funding.

Required

Explore the validity of the four directors' opinions concerning the change in capital structure.

(12 marks)

(Total 20 marks)

Question 14   36 mins

Mr James used to be a university lecturer. Five years ago he set up a private college, Total Education plc, which offers university level degrees in Management and Finance. Students have to study for three years to complete their degree. The academic year starts on 1st September each year and ends on 31st August, and they pay fees of £6,000 per academic year. The students pay half of each year's fee on 1st December during the academic year and the remaining half of the fee on 1st March during the academic year. The college is based in London and it does not provide any accommodation for the students. The college has grown in size and the number of students enrolled on the degree courses totalled 600 as at the start of September 2014. Major expenses for the college are staff salaries (both academic and administrative staff), and rental of premises. Mr James had never run his own company before and he is unsure whether the working capital position of the company is a matter for concern.

The following information has been provided about the company:

TOTAL EDUCATION PLC

SUMMARY OF THE CONSOLIDATED STATEMENT OF COMPREHENSIVE INCOME FOR THE YEAR ENDED 30th OCTOBER

	Note	2014 £'000	2013 £'000
Revenue		3,060	2,850
Cost of sales		(340)	(320)
Gross profit		2,720	2,530
Administrative expenses	1	(2,450)	(2,260)
Operating profit		270	270
Finance costs – interest payable		(92)	(90)
Profit before taxation		178	180
Taxation		(40)	(45)
Profit for the year		138	135

Note 1: Administrative expenses

Administrative expenses includes staff costs.

TOTAL EDUCATION PLC

EXTRACTS FROM THE CONSOLIDATED STATEMENT OF FINANCIAL POSITION AS AT 30th OCTOBER

	Note	2014 £'000	2013 £'000
ASSETS & LIABILITIES			
Non-current assets			
Property, plant & equipment		585	547
Current assets			
Inventories		35	38
Trade and other receivables	2	667	543
Cash and short term deposits		45	36
		747	617
Total assets		1,332	1,164

Current liabilities

		2014	2013
Bank loans and overdrafts		(110)	(92)
Trade and other payables	3	(32)	(25)
Current tax liabilities		(40)	(25)
		(182)	(142)

Non-current liabilities

Corporate bonds		(865)	(910)
Other liabilities		–	–
		(865)	(910)
Total liabilities		**(1,047)**	**(1,052)**
Net assets		**285**	**112**

Note 2: Trade and other receivables

	2014	2013
	£'000	£'000
Trade debtors	600	510
Other debtors and prepayments	67	33
	667	543

Note 3: Trade and other payables

	2014	2013
	£'000	£'000
Trade payables	29	23
Other creditors and accruals	3	2
	32	25

Required

Prepare a report for Mr James evaluating the working capital position of Total Education plc. Your report should include any calculations you consider appropriate. **(20 marks)**

May 2014 (Adapted)

Question 15   72 mins

Drywear plc is a UK company that manufactures high quality men's shirts. Currently the shirts are only sold in the UK. The shirts have become very popular due to the unusual pattern designs and the directors think it may be worthwhile setting up a subsidiary to manufacture and sell the shirts in Australia, as this new market could generate additional profits for the company. Therefore, the company is considering a new three-year project in Australia. The directors have no real knowledge of the shirt market in Australia, but have estimated that over the next three years the sales demand for shirts in Australia would be as follows:

Year	Sales demand
1	50,000 shirts
2	60,000 shirts
3	80,000 shirts

The Australian currency is the Australian dollar (AUD). The selling price per shirt would be AUD49. The materials for each shirt would be purchased in the UK at a cost of £15 per shirt. The material cost is payable at the end of each year. The company would rent factory premises at a rental cost of AUD50,000 per year payable at the start of each year.

The management team at the factory would be paid a total of AUD200,000 per year. 30 employees would be hired to manufacture the shirts and the salary cost for each employee would be AUD35,000 per year. Equipment would be purchased for the factory in the UK and at a cost of £40,000. Energy costs are estimated at AUD15,000 for the first year and increasing by 10% per year thereafter.

The company has already carried out some marketing in Australia to increase awareness of the brand. The cost of this amounts to AUD20,000 and the sum is payable now. Further marketing costs of AUD50,000 would be incurred each year should the venture go ahead. Three UK-based managers would visit the company at the start of each year. The cost of each visit is estimated at £10,000.

The current spot rate is AUD1.5606 to the £. It is expected that the exchange rate will change in the future, and it has been estimated that the inflation rate in the UK will be 1% per year and the inflation rate in Australia will be 3% per year.

Tax in Australia would be payable for the business one year in arrears and at a rate of 25%. If the net cashflow for any year is negative then you should assume that zero tax will be paid on this cashflow, and that the negative cashflow will be used to reduce the next available positive cashflow when calculating tax on that positive cashflow.

When evaluating previous business ventures the company has used a discount rate of 10%.

As an alternative to manufacturing the shirts in Australia the company has thought that it might manufacture the shirts in country X. Country X is reasonably close to Australia, and the cost of labour is much lower. The shirts would then be transported to Australia for sale. This country has experienced poor economic growth in the past and the economy remains relatively under-developed. The current government has been in office for only six months, but already many people in the country are unhappy that economic growth is negative and the inflation rate is high. Additionally, many people believe that senior government officials have been awarding government contracts to friends. Government borrowings are high and the credit rating of government debt is poor. The financial services sector is small relative to the size of the economy and the exchange rate volatile. There are some overseas companies who have established subsidiaries in the country, but they are concerned that the government might impose restrictions on remittances of profit back to their home countries.

Required

(a) Prepare calculations to evaluate whether it is worthwhile undertaking the new venture in Australia. State any assumptions you have made in your calculations. **(16 marks)**

(b) Advise the directors of any risks associated with this new venture to manufacture and sell the shirts in Australia. **(12 marks)**

(c) Advise the directors on the potential level of political risk in respect of country X. **(12 marks)**

(Total 40 marks)

Question 16   36 mins

The Furniture People plc is a listed company that manufactures furniture for sale to department stores in the UK. The company has been in existence for fifty years and was initially set up by the Smith family. The Smith family still own a proportion of the shares, although there are no longer any family members on the board of directors.

The profit has been declining over the last five years as it has been a very difficult economic environment. In the most recent year the profit (before interest and taxation) was £1.9m; whereas five years ago the profit (before interest and taxation) was £2.5m. It is difficult to predict whether or not the economic environment will decline further in the near future.

Currently, the furniture the company manufactures is inexpensive for customers to purchase and this is because it is not of the highest quality. The directors think that they can stop the decline in profits by adding a new range of furniture that would be of very high quality. This new range would sell at much higher prices and would appeal to customers who have high earnings. The directors believe the spending patterns of these customers are less likely to be affected when the economic environment is difficult.

To manufacture and market this new range of furniture the company needs to raise extra capital of £10m. £7m of this capital would be used to purchase a new factory, and the remainder would be used to fund additional working capital requirements and to market the new range of furniture. The directors estimate this will generate additional profit (before interest and before taxation) of £0.85m per year. If this new range of furniture is successful then the directors will look to expand the company into other new areas.

The current capital structure of the company comprises both debt and equity. The company has long-term debt of £20m which is secured against the land and buildings it owns. The interest rate on this debt is fixed at 8% per annum and the principal is due for repayment in twelve years. There are 15m shares in issue with a market value of £1.75 per share. The average debt:equity ratio of similar companies is 95%.

The directors are considering raising the extra capital of £10m through secured debt. This debt would be at a floating rate of interest. In recent years interest rates have been relatively stable and the directors seem unconcerned that the debt is not at a fixed rate. Currently, the interest rate applicable to floating rate debt for this company would be 7.5% per annum. The company pays corporation tax at a rate of 20%.

Required

The directors of the company are aware that they need to consider the impact that raising additional debt may have upon the company's capital structure. They have asked you to prepare a report evaluating the proposed financing choice. In preparing the report you should:

(1) Include any calculations that you consider appropriate,
(2) Advise of any further information that would be helpful, and
(3) Advise of any assumptions you have made. **(20 marks)**

Question 17   36 mins

Heston plc is a UK company that manufactures mobile phone accessories. It needs to purchase materials from the USA. These materials are from a single supplier and the total cost is $225,000. The payment date has been agreed as 1 August 2014.

The company wishes to hedge the exchange rate risk using currency futures contracts. The spot rate is 1.5272 – 1.5298 $/£. Futures contracts are available today as follows:

GBP/USD futures:

Settlement date	Price
June	1.5217
September	1.5204

The contract size for these futures is £62,500 and the tick size $0.0001.

The directors of Heston plc are also considering diversifying their operations by undertaking a new project. This project would involve manufacturing clothing. The expected returns from the project would depend upon the state of the economy and have been estimated as follows:

State of the economy	Probability	Expected return from the project
Weak	0.1	-6%
Satisfactory	0.7	+10%
Strong	0.2	+20%

The directors have estimated that the overall expected return from the company excluding the project is 9% and that the standard deviation of these returns is 3%. If the project were to be taken on then it would represent 40% of the total company size. The correlation co-efficient of the returns from the company excluding the project and the project has been estimated to be -0.4.

Required

(a) Prepare calculations that evaluate the outcome of the hedge for Heston plc assuming that on 1 August 2014 the spot rate is 1.5532 – 1.5569 and the price for September futures contracts is 1.5514. **(8 marks)**

(b) Prepare calculations to evaluate whether it is worthwhile Heston plc accepting the project diversifying its operations and advise the directors whether they should accept the project.
(12 marks)

(Total 20 marks)

Question 18   36 mins

Mr Sykes is considering purchasing the entire share capital of Fulford plc. Fulford plc has been in existence for fifteen years and operates five small supermarkets. The standard of customer service in each supermarket is very high and this has resulted in a very loyal customer base. Staff satisfaction is good and, consequently, the staff turnover rate is relatively low. Fulford plc differentiates itself from other supermarkets by offering unusual food products in addition to a standard range of food products.

The following financial information has been provided:

FULFORD PLC

SUMMARY OF THE CONSOLIDATED STATEMENT OF COMPREHENSIVE INCOME FOR THE FINANCIAL YEAR ENDED 31 MARCH 2014

		£'000
Revenue		8,765
Cost of sales		(6,562)
Gross profit		2,203
Administrative & distribution costs		(974)
Operating profit		1,229
Finance costs – interest payable		(315)
Profit before taxation		914
Taxation		(204)
Profit for the year	Note 1	710

FULFORD PLC

EXTRACTS FROM THE STATEMENT OF FINANCIAL POSITION AS AT 31 MARCH 2014

		£'000
ASSETS & LIABILITIES		
Non-current assets		
Property, plant & equipment	Note 2	4,332
Intangible assets		–
		4,332
Current assets		
Inventories	Note 3	176
Trade and other receivables	Note 4	742
Cash and short-term deposits		1,722
		2,640
Total assets		6,972
Current liabilities		
Unsecured bank loans		(603)
Trade and other payables	Note 5	(1,548)
Current tax liabilities		(256)
		(2,407)
Non-current liabilities		
Corporate bonds		(1,827)
Provisions		(94)
		(1,921)
Total liabilities		(4,328)
Net assets/(liabilities)		2,644

Note 1

Over the last five years the profit for the year has been increasing at an average rate of 6% per year.

Note 2

Property, plant and equipment figure includes property that is showing on the statement of financial position at £3,722,000. However, this property has a current market value of £3,965,000.

Note 3

Within inventories there is some obsolete stock totalling £23,000.

Note 4

There are no trade receivables.

Note 5

Trade payables amount to £660,000.

Fulford plc is not listed on a stock exchange. Two listed companies that operate the same type of business as Fulford plc have current price-earnings (P-E) ratios of 12 and 15 respectively.

Required

Mr Sykes has asked you to prepare a report. In the report Mr Sykes requires you to: (1) prepare calculations valuing Fulford plc on two different bases, (2) advise on any issues that he should be aware of in respect of the valuations, and (3) evaluate the working capital position of Fulford plc. Within the report you should also state any assumptions you have made in respect of any calculations. **(20 marks)**

November 2013 (Adapted)

Question 19   72 mins

Pink Bottle is a drinks producer based in Malaysia. A large supermarket company, also based in Malaysia, has asked Pink Bottle to manufacture a new drink that will be sold exclusively by the supermarket.

Pink Bottle developed the new drink during the last year. To do this it had to employ an extra member of staff to assist the existing product development team. This extra member of staff was employed on a one year contract and paid a salary of MYR90,000.

The new drink is made from two ingredients as follows:

Ingredient	Quantity of ingredient needed to make one bottle of product	Cost of ingredient
F	2 litres	This ingredient has to be imported from the United Kingdom at a cost of £0.10 per litre
G	10 grams	This ingredient can be bought in Malaysia at a cost of MYR0.05 per gram

Pink Bottle supplies all its drinks in a very distinctive bottle. The cost of each bottle is MYR0.35

The supermarket has provided Pink Bottle with an initial three-year contract to supply the following number of bottles of the new drink each year:

Year	Number of bottles
1	5,000,000
2	6,000,000
3	8,000,000

The supermarket will pay MYR2.50 per bottle to Pink Bottle.

After Year 3 the supermarket will review how the product is selling and may then decide to offer an extension to the contract. However, it can also decide not to renew the contract at this point.

To fulfil the contract Pink Bottle would need to rent additional factory space. The first year's rent would be MYR200,000 and this would then increase by 5% per year. Pink Bottle would also have to purchase machinery for the factory at a cost of MYR1,500,000. It is estimated this machinery could be sold at the end of the three years for MYR600,000.

Additional staff would need to be employed by Pink Bottle. Forty staff would be employed to manufacture the new drink and they would each be paid a salary of MYR50,000 per year. Three managers would also need to be employed and they would each be paid a salary of MYR120,000 per year.

It has been estimated that the following costs would also be incurred:

Cost	Note
Energy	Total energy costs in Year 1 are MYR60,000. These energy costs are expected to increase by 8% per year.
Packaging	The bottles are packed in boxes of 10 bottles. Each box costs MYR1.50.
Transport	Transport costs in Year 1 are MYR80,000. In Years 2 and 3 these transport costs are expected to increase in proportion with the number of bottles sold in these Years.

Corporation tax will be payable at a rate of 25%. You should assume that this tax is paid one year in arrears based upon the net cashflow for each year. If the net cashflow for any year is negative then you should assume that zero tax will be paid on this cashflow, and that the negative cashflow can be used to reduce the next available positive cashflow when calculating corporation tax on that positive cashflow.

The current exchange rate is MYR1 = £0.2056. It has been estimated that the rate of inflation in Malaysia will be 1.5% per year for the foreseeable future and the rate of inflation in the UK is expected to be 3.5% per year for the foreseeable future.

Pink Bottle has a cost of capital of 11%.

Required

(a) Prepare calculations to evaluate whether it is worthwhile for Pink Bottle to enter into the contract and on the basis of these calculations advise the directors whether the contract should be entered into. State any assumptions you have made in your calculations. **(20 marks)**

(b) Advise the directors of any risks that may be associated with the calculation evaluating whether the contract is worthwhile. **(10 marks)**

(c) In financial management it is usually assumed that the objective of the firm is to maximise shareholder wealth. The four directors of the Pink Bottle company have been discussing the contract and they all think the contract should be accepted. The different reasons they provide for accepting the contract are as follows:

Director A: 'I think we should take on the contract because it will increase our sales.'

Director B: 'The supermarket contract would be good for our reputation.'

Director C: 'If we take on the supermarket contract we can provide employment to new staff for at least the next three years. It is good to be able to provide this employment.'

Director D: 'I think that we should accept the contract. If we do not then the supermarket company may offer it to a competitor.'

Required

Explore whether the reasons the four directors provide for accepting the contract might have any connection to the assumed objective of maximisation of shareholder wealth. **(10 marks)**

(Total 40 marks)

Question 20   36 mins

Green plc is a company that manufactures furniture and is based in the UK. The company has just won an order to supply a significant quantity of furniture to a customer based in the USA. The customer requires invoicing in US dollars and the order value is $500,000. The customer will pay for the furniture in three months' time in February 2014. Green plc is unsure whether to hedge the exchange rate risk using currency options or a forward exchange contract.

The finance director of Green plc has ascertained that currency options are available on an exchange in the USA. The options contracts have a standard size of £31,250 and the premiums payable (in cents per pound) are set out below for a range of exercise prices:

Exercise price	Calls			Puts		
	December	January	February	December	January	February
1.6000	4.65	4.83	5.02	0.97	1.24	1.56
1.6100	4.32	4.43	4.75	1.35	1.67	1.85

	Calls			Puts		
Exercise price	December	January	February	December	January	February
1.6200	3.96	4.17	4.44	1.65	1.92	2.04
1.6300	3.02	3.52	3.79	1.99	2.36	2.78

Further information provided is:

Spot rate   1.6154 – 1.6179

3 month forward rate   1.6302 – 1.6315

The finance director has no knowledge of how to hedge exchange rate risk and has no time to learn about the different hedging methods. His view is that the company should completely remove the risk. Further, the finance director does not think the company will receive any more overseas orders and he wants to use a hedging method that is inexpensive.

Required

(a) Calculate the outcome for the company if the spot rate in February 2014 is $1.6857 – $1.6864 and the company had chosen to hedge the exchange rate risk using currency options with an exercise price $1.6200. **(10 marks)**

(b) Calculate the outcome for the company if the spot rate in February 2014 is $1.6857 – $1.6864 and the company had chosen to hedge the exchange rate risk using a forward exchange contract. **(2 marks)**

(c) Advise the finance director of Green plc whether he should hedge the exchange rate risk using currency options or a forward exchange contract. **(8 marks)**

(Total 20 marks)

Question 21   36 mins

Treet plc is a retailer selling clothing through its own shops, catalogues and online. Customers purchasing clothing through catalogues or online set up an account and this allows them an interest-free period of credit of 30 days. If the customer does not pay the account in full at the end of the interest-free period, interest is charged on the account and minimum monthly payments must be made. Each account has a credit limit set dependent on the financial position of the customer and their credit history.

A much wider range of clothing is offered for sale through catalogue and online sales compared to the stores. There has been a strategy of focusing upon increasing the sales of clothing through catalogue and online sales in the last year. As a part of this strategy the company decided to close 60 stores during September 2012. This left the company with 135 stores.

The company has to be able to respond to changing trends and has to anticipate in advance what clothing will be fashionable for the Spring-Summer selling period and for the Autumn-Winter selling period. This means that it has to work closely with suppliers to ensure that products are well designed and of good quality. It also has to ensure that suppliers are able to deliver products on time.

This sector is very competitive and a number of senior accounting staff left the company in October and November 2012 to work for competitors. At the same time a number of staff responsible for management of customers' accounts also left. It has taken some time to replace these staff. The remaining accounting and customer accounts staff have had to manage as best they can until replacements were eventually recruited.

The following information has been provided about the company:

TREET PLC

SUMMARY OF THE CONSOLIDATED STATEMENT OF COMPREHENSIVE INCOME FOR THE YEAR ENDED 30 SEPTEMBER

	Note	2013 £m	2012 £m
Revenue	1	1,065	1,201
Cost of sales		(798)	(889)
Gross profit	2	267	312
Distribution costs		(108)	(121)
Administrative expenses		(75)	(83)
Operating profit		84	108
Finance costs – interest payable		(15)	(18)
Profit before taxation		69	90
Taxation		(18)	(21)
Profit for the year		51	69

TREET PLC

EXTRACTS FROM THE CONSOLIDATED STATEMENT OF FINANCIAL POSITION AS AT 30 SEPTEMBER

	Note	2013 £m	2012 £m
ASSETS & LIABILITIES			
Non-current assets			
Property, plant & equipment		297	279
Intangible assets		23	23
		320	302
Current assets			
Inventories		138	82
Trade and other receivables	3	212	184
Cash and short term deposits		23	54
		373	320
Total assets		693	622
Current liabilities			
Bank loans and overdrafts		(7)	(4)
Trade and other payables	4	(124)	(86)
Other financial liabilities		(9)	(12)
Current tax liabilities		(32)	(21)
		(172)	(123)
Non-current liabilities			
Corporate bonds		(164)	(152)
Provisions		(8)	(6)
Other liabilities		(54)	(97)
		(226)	(255)
Total liabilities		(398)	(378)
Net assets		295	244

Note 1: Revenue

	2013 £m	2012 £m
Retail revenue from stores	455	605
Catalogue and online revenue	610	596
	1,065	1,201

Note 2: Gross profit

	2013 £m	2012 £m
Retail gross profit from stores	79	127
Catalogue and online gross profit	188	185
	267	312

Note 3: Trade and other receivables

	2013 £m	2012 £m
Trade and customer debtors	221	163
Less: allowance for doubtful debts	(36)	(15)
	185	148
Other debtors and prepayments	27	36
	212	184

Ageing of trade and customer debtors

	2013 £m	2012 £m
Current	43	33
0-30 days	47	55
30-60 days	43	23
60-90 days	14	8
90-120 days	13	9
Over 120 days	25	20
	185	148

Note 4: Trade and other payables

	2013 £m	2012 £m
Trade payables	89	47
Other creditors and accruals	35	39
	124	86

Required

Prepare a report for the directors of Treet plc evaluating the working capital position of the company. Your report should include any calculations you consider appropriate. **(20 marks)**

Question 22   36 mins

Jane Smith and Clare Brown are the directors of a company they set up ten years ago. In the first four years of trading the company made losses, although subsequently it has made profits. The company is in the travel industry. It arranges hotel accommodation and flights for customers who pay an inclusive price for their holiday. The company has to estimate the demand for the holidays in advance as it has to pre-book hotel rooms and flights. The company operates from rented premises in London and has a turnover of £10m. Jane Smith had previous experience working in the travel industry and wanted to set up her own company as she is highly entrepreneurial and felt that she could become wealthy if she had her own business. Clare Brown was a friend who had prior accounting experience, but she is much more cautious than Jane and less entrepreneurial.

The company currently operates in the sector of the market selling holidays to families. This sector of the market is very competitive and families are looking for value for money.

Currently, the company is financed solely by equity. This equity is owned by the two directors and each owns 50% of the shares. The directors are considering whether it may be appropriate to raise further finance as they think that in the near future they may expand the company and commence operating in the luxury travel sector for wealthy customers.

The company could potentially access further equity via the capital markets, but Jane Smith believes that they should introduce long-term borrowings into the company as the interest is tax deductible. Clare Brown thinks that introducing long-term debt into the company is risky and she is worried about the consequences of not being able to pay interest on the borrowings.

Required

You are required to prepare a report advising the directors on whether they should introduce long-term debt into the capital structure of the company. The report should also discuss any further information that would be helpful in advising the directors. **(20 marks)**

Practice Exam answer bank

May 2018 (Adapted)

Question 1

This question tests candidates' understanding of the financing decisions of a firm and determination of capital requirements Factors influencing the choice of capital structures (LO1)

- Cost: cost of different sources of finance will vary over time due to changes in interest rates.
- Duration: Principle of maturity matching ie asset and liability maturities should be matched and finance should be raised according to the maturity of the asset(s) to be purchased.
- Borrowing capacity: the firm's ability to borrow additional loan.
- Risk: How uncertain is the environment in which the business operates?
- Flexibility: How flexible is the source of finance? Short-term loans may be flexible. It may be difficult to repay long-term loans before maturity period.

Firm Size: It is thus argued that large firms tend to be well diversified and hence are less likely to go bankrupt. Therefore, lower expected bankruptcy costs enable large firms to take on more debts. Simply large companies may have the assets to back debt capital whereas small company may not.

The nature of the company's industry and assets: If the company's value is largely in tangible assets, more borrowing is sustainable than if the same value is dependent upon intangibles. Industry gearing ratios are useful to see the amount of borrowing which other similar companies have been able to sustain. For example, retailers such as supermarkets may borrow less compared to manufacturing/ engineering firms and utility firms.

- Ownership and control: If owners fear loss of control they may prefer debt / borrowing to new issuance of equity as this dilutes existing shareholders' control. Therefore the attitude of the owners to risk, that is, If owners are risk averse, they will prefer less risk to more risk for a particular expected rate of return.
- The attitude of the management to risk: Although managers are employed to operate the business on behalf of the owners and should serve the owners' best interests, they may object to high level of gearing if they feel that this places their income and job security at risk.
- Tax benefits accruing to the company in question as a result of borrowing.
- Culture: The origins and cultures of the owners. For example, entrepreneurs from India, Mediterranean Europe tend to borrow more compared to their counterparts in Britain and sub-Saharan Africa.
- Firm Growth opportunities. Rate of growth in firm sales or assets.
- Level of corporate profits. Companies with high levels of profits may be able to borrow more compared with companies with low profits.

Mechanism / Techniques for deciding capital structure

Main techniques include:

- Examine average borrowing ratios of companies in similar lines of business
- Financial planning (detailed examination of the company's future cash flow expectation (including those associated with the borrowing alternatives under consideration) so as to decide upon the best financing method

Additional areas where credit might be given, note this is not an exhaustive list:
- Industry Growth/Opportunities
- Reputation of senior managers/Executive management
- Collateral security availability
- Earnings volatility. The variability of corporate earnings over time.
- Financial Restructuring

Question 2

This question tests candidates' ability on company valuation, determinants and comparison of valuation methods (LO3); To calculate the cost of capital using the Capital Asset Pricing Model (LO2)

Report:

To: Blackpool plc
Subject: Valuation of Golden Tulip Ltd.
From: Financial Advisor
Date

(a) (i) **Net assets liquidation method**

$$\text{Price per share} = \frac{\text{Total assets at net realisable values} - \text{total liabilities}}{\text{No of ordinary shares}}$$

$$\text{Price per share} = \frac{(485 + 40 + 125 + 135 + 140) - (266 + 180)}{100}$$

479/100 = £4.79
Total market value: £479 million

(ii) **Free cash flow basis**

$$\frac{\text{Discounted free cash flows} - \text{long-term liabilities}}{\text{No of ordinary shares}}$$

$$\frac{693.206 - 180.0}{100.0}$$

Price per share = **513.206**/100.0 = £5.13
Total market value of the company = **£513.206 million**

Cost of capital using CAPM

Risk free rate of return = 7%
Market Return = 11%
Beta = 1.25
Using the CAPM: $r_E = R_F + (R_M - R_F)\beta$
12% = 7 + (11 − 7)1.25

Working:

Year	Cash flows	Disc rate (12%)	Disc cash flows
2018	97.0	0.893	86.621
2019	115.0	0.797	91.655
2020-2027	130.0	3.961	514.930
			693.206

P/E Ratio

Market value per share (Po) = P/E × earning per share

EPS = Profit before Tax / Number of ord. Shares

215.0 / 100.0 = 2.15

(iii) Price per share: 2.15 × 10.0 = 21.5
Total market value of the company = **£2,150,000**

Merger may fail for a number of reasons including:

(i) **Human Resource Issues:**

- Poor consultation/communication with employees and their representatives
- The nature of the combination process - such as the secrecy that shrouds negotiations
- It is important to raise people's awareness of and capacities to respond to the normal and to-be-expected stresses and strains of living through a combination

(ii) **Over-optimisation**

- Acquirers often pay too much for their targets as a result of flawed evaluation process that overestimates the likely benefits
- Managers are over-optimistic about market economics, the competitive position and the operating synergies available

(iii) **Failure of integration management**

- Improper planning and execution of the integration process
- Problem of following the prepared integration slavishly

(iv) **Misguided strategy**

- The selection of a suitable organisational bedfellow is a major financial decision. Selection decisions are generally driven by financial and strategic considerations
- Often many acquirers select poor targets
- Strategic plan turned out to be value destroying rather than value creating

(v) **Cultural issues**

- Shared beliefs and values that govern societies. It focuses on the complex interaction between the existing type of premarital culture of the partners and the terms and interpretation of the type of marriage contract the parties believed they had entered.
- Establishing the desired relationship between the two companies depends on the cultures of two organisations.
- Many organisational alliances fail to meet expectations because the cultures of the partners are incompatible.
- The degree of congruence between the acquirer and the acquired organisations in respect of cultures may either facilitate or hinder the implementation of the merger.

Additional areas where credit might be given, note this is not an exhaustive list:

- **Government policies/legislation**

Question 3

(i) This question tests candidates' understanding of alternative sources of finance for international investments (LO4).

(ii) Discuss the factors/risks faced by multinational enterprises in the international business environment (LO4).

(a) Methods to pay for foreign investments

- Export domestic capital: Use the firm's own internal funds to finance investment overseas.
- Borrow in foreign country to reduce foreign exchange risk. This may include bond issues and long-term loans.
- Engage swaps deal: This may include equity and/or interest rates swaps.

Factor which influence the choice

- Cost: Borrow where interest rates are lowest.
- Foreign Exchange Risk consideration.

(b) **Risk associated with foreign investments**

- Devaluation Risk
- Inflation rate of the host country
- Political / country risk: assessing economic opportunity against political odds, tax regime, economic analysis, debt ratio and domestic borrowing levels. Political Risk of the host country: nationalisation and the chance that political climate may deteriorate.
- Exchange risk such as operating and translation risks. This is due to the fluctuations or daily currency movement.
- Restrictions on remittance of funds.

Dealing with the risk

Matching

- This technique can be used to reduce the amount of translation or transaction risk faced by a company. To mitigate transaction risk, a company investing in a foreign market should borrow funds denominated in the currency of the country in which it is investing to match its income generation in that country.

Forward market hedge

- Foreign exchange contracts that enable companies to fix in advance future exchange rates on an agreed quantity of foreign currency, for delivery or remittances to pay dividend/interests on an agreed date.

Swaps

- A swap is an agreement between two parties (ie, counterparties), that exchange sets of cash flows over a period of time in future. Shanghai Electronics can enter into swap agreement with a swap bank to provide the foreign capital needed for the investment.

Futures

- Futures hedge: Enter Futures market to hedge against payables and receivables through purchase and sale of futures contracts.

Currency option hedge

- Options give the holder the right to buy or sell a foreign currency at a set price on or before a specified date to hedge against payables and receivables.

Additional areas where credit might be given, note this is not an exhaustive list:

Risk Associated with foreign investment

- Culture of the host country: language, corruption & rule of law/Contract enforcement

Managing Risk

- Money market hedge: involves taking a money market position to cover future payables and receivables
- Leading and lagging: pay before the currency appreciates or delay payment if expect foreign currency to appreciate
- Exported capital using internal funds or equity issues in the home country to reduce devaluation risk

November 2017 (Adapted)

Question 4

This question tests the candidates' ability to:

(i) To calculate the cost of capital using the Weighted Average Cost of Capital (LO1) and Net Present Value (LO2).

(ii) Discuss the factors/risks faced by multinational enterprises in the international business environment (LO4).

(iii) This question tests the candidates' understanding in respect of risk management strategies and the differences between financial futures and options (LO4).

(a) **WACC**

Ordinary share capital	$25 \times 10.0 = 2.50$
Preference share capital	$15 \times 9.40 = 1.41$
Debenture stock	$15 \times 10.0 = 1.50$
Retained profit	$45 \times 8.0 = 3.60$
WACC	9.01%

(b) **New Haven Devices**

	0	2018	2019	2020
	£	£	£	£
Licence fee	(100,000)			
Sales		320,000	470,000	540,000
Manufacturing costs		(160,000)	(240,000)	(270,000)
Marketing costs		(100,000)	(120,000)	(130,000)
Net profit +		60,000	110,000	140,000
Royalty		(12,800)	(21,150)	(24,300)
Inventory		(40,000)	(5,000)	–
Net cash flows	(100,000)	7,200	83,850	115,700
Discount Factor (9%)	1.000	0.977	0.842	0.772
Present values	(100,000)	7,034	70,601.7	89,320.40

NPV = 66,956.1

Workings

(1) *Calculation: Royalty calculations*

4% of 320,000 = 12,800
4.5% of 470,000 = 21,150
4.5% of 540,000 = 24,300

(2) *Inventory requirements*

Additional production in year 1 to meet year 2 sales level is equivalent to 2 months (1/6) of year 2 manufacturing costs of 240,000, ie extra 40,000 of cash flows.

Year 2 – 1/6 of 270,000 = 45,000. However, 40,000 of that requirement will already be satisfied in year 1 and hence, only the extra 5,000 represents the cash outflow in year 2.

In year 3, the assumption is that inventory is reduced to zero.

Hashimoto Ltd

	0 £	2018 £	Years 2019 £	2020 £
Workshop	(75,000)			
Sales		270,000	625,500	1,008,000
Operating costs		(25,000)	(25,000)	(25,000)
Purchases		(225,000)	(360,000)	(630,000)
Sundry expenses		(70,000)	(122,000)	(189,000)
Net cash flows	(75,000)	(50,000)	118,500	164,000
Discount Factor (9%)	1.000	0.917	0.842	0.772
PV	(75,000)	(48,850)	99,777	126,608

NPV = 102,535

Workings

(1) Sales calculations

400 × 675 = 270,000
900 × 695 = 625,500
720 of 1,400 = 1,008,000

(2) Purchases calculations

500 × 450 = 225,000 (year 1)
800 × 450 = 360,000 (year 2 -100 excess from year 1)
1,400 × 450 = 630,000 (year 3)

Summary

On the basis of the foregoing assessment and given that there is no shortage of investment funds, project 2 is preferred to project 1 since it generates a higher NPV for the company.

(c) **Foreign risk exposure**

Types of foreign exchange risks

Transaction exposure

(1) Gains or losses may result from the settlement of transactions whose payment terms are stated in a foreign currency. Transaction exposure refers to the potential change in the value of outstanding obligations due to changes in the exchange rate between the inception of a contract and the settlement of the contract.

Economic Exposure

(2) Also called operating exposure, competitive exposure, or revenue exposure, measures the impact of an exchange rate change on the net present value of expected future cash flows from a foreign investment project.

Translation exposure (accounting exposure)

(3) Measures the effect of an exchange rate change on published financial statements of a firm. The accounting rules in many countries require the home country of the company to prepare consolidated financial statements.

Here, companies translate financial statement items from a foreign currency into their home country in order to prepare consolidated financial statements or compare financial results

Internal and external hedging techniques

Netting

This involves associated companies which trade with each other setting off inter-company debts. This helps to reduce transaction risk.

Matching

This technique can be used to reduce the amount of translation or transaction risk faced by a company. To mitigate transaction risk, a company investing in a foreign market should borrow funds denominated in the currency of the country in which it is investing to match its income generation in that country.

Forward market hedge

Foreign exchange contracts that enable companies to fix in advance future exchange rates on an agreed quantity of foreign currency, for delivery or purchase on an agreed date.

Swaps

A swap is an agreement between two parties (ie counterparties), that exchange sets of cash flows over a period of time in future. Lincoln can enter into swap agreement with a swap bank to provide the foreign capital needed for the investment.

Good answers should point out that companies can easily hedge translation and transaction exposures, because these risks are based on projected foreign currency cash flows. However, it is difficult for companies to hedge economic exposure because the scope of economic exposure is broad. As a result, finance managers should assess economic exposure comprehensively. Simply put, finance managers should be aware that techniques such as forward market, money market, options, lead and lag etc are not enough for hedging economic exposure.

Strategies such as production, marketing and financing diversification are more effective means for hedging economic exposure. These strategies should be discussed in full.

> Additional areas where credit might be given, note this is not an exhaustive list:
> - **Futures hedge:** enter futures market to hedge against payables and receivables through purchase and sale of futures contracts.
> - **Money market hedge:** involves taking a money market position to cover a future payables and receivables.
> - **Currency option hedge:** gives the holder the right to buy or sell a foreign currency at a set price on or before a specified date to hedge against payables and receivables.
> - **Leading and lagging:** pay before the currency appreciates or delay payment if expect foreign currency to appreciate.

Question 5

This question tests candidates' ability on company valuation, determinants and comparison of valuation methods (LO3).

Report:

To: Fast Lane Ltd
Subject: Valuation of Executive Car Maintenance Ltd
From: AIA student
Date: 1 July 20X7

(a) (i) **Net assets liquidation method**

$$\text{Price per share} = \frac{\text{Total assets at net realisable values} - \text{total liabilities at market values}}{\text{No of ordinary shares}}$$

$$\text{Price per share} = \frac{(265 + 25 + 57 + 120 + 43.2 + 271.6) - (346.2 + 77.5)}{180.9}$$

358.1/180.9 = **£1.979**

Total market value: £358.1 million

(ii) **Free cash flow basis**

$$\frac{\text{Discounted free cash flows} - \text{long-term liabilities}}{\text{No of ordinary shares}}$$

$$\frac{537.578 - 77.5}{180.9}$$

Price per share = **460.078**/180.9 = **£2.54**

Total market value of the company = **£460.078 million**

Working:

Year	Cash flows	Disc rate (10%)	Disc cash flows
1	67.0	0.909	60.903
2	70.0	0.826	57.82
3-10	95.0	4.409	418.855
			537.578

P/E Ratio

Market value per share (P_0) = P/E × earning per share
EPS = Profit after tax/number of ord. shares
83.4/180.9 = 46.1 Pence

(iii) **Price/earning ratio = market price/EPS**

5.80/46.1 = 12.58

Price per share: 46.1 × 12.58 = 5.799
Total market value of the company = **£1,049.22 million**

(iv) **Dividend yield basis = gross dividend per share/market value per share**

Div. per share = 17.2/180.9 = 0.0951

Dividend yield = dividend per share/market price
= 9.51/5.80 = 1.64 or 1.6395

Market value = $\dfrac{9.51(100/80)}{1.6395}$

= £7.25

Total market value of the company = **£1,311,525 million**

(b)
- Liquidation method is more likely to reflect a conservative value. This is because it fails to take account of the business as a going concern. Normally, the going concern value of a business will be higher than the sum of the individual values of the assets when sold piecemeal, because of the benefits of combining the assets. Net realisable values represent a lower limit of the current market value of asset held. Using net realisable values can pose a number of practical problems. For example, if the asset is unique, such as a custom-built piece of equipment, it may be particularly hard to obtain a reliable value. Realisable values can differ according to the circumstances of the sale.

- Dividend yield ratio relates the cash return from dividends to the current market value per share. Dividends represent only part of the earnings stream of a business, and to value shares on this basis may be misleading. The valuation obtained will be largely a function of the dividend policy adopted (which is at management's discretion) rather than the earnings generated. Lastly, the share value of unlisted company is not known and hence this ratio cannot be applied.

- P/E ratio method relates the current share price to the current earnings of the business. It is commonly used to assess the owners' appraisal of share value. The P/E ratio reflects the market's view of the likely future growth in earnings. In other words, it measures the amount that investors are willing to pay for each dollar of a firm's earnings. The higher the P/E ratio, the more highly regarded are the future growth prospects. However, this method is a view as mechanical exercise. Moreover, unlisted companies cannot apply this method to value shares. An unlisted company can use the P/E of similar business with similar risk and growth characteristics but there may be differences in accounting policies.

- Free cash flow method involves using cash flows to be generated by a business over time. However, in practice, there are problems associated with how the figures in cash flows are estimated. The discretionary policies of management concerning new investment will have a significant influence on the free cash flows figure calculated.

(c)
- It takes into account the net benefits flowing from the investment, the time value for money and the level of return required by investors. However, price per share using this method appears lower than the current market price and the share prices given by P/E and dividend yield method. It is better that the highest price (£7.05) given by dividend yield method is used.

Additional areas where credit might be given, note this is not an exhaustive list:
- **Calculation of EPS figure to be used may be distorted by the accounting policy adopted by the firm to arrive at profit.**
- **Candidates who settle for the free cash flow figure should be marked correctly.**

PRACTICE EXAM ANSWER BANK

Question 6

This question tests candidates' ability to: (i) calculate and assess the implications of liquidity position of a firm and (ii) Evaluate the suitable sources of finance for effective working capital management (LO5).

(a) **Liquidity position**

Current ratio = Current asset/Current liabilities
306,000/285, 000 = 1.07:1

Acid test ratio = Trade receivables/current liabilities
163,000/285,000 = 0.57:1

The liquidity position of the business appears low. The current ratio is about 1:1 whereas acid test ratio is around 0.6. This suggests that the business is insufficiently liquid to meet its short-term obligations. The above also indicates why the company has overdraft of £140,000.

(b) **Average Stock turnover period:** $\frac{\text{Opening stock } + \text{ Closing stock}/2}{\text{Cost of sales}}$

$$\frac{225 + 243}{423}$$

= 0.553191489 × 360 days   = 199.0

Add: Average settlement period for receivables

$\frac{\text{Trade receivables} \times 360}{\text{Credit sales}}$

$\frac{163 \times 360}{552}$

0.2952289855 × 360   = 106.3
                                                                                          305.3

Less: Average settlement period for creditors:

$\frac{\text{Trade payables} \times 360}{\text{Credit purchases}}$

$\frac{145 \times 360}{441}$

0.328798185 × 360   = 118.3

Operating credit cycle   187

The company can reduce the operating cash cycle in a number of ways. The average stockholding period seems quite long. At present average stocks held represent almost six and a half months' sales. This may be reduced by reducing the level of stocks held.

Similarly, the average settlement period for debtors seems long at more than three months' sales. This may be reduced by imposing tight credit control, offering discounts, charging interests on overdue accounts, and so on. However, any policy decisions concerning stocks and debtors must take account of current trading conditions.

The operating cash cycle could also be reduced by extending the period of credit taken to pay suppliers.

(c) **Benefits**
- Flexibility: Overdraft is a flexibility form of borrowing and size can be increased or decreased according to the financing requirements of the business.
- Easy to arrange as little or no formality is required. It can be agreed by a telephone call.
- Interest rates may vary according to the creditworthiness of the customer.

Drawbacks
- Re-payable on demand as overdrafts are self-liquidating. This may be problematic for illiquid business.
- It is short-term and may be expensive if borrowing for fixed assets.

Alternative sources of finance
- Use of general reserves. The company has general reserves of £158,000 and therefore would save cost by using some of them instead of overdraft.
- Term Loan: May be cheaper compared to overdraft as interest is fixed.

> Additional areas where credit might be given, note this is not an exhaustive list:
> - Trade credit
> - Issue of short-term debt instruments such as commercial papers

May 2015 (Adapted)

Question 7

This question tests the candidate's ability to:

(i) Calculate the net present value of a project including an overseas element (LO2)

(ii) Use purchasing power parity to calculate future exchange rates (LO4)

(iii) Evaluate the uncertainties associated with business planning (LO1 and LO2)

(iv) Calculate the outcome of hedging using futures contracts (LO4)

(a) Purchasing power parity to calculate future exchange rates:

Year 1: $1.75 \times \frac{1.01}{1.02} = 1.73$

Year 2: $1.73 \times \frac{1.01}{1.02} = 1.71$

Year 3: $1.71 \times \frac{1.01}{1.02} = 1.69$

Year 4: $1.69 \times \frac{1.01}{1.02} = 1.67$

PRACTICE EXAM ANSWER BANK

		Time			
	0	1	2	3	4
	$	$	$	$	$
Sales volume		5,000	6,000	6,500	
Sales price		800	800	850	
Total revenue		4,000,000	4,800,000	5,525,000	
Sales personnel		-300,000	-300,000	-300,000	
Marketing campaign	-150,000	-150,000	-150,000		
$ total	-150,000	3,550,000	4,350,000	5,225,000	
Exchange rate	1.75	1.73	1.71	1.69	
Amount in £	-85,714	2,052,023	2,543,860	3,091,716	
Marketing and branding company (ignore)					
Factory rent		-70,000	-70,000	-70,000	
Salaries (70 at £20,000 rising at 5%)		-1,400,000	-1,470,000	-1,543,500	
Managers' salary (ignore)					
Machinery		-50,000	-60,000	-70,000	
Factory running costs		-12,000	-12,000	-12,000	
Material and shipping costs (working 1)		-750,000	-900,000	-975,000	
	-155,714	-229,977	31,860	491,216	
Tax at 25%		0	0	0	-34,346
Net cashflow	-155,714	-229,977	31,860	491,216	-34,346
Discount factor 11%	1.000	0.901	0.812	0.731	0.659
Present value	-155,714	-207,209	25,870	359,079	-22,634
Net present value	**-608**				

NPV is negative:
Do not enter into contract - shareholder wealth decreased

	Time		
	1	2	3
Working 1			
Sales volume	5,000	6,000	6,500
Material cost per table	120	120	120
Shipping cost per table = £1,500/50	30	30	30
	150	150	150
Overall total (£)	750,000	900,000	975,000

(b) There are a number of potential risks the company faces in respect of this new venture. Risk is a normal feature of any business project and is not necessarily to be avoided as it brings the potential for profit. However, it is important the company knows what risks it faces as it can look to manage those risks and this knowledge may cause the company to require further information to aid in its decision making. This is especially the case for this project for whilst it has a negative net present value it is relatively small and this can imply a company must think carefully before deciding what to do.

The company has only ever sold items in the UK. This will be a new thing selling to the USA. The company really needs to know whether the product is attractive to the USA market. The marketing and branding company figures suggest this is the case, but this is crucial and the directors of Gorforth plc may want further assurance that the projected sales figures are realistic.

The directors of Gorforth are going to oversee the project. But this is problematic as they have had no experience of the USA market. Further, this issue may be exacerbated because they will be physically remote from the USA and it can be very difficult to manage remotely.

The sales personnel are going to be UK people, but living in the USA. This sounds to be a good idea. However, the cultures of the two countries are very different and the directors must ensure the sales personnel are culturally astute and can operate effectively in the USA. Further, they should be specialists in the market that Gorforth plc operates in.

The project exposes the company to exchange rate risk. Depending on how exchange rates move in the future this could either benefit the business or add an extra cost. The purchasing power parity calculation is not necessarily a good guide to actual future exchange rates. Therefore, the company could consider hedging this risk using an appropriate hedging instrument such as forward contracts.

The cashflows are all estimates. This is inevitable as no company can predict the future precisely, but Gorforth plc needs to assess how likely it is these cashflows will arise. It may also want to undertake some sensitivity analysis to assess how critical each cashflow is. It may then focus on trying to put additional efforts into attempting to get more accurate estimates of these.

The cost of capital is based on an out of date calculation. This is important as the cost of capital is used as the discount rate for calculating the net present value. The capital structure has changed and this can affect the cost of capital. In addition, if the business risk of the project is different to the business risk of the current operations then this will also affect the cost of capital figure. If the cost of capital is lower than 11% the net present value will be greater; however, if it is higher the project net present value will be lower. It may be worth the company either re-calculating the cost of capital or in calculating the internal rate of return (IRR) for the project. The IRR will tell the directors when the net present value is going to change from positive to negative.

(c) The company requires September contracts with rate $1.6192

Number of contracts required = $315,000/$1.6192 = £194,541/£62,500 = 3.1 (ie 3 contracts).

On 1 July:

Tick movement = ($1.6192 – $1.5697)/$0.0001 = 495 ticks.
Tick value = £62,500 × $0.0001 = $6.25.
Loss on futures = 3 contracts × $6.25 × 495 ticks = $9,281.25.

Overall: receipt less futures loss = $315,000 - $9,281.25 = $305,718.75.
In sterling the net receipt is $305,718.75/$1.5693 = £194,812.

Question 8

This question tests the candidate's ability to:

(i) **Calculate cost of capital for a company (LO1)**

(ii) **Advise on company dividend policy (LO1)**

(a) Total market value of equity = 40m shares × £2.82 = £112.8m

Growth rate of dividends = $\sqrt[4]{\frac{9.60m}{8.40m}} - 1 = 0.034 = 3.4\%$

$$ke = \frac{D_0 \times (1+g)}{P_0} + g$$

$$ke = \frac{9.60m \times (1 + 0.034)}{112.8m} + 0.034 = 12.2\%$$

The cost of the irredeemable debt is:

$$kd = \frac{i}{P_0}(1-t)$$

$$kd = \frac{50m \times 7\% \times (1-20\%)}{60m} = 4.67\%$$

The market value of equity = £112.8m.
The market value of debt is £60m.
Total market value is £112.8m + £60m = £172.8m.

The WACC is:

$$\left(\frac{112.8m}{172.8m} \times 12.2\%\right) + \left(\frac{60m}{172.8m} + 4.67\%\right) = 9.58\%$$

(b) It is the responsibility of directors to decide upon the dividend paid to shareholders. This is an important decision as shareholders will normally (but not always) expect to receive dividends as a reward for investing risk capital in the business. If shareholders are not happy with the level of dividend then they may decide to sell their shares in the company. This area is contentious and different views are held as to what might be deemed an appropriate dividend policy. In recent years the company has been paying a dividend that has increased year on year and by approximately the same growth rate. Therefore, the apparent policy has been to pay a consistently growing dividend. However, this is only based on the dividend figures presented for this year and the previous four years.

Director A wanted to cut the dividend and use the cash to fund a project. There have been arguments proposed (initially by Modigliani and Miller) that suggest the key decision for a company is the investment decision. That is, if a project is available that has a positive net present value it should be invested in as it will add to shareholder wealth. Dividends are simply a residual, in the sense that once all positive NPV projects have been invested in then the remainder of any cash can be paid out to shareholders in the form of dividends.

Director A's dividend irrelevancy stance implies that dividends will fluctuate depending on whether projects are available. It is argued this does not matter to shareholders as they will gain through an increase in market value because of the project returns. However, Director B may be correct that the company has attracted loyal shareholders. Sometimes it is stated that firms attract a particular clientele in respect of their dividend policy as the shareholders have a preferred payout ratio. If the company now starts to deviate from the past dividend policy then shareholders may become upset and move to other firms that can satisfy their preference.

Director C is correct to point out that the project prospects are important. If the project cannot provide a positive net present value then the return is insufficient for shareholders and the project should not be invested into. It is then preferable to return cash to shareholders in the form of dividends as they will not want the company destroying shareholder wealth. There is another aspect regarding prospects that can impinge on dividend policy. Namely, dividends and dividend policy can send signals to the market about the future. A cut in dividends can potentially signal that the company's prospects are weak. Therefore, if a cut in dividend was made the company might need to clearly communicate that it is because a good project is available and not because the company is struggling.

Director D mentions that taxation issues may impinge on the dividend decision. However, it may be less to do with complications regarding tax and more to do with shareholders having a preference for dividends or capital gains depending on the relative tax rates for income tax and capital gains tax. This links back to ideas regarding the clientele effect, as taxation may be driving this. Hence, the company might also need to think whether this taxation issue is likely to be problematic.

Question 9

This question tests the candidate's ability to:

(i) **Advise on reasons for companies engaging in acquisitions (LO3)**

Report

To: Directors
Subject: Advice on acquisition of Diamond Watches
From: XXXX
Date: XXXX

There are a range of reasons why a company may choose to engage in an acquisition of another company. Before engaging in an acquisition it is important to assess whether the acquisition fits strategically with existing activities. Therefore, it is important that you carefully consider whether the acquisition of Diamond Watches is appropriate and particularly as many acquisitions subsequently fail to add value.

Diamond Watches operates in the same industry as Timepiece plc. Therefore, you have knowledge of this industry and, hence, you are more likely to manage Diamond Watches successfully post-acquisition. Currently, you are reliant on a particular segment of the watch market – the 18-30 age group and at the less expensive end of the market – and it appears your market share is unlikely to grow in this segment. Diamond Watches sells to a different age range and in the more expensive part of the watch market. Therefore, the acquisition will give you the possibility of expanding your operations and might enable you to be less reliant on one market segment. This is potentially beneficial for risk diversification. Hence, should your current watch brand portfolio become less fashionable then you will have reduced your dependence on this segment of the market and will have an income stream that derives from a different segment.

The diversification might also impact on the quality of your earnings. At present you rely on earnings solely from the one market segment and as there is a fashion element to this market there is a potential volatility inherent in the earnings as fashions change and potentially quite rapidly. Diamond Watches are bought on the basis of quality for the most part and, therefore, are not subject to fashion to the same extent. Hence, the earnings from Diamond Watches may be less likely to fluctuate. Additionally, as Diamond Watches are selling to a clientele who are relatively wealthier this may protect the company's earnings from the effects of economic downturns; whereas sales of your watches could be more susceptible to changes in the economy. Therefore, this acquisition could add further stability to your earnings.

As the companies operate in the same industry then there is likely to be some scope for synergistic benefits and operating economies to be achieved. This would improve the overall earnings of the companies when combined post-acquisition. Synergies might be achieved through sharing overlapping functions, for example, in finance, manufacturing or sales and distribution. Diamond Watches is innovative in respect of its manufacturing processes and this might suggest that your company could introduce techniques that would result in cost efficiencies occurring. However, as you sell to different shops and a different range of customers then there does not appear to be scope to cross-sell products.

The two management teams appear to have particular strengths that could also bring benefits beyond the innovation in manufacturing processes noted above. There are possible issues regarding product reliability for your watches. However, Diamond Watches has an especial focus on quality. Therefore, you may be able to use the acquisition as an opportunity for learning from their management how best to ensure quality systems can be implemented. Reciprocally, one of your strengths is in the creative design, branding and advertising of watches. A possible weakness at Diamond Watches is that the branding and marketing is weaker and should you transfer your skills to their products this could have a positive impact on their sales. Similarly, as they currently focus on quality rather than design, then there may be scope to add value by improving design.

You could choose to expand internally rather than through an acquisition. However, it appears that this could have difficulties. There is a shortage of skilled staff and by buying Diamond Watches you avoid this problem. If you were to establish a new manufacturing facility then an additional cost would be incurred in respect of training non-specialist staff and in the deployment of time by current managers. Therefore, the acquisition might be less expensive than internal expansion.

The company is now receiving low interest amounts on the cash pile it has invested. Therefore, it might be appropriate to use the cash to acquire Diamond Watches. However, we do not know whether the cash pile is sufficiently large to acquire Diamond Watches. Further, it is only worthwhile acquiring the company if the return on the acquisition is sufficient taking account of the risk involved. If the return is insufficient then it would be better to return the cash to shareholders by paying a special dividend or by repurchasing some shares.

Question 10

This question tests the candidate's ability to:

(i) **Prepare calculations to value a business (LO3)**

(ii) **Evaluate the working capital position of a company (LO5)**

Report

To: Mrs Smith and Mr Grace
Subject: Valuation of Hope plc and evaluation of working capital position
From: XXXX
Date: XXXX

This report provides valuation calculations on two bases for Hope plc, evaluates the working capital position and advises on further information that should be sought before deciding whether to proceed with the management buy-in.

(1) *Valuations*

Valuation on a net assets basis

	£m
Net assets as per statement of financial position	2.7
Adjustment for property (£2.5m - £1.7m)	0.8
Total valuation	**£3.5m**

Valuation on an earnings basis

The earnings of the business for the last three years have been decreasing. The valuation could be based on average earnings but the current year earnings are likely to be more appropriate = £0.4m

P/E ratios are provided for two competitors and the average = (12 + 10)/2 = 11

A further assumption is that the P/E ratio should be reduced by 40% to 6.6 to reflect that Hope plc is unquoted.

Therefore, the total valuation = 6.6 × £0.4m = £2.64m

(2) *Evaluation of the working capital position*

Using standard ratio analysis the following calculations have been prepared to evaluate the working capital position:

Ratio	2015
Current ratio	1.6m/1.3m = 1.23
Quick ratio	1.6m − 0.3m/1.3m = 1.00
Receivables days	(0.4m × 365)/4.6m = 31.7 days
Stock turnover	(0.3m × 365)/2.1m = 52.1 days
Payables days	(0.5m × 365)/2.1m = 86.9 days
Operating cycle	31.7 + 52.1 − 86.9 = −3.1 days

There is no especial reason why the working capital ratios for the printing industry cannot be interpreted in a standard manner.

The current ratio appears low at 1.23:1, whereas the norm for this ratio would be 2:1. However, the quick ratio is as per the norm. Overall, there does not appear any cause for concern in respect of these two ratios.

Similarly, there does not appear to be any reason to be concerned about the receivables days. The norm for this measure is that debts from customers would be collected in approximately 30 days and Hope plc has a collection period only marginally longer than this.

Stock turnover at 52 days is higher than might be expected as the norm for this is 30 days. This may need further investigation. The implication is the company is holding too high a stock level and it may need reducing.

The period of time taken to pay creditors is of greatest concern as the company is paying suppliers only after 86 days. This is a long period for suppliers to have to wait and standard credit terms would be 30 days. It is important to ascertain if this is due to Hope plc having difficulty paying on time as it can potentially indicate liquidity issues. This is the primary reason for the negative operating cycle.

(3) *Further information you should seek*

Before proceeding I advise that the following information should be sought:

What is the likely attitude of the third family member should you approach the company? As this family member is unsure whether to sell their shares this may make the negotiation of an appropriate value protracted. Further, they may decide that they do not want to sell. We do not know what level of dividends shareholders have been receiving and this might also be a factor in determining whether the third shareholder would consider selling.

How will the employees react? As you would be coming into the company as external managers then employees may react strongly to the buy-in. This can be difficult if key employees choose to leave. The reaction of employees may be further exaggerated should you want to make substantial changes to halt the profit decline.

Nov 2014 (Adapted)

Question 11

This question tests the candidate's ability to:

(i) Calculate the net present value of a project (LO1)
(ii) Evaluate the uncertainties associated with business planning (LO1 and LO2)
(iii) Advise on operating in an international business environment (LO4)
(iv) Advise on the setting of company objectives (LO1)

(a)

Cashflows	0 £	1 £	2 £	3 £	4 £
Sales revenue (working 1)		29,400,000	54,000,000	3,900,000	
Development cost (ignore sunk cost)					
Rent		-400,000	-400,000	-400,000	
Employees (500 at £25,000)		-12,500,000	-12,500,000	-12,500,000	
Managers (ignore not incremental)					
Material cost (working 2)		-15,300,000	-30,600,000	-2,550,000	
Energy		-55,000	-55,000	-55,000	
Marketing	-150,000	-90,000			
Net cashflow before taxation	-150,000	1,055,000	10,445,000	-11,605,000	
Taxation at 20%		30,000	-211,000	-2,089,000	2,321,000
Net cashflow after taxation	-150,000	1,085,000	10,234,000	-13,694,000	2,321,000
11% discount factor	1	0.901	0.812	0.731	0.659
Present value	-150,000	977,585	8,310,008	-10,010,314	1,529,539

Net Present Value   £656,818

The positive NPV indicates shareholder value will be increased and the project is worthwhile.

Working 1	1	2	3
Number of televisions sold	60,000	120,000	10,000
Selling price	490	450	390
Sales revenue (£)	29,400,000	54,000,000	3,900,000
Working 2	1	2	3
Number of televisions sold	60,000	120,000	10,000
Material cost per television	255	255	255
Total material cost (£)	15,300,000	30,600,000	2,550,000

(b) Any new project will involve risk as it is concerned with the future. There will be some risks that are generic to any new project, but there will also be risks that are specific and dependent upon the nature of the project and the company that is taking on the project. It is important that the company considers any risks as these may have a significant impact on the eventual project.

The new product is described as likely to become obsolete within three years and this is because of new innovations coming along. It can be very difficult to assess how soon any technology will be overtaken and superseded. Therefore, assessing the likely length of the product life is extremely difficult.

It is stated that Stark plc needs to employ staff who can learn advanced manufacturing techniques and can be highly productive. This implies that should it prove difficult employing staff of appropriate calibre then this may impact adversely on the project outcome.

The figures included in the net present value calculation are all estimates of future values. It is not possible to predict the future with accuracy and, if any actual cashflows differ from these estimates, then this will affect the eventual net present value.

There is no information about what constitutes the company's cost of capital. A company may use its existing weighted average cost of capital as the discount rate for projects, but this may not be an appropriate rate to use. The project risk may differ from the existing company risk, or the capital structure may alter when the project is taken on.

(c) Foreign direct investment (FDI) can be advantageous to a company and in the case of Stark plc then it may result in improved profitability as the labour cost in the target country is judged to be lower than in the UK. Additionally, FDI can have advantages for the host country, but it is also the case that the host country may be averse to FDI as it can also have demerits. Therefore, it is appropriate for the company to be able to set out the advantages for the host country.

The company will create 500 new jobs in the country. This is a significant number of jobs to create. Relatedly, this may help in stimulating the economy if this results in other companies becoming confident enough to follow this lead.

Stark plc is a highly innovative company that develops and manufactures technologically advanced products. Therefore, the host country may benefit from the transfer of technological know-how. This may eventually aid the country in developing in related industries.

The company will be training the staff. This will increase the skill level of the local workforce. The workforce will also have exposure to advanced manufacturing techniques. Should the workforce move to other local companies they can transfer this knowledge.

The company is profitable and can afford to invest capital in the new venture. Therefore, the host country will be importing capital which is an important resource.

(d) Report

To: Directors – Stark plc
Subject: Company objectives
From: XXXX
Date: XXXX

Companies need to establish objectives as this then guides their planning and enables them to monitor whether they are achieving the objectives. It is common that the prime objective is to maximise profit. However, there are a range of non-financial objectives that can also be pursued and these will not necessarily compromise the objective of maximising profit; rather, they can aid in achieving this prime objective.

The company needs to employ staff for all its operations who are capable of learning new techniques and can be highly productive. Therefore, if it provides a good salary level and working conditions of a high standard it is more likely to recruit staff who have these capabilities. These staff are also likely to be better motivated and to remain with the company. Overall, this should aid the company in achieving higher profits than a demotivated workforce that lacks loyalty and commitment.

The company might also give consideration to its responsibilities towards customers. If it adopts an objective of achieving high customer care levels, including aftersales service, then this may result in high levels of brand loyalty and repeat business. The technologically advanced markets the company operates in are likely to be competitive and having loyal customers can be beneficial for profits.

The products made are technologically advanced and, therefore, it is likely that the company is connected to suppliers who have the capability to manufacture components that are both of the highest quality and similarly state of the art. Having an objective of maintaining good relationships with suppliers can be good for the company's profits as the suppliers are likely to then ensure they deliver components of appropriate quality and on time. Thus, production can be maintained as can the quality of the final product.

Many companies are active in engaging in their corporate social responsibilities. This can range from ensuring compliance with laws to being environmentally responsible. This might be considered a cost to the company. However, it can also enhance the reputation of the company and lead to greater take-up of products by customers. If this occurs then profits can be positively impacted.

Question 12

This question tests the candidate's ability to:

(a) **Prepare calculations to value a business and advise on the difficulties inherent in these calculations (LO3)**

(b) **Advise on post-acquisition problems (LO3)**

Report

To: Senior managers – Finance Jobs plc
Subject: Acquisition of People Ltd
From: XXXX
Date: XXXX

This report advises on the valuation of People Ltd by providing a range of valuations that have been calculated on three different bases. It also advises on potential integration issues should you decide to acquire People Ltd. These integration issues should not be under-estimated as it is common for acquisitions to fail.

Valuation on a net assets basis

	£
Net assets as per statement of financial position	201,000
Adjustment for office equipment (£210,000 - £132,000)	(78,000)
Adjustment for trade receivables	(9,000)
Total valuation	**£114,000**

Valuation on an earnings basis

The earnings of the business for this year = £84,000.

P/E ratios are provided for a listed recruitment company = 12.

A further assumption is that the P/E ratio should be reduced by 40% to 7.2 to reflect that People Ltd is unquoted.

Therefore, the total valuation = 7.2 × £84,000 = £604,800.

Valuation on dividend yield

The dividends have not increased over the last three years = £8,000. This is a zero growth rate.

The cost of equity in respect of the company is not known. Therefore, as an approximation take the cost of equity for Andover plc = 9%.

The total valuation = £8,000/9% = £88,889.

Potential issues

There are a number of potential issues associated with the integration of People Ltd should it be acquired. The two companies are both recruitment companies and, therefore, your company is not moving into a different industry sector. However, the recruitment sectors the two companies operate in are different. You have knowledge of the banking and finance sector, but People Ltd is focused on the charity sector. The clients in the two sectors may have very different expectations concerning any recruitment agency they employ.

Further, you are focused upon recruiting accounting and finance specialists, whereas People Ltd recruits across the range of management positions. Therefore, there are differences that need to be recognised in the types of employees being recruited. The employees of People Ltd will understand their 'market' and you may need to rely on their expertise.

Finance Jobs plc is London-based whereas People Ltd operates across the UK. This gives you the opportunity to expand geographically as well as in size. However, you will need to be prepared to spend time visiting these UK operations to facilitate the integration. Connectedly, there may be an issue of control. It is potentially more difficult to control operations when the geographic spread is wider.

The employees in the two companies are working in very different cultures. In your company the employees have to be dynamic and prepared to win business. You motivate the employees by offering financial rewards. The employees in People Ltd are not financially-motivated. They are motivated because of a desire to assist the charities and the working atmosphere is supportive. Therefore, a potential clash of cultures could result.

There is also a great difference in the underlying motivation of the directors in the two companies. You are highly entrepreneurial and likely to be profit-motivated. Mary Storey is looking to help the charities meet their aims. To this end she does not charge a 'full' fee. Therefore, the two companies have a different ethos. Mary does look to save costs, which may accord with your views. However, she does so by renting cheap premises. This would be unlikely to fit with your current client-base.

Question 13

This question tests the candidate's ability to:

(i) **Draw on finance theory to calculate the effect of changing capital structure on the value of a company (LO1 and LO3)**

(ii) **Explore the different capital structure theories (LO1)**

(a) Market value (using Modigliani & Miller)

$MV(g) = MV(u) + (t \times MVdebt)$
$MV(g) = £20m + (£7m \times 25\%)$
$MV(g) = £21.75m$

(b) Weighted average cost of capital (using Modigliani & Miller)

$$WACC(g) = ke_0 \times (1 - \frac{Dt}{E+D})$$

$$WACC(g) = 11\% \times (1 - \frac{[25\% \times £7m]}{£21.75m})$$

$WACC(g) = 10.11\%$

(c) There are differing ideas concerning capital structure. The theories developed in this area are the static trade-off model, Modigliani and Miller (without and with taxation, and incorporating financial distress), and pecking order theory. There is no definitive answer to the best capital structure and this makes it difficult to provide precise guidance to companies on this matter.

The first director suggests that debt is appropriate as interest is tax deductible. This is correct and because of this tax benefit, the effective interest cost of debt is reduced. Debt is cheaper than equity anyway because of the relative risk position of debtholders and shareholders, and this tax advantage does reduce the cost of debt even further below the cost of equity. This is not in any sense a contentious issue and is incorporated in the static trade-off model and Modigliani and Miller models.

However, what the first director neglects to mention is the matter raised by the second director. Namely, if debt is introduced then shareholders are unlikely to ignore this. They are impacted because the company now has interest payments to meet and these are met before the directors consider whether a dividend should be paid. Therefore, the introduction of debt affects the risk position of shareholders via the introduction of financial or gearing risk. If the shareholders' risk is increased then we would expect them to require a higher return. The difficulty is it is uncertain to what extent the shareholders' return will increase.

The static trade-off model suggests that at low levels of gearing, when debt interest is relatively small, we might expect the required return of equity holders to increase by only a small amount. However, as the level of gearing rises then the trade-off model suggests the increase in the required return of equity holders becomes more pronounced and this negates the introduction of the cheaper form of finance, debt. This results in a U-shaped WACC curve. Modigliani and Miller (with taxation) suggest the rise in the shareholders' required return is at a constant rate. The result (with taxation) is that WACC constantly falls as the cheaper finance (debt) is introduced.

Which of these is correct? The third director asks what happens if the company over borrows and it has been suggested that Modigliani and Miller (with taxation) neglect this effect. Namely, as gearing rises to higher levels the risk of the company finding it difficult to meet interest payments becomes a real danger. This situation of financial distress impacts on companies in different ways. Suppliers may want cash up-front and refuse to offer credit. The reputation of the company may suffer. Additionally, the cost of borrowing additional debt is likely to rise as lenders are concerned about the credit risk. It has been suggested this rise in the cost of debt at higher levels of gearing will increase the WACC under Modigliani and Miller's (with taxation) model at these higher levels of gearing. Hence, the static trade-off model and Modigliani and Miller model may be similar after all.

However, an alternative theory is pecking order theory. This suggests raising finance in a particular order: (1) use internal cash, (2) use debt and (3) lastly, use equity. This is partly according with the view of the fourth director. Namely, this director prefers debt over equity because of issue costs and that it is more onerous to raise equity. This theory has also been allied to ideas of signalling; associating equity issues with directors having bad news. Overall, however there is some accord with the three theories in that they do suggest it is reasonable to bring debt into a company's capital structure in moderation.

Question 14

This question tests the candidates ability to:

(i) **Evaluate the working capital position of a company (LO5)**

Report

To:	Mr James
Subject:	Evaluation of working capital
From:	XXXX
Date:	XXXX

It is important that the college manages its working capital position effectively. If the working capital position is not managed well this can have important implications for the company's cashflow (liquidity) and profit. There are a number of ratios that can assist in the evaluation; however, to interpret the ratios it is important to take into account the company's situation and that it operates in the education industry.

Using standard ratio analysis the following calculations have been prepared:

Ratio	2014	2013
Current ratio	747/182 = 4.10	617/142 = 4.35
Quick ratio	747-35/182 = 3.91	617-38/142 = 4.08
Receivables' days	(600 × 365)/3,060 = 71.6 days	(510 × 365)/2,850 = 65.3 days
Stock turnover	(35 × 365)/340 = 37.6 days	(38 × 365)/320 = 43.3 days
Payables days	(29 × 365)/340 = 31.1 days	(23 × 365)/320 = 26.2 days
Operating cycle	71.6 + 37.6-31.1 = 78.1 days	65.3+43.3-26.2 = 82.4 days

The trend of the ratios from 2013 to 2014 is that they have remained relatively stable. This can be a good thing if the ratios indicate sound working capital management is occurring, or a bad thing if the ratios depict poor management of working capital. Therefore, it is necessary to look at each ratio in turn to make this judgement.

The current ratio is 4.1: 1 in 2014 and slightly higher at 4.35 : 1 in 2013. Typically, we might expect a ratio of 2:1 and these are well above this. Similarly, the quick ratio is well above a standard 1:1. These ratios are used as indicators of liquidity problems and as both are well above the standard figure suggest liquidity is not problematic. Indeed some may argue they are too high. However, as this is an education company then we need to be careful in respect of this interpretation. Major components of current assets and current liabilities are inventories, trade debtors and trade payables. The next three ratios consider these in the context of the industry your company operates in.

The receivables days have increased slightly to 71.6 days from 65.3 days. Initially, this might be interpreted as indicating two matters. First, that the number of days is too high as it is indicating how long it takes for debtors to pay the company. Second, that the number of days has increased from 2013 to 2014 may indicate that the company is not collecting monies due quite as efficiently in 2014. However, in your company the debtors are the students and the fees they are paying. The fee per year is £6,000 and this equates to £500 per month. Therefore, as at 31st October because the students only pay the first instalment on 1st December then they owe two months' fees. Consequently, the figures calculated are approximately correct in this respect. That they are not exactly two months is due to two things. First, it can be seen from the revenue figures that the number of students enrolling at the college is increasing. Consequently, the debtors at 31st October are for the current year's intake, but the revenue mainly relates to last year's intake. Second, there may be some bad debts deducted in respect of students unable to pay fees. It is worth considering whether students should have to pay the first instalment (and also the second instalment) earlier in the academic year as this will be better for your cashflow and may help in respect of bad debts.

Stock turnover period has decreased slightly from 43.3 days to 37.6 days in 2014. Normally, we might expect a standard period for stockholding to be 30 days, and this is slightly higher. However, the nature of the business needs consideration again. Total stocks are very low compared to the size of the business at £35,000 in 2014 and £38,000 in 2013. This might be expected as you do not make or sell a physical product. Education requires minimal stocks and you need not attend too closely to monitoring stocks. The reason that the stockholding period calculation appears high is the cost of sales figure is also relatively low. This is because major costs in your business are the staff costs and these appear to have been included in administrative expenses.

Payables period has increased from 26.2 days to 31.1 days. This ratio indicates how long your business is taking to pay creditors. As it has increased this sometimes indicates a company is making creditors wait longer for payment because of cashflow problems. However, the increase is marginal in your company and, similar to inventories you need to recognise that trade payables are very small in your business context and, again, the small cost of sales figure amplifies this ratio.

Given the above comments you should be able to recognise that the operating cycle is not terribly meaningful. This is because it is a combination of the three ratios just discussed. As mentioned above the most important item in all of the three ratios is the trade debtors figure. That is, it has most impact on the company's cashflow and, hence, on its liquidity. Therefore, this should be focused upon in managing working capital.

May 2014 (Adapted)

Question 15

This question tests the candidate's ability to:

(i) **Calculate the net present value of a project including an overseas element (LO2)**

(ii) **Use purchasing power parity to calculate future exchange rates (LO4)**

(iii) **Evaluate the uncertainties associated with business planning (LO2)**

(iv) **Assess political risk (LO4)**

(a) Purchasing power parity to calculate future exchange rates:

PRACTICE EXAM ANSWER BANK

$$\text{Year 1}: 1.5606 \times \frac{1.03}{1.01} = 1.5915$$

$$\text{Year 2}: 1.5915 \times \frac{1.03}{1.01} = 1.6230$$

$$\text{Year 3}: 1.6230 \times \frac{1.03}{1.01} = 1.6551$$

$$\text{Year 4}: 1.6551 \times \frac{1.03}{1.01} = 1.6879$$

	0 AUD	1 AUD	2 AUD	3 AUD	4 AUD
Shirt sales		50,000	60,000	80,000	
Selling price per shirt		49	49	49	
Sales revenue		2,450,000	2,940,000	3,920,000	
Rent	-50,000	-50,000	-50,000		
Management team		-200,000	-200,000	-200,000	
Employees (30 at AUD35,000)		-1,050,000	-1,050,000	-1,050,000	
Energy		-15,000	-16,500	-18,150	
Ignore sunk marketing costs	0				
Marketing costs		-50,000	-50,000	-50,000	
UK costs in AUD (Working 1)	-78,030	-1,209,540	-1,476,930	-1,986,120	
	-128,030	-124,540	96,570	615,730	
Tax at 25%					-114,933
Net cashflow in AUD	-128,030	-124,540	96,570	615,730	-114,933
Converted to £	-82,039	-78,253	59,501	372,020	-68,092
Discount factor 10%	1	0.909	0.826	0.751	0.683
Present value	-82,039	-71,132	49,148	279,387	-46,507
Net present value	**128,857**				

	0 £	1 £	2 £	3 £
Working 1				
UK costs:				
Equipment	40,000			
Visits	10,000	10,000	10,000	
Materials (at £15 per shirt)		750,000	900,000	1,200,000
Total in £	50,000	760,000	910,000	1,200,000
Exchange rate (working)	1.5606	1.5915	1.6230	1.6551
Total in AUD	78,030	1,209,540	1,476,930	1,986,120

(b) There are always risks associated with any business venture. However, the types of risks and the level of risk will vary dependent upon the venture and many other factors.

It is always difficult operating in a new market and in this situation the company is not only hoping to sell its products in Australia, but it is also setting up a manufacturing operation. There will likely be differences between the UK and Australia in respect of culture and the like. The directors have no knowledge of Australia and this increases the risk.

The shirt sells in the UK because of the unusual design. The directors need to be confident this will also be popular in Australia. Clothing tastes can differ markedly. Also that the shirt is high quality may not be as important to Australian consumers, and they may be more concerned about selling price. This is important as the sales figures are key in the net present value calculation.

Of course, all the figures in the net present value calculation are estimates. This is always the case as it is not possible to predict the future. If any cashflows deviate from these estimates then the true net present value will also differ.

There is no explanation given as to how the discount rate used in the project has been arrived at. Companies may sometimes use their weighted average cost of capital as the discount rate for projects, but this may be an inappropriate rate to use. The project risk may differ from the existing company risk, or the level of gearing may change when the project is taken on.

There are cashflows both in Australian dollars and in British pounds. Therefore, this exposes the business to exchange rate risk. Depending on how exchange rates move in the future this could either benefit the business or add an extra cost. The company could potentially hedge this risk using an appropriate hedging instrument.

(c) There are a number of factors that can be examined to aid in assessing the level of political risk in a country. These may be macro- and micro-factors. Information has been provided that facilitates an assessment of the potential level of political risk. However, it should be noted that the information is relatively brief and further information is needed to improve the accuracy of the assessment.

In the past economic growth has been poor, and the economy is under-developed. This suggests higher levels of political risk would apply. Further, it is stated that the economic growth rate is negative at present and this is also a strong indicator of a struggling economy. Coupled with this the inflation rate is high, which is also indicative of higher political risk.

The political state of affairs is problematic too and suggestive of higher political risk. The current government has been in office for only a short period of time (six months) and already the population is disgruntled with those in office. Therefore, there are signs of political instability. There is also a possibility of corruption in the political elite. This potential problem related to political ethics is also causing unrest and this is exacerbating the political instability.

Government debt levels are high and the credit rating attached to this debt is poor. It is unsurprising given the economic position of the country, that the external credit rating agencies are concerned about the government's ability to repay its debt. Relatedly, the financial services sector has developed only to a limited extent and the exchange rate is volatile. These factors all support the notion that there is high political risk.

Particularly worrying is the concern that the government may block remittances. This does not appear to have happened yet and may be unsubstantiated. However, should it occur then this would be a serious matter and might impact significantly on overseas companies operating in country X. Again, it confirms that there is a relatively high level of political risk in country X.

Question 16

This question tests the candidate's ability to:

(i) **Evaluate financing options (LO1)**

(ii) **Evaluate the effect of financing options upon capital structure (LO1)**

Report:

To: Directors – The Furniture People plc
Subject: Evaluation of financing choice
From: XXXX
Date: XXXX

The financing option you are considering is to bring further debt into the company's capital structure. This will increase the gearing level of the company. An alternative is to use equity, and there are advantages and disadvantages in both cases. This report focuses upon evaluating your current view that debt is the more appropriate choice.

At present the company has a debt:equity ratio of 76.2%.

This is calculated as follows:

Debt = £20m

Equity = 15m shares × £1.75 = £26.25m

Debt:equity ratio = 20m/26.25m = 76.2%.

If the company raises an additional £10m by debt then this debt:equity ratio changes to 30/26.25 = 114.3%.

This assumes the market value of equity is unchanged.

It can be difficult to know whether there is an appropriate debt:equity for any company. However, companies will often compare their ratio to the industry average which in this case is 95%. Therefore, your company's debt:equity ratio is at present below this industry average, but should you raise the amount of £10m through debt then you will be above the industry average. This may be interpreted by stakeholders and the market as inappropriate. That is, there may be concerns that the company has too much long-term debt. Therefore, it would be sensible if you could ascertain the likely market reaction.

A key issue that may cause an adverse market reaction relates to the affordability of debt interest. Debt interest must be paid each year (unlike dividends) and the company needs to ensure it has sufficient profits to do so. The profit in the last year was £1.9m and it is anticipated the new venture would generate profits of £0.85m. If we consider the interest payments based on these then the position is as follows:

		Current situation £m	After raising £10m debt £m
Profit	(£1.9m + £0.85m)	1.9	2.75
Interest	(£20m at 8% + £10m at 7.5%)	(1.6)	(2.35)
Profit after interest		0.3	0.4
Tax at 20%		(0.06)	(0.08)
Profit after interest and after tax		0.24	0.32

These calculations indicate that the new debt is affordable. However, it needs to be recognised that this new debt is at a floating rate of interest and the 7.5% interest rate may fluctuate in the future. If it falls then that is not an issue; however should it rise then this can impact on the affordability. A 1% rise in the rate will result in additional interest payments of £100,000 per year. A further uncertainty is the profit figure. The profits from the present operations have been in decline and may continue to do so, and the profits from the new venture are estimated. Some further sensitivity analysis may help in deciding whether affordability of interest is an issue.

Connected to affordability of interest is the issue of financial distress. If the level of debt is considered too high and there is a risk of financial distress, then there are indirect costs associated with this that might adversely impact the company. The new venture is to manufacture higher quality furniture and this implies the company wishes to change its reputation. If there is the possibility of financial distress this may impact adversely upon reputation. Financial distress can have other indirect impacts upon, for example, supplier relationships and customer relationships.

The company must also consider whether it is able to provide security for the debt. It is already securing current debt against land and buildings it owns. It is not known to what extent it has other available assets for security. The factory it intends to purchase may be suitable as security, but it will not provide all the security necessary as its value (£7m) is less than the total loan (£10m).

One reason why debt may be used as a source of finance relates to cost. The cost of debt will normally be below the cost of equity, and interest payments on debt are tax allowable further reducing the cost of debt. The company pays corporation tax and can use this tax advantage of debt. However, taking on more debt will normally cause the cost of equity to rise. Therefore, it would be useful if the company is able to estimate how cost of equity may be impacted by the new venture and the debt financing. The effect on the overall weighted average cost of capital can then be estimated.

The directors mention that they may look for further ventures should this one be successful. Any new projects will also require finance. Therefore, the company needs to consider whether it would like to build 'financial slack' into its capital structure. It may want to have spare borrowing capacity as this will enable it to fund any new projects using debt finance. This can be important if a project needs finance quickly; raising equity is typically a slower process. A further issue that will need consideration is in respect of repaying any long-term debt. The company must ensure it has planned replacement funding for the current debt and any new debt raised.

It would also be useful to know if control issues need to be considered. A debt issue would not affect the level of shareholder control. The directors may not be personally concerned about this, but they may want to take into account any preferences and possible reactions of shareholders.

Question 17

This question tests the candidate's ability to:

(i) **Calculate the outcome of hedging using futures contracts (LO4)**

(ii) **Calculate the outcomes of accepting a project under portfolio theory (LO4)**

(a) The company requires September contracts with rate $1.5204.

Number of contracts required = $225,000/$1.5204 = £147,987/£62,500 = 2.4 (The company can only enter into a whole number of contracts = 2 contracts).

On 1 August:

Tick movement = $1.5514 – $1.5204/$0.0001 = 310 ticks.
Tick value = £62,500 × $0.0001 = $6.25.
Loss on futures = 2 contracts × $6.25 × 310 ticks = $3,875.00.
Overall: payment plus futures loss = $225,000 + $3,875 = $228,875.

In sterling the overall payment is $228,875/$1.5532 = £147,357.

(b) Expected return and standard deviation for the project:

Probability (P)	Returns (R)	Probability × returns	$R - \check{R}$	$(R - \check{R})^2$	$P(R - \check{R})^2$
0.1	−6	−0.6	−16.4	268.96	26.896
0.7	10	7.0	−0.4	0.16	0.112
0.2	20	4.0	9.6	92.16	18.432
	$\check{R}$	10.4			45.44
				σ	6.74

The company and project combined expected return is:

	Expected return ($\check{R}$)	Standard deviation (σ)	Weightings (W)	$W \times \check{R}$
Company	9	3	0.6	5.4
Project	10.4	6.74	0.4	4.16
			Combined $\check{R}$	9.56

Using the equation for two-asset portfolio the combined standard deviation can be calculated:

$\sigma^2 = (0.6 \times 3)^2 + (0.4 \times 6.74)^2 + (2 \times 0.6 \times 0.4 \times 3 \times 6.74 \times -0.4) = 6.626$.

Standard deviation (σ) = 2.574.

Therefore, when compared:

	Expected return	Standard deviation
Company	9%	3%
Combined company with project	9.56%	2.574%

Hence, taking on the project increases the expected return and reduces risk (standard deviation). Therefore, it is a worthwhile project.

Question 18

This question tests the candidate's ability to:

(i) **Prepare calculations to value a business and advise on the difficulties inherent in these calculations (LO3)**

(i) **Evaluate the working capital position of a company (LO5)**

Report

To: Mr Sykes
Subject: Fulford plc – valuation of company and evaluation of working capital position
From: XXXX
Date: XXXX

Valuation on two different bases

The information provided permits a valuation of the company on a net assets basis and on an earnings basis as follows:

Valuation on an assets basis.

The net assets of the company are £2,644,000 but adjustments need to be made to this figure as follows:

	£
Net assets	2,644,000
Property (£3,965,000 – £3,722,000)	243,000
Inventories	(23,000)
Valuation	£2,864,000

The adjustments to make to this are for the property and inventories values as stated in the question, to bring them to their current value. This assumes the other items on the statement of financial position are reflecting realisable values. In practice it can be difficult to determine realisable values.

Valuation on an earnings basis:

The earnings of the company for the current year are £710,000.

The P-E ratios for two listed supermarket companies average as follows:

(12 + 15)/2 = 13.5.

We need to reduce this average P-E ratio to reflect that the shares in Fulford plc are not listed and, hence, are not as marketable. If we reduce this by 40% then the adjusted P-E is 8.1.

Therefore, the valuation = £710,000 × 8.1 = £5,751,000.

It is important to note that the adjustment required for the P-E ratio is highly debatable. It is difficult to know how a listing impacts upon company valuation.

The company earnings have been increasing in recent years. As you would be purchasing the right to the future earnings of the company then, should future earnings also be increasing, the above calculation will undervalue the company.

Evaluation of working capital

There are a number of ratios that can assist in the evaluation of working capital. However, to interpret the ratios it is important to take into account the company's situation and the industry it operates in.

	2014
Current ratio	2,640/2,407 = 1.10
Quick ratio	(2,640 – 176)/2,407 = 1.02
Trade receivables' days	No trade receivables = 0 days
Stock turnover	(176 × 365)/6,562 = 9.8 days
Trade payables period	(660 × 365)/6,562 = 36.7 days
Operating cycle	0 + 9.8 – 36.7 = –26.9 days

The current ratio and quick ratio are both similar and just above 1:1. It is to be expected that they will be similar for a supermarket as the inventories are relatively low as explained below. Additionally, although a typical current ratio might be 2:1, a supermarket would normally have a ratio nearer to 1:1 as it will have no (or few) trade receivables as explained below. Therefore, these ratios are both appropriate for the company.

The receivables days are zero as the company has no trade receivables. There are no trade receivables as a supermarket is a cash-based business. This is advantageous for cashflow.

The stock turnover is 9.8 days and, again, this would be expected in a supermarket. Many of the items held in stock are perishable and with limited shelf life. Therefore, this figure is appropriate.

The trade payables period of 36.7 days represents the time taken to pay suppliers. This is slightly high, as a typical payment period would be 30 days. However, it is only marginally higher than expected.

The result is that the operating cycle is negative. This is highly advantageous for cashflow as the supermarket has sold products and received the cash for the sales, before needing to pay suppliers. Therefore, suppliers are financing the business. This is typical for this industry and, overall, the working capital position of the company is sound.

November 2013 (Adapted)

Question 19

This question tests the candidate's ability to:

(i) **Calculate future exchange rates using purchasing power parity (LO4)**

(ii) **Calculate the net present value of an overseas project (LO2)**

(iii) **Advise on risks associated with investment projects (LO4)**

(iv) **Explore the connection between the objective of maximisation of shareholder wealth and alternative objectives (LO1)**

(a) Workings for exchange rate calculation – using purchasing power parity:

Year 1

Expected exchange rate = $0.2056 \times \frac{(1+3.5\%)}{(1+1.5\%)} = 0.2097$

Year 2

Expected exchange rate = $0.2097 \times \frac{(1+3.5\%)}{(1+1.5\%)} = 0.2138$

Year 3

Expected exchange rate = $0.2138 \times \frac{(1+3.5\%)}{(1+1.5\%)} = 0.2180$

	Time				
	0	1	2	3	4
	MYR	MYR	MYR	MYR	MYR
Sales of bottles		5,000,000	6,000,000	8,000,000	
Sales price bottle		2.5	2.5	2.5	
Total revenue		12,500,000	15,000,000	20,000,000	
Cost of ingredient F (working 2)		-4,768,717	-5,612,722	-7,339,450	
Cost of bottles, ingredient G and packaging (Working 1)		-5,000,000	-6,000,000	-8,000,000	
Factory rent (5% increase per year)		-200,000	-210,000	-220,500	
Staff – manufacturing (40)		-2,000,000	-2,000,000	-2,000,000	
Staff – management (3)		-360,000	-360,000	-360,000	
Energy (8% increase per year)		-60,000	-64,800	-69,984	
Transport (increasing to proportionate to sales)		-80,000	-96,000	-128,000	

	Time				
	0	1	2	3	4
	MYR	MYR	MYR	MYR	MYR
Machinery cost	-1,500,000				
Machinery sale				600,000	
	-1,500,000	31,283	656,478	2,482,066	
Tax at 25%			0	0	-417,457
Net cashflow	-1,500,000	31,283	656,478	2,482,066	-417,457
Discount factor 11%	1.000	0.901	0.812	0.731	0.659
Present value	-1,500,000	28,186	533,060	1,814,391	-275,104

Net present value (MYR) 600,532

NPV is positive:
Enter into contract – shareholder wealth increased

Ignore employee cost associated with development

	Time		
	1	2	3
Working 1			
Cost of bottles, ingredients and packaging			
Number of bottles of drink produced	5,000,000	6,000,000	8,000,000
Ingredient G (10 grams × MYR0.05 per gram)	0.5	0.5	0.5
Bottle cost	0.35	0.35	0.35
Packaging (MYR1.5 per box and 10 bottles per box)	0.15	0.15	0.15
Total – ingredient G, bottle and packaging – per bottle	1	1	1
Overall total	5,000,000	6,000,000	8,000,000

	Time		
	1	2	3
Working 2			
Ingredient F			
Number of bottles of drink produced	5,000,000	6,000,000	8,000,000
Ingredient F			
Ingredient F (£0.1 per litre × 2 litres per bottle)	0.2	0.2	0.2
Total ingredient F cost in £	1,000,000	1,200,000	1,600,000
Exchange rate	0.2097	0.2138	0.2180
Total ingredient F cost in MYR	4,768,717	5,612,722	7,339,450

(b) There are a number of risks that might be associated with the calculations evaluating whether the project is worthwhile. These could include:

UK exchange rates may not conform to the projected exchange rates as predicted by purchasing power parity. This could have either a positive or negative impact upon the net present value dependent on the actual exchange rates in the future.

All costs are estimates and these may be found to be incorrect in the future. For some of these costs estimates have also been made of future increases and these may be found to be inaccurate. Again, this could have either a positive or negative impact upon the net present value

The company is using its cost of capital to discount the project flows. This may be an inappropriate rate to use and particularly if either the business risk of the project differs from the business risk of the company's existing activities or the project is financed in a manner that alters the current capital structure. Further it may have been calculated incorrectly.

Taxation flows are dependent upon taxation rates in the country the company is situated. If the government alter taxation rates or rules as to how taxation should be calculated or paid then this may have a positive or negative impact upon the net present value.

The amounts payable by the supermarket are stipulated in the contract. There is the risk that any company deviates from a contract. Legal recourse may then become possible, but it is not necessarily the case that legal challenges will be successful and even if they can there is likely to have been disruption to the cash inflows.

(c) The reasons the four directors provide for accepting the contract are very different and relate to:

1. Increasing sales,
2. Enhancing reputation,
3. Provision of employment opportunities, and
4. Blocking out competitors.

If we examine each of these in turn then a connection can be made in each case to the normally assumed objective of maximisation of shareholder wealth.

Director A considers increasing the company's sale figure of great importance. Shareholder wealth can be positively impacted when a company increases its sales, but only if the project returns are sufficient to more than satisfy the required return of the providers of capital. A situation can be envisaged whereby a project is taken on and sales increased, but its returns are inadequate and this would negatively impact shareholder wealth.

Director B believes that the contract will enhance reputation. If reputation is enhanced this can potentially lead to increased shareholder wealth and in different ways. For example, the enhanced reputation may lead to other companies approaching Pink Bottle with offers of contracts to develop new drinks. Enhanced reputation might also lead to providers of capital reviewing their assessment of the risk level of the company downwards. In turn this would result in those providers of capital lowering their required returns, leading to a positive effect on shareholder value. However, reputation is a difficult concept and companies' reputations can fluctuate over time. For example, if there is a positive effect on reputation for Pink Bottle by taking on the contract, this effect may only exist for a limited time.

Director C thinks that the contract is beneficial because it provides employment opportunities and this is a very worthy aim. However, if the company accepts the contract simply because it employs extra staff it can mean that the company may be taking on a project that either happens to increase shareholder wealth, or happens not to, depending on the project returns and the cost of capital. A tentative argument could be proposed that if the employees are grateful to be employed, then they will work hard and this efficiency may be more likely to result in the generation of shareholder wealth. However, it could equally be argued that if they believe their contracts will be terminated after three years then there is no incentive to work hard.

Director D thinks that it is a good idea to accept the project as this ensures it is not offered to a competitor. However, it could be that if the project provides inadequate returns then it is better to allow a competitor to take it on, as it will have adverse consequences for shareholder wealth in the competitor. A counter-argument might be that if it is thought that this contract will lead to further contracts in the future, then acceptance of a contract that diminishes shareholder wealth is worthwhile if it is thought that the follow-on contracts that the company receives will more than compensate for this in respect of adding to shareholder wealth.

Question 20

This question tests the candidate's ability to:

(i) **Calculate the outcome of hedging using currency options and forward exchange contracts (LO4)**

(ii) **Advise on the selection of an appropriate currency hedging method (LO4)**

(a) Amount the company is hedging in £ based on exercise price $1.62:

$500,000/$1.62 = £308,642.

Therefore, number of contracts = £308,642/£31,250 = 9.9 contracts; 10 contracts when rounded.

The company needs call options = right to buy £.

The cost (premium) for February option contracts with exercise price $1.62 is 4.44 cents per pound = total = 10 contracts × 4.44/100 × 31,250 = $13,875.

At spot rate the contracts cost $13,875/1.6154 = £8,589.

If the exchange rate in February is $1.6857 – $1.6864?

Exercise the option at $1.6200 = £31,250 × 10 contracts = £312,500 × $1.6200 = $506,250.

The receipt from the customer = $500,000, hence $6,250 needs to be purchased at February spot rate = $6,250/$1.6857 = £3,708.

In total:

	£
Option premium paid	(8,589)
£ received under options contracts	312,500
Purchase of surplus $	(3,708)
Net receipt	£300,203

(b) Under the forward exchange contract the company would exchange the $ at the forward rate of $1.6315.

Therefore, the sterling receipt for the company would be $500,000/$1.6315 = **£306,466**

(c) A forward exchange contract is where a company enters into a contract with a bank to buy or sell an agreed amount of currency on an agreed future date and with the exchange rate agreed today. This will eliminate all the exchange rate risk for the company which is what the finance director requires.

Forward contracts are simple to understand and enact, and this is also appropriate for the finance director as he is unfamiliar with hedging techniques and has no time to learn about them. As there are unlikely to be further overseas contracts this reinforces this.

Forward exchange contracts are available on most currencies and this will certainly include £/$ contracts.

Options contracts and fundamentally different to forwards as they give the right, but not the obligation, to buy or sell a currency at an agreed rate in the future. Hence, the company can hedge against adverse currency movements whilst participating in favourable exchange rate movements. Therefore, options would also eliminate the risk.

This flexibility has to be paid for and the company will have to pay an upfront premium. Options are available both through exchanges and over the counter from financial firms, and £/$ contracts will certainly be available. This runs counter to the director's desire for an inexpensive hedging method.

Also, options are not quite as straightforward as forward contracts and this makes them less suitable for the finance director's use.

Question 21

This question tests the candidate's ability to:

(i) **Evaluate the working capital position of a company (LO5)**

Report

To: Directors – Treet plc
Subject: Evaluation of working capital
From: XXXX
Date: XXXX

It is important that the company manages its working capital position effectively. If the working capital position is not managed well this can have important implications for the company's cashflow (liquidity) and profit. There are a number of ratios that can assist in the evaluation; however, to interpret the ratios it is important to take into account the company's situation and the industry it operates in.

Ratio	2013	2012
Current ratio	373/172 = 2.17	320/123 = 2.60
Quick ratio	(373 – 138)/172 = 1.37	(320 – 82)/123 = 1.93
Receivables' days	(185 × 365)/1,065 = 63.4 days	(148 × 365)/1,201 = 45.0 days
Stock turnover	(138 × 365)/798 = 63.1 days	(82 × 365)/889 = 33.7 days
Payables payment	(89 × 365)/798 = 40.7 days	(47 × 365)/889 = 19.3 days
Operating cycle	63.4 + 63.1 – 40.7 = 85.8 days	45.0 + 33.7 – 19.3 = 29.4 days

The trend in all of the ratios is that they depict a worsening position in respect of the working capital position of the company. This may be connected to the staff shortages in the accounting department as a lack of monitoring of the working capital position may have occurred.

The current ratio is well above 2:1 and the quick ratio is well above 1:1 and, therefore, both these ratios appear to be sound. They suggest that the liquidity of the company is sound on an overall basis.

However, the other three ratios – receivables' days, stock turnover days and payables payment days – are of greater concern. The receivables' days have increased from 45 to 63 days (approximately). To understand this figure it is important to consider the two different parts of the business. The retail part of the business is based upon cash sales. Therefore, it does not impact upon the receivables figures. The receivables figures relate to catalogue and online sales. That this is increasing suggests that customers are paying more slowly. The company is compensated for longer payment periods as customers are charged interest. However, the company needs to be careful that this does not indicate that they are lending to customers who are less able to pay. The increase in doubtful debts and the movement in the aged debtors from 2012 to 2013 suggest that there may be an issue in this respect. Two factors may have impacted on this:

1. That the number of staff responsible for management of customers' accounts was depleted for a period (which may have affected credit vetting and debt monitoring); and

2. The strategy of focusing on catalogue and online sales will have placed greater demands on the customer accounts department.

The strategy may have been decided by consideration of gross profit margins. The figures below indicate that gross profit percentages are higher for catalogue and online sales. The strategy has increased revenue per store. However, the implications of the strategy for management of working capital need thinking through carefully.

Gross profit margins	2013	2012
Retail revenue	79/455 = 17.4%	127/605 = 21.0%
Catalogue and online revenue	188/610 = 30.8%	185/596 = 31.0%
Overall	267/1,065 = 25.1%	312/1,201 = 26.0%

Average annual revenue per store	2013	2012
	£455m/135 = £3.4m per store	£605m/195 = £3.1m per store

Stock turnover days have increased significantly from 2012 to 2013. At January 31st 2013 there is the equivalent of 63 days inventory. This may suggest that the company's predictions for fashion trends were poor relative to the previous year. This may mean that the remaining stock will need to be sold at discounted prices if the company is not to be left with this stock.

Payables days were relatively low in 2012 at 19 days. This is very prompt payment for creditors as it may be normal to pay after 30 days. In 2013 the period lengthened to 40 days. This may suggest that the company is making suppliers wait a little longer than normal. This could be due to the accounting department being under-staffed and having fallen behind with payments. It could be a more deliberate measure to make suppliers wait longer for payment as a balance to the increase in receivables days and stock turnover days. This may be the case as the operating cycle has lengthened considerably, even taking into account the longer payables payment period. The company will need to take care that this does not upset suppliers as they are reliant upon them for prompt delivery of items.

Question 22

This question tests the candidate's ability to:

(i) **Advise on the capital structure of a company (LO1)**

Report

To: Jane Smith, Clare Brown
Subject: Advice on company financing
From: XXXX
Date: XXXX

You are seeking to raise further finance and uncertain whether to raise this finance through equity or using borrowings (debt). It needs to be stated at the outset there are different views concerning capital structure and there is not an ideal capital structure. There are alternative theories as to how a company should be financed and there are a number of practical considerations that need to be taken into account. Consequently, there is not one perfect solution to this issue.

Traditional theory and trade-off theory would both suggest that introducing debt into the company would be appropriate. The reason being that debt is relatively cheaper than equity as it is a less risky proposition. As Jane has noted one aspect of this is that debt interest is also tax-deductible and this reduces the cost of debt further. Therefore, the implication is that introducing debt would reduce the overall cost of capital for the company. However, the company must be careful not to introduce too much debt as then the company may struggle to meet its interest commitments. Clare is concerned about this occurring. This is related to the idea of financial distress whereby companies need to ensure they do not become too highly geared as then the overall cost of capital starts to rise. Consequently, there is an optimal range for debt although it is not always easy to know where this is.

If you are looking to take on debt then one approach to thinking about what may be the appropriate balance between debt and equity is to look at current industry average for gearing levels. Aiming to create a capital structure that fits with peer companies is one way of overcoming this problem of not knowing where the optimal range is. Therefore, if you have industry gearing data this would be helpful to review.

Pecking order theory suggests that companies should use debt before equity as a financing method. The rationale being that debt is less costly to issue than equity. Further, the use of debt may send a positive signal to the market. This latter point is discussed further below.

You also have to take into account a range of practical issues. One of these concerns the profit situation of the company. By taking on debt you are committing to paying the debt interest as it falls due. This is unlike dividends that can be varied each year. Therefore, the company must have sufficient cash and profits each year to meet this commitment. The company is now profitable but I would need to know what levels of profit it has achieved in the past to be able to advise on how much debt interest the company might be able to afford. If the debt is being used to finance the expansion then forecasts of profits from the new venture would also be required as these would be available to meet interest payments. It should also be borne in mind that the tax advantage of debt only applies if the company has profits and, hence, pays taxes.

Further, in respect of meeting the debt interest commitments you need to consider the likely volatility of profits in future years. If profits are more volatile and likely to fluctuate then this indicates that companies need to maintain lower levels of debt to ensure affordability in years when profits are poor. It would be helpful to know how volatile the profits are in both its current market sector and in the sector it is expanding into. The company is currently operating in a very competitive market sector and the profits from this may be more volatile than the luxury sector. This is because the current sector is very price sensitive and families may not book holidays if, for example, there is a recession and they have less money available for non-necessary items. This is less likely to be the case for luxury holidays and this could indicate that debt finance would be suitable for this venture.

If you do decide to use debt then security may be required. The company does not appear to have any security as it does not own its premises and it is unlikely to have any other significant physical assets. Therefore, it would need to be ascertained whether debt is available that does not require security. You will have to pay greater interest on such debt as it is a more risky proposition for the lender(s).

Your own views are important in selecting a method of finance. Jane has a preference for debt. It is stated that this is based on her consideration that debt is a cheaper source of finance. However, it might also be indicative of her having a more entrepreneurial view of the world. This suggests Jane is more willing to take on risks and is less concerned about the fact that debt interest is a fixed commitment. Further, Jane may also be thinking that introducing equity would dilute their shareholdings with associated implications for control of the company and the value obtained should they sell the company in the future. This can be compared to Clare's more prudent approach to the business. It is perhaps useful for Clare to bear in mind that debt is a normal feature of company financing.

Indeed, the use of debt can send a very positive signal to the market. The message it conveys is that the directors have confidence in the profitability of the company and for that reason are willing to take on debt to expand. It would be helpful to know how you think the company is viewed by those outside the firm and for your views on the likely reaction of the market if you were to expand the company into the new market sector.

Finally, when companies are seeking additional finance they need to think about market conditions and what types of finance are actually available at the time. Knowing current conditions for accessing debt and equity would be very helpful. Relatedly, it should be noted that it can be useful if companies leave some spare debt capacity. This then permits them to potentially access debt at short notice and this can be useful if good project opportunities become available but at short notice. Therefore, knowing whether you are likely to look for other new ventures would be very useful.

Exam question bank

1 Twitten plc [November 2021]

Twitten plc is a UK company in the industrial chemicals sector. It manufactures a range of chemical products, the most important of which is called MDX20. Twitten plc's primary financial goal is to maximise shareholder wealth.

Twitten plc's long-term funding comprises:

- 100 million ordinary shares quoted on the London Stock Exchange at £6.40 ex-div. The cost of equity is 17%.
- A £200 million irredeemable debenture trading ex-interest at 80% of its nominal value. The post-tax cost of debt is 7%.

Twitten plc is considering the purchase of a patent for €20 million. The patent was developed by a Spanish research company, Raclo SA. The purchase will take place on 31 December 2021 but the price will be payable in two equal instalments on 31 December 2021 and 31 December 2022.

The investment will be financed using currently available internal funds. Twitten plc estimates that the patent will have a useful life of five years, during which the patent will generate the following financial benefits for Twitten plc:

- Patent royalty income of €1,000,000 each year in money terms.
- MDX20 manufacturing cost savings of £4,200,000 each year in real terms.

In accordance with the UK's double taxation treaty with Spain, the patent royalties are only taxable in the UK. Twitten plc pays corporation tax in the UK on its profits at a rate of 19%, payable in the year the profits arise. The cost of the patent (translated to sterling at the exchange rate at purchase) qualifies for tax-allowable amortisation on a straight-line basis.

New capital investments are only accepted by Twitten plc if they meet all the following criteria:

- A net present value (NPV) of its relevant cash flows of at least zero based on Twitten plc's current weighted average cost of capital;
- A payback period (PBP) of no more than 3 years; and
- An accounting rate of return (ARR) of 22% per annum based on pre-tax profits and average investment;
- For investment appraisal purposes, the current exchange rate is €1.1635. This exchange rate is expected to move in line with the purchasing power parity theory. Inflation in the Euro-zone is 0.7% per year and in the UK it is 1.1%.

Market data

Spot exchange rate (€/£)	€1.1631 – 1.1640
1 year forward exchange rate (€/£)	€1.1585 – 1.1595

12-month money market rates	%p.a.
Deposit: £	1.00%
Deposit: €	0.80%
Borrowing: £	1.25%

Twitten plc has a small treasury function with system capabilities to make currency hedging decisions. With large foreign exchange payments, making lead payments are also considered as a means of hedging currency risk.

Required

(a) Calculate Twitten plc's weighted average cost of capital and justify its use as a discount rate in the appraisal of the Raclo patent. **(7 marks)**

(b) Evaluate the investment in the Raclo patent against Twitten plc's investment appraisal criteria and make a recommendation based on whether it maximises shareholder wealth. Ignore hedging for this part of the requirement. **(19 marks)**

(c) Assess Twitten plc's currency risk exposure in relation to the Raclo patent, making reference to transaction, translation and economic risk. No calculations are required for this part of the requirement. **(5 marks)**

(d) Calculate, providing supporting explanation, the total sterling cost of the patent, assuming Twitten plc buys it and hedges the currency risk in the most appropriate way. **(9 marks)**

(Total 40 marks)

2 Stannich Ltd [November 2021]

Stannich Ltd manufactures and sells quality and customised furniture to retailers. Its draft financial results for the year ended 30 September 2021 along with the budgeted financial statements for the period are as follows:

Statement of profit or loss

	Note	Actual $000	Budget $000
Sales revenue	1,2	15,222	10,546
Cost of sales		(10,679)	(7,921)
Operating profit		4,543	2,625
Interest		(314)	(221)
Profit before tax		4,229	2,404
Taxation		(634)	(361)
Profit after tax		3,595	2,043

Statement of financial position

	Note	Actual $000	Actual $000	Budget $000	Budget $000
Non-current assets	2		10,177		5,965
Current assets					
Inventory	3,4	1,272		651	
Trade receivables	4,5	1,752		867	
Cash		0		5	
			3,024		1,523
Current liabilities					
Bank overdraft	6	543		12	
Trade payables	4	965		651	
Tax payable		634		361	
			(2,142)		(1,024)
Long-term payables			(3,750)		(2,750)
			7,309		3,714
Share capital			50		50
Retained profits			7,259		3,664
			7,309		3,714

Notes

1. A new sales team was put in place in January 2021 in order to expand Stannich Ltd's customer base. The sales team was given significant autonomy on pricing and credit terms.

2. Investment was made in Stannich Ltd's factory to expand its production capacity to cope with the additional demand. This was financed by a £1million loan payable in three years.

3. At the beginning of the year, Stannich Ltd had a backlog of outstanding customer orders. This refers to orders which had been received from customers, but which had not been completed in Stannich Ltd's factory. This backlog on 30 September 2021 was approximately 80% higher in value than the equivalent backlog a year earlier.

4. Targets for working capital periods were set in the budget as follows:

	Budget (days)
Receivables payment period	30
Inventory turnover period	30
Payables payment period	(30)
Working capital cycle	30

5. A proposal has been made by the sales manager as follows:

    (a) Like many furniture manufacturers, Stannich Ltd should charge a 10% deposit from its customers on acceptance of a customer order, and

    (b) Offer a 2% discount to customers who pay for their furniture within ten days of the invoice date. Based the sales manager's experience, 25% of customers would take advantage of the discount.

6. Stannich Ltd's overdraft is at its maximum level and pays 9.5% interest on its overdraft.

Required

(a) Evaluate the extent of Stannich Ltd's success in achieving its target working capital cycle set in the budget. For each element of working capital, explain any potential reasons for differences between actual and budget and their impact on Stannich Ltd's cash position. Include calculations as appropriate. **(8 marks)**

(b) Evaluate, with supporting calculations, the impact on Stannich Ltd's profit and working capital of the sales manager's proposal and recommend any relevant action you consider appropriate for Stannich Ltd. **(12 marks)**

(Total 20 marks)

3 Scotswood plc [November 2021]

Scotswood plc operates in the manufacturing sector. It has had one wholly owned subsidiary, Redheugh Ltd, for many years. The directors of Scotswood plc have decided to restructure its product portfolio and have decided to sell Redheugh Ltd. They have also identified a potential acquisition target, Ouseburn Ltd, which is considered a more appropriate fit with Scotswood plc. The acquisition, if it goes ahead, will be financed by the sale of Redheugh Ltd.

Industry information

The quoted companies in the industry in which all the above companies operate:

- Have an average price-earnings (P/E) ratio of 12.3.
- Have an average cost of equity of 10%.
- Have an average working capital to sales ratio of 13%.
- Spend, on average, 8% of annual sales revenue expenditure on replacement and renewals of non-current assets.

Corporate tax is payable on company profits at 15%.

Redheugh Ltd

Redheugh Ltd has 600 million ordinary shares in issue. In the year ended 30 November 2021, Redheugh Ltd had earnings after tax of £450 million and free cash flow to equity of £480 million. Earnings and free cash flows to equity have been reasonably constant for the last four years and are expected to remain so for the foreseeable future under Scotswood plc's management.

An unconnected company, Benwell plc has expressed an interest in acquiring the entire share capital in Redheugh Ltd. Benwell plc has made two alternative offers to Scotswood plc for the shares:

(1) Cash of £9.20 for each ordinary share in Redheugh Ltd, or
(2) 3 newly issued ordinary shares in Benwell plc for every 2 ordinary shares in Redheugh Ltd.

Both offers are conditional on the whole of the share capital being transferred to Benwell plc. Benwell plc is quoted on a major stock exchange where its 1 billion ordinary shares are currently trading at £6.50 each.

Offer 2 is conditional on Scotswood plc retaining its new shares in Benwell until 31 December 2023.

Ouseburn Ltd

In the year ended 31 October 2021, Ouseburn Ltd generated profit before tax of £145 million as follows:

	Note	£m
Revenue	1,3	300
Operating expenses	2	(125)
Operating profit		175
Finance costs	4	(30)
Profit before tax	1,3	145

Notes

1. Revenue and free cash flows are expected to grow at 3% each year for the foreseeable future.
2. Depreciation of £35 million is included in the operating expenses.
3. The industry average working capital to sales ratio and expenditure on renewals and replacement non-current assets is typical of Ouseburn Ltd.

4   Finance costs relate to a £600 million long-term loan repayable in 12 years.

5   Ouseburn Ltd's weighted average cost of capital is assumed to be 8%.

Required

(a) Calculate the valuation of Redheugh Ltd's share capital, Redheugh Ltd's P/E ratio and Redheugh Ltd's cost of equity implicit in each of Benwell plc's offers. For offer 2 only, calculate the percentage shareholding Scotswood plc would have in Benwell plc if this offer were accepted.

(9 marks)

(b) Critically analyse the two offers made by Benwell plc and recommend, with reasons, which (if either) should be accepted   **(5 marks)**

(c) Calculate an appropriate value of Ouseburn Ltd based on free cash flows to the company.

(6 marks)

(Total 20 marks)

4 Saturna plc [November 2021]

Extracts from Saturna plc's statement of financial position as at 30 November 2021 is as follows:

	Note	£m
£1 ordinary shares	1	55
Reserves		875
6% redeemable debenture	2	100

Notes

1. Saturna plc's shares are quoted on a major stock exchange where they are trading at £7.22 each.

2. Saturna plc issued a fixed-rate 6% debenture in 2011 with a nominal (par) value of £100 million to a private investor (it is not quoted on the stock exchange). It is due to be redeemed at a 6% premium on 30 April 2032, although the debenture instrument specifies that it can be redeemed early at any time after 30 November 2022 for its fair value. The redemption yield on debentures such as this one is currently 5% per annum.

Because Saturna plc can borrow at significantly lower rates today compared to 2011, the treasurer of Saturna plc is proposing that the company buys back the debenture on 30 November 2022.

To refinance the loan, the treasurer of Saturna plc intends to borrow £120 million on 30 November 2022 for two years. This can be arranged via a fixed rate loan bearing interest of 4.5% or at a floating rate of SONIA + 4%. SONIA is currently at 0.2% but is likely to rise to 0.6% by 30 November 2022.

Two options have been identified in respect of the management of interest rates in respect of the new debt:

(1) Standard 3-month £500,000 interest rate futures contracts are available today as follows:

	£
December 2021	99.75
March 2022	99.70
June 2022	99.65
September 2022	99.65
December 2022	99.60

(2) Saturna plc can enter into an interest rate swap with Jupitus plc. Jupitus plc can borrow £120m for two years at a fixed interest rate of 5.6% or at a floating rate of SONIA + 4.8%. Arrangement fees are charged on each party at 0.65% per year of the amount borrowed.

Saturna plc pays corporate tax at 19% on its taxable profits. The risk-free rate of return is 0.2% and the market rate of return is 6.7%. Saturna plc's equity beta is 0.95.

Required

(a) Calculate Saturna plc's financial gearing percentage using market values and its weighted average cost of capital as at 30 November 2021. **(8 marks)**

(b) Prepare calculations which illustrate the interest rate hedge on the futures market, assuming interest rates move as expected. State whichever reasonable assumptions necessary. **(8 marks)**

(c) Calculate Saturna plc's saving in finance costs in pounds resulting from the interest rate swap. State whichever reasonable assumptions necessary. **(4 marks)**

(Total 20 marks)

5 Matti Fortuna Gyms SA [May 2022]

Matti Fortuna Gyms SA (MFG) is a company headquartered in Paris, France, which operates a successful chain of gyms in France. Its functional currency is the Euro (€). MFG was founded by former footballer, Matti Fortuna.

MFG's brand is distinctive and based on giving its members a comprehensive and effective, but standard gym experience.

Its members are diverse in terms of age, gender and ethnicity. The monthly membership fee is €25 per month for 24-hour access to the gyms, throughout the year.

The directors of MFG decided to expand into the UK, and have identified two possible methods of doing so:

Method 1:	Acquire properties around the UK and convert them into brand new MFG gyms which will be opened to the public on 1 June 2023 (see Exhibit 1).
Method 2:	Acquire shares in Stennerham Ltd, a UK company which operates a chain of fitness and leisure clubs (see Exhibit 2).

MFG is a listed company with 400 million ordinary shares in issue. Matti Fortuna, owns 20% of the shares. The shares are currently quoted at €1.84 each.

Required

(a) For method 1, shown below in exhibit 1, calculate the after-tax net present value (NPV) in Euros as of 31 May 2022 and conclude on its financial acceptability. **(14 marks)**

(b) For Method 1 shown below in exhibit 1, explain and critically appraise your colleagues' approach and assumption when selecting the 12 London properties. **(6 marks)**

(c) For method 2, shown below in exhibit 2, as far as the available information permits, calculate

   (i) a share price for Stennerham Ltd using the free cash flows method;

   (ii) Matti Fortuna's percentage shareholding in MFG assuming a share for share exchange is used to finance the acquisition. **(13 marks)**

(d) Evaluate the main financial and non-financial benefits and risks for MFG of method 2 in comparison to method 1. **(7 marks)**

(Total 40 marks)

Exhibit 1 – Method 1 – Brand new gyms

Method 1 involves the purchase of 265 UK properties between 1 June 2022 and 1 June 2024. Each will be converted and used as a gym.

Your colleague has correctly prepared the following projections of the relevant sterling cash flows arising from this investment.

	31 May						
	2022	*2023*	*2024*	*2025*	*2026*	*2027*	*2028*
	£m	£m	£m	£m	£m	£m	£m
Operating cash flows	0	19.25	106.25	265	265	265	265
Purchase of properties	(7.18)	(18.45)	(28.70)				
Purchase of equipment	(1.40)	(3.60)	(5.60)				

The gym equipment has a six-year useful life and qualifies for tax-deductible capital allowances at 18% on a reducing balance basis. At the end of its life the equipment is gifted to local charities for zero proceeds.

MFG will pay UK corporation tax at 25% on its UK profits, payable at the end of the year to which it relates. No further tax will be payable in France on the profits of the UK gyms.

Money market interest rates in the UK are 1% in the UK and 1.2% in France.

Investment appraisal process

- MFG appraises investments over a six-year period by calculating a Euro NPV after tax.
- MFG appraises investments by discounting Euro cash flows at a Euro weighted average cost of capital of 10%.
- Assume a 31 May year end and today is 31 May 2022.
- Current spot exchange rate is £1 = €1.1500
- Ignore inflation

London gyms

In the first year of this investment, the £7.18m property cost includes the cost of 12 properties located in the capital of the UK, London. Although approximately 20 suitable properties were identified in London by MFG, the directors decided to limit the initial investment in London properties to £4 million. This was because London property prices are more expensive than in other UK locations.

In order to decide which properties were to be selected, your colleagues in the finance department made recommendations to the directors, based on their profitability index and the assumption that the investment in each gym could be proportionately scaled down.

Exhibit 2 – Method 2 – Acquisition of Stennerham Ltd

Method 2 involves the acquisition of 100% of the ordinary shares in a UK company, Stennerham Ltd.

Stennerham Ltd operates a chain of 12 clubs, located across the south of the UK. All Stennerham clubs have state of the art gyms with equipment renewed every three to four years. The clubs all have swimming pools, squash and tennis courts. Annual membership fees are £2,200 on average.

Stennerham members are generally affluent individuals with an average age of 46.

Stennerham Ltd has 1 million ordinary shares in issue.

The following is an extract of Stennerham Ltd's management accounts for the year ended 31 March 2022.

	Note	£000
Profit before interest and tax (PBIT)	1,2	29,600
Finance costs	3	(4,000)
Profit before tax		25,600

Notes

1. Profit before interest and tax is after a depreciation charge of £2.5 million per year.
2. Without opening new clubs, it is expected PBIT will be stable in perpetuity.
3. Finance costs represent interest on long term bank loans totalling £50 million. These loans are due for repayment between 2028 and 2035.
4. Based on Stennerham Ltd's return on shareholders' funds, it has a cost of equity of 12% and a weighted average cost of capital of 10.65%.

6 Pax Ltd [May 2022]

Pax Ltd is a manufacturing company established in 2012. It has a number of research and development (R&D) programmes underway which aim to make its manufacturing activities more efficient.

Pax Ltd experienced significant sales growth until 2020. However, the company's profit is modest and its lack of liquidity has meant that some of its R&D programmes have been temporarily suspended.

The following is a forecast in respect of the year ending 30 June 2023.

	Note	£m
Sales revenue	1	540.00
Cost of sales		(305.70)
Other operating costs		(222.20)
Operating profit		12.10
Finance costs	2	(4.10)
Earnings before tax		8.00
Tax at 25%		(2.00)
Earnings after tax	3	6.00

Notes

1. The target receivables collection period in the year ending 30 June 2023 is 36.5 days.
2. Pax Ltd took out a ten-year secured loan with its bank in 2017. It also uses an unsecured overdraft with the same bank. The overdraft facility has been, and is expected to continue, at its maximum level throughout the year ending 30 June 2023. It has been used as a permanent source of finance and is included in any gearing calculation.
3. The directors believe a price/earnings (P/E) ratio of 8.33 would be appropriate to calculate the value of Pax Ltd's equity share capital.

The directors are considering two proposals.

Proposal 1 – Settlement discount

- Offer a 2% discount to customers who pay their invoices in full in 15 days
- 20% of Pax Ltd's customers are expected to take up the offer, the remainder will pay in 36.5 days (the target receivables collection period).

Proposal 2 – Refinancing

- Pax Ltd's bank proposed a £25 million loan repayable in five years. Like the existing loan it will be secured against Pax Ltd's main factory, which is worth £200m.

- The loan would be used to repay its overdraft in full and also to acquire some new machinery which will save £2.6m in operating costs.

Required

(a) Calculate Pax Ltd's forecast financial gearing (market value of debt as a percentage of market value of debt plus equity (D/(D+E)) as of 30 June 2023, assuming neither proposal is accepted.

(3 marks)

(b) Calculate Pax Ltd's projected earnings after tax, the market value of its equity and its gearing ratio if proposal 1 is implemented (but not proposal 2). **(11 marks)**

(c) Evaluate the factors for Pax Ltd to consider when deciding on the suitability of proposal 2 as a source of finance for the company. No calculations are necessary. **(6 marks)**

(Total 20 marks)

7 Denny Ltd [May 2022]

The FLP group consists of:

- Jabasi Inc, the parent company, based in USA whose currency is the US dollar ($)
- Denny Ltd, a UK subsidiary, whose currency is the Pound (£); and
- Gamlar AB, a Swedish subsidiary which uses the Krona (SEK)

In addition to sales to external customers, the three companies trade in goods and services with each other. Each company has its own treasury function and policies, including hedging policies. However, it is group policy that intra-group balances payable/receivable are settled using a process of multilateral netting. Settlement payments due as a result of the netting will take place on 31 July 2022.

The exchange rates used for the netting are agreed at the beginning of each year. The rates agreed on 1 October 2021 for the year ending 30 November 2022 are as follows:

- $1 = £0.87
- $1 = SEK10.23

In the quarter ending 31 May 2022, the three companies have had intra-group trading.

The intra-group balances on 31 May 2022 are expected to be as follows:

			Sales to	
		Denny	Jabasi	Gamlar
Sales from	Denny £m		14.4	22.4
	Jabasi $m	10.1		1.4
	Gamlar SEKm	117.8	88.8	

Market data

	31 May price	31 July price
Spot prices	$1 = £0.8600 – 0.8700	$1 = £0.8622 – 0.8732
Sterling futures contract (September contract size £62,500, price $ per £)	$1.1520	$1.1610

EXAM QUESTION BANK

	Deposit	Borrowing
US ($) interest rates (2 months, p.a)	5.00%	5.50%
UK (£) interest rates (2 months, p.a)	5.25%	5.75%

Required

(a) Calculate the net payments and receipts expected in dollars on 31 July 2022 as a result of the multilateral netting. Evaluate the benefits and risks arising for Denny Ltd from the multilateral netting process. **(7 marks)**

(b) Develop, with supporting calculations, an explanation of how a money market hedge would be performed by Denny Ltd to manage transaction risk associated with its expected cash flow on 31 July 2022. **(7 marks)**

(c) Calculate the sterling value of the cash flow expected on 31 July 2022 if it is hedged on the currency futures market. **(6 marks)**

(Total 20 marks)

8 Mankita Group [May 2022]

You work as a financial analyst for Mankita plc, the parent company of the Mankita Group which consists of more than 30 international companies. You have received the following emails from colleagues working for the Mankita Group.

Email 1 – from your manager in Mankita plc

In the next few months, the Mankita Group will acquire two new subsidiaries, FJJ plc and Telatela plc, which are in the same industry sector. I have been asked by the group chief executive to estimate their weighted average costs of capital (WACCs). The available data is as follows:

FJJ plc

- Pays annual dividends of £0.12 per share and earnings per share of £0.48. Retained profits are reinvested to fuel growth in FJJ plc's business.
- Has 350 million ordinary shares quoted on a stock exchange at £1.36 and no debt.
- Yield on new investments has been consistently between 14% and 20% per year.
- Operating gearing, measured as Contribution/Operating profit is 177%.

Telatela plc

- Has a debt to equity ratio of 2:5 based on market values.
- The post-tax cost of debt is 6%.
- Equity beta of 1.15.
- Market rate of return is 13% and the market premium for risk is 10%.
- Operating gearing is 144%.

Email 2 – from your colleague in the production department of one of Mankita plc's subsidiaries

TYR559 is the main component in a number of our products. We use it at a constant rate of 10,000 units per day, 360 days per year. Each unit has a purchase cost of £5,000 and, because TYR559 needs to be kept at a certain temperature, we have to pay our supplier a fixed fee of £26,000 per delivery and deliveries can only be in batches of 1,000. Each unit costs approximately £500 to store for a whole year.

At present, each order is for 100,000 units but we've had difficulty finding appropriate storage facilities. Our finance director has asked what savings we can make if we ordered using the economic order quantity (EOQ) model.

Required

(a) Calculate the weighted average costs of capital (WACC) of both FJJ plc and Telatela plc. Also, identify and develop possible reasons why the two companies' costs of equity and WACC may be different. **(11 marks)**

(b) Calculate the inventory-related cost savings resulting from changing the order quantity for TYR559. **(9 marks)**

(Total 20 marks)

9 Melona Inc [November 2022]

Assume it is November 2022.

Melona Inc was established in 2016 to develop an application used in mobile phones, called Misca (the Misca app). The Misca app was successful and generated significant profits from 2018 to 2021 onwards. Although the app has been updated regularly to improve its functionality, Melona Inc's revenue from the Misca app has started to fall in 2022. This is because alternative apps have begun to appear that are more innovative and easier to use.

Melona Inc's forecast earnings for the year ending 31 December 2022 is as follows:

	Note	$m
Revenue	1	41.0
Fixed costs		(14.0)
Depreciation, amortisation and other non-cash expenses		(5.0)
Earnings before interest and tax (EBIT)		22.0
Dividends from Doctim Inc	2	3.0
Finance charges	3	(2.0)
Taxation	4	(5.8)
Earnings after tax		17.2

Notes

1. Melona Inc's revenue comes from sales of the Misca app. It has no other sources of operating income. In 2023 it is expected to be 7% lower than in 2022 and is expected to fall by a further 15% in 2024 unless new sources of revenue are secured.

2. Doctim Inc is a technology-development company. Melona Inc owns 10% of the ordinary share capital in Doctim Inc.

3. Melona Inc borrowed $25 million to fund the development of the Misca app. The annual interest rate is 8% and the interest is payable quarterly in arrears. The entire $25 million is repayable on 31 December 2023. The forecast cash balance on 31 December 2022 is nil.

4. Taxation is payable at 25% of earnings before tax, at the end of the year to which it relates.

Doctim Inc

Doctim Inc, a software development company, was established in 2015 in a country called Jordak, by two software engineers, who are still directors. Their reputation for innovation and quality was quickly established. As a result, the company attracted funding from several equity investors which financed the company's growth. One of these investors was Melona Inc, which acquired a 10% stake in Doctim Inc for $100,000.

The development of the Melona Inc's Misca app was outsourced to Doctim Inc in 2016 and 2017 as it did not have its own research and development function. Since then, Doctim Inc has been responsible for the maintenance and updating of the app. Melona Inc pays Doctim Inc $3 million each year for the maintenance of its app.

Doctim Inc was listed on the Jordak stock exchange in 2019. The Jordak stock exchange is highly regulated. The Jordak government must own a stake of between 10% and 20% in every company listed on the stock exchange. For that reason, Doctim Inc is owned by the government, the two founding shareholders, Melona Inc and four other companies. None of whom has bought or sold any shares in Doctim Inc for over a year.

Trading in shares on the Jordak stock exchange is a lengthy and costly process. Taxation is charged on both purchases and sales of shares. Large transactions in shares must, in some cases, be approved by the stock market authority which is controlled by the Jordak government in advance.

The directors of Melona Inc are considering selling the 10% stake in Doctim Inc on 1 January 2023 in order to set up its own development function so it can develop and maintain new applications. The finance director has argued that the market valuation quoted on the Jordak stock exchange cannot be relied upon to give a fair value.

Doctim Inc's recent financial results and position, along with forecasts for the next few years and other relevant information are as follows:

Year ended 31 December	2020 Actual $m	2021 Actual $m	2022 Forecast $m	2023 Forecast $m
Earnings before interest and tax	46.0	51.5	57.7	64.6
Finance costs	(2.5)	(2.5)	(2.5)	(2.5)
Taxation	(8.7)	(9.8)	(11.0)	(12.4)
Earnings after tax	34.8	39.2	44.2	49.7
Dividends paid	-	-	(30.0)	(33.6)
Retained earnings	34.8	39.2	14.2	16.1
Tangible assets	1.4	0.8	1.6	1.7
Intellectual property	209.0	234.0	259.0	284.0
Liabilities	(50.0)	50.0)	(50.0)	(50.0)

Other information

- Earnings before interest and tax includes a charge of $20 million for amortisation of intellectual property.

- Capital expenditure on new development projects will be $80 million per year on average.

- The price to earnings ratios for companies in the same industry sector as Doctim Inc on efficient markets range from 7 to 15.

- Doctim Inc's assumed cost of equity is 20%, and its anticipated growth in earnings is 12%

- The total cost of setting up and running Melona Inc's own development function is expected to be as follows:

	2023 $m	2024 $m
Capital expenditure	40.0	78.0
Revenue expenses	10.0	15.0

Required

(a) Calculate, with supporting explanations, a range of valuations for Doctim Inc's ordinary share capital based on the information available, including a valuation based on free cash flows, and recommend and justify an appropriate valuation for Melona Inc's shareholding. **(22 marks)**

(b) Assuming Melona Inc establishes its own development function on 1 January 2023 and disposes of its shareholding in Doctim Inc on the same day to partially fund it, calculate Melona Inc's cash balances at 31 December 2023 and 2024 and the amount of additional finance required.
(12 marks)

(c) Justify the suggestion of Melona Inc's finance director that the market value of its shareholding in Doctim Inc is unreliable and evaluate the available evidence in the scenario to support the suggestion. **(6 marks)**

(Total 40 marks)

10 Stannerton Ltd [November 2022]

Stannerton Ltd is a UK company which manufactures mobile telephone components in its UK factory. Raw materials and finished goods are stored in a warehouse located on the same site as the factory. The factory and the warehouse are both operating at approximately 90% capacity.

Currently, its sales are mainly to European customers. Its suppliers are almost all located in the UK.

An extract from the financial year just ended shows results as follows:

	£m
Revenue	600.0
Purchases and other cost of sales	(250.0)
Operating profit	350.0

Its working capital cycle is constant through the year as follows:

	Days
Receivables period	45.0
Inventory period	25.0
Payables period	(30.0)
	40.0

Stannerton Ltd has recently won a five-year contract to supply a new Canadian customer, Bomon Inc, with mobile phone components with an annual sales value of C$480 million (C$ = Canadian dollars). The contract will start on 1 January 2023.

The current spot rate between the British pound (£) and the Canadian dollar is C$1 = £0.625. The exchange rate between the pound and the dollar was C$1 = £0.5843 on 1 January 2022.

Sales to Bomon Inc will arise evenly over the year.

In line with the contract, Stannerton Ltd will invoice Bomon Inc at the end of each quarter, i.e 31 March, 30 June, 30 September and 31 December for the sales made in each quarter. The contract specifies that payment will be made in Canadian dollars 90 days following the date on the invoice.

Required

Evaluate, with supporting explanations and calculations, the currency and working capital risks arising from Stannerton Ltd's contract with Bomon Inc. Recommend and justify possible actions which could mitigate these risks. **(Total 20 marks)**

11 Trapling PLC [November 2022]

It is 31 December 2022.

Trapling PLC is a pharmaceutical company. In 2021, it started a research and development (R&D) project aimed at creating new technology which would lead to the launch of three new products to be sold to medical practitioners. The project is under review and the directors are about to make a decision as to whether Trapling PLC will continue the research and launch the new products.

Trapling PLC pays corporate tax on its profits at 30%, payable at the end of the year the profits arise.

The R&D project has already incurred $142 million and is expected to be completed at the end of 2023. Between now and the end of 2023 the R&D project will incur further incremental costs of $16 million. This expenditure is tax-deductible.

On completion of the R&D project, production of the new products will start on 1 January 2024. Production plant and equipment will be bought at a cost of $75 million on 1 January 2024. It will be scrapped for zero proceeds on 31 December 2030. The expenditure on plant and equipment will be 100% tax-deductible in the year it is incurred.

The new products will generate pre-tax cash profits of $40 million in 2024. This will rise to $72 million in 2025 and pre-tax profits will remain at that level until the end of 2030, after which it is likely the new product will need to be replaced or enhanced, so profits after 2030 can be ignored for the purpose of investment appraisal.

It is expected that working capital of 10% of each year's pre-tax profit will be required at the start of each year for liquidity purposes. It is assumed that any working capital will be released at the end of 2030.

A summary of Trapling PLC's cost of capital is as follows:

Weighted average cost of capital	10.912%
Geared cost of equity	16.176%
Ungeared cost of equity	13.360%

If Trapling PLC continues with the project and launches the new products, it will borrow $100 million immediately for eight years at an interest rate of 4%.

Required

(a) Appraise the financial viability of Project JJX by calculating its adjusted present value (APV) at the 31 December 2022 assuming Trapling PLC launches the new product itself after the development phase is complete. **(15 marks)**

(b) Explain and justify the use of the APV as a decision-making technique in the specific circumstances of this project. **(5 marks)**

(Total 20 marks)

12 Kraddassian Broadcasting Corporation [November 2022]

Assume today is 30 November 2022.

The Kraddassian Broadcasting Corporation (KBC) is a national broadcaster in the country of Kraddassia. It spends $400 billion each year on providing television, radio and other online broadcasts aimed to entertain, inform and educate the Kraddassian population. The cost of producing the broadcasts can vary greatly depending on their nature.

The KBC's activities are funded primarily by the Kraddassian government. In the financial year ending 31 December 2023, the government will provide $360 billion to pay for the KBC's operations, the payments will be spread over the year and will be scheduled based on the Baumol model. The first payment will take place on the 1 January 2023.

Public authorities in Kraddassia have a cost of capital of 5% and the KBC earns an interest rate of 3% on its cash deposits. The fixed cost of administering and executing each payment to the KBC is $0.1 billion.

The KBC anticipates having to borrow $5 billion on 31 May 2023 for six months. The directors of the KBC are keen to hedge against interest rate risk associated with this borrowing.

A bank has offered a $5billion 6-12 forward rate agreement at 5.25%.

On the futures market the following 3-month $0.5bn contracts are available:

	Price
December	94.75
March	94.65
June	94.45
September	94.25

Assume interest rates on 31 May 2023 will be 6% and closing futures price on that date is 93.90.

Required

(a) (i) Calculate the amounts and dates of the government's payments to the KBC in 2023.

(ii) Evaluate the decision to use the Baumol model to determine the amount and timing of each payment. Your evaluation should include an illustration of the cost savings that the model can generate and also an explanation of why it may not be useful in KBC's case **(10 marks)**

(b) Calculate the outcome of each hedging strategy in respect of the loan due to be taken on 31 May 2023. **(10 marks)**

(Total 20 marks)

13 Verity Trading Ltd [May 2023]

Verity Trading Ltd is a UK company which manufactures chemicals for the food industry.

It has a post-tax weighted average cost of capital of 12% and pays tax on its profits at 25% at the end of the year in which the profits arise.

Verity Trading Ltd operates a continuous manufacturing process. Production can be slowed from day to day but due to the technology involved, it is not practical to stop the manufacturing process without incurring large operating costs and lost sales. Sufficient inventory of raw materials is maintained to support two days of production, in order to minimise the risk of stoppages.

On average, each unplanned stoppage costs approximately £150,000.

Chemical XC337 is used in almost all of Verity Trading Ltd's products. The following table shows data on Verity Trading Ltd's usage and purchase price of XC337.

	2021 Actual	2022 Actual	2023 Forecast	2024 onwards Forecast
XC337 usage (tonnes)	7,250	8,500	9,750	10,725
Cost per tonne (£)	255	275	280	300

The forecast cost per tonne is based on the assumption that Verity Trading Ltd renews a supply contract with its current supplier, Yello Ltd, which is a UK supplier. Relevant details are as follows:

- Yello Ltd began supplying chemical XC337 to Verity Trading Ltd on 1 January 2021. The contract covered a supply period until 31 December 2023.

- The deliveries from Yello Ltd are scheduled according to the economic order quantity (EOQ) which is agreed between Verity Trading Ltd and Yello Ltd at the beginning of each year.

- Verity Trading Ltd pays for the deliveries at the end of each quarter.

- Since 1 January 2021, Yello Ltd has made deliveries as follows:

	2021	2022
On time (% of deliveries)	81%	76%
Up to 2 days late (% of deliveries)	13%	18%
Up to 5 days late (% of deliveries)	6%	6%

Chemical XC337 is highly toxic and requires very specific conditions for its delivery and storage. The cost of ordering chemical XC337 from Yello Ltd is in the form of a delivery charge. Yello Ltd charges £27,500 per delivery.

The incremental cost of holding a tonne of chemical XC337 is £6,000. This is the same regardless of the supplier.

Alternative supplier

Verity Trading Ltd has received a bid from an alternative supplier based in Bergen, Norway. The supplier is Nordqvistan ASA ("NQ ASA") and has offered to supply chemical XC337 for three years starting from 01 January 2024.

NQ ASA has been manufacturing and supplying chemicals, including chemical XC337 for many years. It has built a reputation for safe working practices in a traditionally hazardous chemical manufacturing environment. NQ ASA's own suppliers are thoroughly audited for socially responsible practices and terminate supply contracts with any supplier whose practices are deemed unsafe or exploitative. It is also known in the industry for its strong research and development programmes aimed at reducing waste products from its processes.

NQ ASA's bid is as follows:

- Supply chemical XC337 to Verity Trading Ltd for 4,100 Norwegian Krone (NOK) per tonne.

- There will be no delivery charge.

- NQ ASA will integrate its information systems with those of Verity Trading Ltd so that NQ ASA can monitor inventory levels and automatically dispatch chemical XC337 when needed. Average inventory levels will be maintained at 150 tonnes.

- NQ ASA will fully reimburse any cost incurred by Verity Trading Ltd caused by production stoppages due to late deliveries.

- The system integration will allow Verity Trading Ltd to pay immediately for each delivery. Payment will be in Norwegian Krone.

- The cost of system integration will be borne by Verity Trading Ltd and will be $500,000 payable in US dollars (USD) on 31 December 2023. The cost of system integration is deductible from Verity Trading Ltd's taxable profits.

The current spot and forecast exchange rates are as follows:

	24 May 2023	31 December 2023	31 December 2024 onwards
£1 = NOK	11.75	11.10	10.85
£1 = USD	1.20	1.15	1.12

Exchange-traded sterling futures with an expiry of 31 December 2023 are available in standard contract sizes of £62,500 at a futures rate of $1.1510.

Required

(a) Assuming the contract with Yello Ltd is renewed on 1 January 2024, calculate:

    (i) The economic order quantity for chemical XC337 in 2024;

    (ii) The annual ordering, holding and purchasing costs associated with chemical XC337 in 2024. **(12 marks)**

(b) Assess the appropriateness of the economic order quantity for determining the amount and timing of deliveries of chemical XC337 to Verity Trading Ltd. **(5 marks)**

(c) Assuming the payment for system integration on 31 December 2023 is fully hedged using currency futures, calculate the net payment in pounds sterling. **(5 marks)**

(d) Critically analyse the proposal to switch to Nordqvistan ASA as the suppliers of chemical XC337. Your analysis should include a calculation of the net present value (NPV) in pounds sterling of the proposal as well as an assessment of its advantages and risks. **(18 marks)**

(Total 40 marks)

14 Pinguo Ltd [May 2023]

Today is 1 June 2023.

Pinguo Ltd is an investment company set up in 2015 by Saskia Jaxman to hold her significant property portfolio. Since 2015, Saskia has acquired other investments using Pinguo Ltd as an investment-holding vehicle. She also gifted 10% of the share capital to her husband, Goran, in 2018.

Pinguo Ltd has no trading activity, and no other assets other than its investments, no employees other than Saskia and Goran who are directors as well as shareholders.

Saskia and Goran have decided to divorce and, as part of the divorce settlement, Saskia has agreed to transfer $1 million to Goran on 1 June 2023. Saskia has identified two options to finance the transfer:

(1) Transfer Pinguo Ltd shares with a value of $1 million to Goran.

(2) Have Pinguo Ltd dispose of enough of its quoted investments and use the proceeds (net of 12% legal fees and taxes payable by Pinguo Ltd) to declare a dividend for Saskia of $1 million which she will transfer to Goran.

Pinguo Ltd's investments and their market and book values as at 1 June 2023 are as follows:

	Market value $m	Book value $m
Property	4.2	3.6
Quoted investments	3.1	3.1
Bonds and cash deposits	0.5	0.5
	7.8	7.2

Pinguo Ltd's long-term capital structure comprises 4 million $1 ordinary shares and a number of long-term loans with an average interest rate of 8% per year. Pinguo Ltd's cash balance is nil.

Pinguo Ltd's recent and forecast investment income is as follows:

Years ending 30 June	2021 Actual $,000	2022 Actual $,000	2023 Forecast $,000
Rental income (net of related expenses)	420	440	490
Dividend income	465	205	553
Interest income on bonds and cash deposits	18	18	18
Net gains/(losses) on disposal of investments	362	-20	190
Total investment income	1,265	643	1,251
General overheads and management expenses	-200	-200	-200
Finance costs (interest)	-96	-144	-144
Profit before tax	969	299	907
Taxation	-145	-45	-136
Earnings after tax	824	254	771

The investments held by Pinguo Ltd are unrelated to each other. The following assumptions can be made in relation to the year ending 30 June 2024:

- No investments will be sold or acquired in the year ending 30 June 2024
- The income from Pinguo Ltd's remaining investments is expected to be in line with that of the year ending 30 June 2023.
- There is no expected change in Pinguo Ltd's capital structure or effective tax rate in the year ending 30 June 2024.

Required

(a) Assuming option 1 is chosen and Saskia decides to transfer shares in Pinguo Ltd to Goran:

  (i) Calculate the value of Saskia's current shareholding in Pinguo Ltd using the assets basis.

  (4 marks)

  (ii) Calculate the price to earnings (P/E) ratio implicit in the assets-basis value. **(1 mark)**

  (iii) Justify the use of the assets basis to value Saskia's shares in Pinguo Ltd, rather than an earnings basis; and **(6 marks)**

  (iv) Using the assets basis, calculate how many shares Saskia would have to transfer to Goran on 30 June 2023. **(2 marks)**

(b) Assuming option 2 is chosen, calculate, with supporting explanations:

  (i) The value of quoted investments to be sold
  (ii) Pinguo Ltd's forecast dividend income for the year ending 30 June 2024. **(7 marks)**

  (Total 20 marks)

15 Portshead plc [May 2023]

Today is 1 June 2023.

Portshead plc is a company quoted on a major stock exchange in the country of Kardasia. It was established by the Portshead family in 2003 and admitted to the stock exchange in 2018. Portshead plc has 350 million ordinary shares in issue trading at $9.90 per share. This has grown steadily since 1 June 2018 when it was $4 per share but share price growth is likely to be 1% for the next five years.

When it was listed on the stock exchange, the Portshead family members retained a total of 96.25 million ordinary shares between them.

According to Kardasian company law, a shareholder or group of shareholders with at least 26.5% of the ordinary share capital can be represented on the board of directors and also prevent certain key decisions about their company's management and strategy.

On 1 June 2015, prior to its listing, Portshead plc issued some 7% convertible loan stock to a small number of private investors for 110% of nominal value. The loan stock is not quoted on the stock exchange. It has a nominal value of $50 million. The earliest date for conversion is 31 December 2028. On 1 June 2028, holders of this convertible loan stock have the option but not the obligation to either redeem the loan stock at par or convert it into 25 ordinary shares in Portshead plc for every $100 of loan stock. Yields on similar convertible instruments are currently 10%. Portshead plc pays tax on its profits at a rate of 25%.

Leia Portshead is the Portshead family's representative on the board of directors. She is concerned about the prospective conversion of this loan stock and has asked for your help in understanding its consequences and suggests that the Portshead family members are willing to purchase the convertible loan stock now to prevent the conversion.

Required

(a) Calculate, with supporting explanations, the Portshead family's current shareholding percentage in Portshead plc and their expected shareholding after the prospective conversion in 2028 for each of the following scenarios:

 (i) The family buys the convertible loan stock immediately.
 (ii) The family does not buy the loan stock. **(6 marks)**

(b) Report on the significance of each of your calculations in a)(i) and a)(ii) for the Portshead family.
 (2 marks)

(c) Calculate the value of the convertible loan stock. **(7 marks)**

(d) Develop and justify an alternative strategy for the Portshead family to prevent the dilution of the family's shareholding. **(5 marks)**

(Total 20 marks)

16 Brandin Co [May 2023]

Today is 1 June 2023. SONIA is currently at 3.75%.

Brandin Co will borrow £75 million on 30 November 2023 for a period of ten months at a rate 5% above SONIA. This represents an increase in Brandin Co's borrowings, and it will be renewed every ten months, so it is permanent financing.

Three-month £125,000 interest rate futures contracts, expiring on 31 December 2023, are available at a price of 95.55.

On 30 November 2023, SONIA is at 4.95%.

As well as this debt, Brandin Co also has a debenture redeemable on 31 May 2025 with a nominal value of £100 million. It is trading at 101% of nominal value and its post-tax cost of debt is 6.4%

Brandin Co has 72.5 million ordinary shares in issue, trading at £5 per share. The cost of equity is 14.5%

Brandin Co pay tax on its profits at 19%.

Required

(a) Calculate, with supporting explanations of basis risk, the closing price of a December interest rate futures contract on 30 November 2023. **(4 marks)**

(b) Calculate the net interest payable by Brandin Co on its loan, taking into account the futures hedge and calculate the annualised effective interest rate for the loan. **(10 marks)**

(c) Calculate Brandin Co's weighted average cost of capital on 30 November 2023. **(6 marks)**

(Total 20 marks)

17 Falstone PLC. [November 2023]

You work as a financial controller for Falstone PLC, a software development company based in a country in the eurozone. You have received two emails this morning. The first is about the investment appraisal of a potential new product, codenamed Project Sadie. The second email relates to a company in which Falstone PLC holds a 10% shareholding.

Email 1 from Management Accountant - Project Sadie

The net present value (NPV) of Project Sadie is €9.02 million, which suggests a viable project.

I have attached the following to this email:

Attachment 1	The original data provided by the Product Development department and the corporate Treasury.
Attachment 2	My calculation of the NPV.
	The Product Development director wrote to me and said that the data from the Treasury department was wrong and gave me alternative assumptions to use when preparing the NPV. See the calculation for more details.
	I would also like you to review my calculations on inflation and capital expenditure as I am not sure if they are correct.

Attachment 1: Data and assumptions for Project Sadie

The project will begin on 1 January 2024 and will generate revenue in the three years to 31 December 2026 when the new product will be withdrawn. The new product, which uses existing technology, will be sold to one single client based in the United States over the three-year period. Revenue will be in US dollars ($) as follows:

Year ending	31.12.2024	31.12.2025	31.12.2026
Contract fee in dollars	$42.0m	$60.0m	$65.0m

Exchange rate projections ($/(€))

The best-case and worst-case scenarios and their probabilities for the exchange rate between the dollar and the euro have been identified as follows.

	01.01.2024	31.12.2024	31.12.2025	31.12.2026
1 € = USD (40% probability)	1.1000	1.1200	1.1250	1.1290
1 € = USD (60% probability)	1.1100	1.1450	1.1560	1.1900

Costs:

	€m	Notes
Maintenance Cost	€16m a year for three years	This is subcontracted to a reliable third party and the fee will not be affected by inflation.
Incremental Fixed costs	€14m a year in real terms	This will be subject to inflation at the following rates: 2024: 8% 2025: 6% 2026: 4%
Capital expenditure: equipment	€40m on 1 January 2024	This will qualify for capital allowances at 15% per year on a reducing balance basis and will be disposed of on 31 December 2026 for €5m.

Capital structure:

- Falstone PLC has 750 million ordinary shares in issue valued at €3.69 each. The most recent dividend was €0.45 per share and this is expected to grow at 4% per year for the foreseeable future.

- Falstone PLC is also financed with a €500m 6.67% debenture redeemable at par in five years. It is trading at 83% of its nominal value.

- Falstone PLC pays tax on its taxable profits at 25% which is payable at the end of the year in which the profits arise.

- Project Sadie is considered a marginal project and the current weighted average cost of capital is an appropriate discount rate.

Attachment 2: NPV of Project Sadie.

	Note	01.01.2024	31.12.2024	31.12.2025	31.12.2026
Time		0	1	2	3
		€m	€m	€m	€m
Contract fee in dollars			42.00	60.00	65.00
Exchange rate	1		1.1000	1.1200	1.1250
Contract fee in euros			38.18	53.57	57.78
Maintenance			(16.00)	(16.00)	(16.00)
Incremental fixed costs			(15.12)	(15.12)	(15.12)
			7.06	22.45	26.66
Capital expenditure		(40.00)			5.00
		(40.00)	7.06	22.45	31.66
Tax at 25%		10.00	(1.77)	(5.61)	(7.92)
		(30.00)	5.29	16.84	23.74
Discount factors at 7%	2	1.000	0.935	0.873	0.816
		(30.00)	4.95	14.70	19.37
Net present value (€m)		9.02			

Notes

1 The Product Development director instructed me to use these forward exchange rates, saying that any other estimates provided by the Corporate Treasury department are irrelevant.

2 The Product Development director instructed me to use 7% as this was closer to the interest rate that Falstone PLC pays on its debt.

Email 2 from Corporate Treasury - Kielder PLC rights issues.

Kielder PLC has 3,000,000 ordinary shares of €1 each, which are at present selling for €5.20 per share. It plans to do a 1 for 4 rights issue at £4.00 per share.

Falstone owns 10% of the shares in Kielder PLC.

Required

(a) (i) Critically analyse the net present value calculation for Project Sadie and explain where the technical errors are, why they are errors and what alternative approach was necessary.

Calculations are not required for this part of the question and will not be rewarded.

(8 marks)

(ii) Evaluate the ethical issues arising from the product development director's intervention in the project evaluation. **(3 marks)**

(b) Calculate the weighted average cost of capital for Falstone PLC and recalculate the net present value of Project Sadie and either confirm or restate the management accountant's conclusion about the suitability of Project Sadie. **(20 marks)**

(c) Calculate with supporting explanations Kielder plc's theoretical ex-rights price and the impact on Falstone plc's wealth as a Kielder plc shareholder of selling all of its rights.

(9 marks)

(Total 40 marks)

18 KAM Group. [November 2023]

The KAM Group of companies consists of three companies based in Europe: Kaarija Oyj, Alessa ASA and Muller Ltd. There is substantial trading in goods and services between the three companies (inter-company trade). The companies are based in different countries and their domestic currencies are the euro (€), Norwegian krone (NOK) and the pound (£).

Each company settles its outstanding inter-company payables at the end of the quarter following the quarter of the transaction. The outstanding balances at the end of the quarter ended 30 September 2023 will therefore be settled on 31 December 2023. Those balances are as follows:

In each currency			Sales to		
			Kaarija Oyj	Alessa ASA	Muller Ltd
Sales from	Kaarija Oyj	€m		39.0	9.0
	Alessa ASA	NOKm	725.0		166.0
	Muller Ltd	£m	40.0	90.0	

Balances are stated and paid in the currency of the seller. The current policy of KAM Group is that each company is responsible for managing its own currency risk.

Muller Ltd is a UK company. It intends to use forward contracts to hedge the settlement of its outstanding balances with the other two companies. Relevant forward rates are as follows:

	31 December 2023
£1 = €	1.13 – 1.14
£1 = NOK	9.99 – 10.21

KAM Group headquarters has announced that, with immediate effect, inter-company balances will be settled by multilateral netting. Balances will be translated into and settled in euros at the following rates as determined by the central treasury department:

£1 = €	1.15
£1 = NOK	11.75

Required

(a) Under the currency policy where each company is responsible for managing its own currency transaction risk:

    (i) Calculate Muller Ltd's net payment or receipt in pounds on 31 December 2023 in respect of its inter-company balances, using forward contracts. **(4 marks)**

    (ii) Develop an account of how Muller Ltd could use sterling futures contracts to hedge its currency transaction risk in respect of its inter-company balances. No calculations are required for this part of the requirement. **(6 marks)**

(10 marks)

(b) Calculate Muller Ltd's net payment or receipt in pounds under the new policy of multilateral netting and report on whether the new policy would be beneficial for Muller Ltd. **(10 marks)**

(Total 20 marks)

19 Dastee Co. [November 2023]

Today is 30 November 2023.

Dastee Co requires $50 million to finance a research and development (R&D) project.

Dastee Co holds a convertible debenture which was issued by another company, Grensch Co. Grensch Co is an unlisted company so neither the debenture nor its shares are quoted on a stock exchange.

The directors of Dastee Co have decided that the Grensch Co debenture will be sold immediately and if the proceeds are insufficient to fund the R&D project it will borrow the shortfall from a commercial bank.

The Grensch Co debenture.

Grensch Co issued the convertible debenture on 1 December 2014. Its nominal value was $100 million, of which $35 million is currently held by Dastee Co.

Interest is paid at 7.2% of the nominal value to Dastee Co and other debenture holders on 30 November each year.

On 30 November 2034, debenture holders may choose between the following two options:

- Redeem the debenture at par; or
- Convert the debenture into 40 ordinary shares in Grensch Co.

Current market yields on debentures of a similar risk profile are estimated at 9%.

Grensch Co.

Grensch Co has 600 million ordinary shares in issue. Although the shares are not quoted, it is widely expected that Grensch Co will experience annual growth in value of 4% for the foreseeable future.

In its most recent financial statements, Grensch Co reported earnings before interest and tax of $228.67 million and an interest cover of 7. It pays tax on its profits at 22%.

Grensch Co operates in an industry where the average price-earnings ratio for quoted companies is 14.

Required

With supporting explanations, calculate the value of the debentures held by Dastee Co's and how much it will need to borrow to fund its R&D project. **(20 marks)**

20 HJQ Inc [November 2023]

HJQ Inc is a consultancy providing services to a wide range of business customers. HJQ Inc's management accounts show the following results for its year ended 30 November 2023.

	Note	2023 $m
Sales turnover		396
Operating expenses	1, 2	(151)
Profit before tax		245
Finance charges	3	(67)
Profit before tax		178
Tax at 25%	4	(45)
Profit after tax		133

Notes

1. 85% of the operating expenses are fixed. 15% of these costs vary directly with sales revenue.

2. Depreciation is $20 million and this equates approximately to the annual investment in non-current assets. There are no significant non-cash expenses.

3. Finance charges represent interest payable on a long-term loan repayable in ten years. The cash balance at 30 November 2023 is nil.

4. Tax is paid at the end of the year in which the profits arose.

HJQ Inc has receivables period of 42 days and it pays its suppliers after 37 days on average. It has no inventory.

Plans for improvement:

The directors of HJQ Inc have approved a strategy for improving the financial performance of the company. The result of the strategy will be:

- Sales turnover will increase by 10% per year in 2024, 2025 and 2026.
- Fixed costs will remain at 2023 levels until the end of 2026.
- Working capital periods will be as follows.

	2024 Days	2025 Days	2026 Days
Receivables period	35	30	30
Payables period	35	35	35

HJQ Inc has a cost of equity of 13%.

From 2027 onwards, the earnings of HJQ Inc will stabilise at 2026 levels. Because of the rapid growth anticipated, the directors are worried about the risk of overtrading.

Required

(a) (i) Calculate HJQ Inc's forecast earnings before tax for the years ending 30 November 2024, 2025 and 2026 based on the company's anticipated performance improvements. **(4 marks)**

    (ii) Calculate HJQ Inc's forecast operating cycle and net working capital at 30 November 2024, 2025 and 2026. **(4 marks)**

(b) Calculate HJQ Inc's forecast cash balance on 30 November 2024, 2025 and 2026. **(7 marks)**

(c) Recommend to the directors TWO further pieces of information that would be useful to assess the risk of overtrading in the next three years. **(2 marks)**

(d) Calculate a discounted cash-based valuation for HJQ Inc. **(3 marks)**

(Total 20 marks)

Exam answer bank

1 Twitten plc

This subject is taken from 'The Financial Environment and Capital Requirements and Consequent Costs', 'The Investment Decision' and 'International finance and interest rate risk'.

Learning Outcomes

LO1, LO2 and LO4

This question requires candidates to evaluate the suitability of a weighted average cost of capital to appraise a specific investment opportunity. Then it requires the evaluation of the investment against four criteria and a recommendation based on the organisation's primary financial goal of shareholder wealth maximisation. The question also integrates currency risk into the scenario and requires candidates to assess the currency risk associated with the decision in question as well as proposing a hedge for a specified foreign currency payment.

(a) Market value of equity = 100 million shares × £6.40 = £640m

Market value of debt = 80% × £200 million = £160m

WACC = 17% × 640/800 + 7% × 160/800 = 15%

The WACC is suitable to use in the appraisal of the Raclo patent because:

- The WACC is an average of the expected returns for Twitten plc's investors ie its shareholders and its lenders. Accepting only investments with positive NPVs after discounting at the WACC ensures that investors' requirements are met.

- The investment is small. It is worth £17.2m (€20m) in a company whose market capitalisation is £800m, so represents approximately 2% of its asset base.

- Twitten plc's business risk does not change as a result of the investment in the patent. The patent is on technology which the directors believe can bring efficiencies to its existing processes.

- The investment is financed out of the internal funds available to Twitten plc so its financial risk is not altered by the investment.

(b) (i) Net present value

	2021	2022	2023	2024	2025	2026
Investment (€)	(10,000.0)	(10,000.0)				
Patent royalties (€)		1,000.0	1,000.0	1,000.0	1,000.0	1,000.0
	(10,000.0)	(9,000.0)	1,000.0	1,000.0	1,000.0	1,000.0
Exchange rate	1.1635	1.1589	1.1543	1.1497	1.1452	1.1407
Sterling equivalent	(8,594.8)	(7,766.0)	866.3	869.8	873.2	876.7
Cost savings (inflate at 1.1%)		4,246.2	4,292.9	4,340.1	4,387.9	4,436.1
	(8,594.8)	(3,519.8)	5,159.2	5,209.9	5,261.1	5,312.8
Tax at 19%		(970.7)	(980.3)	(989.9)	(999.6)	(1,009.4)
Tax saving on amortisation		653.2	653.2	653.2	653.2	653.2
	(8,594.8)	(3,837.3)	4,832.1	4,873.2	4,914.7	4,956.6
Discount factors at 15%	1.000	0.870	0.756	0.658	0.572	0.497
	(8,594.8)	(3,338.4)	3,653.1	3,206.6	2,811.2	2,463.4
Net present value	201.1					

Working 1: forecast exchange rates

The € cash flows are patent receipts, the appropriate exchange rate to use is therefore the sell rate.

Year 1 (2022) rate = €1.1635 × 1.007 ÷ 1.011 = €1.1589
Year 2 (2023) rate = €1.1589 × 1.007 ÷ 1.011 = €1.1543
Year 3 (2024) rate = €1.1543 × 1.007 ÷ 1.011 = €1.1497
Year 4 (2025) rate = €1.1497 × 1.007 ÷ 1.011 = €1.1452
Year 5 (2026) rate = €1.1452 × 1.007 ÷ 1.011 = €1.1407

Working 2: tax saving on amortisation

Amortisation of the sterling cost over a five-year period
Qualifying cost = €20,000,000/1.1635 = £17,189,514
Annual amortisation × 1/5 = £3,437,903
19% × £3,437,903 = £653,201

(ii) Payback period

	2021	2022	2023	2024	2025	2026
Period	0	1	2	3	4	5
Net cash flows (£m)	(8,594.8)	(3,837.3)	4,832.1	4,873.2	4,914.7	4,956.6
Cumulative (£m)	(8,594.8)	(12,432.0)	(7,599.9)	(2,726.7)	2,188.0	7,144.5

The cumulative net cash flows turn positive in the fourth year.

(iii) Accounting rate of return

	1	2	3	4	5
	2022	2023	2024	2025	2026
Total patents	1,000.0	1,000.0	1,000.0	1,000.0	1,000.0
Exchange rate	1.1589	1.1543	1.1497	1.1452	1.1407
Patents (£ equivalent)	862.9	866.3	869.8	873.2	876.7
Cost savings (£m – from NPV)	4,246.2	4,292.9	4,340.1	4,387.9	4,436.1
	5,109.1	5,159.2	5,209.9	5,261.1	5,312.8
Average increase in sterling profits	5,210.4				

Average investment
Sterling value of the patent on purchase (W2) = £17,189,514
Average carrying value over the five year period = (£17,189,514 + 0)/2 = £8,594,757.
ARR = £5,210.4 ÷ £8,594.8 = 60.6%

Conclusion and recommendation

Of the three criteria, two are satisfied (the NPV and the ARR), however the PBP is longer than 3 years so the investment is not acceptable against Twitten plc's current decision-making policies.

However, in order to maximise shareholder wealth, it is only the NPV criteria that needs to be satisfied, so the recommendation to the Twitten plc board is to consider whether the PBP requirement in this case may be waived in favour of a suitable and viable investment opportunity.

(c) **Transaction**

This is the risk that the sterling value of the payments and receipts in Euros is increased or reduced by movements on the exchange rate between the two currencies.

Twitten plc has transaction risk exposure resulting from two aspects of this investment:

- The payment in Euros of the second instalment on the purchase of the patent, and
- The receipt of patent royalties in Euros

Although it is not clear what the pattern of receipts will be (eg. many small receipts or fewer larger ones), the payment of the second instalment is a large figure, expected to take place a considerable time after the contract for the purchase has been agreed. The transaction risk can be considered large.

Translation risk

This is the risk that the organisation will make accounting gains or losses when foreign branches or subsidiaries are translated into sterling in the statement of financial position at the end of each accounting period. Here the patent will be held at original cost (translated at the original spot rate) and won't be retranslated, so there is little/no translation risk.

Economic risk

This is the long-term risk to the NPV of Twitten plc's cash flows resulting from engaging in overseas transactions. If the Euro weakens as assumed in the NPV calculation, it can be seen that the sterling value of Twitten plc's income stream diminishes as time progresses.

(d) Assuming Twitten plc pays €20 million for the Raclo patent in two instalments and its payments for the acquisition are hedged in the most beneficial way, calculate the sterling cost of the patent, providing supporting explanation.

(i) Using a one-year forward the cost of the patent would be £17,229,565 as follows:

	£
Instalment 1	
€10 million ÷ €1.1631	8,597,713
Instalment 2	
€10 ÷ €1.1585	8,631,852
	17,229,565

(ii) A money market hedge can be used as follows:

On 31 December 2021, deposit (€10,000,000 ÷ 1.008) = €9,920,635.
In order to do this Twitten plc will borrow (€9,920,635 ÷ €1.1631) = £8,529,477.
The repayment of this borrowing, with interest, will be (£8,529,477 × 1.0125) = £8,636,095.

The total cost of the patent will therefore be:

	£
Instalment 1	
€10 million ÷ €1.1631	8,597,713
Instalment 2	8,636,095
	17,233,808

(iii) Lead payment

Based on expected movements in the €/£ exchange rate, the Euro is expected to weaken which makes the payment smaller in sterling. However, it is also possible that the exchange rate moves in the opposite direction, meaning the payment in pounds will be larger.

However, bringing the payment of instalment 2 to an earlier date will have a time-value of money implication and reduces the NPV of the investment.

Insofar as the exchange rate risk is unacceptable then the forward contract is recommended to fix the payment in sterling at its lowest cost.

> Additional areas where credit might be given, note this is not an exhaustive list:
> - Marks will be given for any relevant additional points

2 Stannich Ltd

This subject is taken from 'Working capital management' and 'The Financial Environment and Capital Requirements and Consequent Costs'

Learning Outcomes

LO1 and LO5

The question requires candidates to understand the impact of allowing working capital to get out of control, even if it leads to higher profitability. It requires the evaluation of whether working capital goals have been met as well as the evaluation of proposals made to improve the situation. The candidate is also expected to recognise the need for new long-term finance in the scenario.

(a) The working capital cycle of Stannich Ltd

The operating cycle at 30 September 2021 is 52 days, calculated as follows:

	Actual Days	Budget Days
Receivables' payment period (1,752/15,222 × 365)	42	30
Inventory turnover period 1,272/(15,222-4,543) × 365	43	30
Payables payment period (965/(15,222-4,543) × 365	(33)	(30)
	52	30

Receivables payment period (RPP)

The RPP is longer than budget by 12 days and this represents one of two main reasons for the longer working capital cycle. A longer RPP suggests that customers are paying for their furniture much later than anticipated in the budget. As a result, Stannich Ltd is investing more of its liquid resources in receivables which is having an adverse impact on its cash position.

If receivables payment periods were reduced to budgeted levels, this would release cash approximately equivalent to 12 days of sales revenue (12/365 × $15,222,000), ie $500,450.

Inventory turnover period (ITP)

The ITP is longer than expected by 13 days. This means that there is six weeks of production in inventory, rather than just four.

Given that there appears to be a significant backlog in unfulfilled customer orders, this is likely to be a build-up in raw materials and work in progress rather than finished goods, due to difficulties in dealing with increased orders.

This is putting adverse pressure on Stannich Ltd's liquidity. If the inventory turnover period were reduced to budgeted levels, this would release cash approximately equivalent to 13 days of cost of sales (13/365 × [$15,222,000 – $4,543,000]), ie $380,348.

Payables payment period (PPP)

The PPP is broadly in line with the budget. It is three days longer than budget which means that it is taking approximately three days longer to settle its debts with suppliers than expected. This slight delay is offsetting to a small degree, the longer receivables and inventory period.

(b) **Deposit**

This will mean that 10% of all sales will be collected six weeks earlier than is currently the case.

This will release approximately $175,000 (42/365 × 10% × $15,222k or 10% of receivables) of working capital and will enable Stannich Ltd to pay off its overdraft.

However, given that the success in building sales appears to be at least partly due to the longer credit period offered to customers, there is a risk that the deposit will result in the loss of some of the new customer base.

Deposit and discount together

The proposed deposit and discount would generate a net loss of $23,000 for Stannich Ltd.

This is calculated as follows:

	$000	$000
Value of the deposit		
10% × $15,222		1,522
Sales on credit		13,700
Total sales revenue		15,222
Receivables will be		
25% × $13,700 × 10/365	94	
75% × $13,700 × 42/365	1,182	
		1,276
Current level of receivables		1,752
Reduction in receivables		476
		× 9.5%
Finance cost savings at 9.5%		45
Discount (2% × 25% × $13,700k)		68
Expected loss		(23)

The reduction in sales revenue due to the discount itself is larger than the saving in finance cost arising because of earlier collection of the receivables.

The benefit of the early settlement may take some time to release the working capital/cash making this solution a little too slow.

Recommendation

It appears that Stannich Ltd is overtrading. Its business, and its investment in non-current assets, have grown quickly without any commensurate increase in long-term funding which has put pressure on the overdraft and put the company's survival is question to some degree. The most important and urgent thing to do is to arrange long-term finance either from the Stannich Ltd shareholders or from a lender (eg the bank).

Based on the information available and the assumptions made, the settlement discount should not be offered.

The deposit is also recommended too. Even if some sales are lost, it is probably a good idea to slow down the expansion until the production issues are resolved and Stannich Ltd can produce its furniture more efficiently, avoiding the build-up of inventory.

> Additional areas where credit might be given, note this is not an exhaustive list:
> - Alternative and reasonable assumptions leading to alternative conclusions and recommendations
> - Marks will be given for any relevant additional points

3 Scotswood plc

This subject is taken from 'Valuation and corporate change'

Learning Outcomes

LO1 and LO5

The question requires the candidate to evaluate two offers received by a takeover target from the perspective of target. It also requires the candidate to calculate a company valuation for a different target using free cash flows.

Offer 1

Valuation of shares = 600 million shares × £9.20 = £5.52 billion (or £5,520 million)

P/E ratio = £5,520m ÷ £450m = 12.26

Cost of equity is arrived at by, first, dividing the valuation by the free cash flows to equity to find the perpetuity factor = £5,520m ÷ £480m = 11.5.

The cost of equity is the inverse of the perpetuity factor = 1/11.5 = 8.7%.

Offer 2

Valuation of the shares = 600 million ÷ 2 RH shares × 3 BW shares × £6.50 = £5,850 million.

P/E ratio £5,850 ÷ £450m = 13.0

Perpetuity factor = £5,850 ÷ £480m = 12.19

Cost of equity = 1/15.39 = 8.2%

Percentage shareholding in Benwell plc

Currently Benwell plc has £1bn shares in issue.

To acquire Redheugh Ltd's share capital, Benwell plc would issue 600m × 3/2 = 900 million shares

Scotswood plc would therefore hold 900m/1,900m shares = 47.4% of Benwell plc's issued share capital.

Based on industry average P/E ratio and cost of equity the valuation of Redheugh Ltd would be approximately £4.8bn to £5.5bn:

- Earnings: 12.3 × £450m = £5,535m
- FCF(E): £480m/0.10 = £4,800m

Therefore, both offers appear generous, given that Redheugh Ltd is an unquoted company with no discernible growth prospects under its current circumstances. Presumably, Benwell plc has identified potential synergies or growth strategies which have made it worthwhile for them to make the offers they have.

Of the two offers, offer 2 is the more generous and implies a P/E ratio above the average of quoted companies within the industry and a much lower cost of equity than the industry average.

However, offer 2 commits Scotswood plc to retaining a significant shareholding in Benwell plc for approximately two years. This would have to be subjected to a due diligence review. But also, it does not provide any immediate finance for the acquisition of Ouseburn Ltd.

It is recommended that offer 2 be accepted based on the offer being favourable compared to industry benchmarks but without the commitment to hold a significant shareholding in Benwell plc.

Free cash flows to the company

	£m
Operating profit	175
Increase working capital (£300 × 13% × 0.03)	(1)
Add: depreciation	35
Less: replacement capex (£300 × 8%)	(24)
Less: tax (15% × £145)	(22)
Free cash flow to the company	163

FCF discounted at the weighted average cost of capital of 8% adjusted for a 3% expected annual growth rate = 163/(0.08 − 0.03) = £3,260 million.

Deduct the debt (£3,260m − £600m) = £2,660 million.

> **Additional areas where credit might be given, note this is not an exhaustive list:**
> - Alternative and reasonable assumptions leading to alternative conclusions and recommendations
> - Marks will be given for any relevant additional points

4 Saturna plc

This subject is taken from 'Valuation and corporate change', 'The Financial Environment and Capital Requirements and Consequent Costs'

Learning Outcomes

LO1 and LO4

The question tests the candidate's ability to calculate the value of a debenture for the purposes of redeeming it early and the weighted average cost of capital. In the face of refinancing the debt, the question also requires the candidate to demonstrate understanding of how the interest rate futures market and interest rate swaps can be helpful in managing interest rates within a large organisation.

(a)

		£m
MV of equity (MVe)	55m shares × £7.22	397.10
MV of debt (MVd)		£m
T1 – 10	Interest £6m × 7.722	46.332
T10	Redemption £106m × 0.614	65.084
		111.416
Gearing (MVd/(MVd+MVe))		**21.9%**
Cost of equity (Ke)	(0.2 + 0.95 × (6.7 − 0.2))	6.375%
Post-tax cost of debt (Kd (1 − t))	5% × (1 − 0.19)	4.05%
WACC	Equity (9.89% × 78.1%)	7.7%
	Debt (4.05% × 21.9%)	0.9%
		8.6%

(b) Interest rate futures

	December 2022	
Contracts		
Number	£120m/£0.5m × 24/3	1,920
Nov 21	Sell contracts	99.6
Nov 22	Buy contracts (assumed)	99.4
	Profit	0.2
Profit (£)	0.2% × 1,920 × £500,000 × 3/12	480,000
Interest payable (SONIA + 4.0)		
	4.6% × £120m × 24/12	
Profit on futures		

(c)

	Saturna plc	Jupitus plc	
Fixed rate	4.5%	5.6%	1.1%
Floating rate	SONIA + 4.0%	SONIA + 4.8%	0.8%
Potential saving			0.3%
less fees			0.13%
Saving to share			0.17%

Assume the saving is shared equally = 0.17%/2 = 0.085% per year, 0.085% × £120m × 2 years = £20.4m each.

Additional areas where credit might be given, note this is not an exhaustive list:

- Alternative presentations of calculations
- Alternative assumption on the split of the saving in part (c), given the two companies appear to have different credit ratings

---

5 Matti Fortuna Gyms SA

Matti Fortuna Gyms SA

Learning Outcomes

LO2 and LO3

This question is taken from the Investment Decision and Valuation and corporate change parts of the syllabus. This question requires candidates to evaluate and make recommendations on two possible ways available to a French company to expand its business into the UK.

(a) For method 1, calculate the after-tax net present value (NPV) in Euros as of 31 May 2022 and conclude on its financial acceptability.

NPV of Option 1 in Euros

	0	1	2	3 31 May	4	5	6
	2022	2023	2024	2025	2026	2027	2028
Operating cash flows	0	19.25	106.25	265	265	265	265
Tax at 25%	-	(4.81)	(26.56)	(66.25)	(66.25)	(66.25)	(66.25)
Properties	(7.18)	(18.45)	(28.70)				
Equipment	(1.40)	(3.60)	(5.60)				
Tax savings on WDA							

	0	1	2	3 31 May	4	5	6
	2022	2023	2024	2025	2026	2027	2028
(Working 1)	–	0.06	0.21	0.47	0.49	0.49	0.59
	(8.58)	(7.55)	45.60	199.22	199.24	199.24	199.34
Exchange rate (× 1.012/1.01)	1.1500	1.1523	1.1546	1.1569	1.1592	1.1615	1.1638
	(9.87)	(8.70)	52.65	230.48	230.96	231.42	231.99
DF at 10% (not adjusted)	1.000	0.909	0.826	0.751	0.683	0.621	0.564
	(9.87)	(7.91)	43.51	173.16	157.75	143.69	130.84

NPV (not adjusted)   631.17

Large, positive NPV indicates a financially acceptable investment

Working 1: Tax saving on sterling WDAs

		2023	2024	2025	2026	2027	2028
Equipment bought 31 May							
2023	1,400,000	252,000	206,640	169,445	138,945	113,935	519,035
2024	3,600,000		648,000	720,000	720,000	720,000	720,000
2025	5,600,000			1,008,000	1,120,000	1,120,000	1,120,000
		252,000	854,640	1,897,445	1,978,945	1,953,935	2,359,035
Tax saving at 25%		63,000	213,660	474,361	494,736	488,484	589,759

The WDA given in May 2028 to the equipment bought in May 2023 is a balancing allowance on disposal equal to cost of £1.4 million less the capital allowances claimed up to the year ending 31 May 2027.

(b) For Method 1, Explain and critically appraise your colleagues' approach and assumption when selecting the 12 London properties.

Capital rationing

My colleagues were dealing with a case of capital rationing as the amount of money available for investment In London was limited. In this case it was soft capital rationing as the directors had decided to limit spend in London presumably to avoid overspend on expensive properties, rather than a lack of available funding.

Profitability index

The probability index can be used to rank the possible investments under consideration. It is calculated as the NPV of the project divided by the initial outlay. It is usually used in order to rank divisible projects. Divisible projects or investments can be scaled down in circumstances where capital is rationed.

Divisibility

The divisibility or scalability of each investment (i.e. each property) is limited. It is quite unlikely that all the properties can be partially acquired; much more likely is that each property for sale can be bought or not bought.

It may be possible to purchase a property and to let part of it out so only part of it is being used as a gym, but this brings additional risks.

Likewise, the equipment bought for each gym is likely to depend on the size of the property it is going to occupy. Scaling down the investment in gym equipment is likely to lose customer goodwill.

Alternative approach

If a decision were made based purely on financial grounds then the possible combinations of property and the combination which generated the highest aggregate NPV could be chosen.

In this case, non-financial factors are likely to be important. Potential non-financial factors affecting the decision would be:

- State of repair
- Geographical coverage
- Safety considerations
- Local amenities like car parks and transport links

(c) Valuation of Stennerham Ltd

Using the WACC:

	Note	£'000
Profit before interest and tax		29,600
Add depreciation	1	2,500
Less capital expenditure on equipment	1	(2,500)
		29,600
Tax at 25%		(7,400)
		22,200
Perpetuity factor (1/0.1065) at WACC		9.39
		208,477
Less debt		(50,000)
		158,477

Note.

Depreciation, as a non-cash flow is added back to profit but, here, is taken as an estimate of the necessary capital expenditure to keep gym equipment up to date. Alternative assumptions could be valid here, e.g. if the cost of replacement equipment is climbing the capex deducted should be higher by roughly 3 years' of inflation.

Alternative calculation, using cost of equity

	£,000
Profit before tax	25,600
Net depreciation and capex	-
Tax at 25%	(6,400)
	19,200
Perpetuity factor (1/0.12) at Ke	8.3333333
	160,000
No deduction for debt (interest already deducted and using ke)	(-)
	160,000

This indicates a share price of £160m/1m = £160/share.

MFG's share price is €1.84, which at today's exchange rate of €1.15 is £1.60 in sterling.

This means that, if a share-for-share exchange is used to finance the acquisition, MFG will have to issue 100 million of its own shares to the Stennerham shareholders.

Matti Fortuna's shareholding will fall from 20% to 16% as follows:

	Before	S4S	After	SH%
Matti Fortuna's shares	80		80	16%
Stennerham shareholders		100	100	20%
Other (existing) shareholders	320		320	64%
	400	100	500	100%

(d) Benefits and risks of method 2

Diversification

Method 2 involves a shift away from the successful strategy of no-frills gyms. This represents diversification for MFG. Diversification can be useful in lowering a company's risk profile. It is limited diversification so does not necessarily involve a drastic departure from what MFG's core competencies.

To counter this, however, it would be useful to retain key senior staff in Stennerham to maintain continuity of operations. Stennerham clubs are quite different in terms of the activities offered and will therefore involve different knowledge and obligations (e.g. health and safety compliance).

Customers

The customers are different. This can be a very good strategy for MFG if they are successful in building a loyal base of affluent customers. Stennerham club members pay approximately seven times for their membership compared to MFG's current members in France. Whlst this makes them attractive as a customer group, they will have more exacting expectations in terms of quality of service.

Speed

Method 2 allows a quicker expansion into the UK. Stennerham clubs are already in operation and seemingly successful. Once the acquisition has been completed, there is no need to enter into a large number of negotiations for the purchase of properties followed by the conversions, recruitment and starting marketing campaigns in a country where MFG is relatively unknown.

Financial outlay

The financial outlay to acquire Stennerham Ltd (£160m not including equipment renewal) is much higher than the financial investment in opening its own gyms (£65m including equipment). This might be expected from investing in an up-market company like Stennerham Ltd compared to a no-frills company. But £160m for 12 clubs compared to £65m for 265 gyms appears very expensive and must therefore be an important part of MFG's strategy to be worthwhile.

Furthermore, when comparing NPVs for each investment over a six-year period, the Stennerham acquisition has a negative NPV, indicating a much slower payback than opening own gyms.

Additional areas where credit might be given, note this is not an exhaustive list:

- Marks will be given for any relevant additional points

6 Pax Ltd

Pax Ltd

Learning Outcomes

LO1, LO3 and LO5

This subject is taken from 'Working capital management' and 'The Financial Environment and Capital Requirements and Consequent Costs' and Valuation and Corporate Change.

The question requires candidates to understand the impact of two proposals on a company and its key financial indicators. The proposals are (1) a settlement discount, a tool often used in management of working capital and (2) a refinancing package. This question therefore synthesises the working capital management and capital requirement and costs elements of the BFM syllabus. Because one of the key indicators used to assess the proposals is gearing based on market values, the candidates must also value the company's share capital, which brings in a third part of the syllabus.

(a) Calculate Pax Ltd forecast financial gearing (market value of debt as a percentage of market value of debt plus equity (D/(D+E)) as at 30 June 2023.

	£m
5% secured bank loan (£2.5m/0.05)	50.00
8% overdraft (£1.6m/0.08)	20.00
Total debt	70.00
Market value of equity (£8m × 8.33)	49.98
Gearing (D/(D+E))	58%

(b) Calculate Pax Ltd's projected earnings after tax, the market value of its equity and its gearing ratio if proposal 1 is implemented (but not proposal 2).

Sales revenue in the year ending June 2023 expected to be (per question) £540 million.
Target receivables period for the year ending June 2023 is 36.5 days.
Target average receivables = 36.5/365 × £540m = £54m
Average receivables period if discount is offered:
(20% × 15 days) + (80% × 36.5 days) = 32.2 days
Average receivables outstanding = 32.2/365 × £540m = £47.64m
Reduction in receivables (and also overdraft) = £54m - £47.64m = £6.36m
Savings in finance cost = £6.36m × 8% = £0.51m
Cost of the discount = 20% × 2% × £540m = £2.16m

Therefore, the market value of equity will fall to £39.17m and gearing will go up to 62%, as follows:

Effect on equity	£m
Earnings before tax per forecast	8.00
Cost of the discount	(2.16)
Finance saving	0.51
Revised EBT	6.35
Tax at 25%	(1.59)
Earnings after tax	4.76
P/E ratio	8.33
Market value of equity	39.67

Effect on gearing	£m
Debt (£70m – £6.36m)	63.64
Equity	39.67
Gearing (D/(D+E))	62%

1. **Secured loan**

   Cost

   The annual cost of the proposed loan is lower than that of the overdraft. However, with overdrafts, the cost of the facility is based on its usage. On days where the overdraft is not being used there is no cost to Pax Ltd. With the loan, even if the funds are not being used, Pax Ltd will be charged interest on the whole facility.

   Availability and use

   However, the loan is larger than the average balance on the overdraft which makes some additional liquidity available to Pax Ltd. As some of the research and development programmes have been temporarily frozen due to lack of funds, the additional funding may make the resumption of the R&D work possible.

   Risk

   Pax Ltd has been relying on the overdraft as a source of permanent finance which is an aggressive and risky approach to financing. Overdrafts can be withdrawn with little notice, whereas a secured loan cannot unless there is a breech of the loan's conditions.

   The company's success in 2020 generated significant sustainable growth in revenue but was not supported by any additional permanent finance. This has led to reduced liquidity and has now posed a significant threat to its research and development programmes.

   Security

   The security that must be offered to the lender does reduce Pax Ltd's flexibility in that it would not be able to sell the property without prior permission from the bank. However, it is unlikely that such permission would be withheld and the value of the property appears well above that of the loan.

Additional areas where credit might be given, note this is not an exhaustive list:
- Marks will be given for any relevant additional points

7 Denny Ltd

Denny Ltd

This subject is taken from 'International finance and interest rate risk'

Learning Outcomes

LO4

This question focuses on international treasury and foreign exchange risk management. It begins with a requirement to calculate cash flows arising as a result of a multilateral netting process. It then tests the candidate's ability to discuss the benefits and risks of the netting for the UK company, one of which will be the large exposure to currency transaction risk as the multilateral netting means they will receive a large sum in foreign currency. The question finishes with two requirements for the candidate to demonstrate understanding of money market hedges and the futures market and how they can be used specifically to manage the transaction risk arising from the netting.

EXAM ANSWER BANK

(a) Multilateral netting calculation

			Sales to			Total
			Denny	Jabasi	Gamlar	
Sales from	Denny	$m		16.6	25.7	42.3
	Jabasi	$m	10.1		1.4	11.5
	Gamlar	$m	11.5	8.7		20.2
	Total payments	$m	(21.6)	(25.3)	(27.1)	(74.0)
	Total receipts	$m	42.3	11.5	20.2	
			20.7	(13.8)	(6.9)	

Denny Ltd will receive $13.8m from Jabasi SA and $6.9m from Gamlar AB on 31 May 2022.

Administration

On 31 July 2022, Denny Ltd will receive two large cash flows from the other companies. There is a smaller administrative burden when the number of cash flows is reduced.

Forex risk - Dollar receipt

By netting off payables and receivables, the overall transaction risk that Denny Ltd is exposed to is reduced.

In Dollars, the value of the receipts is known in advance because the exchange rates used in the netting process are agreed in advance.

However, the rate is agreed up to 14 months before the cash settlement takes place and this can lead to receipts and payments for each subsidiary being on adverse terms compared to the relevant spot rate on the date of the cash settlement.

Forex risk – conversion to sterling

Furthermore, the functional currency of Denny Ltd is sterling, not Dollars. Therefore, there is a large exposure to transaction risk. The €20.7m will have to be converted into sterling.

If the actual exchange rate between the pound and the dollar is different to today's spot rate the amount received in sterling will change. At today's spot rate that would be €20.7 × 0.85 = £17.6m. However, if the pound were to strengthen against the dollar by just one cent before 31 July the sterling value would fall by over £200,000.

Liquidity risk

Denny Ltd must wait two months after the relevant quarter end before receiving cash on the inter-company trading. This means that some of the transactions will have taken place up to five months before settlement. This represents an average receivables period of 3.5 months. The long receivables conversion period means Denny Ltd's cash balance is lower, meaning that it is more likely that it will need financial help from its parent.

Additional areas where credit might be given, note this is not an exhaustive list:
- Compliance risks
- Financial reporting risks
- Marks will be given for any relevant additional points

(b) Money market hedge.

 (i) The receivable is an asset so Denny Ltd would create a dollar liability today by borrowing an amount in dollars for two months at a rate of 5.5% × 2/12 = 0.92%.

 The amount borrowed would be $20.7m/1.0092 = $20,511,296. This is enough, so that in two months, with interest accumulated the amount repayable to the lender would be $20.7m.

 (ii) The dollars borrowed would be converted to sterling at £0.86 per $, generating £17,639,714.

 (iii) The sterling would immediately be deposited for two months and will accumulate interest at a rate of 5.25%×2/12 = 0.88%.

 As the deposit matures in July 2022, the cash, increased by accumulated interest, will be withdrawn by Denny Ltd. This represents the sterling value of the receipt being hedged.

 (iv) Finally, on 31 July 2022, the receipt of $20.7m will be used to repay the dollar loan taken out today.

(c) To hedge a dollar receipt:

Buy September contracts.

Number of contracts: ($20,700,000/1.1520)/£62,500 = 287 contracts (depending on rounding).

Profit on futures market:

	$
Buy	1.1520
Sell	1.1610
Profit per pound	0.0090

Total profit on the futures market:

$0.009 × 287 contracts × £62,500 = $161,438 ($162,000 if contracts rounded to 288).

	$
Underlying transaction	20,700,000
Gain on futures	161,438
	20,861,438
At spot rate	0.8622
	17,986,732

Marking note

If candidate did not round to one decimal place of a million in part (a) the underlying transaction is $20,683,698. The calculation becomes:

Number of contracts ($20,683,698/1.1520)/62,500 = 287

	$
Underlying transaction	20,683,698
Gain on futures	161,438
	20,845,136
At spot rate	0.8622
	17,972,676

Additional areas where credit might be given, note this is not an exhaustive list:

- Marks will be given for any relevant additional points

8 Mankita Group

Mankita Group

This subject is taken from 'The Financial Environment and Capital Requirements and Consequent Costs' and 'Working Capital Management'

Learning Outcomes

LO1 and LO5

This question requires the calculation of two weighted average costs of capital (WACCs), including the cost of equity (k_e). Although the companies are in the same industry they have different k_e and WACCs. The question therefore asks the candidates to suggest possible reasons for the differing costs in order to test understanding of how ke and WACC behaves in relation to risk.

The question also requires calculations using the Economic Order Quantity model to evaluate the savings resulting from a shift in purchasing policy.

(a) Weighted average costs of capital

FJJ plc

Cost of equity (ke) = $\frac{d_0(1+g)}{p_0} + g$

g = rb

r = return on new investments = average appears to 17% (i.e. (14+20)/2).

b = profit retention rate = (48-12)/48 = 75%

estimated growth = 0.17 + 0.75 = 12.75%

ke = $\frac{12(1.1275)}{136}$ + 0.1275 = 22.7%

If FJJ plc has no gearing then the cost of equity is also the weighted average cost of capital, i.e. 22.7%.

Telatela plc

Ke = $r_f + \beta(r_m - r_f)$

i.e. (13-10)% + 1.15 × 10% = 14.5%

kd = 6%

WACC = 14.5% × 5/7 + 6% × 2/7 = 12.1%

Possible reasons for differences in costs of capital

(1) The cost of capital measures the amount of return or yield that a company's investors require in return for their financial contribution. Generally, the required return, and therefore the cost of capital depends largely on the risk to which its investors are exposed by their investment in that company. For higher risk companies, higher returns are expected by the investors and therefore the cost of capital is higher. As both companies are in the same industry sector, there must be company-specific reasons for the differing risk-profiles causing differences in the costs of capital.

(2) FJJ is apparently experiencing or expecting high-growth. This may be because it is at an earlier stage in its life cycle than Telatela plc, or it has more innovative products. Whatever the cause of the more rapid growth in FJJ, it makes it less stable and puts investors' capital at greater risk, which brings about a higher cost of capital.

(3) FJJ has higher operating gearing than Telatela. This means that its cost base is more fixed. This can cause more fluctuations in the company's cash flows from period to period. Higher fixed costs mean that profitability increases more in good years but it declines more than proportionately in years where sales revenue falls. This fluctuation is generally perceived as more risky.

Additional areas where credit might be given, note this is not an exhaustive list:

- Higher financial gearing in Telatela plc might have increased the cost of equity but, in accordance with the traditional theory of gearing, the higher level of debt can bring down the overall WACC.
- Marks will be given for any relevant additional points relating to risk

---

(b) TYR559

Costs of the current purchasing strategy

Ignore purchasing costs as they do not change if the order quantity changes, therefore they are not relevant.

Annual demand (D) = 360 × 10,000 units = 3.6m

Holding costs $(C_h \times Q/2)$ = £500 × 100,000/2 = £25,000,000

Ordering costs $(C_o \times D/Q)$ = £26,000 × 3,600,000/100,000 = £936,000

In total = £25,936,000

If EOQ is adopted as the order size, the standard order would be:

$\sqrt{\frac{2C_oD}{C_h}} = \sqrt{\frac{2 \times 26,000 \times 3,600,000}{500h}}$ = 19,000 (rounded to nearest 1,000)

Holding costs $(C_h \times Q/2)$ = £500 × 19,000/2 = £4,750,000

Ordering costs $(C_o \times D/Q)$ = £26,000 × 3,600,000/19,000 = £4,926,316

Total = £9,676,316

Saving = £16,259,684

9 Melona Inc

This subject is taken from 'The Financial Environment and Capital Requirements and Consequent Costs'.

Learning Outcomes

LO1 and LO3

Chapters

3 Capital markets and government policy
5 Financial planning and forecasting
13 Valuation of companies

This question requires candidates to use the information available to determine a reasonable valuation for a minority shareholding in a company. The question requires candidates to understand the role of the financial manager in determining capital requirements. It also requires an understanding of the factors which may affect the efficiency of a stock market an how that might impact the valuation of a company listed on it.

(a) Range of valuations for a 10% stake in Doctim
Valuations are based on a 100% holding and then adjusted.
Based on projected free cash flows
Projected earnings after tax are as follows:

	2023 Forecast $m
Earnings after tax	49.7
Amortisation (non-cash)	16.0
Melona Inc maintenance ($3m × (1-0.2))	(2.4)
Free cash flow	63.3
Discount factor at 20% and growth rate of 12% (1/(0.2-0.12))	12.5
Value of 100% equity stake	791.3

This is the present value of the Doctim Inc's projected cash flows, using the shareholders' required return (cost of equity) as a discount rate.

Based on the above valuation, a 10% shareholding would be valued at $79.1m.

However, a 10% shareholding is a small minority interest so a discount to this value would be appropriate. Assuming a discount of 25% for lack of control, the value would be ($79.1m × 75%) $59.3m.

Earnings valuation

The current levels of earnings attributable to the ordinary shareholder is $44.2m. We can multiply this by an appropriate price-earnings ratio to estimate a valuation.

The price-earnings ratio tends to be greater when growth prospects and reputation are enhanced. Because Doctim Inc and its directors have a good reputation for reliability and quality, we should reflect this by using a ratio towards the top end of the range given, say 12.5.

Based on that logic, a 100% stake would be worth 12.5 × $44.2m, ie. $552.5.

Once again, this should be discounted to reflect the small minority holding that Melona Inc owns. Accordingly the 10% stake could be valued at 10% × $552.5m × 75% = $41.4m.

A dividend valuation would be based on the present value of the future dividends that Melona Inc would receive from Doctim Ltd ie. ($3m × 1.12)/(0.2 − 0.12) = $42m.

This is often an appropriate valuation for a minority shareholding.

Based on value of the assets held by Doctim, the 10% stake would be worth:

	$m
Tangible assets	1.6
Intellectual property	259.0
Liabilities	(50.0)
	210.6
10%	$21.1m

This is very low as it does not reflect the growth prospects of Doctim Inc.

Based on the calculations above, the range (ignoring the asset valuation) is $41m, $42m to $59m. Given that the cash flow valuation is calculated based on a growing perpetuity formula and it is unrealistic to expect the company to grow eternally at 12% per year, we should recommend a figure towards the lower end of that range ie $45m.

Additional areas where credit might be given, note this is not an exhaustive list:

- Marks will be given for any relevant additional points

(b) Earnings projections:

	2022 $m		2023 $m		2024 $m
EARNINGS					
Revenue	41.0	× 93% =	38.1	× 85%	32.0
Fixed costs	(14.0)	+ 10.0 – 3.0	(21.0)	+ 5.0 – 3.0	(23.0)
Non-cash expenses	(5.0)		(5.0)		(5.0)
EBIT	22.0		12.1		4.0
Dividends from Doctim Inc	3.0		-		-
Finance costs	(2.0)		(2.0)		(2.0)
Taxation	(5.8)		(2.5)		(0.5)
Earnings after tax	17.2		7.6		1.5

Cash position

CASH	2023	2024
Cash balance b/f	0.0	(7.4)
Earnings after tax	7.6	1.5
Add back non-cash items	5.0	5.0
Capital expenditure	(40.0)	(78.0)
Repayment of existing loan	(25.0)	
Proceeds on sale of Doctim Inc	45.0	
Cash deficit	(7.4)	(78.9)

Borrowing of at least $7.4m would be required by the end of 2023 with a further $71.5m required by the end of 2024.

Additional areas where credit might be given, note this is not an exhaustive list:

- Marks will be given for any relevant additional points

(c) The finance director is suggesting that the stock market on which Doctim Inc is listed is inefficient.

This means that information which is relevant to the value of Doctim Inc is, at best, only partially reflected in the company's quoted market value.

There is some evidence to suggest that this is the case.

(i) The share price in Doctim Inc did not change when the financial irregularities were revealed. The lack of controls which lead to the irregularities would be seen by rational investors as too risky and would lead to a drop in share price if Doctim Inc was listed on an efficient market.

(ii) The Jordak government appear to be a dominant participant in the market. This is because each company quoted on the stock market has to be at least 40%-owned by the government or one of its agents. This means that free movement of securities from buyer to seller is impeded.

(iii) Similarly, buying and selling securities in companies listed on the Jordak stock market is hindered by the high taxes charged on both buyers and sellers. This means that rational investors may be deterred from entering transactions even when they believe the available information suggests they should do.

> **Additional areas where credit might be given, note this is not an exhaustive list:**
> - Marks will be given for any relevant additional points

10 Stannerton Ltd

This subject is taken from 'International Finance and Interest Rate Risk' and 'Working Capital'.

Learning Outcomes

LO4 and LO5

This question requires the candidate to appreciate the advantages and drawbacks of an overseas expansion which brings a significant growth in profitability but also significant working capital and currency risk.

The relevant chapters are

- Chapter 16 Foreign currency risk
- Chapter 17 Foreign exchange risk: options
- Chapter 20 Management of working capital

Relevant material can also be sourced from:

- Chapters 21 and 22

Transaction risk

The payments made by Bomon Inc will be in Canadian dollars which is not the home currency of Stannerton Ltd. This means that currency transaction risk arises as the exchange rate between the pound and the Canadian dollar may move and affect the sterling value of the cash flows received by Stannerton Ltd.

Each quarterly invoice will be C$120 million so a movement of just 1 pence to the dollar will cost Stannerton Ltd £1.2 million when the receipts are converted to sterling.

Exchange rate movements would have an adverse effect (ie downside risk) if the Canadian dollar weakened against the pound.

For example, at today's spot rate of C$1 = £0.625, a receipt of $C120 million would be converted into £75 million. If the Canadian dollar weakened to (say) £0.60, the receipt would be converted into £72 million, giving a loss of £3 million.

In order to mitigate transaction risk Stannerton Ltd could renegotiate the contract so the receipts are in sterling. This would remove the transaction risk for Stannerton Ltd altogether, but will transfer it to Bomon Inc, so the risk for Stannerton Ltd becomes a commercial one as Bomon Inc may not agree to accepting the transaction risk without a renegotiation of the contract price.

Alternatively, a range of hedging techniques are available to mitigate or even remove the transaction risk for each receipt expected by Stannerton Ltd. For example, a forward contract can be used whereby Stannerton Ltd can fix the exchange rate that will apply to a particular receipt months in advance of the actual receipt.

Economic risk

There is also some economic risk arising from the currency of the contract. Since the beginning of 2022, the Canadian dollar has strengthened by 7%. If this was a long-term trend then the revenue from this contract in 2023 would be increased by (C$480 million × 0.625 × 0.07 =) £21 million.

It is unlikely at present that any of Stannerton Ltd's costs are in Canadian dollars. It would be useful from a forex risk perspective if some of the cost base was in Canadian dollars (eg by using Canadian suppliers) as the long-term risk to the dollar revenue would be partially offset by the risk on the dollar costs.

Working capital risks

The credit period of 90 days is twice as high as that given to Stannerton Ltd's existing clients. On average C$120 million dollars of receivables will be outstanding. In sterling this is C$120 × 0.625 = £75 million. The current level of receivables is 45/365 × £600 million = £74 million, so the receivables will more than double, which puts Stannerton Ltd's liquidity under pressure.

It appears that an increase in receivables would have to be appropriately financed. As the new contract will lead to a permanent or long-term increase in receivables, permanent or long-term finance will be necessary.

The large increase in production resulting from the Bomon contract is likely to cause capacity difficulties in the factory and warehouse. Sales and production are about to increase by 50% but both the production and storage facilities are already at 90% so Stannerton Ltd will be taken to 135% of current capacity.

Lack of appropriate storage can lead to damage or loss of inventory.

Lack of sufficient manufacturing space can lead to delays in production and stockouts.

New production and storage facilities should be bought or leased.

Lack of appropriate storage can lead to damage or loss of inventory.

> **Additional areas where credit might be given, note this is not an exhaustive list:**
> - Overtrading risks
> - Other hedging techniques
> - Other means of dealing with the risks
> - Marks will be given for any relevant additional points

11 Trapling PLC

This subject is taken from 'The Investment Decision'

Learning Outcomes

LO2

The question requires candidates to understand the role of the financial manager in making investment decisions which could lead to changes in the organisation's capital structure. Here the gearing of Trapling PLC is increasing as a result of a new project, so the APV would be appropriate.

The relevant chapters are:

- Chapter 8 Investment decisions
- Chapter 10 The Capital Asset Pricing Model
- Chapter 11 Capital structure and advanced valuation techniques

(a)

	T1 2023	T2 2024	T3 – 8 2025 – 2030	T8 2030
Pre-tax profits		40.00	72.00	
Development expenditure	(16.00)			
Tax at 30%	4.80	(12.00)	(21.60)	
Plant and machinery	(75.00)			
Capital allowances		22.50		
Working capital	(4.00)	(3.20)		7.20
	(90.20)	47.30	50.40	7.20
Discount factor at 13.36%	0.880	0.774	3.038	0.359
	(79.38)	36.61	153.12	2.58
Base NPV	112.93			
Tax savings				
4% × $100m × 30% = $1.2m				
× 6.733	8.08			
APV	121.01			

(b) The adjusted present value involves the calculation of a project's net present value using the ungeared cost of equity of the organisation undertaking it.

This gives a base NPV which completely ignores the impact of the organisation's debt capital.

Because interest payable attracts tax relief, the base NPV must be adjusted for the present value of the tax savings resulting from the interest payable on that finance.

It is based on Modigliani & Miller's theory that the value of a geared company (or project) is the same as that of an ungeared equivalent plus the tax savings resulting from the interest payable.

It is best used to evaluate projects which increase the organisation's borrowing (or borrowing capacity).

Additional areas where credit might be given, note this is not an exhaustive list:

- Marks will be given for any relevant additional points
- Using discount factors at 13% from the tables would be given full credit.

---

12 Kraddassian Broadcasting Corporation

This subject is taken from 'International finance and interest rate risk' and 'Working Capital'.

Learning Outcomes

LO4 and LO5

The question requires candidates to understand how the Baumol model can be used to schedule regular cash receipts/payments optimally to minimise cost as well as the use of hedging strategies to mitigate interest rate risk.

Relevant chapters are:

Chapter 18 Interest rate risk

Chapter 22 Management of inventories and cash

(a) The fixed cost (f) of transferring the funds is $0.1 billion.
The total amount (S) to be used is $360 billion.
The net interest cost for the government is (5% – 3%) = 2% or 0.02
The optimal periodic transfer to the KBC is determined using the formula.

$$\sqrt{\frac{2fS}{i}}$$

Ie $\sqrt{\frac{2\times 0.1\times 360}{0.02}}$ ie. $60 billion

Over the year, the KBC requires funds of $360 billion, so in total there will be six transfers of $60 billion ($360bn/$60bn).

This means that the payments will be every 2 months as follows

Date	Payment to KBC
1 January 2023	$60 billion
1 March	$60 billion
1 May	$60 billion
1 July 2023	$60 billion
1 September 2023	$60 billion
1 November 2023	$60 billion

The cost of this option is:

Cost of borrowing = 2% × $60 billion/2 = $0.6bn

Cost of transferring = $0.1bn × 360/6 = $0.6bn

Ie $1.2bn

The aim of the Baumol model is to schedule regular cash payments in such a way so that the cost of the funds and the cost of transferring them are optimised.

If the whole $360bn is transferred at once at the beginning of the year. The average amount provided through the year would be larger (360/2 = $180bn) and the government's cost of capital in respect of the funds at 2% would be larger ($180bn × 2% = $3.6bn. On the other hand only one transfer would be necessary and that would cost $0.1bn. So the total cost would be $3.7bn.

It assumes that the cash is used up at a constant rate over time which is unlikely to happen given the variety of programmes made by the KBC.

Additional areas where credit might be given, note this is not an exhaustive list:

- Marks will be given for any relevant additional points

(b) Use of the forward rate agreement (FRA)

The loan would be taken out on 31 May 2023 at an interest rate of 6% for 6 months.

The interest cost would therefore be $5bn × 6% × 6/12 = $0.15 billion.

Because the interest rate is higher than that of the FRA, the KBC would get a FRA receipt from the bank: $5bn × (6% - 5.25%) × 6/12 = $0.01875 billion.

The net interest cost would therefore be $0.13125 bn.

Use of the interest rate futures.

June contracts would be used.

The number of contracts = $5bn/$0.5bn × 6/3 = 20 contracts

Begin by selling the futures contracts (The KBC is a borrower)

Sell contracts 30.11.2022	94.45
Buy contracts 31.05.2023	93.90
Profit on futures	0.55

Profit = 0.55% × 20 contracts × $0.5bn × 3/12 = $0.01375 billion
The interest rate on the loan will be as above $5bn × 6% × 6/12 = $0.15 billion.
So the net interest cost = $0.15bn − 0.01375bn = $0.13625 billion

---

Additional areas where credit might be given, note this is not an exhaustive list:

- Marks will be given for any relevant additional points

---

13 Verity Trading Ltd

This subject is taken from 'The Investment Decision', 'Working Capital Management' and 'International Finance and Interest Rate Risk'.

Learning Outcomes.

LO2, LO4 and LO5.

Chapters:

9 Investment decisions.
16 Foreign exchange risk.
22 The management of inventories and cash.

This question requires candidates to deal with a working capital issue (inventory management) which has a knock-on effect on an organisation's shareholder wealth and a decision which requires an investment appraisal both in financial and non-financial terms. The advantages and risks associated with the proposal in the scenario touch on financial risk as well as business suitability. The NPV expands to LO1 because candidates need to calculate the weighted average cost of capital in order to evaluate the proposal. Finally, the proposal involves international trade so explicitly challenges the students in terms of LO4 too.

(a) EOQ and annual costs - Yello Ltd.

Economic order quantity.

	2024 – 6
Co	27,500
D	10,725
Ch	6,000
EOQ (=Q)	$\sqrt{\dfrac{2 \times 27{,}500 \times 10{,}725}{6{,}000}}$
	314

Annual ordering, holding and purchasing costs

Annual Ordering costs	**2024 – 6**
Cost per order	27,500
Orders (D/Q)	34
Delivery cost (34 × £27,500)	£935,000

Annual holding costs	**2024 – 6**
Holding cost per tonne per year (Ch)	6,000
Safety stock (S) (2/365 × D)	58.767
Average inventory (Q/2)+S	216
Annual cost	£1,296,000

Purchase cost (PD)	**2024**
Price	300
Demand	10,725
Purchase cost (PD)	3,217,500

	2024
Total cost	£5,448,500

(b) Use of EOQ.

EOQ is highly theoretical, based on a number of assumptions which are often unrealistic and difficult to apply to a practical scenario.

In relation to Verity Trading Ltd and XC337, the usefulness of the EOQ model is limited because:

- Production volumes, and therefore daily materials usage, can be varied. EOQ only works as a decision-making technique if the daily (or weekly etc) usage is constant.

- Likewise, the annual demand changes from year to year. From this, we can assume that production is likely to grow throughout the year which further increases the likelihood that usage of chemical XC337 is not constant.

- EOQ also assumes that replenishment of inventory is immediate. This does not happen with the replenishment of XC337 by Yello Ltd. In fact, given Yello Ltd's occasional failure to deliver within 2 days of the target delivery date, it can be assumed that production has had to stop a number of times in 2021 and 2022.

(c) Cost in sterling of the new system assuming a futures hedge.

Number of contracts = ($500,000÷1.1520)/£62,500 = 7 contracts.

Sell	1.1520
Buy	1.1500
Profit	0.0020

Profit = 0.0020 × £62,500 × 7 contracts = $875 or £761 at spot of $1.15.
Cost of the system = $500,000/1.15 = £434,783.
Less profit on futures = £434,783 - £761 = £434,021.

(d) Evaluation of proposal to switch supplier

	31.12.2023	31.12.2024
Time	0	1-3
	£	£
Cost of integration (part (c))	(434,021)	
Cost savings (Working 1)		495,735
Saved shutdown costs (Working 2)		300,000
	(434,021)	795,735
Taxation at 25%	108,505	(198,934)
	(325,516)	596,801
DF at 12%	1.000	2.402
	(325,516)	1,433,516
NPV	1,108,000	

Working 1: Purchase and holding cost	1
NQ ASA cost (NOK)	
Tonnage	10,725
Price/tonne	4,100
Cost (NOK)	43,972,500
Exchange rate	10.85
Sterling equivalent	4,052,765
Holding cost 6,000 × 150	900,000
	4,952,765
Current purchase cost	5,448,500
Incremental cost of switching (£)	495,735

Working 2: shutdown costs	
Yello deliveries more than 2 days late	6%
Total deliveries (part (a))	34
Number of stoppages	2.05

Advantages and risks of switching to Nordqvistan ASA.

Financially, switching appears to be worthwhile. Whilst the price per tonne appears to be higher, the ordering and holding costs are much lower because of the lower average inventory levels expected and the zero delivery charge.

Switching to Nordqvistan ASA appears to be a more favourable option in terms of sustainability. Its safety record means that Verity Trading Ltd's own supply chain is becoming more safety conscious. NQ ASA also has a strong, proven track record in reducing waste which means Verity Trading Ltd's supply chain would become more environmentally sustainable.

The success of the switch depends on the reliability of the information systems used to monitor inventory and place orders. If the IT system goes offline unexpectedly future stoppages would happen.

There is less administrative burden given that Verity Trading Ltd will not need to monitor and order inventory.

Additional areas where credit might be given, note this is not an exhaustive list:

- Marks will be given for any relevant additional points
- Candidates may be rewarded for identifying the earlier payment to the supplier
- Candidates may include comments about currency risk in respect of the payments in Norwegian Krone

14 Pinguo Ltd

This subject is taken from 'International Finance and Interest Rate Risk' and 'Working Capital'.

Learning Outcomes.

LO1 and LO3.

This question requires the candidate to consider two methods of transferring $1 million between two individuals either in the form of a share transfer or as a cash payment funded by a dividend generated by the sale of the company's assets. In considering the first option, candidates need to value the equity in an investment company and also to justify a particular technique for doing so compared to another.

The question develops from there and encourages the candidate to consider the impact of the second option and how that might be affected by market imperfections such as transaction fees and taxes.

The relevant chapters are:

- Chapter 2 sources of finance.
- Chapter 5 Financial planning and forecasting.
- Chapter 13 Valuation of companies.

(a) Value of shares.

(i) Assets valuation.

	$,000
Market value of investments	7,800
Less liabilities (W1)	(1,800)
Net assets at market value	6,000
90% of which	5,400

Working 1: long-term loans attract an interest rate of 8% which equates to a finance charge of $144,000 a year. The loans must be $144,000/0.08 = $1.8m.

(ii) Taking 2023's forecast earnings, the P/E ratio implicit in this valuation is $6m/0.771 = 7.78.

(iii) Use of the assets basis rather than the earnings basis.

The only activity that Pinguo Ltd undertakes is that of holding investments.

Those investments are not related to each other, so do not have any synergistic value enhancing Pinguo Ltd's earning capacity.

The investments could easily exist without the company, so the company does not add any additional value, other than maybe legal protection or as a tax shelter.

It is likely to be difficult to identify a suitable price to earnings (P/E) ratio as a comparable quoted company will not exist. By definition, a quoted company would be much larger than Pinguo Ltd and is unlikely to have a portfolio mix that is approximate to that of Pinguo Ltd.

It is also difficult, based on the data available, to identify a sustainable earnings figure. Pinguo Ltd's gains and losses on disposal are significant (so would need to be included) but fluctuating (so even an average is likely to be too much of an approximation).

(iv) Shares to dispose of:
Each share's value would be $6m/4m shares = $1.50 per share.
Therefore transfer 666,667 shares to Goran.

(b) Saskia is a 90% shareholder and, unless Goran can legally waive his share of the dividend, he would also have to be paid a dividend in line with his 10% holding.

For a dividend to be paid to Saskia of $1m, the total dividend would have to be $1m/0.9 $1,111,111.

To cover legal fees and taxes, we need to gross up the $1,111,111 by dividing it by (1 − 0.12).

$1,111,111/0.88 = $1,262,626 worth of investments which should be disposed of.

The current portfolio of quoted investments held by Pinguo Ltd is $3.1m, so this is a disposal of 40.73% of its quoted shares.

The forecast dividend income for the year ending 30 June 2024 is therefore 40.73% lower than that of the year ending 30 June 2023, i.e. $553,000 × (1-0.4073) = $327,764.

> **Additional areas where credit might be given, note this is not an exhaustive list:**
>
> - Marks will be given for any relevant additional points

15 Portshead plc

This subject is taken from 'The Investment Decision'.

Learning Outcomes.

LO3 and LO1.

The question requires candidates to understand the role of the financial manager in advising on the value of potential investments in contexts where a very specific objective is in play.

The relevant chapters are:

- Chapter 13 Valuation of companies.
- Chapter 1 Financial management and financial objectives.
- Chapter 2 Sources of finance.

(a) Portshead Family shareholding

Current shareholding and position.

The family's current shareholding is 96.25 million shares out of a total of 350 million in issue. This is a 27.5% shareholding.

Conversion.

Each $100 of nominal value can be converted into 32 shares, this means there will be ($50m/100 × 32 shares) = 16m new shares.

Portshead family acquires the convertible loan stock now:

If the family purchases the convertible loan stock today and retains it until June 2028, they will be entitled to the new shares. **[1]** This will bring the family's total number of shares to (96.25m + 16.0m) = 112.25 million shares.

The total issued share capital of Portshead plc will also increase by the number of new shares to (350m + 16m) = 366 million shares.

The family stake will then be 112.25 ÷ 366 = 30.67%.

Portshead family does NOT acquire the loan stock.

The shareholding will be (96.25 ÷ 366.0m) = 26.3%.

(b) If the family purchases the loan stock prior to its conversion, its shareholding remains higher than 26.5% so is ensured representation at board level.

However, if the loan stock is converted by other investors the family's shareholding will be diluted to such an extent that it will no longer entitled by law to board representation.

(c) Value of the convertible loan stock

	Year	Period		Cash flow ($m)	10%	PV
1 June	2024	1	Interest	7	0.909	6.363
	2025	2	Interest	7	0.826	5.782
	2026	3	Interest	7	0.751	5.257
	2027	4	Interest	7	0.683	4.781
	2028	5	Interest	7	0.621	4.347
		5	Conversion	166.56	0.621	103.27
						129.8

Working 1: Conversion value.

The expected share price is expected to grow at 1% between now and 1 June 2028 (5 years) to:
$9.90 \times 1.01^5 = $10.41.
Conversion value = 16 million shares at $10.41 = $166.56.

(d) The Portshead plc shares are quoted on a major stock exchange. This means that there is a free market on which the Portshead family-shareholders can purchase shares in the company. If they are worried about the conversion and its dilutive effect on the family's stake and influence in the company, a number of shares can be purchased relatively easily.

The number of shares they would need to purchase to ensure they had a shareholding of at least 26.5 after the conversion would be:

Shares needed (26.5% × 366m)	96.99 million
Shares currently held	96.25 million
Purchase	0.74 million

This would cost 740,000 × $9.90 = $7.326 million, which is a lot less than what the acquisition of the convertible loan stock would be.

Additional areas where credit might be given, note this is not an exhaustive list:

- To acquire the loan stock would need negotiation as it is not listed, this is likely to take time and, depending on the relative strength of the current holder of the stock, it might be more expensive.

16 Brandin Co

This subject is taken from 'International finance and interest rate risk'.

Learning Outcomes.

LO4 and LO1.

The question requires candidates to illustrate how interest rate futures can be used to mitigate interest rate risk. Then the link between the interest rate risk and the company's weighted average cost of capital is tested.

The relevant chapters are:

- Chapter 18 Interest rate risk.
- Chapter 9 cost of capital.

(a) Closing futures price.

The difference between the implied futures price of the current interest rate and the current futures price is known as basis.

Interest rate now of 3.75% would imply a futures price of £96.25. However, the futures price today is less than that at £95.55. There is a difference of 0.70 or 70 basis points.

Basis is assumed to narrow uniformly until the expiry of the contract.

Today is 1 June 2023 and the expiry is on 31 December 2023, so it will narrow over a seven month period, that is at 10 points per month. When Brandin Co needs to close out the futures hedge on 30 November 2023, there will be one month to expiry so the closing futures basis will be 10 points.

The closing futures price is therefore estimated at (100 − 4.95) − 0.10 = £94.95.

(b) The hedge will be set up by selling interest rate futures.

The number of contracts is calculated as follows:

(£75,000,000 ÷ £125,000) × 10/3 months = 2,000 contracts.
Sell at 95.55.
Buy at 94.95 (per part (a)).
Profit = 60 ticks.
1 tick = 0.01% × 3/12 × £125,000 = £3.125 per tick per contract.
Futures outcome is therefore a profit of £3.125 × 60 ticks × 2,000 contracts = £375,000.

The net outcome re cost of the debt:

Interest payable on actual loan based on closing SONIA:

(4.95% + 5%) × £75,000,000 × 10/12 = £6,218,750
Less the futures outcome (£6,218,750 − £375,000) = £5,843,750.
Effective rate of interest = £5,843,750/£75,000,000 × 12/10 = 9.35%.

(c) Cost of capital

		MV (£m)
Equity	72.5m × 5	362.5
New debt		75.0
Debenture	101% × £100	101.0
		538.5

The WACC is therefore:

14.5% × 362.5/538.5 + 9.35% × (1−0.19) × 75/538.5 + 6.4% × 101/538.5 = 12.02%.

> **Additional areas where credit might be given, note this is not an exhaustive list:**
> - Marks will be given for any relevant additional points

17 Falstone PLC.

This subject is taken from 'The Financial Environment and Capital Requirements and Consequent Costs' and 'The Investment Decision'.

Learning Outcomes LO1 and LO2.

The question requires candidates to understand the mechanics of investment appraisal and to identify and correct errors in a net present value calculation. As part of the correction of the NPV, candidates also had to calculate a weighted average cost of capital.

In this scenario, candidates are also required to understand and show the expected outcome for a shareholder of a rights issue.

(a) (i) Technical issues relating to the appraisal of Project Sadie.

Exchange rates

The director of product development has requested that the dollar revenue be translated into euros at the projected exchange rates which give the more favourable euro equivalent.

This ignores the possibility that the actual exchange rate in the next three years could move more adversely and an expected value should have been calculated to give an average of the potential exchange rates.

Inflation

Only the first year's inflation has been incorporated into the relevant cash flow for incremental fixed costs. The 6% and 4% inflation rates have been ignored.

This means that a relevant cost of the project has been understated and overstates the NPV.

Capital expenditure and tax

Whilst the capital expenditure appears to be recorded correctly in the NPV calculation, there appears to be an error in the tax treatment of the expenditure. The entire expenditure on capital items has been deducted from taxable profits and given tax relief at 25%.

The expenditure should be given tax relief via capital allowances whereby 18% of the unrelieved expenditure is deducted from profits. This overstates the positive NPV of Project Sadie.

Discount rate

The discount rate to be used on this project should be Falstone PLC's weighted average cost of capital. The use of 7% (the interest rate on the planned loan) does not reflect the return expected by the shareholders and existing lenders which provide Falstone PLC's capital.

(ii) **Ethical issues**

It appears that the product development director's intervention has meant that the NPV has been overstated. This is misleading for their colleagues on the board who will be deciding whether Project Sadie should proceed.

Mojobank plc will also make a decision about lending to Falstone PLC partly based on the NPV calculation, which means that the PD director's behaviour is potentially criminally fraudulent too.

> **Additional areas where credit might be given, note this is not an exhaustive list:**
> - Reference to fundamental principles
> - Ethical conflict resolution

(b) Correct net present value of Project Sadie

	01.01.2024	31.12.2024	31.12.2025	31.12.2026
	0	1	2	3
	€m	€m	€m	€m
Contract fee in dollars		42.00	60.00	65.00
Exchange rate (W1)		1.1350	1.1436	1.1656
Contract fee in euros		37.00	52.47	55.77
Subcontractor's fee		(16.00)	(16.00)	(16.00)
Incremental fixed costs		(15.12)	(16.03)	(16.67)
		5.88	20.44	23.10
Tax at 25%		(1.47)	(5.11)	(5.78)
Capital expenditure	(40.00)			5.00
Capital allowances (W2)		1.50	1.28	5.98
	(40.00)	5.91	16.61	28.30
Discount factors at 16% (W3)	1.000	0.862	0.743	0.641
	(40.00)	5.09	12.34	18.14
Net present value	(4.43)			

Negative NPV suggests non-viable project

Working 1: Exchange rate projections ($/(€))

	01.01.2024	31.12.2024	31.12.2025	31.12.2026
1 € = USD (40% probability)	1.1000	1.1200	1.1250	1.1290
1 € = USD (60% probability)	1.1100	1.1450	1.1560	1.1900
	1.1060	1.1350	1.1436	1.1656

Working 2: capital allowances

		TWDV	Tax at 25%
Time 0	Cost	40.00	
Time 1	WDA at 15%	–6.00	1.5
		34.00	
Time 2	WDA at 15%	–5.10	1.28
		28.90	
Time 3	Balancing adjustment	–23.90	5.98
		5.00	

Working 3: weighted average cost of capital

Equity

Cost of equity = (45 × 1.04)/369 + 0.04 = 16.68%

Value of equity = 750m shares × €3.69 = €2,767.5m

Debt

Cost of debt = internal rate of return on debenture cash flows

	€m	5%	PV €m	10%	PV €m
Market value	(415.00)	1.000	(415.00)	1.000	(415.00)
Interest 6.67% × €500m × (1 – 0.25)	25.00	4.329	108.24	3.791	94.77
Redemption value	500.00	0.784	391.76	0.621	310.46
			85.00		(9.77)

IRR = 5 + 85/(85+9.77) × (10 – 5) = 9.48%

Weighted average cost of capital

	k	MV	%	WACC
Equity	16.68	2767.5	0.870	14.50
Debt	9.48	415.0	0.130	1.24
		3182.5		15.74

Say 16% for investment appraisal purposes.

(c) Kielder PLC - rights issue

The theoretical ex-rights price (TERP) is as follows

	€
4 shares at €5.20	20.80
1 share at €4.00	4.00
5 shares at	24.80
TERP = €24.80 / 5	4.96

Value of a right = TERP less the rights price = €4.96 - €4.00 = €0.96.
Falstone PLC holds 300,000 shares so has the right to buy 75,000 new ones.
Falstone PLC's existing shares will be worth 300,000 × €4.96 = €1.488m.
It will sell its rights for 75,000 × €0.96 = €72,000.
Its cum-rights shareholder wealth was 300,000 × €5.20 = €1,560,000.
Its ex-rights shareholder wealth is unchanged at €1,488,000 + €72,000 = €1,560,000.

18 KAM Group.

This subject is taken from 'International finance and interest rate risk' (Chapter 16).

Learning Outcomes LO4.

The question requires candidates to understand the cash flows resulting from inter-company trading in an international context. Two options for the settlement of cross-border balances are considered and concluded on. A narrative element is included whereby candidates must set out how a futures hedge may be useful in this context.

(a) (i) Muller Ltd's net payment or receipt in pounds.

If the current policy of using currency forward contracts is used, Muller Ltd's anticipated cashflows on 31 December 2023 would be as follows:

		£m
To Kaarija Oyj	€9.0m ÷ 1.13	(8.0)
To Alessa ASA	NOK 166.0m ÷ 9.99	(16.6)
From Kaarija Oyj and Alessa ASA	£40m + £90m	130.0
		105.4

(ii) Use of futures contracts

Muller Ltd's receipts will be in sterling which is the company's home currency so no hedging is necessary in this respect.

A futures hedge would be used by Muller Ltd to mitigate the currency transaction risk associated with its payments in euros and NOK.

If sterling futures are available to cover both the euro and NOK payments, this means that Muller Ltd would sell sterling futures today.

On 31 December 2023, Muller Ltd would close the hedge by buying the same number of futures contracts.

If the exchange rate has moved adversely against Muller Ltd this should generate a profit on the futures market which would offset the higher payments due to the other two companies.

(b) Multilateral netting.

Working

In each currency

			Sales to			
			Kaarija Oyj	Alessa ASA	Muller Ltd	Exch rate
Sales from	Kaarija Oyj	€m		39.0	9.0	1.00
	Alessa ASA	NOKm	725.0		166.0	11.75
	Muller Ltd	£m	40.0	90.0		1.15

In Euros

			Sales to			Total
			Kaarija Oyj	Alessa ASA	Muller Ltd	Exch rate
Sales from	Kaarija Oyj	€m	–	39.0	9.0	48.0
	Alessa ASA	€m	61.7	–	14.1	75.8
	Muller Ltd	€m	34.8	78.3	–	113.1
	Total payments €m		(96.5)	(117.3)	(23.1)	(236.9)
	Total receipts €m		48.0	75.8	113.1	
	Net cash flows		(48.5)	(41.5)	90.0	

Muller Ltd would receive a total of €90.0m, €48.5m from Kaarija Oyj and €41.5m from Alessa ASA.

Translated to sterling at the forward rate of £1 = 1.14 is £102.6m.

The new policy of multilateral netting would not be beneficial for Muller Ltd.

19 Dastee Co.

This subject is taken from 'Valuation and corporate change'.

Learning Outcomes LO3.

The question requires candidates to understand value a convertible debenture issued by an unlisted company. Candidates were expected to realise that a share valuation is also necessary given that there is a possibility for the debenture to be converted to ordinary shares.

Cash proceeds from sale of convertible debenture.

The market value of a convertible debenture is estimated as the present value of the expected cash flows for its investors.

The discount rate is the market yield on debentures of a similar risk profile. In this case that is given as 9%.

Period		$ per $100
1 – 11	Interest per $100 debenture (6.804 × $7.20)	48.99
11	Terminal value [$121.60 (w1) × 0.388]	47.18
	Market value of the debenture	96.17

Dastee Co's debenture is worth 96.17% × $35 million = $33.66m.

A further $16.34 million will have to be borrowed to pay for the acquisition of its investment.

Working 1 Terminal value of the debenture

As the holders of the debenture have a choice between (1) redeeming the debenture at par and (2) converting the debenture into ordinary shares, the market value of the debenture today depends on the market's expectation as to which of these options the investors will choose.

Under option 1 the investor will be entitled to $100 per debenture (ie its par value).

Under option 2 the investor will be entitled to convert each $100 debenture into 40 ordinary shares in Grensch Co.

Grensch Co is not a listed company so the market value of its shares must be estimated.

The average price-earnings (P/E) ratio for Grensch Co's industry is 14. This can be reduced by (say) 30% to reflect the restricted marketability of the shares due them being unlisted this gives us a P/E ratio of 9.8.

The current level of earnings after tax is $196m × (1 – 0.22) = $152.88m:

	$
Earnings before interest and tax	228.67
Finance charges (£228.7m/7)	(32.67)
	196.00
Tax at 22%	(43.12)
	152.88

The P/E ratio is applied to the post-tax earnings to give a total value (9.8 × $152.88) $1,498.2m.

Divided by 600 million ordinary shares in issue, this gives a share value of $1,498.2/600 = $2.50.

If the share price is expected to rise by 4% each year for 5 years and then remain stable, this means the share price on 31 December 2034 will be $2.50 × 1.04^5 = $3.04.

The conversion value of Grensch Co's convertible debenture is therefore 40 × $3.04 = $121.60, which is preferable to its redeemable value at par ($100), so the assumption is that the conversion will take place.

20 HJQ Inc

This subject is taken from 'Working capital management'.

Learning Outcomes LO5.

The question requires candidates to understand the nature and importance of working capital management for liquidity purposes and how that interacts with a company's earnings and its valuation.

(a) (i) Earnings before tax 2024 – 2026

	Current 2023 $m		Forecast 2024 $m		Forecast 2025 $m		Forecast 2026 $m
Sales turnover	396	×1.1=	436	×1.1=	480	×1.1=	528
Variable operating expenses	(23)	×1.1=	(25)	×1.1=	(28)	×1.1=	(31)
Fixed operating expenses	(128)		(128)		(128)		(128)
Profit before tax	245		283		324		369

(ii) Working capital 2023 – 2026

	Current 2023 Days	Forecast 2024 Days	Forecast 2025 Days	Forecast 2026 Days
Receivables	42	35	30	30
Payables	(37)	(35)	(35)	(35)
Operating cycle	5	–	(5)	(5)
	$m	$m	$m	$m
Receivables balance	46	42	39	43
Payables balance	(15)	(15)	(15)	(15)
Net working capital	31	27	24	28

(b) Forecast cash balances 2024 – 2026

	$m	$m	$m
Profit after tax	162	193	226
Movement in working capital	4	3	(4)
	166	196	222
Cash balance b/f	(56)	110	306
Cash balance c/f	110	306	528
Current assets	152	345	571
Current liabilities	15	15	15
Current ratio	10	23	38

(c) Overtrading

To assess the risk of overtrading between 2024 and 2026, the information that would be useful is as follows:

- To what extent does the expansion require new investment in non-current assets?
- To what extent will new investment be financed by long-term capital rather than short-term finance/credit?

(d) Cash flow valuation

	2024 $m	2025 $m	2026 $m
Profit after tax	162	193	226
Movement in working capital	4	3	(4)
	166	196	222
Perpetuity factor (1/0.13)			7.69231
Discount factors at cost of equity (13%)	0.885	0.783	0.783
	147	153	1,337

Valuation ($m) 1,637

EXAM ANSWER BANK

Mock Exam questions and answers

AIA PROFESSIONAL QUALIFICATION

PROFESSIONAL 2

BUSINESS AND FINANCIAL MANAGEMENT

TUESDAY 14th MAY 2019 (ADAPTED)

Time allowed – 3 hours

Answer ALL questions

Present Value and Annuity Tables are printed at the end of the paper.

You are allowed an additional 15 minutes reading time before the exam begins.

1. NAZ Electronics plc is a US based freezer manufacturer and is evaluating its current market position in the European Union (EU) following an announcement of 25% common external tariff on US freezers imported into the EU. The management of NAZ believes that this tariff imposition by the European Commission will reduce the company's profits on its exports to Spain. Therefore, the company is considering the establishment of a freezer manufacturing plant in Barcelona, Spain.

   NAZ wants to invest a total capital of 2,000,000 Euros financed entirely with common stock, all of which will be owned by the parent company. In addition, working capital of €150,000 will be required and this will be recovered at the end of the project's five-year life. The company uses the straight-line method of depreciation and it is expected that the plant will have a scrap value of €500,000 at the end of the life of the project. The table below provides a summary of the company's annual possible sales and fixed cost forecast for the next 5 years as follows:

Year	2020	2021	2022	2023	2024
Sales (units)	5,000	5,500	6,500	7,000	7,500
Fixed costs	€125,000	€140,000	€162,500	€185,000	€220,000

   The freezer would be sold at a price of €250 per unit and this price is expected to rise in line with inflation at 3.0%. The following data, based on the current prices, are given as follows:

	Cost per unit €
Costs of the local materials	50
Other materials purchased from the parent	20
Labour cost	40
Overheads: Variable	10

   Local materials, labour and variable overheads costs are expected to grow at the constant rate of 2.5% per annum for the next 5 years because of inflation. However, the cost of material from the parent company will rise by 2% per annum

   The current exchange rate is €0.90 per US dollar. The Spanish inflation rate is expected to remain at a relatively high rate of 5.0% per annum compared to the US inflation rate of only 3.0% per annum. The risk free rate is 7% and the market return is 13.0%. The company's finance director estimates the beta of this project to be 1.5. The country risk premium for Spain is 1%. There is no restriction on cash flow repatriation.

   Corporate tax in Spain is 30% and is payable at each year end without delay. Because of a double-taxation between the US and Spain, NAZ will have to pay tax on the project in Spain.

   Required

   (a) Calculate the cost of capital and evaluate whether it is worthwhile to undertake this project in Euros and US dollars. **(26 marks)**

   (b) The management of NAZ Electronics plc recognise that there will be risks attached to the new project should they decide to accept it. You are required to advise the directors of what the principal risks might be in respect of the new project. **(10 marks)**

   (c) Advise management how to manage these risks. **(4 marks)**

   (Total 40 marks)

MOCK EXAM QUESTIONS

2. You are corporate finance director of Jubilee plc - a US based company which has to pay a supplier in the United Kingdom for imported components in 90 days' time. The payment is to be made in the currency of the supplier. The payment amounts to £2 million and since this is a future currency liability you need to decide which hedging strategy should be used.

Your analysts provide you with the following information on which to evaluate the possibilities:

1. Spot rate of £1 today = $1.50
2. 90 day forward rate of £1 =$1.48
3. A call option on pound sterling that expires in 90 days has an exercise price of $1.485 and a premium of $0.025 (The option can only be exercised at the end of the period).
4. Forecasted future spot rates in 90 days are:

Forecast	Probability
$1.45	20%
$1.47	70%
$1.51	10%

Current interest rates are:

	UK	US
90 day deposit rate	4.5%	4.5%
90 day borrowing rate	5.0%	5.0%

Required

(a) Provide your assessment and advise management of Jubilee plc on using the following three hedging strategies.

    (i) Not to hedge at all;
    (ii) Forward contract hedge; and
    (iii) Option hedge. **(12 marks)**

(b) The executive management of Jubilee is trying to decide on the best hedging strategy to choose. Advise the executive management on:

    (i) the main differences between forward contract and options contract; and
    (ii) the advantages and disadvantages of options contract and forward contract.

(8 marks)
(Total 20 marks)

3. The directors of DTT plc are proposing to make a takeover bid for Yummy Ltd, a food retailer with ten superstores in the West of Scotland. The bid has not yet been made public. The most recent accounts of Yummy Ltd are as follows:

SUMMARY OF THE STATEMENT OF INCOME
FOR THE YEAR ENDED 31 DECEMBER 2018

	£
Revenue	1,130,000
Profit before interest and taxation	215,000
Interest charges	40,000
Profit before taxation	175,000
Corporation tax	25,000
Profit after taxation	150,000
Dividend paid	44,000
Profit for the year	106,000

EXTRACTS FROM THE STATEMENT OF FINANCIAL POSITION AS AT 31 DECEMBER, 2018

	£	£
Fixed Assets		
Freehold premises at cost	240,000	
Less Accumulated Depreciation	40,000	
		200,000
Motor van at cost	310,000	
Less Accumulated Depreciation	27,000	
		283,000
Fixtures & Fittings at cost	170,000	
Less accumulated depreciation	20,000	
		150,000
Total Fixed Assets		633,000
Current Assets		
Inventories	320,000	
Trade & other receivables	20,000	
Cash at bank	44,000	
		384,000
Total Assets		1,017,000
Current Liabilities:		
Trade & other payables	200,000	
Accrued expenses	34,000	
	234,000	
Long-term Liability		
14% loan stock	114,000	
Total liabilities		(348,000)
Total Assets less total liabilities		**669,000**
Capital and reserves		
Ordinary share at £1.5 each	600,000	
General reserve	69,000	
		669,000

The following additional information is also available:

1. The realisable value of inventories is believed to be 90% of its book value as the inventory figure includes some unsaleable inventories.

2. DJ Ltd - An independent valuer - has estimated the current realisable values of the assets of the company as follows:

	£
Freehold premises	215,000
Motor van	280,000
Fixtures & Fittings	155,000

3. Five per cent of the debtors figure will never be collected.

4. For the remaining assets, the balance sheet values were considered to reflect their current realisable values.

5. Lee Ltd is listed on the Stock Exchange and is in the same line of business as Yummy Ltd. Lee Ltd has a price/earnings ratio of 7.

6. The free cash flows of the business over the next 5 years are estimated as follows:

Year
2019   £70,000
2020   £85,000
3-5   £102,000

In recent years, Lee Ltd has appraised investments using a discount rate of 10%.

Required

As an Accounting Consultant, you have been asked by the directors of DDT plc to prepare a report. Your report should include:

(a) Calculation of the value of Yummy Ltd using the following methods: Net assets liquidation basis; free cash flow basis; and price/earnings ratio basis. **(12 marks)**

(b) Evaluate why the statement of financial position generally has limited usefulness for estimating the value of a firm. **(8 marks)**

(Total 20 marks)

4. The accounts of Freeman Ltd, a distributor of baby foods, are provided below for the year ended 31 May 2018 as follows:

SUMMARY OF THE STATEMENT OF INCOME
FOR THE YEAR ENDED 31 MAY 2018

	£
Revenue	4,820,000
Operating profit	1,200,000
Finance costs (net of finance income)	(400,000)
Profit before taxation	800,000
Taxation	(300,000)
Profit for the year	500,000

EXTRACTS FROM THE STATEMENT OF
FINANCIAL POSITION AS AT 31 MAY, 2018

	£	£
ASSETS & LIABILITIES		
Fixed Assets		
Freehold premises net of depreciation		1,800,000
Fixtures and fittings net of depreciation		820,000
Motor vans net of depreciation		1,020,000
Current Assets		
Inventories	366,000	
Trade & other receivables	364,000	
Cash	24,000	
		754,000
Total Assets		4,394,000
Current Liabilities		
Unsecured bank loans	(540,000)	
Trade & other payables	(400,000)	
Corporation tax	(104,000)	
		(1,044,000)
Long-term Liabilities		
Corporate bonds		(650,000)
Total Assets less Liabilities		**2,700,000**

	£	£
Capital & Reserves		
Ordinary share capital		2,000,000
Preference share capital		650,000
General reserves		50,000
		2,700,000

Notes:

1. The inventories as at 1 June 2017 amounted to £200,000.

2. Trade receivables and trade payables as at 31 May 2018 amounted to £350,000 and £250,000 respectively.

3. For the financial year ended 31 May 2018, the cost of sales amounted to £2,600,000.

4. Credit sales and credit purchases amounted to 2,000,000 and £2,500,000 respectively for the financial year ending 31 May 2018.

Required

(a) Calculate the relevant ratios and evaluate the working capital position of Freeman Ltd.

(11 marks)

(b) The management of Freeman Ltd is planning to adopt a just-in-time system to manage the inventories. As an accountant, evaluate the main arguments for and against adopting a just-in-time approach by Freeman Ltd. **(Total 20 marks)**

[End of question paper]

[Present Value and Annuity Tables are printed on pages 8 to 12]

PRESENT VALUE TABLES
DISCOUNT RATES %

YEARS	1	2	3	4	5	6	7	8	9
1	0.990	0.980	0.971	0.962	0.952	0.943	0.935	0.926	0.917
2	0.980	0.961	0.943	0.925	0.907	0.890	0.873	0.857	0.842
3	0.971	0.942	0.915	0.889	0.864	0.840	0.816	0.794	0.772
4	0.961	0.924	0.888	0.855	0.823	0.792	0.763	0.735	0.708
5	0.951	0.906	0.863	0.822	0.784	0.747	0.713	0.681	0.650
6	0.942	0.888	0.837	0.790	0.746	0.705	0.666	0.630	0.596
7	0.933	0.871	0.813	0.760	0.711	0.665	0.623	0.583	0.547
8	0.923	0.853	0.789	0.731	0.677	0.627	0.582	0.540	0.502
9	0.914	0.837	0.766	0.703	0.645	0.592	0.544	0.500	0.460
10	0.905	0.820	0.744	0.676	0.614	0.558	0.508	0.463	0.422
11	0.896	0.804	0.722	0.650	0.585	0.527	0.475	0.429	0.388
12	0.887	0.788	0.701	0.625	0.557	0.497	0.444	0.397	0.356
13	0.879	0.773	0.681	0.601	0.530	0.469	0.415	0.368	0.326
14	0.870	0.758	0.661	0.577	0.505	0.442	0.388	0.340	0.299
15	0.861	0.743	0.642	0.555	0.481	0.417	0.362	0.315	0.275

PRESENT VALUE TABLES
DISCOUNT RATES %

YEARS	10	11	12	13	14	15	16	17
1	0.909	0.901	0.893	0.885	0.877	0.870	0.862	0.855
2	0.826	0.812	0.797	0.783	0.769	0.756	0.743	0.731
3	0.751	0.731	0.712	0.693	0.675	0.658	0.641	0.624
4	0.683	0.659	0.636	0.613	0.592	0.572	0.552	0.534
5	0.621	0.593	0.567	0.543	0.519	0.497	0.476	0.456
6	0.564	0.535	0.507	0.480	0.456	0.432	0.410	0.390
7	0.513	0.482	0.452	0.425	0.400	0.376	0.354	0.333
8	0.467	0.434	0.404	0.376	0.351	0.327	0.305	0.285
9	0.424	0.391	0.361	0.333	0.308	0.284	0.263	0.243
10	0.386	0.352	0.322	0.295	0.270	0.247	0.227	0.208
11	0.350	0.317	0.287	0.261	0.237	0.215	0.195	0.178
12	0.319	0.286	0.257	0.231	0.208	0.187	0.168	0.152
13	0.290	0.258	0.229	0.204	0.182	0.163	0.145	0.130
14	0.263	0.232	0.205	0.181	0.160	0.141	0.125	0.111
15	0.239	0.209	0.183	0.160	0.140	0.123	0.108	0.095

DISCOUNT RATES %									
YEARS	18	19	20	21	22	23	24	25	26
1	0.847	0.840	0.833	0.826	0.820	0.813	0.806	0.800	0.794
2	0.718	0.706	0.694	0.683	0.672	0.661	0.650	0.640	0.630
3	0.609	0.593	0.579	0.564	0.551	0.537	0.524	0.512	0.500
4	0.516	0.499	0.482	0.467	0.451	0.437	0.423	0.410	0.397
5	0.437	0.419	0.402	0.386	0.370	0.355	0.341	0.328	0.315
6	0.370	0.352	0.335	0.319	0.303	0.289	0.275	0.262	0.250
7	0.314	0.296	0.279	0.263	0.249	0.235	0.222	0.210	0.198
8	0.266	0.249	0.233	0.218	0.204	0.191	0.179	0.168	0.157
9	0.225	0.209	0.194	0.180	0.167	0.155	0.144	0.134	0.125
10	0.191	0.176	0.162	0.149	0.137	0.126	0.116	0.107	0.099
11	0.162	0.148	0.135	0.123	0.112	0.103	0.094	0.086	0.079
12	0.137	0.124	0.112	0.102	0.092	0.083	0.076	0.069	0.062
13	0.116	0.104	0.093	0.084	0.075	0.068	0.061	0.055	0.050
14	0.099	0.088	0.078	0.069	0.062	0.055	0.049	0.044	0.039
15	0.084	0.074	0.065	0.057	0.051	0.045	0.040	0.035	0.031

DISCOUNT RATES %								
YEARS	27	28	29	30	31	32	33	34
1	0.787	0.781	0.775	0.769	0.763	0.758	0.752	0.746
2	0.620	0.610	0.601	0.592	0.583	0.574	0.565	0.557
3	0.488	0.477	0.466	0.455	0.445	0.435	0.425	0.416
4	0.384	0.373	0.361	0.350	0.340	0.329	0.320	0.310
5	0.303	0.291	0.280	0.269	0.259	0.250	0.240	0.231
6	0.238	0.227	0.217	0.207	0.198	0.189	0.181	0.173
7	0.188	0.178	0.168	0.159	0.151	0.143	0.136	0.129
8	0.148	0.139	0.130	0.123	0.115	0.108	0.102	0.096
9	0.116	0.108	0.101	0.094	0.088	0.082	0.077	0.072
10	0.092	0.085	0.078	0.073	0.067	0.062	0.058	0.054
11	0.072	0.066	0.061	0.056	0.051	0.047	0.043	0.040
12	0.057	0.052	0.047	0.043	0.039	0.036	0.033	0.030
13	0.045	0.040	0.037	0.033	0.030	0.027	0.025	0.022
14	0.035	0.032	0.028	0.025	0.023	0.021	0.018	0.017
15	0.028	0.025	0.022	0.020	0.017	0.016	0.014	0.012

CUMULATIVE PRESENT VALUE TABLES
DISCOUNT RATES %

YEARS	1	2	3	4	5	6	7	8	9
1	0.990	0.980	0.971	0.962	0.952	0.943	0.935	0.926	0.917
2	1.970	1.942	1.913	1.886	1.859	1.833	1.808	1.783	1.759
3	2.941	2.884	2.829	2.775	2.723	2.673	2.624	2.577	2.531
4	3.902	3.808	3.717	3.630	3.546	3.465	3.387	3.312	3.240
5	4.853	4.713	4.580	4.452	4.329	4.212	4.100	3.993	3.890
6	5.795	5.601	5.417	5.242	5.076	4.917	4.767	4.623	4.486
7	6.728	6.472	6.230	6.002	5.786	5.582	5.389	5.206	5.033
8	7.652	7.325	7.020	6.733	6.463	6.210	5.971	5.747	5.535
9	8.566	8.162	7.786	7.435	7.108	6.802	6.515	6.247	5.995
10	9.471	8.983	8.530	8.111	7.722	7.360	7.024	6.710	6.418
11	10.368	9.787	9.253	8.760	8.306	7.887	7.499	7.139	6.805
12	11.255	10.575	9.954	9.385	8.863	8.384	7.943	7.536	7.161
13	12.134	11.348	10.635	9.986	9.394	8.853	8.358	7.904	7.487
14	13.004	12.106	11.296	10.563	9.899	9.295	8.745	8.244	7.786
15	13.865	12.849	11.938	11.118	10.380	9.712	9.108	8.559	8.061

CUMULATIVE PRESENT VALUE TABLES
DISCOUNT RATES %

YEARS	10	11	12	13	14	15	16	17
1	0.909	0.901	0.893	0.885	0.877	0.870	0.862	0.855
2	1.736	1.713	1.690	1.668	1.647	1.626	1.605	1.585
3	2.487	2.444	2.402	2.361	2.322	2.283	2.246	2.210
4	3.170	3.102	3.037	2.974	2.914	2.855	2.798	2.743
5	3.791	3.696	3.605	3.517	3.433	3.352	3.274	3.199
6	4.355	4.231	4.111	3.998	3.889	3.784	3.685	3.589
7	4.868	4.712	4.564	4.423	4.288	4.160	4.039	3.922
8	5.335	5.146	4.968	4.799	4.639	4.487	4.344	4.207
9	5.759	5.537	5.328	5.132	4.946	4.772	4.607	4.451
10	6.145	5.889	5.650	5.426	5.216	5.019	4.833	4.659
11	6.495	6.207	5.938	5.687	5.453	5.234	5.029	4.836
12	6.814	6.492	6.194	5.918	5.660	5.421	5.197	4.988
13	7.103	6.750	6.424	6.122	5.842	5.583	5.342	5.118
14	7.367	6.982	6.628	6.302	6.002	5.724	5.468	5.229

DISCOUNT RATES %									
YEARS	18	19	20	21	22	23	24	25	26
1	0.847	0.840	0.833	0.826	0.820	0.813	0.806	0.800	0.794
2	1.566	1.547	1.528	1.509	1.492	1.474	1.457	1.440	1.424
3	2.174	2.140	2.106	2.074	2.042	2.011	1.981	1.952	1.923
4	2.690	2.639	2.589	2.540	2.494	2.448	2.404	2.362	2.320
5	3.127	3.058	2.991	2.926	2.864	2.803	2.745	2.689	2.635
6	3.498	3.410	3.326	3.245	3.167	3.092	3.020	2.951	2.885
7	3.812	3.706	3.605	3.508	3.416	3.327	3.242	3.161	3.083
8	4.078	3.954	3.837	3.726	3.619	3.518	3.421	3.329	3.241
9	4.303	4.163	4.031	3.905	3.786	3.673	3.566	3.463	3.366
10	4.494	4.339	4.192	4.054	3.923	3.799	3.682	3.571	3.465
11	4.656	4.486	4.327	4.177	4.035	3.902	3.776	3.656	3.543
12	4.793	4.611	4.439	4.278	4.127	3.985	3.851	3.725	3.606
13	4.910	4.715	4.533	4.362	4.203	4.053	3.912	3.780	3.656
14	5.008	4.802	4.611	4.432	4.265	4.108	3.962	3.824	3.695
15	5.092	4.876	4.675	4.489	4.315	4.153	4.001	3.859	3.726

DISCOUNT RATES %								
YEARS	27	28	29	30	31	32	33	34
1	0.787	0.781	0.775	0.769	0.763	0.758	0.752	0.746
2	1.407	1.392	1.376	1.361	1.346	1.331	1.317	1.303
3	1.896	1.868	1.842	1.816	1.791	1.766	1.742	1.719
4	2.280	2.241	2.203	2.166	2.130	2.096	2.062	2.029
5	2.583	2.532	2.483	2.436	2.390	2.345	2.302	2.260
6	2.821	2.759	2.700	2.643	2.588	2.534	2.483	2.433
7	3.009	2.937	2.868	2.802	2.739	2.677	2.619	2.562
8	3.156	3.076	2.999	2.925	2.854	2.786	2.721	2.658
9	3.273	3.184	3.100	3.019	2.942	2.868	2.798	2.730
10	3.364	3.269	3.178	3.092	3.009	2.930	2.855	2.784
11	3.437	3.335	3.239	3.147	3.060	2.978	2.899	2.824
12	3.493	3.387	3.286	3.190	3.100	3.013	2.931	2.853
13	3.538	3.427	3.322	3.223	3.129	3.040	2.956	2.876
14	3.573	3.459	3.351	3.249	3.152	3.061	2.974	2.892
15	3.601	3.483	3.373	3.268	3.170	3.076	2.988	2.905

Formulae Sheet

Ke (i) $\quad E(r_1) = r_1 + [E(r_m) - r]\beta$

(ii) $\quad \dfrac{D_1}{P_0} + g$

WACC $\quad Ke_g \dfrac{E}{E+D} + Kd(1-t)\dfrac{D}{E+D}$

or $\quad Ke_0 \left(1 - \dfrac{Dt}{E+D}\right)$

2 asset portfolio $\sigma_p = \sqrt{\sigma_a^2 x^2 + \sigma_b^2 (1-x)^2 + 2x(1-x)p_{ab}\sigma_a\sigma_b}$

Purchasing power parity $\quad \dfrac{i_f - i_{uk}}{1 + i_{uk}}$

Corporate Beta $\quad \beta a = \beta e \dfrac{E}{E + D(1-t)} + \beta d \dfrac{D(1-t)}{E + D(1-t)}$

AIA PROFESSIONAL QUALIFICATION

PROFESSIONAL 2

BUSINESS AND FINANCIAL MANAGEMENT

MODEL ANSWERS

TUESDAY 14th MAY 2019 (ADAPTED)

> Valid alternative points, whether or not they are shown in the Model Answers, will be given credit where appropriate.

CREATING WORLD CLASS ACCOUNTANTS

MOCK EXAM ANSWERS

1. This subject is taken from 'The Financial Environment and Capital Requirements and Consequent Costs' and 'The Investment Decision'

   The question requires candidates to understand the role of the financial manager in determining capital requirements and capital structure and managing relationships with relevant stakeholders. In addition, candidates are required to critically appraise a long-term investment.

   Learning Outcomes

   LO1 and LO2

   (a) **Calculation of cost of capital**

   Risk free rate of return = 7%
   Market Returns = 13%
   Beta = 1.5
   Country risk premium = 1.0%

   Using the CAPM: $r_E = R_F + (R_M - R_F)\beta$
   7 + 13-7(1.5) = 16%
   Project cost of capital = 16 + 1.0 = 17%

   Workings

   Estimation of the cash flows for:

   Inflating local material costs by 2.5% per year:

   Year 1: material costs = 50 = €50
   Year 2: material costs = 50 × 1.025 = €51.25
   Year 3: material costs = 51.25 × 1.025 = €52.53
   Year 4: material costs = 52.53 × 1.025 = €53.84
   Year 5: material costs = 53.84 × 1.025 = €55.19

   Inflating material costs purchased from parent by 2.0% per year:

   Year 1: material costs = 20 = €20.00
   Year 2: material costs = 20 × 1.02 = €20.4
   Year 3: material costs = 20.4 × 1.02 = €20.81
   Year 4: material costs = 20.81 × 1.02 = €21.23
   Year 5: material costs = 21.23 × 1.02 = €21.65

   Inflating labour cost by 2.5% per year

   Year 1: labour cost = €40.00
   Year 2: labour cost = €40.00 × 1.025 = €41.00
   Year 3: labour cost = €41.00 × 1.025 = €42.03
   Year 4: labour cost = €42.03 × 1.025 = €43.08
   Year 5: labour cost = €43.08 × 1.025 = €44.16

   Inflating variable costs by 2.5%

   Year 1: €10.00 = €10.0
   Year 2: €10.00 × 1.025 = €10.25
   Year 3: €10.25 × 1.025 = €10.51
   Year 4: €10.51 × 1.025 = €10.77
   Year 5: €10.77 × 1.025 = €11.04

   Inflating selling price by 3.0%

   Year 1: selling price 250 = €250.0
   Year 2: selling price = 250 × 1.03 = €257.5
   Year 3: selling price = 257.5 × 1.03 = €265.23

Year 4: material costs = 265.23 × 1.03 = €273.19
Year 5: material costs = 273.19 × 1.03 = €281.39

Depreciation
Cost of plant = 2.0 million
Scrap value = 0.5
Life span = 5 years

Depreciation provision per annum = (2.0-0.5)/5 = 0.3

Estimating operating cash flow in Euros

Years	1	2	3	4	5
Selling price	250.00	257.50	265.23	273.19	281.39
Local material	(50.00)	(51.25)	(52.53)	(53.84)	(55.19)
Other material	(20.00)	(20.40)	(20.81)	(21.23)	(21.65)
Labour cost	(40.00)	(41.00)	(42.03)	(43.08)	(44.16)
Variable cost	(10.00)	(10.25)	(10.51)	(10.77)	(11.04)
Contribution	130.00	134.6	139.35	144.27	149.35
Units sold	5,000	5,500	6,000	6,500	7,000
Contribution	650,000	740,300	836,100	937,755	1,045,450
Fixed cost	(125,000)	(140,000)	(162,500)	(185,000)	(220,000)
Operating CF	525,000	600,300	673,600	752,755	825,450
Depreciation	(300,000)	(300,000)	(300,000)	(300,000)	(300,000)
PBT	225,000	300,300	373,600	452,755	525,450
Tax (30%)	(67,500)	(90,090)	(112,080)	(135,826.5)	(157,635)
PAT	157,500	210,210	261,520	316,928.5	367,815

Net present value analysis in Euros

Year	0	1	2	3	4	5
Capital	(2,000,000)					
Working cap.	(150,000)					150,000
Scrap value						500,000
Operating CF		525,000	600,300	673,300	752,755	825,450
Taxation	-	(67,500)	(90,090)	(112,080)	(135,826.5)	(157,635)
NCF	(2,150,000)	458,000	510,210	561,220	616,928.5	1,317,815
DCF 17%	1.000	0.855	0.731	0.624	0.534	0.456
PV	(2,150,000)	391,590	372,963.51	350,201.28	329,439.82	600,923.64

Initial outlay = (2,150,000.00)
Present value of cash flows = 2,045,118.25
NPV = (104,881.75)

The project has a negative NPV and therefore not viable.

Forecasting exchange rate using PPP

$$\text{Purchasing Power Parity: PPP} = \frac{(1+\text{Infl in Spain})}{(1+\text{Infl in US})}(\text{Spot rate in Euros})$$

Inflation rate in Spain = 5.0%
Inflation rate in US = 3.0%
Spot rate = €0.90 per $1.00

Year 1: $= \dfrac{1+.05}{1+.03} \times 0.90 = 0.9175$

Year 2: $\left(\dfrac{1.05}{1.03}\right)^2 \times 0.90 = 0.9353$

Year 3: $\left(\dfrac{1.05}{1.03}\right)^3 \times 0.90 = 0.9535$

Year 4: $\left(\dfrac{1.05}{1.03}\right)^4 \times 0.90 = 0.9720$

Year 5: $\left(\dfrac{1.05}{1.03}\right)^5 \times 0.90 = 0.9908$

Cash flow Conversion on US Dollars

Year	0	1	2	3	4	5
CF	(2,150,000)	458,000	510,210	561,220	616,928.5	1,317,815
ER	0.90	0.9175	0.9353	0.9535	0.9720	0.9908
TCF	(2,388,889)	499,183	545,504	588,589	634,700	1,330,051
DCF 17%	1.000	0.855	0.731	0.624	0.534	0.456
PV	(2,388,889)	426,801	398,763	367,280	338,930	606,503

Initial outlay in dollars = $(2,388,889)
Present value of cashflow in dollars = $2,138,277
Net present value = (250,612)

The project is not viable

(b) From: Accountant
    To: Management of NAZ plc
    Subject: Report of potential risks facing NAZ plc

I submit my report regarding the possible risks that NAZ will face in establishing its presence in Spain.

The management are correct to assert that the new venture will entail risks. Risks will be present for any potential new venture and companies need to be aware of these risks. It may be possible to hedge some of these risks or to implement relevant controls to limit their impact. However, uncertainty will still remain as it is not likely that all risks can be hedged. The principal risks are set out below.

1. The company will be moving into a new country as it currently does not have any operations in Spain. This potentially brings with it the risk that the company may make mistakes in the set up and running of the manufacturing process or that supply chains and working patterns are different.

2. The company is also exposed to financial risk as a large amount of capital resource is required to undertake this investment compared with exporting. This comes with additional cost of financing and the risk that NAZ cannot raise sufficient finance.

3. The company will be establishing a manufacturing unit in Spain and, therefore, it will be exposed to exchange rate risk. Purchasing power parity formula has been used to calculate future exchange rates, but this only provides an estimate of the future rates and these estimates may be incorrect. The company does have the possibility of eliminating some, or

possibly all, of the exchange rate risk by using appropriate exchange rate hedging techniques such as forward exchange contracts.

4. The cashflows have been discounted at an estimated company's cost of capital of 17%. However, this may alter in the future. If the company's risk alters by taking on this new venture then this would impact on the cost of capital. Similarly, if the company's gearing level alters in the years ahead then this can impact on the cost of capital. If the company becomes riskier then this would increase the cost of capital and reduce the net present value of the project.

5. Another principal source of risk is the future cashflow estimates. It can be very difficult to estimate future cashflows, even into the near future. The company cannot know for certain the future cost of materials, labour and the like. It may be possible to mitigate against some of this risk by entering into long-term agreements with suppliers. This would certainly be likely to be feasible in respect of the rental of the factory. However, it may be harder in respect of costs such as material and labour.

6. NAZ is also exposed to geographical separation and cultural risk. The geographical separation of the parent company from its subsidiaries add to the problems of management control of the group of companies as a whole. Separation may exacerbate problems caused by language and cultural differences.

How to manage these risks

1. Use of hedging techniques such as futures, options, forward contracts and matching to overcome exchange risks, interest rates risk and rising inflation rates.

2. Hiring local employees to bridge differences in culture.

3. Forming strategic alliances with local distributors to enhance channels of distribution for the firm's products.

4. Careful planning of the entire phases of the capital investment process, paying attention to the following: sources of financing the project; an assessment of the political climate in the host country (Spain); cash flow estimation; the required rate of return; risk analysis and expenditure control.

Additional areas where credit might be given, note this is not an exhaustive list

- Differences in reporting and enforcement standards may affect the cost of doing business.

---

2. **This subject is taken from 'International Finance and Interest Rate Risk'**

    Candidates are required to critically appraise the economic and financial consequences of global company operations.

    Learning Outcome

    LO4

    Subject Area Covered

    International Finance

    1. No hedge, that is, purchase £2 million at the spot rate in 90 days' time.

Forecast spot rate	cost in US$	Probability
$1.45	$2.90 million	20%
$1.47	$2.94 million	70%
$1.51	$3.02 million	10%

    2. Forward Hedge: Purchase sterling 90 days forward

Dollar cost = £2 million × forward rate of £
= £2 million × $1.48 = $2.96 million

3. Option hedge, that is purchase a call option

90 day Spot rate	Option premium	Exercise option?	Dollar cost	Probability
$1.45	$0.025	No	$2.95m	20%
$1.47	$0.025	No	$2.99m	70%
$1.51	$0.025	Yes	$3.02m	10%

Calculation of option price

$1.45 + $0.025 = $1.475
$1.47 + $0.025 = $1.495
$1.485 + $0.025 = $1.51

Dollar Cost

$1.475 × 2 millon = $2.95 million
$1.495 × 2 million = $2.99 million
$1.51 × 2 million = $3.02 million

If you compare the three strategies, it is clear that there is 90% probability that the cheapest hedging strategy is "not to hedge at all" since the hedging cost is lower than forward hedge or option hedge. However, if you are risk averse, then the forward hedge appears superior.

(b) Main difference

Forward contracts lock in the exchange rate that will apply to a particular transaction in the future. On the other hand, options provide insurance that the exchange rate will not be worse than some level.

Advantages and Disadvantages

The advantage of a forward contract is that uncertainty is eliminated as far as possible. The disadvantage is that the outcome with hedging can be significantly worse than the outcome with no hedging. This disadvantage is not as marked with options as the downside risk is limited. However, unlike forward contracts, options involve an up-front cost.

Additional areas where credit might be given, note this is not an exhaustive list

- Under forward contracts, the defaulting party can be sued.
- Under options contract, the decision to buy/(sell) or not to buy/(sell) is optional.

---

3. **This subject is taken from 'Valuation and Corporate Change'**

Candidates are required to critically appraise the operations of two business organisations.

Learning Outcome

LO3

Subject Area Covered

Valuation and corporate change

MOCK EXAM ANSWERS

(a) (i) Net assets liquidation Method

$$\text{Price per share} = \frac{\text{Total assets at net realisable values} - \text{total liabilities at market values}}{\text{No of ordinary shares}}$$

$$\text{Price per share} = \frac{(215 + 280 + 155 + 288 + 19 + 44) - (348)}{400}$$

= £1.63

Total value 1.63 × 400,000 = **£652,000**

Workings:
Inventories = 90/100 × 320,000 = 288,000
Trade receivables = 95% of 20,000 = 19,000

(ii) **Price/earning ratio = Market price/EPS**

EPS = Profit after tax/No. of shares
EPS= 150,000/400,000 = 0.375
Market price per share = P/E × EPS 0.375 × 6 = £2.25
Total value: 2.25 × 400,000 = £900,000

(iii) Free cash flow basis:

$$\frac{\text{Discounted free cash flows} - \text{long-term liabilities}}{\text{No of ordinary shares}}$$

$$\frac{453,304 - 114,000}{400.0}$$

Price per share = 339.304/400.0 = £0.85

Total market value of the company = **£340,000**

Year	Cash flow	Discount rate (10%)	Present value
2019	70,000	0.909	63,630
2020	85,000	0.826	70,210
2021	102,000	0.751	76,602
2022	102,000	0.683	69,666
2023	102,000	0.621	63,342
2024	102,000	0.564	57,528
2025	102,000	0.513	52,326
			453,304

(b) The use of balance sheet values for valuing the value of the firm is straightforward and the data required for the valuation process are easy to obtain. However, balance sheet values have limited usefulness for estimating the value of a firm for the following reasons.

(i) Book values represent historic values as intangible assets such as goodwill and brand names may not be included in the balance sheet and hence are ignored in the valuation process.

(ii) The values of assets shown in the balance sheet are historic costs (less depreciation to date) and these figures may be below the current market values of the assets

(iii) Book values of assets recorded in the balance sheet ignore inflation

(iv) Balance sheet values ignore investment risk associated with the business

---

Additional areas where credit might be given, note this is not an exhaustive list
- The use of book values may lead to under-valuation in acquisition transactions.

4. **This subject is taken from 'Working Capital Management'**

Candidates are required to critically appraise the working capital management practices of an organisation and make appropriate recommendations

Learning Outcome

LO5

Subject Area Covered

Working Capital Management

(a) (i) **Liquidity position:**

Current ratio: current asset/Current liabilities
754,000/1,044,000 = 0.72:1
Acid test ratio: Trade receivables/current liabilities
388,000/1,044,000 = 0.37:1

(ii) **Stock turnover period:** Closing <u>inventory</u>

Cost of sales

$$\frac{366}{2,600}$$

= 0.141 × 365 days = 51.38 days

(iii) **Settlement period for receivables**

$$\frac{\text{Trade receivables} \times 365}{\text{Credit sales}}$$

$$\frac{350 \times 365}{2,000}$$

0.135 × 365 = <u>63.88 days</u>

(iv) **Settlement period for creditors:**

$$\frac{\text{Trade payables} \times 365}{\text{Credit purchases}}$$

$$\frac{250 \times 365}{2,000}$$

= <u>36.5 days</u>

(v) **Operating credit cycle =**
51.38 + 63.88 − 36.5 = 78.76

Comments:

The liquidity position of the business appears weak. The current ratio is about 0.7:1 whereas acid test ratio is around 0.37:1. Ideally, the current and acid test ratios should be 2:1 and 1:1 but can vary from industry to industry. Our analyses suggest that the business is insufficiently liquid to meet its short-term obligations.

The stock turnover at 51 days is higher than the norm of 30 days. As this business is in the food industry, it is expected that the stock turnover should even be lower than 30 days as food items have limited life on the shelf. Further investigation appears warranted to help find ways of reducing the length of time stock is held.

MOCK EXAM ANSWERS

The receivable days (about 64 days) appears high. At present, it takes over two months to receive credit cash from customers raising concerns in respect of how the business finances its stock purchases and credit control policies. This may be reduced by imposing tight credit control, offering discounts, charging interests on overdue accounts, and so on. However, any policy decisions concerning stocks and debtors must take account of current trading conditions.

The period taken to pay creditors (37 days) is significantly lower than the period taken by customers to settle their debts. This has implications for finance costs of the firm as managers may borrow from banks to pay suppliers. The operating cash cycle could also be reduced by extending the period of credit taken to pay suppliers.

(b) Just-in-time procurement describes a policy of obtaining goods from suppliers at the latest possible time and avoiding the need to carry any materials or stock. This is essential for retailers as holding idle inventories have cost and implications for firm's profitability and competitive advantage.

The main arguments for JIT include:

(i) Reduction in stockholding costs

(ii) Reduced security costs

(iii) Improved labour productivity

(iv) Reduced inventory levels mean that a lower level of investment in working capital will be required

On the other hand, the following are arguments against JIT

(i) Reliance on suppliers to deliver stocks of right quality and quantity at the agreed times may mean entrusting key part of Freeman's operations into the hands of suppliers. This is risky.

(ii) Failure to do so could lead to loss of customers.

(iii) Another cost associated with JIT approach is that suppliers will be required to hold stock for the business and consequently may recoup this additional cost through increased prices.

(iv) JIT may involve a large number of small deliveries to be made thereby increasing transaction costs.

(v) The close relationship necessary between the business and its suppliers may prevent the business from taking advantage of cheaper sources of supply if they become available.

Additional areas where credit might be given, note this is not an exhaustive list
- Reduced the impact of theft/fire /warranty cost by not holding too much inventories.

MOCK EXAM ANSWERS

Index

Note. **Key Terms** and their page references are given in **bold**.

Acceptability, 190
Acceptance credits, 517
Accountability, 79
Accounting rate of return (ARR), 175, 307
Acid test ratio, 109, **482**
Acquisitions, 340
Adjusted cost of capital, 266
Adjusted present value, 261
Adjustments, 319
Agency relationship, 13
Allocative efficiency, 76
Alpha value, 231
Alternative Investment Market (AIM), 68
Amalgamations, 340
Appraisal schemes, 292Arbitrage, 257, 386
Arbitrage pricing model, 237
Argenti, 118
ARR method of share valuation, 307
Asset turnover, 107
At the money, 419
Average production (work-in-progress) period, 482
Average stock, 528

BACS, 535
Bad debt risk, 504
Bad debts, 499
Balance sheet based forecast, 120
Balanced portfolio, 227
Bank lending, 67
Bank of England, 17
Base currency, 378
Base rate, 442
Basis, 398
Basis risks, 450
Baumol model, 537
Beaver, 117
Benefits intangible, 183
Beta factor, 229, 233, 234, 235
Bilateral netting, 383
Bills of exchange, 517
Blocked funds, 285
Bonds, 36
Bonus issue, 162
Bootstrapping, 348
Borrowing, 120
Bottom-up planning, 90
Buffer, 533
Buffer safety inventory, 528
Bulk discounts, 530

Business failure, 117, 488
Business plan, 123
Business risk, 146, 147, 271
Buy-in, 366

Cap, 456
Capital allowances, 186
Capital asset pricing model, 226
Capital expenditures, 174
Capital gains, 158
Capital gearing, 244
Capital investment decisions, 237
Capital markets, 68
Capital structure, 53, 57
Capitalisation issue, 162
Career management, 292
Cash budget, 119, 534
Cash cows, 96
Cash cycle, 480
Cash flow, 480
Cash flow forecasts, 489
Cash flow problems, 533
Cash flow ratio, 108
Cash-rich companies, 96
Centralised treasury department, 543
Certificates of deposit (CDs), 543
City Code on Takeovers and Mergers, 343
Clientele effect, 158
Closing out a futures contract, 399
Collar, 431, **456**
Collecting debts, 500
Commercial banks, 67
Communications, 292
Competition and Markets Authority, 351
Competitive advantage, 290
Contested takeover bids, 344
Contingencies, 116
Contingency funding, 120
Contingency plans, 129
Contract price, 397
Contract size, 397
Control systems, 291
Conversion premium, 38, 331
Conversion value, 38
Convertible bonds, 38
Convertible loan stock, 330, **345**
Convertible securities, 142, 330
Corporate governance, 78
Corporate mentoring, 354
Corporate objectives, 6
Corporate strategy, 6

INDEX

Correlation between investments, 214
Cost of capital, 55, 136, 143
Cost of debt, 271
Cost of equity, 137
Cost of floating rate debt, 142
Cost of preference shares, 140
Coupon, 37
Covenants, 330
Credit control, 499
Credit creation, 66
Credit insurance, 505
Credit ratings, 509
Credit reviews, 510
Credit utilisation report, 512
Creditors, 515
Creditors' turnover, 110,, **483**
Creditworthiness, 500
Cultural differences, 290
Cultural risks, 290
Culture shock, 292
Currency future, 395, 397
Currency option, 418
Currency options, 389, 430
Currency risk, 283, 380
Current ratio, 109, **481**

Day-of-the-week effects, 233
Debentures, 328
Debt collection policy, 500
Debt ratios, 107
Debtors, 499
Debtors age analysis, 511
Debtors' payment period, 482
Debtors turnover, 498
Deep discount bonds, 37
Demerger, 360
Denationalisation, 77
Deposit, 398
Deregulation, 76
Derivative, 395, 441
Direct quote, 378
Discount, 269, 530
Discount rate, 143
Discounted cash flow, 175
Discounted future cash flows method of share valuation, 308
Distribution systems, 290
Diversification, 217
Divestment, 360, 361
Dividend cover, 113
Dividend decisions, 4, 24
Dividend growth model, 138, 322
Dividend valuation model, 137, 232

Dividend yield, 111
Dividend yield method of share valuation, 321
Dividends, 542
Double taxation, 286
Double taxation agreement, 20
Drucker, 91
Du Pont system of ratio analysis, 105

Earnings growth model, 308
Earnings method of valuation, 303
Earnings per share, 7, 111
Earnings yield valuation, 307
Earn-out arrangements, 347
Economic exposure, 380, **408**
Economic order quantity, 526
Economic order quantity (EOQ), 526
Economic policy, 15
Economic value added, 313
Economy, 22
Effectiveness, 22
Efficiency, 22
Efficient market hypothesis, 72
Enhanced scrip dividends, 162
Equity finance, 43
Events after the reporting period, 116
Exchange controls, 285
Exchange rate, 376
Exchange-traded options, 419
Exercise price, 332, 418
Expatriate staff, 291
Expectations, 444
Expected cash flows, 534
Expected return of a portfolio, 213
Export credit insurance, 514

Factoring, 505
Fairness, 79
Feasibility, 190
Finance house deposits, 542
Financial control, 4
Financial future, 395
Financial intermediary, 65
Financial management, 4, 23
Financial obligations, 115
Financial planning, 4
Financial risk, 53, 147, 271
Financing a subsidiary, 282
Financing decision, 23
Fintech, 70
Fisher effect, 388
Fixed charge, 40
Float, 535
Floating charge, 40

Floating rate debt, 142
Floating rate debt capital, 147
Floor, 456
Forecast, 119, 123
Foreign currency, 418
Foreign currency quotations, 378
Foreign exchange (FX) markets, 377
Foreign exchange constraints, 20
Foreign exchange risk management, 544
Forward exchange contract, 389
Forward rate, 376
Free cash flow, 309
Fundamental theory of share values, 138, 322
Futures, 395, 396

Gap analysis, 125, 445
Gap analysis of interest rate risk, 445
Geared betas, 268
Gearing, 8, 53, 57, 107, 160, 164, 244, 305
Gearing of a company, 268
Gearing ratio, 53, 57, 107
Gilt-edged securities, 442
Going private, 164, 366
Gordon's growth model, 139
Government, 14
Government incentives, 77
Grants, 77
Green finance, 57

Hedge efficiency, 399
Hedge ratio, 454
Hedging, 544
Hedging of risks, 379
Human resources, 291

Immediate delivery, 376
Import quotas, 283
In the money, 419
Independence, 79
Indirect quote, 378
Inflation, 15, 114, 183
In-house credit ratings, 509
Initial margin, 398
Initial public offering (IPO), 44
Innovation, 79
Institutional investors, 70
Insurance, 435
Integrity, 79
Interest cover, 108
Interest rate futures, 448
Interest rate guarantee, 455
Interest rate guarantee (IRG), 455

Interest rate option, 455
Interest rate parity, 386, 387
Interest rate swap, 468
Interest rates, 16
Interest yield, 111, 329
Internal rate of return, 175
International CAPM, 235
International investment appraisal, 194
Inventories, 526
Inventory days, 532
Inventory level, 528
Inventory turnover, 482, 532
Inventory turnover period (Finished goods), 482
Investing surplus cash, 541
Investment decisions, 5, 23
Investors in Industry, 341
Invoice currency, 381
Invoice discounting, 507
Irredeemable debentures, 329
Irredeemable debt, 140
Issue costs, 264
Issue price for a rights issue, 47

Judgement, 79
Junior debt, 346
Just-in-time procurement, 531

Keynes, 532

Lagged payments, 383
Law of one price, 196
Lead payments, 383
Leasing, 34
Legislation, 15
Liquidation, 361
Liquidity, 160
Liquidity preference, 442
Liquidity ratios, 108, 117, 488
Listing, 43
Litigation risks, 288
Loan note, 37
Loan stock, 328
Local authority deposits, 542
Local managers, 291, 292
Long range planning, 8
Long-term capital, 68
Long-term commitments, 116
Long-term creditors, 14
Long-term objectives, 90
Long-term strategic planning, 91

INDEX

Management buy-in, 366
Management buy-out, **362**
Management charges, 285
Management control, **97**
Marginal cost of capital, 147
Market failure, **74**
Market risk, **226**
Market segmentation theory, 444
Market value added, 321
Marking to market, 398
Markowitz, 213
Matching assets and liabilities, 382
Matching receipts and payments, 382
Maturity mismatch, 452
Maximax, 209
Maximin, 210
Maximum level, **528**
Media, 290
Merger, **340**
Mergers, 340
Mezzanine finance, 346
Miller-Orr model, 538
Minimax regret, 210
Minimum level, **528**
Modigliani and Miller (MM), 55, 159, 250, 268
Monetary Policy Committee, 17
Money market hedge, 391
Money markets, 68
Monopoly, **75**
Multilateral netting, 383

Negotiated options, 419
Net assets method of share valuation, 301
Net operating income approach, 247
Net present value, 148, 175
Net present value (NPV) approach, 312
Net working capital, **480**
Netting, **383**
Non-financial objectives, 10
Non-relevant costs, 181
Non-systematic risk, **226**

OECD Model Agreement, 20
OECD Principles of Corporate Governance 2004, 79
Official aid schemes, 77
Operating gearing, 108
Operational control, **97**
Operational planning, **97**
Opportunity cost of capital, 266
Optimal hedge ratio, 454
Option, **418**

Option forward exchange contracts, 389
Option to abandon, 191
Option to follow-on, 191
Option to wait, 191
Options theory, 435
Ordinary shares, 43
Organisation for Economic Co-operation and Development (OECD), 79
Out of the money, 419
Outside managers, 366
Over the counter (OTC) options, 419
Over-capitalisation, 484
Overdraft, 31, 67
Overdraft facility, 533
Overseas factor, 514
Overseas taxes, 19
Overtrading, 484
Ownership and management, 79

P/E ratios, 217
Payables payment period, **483**, **518**
Payables turnover, **518**
Payables turnover period, **483**
Payback, 175
Pecking order theory, 246
Personal taxation, 158
Philadelphia Stock Exchange, 419
Placing, 45
Planning, 174
Planning period, 92
Political risk, **283**
Pooling, 447
Pooling of risks, 379
Portfolio, 218
Portfolio management, 234
Portfolio theory, 213
Post balance sheet events, 116
Post-acquisition integration, 352
Potential or contingent liabilities, 116, 118
Precautionary motive, 533
Preference shares, 140
Price/Earnings ratio, 111, 304
Principles-based governance, **80**
Private companies, 140
Privatisation, 77
Probability distribution, 126
Probity, **79**
Profit margin, 106
Purchase, **340**
Purchasing power parity, **196**, 387

Quantity discounts, 530
Quick ratio, 109, **482**

Rappaport, 312
Ratio analysis, 104
Ratio pyramids, 105
Rational model, 91
Raw materials inventory holding period, 482
Real options, 191
Receivables' days, 482
Receivables' payment period, 482
Receivables turnover, 498
Recruitment and training, 292
Redeemable debentures, 329
Redeemable debt, 115
Redemption, 41
Reference currency, 378
Regulation of markets, 74
Relevant costs, 181
Reorder level, 527
Reporting, 11
Reputation, 79
Residual theory, 156
Residual theory of dividend policy, 159
Responsibility, 79
Restrictive practices, 76
Retained earnings, 156, 160
Return on capital employed (ROCE), 106
Return on investment, 174
Reverse takeover, 340
Reverse yield gap, 444
Risk, 208
Risk averse, 210
Risk management, 379
Risk of a portfolio, 214
Risk seeker, 209
Royalty, 285
Rules-based governance, 80

Safety stock, 528
Sale and leaseback, 35
Sales growth, 107
Savings, 183
Scepticism, 79
Scrip dividend, 162
Scrip issue, 52, **162**
Secondary ratios, 106
Sell-off, 361
Sensitivity analysis, 211
Separation of ownership and management, 79
Settlement date, 397, 400
Settlement discount, 503
Share capital and reserves, 115
Share exchange, 345
Share ownership, 15

Share prices, 156, 232
Share repurchases, 164
Share valuation, 300
Share warrants, 435
Shareholder value analysis, 312
Shareholders and management, 13
Shareholders' preferences between risk and return, 217
Short-term capital, 68
Short-term debt instruments, 543
Short-term deposits, 542
Short-term finance, 515
Short-term interest rate futures, 449
Short-term investments, 542
Short-term loans, 32
Short-term objectives, 90
Signalling, 161, 162
SONIA, 442
Spare debt capacity, 264
Special dividend payment, 542
Speculative motive, 533
Spin-off, 361
Spot rate, 376
Stakeholder groups, 92
Stakeholders, 12
Static trade-off theory, 245
Stock days, 532
Stock Exchange, 68
Stock Exchange introduction, 45
Stock market ratios, 105, 111
Stock split, 52, **163**
Stock turnover, 482
Stockless production, 531
Stocks, 526
Strategic analysis, 92
Strategic cash flow planning, 96
Strategic choice, 94
Strategic control, 98
Strategic fund management, 97, 120, 489
Strategic options evaluation, 94
Strategic options generation, 94
Strategic planning, 91
Strategic planning and control, 97
Strategy, 5
Strategy selection, 94
Subscription rights, 332
Subsidy, 265
Suitability, 189
Super-profits method of share valuation, 323
Surplus cash, 541
Synergy, 340
Synthetic forward, 391
Systematic risk, 146, 217, **226**, 268

Tactical control, 98
Tactical or management control, 97
Tactical planning, 97
Tactics, 97
Takeover, 300, 340
Takeover bid, 342
Targets, 8
Tariffs, 283
Tax havens, 286
Tax shield, 262
Tax shield exhaustion, 257
Taxation, 18, 19, 185
Teacher, 354
Term currency, 378
Theoretical ex rights price (TERP), 48
Tick, 397, 450
Tick size, 397
Tie-breaker clauses, 20
Top-down planning, 90
Trade bill, 517
Trade credit, 515
Traded interest rate options, 457
Traded options, 419
Trading cycle, 480
Traditional view of dividend policy, 159
Traditional view of WACC, 248
Training programme, 292
Transaction exposure, 380
Transactions motive, 532
Translation exposure, 380, **410**
Transparency, 79
Treasury bills, 442, 543

Treasury management, 543
Turnover periods, 109

Uncertainty, 126, 211
Underwriters, 46
Ungeared betas, 268
Unsystematic risk, 226

Value drivers, 312
Value for money, 22
Value of rights, 48
Variation margin, 398
Venture capital, **41**, 363

Warrant, 332
Weighted average cost of capital, 55, 143
What if questions, 126
White knight, 344
Witholding tax, 20
Working capital, 108
Working capital cycle, **480**
Working capital requirement, 487

Yield curve, 443

Zero cost collar, 456
Zero coupon bonds, 38